GREAT CHRISTIAN JURISTS IN FRENCH HISTORY

French legal culture, from the Middle Ages to the present day, has had an impressive influence on legal norms and institutions that have emerged in Europe and the Americas, as well as in Asian and African countries. This volume examines the lives of twenty-seven key legal thinkers in French history, with a focus on how their Christian faith and ideals were a factor in framing the evolution of French jurisprudence. Professors Olivier Descamps and Rafael Domingo bring together this diverse group of distinguished legal scholars and historians to provide a unique comparative study of law and religion that will be of value to scholars, lawyers, and students. The collaboration among French and non-French scholars, and the diversity of international and methodological perspectives, gives this volume its own unique character and value to add to this fascinating series.

Olivier Descamps is a professor of law and legal history at the Panthéon-Assas University in Paris, France, and managing director of the Institute of Legal History of the French National Center for Scientific Research (CNRS) in Paris. A specialist in legal history, canon law, and comparative law, he has authored or edited five books, including *Les sources du droit à l'aune de la pratique* (2018) and *Le statut du magistrat* (2019). Professor Descamps is coeditor of the *Revue historique de droit français et étranger*, one of the leading journals in legal history worldwide.

Rafael Domingo is the Spruill Family Research Professor at Emory University in Atlanta, USA, and ICS Professor of Law at the University of Navarra, Spain. A specialist in legal history, legal theory, ancient Roman law, and comparative law, he has authored or edited more than twenty books, including *The New Global Law* (Cambridge University Press, 2010), *God and the Secular Legal System* (Cambridge University Press, 2016), *Roman Law: An Introduction* (2018), and *Great Christian Jurists in Spanish History* (Cambridge University Press, 2018).

Law and Christianity

The Law and Christianity series publishes cutting-edge work on Catholic, Protestant, and Orthodox Christian contributions to public, private, penal, and procedural law and legal theory. The series aims to promote deep Christian reflection by leading scholars on the fundamentals of law and politics, to build further ecumenical legal understanding across Christian denominations, and to link and amplify the diverse and sometimes isolated Christian legal voices and visions at work in the academy. Works collected by the series include groundbreaking monographs, historical and thematic anthologies, and translations by leading scholars around the globe.

Books in the Series

Great Christian Jurists and Legal Collections in the First Millennium Philip L. Reynolds

English Ecclesiastical Lawyers: A History of Their Life and Work R. H. Helmholz

Law, Love, and Freedom: From the Sacred to the Secular Joshua Neoh

Great Christian Jurists in French History Olivier Descamps and Rafael Domingo

Church Law in Modernity: Toward a Theory of Canon Law Between Nature and Culture Judith Hahn

Common Law and Natural Law in America: From the Puritans to the Legal Realists Andrew Forsyth

Care for the World: Laudato Si' and Catholic Social Thought in an Era of Climate Crisis edited by Frank Pasquale

Church, State, and Family: Reconciling Traditional Teachings and Modern Liberties John Witte, Jr.

Great Christian Jurists in Spanish History Rafael Domingo and Javier Martínez-Torrón

Under Caesar's Sword: How Christians Respond to Persecution edited by Daniel Philpott and Timothy Samuel Shah

God and the Illegal Alien Robert W. Heimburger

Christianity and Family Law John Witte, Jr. and Gary S. Hauk

Christianity and Natural Law Norman Doe

Great Christian Jurists in English History edited by Mark Hill, QC and R. H. Helmholz

Agape, Justice, and Law edited by Robert F. Cochran, Jr. and Zachary R. Calo

Calvin's Political Theology and the Public Engagement of the Church Matthew J. Tuininga

God and the Secular Legal System Rafael Domingo

How Marriage Became One of the Sacraments Philip L. Reynolds

Christianity and Freedom (Volume I: Historical Perspectives, Volume II: Contemporary Perspectives) edited by Timothy Samuel Shah and Allen D. Hertzke

The Western Case for Monogamy Over Polygamy John Witte, Jr.

The Distinctiveness of Religion in American Law Kathleen A. Brady

Pope Benedict XVI's Legal Thought Marta Cartabia and Andrea Simoncini

Great Christian Jurists in French History

Edited by

OLIVIER DESCAMPS

Panthéon-Assas University

RAFAEL DOMINGO

Emory University and University of Navarra

CAMBRIDGE
UNIVERSITY PRESS

University Printing House, Cambridge CB2 8BS, United Kingdom

One Liberty Plaza, 20th Floor, New York, NY 10006, USA

477 Williamstown Road, Port Melbourne, VIC 3207, Australia

314–321, 3rd Floor, Plot 3, Splendor Forum, Jasola District Centre,
New Delhi – 110025, India

79 Anson Road, #06–04/06, Singapore 079906

Cambridge University Press is part of the University of Cambridge.

It furthers the University's mission by disseminating knowledge in the pursuit of
education, learning, and research at the highest international levels of excellence.

www.cambridge.org
Information on this title: www.cambridge.org/9781108484084
DOI: 10.1017/9781108669979

First published 2019

Printed and bound in Great Britain by Clays Ltd, Elcograf S.p.A.

A catalogue record for this publication is available from the British Library.

Library of Congress Cataloging-in-Publication Data
NAMES: Descamps, Olivier, 1969- editor. | Domingo, Rafael, 1963- editor.
TITLE: Great Christian jurists in French history / edited by Olivier Descamps,
Université Panthéon-Assas, Paris and Rafael Domingo, Emory University, Atlanta and
University of Navarra, Spain.
DESCRIPTION: Cambridge, United Kingdom ; New York, NY, USA : Cambridge University Press,
2019. | Series: Law and Christianity | Includes bibliographical references and index.
IDENTIFIERS: LCCN 2018061693 | ISBN 9781108484084 (hardback : alk. paper) |
ISBN 9781108705752 (pbk. : alk. paper)
SUBJECTS: LCSH: Christian lawyers–France–Biography. | Judges–France–Biography. |
Law teachers–France–Biography. | Law–France–Christian influences–History. |
Law and Christianity–History.
CLASSIFICATION: LCC KJV251 .G744 2019 | DDC 340.092/8744–dc23
LC record available at https://lccn.loc.gov/2018061693

ISBN 978-1-108-48408-4 Hardback

To Jean Gaudemet (1908–2001),
in memory

Contents

Contributors

Frédéric Audren, Research Professor, French National Center for Scientific Research (CNRS); and Researcher at the European Study Center (CEE-CNRS), Paris, France.

Julien Barroche, Research Fellow, National Institute for Oriental Languages and Civilization (INALCO), Paris, France.

Brigitte Basdevant-Gaudemet, Professor Emerita of Law and Religion, University of Paris-Saclay, Paris, France.

Isabelle Brancourt, Senior Research Fellow, Institute for History of Representations and Thoughts in Modernities (IHRIM), French National Center for Scientific Research (CNRS), Lyon, France.

Luisa Brunori, Research Fellow, Center for Judicial History, University of Lille, France.

Anne-Sophie Chambost, Professor of Law and Legal History, Jean Monnet University, Saint-Etienne, France.

Orazio Condorelli, Professor of Canon Law and Ecclesiastical Law, University of Catania, Italy.

Kathleen G. Cushing, Reader in Medieval History, Keele University, UK; and President of the *Iuris canonici medii aevi consociatio* (ICMAC).

Wim Decock, Assistant Professor of Legal History, Universities of Leuven and Liège, Belgium; Affiliate Researcher, Max Planck Institute for European Legal History, Frankfurt am Main, Germany.

Olivier Descamps, Professor of Law and Legal History, Panthéon-Assas University (Paris II); and Managing Director of the Institute of Legal History, French National Center for Scientific Research (CNRS), Paris, France.

Rafael Domingo, Spruill Research Professor of Law, Emory University, Atlanta, GA, USA; and Professor of Law and ICS Research Professor, University of Navarra, Spain.

David Gilles, Associate Professor of Law, University of Sherbrooke, Quebec, Canada.

Mary Ann Glendon, Learned Hand Professor of Law, Harvard University, Cambridge, MA, USA; and former United States Ambassador to the Holy See.

Laetitia Guerlain, Assistant Professor of Legal History, University of Bordeaux, France.

Christian Hattenhauer, Professor of Law and Legal History, University of Heidelberg, Germany.

Nicolas Laurent-Bonne, Professor of Law and Legal History, University of Clermont-Auvergne, France.

Daniel Lee, Assistant Professor of Political Science at the University of California, Berkeley, CA, USA.

Yves Mausen, Professor of Law and Legal History, University of Fribourg, Switzerland.

Matthew C. Mirow, Professor of Law, Florida International University College of Law, Miami, FL, USA.

Kenneth Pennington, Kelly-Quinn Professor of Ecclesiastical and Legal History, Catholic University of America, Washington, DC, USA.

Paul J. du Plessis, Professor of Roman Law, University of Edinburgh, Scotland.

Xavier Prévost, Professor of Law and Legal History, and Managing Director of the Research Institute Montesquieu, University of Bordeaux, France.

Christof Rolker, Professor of Historical Basic Sciences, University of Bamberg, Germany.

Marco Sabbioneti, Research Fellow, Institute for Study of Legal Science, University of Florence, Italy.

Mathias Schmoeckel, Professor of Law and Legal History, University of Bonn, Germany.

William Sweet, Professor of Philosophy and Director of the Center for Philosophy, Theology, and Cultural Traditions, Saint Francis Xavier University, Nova Scotia, Canada.

John Witte, Jr., Robert W. Woodruff Professor of Law, McDonald Distinguished Professor, and Director of the Center for the Study of Law and Religion, Emory University, Atlanta, GA, USA.

Acknowledgments

The editors of this volume are deeply grateful to John Witte, Jr., the Robert W. Woodruff Professor of Law, McDonald Distinguished Professor, and director of the Center for the Study of Law and Religion at Emory University, for his leadership in the development of this project on Great French Christian Jurists. They are also grateful to Gary S. Hauk, senior editorial consultant of the Center for the Study of Law and Religion at Emory University, for his acute and professional attention to the preparation of the final manuscript. They owe a special word of thanks to John Berger, senior editor at Cambridge University Press, for his committed editorial assistance. Finally, yet importantly, the editors want to express their warm thanks to the McDonald Agape Foundation for its generous support in making this volume possible.

Introduction

OLIVIER DESCAMPS AND RAFAEL DOMINGO

This book aims to illustrate the fertile interactions and lasting synergies between Christianity and law in French history by exploring the contributions that brilliant legal figures have made over the centuries to juridical ideas and institutions. The volume is part of a larger project on Christian jurists in world history led by John Witte, Jr., director of the Center for the Study of Law and Religion at Emory University. The first two volumes, on English and Spanish Christian jurists, have already been published.[1] This volume on French Christian jurists is thus the third in a series projected to include at least seven more.

Like the other volumes in the collection, this one is biographical, juridical, ecumenical, and global in character. The biographical dimension emphasizes not only the great legal contributions of each jurist but also his or her links to Christianity. The juridical dimension highlights the impact of each jurist on public and private law and justice, whether from inside the legal profession or from a broader philosophical, theological, or intellectual tradition. The ecumenical dimension shows Christianity as a unity, taking into consideration the way different churches and denominations are part of a whole. Finally, the global dimension emphasizes that each volume in this series on great Christian jurists illustrates the distinctive contributions of different nations to the global conversation about law and Christianity.

This volume on French Christian jurists examines the lives of twenty-seven key legal thinkers in French history, particularly the ways their Christian faith and ideals were a factor in framing the evolution of law and justice.

[1] See Mark Hill and R. H. Helmholz (eds.), *Great Christian Jurists in English History* (Cambridge, New York: Cambridge University Press, 2017); and Rafael Domingo and Javier Martínez-Torrón (eds.), *Great Christian Jurists in Spanish History* (Cambridge, New York: Cambridge University Press, 2018).

All chapters have been written by distinguished legal scholars and historians, mainly from France but also from Belgium, Canada, Germany, Italy, Spain, Switzerland, the United Kingdom, and the United States. The collaboration among French and non-French scholars, and the diversity of international and methodological perspectives, gives the volume its unique character and value.

The expression *Christian jurist* has to be understood broadly to include not only civil and canon lawyers but also theologians, philosophers, and political thinkers who contributed decisively to building up the edifice of justice and law. A global and intercultural historical project, as this one aspires to be, cannot maintain a single, narrow understanding of the idea of jurist but must be inclusive. Reality is a single whole, and its legal dimension is just one among many dimensions. Often, in history, the legal dimension has been more intensely affected and influenced by other dimensions of human existence – moral, philosophical, historical, theological, spiritual, sociological, or economic – than by actors engaged exclusively within the artificial limits of the legal dimension. The term jurist, then, refers here to anyone involved with law and justice in the broadest sense.

Behind many legal developments, one finds Christian ideals as they were interpreted at a given time. And behind those ideals, one often finds a particular Christian legal thinker or practitioner who, perhaps unintentionally, left an indelible mark on our legal culture. This volume deals with these Christian jurists. How is it possible not to see, for instance, the Christian contribution to individual rights and liberties inherent in some of John Calvin's ideas; the Christian contribution to the French Civil Code arising from the brilliant works of Jean Domat, Robert-Joseph Pothier, or Jean-Étienne-Marie Portalis; the Christian contribution to the Universal Declaration of Human Rights latent in the ideas of Jacques Maritain; or the Christian contribution to the European process of integration shaped by Robert Schuman?

The selection of French Christian jurists for this volume has not been easy, owing to their great number and the distinctiveness of French law. Several considerations determined the selection. The first had to be the historical starting point. Since other volumes of the same series also examine Christian influences in legal thought of the first millennium,[2] our volume includes only the main periods of the second millennium – the medieval period of civil and canon law, the French modern period, and the contemporary age.

[2] See Philip L. Reynolds (ed.), *Great Christian Jurists and Legal Collections in the First Millennium* (Cambridge University Press, 2019).

The second consideration has been the interest in covering all periods of French history. Some periods – for instance, that of the French Revolution and afterwards – have fewer original Christian thinkers; in other periods, such as that of French humanism, most French legal scholars and practitioners were Christians (Catholic or Protestant); in still other periods, like the brilliant epoch at the end of the nineteenth century, notable legal figures included both Christians and non-Christians, as was also true of the twentieth century. In general, after the French Revolution, Christian contributions to French law and legal theory became more moderate, understated, and subtle, but even so, Christians continued to offer important contributions to law and justice as legal theorists of public law, canonists, legal historians, and legal philosophers.

The third consideration was the desire to cover different disciplines of the law. This volume would be justified if it did no more than assess the great contribution of French Christian jurists to, say, French civil law or canon law. This volume, however, aims to reflect the extent and variety of topics in which the interaction between law and Christianity has taken place (e.g., legal history, codification, constitutionalism, human rights, public law, legal sociology).

Finally, the fourth consideration concerns the reasonable editorial limits of the series in both the length of the volume and the number of selected jurists. Originally intending to limit the volume to twenty-five jurists, we raised the number to twenty-seven in view of the learned opinions and persuasive suggestions of contributors.

Of the twenty-seven selected jurists in this volume, six flourished during the second half of the sixteenth century, and nine lived during the nineteenth and twentieth centuries. The period of French humanism, when France snatched preeminence in legal scholarship from Italy to make the University of Bourges the leading law school in Europe, and the period of the late nineteenth century, when the science of public law was systematized, were momentous in legal creativity and imagination. Probably these periods exceed in importance the era of drafting the French civil code, although the civil code, without a doubt, has had the most global impact in French legal history.

All of the selected jurists were brilliant French Christian legal thinkers or actors. Yet many very important legal scholars – especially humanists of the sixteenth century, such as François Baudouin, Guillaume Budé, François Douaren, Michel de l'Hôpital, Pierre Grégoire, Antoine Loysel, and Pierre Pithou, to mention some of them – have been left out because they did not meet all of our criteria. Our volume is not a dictionary of jurists,[3] in which

[3] For a dictionary on French jurists, see Patrick Arabeyre, Jean Louis Halpérin, and Jacques Krynen (eds.), *Dictionnaire historique des juristes français: XIIe–XXe siècle* (Paris: Presses

everybody and everything interesting must be alphabetically collected. It is, rather, a sample of the enormous and enduring interaction between law and Christianity in French culture.

FRENCH CHRISTIAN JURISTS IN THE MIDDLE AGES

In the twelfth and thirteenth centuries, the kings of French lands developed a feudal court system. Legal standards and the rule of the courts varied greatly between the north and the south. In northern French lands, customary law (*droit coutumier*) predominated. Customary law was the result of a complex process of legal development. It was an amalgam of Frankish capitularies, Germanic customary law, and canon law. Universities offered the study of Roman law, but its role was rather secondary and not very important in the northern courts. In the south of France, however, the written law (*droit écrit*) predominated.[4] Written law was the Roman law of the rediscovered Justinian *Corpus iuris*, adapted as a customary system and often modified by local statutes. In sum, in the north customary law prevailed over Roman law. In the south, however, the opposite obtained. This division of French lands into two portions was emphasized by Pope Honorius III, who in his famous decretal *Super speculum* (1219) banned the teaching of Roman law in the University of Paris in order not to entangle clerics in secular matters. Cultural exchanges between the south of France, with its concentration of important law schools, and Italy were very common. Some Italian professors taught in French schools, and many French students went to Bologna.

Ivo of Chartres (Chapter 1), bishop of Chartres and one of the *founding fathers* of classical canon law, was a solid rock on which to begin building our project. The most learned canonist of his time, Ivo lent a critical voice of moderation in the investiture crisis. The three "Ivonian collections" have a notable place among the canon-law collections before the *Decretum Gratiani* (*c.* 1140). The author of this chapter, Christof Rolker, points out Ivo's conception that canon law, as an expression of God's mercy and justice, must be

Universitaires de France, 2013). From a global perspective, including dozens of French jurists, see Rafael Domingo (ed.), *Juristas Universales*, 4 vols. (Madrid, Barcelona: Marcial Pons, 2004).

4 For a further explanation, see Manlio Bellomo, *The Common Legal Past of Europe: 1000–1800*, 2nd edn, trans. Lydia G. Cochrane (Washington, DC: Catholic University of America Press, 1995), 101–06. For a general overview, see R. C. van Caenegem, *An Historical Introduction to Private Law*, trans. D. E. L. Johnston (Cambridge: Cambridge University Press, 1992); and O. F. Robinson, T. D. Fergus, and W. N. Gordon, *European Legal History*, 3rd edn (Oxford: Oxford University Press, 2000).

applied in the spirit of charity. Ivo thus made a key contribution to the emerging field of canon law as a distinct discipline and to the development of the concept of law in general in Western legal culture.

Stephen of Tournai, our second selected jurist (Chapter 2), studied law in Bologna under the civil-law teacher Bulgarus, ten to fifteen years after Master Gratian had taught there. Named bishop of Tournai, Stephen authored a fully elaborated exposition (*summa*) on the *Decretum Gratiani* (*Summa in decretum Gratiani*), based on similar works prepared in Italy by Paucapalea, Rufinus, and Rolandus. In his *Summa*, Stephen used Roman law frequently to resolve canonical issues. In this chapter on Stephen, Kenneth Pennington aptly criticizes Johann Friedrich von Schulte's edition of Stephen's *Summa* and explains why his vision of the relationship between Roman law and canon law was so important for the development of canonical jurisprudence.

Orazio Condorelli introduces Guillaume Durand in Chapter 3. A student at Bologna, professor at Modena, and later bishop, Durand worked for the Roman Curia for a long time and in the papal government of Romagna. A practical-minded man and good administrator, Durand wrote a famous and widely read treatise on liturgy. It was the *Speculum iudiciale*, however, that gave him a worldwide reputation, including the nickname of Speculator. The *Speculum* represents the peak of the so-called *ordines iudiciarii*, that is, treatises devoted to the exposition of civil and criminal procedures.

Chapters 4 and 5 refer to two famous civil lawyers of the School of Orléans, also called Ultramontani by the Italians: Jacques de Revigny and Pierre Belleperche. Both shaped the renewal of Roman law teaching, and both rivaled the Glossators of Bologna in their mastery of the *Corpus iuris*. Influenced by French Scholasticism, Revigny and Belleperche gave legal reasoning a relevant role. Both were interested in practical questions, and both are considered precursors of the Italian school of commentators (*mos italicus*), which reached its peak with Bartolus de Saxoferrato and Baldus de Ubaldis.

In his chapter on Revigny (Chapter 4), Paul du Plessis explains the importance of Revigny's writings for understanding the interaction between Roman law and customary law during the thirteenth century. Focusing on the methods and approaches to research and teaching by scholars at Orléans, du Plessis evaluates the broader significance of the School of Orléans for successive generations of legal scholars in Italy and elsewhere.

Yves Mausen introduces Pierre de Belleperche in Chapter 5. Nicknamed the king of the legists (civil lawyers), Belleperche approached law systematically, emphasizing the internal harmony of the Justinian *Corpus iuris* as well as some moral principles. Although less innovative than Jacques de Revigny,

Pierre de Bellepeche was probably more influential. According to Mausen, however, despite Belleperche's station as a bishop, religion had little impact on his legal thinking. "If his religious convictions had any implications at all for his actions as a jurist," Mausen concludes, "they would consist precisely of his efforts for promoting social peace by strengthening royal power. To this extent, he can possibly be seen as devoted to a certain Realpolitik." Pierre de Belleperche was the last great French professor at Orléans. After he died in 1308, Italian doctrine came to dominate the French schools during the fourteenth century. In fact, our volume includes no French Christian jurist of the fourteenth century.

CHRISTIAN JURISTS OF MODERN FRANCE

After the invasion of the Italian peninsula by King Charles VIII of France, in 1494, the artistic and literary atmosphere of the Italian Renaissance influenced French culture. The legal field was no exception. The Italian jurist Andrea Alciato (1492–1550) became the forerunner of French humanism by introducing the historical method into legal teaching. He taught at Avignon (1518) – where he met the philologist and Hellenist Guillaume Budé (1467–1540), father of the French Renaissance – and at Bourges (1528), the leading university of Europe at that time. Distinguished professors at Bourges included Éguiner-François Baron (1495–1550), François Douaren (1509–1559), François Baudouin (1520–1573), Jacques Cujas (1522–1590), François Hotman (1524–1590), and Hugues Doneau (1527–1591).

Sixteenth-century French humanism provided Roman law a new intellectual framework. Fascinated by classical antiquity and historicism, the humanists approached the *Corpus iuris* in a different way than the medieval glossators and commentators (*mos italicus*). French humanism applied historical and philological methods to understand the meaning of legal texts in their historical context (*mos gallicus*). Humanists accepted the *Corpus iuris* for its technical skills and the quality of its pure arguments (*imperium rationis*), but not as a traditional source of legal authority (*ratio imperii*). As Franz Wieaker points out, the humanist "called for sources which were pure rather than traditional, for the recognition of the ideal rather than logical attestation of the authoritative, for system rather than exegesis."[5] For these reasons, humanists reproached medieval scholars for having corrupted ancient Latin through their barbaric linguistic abuses, their ignorance of Greek, and

[5] Franz Wieacker, *A History of Private Law in Europe*, trans. Tony Weir (Oxford: Clarendon Press, 1995), 64–65.

their anachronistic interpretations of the legal texts in adapting them to the needs of medieval society.

Reading this volume helps understand the significant connections among legal humanism, the Calvinist reformation, the University of Bourges, and the *mos gallicus*. Humanism is a many-branched cultural movement; Calvinism, a religious reform movement; the *mos gallicus*, a legal method to interpret the ancient sources; and the University of Bourges, a venerable French university. These four realities are quite varied, but they are all interconnected. Thus, for example, the reformer Calvin studied in Bourges and highly admired the humanist Budé. Many professors of Bourges (e.g., Hotman and Doneau) were Huguenots (French Calvinists) and, as result of the devastating Wars of Religion (1562–1598), were compelled into exile and taught at German and Dutch universities. The *mos gallicus* was not a Protestant method of interpretation (notable Catholics followed the French method), but it was important in the development of the Reformation.

Along with the flourishing of a great school of Roman law, legal humanism also stimulated the opposite: a nationalist reaction in defense of French national law against Roman law. The first book on French law written in French was published in that era. Charles Dumoulin, François Hotman, Guy Coquille, Louis Le Caron (who promoted the notion of French law), and René Choppin are some representatives of this French legal nationalism that culminated with the growing unification and later codification of French law under Napoléon.

Our six selected jurists of the sixteenth century are, chronologically, Charles Dumoulin, John Calvin, Jacques Cujas, François Hotman, Hugues Doneau, and Jean Bodin. In Chapter 6, Wim Decock introduces Charles Dumoulin as one of the most influential jurists in French history and a precursor to French national law. A man of strong character, nationalistic convictions, and Bartolist methods, Dumoulin exercised humanist intellectual attitudes. A fervent follower of Gallicanism, Dumoulin advocated for national churches instead of a universal ecclesiastical governance in a way compellingly similar to his primary efforts to distinguish clearly between the tradition of Roman law, which is universal, and the tradition of customary law, which is particular. As Decock explains, Dumoulin paved the way for the idea that French customary law, and not Roman law, should be considered the general law applicable within the French kingdom, thus disintegrating the hitherto unbreakable unity between Roman law and common law.

In Chapter 7, John Witte, Jr. vindicates the legal figure of John Calvin as a defender of the state rule of law, democratic process, and individual liberties. According to Witte, Calvin was primarily a Christian jurist who provided the legal theoretical framework for the constitutional protection of freedom of conscience and free exercise of religion and a solid constitutional theory of republican government. Witte analyzes how Calvin and Calvinists based their doctrine of religious and civil rights on the Decalogue and established a strong connection between the idea of human rights and the rights of persons to do their duties as bearers of God's image.

In Chapter 8, Xavier Prévost introduces the reader to Jacques Cujas, the leading legal historian and most notable expositor of French humanism. A prolific author of remarkable clearness and precision, in his ten-volume *Opera omnia* Cujas dealt with a great variety of topics of Roman law, canon law, feudal law, and French customs and legislation. Cujas also devoted himself to the exegesis and publication of Roman legal sources, such as the *Collatio legum Mosaicarum et Romanarum*, a private comparative collection of Jewish and Roman sources of the fourth century, and the *Consultatio veteris cuiusdam iurisconsulti*, a fifth-century Roman legal treatise. He recovered and published part of the Theodosian Code (438 CE), a legal body of around twenty-five hundred imperial constitutions created from 306 to 437 CE. In 1566, Cujas published the first critical edition of the *Libri feudorum*, a twelfth-century collection of feudal customs. Cujas refused to take any part in the religious wars which filled all the thoughts of his contemporaries. His usual answer to those who asked him about the topic became famous: the conflict "has nothing to do with the edict of the praetor!" (*Nihil hoc ad edictum praetoris!*).

In Chapter 9, Mathias Schmoeckel introduces the controversial character of François Hotman, Calvin's secretary and translator, a champion of the Calvinist cause, and one of the most influential Calvinist lawyers of sixteenth-century France. A radical thinker and theorist who later became more moderate, Hotman in his famous work *Franco-Gallia* (1573) advocated for representative government and an elective monarchy. His work was a precursor to the doctrine of the separation of powers, and, along with Dumoulin, Hotman was a key figure in the development of French national law.

Another Calvinist lawyer was Hugues Doneau (Chapter 10). Like Hotman, Doneau escaped the massacres of St Bartholomew's Day (1572). Cujas's scientific and personal opponent, Doneau was the leader of the most dogmatic branch of legal humanism, which focused on the systematic foundations of the law. In his *Commentaries on Civil Law*, Doneau systematized the Roman civil law as it was applied in his time. Christian Hattenhauer, author of this chapter, explores the similarities between Doneau's approach and the rational approach of the German school of pandectists in the nineteenth century. According to Hattenhauer, Doneau's central innovation consisted in interpreting private law by putting the human person as a whole at its heart. Contrary to the *Institutes* of Gaius and Justinian, divided into persons, things, and legal actions, the notion of *person* in Doneau's view should be the unique starting point of any legal development. Doneau oriented the restructuring of Roman law toward subjective rights, moving from a civil law excessively dependent on legal procedures to a more substantive and dogmatic civil law. Nineteenth-century German scholars used Doneau's basic concepts of civil law to build up their system of pandects. As an example, Doneau was a source of inspiration in the dogmatic grounding of the unique characteristic in German law, the so-called abstraction principle (*Abstraktionsprinzip*).

Daniel Lee explores in Chapter 11 the singular and still crucial contribution of Jean Bodin to law and political theory. Humanist and jurist, Bodin is especially celebrated for his *Six livres de la république* (1576), an impressive treatise on comparative law and politics which paved the way for the scientific study of public law in its modern framework. His theory of sovereignty constituted the first systematic analysis of the idea of absolute and indivisible power, and it is key to understanding the original structure of nation-states, national legal systems, and the international legal order. Bodin held that the prerogatives of sovereignty cannot be divided but only delegated, and therefore should be concentrated in a single person or group of persons. The absolute power of the king was limited by the law of nature and the divine law of God that are universally binding on all human beings, including the sovereigns.

Over the course of the seventeenth century, France continued the process of nationalization of its law, led more by judges and lawyers of the Parliament of Paris than by legal scholars. A French common law (*droit commun de la France*) arose based on customs, *droit écrit*, royal ordinances, and case law from the parliaments. French jurists tried to deal with this plurality of sources of French law by providing a unified and coherent systematization. The second part of the seventeenth century was dominated by the central figure of King Louis XIV, the "Sun King" (r. 1643–1715). During his reign of more than seventy years, one of the longest in world history, he consolidated the growing centralization of the sovereign nation-state and perfected the practice of royal absolutism, which endured until the French Revolution. Louis XIV issued the Great Ordinances (*Grandes Ordonnances*), including the civil ordinance on the reformation of justice (1667), the criminal ordinance (1670), the commercial ordinance (1673), and the maritime ordinance (1681). Each ordinance provided the complete and systematic regulation of a certain legal field, with exclusive jurisdiction for that specific area. In 1685, Louis issued the Edict of Fontainebleau and revoked the religious toleration that the Edict of Nantes had guaranteed the Huguenots for more than eighty years. Protestant churches and schools were closed, and Huguenots were forced to leave France or convert to Catholicism. The Ordonnances of the eighteenth century – including, among others the ordinance on donations (1731), the ordinance on wills (1735), and the ordinance on substitutions (1747) – can be regarded as precursors of the French process of codification. The selected jurists from this period are Jean Domat (1665–1696), Henri François d'Aguesseau (1668–1751), and Robert-Joseph Pothier (1699–1772).

Written by David Gilles, Chapter 12 explores the life and works of Domat and his desire to construct both a civil law and a public-law system inspired by natural law and Christian principles. A Jansenist and a libertarian, as well as a close friend of Descartes, Domat believed that, although Roman law contains natural law, the great principles illuminating natural law had been lost. According to Gilles, Domat's originality lay in his effort to reconcile Christian thought with modern rationalism, and to reconcile the divine foundation of the legal system with his resolution to create a purely rational and geometric law. Louis XIV regarded Domat's contribution so highly that the Sun King sponsored his publications and paid him a pension for life.

In Chapter 13, Isabelle Brancourt approaches the figure of chancellor Henri François d'Aguesseau, a radical Gallican recognized and even applauded by the philosophers and free thinkers of the French Enlightenment. Chancellor of France three times between 1717 and 1750, an enlightened intellectual, and a notable and loyal administrator, d'Aguesseau carried out important reforms of the French legal system. He contributed to the law first by clarifying and simplifying legal standards in light of a very innovative and fresh interpretation of the corpus of the law. He sought full harmony between natural law and civil law and rejected any positive law contrary to natural reason. From a political point of view, he promoted legal uniformity as a necessary condition for the right development of sovereign government, and, ultimately, he served legal absolutism.

In Chapter 14, Olivier Descamps explores Robert-Joseph Pothier's contribution to the legal realm. One of the most celebrated jurists of French legal history, Pothier is consider the "French Papinian" and the father of the Civil Code. Appointed in 1749 by Chancellor d'Aguesseau as professor of French law at the University of Orléans, Pothier wrote treatises on Justinian law and French law that dominated the development of French private law, especially in the area of obligations. Pothier is for French law what William Blackstone is for English law, James Kent for American law, and Emer de Vattel for international law: the great writer of the first systematic treatise in accordance with the standards of the Age of Reason. Pothier was not very innovative, but he had an encyclopedic knowledge and a great capacity for conceptual clarity and precision. As Descamps explains, Pothier made law of obligations the cornerstone of the private law, including contracts of marriage.

Inspired by liberal principles and radical ideas, the French Revolution (1789–1799) deeply changed the course of modern French and Western history. The French Revolution overthrew absolute monarchy and established the French Republic (1792), which culminated with the Napoleonic era (1799–1815). By declaring the Rights of Man and of the Citizen (1789) and abolishing privileges of the nobility and the clergy, the Revolution sought to establish a free and equal society under the same unified legal system. In 1790, the Assembly passed the Civil Constitution of the Clergy, which subordinated the Roman Catholic Church in France to the French government. In the years following the Revolution, however, churches were closed and converted into storage places, warehouses, or even stables, and religious worship was suppressed. Streets and places lost their Christian names, and the Gregorian calendar was replaced by a revolutionary one, which dated from the founding of the French Republic.

CHRISTIAN JURISTS OF CONTEMPORARY FRANCE

The Napoleonic era, comprising the Consulate (1799–1804) and the Empire (1804–1815) was decisive for the history of France. Indeed, Bonaparte, who became emperor in 1804, established a new society, new administrative structures, and legal institutions that are still present in twenty-first-century France. By his numerous military conquests in Europe, he imposed the French model throughout the Continent in various ways.

One of the essential contributions of the Napoleonic era was codification. In August 1800, Napoléon appointed a commission composed of four brilliant lawyers, whose mission was to draw up a civil code for all of France.[6] Among these eminent members, Jean-Étienne Portalis (1746–1807) stands out. In Chapter 15, Nicolas Laurent-Bonne introduces the controversial figure of Portalis, both a Gallican Catholic and a liberal Freemason, a great defender of religious peace, and a leading jurist during the preparation of the Civil Code and the implementation of the Concordat. "His clear Gallicanism," Laurent-Bonne concludes, "his political and religious liberalism, his incessant references to the school of modern natural law and the philosophy of Hume and Locke, his defense of Protestants and religious liberties as well as the

[6] For an overview in English, see Jean-Louis Halpérin, *The French Civil Code*, trans. Tony Weir (Austin: University of Texas Press, 2006).

philosophical spirit and reason, and his stigmatizing of unjust privileges invite the drawing of a more nuanced image of an Enlightenment man."

While the Civil Code was promulgated in 1804, the work of codification continues in other decisive areas of law (commercial law, civil procedure, criminal procedure, criminal law). The phenomenon of codification, which is European in character, opened a new methodological era with the School of Exegesis, which proposed a literal interpretation of the texts. The law established in the Civil Code, a reconciliation between the law of ancient France and the achievements of the Revolution, was clearly secularized. Moreover, Bonaparte continued the action of the first revolutionaries on the religious question by making the Catholic Church a public service. He restored religious peace after the persecutions of the Terror (1793–1794) and the hostility of the Directory. Napoléon negotiated with Pope Pius VII a new Concordat based on the principles of Gallicanism, including the appointment of bishops by the head of state and police control over clerics. Organizing Protestant and Jewish religious communities as well, Bonaparte succeeded in establishing religious pluralism. The Concordat, signed on July 15, 1801, in Paris by Napoléon and Pope Pius VII, confirmed the national reconciliation between revolutionaries and Catholics and restored the civil status of the Roman Catholic Church, no longer as a state church but as the majority church of France.

The nineteenth century in France was full of wealth and development in many different fields. Politically, a welter of regimes followed each other (the Empire, the Bourbon restoration, the July Monarchy, the Second Republic, the Second Empire, and the Third Republic). Constitutions and constitutional charters varied according to the institutional system chosen. These changes raised questions and often prompted a critical look at French institutions. It is not surprising that Alexis de Tocqueville, a classical liberal and passionate defender of liberty, obtained from the July Monarchy a mission to examine prisons and penitentiaries in the United States. This was the genesis of his famous two-volume *Democracy in America* (1835 and 1840), in which he explored the success of the republican representative government in the young nation. As Mary Ann Glendon points out in Chapter 16, Tocqueville was "particularly noted for his insistence on the roles of law and culture in maintaining a free, democratic society; his emphasis on the importance of the mediating institutions in which civic character and competence are formed; and his profound but tragic insight that democracy not only depends on certain conditions but helps to shape those conditions, sometimes in ways that threaten the very habits, attitudes, and institutions on which its health depends."

The alternation of political regimes among monarchy, republic, and empire accompanied a period of industrial revolution with disastrous social consequences. The Catholic Church played a crucial role in the area of education and welfare, but the Church had reservations about some social and intellectual developments. Pope Pius IX (1846–1878), the longest-serving pontif in the history of the papacy, condemned fundamental errors plaguing the modern age in his encyclical letter *Quanta cura* (1864), including a *Syllabus of Errors* inserted as an index. The document met with a mixed reception among French Catholics and divided them.

A decisive moment of the French nineteenth century was the Battle of Sedan (in northeastern France) in 1870, during the Franco-Prussian War. Napoléon III was captured and the French army decisively defeated. This painful episode for France, which ultimately lost Alsace and Lorraine (1871), was also the starting point for establishing a new political regime, the Third Republic. It took ten years to finally stabilize the new republican regime. Uncertainty and hesitations about the best form of government (monarchy or republic) testified to the division of French society. The legacy of the French Revolution pitted conservatives against republicans. Soon, an opposition between secular and clerical republicans focused on religious congregations. The number of members of religious congregations in France had notably changed in the previous century. They numbered 80,000 in 1789, 13,000 in 1808 (because of the Revolution), and 160,000 in 1878. By a decree of March 29, 1880, the Society of Jesus (the Jesuits) was dissolved and ordered to disperse within three months. A second decree on the same day ordered the closure of unauthorized congregational educational institutions within six months: as a result, more than 250 convents were closed, and more than 5,000 members of religious congregations were expelled. Attacks against congregations and religious repression were more pressing with the enactment of the law of December 4, 1902, which criminalized unauthorized congregations. The law of July 7, 1904, banned congregations from teaching and set a ten-year deadline for closing institutions. This law was one of the main causes of the rupture of the diplomatic relations between France and the Holy See. In 1905 the *Law on the Separation of the Churches and the State*[7] was passed by the Chambers of Deputies. It consecrated the principle of state secularism in France (*laïcité*).

Another fracture emerged in France in the same period between 1894 and 1906. This was the Dreyfus affair. In 1894, a Jewish French artillery officer,

[7] Loi du 9 décembre 1905 concernant la séparation des Églises et de l'État.

Alfred Dreyfus, was accused of delivering secret documents to the Germans. He was arrested for treason and espionage, convicted in a secret court-martial, stripped of his army rank, and sentenced to deportation and life imprisonment. The influential open letter titled *J'accuse*, in which Émile Zola accused the French government of anti-Semitism and jailing Dreyfus without evidence, aroused strong opposition between Dreyfusards and anti-Dreyfusards. Against a backdrop of anti-Semitism and anti-German sentiment, the case was finally retried, and Dreyfus was completely exonerated in 1906.

In this complex and divided French society, jurists did not remain insensitive. This was true of Paul Viollet, introduced by Anne-Sophie Chambost in Chapter 17. A Dreyfusard and moderate republican, Viollet devoted himself to establishing the League of Human Rights and the creation of the Catholic Committee for the Defense of Rights. Chambost believes that "in his many commitments as a Catholic, as much as in his scholarly works as a legal historian, Viollet always challenged every border: disciplinary, professional, religious, and political. In this way, he endorsed throughout his life what he considered to be the function of an intellectual in the French Republic, fully conscious that democratic progress, still vulnerable, had to be firmly protected."

The difficulty for many Christian jurists was to reconcile the universal church with the epoch made up of unprecedented technical and scientific progress but also of political and social evolutions not in agreement with a traditional Catholic France. Such reconciliation was the work of the great canon-law historian Paul Fournier, introduced by Brigitte Basdevant-Gaudemet and Rafael Domingo in Chapter 18. Fournier denounced both the rigor of the anticlerical policy and the resistance of monarchist and uncompromising Catholic circles. Pope Leo XIII invited French Catholics to rally in behalf of the Republic in 1892 in ways compatible with the principles of Catholicism. Lawyers worked to defend this rally while proposing legal solutions with a strong social impact in accordance with the social doctrine of the Church.

In Chapter 19, Marco Sabbioneti introduces Raymond Saleilles. As Sabbioneti explains, in a rapidly evolving sociopolitical context and at the height of the so-called *crise allemande* of French culture, Saleilles tried to "redesign French legal culture from within." He saw the connection between social need and legal development, and he proposed an updated legal method, which clarified much more through its immediate applications than through the constructing of complete treatises of general theory. A comparative lawyer, Saleilles understood comparative law as a potential source of a "common law of civilized humanity."

Rallying the Republic but not accepting moral relativism was one of the aspects of Maurice Hauriou's thought, introduced by Julian Barroche in Chapter 20. Working from recent developments of social science, Hauriou vigorously expressed convictions that he nourished with historical analysis based on his initial discipline of the history of law. He defended the reference to and the value of a natural law of divine origin. He rejected socialism and individualism, which were already threatening the Third Republic.

Hauriou, whose contribution to administrative law was massive, entered into controversies with Léon Duguit, introduced in Chapter 21 by M. C. Mirow. Duguit proposed a theory of the nation-state and developed the notion of public service. Moreover, it is in connection with this notion that he analyzed the relations between the church and the state. He considered the former as a public service of the latter. A feature common to both Hauriou and Duguit was their neo-Thomism, which Pope Leo XIII supported, especially in his encyclical *Aeterni Patris* (1879), and which was a bulwark against the modernism already condemned by Pius IX.

Criticism of modernity was still one of the points of Georges Ripert's thought, introduced in Chapter 22 by Frédéric Audren. A conservative but also a firm opponent of natural law, Ripert advocated for the inspiration of the legal system by Christian moral principles, especially in the area of the law of obligations. Audren considers Ripert's approach paradoxical since he was "a positivist by reason and a realist by conviction." According to Audren, Ripert "was doubly realistic: in his analysis of the forces that make and break the law, but also in his proposal to monitor the *moral* activity of lawyers, that is, the impossibility for them to act without reason. All of this constituted a strange modernity (not to say modernism) for a jurist who, to this day, still incarnates reactionism."

Neo-Thomism was also at the center of Jacques Maritain's political and legal thought. Introduced by William Sweet in Chapter 23, Maritain defended a humanism that expresses itself in the emerging notion of human rights. He also supported the idea of the importance of morality in law, and put the person at the center of his philosophy. As Sweet explains, Maritain's influence has been very deep and spread around the world. One can see Maritain's doctrinal impact in the Universal Declaration of Human Rights, in some national and international declarations of rights, as well as in the preamble to the Constitution of the Fourth Republic in France (1946). The Christian democratic movement in Italy, Belgium, and Chile was indebted to Maritain's social and political philosophy. His writings also had a great impact on the social teaching of the Catholic Church, especially in some writings of Pope Paul VI.

In this interwar period, the European idea, which already had a long history, was undergoing remarkable progress under the impetus of numerous projects. Under the auspices of the League of Nations, Aristide Briand proposed the creation of a European federation to maintain peace in Europe. Unfortunately, Fascism and Nazism swept away these ideas and developed outrageous nationalism. Even during the Second World War, however, proposals for European projects emerged. Governments in exile were already making contact with each other and thinking about the postwar period. Yet it would take until the end of the Second World War for the birth of a European movement promoting European integration. Winston Churchill supported the idea of the United States of Europe, already mentioned by Victor Hugo in the nineteenth century. The implementation of European integration owes a debt to the courage and imagination of some men who shared the Catholic faith. Among them, Robert Schuman, introduced in Chapter 24 by Rafael Domingo, played a decisive role with a plan he proposed in 1950 which allowed the creation of the first European community, the European Coal and Steel Community (1951).

New developments arose in a French society undergoing reconstruction during the postwar years. Among the Catholic jurists of that time, Gabriel Le Bras, introduced by Kathleen Cushing in Chapter 25, occupied a place of honor. A student of Paul Fournier, Le Bras was at the origin of the creation of sociology of religion as a new academic discipline whose success has not faltered since the 1940s. Moreover, as Cushing points out, "Le Bras helped to pioneer a scientific approach to the study of canon and Roman law through meticulous attention to the manuscripts and their historical contexts and a collective approach for understanding the church through its institutions and *religion vécue* (lived religion)."

With the advent of the Fifth Republic in 1958, French society continued its evolution marked by economic progress. The principle of *laïcité* was consecrated in the first article of the new Constitution: "France shall be an indivisible, secular (*laïque*), democratic and social Republic. It shall ensure the equality of all citizens before the law, without distinction of origin, race or religion. It shall respect all beliefs. It shall be organized on a decentralized basis."

During the 1960s, in addition to the *aggiornamento* of the Catholic Church with the Second Vatican Council (1962–1965), social evolution led the French legislature to important legal reforms, notably in family law. Jean Carbonnier, introduced in Chapter 26 by Laetitia Guerlain, was the leading jurist of all family-law reforms between 1964 and 1975. An eminent civil lawyer and sociologist, he contributed through his reform projects to the liberalization of the family. As a Protestant, he believed that human nature is originally corrupt; however, he did not derive from this belief the necessity of the law. On the contrary, he thought that well-balanced societies need only a minimum of laws of high quality. What Le Bras did by promoting sociology of religion as a specific discipline, Carbonnier did in relation to the sociology of law.

Another well-known jurist, Michel Villey, introduced in Chapter 27 by Luisa Brunori, advocated for the teaching of philosophy of law in French law schools. A devout Catholic, a passionate Aristotelian, and an expert on Thomas Aquinas, Villey opposed the individualistic trends of French society, the false idols and ideas of his epoch, and he especially criticized the dominant legal positivism. He tackled the notion of human rights, since he considered that the excessive and sometime frivolous multiplication and recognition of rights was going to devalue the very idea of right. He remained attached for life to the Greco-Roman classical approach to justice: "to render to each one his or her own" (*suum cuique tribuere*).

CONCLUSION: FRENCH CHRISTIAN JURISTS AT THE HEART OF ALL LAW REVOLUTIONS

The Christian contribution to French law is enormous, as is the French Christian contribution to Western legal systems and to the idea of law in general. French Christian jurists have been present at the birth of medieval canon law and the European *ius commune*. In the sixteenth century, they were also present at the birth of the first legal systematization of private law, the birth of the *mos gallicus* as a method of legal development, the birth of the idea of French law, the birth of the nation-state, individual rights and liberties, and especially the birth of religious freedom. French Christian Jurists helped set in motion the period of codification in the eighteenth century, the movement for constitutionalism in the nineteenth century, the systematization of public law at the turn of the twentieth century, the foundation of legal sociology, the movement of human rights, and the European integration in the twentieth century. In sum, French Christian jurists have been present at the beginning of all Western legal revolutions from the Middle Ages to our day.[8]

Even French *laïcité*, a hallmark of the French legal system, exudes a certain Christian aroma, since *laïcité* is the final product of the long history and evolution of church–state relations in France. *Laïcité* is a way of understanding religious freedom, and religious freedom in its deepest sense, not just mere religious toleration, is a distinctly Christian idea. In this sense, the implementation of French *laïcité* would have been very problematic in a country with

[8] See Harold Berman, *Law and Revolution*, 2 vols. (Cambridge, MA: Harvard University Press, 1986, 2006), and Jean-Louis Halpérin, *Five Legal Revolutions since the Seventeenth Century* (Heidelberg, New York: Springer, 2014).

non-Christian roots (e.g., a Jewish- or a Muslim-rooted country). Paraphrasing the great comparative law scholar and legal historian Harold Berman, we conclude this introduction by saying that French law, and by extension Western law, is a secular Christian theology, which often makes no sense because its Christian theological presuppositions are no longer accepted.[9]

[9] Berman, *Law and Revolution*, vol. 1, 165.

1

Ivo of Chartres (Yves de Chartres)

(c. *1040–1115*)

CHRISTOF ROLKER

Ivo of Chartres was famous as a teacher, pastor, scholar, and a central figure in many secular and ecclesiastical affairs of his time; after his death, he was widely remembered as a voice of moderation in an age of often extreme partisanship and polemics. Many legal scholars and historians alike – including Stephen of Tournai, Esmein, Fournier, Le Bras, and Gaudement – studied and often praised his wide-ranging work.

Ivo was born around the year 1040 in or near Chartres to a family of relatively low status.[1] Having entered religious life early, he became the first provost of St Quentin near Beauvais in 1067. Ivo took care of the spiritual and secular welfare of this community of regular canons, which soon was seen as a model for other houses. In 1090, he became bishop of Chartres, a position that yielded considerable prestige but also involved him in a number of conflicts. In his first years, Ivo faced opposition from powerful local nobles and from his metropolitan, Archbishop Richer of Sens, who regarded Ivo as an interloper and tried to have his predecessor as bishop reinstalled. This issue was not fully resolved when, in 1092, Ivo began severely and repeatedly to censure King Philip I of France for having repudiated his wife, Berta, and having begun an adulterous relationship with Bertrada of Montfort. On top of all this, Ivo in 1096 chose to oppose the claims of the powerful papal legate, Hugh of Lyon, which was to have far-reaching authority in the affairs of the French church.

These were bitter and sometimes violent struggles, yet they should not make one overlook how swiftly at times all parties were able to cooperate again, if only because of overlapping lines of conflict. For example, Ivo may have strongly disagreed with Hugh of Lyon over the question of Lyonnais primacy,

[1] For Ivo's biography, see Rolf Sprandel, *Ivo von Chartres und seine Stellung in der Kirchengeschichte* (Stuttgart: Hiersemann, 1962), esp. 5–8; and Christof Rolker, *Canon Law and the Letters of Ivo of Chartres* (Cambridge: Cambridge University Press, 2010), 1–24.

but at the same time, both prelates worked together in the king's marriage circumstances. This matter in turn did not stop King Philip and Ivo from joining forces, sometimes against Hugh, to support the same candidates in a number of episcopal elections, including important sees like Sens and Paris. Finally, in at least one case (at Orléans in 1096), Hugh and Philip jointly supported a candidate Ivo thought utterly unfit for office.

Ivo's works were written during, and visibly shaped by, these and other affairs. Above all, this is true of his letters, numbering some 280, which he exchanged with popes, kings, queens, bishops, papal legates, priests, abbots, monks, lords, and ladies in all of Francia and well beyond.[2] Many of these letters are in fact elaborate tracts on theological, legal, and political questions, and already in his lifetime were read, copied, and collected widely. In these letters, Ivo drew on an impressive range of biblical, patristic, synodal, papal, or other authorities and historical precedence to shed light on contemporary questions, whether the royal marriages, the censure of a runaway monk, or the reconsecration of an altar after construction work on a church. Ivo was able to do so not least because over the years he compiled a massive collection today known as his *Decretum*, which covers canon law in the widest possible sense. Ivo also wrote an elaborate introduction to the *Decretum*, normally known simply as his Prologue, which circulated extremely widely in medieval Europe. This Prologue was also attached to several other canon-law collections, including two closely related to his *Decretum*, namely the *Tripartita* and the *Panormia*, which mainly for this reason were attributed to Ivo from early on. Modern scholarship cannot confirm that Ivo compiled (or even knew) the *Panormia*, but it is very possible that he was involved in compiling the *Tripartita*. Taken together, the three "Ivonian collections" have a crucial place among the so-called pre-Gratian canon-law collections.[3] The influential *Decretum* was one of the largest canonical collections of the Middle Ages, introducing into canon law a large number of authorities found in earlier collections. Much of this material was taken into other collections, including

[2] For the sake of convenience, all references to Ivo's letters are to the Patrologia Latina edition: Jean-Paul Migne, edn. *Sancti Ivonis Carnotensis Episcopi Opera Omnia*, 2 vols. (Paris: 1854/55). For the manuscript tradition and provisional editions of some letters, see ivo-of-chartres.github.io/.

[3] Martin Brett, "The Sources and Influence of Paris, Bibliothèque de l'Arsenal 713," in *Proceedings of the Ninth International Congress of Medieval Canon Law. Munich, 13–18 July 1992*, edn. Peter Landau and Jörg Müller (Vatican City: Biblioteca Apostolica Vaticana, 1997); "Creeping up on the Panormia," in *Grundlagen des Rechts. Festschrift für Peter Landau*, edn. Richard H. Helmholz, et al. (Paderborn: Schöningh, 2000); Anders Winroth, *The Making of Gratian's Decretum* (Cambridge: Cambridge University Press, 2000); Detlev Jasper and Horst Fuhrmann, *Papal Letters in the Early Middle Ages* (Washington, DC: Catholic University of America Press, 2001).

Tripartita and *Panormia*, both of which (especially the *Panormia*) were copied very widely. By around 1140, they were among the most important sources of Gratian's *Concordia discordantium canonum*, arguably the most important medieval canon-law collection.

MAJOR THEMES AND CONTRIBUTIONS

Variety of themes

In his letters, collections, sermons, and other writings, Ivo covered a remarkably broad array of topics. His letters show how fellow bishops and others turned to Ivo for advice on diverse matters. Often, Ivo's replies are, or contain, carefully composed legal opinions peppered with canonical authorities to bolster his own argument – and significantly, often with canons that may be quoted to support a different conclusion. Sometimes, he would carefully select and quote a whole range of possible answers from the tradition but leave the decision ultimately to the reader. The same can indeed be said of his *Decretum*, which, on a much larger scale than his letters, brings together authorities from various backgrounds on almost every aspect of Christian life. Characteristically for Ivo, he did not strive to select only authorities supporting specific doctrines, but rather presented his reader with the full range of positions found in canonical writings from the earliest times of the church to his own days. As a result, the *Decretum* grew into a very substantial collection of some 3,700 canons, enough to fill more than 330 folios (as in the Canterbury copy). The individual books focus on baptism and confirmation (book 1), the Eucharist (book 2), the church both as a community and as a building (book 3), feasts and fasting (book 4), holy orders and ecclesiastical hierarchy (book 5), clerical discipline (book 6), monks and monasteries (book 7), sexuality, marriage, and virginity (books 8 and 9), various crimes including murder (book 10), sorcery (book 11), perjury (book 12), theft (book 13), excommunication (book 14), penance (book 15), lay matters (book 16), and speculative theology (book 17). Many of these books are very substantial and often cover more issues than the above list would suggest. Book 4, for example, also contains a synodal order; in book 12 one finds the famous tract of Fulbert of Chartres on feudal oaths but also a complete subsection on the legal status of Jews; book 13 treats procedure in general; among other lay matters, book 16 deals with the role of the king in the church, serfdom, and (in surprising detail) the law of obligations. Book 15, finally, covers multiple transgressions and the penitential tariffs they carry, making it a collection within the collection. Bringing order to so many proof texts on such a diversity of issues was in itself a monumental task, and while modern jurists (especially Paul Fournier) sometimes thought the *Decretum* lacked doctrinal unity, many canon lawyers highly praised Ivo's *magnum opus*.[4]

The canons are drawn ultimately from diverse sources, including the Bible, the writings of the church fathers, synodal and papal decrees, Roman law, capitularies, and penitential books. The most ancient texts go back to the Old Testament and pre-Christian Roman law, while the most recent ones are papal letters written only some two years before the *Decretum* was finished in or around 1094. Many of the canons Ivo gathered in his *Decretum* could also be found in earlier collections, most notably the widely known collection compiled by Burchard of Worms (d. 1025), which Ivo took as a model for his own compilation. Other canons he took from works like the *Collectio Britannica*, which had little independent circulation. Yet in many cases, Ivo took into his *Decretum* canons not found in any earlier collection. For these materials, he seems to have relied on various florilegia, lost or unknown abridgements, or indeed the original works, suggesting in any case that he took considerable effort to find new materials. As a result, the *Decretum* contains far more excerpts, for example, from the letters of Pope Nicholas I (d. 867) than any earlier collection, and it is the first canonical collection compiled north of the Alps to include excerpts from the Justinian Digest. Most notably, perhaps, Ivo introduced an abundance of patristic material into canon law. About a fifth of the canons of the *Decretum* are taken from the writings of the church fathers, including more than five hundred excerpts from St Augustine alone. Many are not found in any earlier collection, and given the precision with which they are quoted, it seems likely that Ivo here was indeed quoting from these works directly rather than from florilegia.

In the early and high Middle Ages, canon law combined a range of legal, theological, and pastoral aspects, and both Ivo's letters and his *Decretum* give an impression of what this meant in practice. Yet while the wide range of topics covered in these works is characteristic both of medieval canon law and of Ivo's multifold duties as pastor, teacher, judge, and high-ranking prelate, some topics stand out. Among the most important ones, to Ivo and his medieval readers, were the Eucharist, marriage, the relation of royal and ecclesiastical power, and the theme of "mercy and justice" in canon law.

[4] See the lavish praise on Ivo's *Decretum* in the dedicatory letter in *Decretum D. Ivonis Episcopi Carnutensis Septem ac Decem Tomis sive Partibus Constans*, edn. Johannes Molinaeus (Louvain, 1561) [s.p.]. Fournier, in contrast, thought of it more as a preparatory work: Paul Fournier, "Les Collections Attribuées à Yves de Chartres," *Bibliothèque de l'École des Chartes* 57 (1896): 395.

The Eucharist

Although Ivo today is best remembered as bishop of Chartres and (certainly since Fournier's groundbreaking studies) for his role in legal history, it was as provost of St Quentin that he established his reputation as a teacher and scholar, in particular for his teaching on the sacraments. The only extant work from this time is a small tract on the Eucharist often transmitted with his letters and therefore known as letter 287.[5] It belongs to the growing literature on the Eucharist written since the mid-eleventh century, often in the form of refutations of Berengar of Tours (d. 1088), whose teachings had been condemned by several synods from the 1050s but continued to influence the debate for more than a century. Short as it is, Ivo's tract contains a number of theological proof texts (mainly taken from the writings of St Augustine and St Ambrose). Some of them are also found in Lanfranc's Eucharist tract, which may well have been one of Ivo's sources; interestingly, though, Ivo provides fuller quotations than Lanfranc. Indeed, Ivo can be shown to have compiled a florilegium of patristic authorities specifically in preparation of his tract, and almost certainly went through full versions of the relevant patristic writings in this context. The proof texts Ivo was able to quote apparently were seen as a welcome contribution to the ongoing debate; this at least is suggested by the wide reception of Ivo's materials in canonical and theological works of the twelfth century (e.g., by Alger of Liège, Abelard, Gratian, and Peter Lombard). In addition, these excerpts also had a very direct role to play in the genesis of Ivo's own canonical collection. The Eucharist florilegium Ivo prepared at St Quentin is preserved as part of his *Decretum*, as the first ten canons (in the modern numbering) of book 2, containing some forty excerpts and covering about ten folios in the manuscripts. It is the earliest datable part of the *Decretum* and may well have been Ivo's starting point for the whole endeavor. The florilegium certainly has a prominent place in the finished version, not only because it appears at the beginning of the second book but also because Ivo chose to place the books on sacramental theology at the very

[5] See Christof Rolker, "The Earliest Work of Ivo of Chartres: The Case of Ivo's Eucharist Florilegium and the Canon Law Collections Attributed to Him," *Zeitschrift der Savigny-Stiftung für Rechtsgeschichte, kanonistische Abteilung* 124 (2007) (with an edition of the tract). The number refers to its position in the Patrologia Latina edition, which in turn is based on the 1610 edition of Ivo's letters by Juret. Here, it was placed at the end of an otherwise largely chronologically arranged collection of letters from Ivo's time as bishop: François Juret, edn. *Ivonis Episcopi Carnotensis Epistolae. Collatione Multorum Manuscriptorum Codicum Restitutae, Auctae et Emendatae; Eiusdem Ivonis Chronicon de Regibus Francorum* (Paris: 1610), here at 499.

beginning of the whole collection. This was an unusual choice, as many compilers of canon law collections were rather brief on the sacraments of faith and in any case preferred to open with ecclesiastical hierarchy – for example, canons on the relation between the papacy and local churches. Often, compilers selected proof texts supporting their own views of the church. This may also be said of Ivo, not because the opening books of the *Decretum* contain canons on papal primacy or other questions of hierarchy, but rather because he chose to place the sacraments first. For him, the church was not only the complex structure of ecclesiastical orders but above all the community of the faithful, united by the administration and reception of the sacraments.

Marriage

One of the recurring issues in Ivo's correspondence was the law of marriage.[6] The marriage affair of King Philip, mentioned above, was only the most prominent case in which Ivo was entangled. He became involved in other noble marriages, notably those of Philip's daughter Constance, whose first marriage Ivo helped to dissolve and whose second (to Bohemund of Antiochia) he solemnly celebrated at Chartres in 1106. He also was consulted by fellow bishops on many other marriages.

Thanks mainly to his letters, Ivo's view on marriage can be studied in great detail. He very strongly insisted on the importance of consent; a marriage's validity depended on individual consent and not sexual intercourse, parental approval, or, for that matter, the blessing of a priest. Repeatedly, he condemned concubinage, but he did not think that premarital sexual relations were an obstacle to marriage. Rather, he argued that under certain circumstances, such informal unions were clandestine marriages and therefore could not be dissolved, at least not without an ecclesiastical sentence. Indeed, Ivo (like many ecclesiastical judges of his time) was faced with many requests from married couples, and more specifically husbands, to have their marriages dissolved. Many of these cases, at least in Ivo's view, were nothing but attempts at self-divorce, which Ivo in many cases tried to counter. For example, a knight publicly confessed to having committed adultery with his bride's sister before his marriage; he then turned to the ecclesiastical court and claimed his marriage to be invalid. Ivo, who regarded this as a blatant abuse of the law,

[6] For the following, see most recently Philip L. Reynolds, *How Marriage Became One of the Sacraments: The Sacramental Theology of Marriage from its Medieval Origins to the Council of Trent* (Cambridge: Cambridge University Press, 2016), esp. 189–207.

in this and a number of similar cases ruled that the marriage was to be upheld, even if it indeed was begun in violation of church law (as the premarital affair created what later canonists would call affinity from illegitimate intercourse between the knight and a relative of the woman he had committed adultery with). In the case in question, he additionally held that the adulterer could neither accuse nor witness on grounds of infamy. On the other hand, in the case of consanguinity between spouses, Ivo was ready to dissolve existing marriages, although he was well aware that the relevant prohibitions were also used as pretext for self-divorce. The conflict between marriage prohibitions, especially those on grounds of kinship, and the principle of indissolubility, was indeed a general problem of medieval canon law.

Ivo's main contribution to the medieval law of marriage was not so much any new doctrine he developed. What his medieval readers seemed to value was not doctrinal consistency (let alone novelty) but rather his ability to take into account both the circumstances of individual cases and the complexity of the canonical tradition. Ivo's grasp of the relevant documents stemming from secular and ecclesiastical sources covering more than a millennium is indeed impressive. Just as he quoted the relevant, and often contradictory, canons with seeming effortlessness in his own letters, he also used them in his *Decretum*, and often was able to find highly relevant materials overlooked by previous compilers. Among other texts, Ivo introduced into the debate on marriage the so-called *Responsa Bulgarorum* of Nicholas I. This papal letter was hardly known before Ivo's time and was not found in any other collection, but in the twelfth century it quickly became one of the central authorities in the definition of marital consent. Another key authority on marital consent that Ivo frequently quoted in his letters and inserted in his *Decretum* was Justinian's Digest; for centuries, these excerpts on marriage had not been cited, but soon after Ivo introduced them into canon law they became a cornerstone in the church's definition of marriage.

For most medieval readers, then, Ivo's teaching on marriage was known mainly through his letters, while canon lawyers would above all work with the proof texts he had included in his *Decretum*. In addition, Ivo's influence on the nascent discipline of theology can be traced via so-called *sententiae* attributed to him, short statements apparently going back to notes his pupils at Chartres (or perhaps already at St Quentin) took from his teaching. To judge from the transmission of these *sententiae*, Ivo was valued highly in the school of Laon, one of the most important centers of theology in the time before the university. Perhaps the most remarkable evidence for his reputation and influence in this milieu comes from the *Liber Pancrisis*, a large collection of theological sentences mainly from patristic sources but also from a small number of "modern masters" (*magistri moderni*).[7] Not only does the collection contain *sententiae* attributed to Ivo, but he also is highlighted alongside William of Champeaux, Anselm of Laon, and his brother Raoul as one of the modern masters, and Ivo is the only one not directly linked to the cathedral school of Laon where the collection was compiled in the 1140s.

The "discord of regnum *and* sacerdotium*"*

Alongside the understanding of the Eucharist and the definition of marriage, another question vividly in dispute in Ivo's time was the relation between royal (and generally lay) power and the ecclesiastical sphere. Already to some contemporary readers, and to many scholars of the nineteenth century especially, Ivo's position on this issue was of special importance. For example, Sigebert of Gembloux (d. 1112) in his catalogue of ecclesiastical writers mentioned several works of Ivo but highlighted one letter in particular:[8]

> Ivo, bishop of Chartres, wrote to Hugh, archbishop of Lyon and apostolic legate, a letter not of great length but abundant with canonical and catholic proof texts, on the discord of *regnum* and *sacerdotium* and unwonted decrees of the Roman church. He also wrote very useful letters to different friends, and further compiled a great volume of canons.

The letter in question (letter 60 in the modern edition, written in 1097) addressed the question of the role the king could and should have in the appointment of bishops. It was written in a time that had indeed seen deep "discord of *regnum* and *sacerdotium*," and it took up the issue of "unwonted decrees of the Roman church," as the pro-imperial chronicler Sigebert put it. Ivo, who in 1090 had received investiture from King Philip and afterwards was consecrated by Pope Urban II, knew very well how delicate the question of temporal and spiritual power was. By the time he wrote the letter to Hugh, he had already clashed repeatedly with the king. In fact, apparently in this context, he had been imprisoned briefly, had been constrained at least once

[7] On the *Liber*, see Cédric Giraud and Constant J. Mews, "Le *Liber Pancrisis*, un Florilège des Pères et des Maitres Modernes du XIIe Siècle," *Bulletin du Cange* 64 (2006); for context, see Cédric Giraud, *"Per Verba Magistri". Anselme de Laon et Son École au XIIe Siècle* (Turnhout: Brepols, 2010).

[8] Robert Witte, ed., *Catalogus Sigeberti Gemblacensis Monachi de Viris Illustribus. Kritische Ausgabe* (Bern: Lang, 1974), 101–02: Iuo, Carnotensis episcopus, scripsit ad Hugonem, Lugdunensem archiepiscopum et apostolice ecclesie legatum, epistolam non multum prolixam, sed multum canonicis et catholicis testimoniis auctorizatam, pro discidio regni et sacerdotii, et pro inusitatis Romane ecclesie decretis. Scripsit et ad diuersos amicos utiles ualde epistolas; composuit etiam insigne uolumen canonum.

from fulfilling his vassalic duties on account of the king's adultery, and almost constantly faced local nobles who tried to take advantage of his situation by alienating church property. At the same time, in episcopal elections Ivo had occasionally (as in Paris in 1095) supported the same candidates as Philip but sometimes (as in Orléans in 1096) in vain opposed royal candidates he thought unfit for office. On this latter occasion, he complained bitterly how episcopal elections could be influenced by money, sex, and violence.[9] In other words, Ivo was acutely aware that the king's authority over ecclesiastical property and fiefs created obligations that would often conflict with episcopal office, and that it de facto gave the king considerable influence in episcopal successions, not always with desirable results. Nonetheless, in this and other letters, Ivo firmly held that royal influence in episcopal elections and disposal of temporal goods were legitimate. Specifically, he argued that papal prohibitions against lay investiture would not affect this, so long as the king did not try to confer anything spiritual. Defending the bishop-elect of Sens, Ivo wrote:[10]

> That the aforementioned elect received investiture from the hands of the king, we have neither heard from anyone who has seen it nor known

[9] Ep. 66 (PL 162, 85–86): Praeterea sciat vestra sollicitudo, quia cum abbas Burguliensis ore patulo, manibus apertis cum multa securitate ad curiam in Natale venisset ad accipiendum episcopatum, sicut ei illa praedicta regina promiserat; quia animadversi sunt plures et pleniores sacculi nummorum latere in apothecis amicorum istius quam apud abbatem, ille est admissus, iste est exclusus. Et cum abbas quereretur apud regem, quare sic eum delusisset, respondit: Sustinete interim donec de isto faciam proficuum meum, postea quaerite ut iste deponatur, et tunc faciam voluntatem vestram. The abbot Ivo refers to was Baldric, later bishop of Dol (d. 1106). Ivo's appraisal of the ultimately successful candidate John was much more negative; according to Ivo, it was public knowledge that the king had had sexual relations with John (PL 162, 83): De hoc enim rex Francorum non secreto, sed publice mihi testatus est, quod praedicti Ioannis succubus fuerit. Et hoc ita fama per Aurelianensem episcopatum et vicinas urbes publicavit, ut a concanonicis suis famosae cuiusdam concubinae Flora agnomen acceperit. Hoc quod dico clerus approbaret, hoc populus acclamaret, nisi metu regis comprimerentur, vel insidiis Turonensis archiepiscopi terrerentur, qui clericos sibi adversantes clandestinis delationibus curiae tradi facit, aut in exsilium pellendos, aut bonis suis spoliandos. It should be mentioned that Ivo was not neutral in this disputed election, as the third candidate was his pupil Galo.

[10] Ep. 60 (PL 162, 85): Quod autem scripsistis predictum electum investituram episcopatus de manu regis accepisse, nec relatum est nobis ab aliquo, qui viderit, nec cognitum. Quod tamen si factum esset, cum hoc nullam vim sacramenti gerat in constituendo episcopo, vel admissum vel omissum, quid fidei, quid sacre religioni officiat, ignoramus [. . .]. Domnus quoque papa Urbanus reges tantum a coroprali investitura excludit, quantum intelleximus, non ab electione, in quantum sunt caput populi, vel concessione; quamvis octava sinodus solum prohibeat eos interesse electioni, non concessioni. Que concessio sive fiat manu, sive fiat nutu, sive lingua, sive virga – quid refert, cum reges nihil spirituale se dare intendant, sed tantum aut votis petentium annuere, aut villas ecclesiasticas et alia bona exteriora, que de munificentia regum optinent ecclesiae, ipsis electis concedere?

> otherwise. In any case, even if it had been done, we do not know what its performance or absence does to affect faith or holy religion; for this investiture has no sacramental power in the making of a bishop. [. . .] Lord Pope Urban excluded kings only from the corporeal investiture (*investitura corporalis*), as far as we understand, not from the election, in which they act as head of the people, nor the granting (*concessio*); while the eighth synod forbade them only to interfere with the election, not the granting. Whether this granting is done by the hand, or by a nod, or by a word, or by a staff – what does it matter, given that the kings do not think themselves to confer anything spiritual by it, but simply either to signify their assent to the wishes of the faithful, or else to grant to the elect church lands or other external goods which the church holds thanks to royal generosity?

The letter, while read and praised widely, is not easy to understand and in modern times has attracted divergent interpretations.[11] What, for example, was the difference between "investiture" by staff and ring (which Ivo deemed perfectly legitimate) and "corporeal investiture" (which he agreed was forbidden)? One should certainly not read the letter as expressing any consistent "theory" of investiture. In fact, the ambiguities and gaps the letter contains may well have added to its success among prelates who faced the messy realities of episcopal elections in the decades around 1100. For example, both in this letter and elsewhere, Ivo was suspiciously silent on a number of recent decrees against lay investiture. Instead, he quoted an impressive battery of canons against "new statutes" violating ancient law, longstanding custom, and the peace of the realm. While he sharply censored Hugh for taking recourse to such "private laws and new statutes," he stopped short of spelling out which norms precisely he referred to – the privilege of the Lyonnais primacy (which Hugh had obtained from Gregory VII), the decrees of the council of Poitiers (which Hugh had presided over), or perhaps even papal investiture prohibitions?

Whatever Ivo's intention was, these passages invited divergent interpretations, and while Ivo was far from winning universal acceptance (certainly not in Lyon), his letters resonated with readers of very different ideological backgrounds.[12] His indifference towards the symbols used by secular rulers – including ring and staff – is astonishing in the light of contemporary polemic writings on precisely this issue. Much more importantly, however, he was

[11] There is an abundant literature on the letter; see Ian S. Robinson in *The New Cambridge Medieval History*, 7 in 8 vols. (Cambridge: Cambridge University Press, 1995–2005), vol. 4/1, 295–96 (with further references).

[12] For example, both Geoffrey of Vendôme and the Norman Anonymous took up Ivo's arguments. For details, see Rolker, *Canon Law*, 129.

clear that lay influence alone (in particular regarding the transfer of property) was nothing spiritual, and that prohibitions of investiture could and indeed should be dispensed with in many cases. The former point is important, as it cut short any attempt to scandalize traditional elements of episcopal succession as simony, a highly charged term that applied to bribery but also implied heresy. As he demonstrated, accusations of simony had caused much confusion in the French church without addressing the real issue of bribery. The second point was perhaps even more important. Prohibitions of investiture were not part of the eternal law, Ivo explained, and while it may be perfectly legitimate to legislate against lay investiture, such legislation need not, and in many case should not, be enacted. This is a recurring theme in his letters on investiture. In 1097, he argued in rather general terms that prelates could and should use their discretion whether or not to enforce such prohibitions.[13] In 1108, he vehemently argued that the bishop-elect of Reims should be allowed to pay homage to the king, as his predecessors had done, even if this was (as Ivo knew well) precisely what recent papal legislation had sought to suppress; yet in a similar vein to his earlier letter, Ivo argued that such prohibitions could always be dispensed with where necessary.[14] In an even later letter, again directed to Lyon, Ivo repeated many of the arguments found in letter 60, and added that any prohibitions of lay investiture may be applied if and only if this did not lead to schism.[15]

As far as Ivo developed any theory on investiture, then, it mainly consisted in a justification of pragmatic solutions. Whatever the law was, at least in such matters as investiture, bishops and other prelates would always have to take into account older canonical traditions, longstanding custom, and individual circumstances when deciding whether it was feasible or wise to rigorously apply the letter of the law. Taken together, Ivo's letters convey the strong

[13] Ep. 60 (PL 162, 73–74): Quod si hec eterna lege sancita essent, non esset in manu presidentium, ut ea in quibusdam districte iudicarent, quibusdam misericorditer relaxerent, ipsis in honore accepto permanentibus, contra quos ista loquuntur. Nunc vero, quia ea illicita maxime facit presidentium prohibitio, licita quoque eorundem pro sua estimatione remissio.

[14] Ep. 190 (PL 162, 196–97): Sed reclamante curia plenariam pacem impetrare nequivimus, nisi praedictus metropolitanus per manum et sacramentum eam fidelitatem regi faceret, quam praedecessoribus suis regibus Francorum antea fecerant omnes Remenses archiepiscopi, et caeteri regni Francorum quamlibet religiosi et sancti episcopi. Quod persuadentibus et impellentibus totius curiae optimatibus, et si propter mandatorum rigorem minus licebat, factum est tamen, quia ecclesiasticae paci et fraternae dilectioni sic expediebat. Cum enim plenitudo legis sit caritas, in hoc legibus obtemperatum esse credimus, in quo caritatis opus impletum esse cognovimus. Petimus ergo flexis genibus cordis, ut hoc eodem intuitu caritatis et pacis veniale habeat paterna moderatio, quod illicitum facit non aeterna lex, sed intentione acquirendae libertatis praesidentium sola prohibitio.

[15] Ep. 236 (PL 162, 242): Ubi ergo sine schismate auferri potest, auferatur; ubi sine schismate auferri non potest, cum discreta reclamatione differatur.

impression that he himself regarded a rigorous application of the prohibitions the exception rather than the rule.

"Mercy and judgment I will sing to you, O Lord"

The Eucharist, marriage, and episcopal succession are but three examples of how Ivo in his letters and his *Decretum* dealt with contemporary questions by engaging with canonical tradition, which he and many of his readers were convinced had to offer firm guidance on almost any aspect of Christian life. Indeed, Ivo often succeeded in finding appropriate canons from authoritative sources – patristic writers, papal registers, Roman law – including parts of this tradition that had been left dormant for centuries. Yet the drawback of this approach was that the complexity and apparent internal contradictions grew with every addition. This at least may well have been the impression especially for readers of the monumental *Decretum* (in the Canterbury copy, for example, it covers 334 folios). The proof texts Ivo assembled in this collection, as the ones he quoted in his letters, often supported very different solutions to any given question; and compared to the letters, they were not only tremendously more numerous (some 3,760 canons in the modern counting, many of them consisting of more than one authority) but also lacked almost any form of comment that would guide the reader. Working with the *Decretum* in search of clear answers from canonical tradition thus could be a daunting task. For this reason, presumably, Ivo addressed the issue of doctrinal unity (and diverseness) in his Prologue:[16]

> In this, we have been led to caution the prudent reader that if perhaps he should read some things that he may not fully understand, or judge them to be contradictory, he should not immediately take offence but instead should diligently consider what pertains to rigour or moderation, what to justice or mercy. For he did not perceive these things to disagree among themselves who said: "Mercy and judgement I will sing to you, O Lord," and elsewhere: "All the paths of the Lord are mercy and truth."

[16] Bruce Clark Brasington, *Ways of Mercy. The Prologue of Ivo of Chartres: Edition and Analysis* (Münster: Lit, 2004), here at 116: In quo prudentem lectorem premonere congruum duximus, ut si forte que legerit non ad plenum intellexerit, uel sibi inuicem aduersari existimauerit, non statim reprehendat, sed quid secundum rigorem, quid secundum moderationem, quid secundum iudicium, quid secundum misericordiam dicatur diligenter attendat. Que inter se dissentire non sentiebat, qui dicebat: *Misericordiam et iudicium cantabo tibi, Domine* (Ps. 101: 1), et alibi: *Vniuerse uie domini misericordia et ueritas* (Ps. 35: 10). The translation is largely based on Robert Somerville and Bruce Clark Brasington, *Prefaces to Canon Law Books in Latin Christianity: Selected Translations, 500–1245* (New Haven and London: Yale University Press, 1998), here at 134.

Instead of arguing that the contradictions between authorities were only apparent ones, Ivo held that such canons have to be understood as expressions of two distinct yet equally valid traditions in canon law, namely those of mercy and rigor. This duality is a *leitmotif* of his correspondence; dozens of letters allude to this distinction, often quoting the same biblical verses.[17]

Sometimes the law was harsh on account of the "hardness of the hearts"; sometimes it was mild, ready to forgive where there was real contrition. This not only explained the sometimes staggering differences in doctrine and, very tangibly, the different penitential tariffs for the same offence. It also meant, according to Ivo, that the ecclesiastical judge and pastor in every case had to decide himself whether justice or mercy was more appropriate – not only when the law was, or seemed to be, contradictory but indeed always. Great discretion was needed, Ivo wrote, in finding the right balance; ultimately, the guiding principle was the salvation of souls and the love of one's neighbor:[18]

> Every ecclesiastical doctor should thus interpret or moderate ecclesiastical rules so that he may refer to the kingdom of love; nor does he err or sin here, because, concerned for the salvation of his neighbours, he endeavours to achieve the required goal in the holy institutions. Whence the blessed Augustine says when considering ecclesiastical discipline: "Have charity and do whatever you will; if you correct, correct with charity, if you pardon, pardon with charity."

In his correspondence, an abundance of examples for this kind of argument can be found, often in the context of his day-to-day pastorate, where he often preferred an interpretation according to mercy. For example, a monk, having fled four times from his monastery, should be received again, Ivo wrote to his abbot, even if it was against the monastery's rule, "because *mercy rejoices over justice*."[19] One meaning of "mercy", therefore, is "dispensation."[20] Ivo thought

17 Namely letters no. 16, 32, 46, 55, 57, 60–61, 67, 70, 74, 79, 82, 89, 92, 124, 133, 149, 157, 161, 170–71, 180, 185–91, 214, 222, 224, 226, 231, 234, 236, 244, 250, 264, and 279.

18 Brasington, *Ways of Mercy*, here at 116–17: Quicumque ergo ecclesiaticus doctor ecclesiasticas regulas ita interpretatur aut moderatur, ut ad regnum caritatis cuncta que docuerit uel exposuerit referat, nec peccat nec errat, cum saluti proximorum consulens ad finem sacris institutionibus debitum peruenire intendat. Vnde dicit beatus Augustinus de disciplina ecclesiastica tractans: *Habe caritatem et fac quicquid uis, si corripis corripe cum caritate, si parcis parce cum caritate*. The translation is that of Somerville and Brasington, *Prefaces*, here at 134.

19 Ep. 57 (PL 162, 68): quia *superexaltat misericordia iustitiam* (Jas. 2: 13); but see Rule of Benedict, chapter 29.

20 Ivo contrasts *dispensatio* rather than *misericordia* (or both terms) with *iustitia* in epp. 16, 157, 185, 190, 214, 222, 231, and 234.

it often necessary, or at least advantageous, to dispense from precepts and prohibition.[21] In the Prologue, as in his letters, he argued that only rules "sanctioned by the eternal law" and essential for salvation were "immutable";[22] all other rules, including certain biblical precepts and all ecclesiastical legislation, were mutable and therefore, if advisable, could be dispensed with.[23]

His conviction that canonical tradition in its mutability and diversity expressed God's mercy and justice, and that it was always to be applied in the spirit of charity, was perhaps Ivo's most important contribution to the emerging field of canon law as a distinct discipline. Certainly, none of Ivo's works had such a wide circulation for such a long time. Originally written for the *Decretum*, the Prologue also was transmitted separately and as part of various other works. It is found in all major versions of Ivo's epistolary collections, that is, both the smaller collections compiled in his lifetime and those larger ones that in their present form can only have been compiled after his death.[24] The Prologue also was attached to several canonical collections that either directly or indirectly depended on Ivo's *Decretum*; most notably (as far as the number of extant manuscripts is concerned) the majority of *Panormia* copies also contain Ivo's Prologue, and so do the *Tripartita*, the *Collection in Ten Parts*, a short version of Gratian's *Decretum*, and other works. All in all,

[21] Brasington, *Ways of Mercy*, here at 125: Multa quoque principes ecclesiarum pro tenore canonum districtius iudicant; multa pro temporum necessitate tolerant; multa pro personarum utilitate, uel strage populorum uitanda dispensant.

[22] Brasington, *Ways of Mercy*, here at 120–21: Preceptiones immobiles sunt quas lex eterna sanxit, que obseruate salutem conferunt, non obseruate eadem auferunt. Qualia sunt: *Dileges Dominum tuum ex toto corde et proximum tuum sicut teipsum* (Mt. 22: 37–39), et: *Honora patrem tuum et matrem tuam* (Ex. 20: 12), et si qua sunt his similia.

[23] Brasington, *Ways of Mercy*, here at 121: Mobiles uero sunt quas lex eterna non sanxit, sed posteriorum diligentia ratione utilitatis inuenit, non ad salutem principaliter obtinendam, sed ad eam tutius muniendam, quale est illud Apostoli: *Hereticorum hominem post primam et secundam correctionem deuita* (Ti. 3: 10). [. . .] Multa reperies in canonicis institutionibus in hunc modum.

[24] In addition to his edition, see his "Zur Rezeption des Prologs Ivos von Chartres in Süddeutschland," *Deutsches Archiv für Erforschung des Mittelalters* 47 (1991): 173–74 for a list of manuscripts. For discussion, see also Tatsushi Genka, "Zum Prologus des Ivo von Chartres in der Lütticher Handschrift UB 230," in *Von den Leges Barbarorum bis zum Ius Barbarum des Nationalsozialismus. Festschrift für Hermann Nehlsen zum 70. Geburtstag*, edn. Hans-Georg Hermann, et al. (Cologne: Böhlau, 2008). For the four main versions of Ivo's epistolary (the "Jesus," "Rochester," "type I", and "type II" collections, respectively) and a conspectus of the manuscripts containing these or other substantial collections of Ivo's letters, see ivo-of-chartres.github.io/letters.html. A slightly smaller version of Ivo's letters (as found in Heiligenkreuz, Stiftsbibliothek 188 and at least six related manuscripts) contains an abbreviated version of the Prologue.

well above two hundred manuscripts, mainly of the twelfth century, of more than a dozen different works suggest that Ivo's Prologue quickly gained wide popularity in different milieux across Europe.

RECOMMENDED READING

Translations of Ivo's works

Ivo of Chartres, "Prologue." In *Prefaces to Canon Law Books in Latin Christianity: Selected Translations, 500–1245*, edited by Robert Somerville and Bruce Clark Brasington, 121–65. New Haven and London: Yale University Press, 1998.

Secondary literature

Brasington, Bruce Clark. *Ways of Mercy. The Prologue of Ivo of Chartres: Edition and Analysis*. Münster: Lit, 2004.

"Require in Prologo: The Decretists and Ivo of Chartres' Prologue." *Zeitschrift der Savigny-Stiftung für Rechtsgeschichte, kanonistische Abteilung* 87 (2001): 84–124.

Brett, Martin. "The *De Corpore et Sanguine Domini* of Ernulf of Canterbury." In *Canon Law, Religion and Politics: Liber Amicorum Robert Somerville*, edited by Uta-Renate Blumenthal, Anders Winroth, and Peter Landau, 163–82. Washington, DC: Catholic University of America Press, 2012.

"Creeping up on the Panormia." In *Grundlagen des Rechts. Festschrift für Peter Landau*, edited by Richard H. Helmholz, Paul Mikat, Jörg Müller, and Michael Stolleis, 205–70. Paderborn: Schöningh, 2000.

"Finding the Law: The Sources of Canonical Authority before Gratian." In *Law before Gratian: Law in Western Europe c. 500–1100*, edited by Per Andersen, Mia Münster-Swendsen, and Helle Vogt, 51–72. Copenhagen: DJØF Publishing, 2007.

"The Sources and Influence of Paris, Bibliothèque de L'Arsenal 713." In *Proceedings of the Ninth International Congress of Medieval Canon Law: Munich, 13–18 July 1992*, edited by Peter Landau and Jörg Müller, 149–67. Vatican City: Biblioteca Apostolica Vaticana, 1997.

"Urban II and the Collections Attributed to Ivo of Chartres." In *Proceedings of the Eighth International Congress of Medieval Canon Law: San Diego, University of California at La Jolla, 21–27 August 1988*, edited by Stanley Chodorow, 27–46. Vatican City: Biblioteca Apostolica Vaticana, 1992.

Fowler-Magerl, Linda. *Clavis Canonum: Selected Canon Law Collections before 1140: Access with Data Processing*. Munich: Hahn, 2005.

Mews, Constant J. "Law, Theology, and Praxis ca. 1140–1380: New Approaches to the Study of Law and Theology in Medieval Europe." *Journal of Religious History* 37, no. 4 (2013): 435–40.

Rolker, Christof. *Canon Law and the Letters of Ivo of Chartres*. Cambridge: Cambridge University Press, 2010.

"The Earliest Work of Ivo of Chartres: The Case of Ivo's Eucharist Florilegium and the Canon Law Collections Attributed to Him." *Zeitschrift der Savigny-Stiftung für Rechtsgeschichte, kanonistische Abteilung* 124 (2007): 109–27.

"History and Canon Law in the *Collectio Britannica*: A New Date for London, BL Add. 8873." In *Bishops, Texts and the Use of Canon Law around 1100: Essays in the Honour of Martin Brett*, edited by Bruce Clark Brasington and Kathleen Grace Cushing, 141–52. Aldershot: Ashgate, 2008.

2

Stephen of Tournai (Étienne de Tournai)

(1128–1203)

KENNETH PENNINGTON

Stephen of Tournai (Étienne of Tournai or Stephanus Tornacensis) was born in Orléans in 1128.[1] He studied the liberal arts in the Sainte-Croix Cathedral School in Orléans and became a canon regular in the Abbey of St Euverte in Orléans between 1153 and 1158.[2] He went on to Bologna, where he studied Roman law with Bulgarus, who was dubbed the "os aureum" [golden mouth] of mid-century jurisprudence.[3] Stephen never mentioned who his teachers of canon law might have been. He was much too young to have studied with Gratian, who had finished his *Decretum* around 1140 and left Bologna. After finishing his legal studies, Stephen taught at the law school in Bologna. In the 1160s, he returned to Orléans and began a very successful climb up the French ecclesiastical hierarchy. He was elected abbot of St Euverte in 1168, and in 1176 he was moved to the prestigious abbey of Sainte-Geneviève in Paris as abbot. Finally, in 1192 he became the bishop of Tournai, where he remained until his death in 1203.[4]

Lawyers are not commonly known for their literary talents, but Stephen was a superb prose stylist. His letters teem with beautiful word images. He particularly liked to juxtapose similar rhyming words with opposite meanings to make

[1] *Lettres d'Étienne de Tournai: Nouvelle édition*, edn. Jules Desilve (Valenciennes-Paris: Lemaitre-Picard, 1893), Letter 215, p. 267; in a letter dated March 1196, he wrote: "septuagesimum annum biennio minus complevi." Henceforth, his letters will be cited as Desilve with the letter number and pages.

[2] Desilve, Letter 10 to Bishop Hugh of Orléans (1198–1206): "Quadraginta ferme et quinque anni sunt elapsi . . . in ecclesia beati Evurtii habitum religionis suscepimus sub ordine regulari."

[3] Desilve, Letters 44 and 78, pp. 57 and 92, both dated *c.* 1177–78, mention hearing Bulgarus's lectures.

[4] George Conklin, "The Ecclesiology of Stephen of Tournai, 1128–1203 (Canonist)" (PhD dissertation, University of North Carolina, 1987) is the most recent attempt to examine all aspects of Stephen's life and works. The only comprehensive earlier study was Joseph Warichez, *Étienne de Tournai et son temps 1128–1203* (Tournai-Paris: Casterman, 1937).

his points.[5] He also used common proverbs for rhetorical effect to make legal arguments.[6] The Parisian intellectual world bestowed its greatest praise on him when he was asked by Robert, the abbot of Saint Victor, to write an epitaph for the tomb of the bishop of Paris, Maurice de Sully (†1196), who was buried in the Victorine monastery.[7] In addition to his letters, Stephen wrote poetry in which he flaunted his knowledge of ancient literature. His single comment about law in one poem alleges heaven's disdain for law.

> Quia de civilibus et humano iure
> In celesti curia non habentur cure,
> Nec apertum separat ab occulto fure
> Nec vult ut in mutuo veniant usure.
>
> [Because in secular affairs and human law,
> The celestial court has no interest,
> Distinguishing not brazen nor secret thief,
> Caring not that loans usury apply.][8]

Although he wrote a splendid *Summa* on Gratian's *Decretum*, both of Stephen's examples of the legal principles that the celestial court ignores are taken from Roman law's doctrines of theft and contracts.

Stephen's sermons in France were collected by its institutions and his admirers.[8] A Parisian manuscript that still resides in his abbey's library of Sainte-Geneviève contains forty-six sermons arranged mostly according to the liturgical year. Warichez printed a number of excerpts from the sermons and one passage in which Stephen explained elements of the Roman law of property.[9] By and large, however, Stephen put a lot of theology and not much law into his sermons, except, perhaps, for the Pentecostal sermon discussed below. There are eight sermons at the end of the Sainte-Geneviève collection written for the dedication of a church. They very likely represent a sign of

5 Desilve, Letter 46, pp. 59–60, is a good example.

6 Desilve, Letters 85, 87, 91, 294.

7 Desilve, Letters 273, pp. 342–43.

8 Lucien Auvray, "Un Poème rythmique et une lettre d'Étienne de Tournai," *Mélanges Paul Fabre: Études d'histoire du Moyen Âge* (Paris: Alphonse Picard, 1902), 279–91 at 284–90.

8 Stephen C. Ferruolo, *The Origins of the University: The Schools of Paris and their Critics, 1100–1215* (Stanford, CA: Stanford University Press: 1985), 269–77 and 361–64, has a nice sketch of his post-Bologna years, and 362 n. 178 has a list of the manuscripts that contain Stephen's sermons. PL 211.567–76 prints one sermon and the contents of thirty-one more.

9 Warichez, *Étienne de Tournai*, 90 n. 1 from Paris, Sainte-Geneviève, 239 and 616.

Sainte-Geneviève's wealth during Stephen's sixteen years as abbot and his success at establishing dependent churches.[10]

Stephen wrote more than three hundred letters after he returned to France. His legal expertise was in demand by litigants, other clerics, and bishops, and he was involved in a number of court cases.[11] The letters reveal how deeply he became enmeshed in French ecclesiastical affairs. Cardinal Priest Peter of San Crisogono, the papal legate to France, appointed Stephen (*c.* 1175–76) to investigate and gather evidence on the state of the church of Orléans under its notorious bishop Manasses II de Garlande.[12] Peter and Stephen had been old friends, having attended school together in Orléans. After Peter was elevated to cardinal, Stephen wrote a letter to him full of praise and redolent of admiration.[13]

In the first years of Pope Innocent III's pontificate, Stephen, who was by then bishop of Tournai, was involved in several court cases. One of the most important was a dispute between the Countess Matilde and the collegiate church of Seclin, in the diocese of Tournai, over Matilde's right to elect the provost of Seclin. It was a longstanding dispute that eventually made its way to Rome. Innocent's decision was published in many canonical collections.[14] Stephen's letters clearly show that his legal learning was much valued. He also reveals extensive knowledge of Roman and canon law in them. They document his involvement in many legal disputes before he became a bishop. As bishop he would have presided over many cases in his episcopal court.[15]

After Stephen was elected abbot of Sainte-Geneviève (*c.* 1180), Robert de Gallardon, the prior of the Cistercian abbey of Pontigny, asked him about the

[10] Stephen of Tournai, *Sermons* (Paris: Sainte-Geneviève, 1421), fol. 108rb–129va. According to Ferruolo, only one of the sermons in this manuscript appears in the other manuscripts of his sermons. They are in need of an edition. See also Warichez, *Étienne de Tournai*, 81–114, where he lists manuscripts of the sermons in his notes. Also see Johannes Baptist Schneyer, *Repertorium der lateinschen Sermones des Mittelalters für Zeit von 1150–1350* (Beiträge zur Geschichte der Philosophie und Theologie des Mittelalters 43; 11 vols. Münster: Aschendorf, 1969–90), vol. 5, 509–13.

[11] Desilve, Letter 56, pp. 70–71, dated *c.* 1173.

[12] *Decretales ineditae saeculi XII from the Papers of the late Walter Holtzmann*, edn. Stanley Chodorow and Charles Duggan, Monumenta iuris canonici Series B 4 (Città del Vaticano: Biblioteca Vaticana, 1992), no. 6, pp. 11–13.

[13] Desilve, Letter 56, pp. 70–71, *c.* 1173.

[14] *Die Register Innocenz' III. 1: 1. Pontifikatsjahr, 1198/1199, Texte*, edn. Othmar Hageneder and Anton Haidacher, Publikationen des Historischen Instituts beim Österreichischen Kulturinstitut in Rom (Wien: Verlag der Österreichischen Akademie der Wissenschaften, 1964), no. 109, pp. 161–65. Also see Desilve, Letter 9, p. 387.

[15] E.g., Desilve, Letters 1, 2, 3, 16, 36, 38, 70–72, 84, 94, 104, 128, 144, 222, 238, 242, 263, 278, 280, 294.

legal status of three novices who had left the abbey of Grandmont to join the Cistercians at Pontigny. The Grandmont monks, called the "good men," were known for their piety and adherence to a life of poverty. They were far from a dissolute order. That created the legal problem. With their bishop's permission monks were normally permitted to transfer to a monastery with a stricter rule. There could be no doubt that Pontigny was a strict order. Robert asked Stephen whether the novices' original vow at Grandmont bound them to return.

Gratian had treated an analogous problem in Causa 19 of his *Decretum*. Stephen cited a key text of Pope Urban II in Causa 19, in which the pope declared that a monk who transferred to another monastery in spite of his bishop's opposition was permitted to do so because the monk's private law, that is his conscience, trumped public law, that is public authority and law.[16] Stephen argued that the principle of private law that triumphed was the liberty of a person's conscience and was established in the New Testament by 2 Corinthians 17: *ubi autem Spiritus Domini ibi libertas* [where there is the spirit of the Lord, there is freedom]. Stephen's conclusion remained a disputed norm in the canonical jurisprudence on the issue of clerical obedience to superiors until the thirteenth century.[17] In the rest of the letter, Stephen wrote an extended analysis of a cleric's freedom (*libertas*) to follow his conscience:

> By the common law of the canons, clerics should not leave or receive other clerics without the permission of their bishops to whom they owe obedience. By private law, however, which through inspiration of the Holy Spirit is written in their hearts, if they transfer to a monastery or to a body of canons regular, those clerics can be received even if their bishops object. As Pope Urban stated ... "where there is the spirit of the Lord, there is freedom (*libertas*)." [19]

Stephen went on to construct a stout defense of clerical transfers for almost any set of facts. He had already made that very simple point in his *Summa* on Gratian's *Decretum*: "Only those clerics who transfer by reason of true piety

[16] Desilve, Letter 1, p. 5.

[17] See my discussion in *Pope and Bishops: The Papal Monarchy in the Twelfth and Thirteenth Centuries* (Philadelphia: University of Pennsylvania Press, 1984), 101–16.

[19] Desilve, Letter 1, p. 12. This letter also was copied into Dijon, Bibliothèque municipale 189, fol. 3ra–5ra. On fol. 4vb a later scribe provided marginal glosses citing all the texts in C.19 that Stephen had cited in his letter.

(*religio*) and are led by private law cannot be prevented by their bishops."[18] Others became involved in the consciences of the young monks. Peter of Celle wrote two letters to the monks imploring them to remain in the Cistercian monastery.[19] In the end, Stephen sent his letter to Peter, the cardinal bishop of Tusculum, with whom there is some slim evidence he studied in Bologna.[20] Robert de Gallardon had asked the cardinal about the novices' legal status in Stephen's presence. The cardinal instructed Stephen to answer Robert's question.[21] It is clear that Stephen assumed the cardinal would agree with his legal defense of the young monks remaining in Pontigny. It is not clear why the legal troubles of these three young monks attracted such extensive attention. The case is, however, an example how Stephen's expertise could be brought to bear on typical ecclesiastical legal problems.

Stephen's enthusiasm for the idea of clerical *libertas* and his conviction that individuals inspired by the Holy Spirit had a right to freedom of choice are revealed in an undated sermon written for Pentecost in which he embraced again Pope Urban II's concept of private law and explored the concept of *libertas*. Inspired by the story of Pentecost, which he connected with *libertas*, he wrote, "A free understanding is a great grace. The Apostle says, 'where the spirit of the Lord is there is freedom (*libertas*).'"[22] Stephen discerned three dangerous types of *libertas*: "The first freedom (*libertas*) can be said to be freedom of vanity, the second freedom of desire, and the third freedom of power. The first freedom is dangerous, the second is corrupting, and the third wicked"[23] – prose that displayed again his love of rhyming rhetorical

[18] Stephen of Tournai, *Die Summa über das Decretum Gratiani*, edn. Johann Friedrich von Schulte (Giessen: 1891; reprinted Aalen: Scientia Verlag, 1965), 230 does not print the text. Stephen of Tournai, *Summa* to C.19 q.2 *dictum Gratiani ante* c.1 s.v. *Invito vero*: Munich, Bayerische Staatsbibliothek lat. 17162 [=M], fol. 127rb and lat. 14403 [=M1], fol. 83v: "Soli illi qui causa uere religionis transeunt priuata lege ducuntur, et hii ab episcopo inpediri non possunt." As discussed below, Schulte's edition omitted large sections of his text.

[19] *The Letters of Peter of Celle*, edn. and trans. Julian Haseldine (Oxford: Clarendon Press, 2001), Letter 161–62 and Appendix 14, pp. 626–35 and 730–31. Letter 162 is also in Dijon, Bibliothèque municipale 189, fol. 5ra–5rb at the end of Stephen's letter 1.

[20] Werner Maleczek, *Papst und Kardinalskolleg von 1191 bis 1216: Die Kardinäle unter Coelestin III. und Innocenz III*, Publikationen des Historischen Instituts beim österreichischen Kulturisntitut in Rom, Abhandlungen, 6 (Wien: Verlag der österreichischen Akademie der Wissenschaften, 1984), 247 n. 277.

[21] Desilve, Letter 85, p. 100.

[22] Stephen of Tournai, *Sermons* (Paris: Sainte-Geneviève, 1421), fol. 49ra–61rb at 60va: "De hac libertate intelligentie specialiter dicit apostolus ubi spiritus domini ibi libertas."

[23] Ibid., fol. 59r: "Prima libertas dici potest libertas uanitatis, secunda libertas uoluptatis, tertia libertas potestatis. Prima libertas periculosa, secunda uiciosa, tertia maliciosa."

flourishes. Freedom was ambivalent and could be good or bad. After exploring freedom in its many meanings near the end of his sermon, he concludes:

> Then, moreover, freedom (*libertas*) of understanding will be perfect when everyone will be knowledgeable of God, when we will know just as we are known. The freedom of justice is consummated by the will of reason and of the Spirit, sensibility coming with prior consent and excepting no impediment.[24]

In the eleventh and twelfth centuries, liberty was the coin of the realm in the secular and ecclesiastical spheres. Pope Gregory VII touted the liberty of the church, and the barons of England demanded that their liberties be respected and protected.[25] I know of no author in the twelfth or thirteenth centuries who explored the halls of liberty and its meanings as thoroughly as Stephen of Tournai in this sermon.[26] It is clear from his letter and his sermon that his experience outside the classroom and his experience in the French church sharpened his understanding of the issues. He was not yet ready to subject his fellow human beings to the authority of bishops, princes, and the law without their authority being tempered by higher norms and individual consciences.

The dates of Stephen's legal education, teaching, and writing are not certain. Scholars have dated his commentary on Gratian's *Decretum* between 1155 and 1165. Since we have a secure birth date for Stephen of 1128, he normally would have begun studying in Bologna when he was about 20 to 22, roughly from 1148 to 1150. However, we know that he joined St Euverte in Orléans as a canon regular around 1153–55.[27] We can infer from his beautifully crafted letters and sermons that he had extensive training in the liberal arts before he left for Bologna. Perhaps the best but not certain conclusion would be that he did not leave Orléans for Bologna until about 1153. If so, he would have come to Bologna a well-trained and mature 25-year-old.

[24] Ibid., fol. 61ra: "Tunc enim perfecta erit libertas intelligentie quando erunt omnes docibiles Dei, quando cognoscemus sicut et congniti sumus. Tunc etiam consumata erit libertas iusticie cum uoluntati rationis ac spiritus nullo penitus impedimento obstante consensu preambulo sensualitas occurret."

[25] For concepts of *libertas* from the twelfth century onward, see my essay "Ecclesiastical Liberty on the Eve of the Reformation," *Bulletin of Medieval Canon Law* 33 (2016): 185–207.

[26] Ivo of Chartres, *Sermon* 20 for Pentecost dealt with *libertas*, PL 162.592–95; cf. Bernard of Clairvaux, *De gratia et libero arbitrio tractatus*, Chapter 1, PL 182.1003, and Chapter 3, 1005: "triplex sit nobis proposita libertas, a peccato, a miseria, a necessitate ... Dicatur igitur libertas naturae, secunda gratiae, teria vitae vel gloriae." Both may have influenced Stephen's thinking.

[27] Desilve, Letter 215, p. 267.

Stephen was already learned when he arrived in Bologna and fell under the spell of the *os aureum*, Bulgarus.[28] If one may judge by Stephen's comments in his works, Bulgarus made an impression on him that none of his canon law teachers did. Stephen praised Gratian as a great interpreter of canon law in his letters (*magnus ille canonum interpres Gratianus*) and mentioned him frequently in his *Summa*.[29] However, he never called him his master (*magister*). Gratian was always a distant person in Stephen's writings. His extensive use of Rolandus and Rufinus in his *Summa* would justify concluding that he knew not only their works but listened to their lectures in Bologna. He mentioned Rufinus once in his *Summa* as *vir clarissimus* [illustrious man], but this reference is in his commentary on *De consecratione*. The passage might not be his work and is not in all the manuscripts.[30] He could have finished his legal studies around 1157 or 1158 and begun teaching.

It is likely that his *Summa* was a product of his teaching in Bologna and that he wrote a first version of it around 1160. In his comment on Causa 13 question 1, Stephen cited a letter of Pope Hadrian IV (r. December 1154–September 1159) that circulated widely in many decretal collections. He called Hadrian's decretal a "new decree" (*novum decretum*).[31] That comment, together with his remark that "today" Pope Alexander III's election broke the tradition that a new pope should not be elected before the old pope was buried, is persuasive evidence that he wrote his *Summa* while teaching in Bologna and probably at the end of the 1150s or the beginning of the 1160s.[32] The large number of Gratian manuscripts that contain glosses with Stephen's siglum are also proof that the *Summa* is the product of his teaching.[33] Some marginal glosses attributed to him repeat the substance of the comments in the *Summa*. More importantly, only the glosses of teachers grace the margins of legal manuscripts.[34] It is not likely that Étienne wrote his *Summa* or the glosses attributed

[28] Desilve, Letter 44, p. 57: "recolo me fuisse socium vestrum in auditorio Bulgari." See Andrea Padovani, *Perché chiedi il mio nome? Dio, natura et diritto nel secolo XIII*. Il diritto nella storia, 6 (Torino: G. Giappichelli Editore, 1997), 166–69.

[29] Desilve, Letter 1, p. 13.

[30] De con. D.2 c.73, edn. Schulte 275; this text is not in Troyes, Bibliothèque municipale 640.

[31] C.13 q.1, M fol. 101va, edn. Schulte 110.

[32] D.79 c.7, M fol. 37ra, edn. Schulte 102–03.

[33] André Gouron, "Sur les sources civilistes et la datation des Sommes de Rufin e d'Étienne de Tournai," *Bulletin of Medieval Canon Law* 16 (1986): 55–70, reprinted in *Droit et coutume en France aux XIIe et XIIIe siècles*, Variorum Collected Studies Series 422 (Aldershot: Variorum, 1993), no. V, argued for the late date *c.* 1165 while he was in France.

[34] See Rudolf Weigand, *Die Glossen zum 'Dekret' Gratians: Studien zu den frühen Glossen und Glossenkompositionem*, Studia Gratiana 26–27 (Rome: Libreria Ateneo Salesiano, 1991), 586–600 who prints many glosses. Weigand points out that more work has to be done on the paternity of the Ste and St glosses.

to him after he returned to France. His *Summa* and any glosses would not have had avenues to circulate as widely as they did if he had written them in Orléans.[35] If he were a student of law for four to five years in Bologna, that would mean that he taught from about 1159 to 1167, that is, until he moved back to Orléans. He complained about ill health in his letters,[36] and that may be the reason he left Bologna. In any case, he brought his learning in Roman and canon law with him to northern France. All of these dates, except those of his birth and his entering St Euverte, are conjectures but seem most likely from the evidence we have.

Stephen's *Summa* on Gratian's *Decretum* is our primary source for his jurisprudence. Regrettably, Johann Friedrich von Schulte's edition of the *Summa* is a very incomplete and flawed edition. When we compare Schulte's text to the manuscripts, we find that Schulte left out major portions of Stephen's commentary and did not understand the evolution of the text.[37] There is evidence that Stephen made a number of changes to the original text of his *Summa*. A key to understanding the development of his text is the evidence provided by Munich manuscript 17162. It is perhaps the oldest manuscript of his *Summa* and the only manuscript that preserves his first draft.[38] A long text appended to the manuscript contains a revised version of Stephen's comments on Causa 2 question 6. This longer version is found in all the other manuscripts. Since the revised commentary was appended to Munich 17162, there can be no doubt that Stephen wrote this version later and intended that it should replace his original text. The scribe who appended it to his *Summa* in Munich 17162 understood Stephen's intention.[39]

The differences in this section of his *Summa* are many. When Stephen revised his *Summa*, he wrote an introductory tract on appeals to begin Causa 2 question 6 and the short set of glosses at the end of Causa 2 question 6. He labelled his introductory text a *summa* when he referred to it later in Causa

[35] Weigand lists the manuscripts in which Stephen's glosses are found.

[36] Desilve, Letters 47, 155, 250. Warichez, *Étienne de Tournai*, 383–84, citing Letter 172, in which he calls himself a "pusillus homo." However, he uses the word "pusillus"and its derivatives frequently as a term of modesty.

[37] The last analysis of Stephen's manuscripts is Stephan Kuttner, "The Third Part of Stephen of Tournai's Summa," *Traditio* 14 (1958): 502–05.

[38] Weigand, "Studien," 351–52 thought the additions in 17162 that were absent from the later manuscripts might have been added to 17162 later. I argue below that Stephen deleted a text in his revised *Summa* because it conflicted with Bulgarus. Either Weigand or I might be right about some of the texts – or all of them. Only a new edition of the *Summa* in which the editor pays close attention to those passages will resolve the question.

[39] M fol. 181va–184va.

2 question 6.[40] All the other manuscripts known to me have this revised text, which means that the revised text was written early; otherwise it would not have circulated widely. There are other significant textual additions to question 6. For example, in Munich 17162 Stephen did not gloss the excerpt from the *Digest* at C.2 q.6 c.29, but his later version did. Schulte gave a very misleading account of these changes in his edition. Schulte decided to print the longer text he found in seven of his manuscripts and only mentioned the shorter text in Munich 17162 in a note.[41] It is impossible to understand these textual developments from Schulte's notations in his edition.

The reason why Stephen thoroughly revised this section of his *Summa* was that appeals had become a pressing problem for the ecclesiastical courts and in canonical jurisprudence during the second half of the twelfth century. Stephen had written a number of small tracts or *summae* at the beginning of some of the Causae and decided that one was necessary for appeals.[42]

Schulte justified some of his editorial methodology on his belief that Stephen had simply inserted large chunks of text from Paucapalea, Rolandus, and Rufinus into his *Summa*. A comparison of those passages reveals that Stephen most often adapted or altered those texts. He only occasionally copied them word for word. Schulte's edition has made it very difficult to follow Stephen's thought without extensive consultation of the manuscripts. That is particularly unfortunate. His *Summa* was a very important commentary on Gratian in the 1160s and circulated remarkably widely, especially in northern Europe but also, it seems, in Italy into the 1170s and perhaps 1180s. Consequently, for any comprehensive study of Stephen's thought, Schulte's edition must be supplemented by the manuscripts until a new edition is completed.[43]

[40] M1 fol. 46v and fol. 104va (appendix) C.2 q.6 c.41 s.v. *contra ius scriptum*, edn. Schulte p. 185: "Si attendas summam in principio questionis."

[41] Edn. Schulte p. 184 n. 4 and passim.

[42] E.g. Causa 11 on "infamia," Causa 16 q.3 on prescription, C.27 on marriage, C.35 on consanguinity. On the problems that appeals created for the courts, see Stanley Chodorow, "Dishonest Litigation in the Church Courts, 1140–1198," in Kenneth Pennington, Robert Somerville, and Stephan Kuttner, eds., *Law, Church and Society: Essays in Honor of Stephan Kuttner*, The Middle Ages (Philadelphia: University of Pennsylvania Press, 1977), 187–206.

[43] Over thirty manuscripts of Stephen's *Summa* still exist; see the Bio-Bibliographical Guide: amesfoundation.law.harvard.edu/BioBibCanonists/Report_Biobib2.php?record_id=a502. That is an extraordinarily large number. For comparison, we have eighteen manuscripts for Paucapalea, eleven for Rolandus, and twenty-two for Rufinus.

Stephen wrote an extensive prologue to his *Summa* that provides a remarkable window into his thoughts about law and the relationship of law to theology.[44] The twelfth-century decretists commonly prefaced their work with a rather lengthy prologue. Stephen was no exception. Although he borrowed ideas from Ivo of Chartres and his immediate predecessors, Paucapalea, Rufinus, and Rolandus, he began with a novel image. He imagined a theologian and a jurist coming to his *Summa* with their different perspectives:

> If you shall have invited two companions to dinner, you will not serve the same food to their different requests. . . I have invited two friends to dinner, a theologian and a jurist. . . What shall we give and what shall we deny? Do you deny what the other asks?

Because of his education in the schools of Orléans, Stephen was more aware than most jurists of the growing gulf between the disciplines of theology and law. Gratian's *Decretum* was a meal that satisfied theologians and jurists for centuries. Scholars have even debated whether the father of canon law was more a jurist or a theologian.[45] In his last draft, Gratian incorporated a lot of Roman-law texts, but they did not make his thought inaccessible. However, twenty-five years after Gratian had drafted his *Decretum*, the commentaries on it had already been engulfed by the technical terminology and principles of Roman law. It had become more difficult for the educated reader or theologian to enter this thicket of citations and understand the complexities of the arguments. Stephen knew that. He continued:

> If I shall explain the laws in my *Summa* to a learned jurist (*iurisperitus*), he will be vexed. . . If I shall begin to set forth mystical (i.e., anagogical) deeds of the Old and New Testament, the theologian will think my words are useless. Let both step down and let them collude (*colludant*) with each other in a sensible agreement to balance losses [of sophistication] with utility.

Stephen's choice of terminology is striking. Although the term appears in a few other eleventh- and twelfth-century texts, *colludere*, *colludium* is a

[44] The prologue has been given a critical edition by Herbert Kalb, *Studien zur Summa Stephans von Tournai: Ein Beitrag zur kanonistischen Wissenschaftsgeschichte des späten 12. Jahrhunderts*, Forschungen zur Rechts- und Kulturgeschichte 12 (Innsbruck: Universitätsverlag Wagner, 1983), 113–20, and has been translated by Robert Somerville and Bruce C. Brasington, *Prefaces to Canon Law Books in Latin Christianity: Selected Translations, 500–1245* (New Haven, London: Yale University Press, 1998), 194–201.

[45] See Atria A. Larson, *Master of Penance: Gratian and the Development of Penitential Thought and Law in the Twelfth Century* (Washington, DC: Catholic University Press of America, 2013) and John C. Wei, *Gratian the Theologian* (Washington, DC: Catholic University Press of America, 2016).

Roman-law concept that appears often in the *Digest* and the *Codex*. Gratian included one of these texts of the *Digest* in his *Decretum*. Stephen wanted his theological dinner companion to read his *Summa* but also wanted him to spread his intellectual wings.[46] Stephen had no qualms about using Roman law in the church. The canonists, especially Rufinus, had debated the role Roman jurisprudence should play in the ecclesiastical courts in the second half of the twelfth century. Huguccio settled the issue in his great *Summa* and endorsed Étienne's acceptance of Roman law.[47]

In the next section of his prologue, Étienne turned from the metaphor of two diners to the duality of the Christian city:

> In the same city under the same king there are two people. With two people there are two types of life. With two types of life there are two forms of government. From the two forms of government arise two jurisdictions, the city and the church. The king of the city is Christ. There are two peoples and two orders in the church, clerics and laypeople. There are two types of life, the spiritual life and the life of the flesh. There are two types of government, priestly authority and princely power. There are two jurisdictions, divine and human justice, rights, and equity. If each is rendered its due, all things will be harmonious.

The first sentence in Gratian's *Decretum* defined law with a definition that he applied to the entire world: "The human race is ruled by two things, namely, natural law (*ius*) and long observed customs and morals." Stephen expanded Gratian's definition but contracted its breadth by focusing on the city, not the world. He followed Saint Augustine's vision of two cities but transformed the Augustine model of good and evil to focus on the Christian polity divided between the ecclesiastical and the secular. By doing, so Stephen drew sharp lines between ecclesiastical authority and secular power. The two cities were united in their Christian faith and their submission to the kingship of Christ, but separated by the governments that exercised jurisdiction over them. Stephen's "church and state" was not monolithic or unitary.

Stephen turned from human governance to the origins of divine justice, rights, and law (*ius*). A central institution in a system of justice was procedure, that is, how a society determines the guilt or innocence of a person. The jurists

[46] Cod. 7.2.12, 7.16.27, 9.22.15, 9.48.7, 12.63(64).1; Dig. 19.1.13.27, 43.29.3.11, 47.10.15.23, 47.10.17.15, 48.16.1.6; Gratian placed Dig. 48.16.1.6 in his *Decretum* at C.2 q.3 d.p.c.8 and the text from the "Interpretatio" of the Theodosian *Code* C.2 q.3 c.8.

[47] See the fine discussion in Wolfgang Peter Müller, *Huguccio: The Life, Works, and Thought of a Twelfth-Century Jurist*, Studies in Medieval and Early Modern Canon Law 3 (Washington, DC: Catholic University of America Press, 1994), 110–23.

began to experiment with a new system of justice in the middle of the twelfth century that they called the judicial order (*ordo iudiciarius*). These new rules of procedure were meant to replace the Germanic ordeal. Paucapalea was the first to attempt to establish a biblical and theological justification for the new procedure. He connected the Lord's judgment of Adam and Eve in Genesis 3: 12 with the beginnings of court procedure (*ordo iudiciarius*) in his prologue to the *Decretum*. Stephen adopted Paucapalea's trope and expanded it. He pointed out that Adam raised a formal objection (*exceptio*) to the Lord's accusation and shifted the blame from his wife to the serpent or even to the Lord (entrapment). Later in his *Summa*, Stephen became the first jurist to define the essential elements of the *ordo iudiciarius*:

> The defendant shall be summoned before his own judge and be legitimately called by three edicts or one peremptory edict. He must be permitted to have legitimate delays. The accusation must be formally presented in writing. Legitimate witnesses must be produced. A decision may be rendered only after someone has been convicted or confessed. The final decision must be rendered in writing, unless the proceeding was very brief or especially evil.[48]

Stephen added that one could argue that the *ordo iudiciarius* also had its beginnings in the Old Testament, when Moses decreed that the truth could be found in the testimony of two or three witnesses (Deuteronomy 19: 15), or even in the New Testament, when the Apostle Paul said, "If you would have worldly judgments, they should be judged by those who are the most insignificant in the church" (1 Corinthians 6: 4). Paucapalea's and Stephen's argument that the *ordo iudiciarius* had its origins in Paradise, and Stephen's additions of the Old and New Testament texts were embraced by all jurists by the end of the thirteenth century. Later jurists argued that the divine origins of judicial procedure meant that its norms were established by natural law. Consequently, a summons to court, witnesses, and a public decision could not be omitted, even by the emperor or the pope. These principles of due process were encapsulated in the maxim, "Even the devil must be granted a trial."[49]

Just as importantly, the religious, biblical, and theological justification for the new procedure that had already established itself in the ecclesiastical courts made the use of the ordeal for ecclesiastical disputes very problematic. Stephen could categorically state that the ordeal "was from the common

[48] C.2 q.1 s.v. *in manifestis*, text *om.* edn. Schulte, M fol. 57va–57vb.

[49] See the discussion in Kenneth Pennington, *The Prince and the Law: Sovereignty and Rights in the Western Legal Tradition* (Berkeley, Los Angeles, London: University of California Press, 1993), 143–64.

masses and was not introduced and used by those learned in Roman and canon law" in his *Summa*.[50] The *ordo iudiciarius* had triumphed.

After laying out his theory of legislation, in which he described laws as falling into four types – laws that counseled, laws that commanded, laws that gave permission, and laws that prohibited – he turned to the *Decretum* and its compiler in his prologue:

> I will call Gratian the compiler of this work but not the author. He compiled and edited chapters taken from the holy fathers and arranged them. He was not the author or creator, unless perhaps someone wishes to call him an author, since he explicated and explained the opinions of the holy fathers in his paragraphs (i.e. *dicta*).

Stephen did not know Gratian and was not his student. He studied law in Bologna ten to fifteen years after Gratian. He did know how Gratian put the *Decretum* together. And he knew that only one man, Gratian, had done it.

Two manuscripts and a fragment of Stephen's *Summa* contain his glosses to the third part of Gratian's *Decretum*, "De consecratione." Schulte thought the text was Stephen's, but Kuttner argued that an unknown French canonist wrote it. Since the manuscript tradition is complex and not edited adequately, and since neither Schulte's nor Kuttner's argument is conclusive, the question must remain open.[51]

A. J. Carlyle was one of the first scholars to draw attention to Stephen's political thought. He concentrated his analysis on Stephen's theories about law, especially ecclesiastical law, but also Stephen's ideas about custom in secular society. He quoted a text from the *Summa* in which Stephen defined the role of custom in society:

> It does not matter whether custom is written as long as it is supported by reason, or if it is not written as long as it is not contrary to written justice and law (*ius*). But if written law (*ius*) is contrary to custom, and the people who have the power of legislating law (*lex*) and who know that the law (*lex*) is contrary to custom and practice the custom contrary to law (*lex*), in that case custom is preferred to written law (*lex*). It does not matter whether the people declare their will with their consent or with their deeds. The overwhelming consent of everyone in not observing the laws (*lex*), abrogates the laws. However, if they do not know the contrary law (*lex*) it is not abrogated.[52]

[50] C.2 q.5 c.7 s.v. *vulgarem*.
[51] Kuttner, "Third Part," 502–05.
[52] D.1 c.5 s.v. *nec differt*, M fol. 3va, edn. Schulte 9.

Stephen followed Gratian (D.4 statement after c.3), who thought that all law must be approved by the people, and he endorsed a text in the *Institutes* of Roman law (Inst. 1.2.9) that custom imitates law if the people who practice the custom approve it. The power of custom in medieval jurisprudence, however, waned quickly. By the end of the twelfth century, no jurist agreed that custom could abrogate a law promulgated by a prince or legislative body that was contrary to custom. Custom remained an important part of medieval law for centuries, but its authority was greatly limited.

Gratian had raised the question whether the appellate decisions of the Roman Curia had authoritative force, because they were not found in the canons of the early Church (D.19). He argued that they had authority unless earlier papal decrees (*decreta*) or evangelical precepts contradicted them. Stephen granted papal court decisions the same authority as conciliar canons or papal decrees without qualification:

> Because some jurists have said that papal decretal letters (*decretales epistolae*) do not have the force (*vis*) of conciliar canons or papal decrees (*decreta*), this distinction shows that decretals are not of less authority than canons and decrees.[53]

A short time later he states:

> It should be noted that in deciding ecclesiastical cases papal decretals are preferred to fathers of the Church (*expositores sacrorum librorum*). Only the popes have the right to promulgate canons or those decrees that must be considered in the place of canons.[54]

In the second half of the twelfth century, papal decretals were quickly becoming the coin of the realm in canonical jurisprudence. The canonists were slow to work them into their commentaries on the *Decretum*. The earliest glossators cited none or just a few papal decretals. Stephen cited just two.[55] Within twenty years the canonists turned to the *ius novum* of papal decretals frequently. Simon da Bisignano finished his *Summa* on the *Decretum* around 1180 and cited 128 *extravagantes decretales*. The "Age of the Decretal" had begun.

Stephen's attitude towards the jurisprudence of Roman law is particularly intriguing. His writings reveal sophisticated theological training. When he arrived in Bologna, nonetheless, he was captivated by the teaching of

[53] D.19 s.v. *De epistolis*. M fol. 9vb, edn. Schulte 29.

[54] D.20 s.v. *Decretales usque nunc autem queritur*. M fol. 10ra–10rb, edn. Schulte 30.

[55] At D.90 c.10 and C.13 q.1 c.7.

Bulgarus. In his *Summa*, Stephen used Roman law frequently to resolve canonical issues. If we may extrapolate to his entire *Summa* from the evidence of his first version in Causa 2 question 6, Stephen was not very deeply engaged with Roman law when he first wrote his *Summa*. He did not gloss chapter 28 and barely commented on chapter 29, the two most important Roman-law texts in that question. In his revised version, he glossed those two texts and paid close attention to the other Roman-law texts that Gratian included in his *Decretum*.

Another possible example of his grappling with Roman jurisprudence is a gloss he deleted in his revised text. In Causa 11 he had discussed whether a judge could render a decision according to what he knew but for which he had not heard evidence presented in his court. This issue became the subject of extensive juristic commentary in the twelfth and thirteenth centuries. In his first version of the *Summa*, Stephen wrote a long gloss that in certain cases the judge could render a decision according to what he knew but for which he had not heard evidence presented in his court. Bulgarus taught that the judge could not do so under any circumstances.[56] Stephen deleted his contrary gloss when he revised the *Summa*, most likely because he adopted Bulgarus's position.[57] There are many other bits of evidence that give us insight into Stephen's attitude toward Roman law. In his revised *Summa*, he carefully noted when Gratian altered or added words to texts from Justinian's codification.[58] Stephen was not hesitant to criticize Gratian when he thought the Magister misunderstood Roman concepts.[59]

Justinian's Roman law had a pride of place in Stephen's jurisprudence. At Causa 2 question 6, Gratian had added five texts from the *Theodosian Code* (chapters 22–27). In the revised text of his *Summa*, Stephen snorted his displeasure: "All these laws until 'Anteriorum (c.28)' do not have standing today. They are not found in Justinian's codification. We should not pay

[56] For Bulgarus's opinion, see Knut W. Nörr, *Zur Stellung des Richters im gelehrten Prozeß der Frühzeit: Iudex secundum allegata non secundum conscientiam iudicat*, Münchener Universitätsschriften, Reihe der Juristischen Fakultät 2 (München: C. H. Beck'sche Verlagsbuchhandlung, 1967), 18.

[57] C.11 q.1 c.4 s.v. *iudices*, M fol. 88ra, edn. Schulte 212 n.3.

[58] E.g., C.2 q.6 c.29 s.v. *alia civilia* and C.2 q.6 c.31 s.v. *ab observatione*, edn. Schulte 183, *om.* M, the early text.

[59] See Conklin, "Stephen," chapter 1.

much attention to them."[60] It was Roman law, but for Stephen it was not the right kind of Roman law, Justinian's. He made his prejudices explicit in another gloss to a text from the *Theodosian Code* in Causa 11: "That law is from the *Theodosian Code* whose laws are not observed today unless they are found in Justinian's *Codex*."[61] Stephen's implicit point was "Why did Gratian include these texts in his *Decretum*?"

It has been suggested that the theologian whom Stephen invited to dinner in his prologue was the canonist Rufinus, who had an inclination to minimize or even reject the application of Roman jurisprudence in canon law.[62] If Rufinus might have been one of the diners, then it may not be absurd to think that Stephen's imagination pictured the other diner to have been Bulgarus. Stephen saw himself as dining with his old teachers and arbitrating between his two masters. His writings make clear that he inclined towards the majesty of Roman law, but he was far from rejecting theology as a fundamental cornerstone of canonical jurisprudence. He learned at the feet of Bulgarus that ancient Roman jurisprudence had much to offer canon law.

Stephen's vision of the relationship between the two disciplines was the future of canonical jurisprudence. At the end of the twelfth century, every canonist was a Romanist – as well as a jurist who knew a lot of theology. In Stephen's time the maxim did not yet exist that *Legista sine canonibus parum valet, canonista sine legibus nihil* [A Roman law jurist without canon law is a small vessel; a canonist without Roman law is nothing], but the maxim's point was already valid. It is somewhat ironic that a Frenchman would have brought Italian jurists to the dinner table for conversations about ancient Roman jurisprudence.

RECOMMENDED READING

Primary Sources

A listing of Stephen's works, editions, and manuscripts may be seen at: amesfoundation.law.harvard.edu/BioBibCanonists/Report_Biobib2.php?record_id=a502.

Stephen of Tournai. *Die Summa über das Decretum Gratiani*. Edited by Johann Friedrich von Schulte. Giessen: 1891; reprinted Aalen: Scientia, 1965.

[60] C.2 q.6 c.22 s.v. *Propter* M1 fol. 46r, edn. Schulte 181, *om.* M.

[61] C.11 q.1 c.35, s.v. *Quicumque*, M fol. 89vb, edn. Schulte 213.

[62] Kalb, *Studien* 55–56; see Ronald G. G. Knox, "The Problem of Academic Language in Rufinus and Stephan," *Proceedings of the Sixth International Congress of Medieval Canon Law, Berkeley* 1980, Monumenta iuris canonici, Series C 7 (Vatican City: 1985), 109–23.

Lettres d'Étienne de Tournai: Nouvelle edition. Edited by Jules Desilve. Valenciennes, Paris: Lemaitre-Picard, 1893.

Secondary Works

Carlyle, Alexander James. *A History of Mediaeval Political Theory in the West*. 6 vols., especially Volume 2, 180–97. Edinburgh, London: William Blackwood, 1903–36.

Conklin, George. *"The Ecclesiology of Stephen of Tournai, 1128–1203 (Canonist)."* PhD dissertation, University of North Carolina, 1987.

Ferruolo, Stephen C. *The Origins of the University: The Schools of Paris and their Critics, 1100–1215*. Stanford, CA: Stanford University Press, 1985.

Gouron, André. "Sur les sources civilistes et la datation des Sommes de Rufin e d'Étienne de Tournai." *Bulletin of Medieval Canon Law* 16 (1986): 55–70. Reprinted in *Droit et coutume en France aux XIIe et XIIIe siècles*. Variorum Collected Studies Series 422, no. V. Aldershot: Variorum, 1993.

Kalb, Herbert. *Studien zur Summa Stephans von Tournai: Ein Beitrag zur kanonistischen Wissenschaftsgeschichte des späten 12. Jahrhunderts*. Forschungen zur Rechts-und Kulturgeschichte 12. Innsbruck: Universitätsverlag Wagner, 1983.

"Bemerkungen zum Verhältnis von Theologie und Kanonistik am Beispiel Rufins und Stephans von Tournai." *Zeitschrift der Savigny-Stiftung für Rechtsgeschichte*, kanonistische Abteilung 72 (1986): 338–48.

Knox, Ronald G. G. "The Problem of Academic Language in Rufinus and Stephan." *Proceedings of the Sixth International Congress of Medieval Canon Law, Berkeley 1980*, pp. 109–23. Monumenta iuris canonici, Series C 7. Vatican City: 1985.

Kuttner, Stephan. "The Third Part of Stephen of Tournai's Summa." *Traditio* 14 (1958): 502–05.

Pennington, Kenneth, with Wolfgang P. Müller. "The Decretists: The Italian School." *The History of Canon Law in the Classical Period, 1140–1234: From Gratian to the Decretals of Pope Gregory IX*. Edited by Wilfried Hartmann and Kenneth Pennington, pp. 121–73. History of Medieval Canon Law. Washington, DC: Catholic University of America Press, 2008.

Somerville, Robert, and Bruce C. Brasington. *Prefaces to Canon Law Books in Latin Christianity: Selected Translations, 500–1245*. New Haven, London: Yale University Press, 1998.

Viejo-Ximénez, José Miguel. "Esteban de Tournai (Étienne de Tournai, Stephanus Tournacensis)." *Juristas universals*. Edited by Rafael Domingo. 4 vols., 1.359–63. Madrid, Barcelona: Marcial Pons, 2004.

Warichez, Joseph. "Étienne de Tournai et son temps 1128–1203." *Tournai*, Paris: Casterman, 1937.

Weigand, Rudolf. "Studien zum kanonistischen Werk Stephans von Tournai." *Zeitschrift der Savigny-Stiftung für Rechtsgeschichte*, kanonistische Abteilung 72 (1986): 349–61.

3

Guillaume Durand

(c. 1230–1296)

ORAZIO CONDORELLI

BIOGRAPHICAL INTRODUCTION

Guillaume Durand is otherwise known as the *Speculator*, from the title of the work – *Speculum iudiciale* – which earned him the reputation as one of the most authoritative jurists of the European Middle Ages.[1] Thomas Diplovatatius (†1541), tracing Guillaume's biography in the *Liber de claris iurisconsultis*, with keen judgment concluded that, "although Guillaume was French of Provence, nevertheless his genius was nourished in Italy."[2]

Belonging to a family of lower nobility, Guillaume Durand was born in Puymisson, in the diocese of Béziers, around 1230/31, although some historians place his birth a few years later. That he had his first intellectual training between Montpellier and Paris is little more than a hypothesis. In fact, his training as a lawyer and then as a man of government took place in Italy. He studied canon law in Bologna, where he obtained the title of *doctor Decretorum*. His teacher was probably Bernardus Parmensis (†1266), the author of the ordinary apparatus of glosses on the *Liber Extra* of Gregory IX. In the prologue of the *Speculum iudiciale* Guillaume defines himself *inter decretorum professores minimum* [the very least among the professors of *Decretum*];[3] the sentence testifies to a teaching activity on a chair of canon law, perhaps in Bologna, certainly in Modena, approximately in the years 1260–64. In the prologue Guillaume appears – even before as a professor – as

[1] For biographical details, see the works by Falletti, Gaudemet, Roumy, Soetermeer, Viejo-Ximénez, and the essays in the volume *Guillaume Durand, evêque de Mende*, listed below in the Recommended Reading.

[2] Thomas Diplovatatius, *Liber de claris iuris consultis. Pars Posterior*, edn. Fritz Schultz, Hermann Kantorowicz, and Giuseppe Rabotti (Bononiae: Institutum Gratianum, 1968), 174–83, at 182.

[3] I have used the following edition: *Speculi clarissimi viri Gulielmi Durandi*. . ., I–II (Basileae: per Frobenium et Episcopium, 1563), prologue, I, p. 1a.

"subdeacon and chaplain of the pope" (*domini pape subdiaconus et capellanus*), and in other passages he presents himself as *auditor generalis causarum palatii domini pape* [general auditor in the papal curia].[4] This responsibility links the author to the role of a judge that, after a brief period of teaching, he held at the Roman Curia, in the court that was the nucleus from which, in the Avignon period, the Roman Rota originated. In those years the Curia included Henricus de Segusio, whom Urban IV had appointed cardinal of Ostia in 1262. Guillaume calls Henricus *dominus meus*, "my lord": the name is certainly a sign of deference towards a renowned canonist, but at the same time it attests a habit of relationships acquired in the exercise of judicial activity in the Roman Curia.

Guillaume combined with the competence of jurist an undoubted talent as administrator and man of government, which in the following years he placed at the service of the Roman See. Gregory X called him to be part of the papal delegation during the Council of Lyons, in which Guillaume promoted the enactment of some constitutions.[5] In the decades of the 1270s and 1280s, owing to his demonstrated skills and the trust gained at the Apostolic See, Guillaume received numerous charges as administrator of various provinces of the Papal States and as papal legate on missions in central and northern Italy, troubled by the struggles between the factions of the Guelphs and Ghibellines. Contemporary sources and the information that he offers in his works allow us to reconstruct the lines of a very intense life. During the pontificate of Nicholas III, he was sent as legate to Romagna and Tuscany and was *rector et capitaneus generalis* [i.e., general governor] in the Patrimony of St Peter (1278–80). In the early 1280s, during the pontificate of Martin IV, Guillaume first held the charge of vicar *in spiritualibus* [in spiritual matters] of the province of Romagna, and subsequent documentation shows Guillaume engaged in the functions of *rector in temporalibus* [governor in secular matters] in Romagna and *comes et rector generalis* [count and general governor] in Romagna, in Bologna and Urbino, and in the Massa Trabaria.

During his stay in the Roman Curia, Guillaume obtained prebends in the churches of Beauvais and Narbonne. In 1279 Nicholas III conferred on him the deanery of Chartres, with the condition of being ordained presbyter and the obligation to reside there. Martin IV then dispensed with this obligation to

[4] For example, *Speculum*, I.4, *de salariis*, § 2, *de salariis procuratorum et tabellionum*, n. 5 (I, p. 327a).

[5] *In sacrosanctum Lugdun. conc. sub Greg. X Gulielmi Duranti cognomento Speculatoris commentarius*, nunc primum a Simone Maiolo... editus (Fani: apud Iacobum Moscardum, 1569) fol. 1v, v. *Lugdun.*

accommodate Guillaume's stay in Rome for papal service. In April 1285 the chapter of the diocese of Mende, vacant since 1278, elected Guillaume as bishop. Guillaume, however, was held in Italy in the service of the Holy See, so that he was consecrated in 1286 by the archbishop of Ravenna and took effective possession of his diocese only in July 1291. The short stay at Mende was characterized by an intense commitment to the pastoral care of the faithful and the clergy, as well as marked by good relations with King Philip the Fair. But Guillaume's reputation as an excellent administrator was not forgotten at the Roman Curia, and Boniface VIII called him back to Italy with the intention of entrusting him with the episcopal see of Ravenna. Guillaume refused the transfer, yet we find him in the Italian peninsula in 1295, as rector of the Mark of Ancona and Romagna, once again charged with suppressing the rebellions of the cities of Romagna against the government of the Holy See.

Back in Rome, he died on All Saints Day in 1296. He was buried in the Dominican church of Santa Maria sopra Minerva. An epitaph placed on his grave declares incisively the features of his personality and the events of his life.[6] The text celebrates with emphasis his merits as administrator of the Papal States and describes Guillaume as a person who did not hesitate to fight with weapons – "in the manner of a lion" (*more leonis*) – to bring rebel populations back to obedience to the Holy See. *Comes belliger* [warlike count]: with this title the epitaph summarizes these aspects of the personality of Guillaume Durand.

AN OVERVIEW OF GUILLAUME'S WORKS

It may surprise some readers that a man so deeply immersed in practical life was at the same time an extremely prolific writer, deserving of an eminent rank among the medieval authors who distinguished themselves both in legal science and in liturgical science. As far as his legal works are regarded – leaving aside for now the *Speculum iudiciale* and the *Repertorium* – his reputation is also linked to a valuable commentary on the constitutions of the Second Council of Lyons. This work was composed between 1277 and 1289.[7] Although the *apparatus* of Garsia Hispanus was

[6] The epitaph is reported by Diplovatatius, *Liber*, 181–82.

[7] Martin Bertram, "Le commentaire de Guillaume Durand sur les constitutions du deuxième concile de Lyon," in *Guillaume Durand, evêque de Mende (v. 1230–1296). Canoniste, liturgiste et homme politique. Actes de la Table Ronde du C.N.R.S., Mende 24–27 mai 1990*, edn. Pierre-Marie Gy (Paris: Éditions du C.N.R.S., 1992), 95–104.

accepted as the ordinary gloss on the constitutions of Lyons during those two decades, Guillaume Durand's commentary was to be revived in the sixteenth century, when it was printed in Fano by Simone Maiolo (1569).[8]

In the years of quiet spent in Mende, Guillaume devoted himself first of all to laying down the rules of pastoral care, and promulgated the *Instructiones et Constitutiones*, addressed to the priests of the diocese, considered as cooperators in the apostolic office proper to the bishop.[9] Although the *Instructions and Constitutions* are addressed to the clergy, they are of great interest because they reflect the order of Christian life that Guillaume Durand intended to establish and preserve in his diocese.

In those years (1293–95) Guillaume also wrote the *Pontificale*, which in three books outlines the ceremonial and describes the liturgical actions that bishops and prelates must observe in sacred functions. The work is inspired by the *Pontificale Romanum* then in use, rearranging the earlier work with the intention of offering a version of the Roman liturgy that could also be used in other local churches. The *Pontificale* of Guillaume, in turn, served as a model for the revision of the *Pontificale Romanum* ordered in 1485 by Innocent VIII.[10]

The *Rationale divinorum officiorum* is a great treatise on the liturgy.[11] The work was composed between 1286 and 1291. Even in this treatise, Guillaume drew wide inspiration from previous liturgists and was very skilled in collecting the best of what the theological tradition offered him. The *Rationale* stands in the tradition of the allegorical interpretation of the liturgy, proposing to explain the signs and symbols through which the liturgy – which is *lex orandi* in the church – as well as architecture and ecclesiastical art express the mysteries of the Christian religion.

THE *SPECULUM IUDICIALE* IN THE TRADITION OF THE *ORDINES IUDICIARII*

The *Speculum iudiciale* is the work that has given Guillaume Durand an imperishable fame and the nickname of *Speculator*. The *Speculum* is dedicated to Cardinal Ottobono Fieschi, who was elected pope on July 11, 1276

[8] Edition cited above, footnote 5.

[9] *Instructions et constitutions de Guillaume Durand le Spéculateur...*, edn. J. Berthelé and M. Valmary (Montpellier: Imprimerie Delord-Boehm et Matial, 1905).

[10] Edited by Michel Andrieu, *Le Pontifical romain au Moyen Âge*. III. *Le pontifical de Guillaume Durand* (Città del Vaticano: Biblioteca Apostolica Vaticana, 1940).

[11] Guillelmi Duranti, *Rationale divinorum officiorum*, edn. Anselme Davril and Timothy M. Thibodeau, I–III (Turnhout: Brepols, 1995, 1998, 2000).

(taking the name Adrian V), and died a month later, on August 18. The prologue refers to Henricus de Segusio as having died, so the work must have been composed between 1271 and 1276. Scholars have now abandoned the thesis that the work had two subsequent recensions; rather, as happened in many other cases, Guillaume continually updated the work by a process of additions and adjustments.[12] Evidence of this process of composition has been found recently in the ms. Paris, BN, lat. 4255, a codex that reports numerous marginal autograph additions and contains the work in its final version.[13] The circulation of the *Speculum* in law schools was based on the extraordinary usefulness of the work, which immediately gained authority in the milieu of legal science and forensic practice.

The *Speculum iudiciale* represents the peak of the tradition of the *ordines iudiciarii*, that is, those treatises specially dedicated to the exposition of civil and criminal procedure, the first examples of which date back to about the mid-twelfth century.[14] From the beginning, the law of procedure had been the meeting place where civil law and canon law blended together. In this sense, the *ordines iudiciarii* represent an example of integrating the two laws within the system known as *utrumque ius*, or both forms of law: the process outlined in the *ordines iudiciarii* is rightly called the "Romano-canonical process."[15]

The prologue of the *Speculum* is important for understanding the way the author intended the features and the purpose of his work.[16] Speaking of the jurists who preceded him, Guillaume distinguishes them into the two categories of those who had illustrated the "theory of law" (*iuris theorica*) and those who had written works intended for the "practice of law" (*iuris practica*). In

[12] Bertram, "Le commentaire," 265–66.

[13] Vincenzo Colli, "Lo 'Speculum iudiciale' di Guillaume Durand: codice d'autore ed edizione universitaria," in *Juristische Buchproduktion im Mittelalter*, edn. Vincenzo Colli (Frankfurt am Main: Klostermann, 2002), 517–66.

[14] Linda Fowler-Magerl, *Ordo iudiciorum vel ordo iudiciarius. Begriff und Literaturgattung* (Frankfurt am Main: Klostermann, 1984); Franck Roumy, "Les origines pénales et canoniques de l'idée moderne d'ordre judiciaire," in *Der Einfluss der Kanonistik auf die europäische Rechtskultur*. III. *Straf- und Strafprozessrecht*, edn. Mathias Schmoeckel, Orazio Condorelli, and Franck Roumy (Köln, Weimar, Wien: Böhlau, 2012), 313–49.

[15] Knut W. Nörr, *Romanisch-kanonisches Prozessrecht. Erkenntnisverfahren erster Instanz in civilibus* (Berlin, Heidelberg: Springer, 2012).

[16] Knut W. Nörr, "A propos du Speculum iudiciale de Guillaume Durand," *Guillaume Durand*, 63–71. Beatrice Pasciuta, "*Speculum iudiciale* (A *Mirror of Procedure*)...," in *The Formation and Transmission of Western Legal Culture: 150 Books that Made the Law in the Age of Printing*, edn. Serge Dauchy, Georges Martyn, Anthony Musson, Heikki Pihlajamäki, and Alain Wijffels (Cham: Springer, 2016), 37–40; Kenneth Pennington "The Jurisprudence of Procedure," in *The History of Courts and Procedure in Medieval Canon Law*, edn. Wilfried Hartmann and Kenneth Pennington (Washington, DC: Catholic University of America Press, 2016), 125–59, at 151–53.

the first category Guillaume mentions a series of decretists and decretalists, in a list that culminates with Innocent IV and Henricus de Segusio (*dominus meus*), whose memory – says Guillaume, echoing the constitution *Super specula* of Honorius III (X 5.5.5) – shines forever, as the stars of the firmament.[17] According to Guillaume, all of these authors had fully described (*perfectissime*) what pertains to the "theory of law."[18] Guillaume therefore believes that he has little to add to this complex of knowledge – it would be like "adding water to the sea" – and thus he considers it sufficient to refer to his *Repertorium* (*aureum repertorium*), with which he offered a valuable access key to the materials of the legal tradition.[19]

The conspicuous fortune of the *Repertorium*, also known as the *Breviarium*, is testified to by a wide circulation of manuscripts as well as by numerous printed editions, in which the work is transmitted individually or even, starting with the Lyon edition of 1577, together with the *Speculum iudiciale*.[20] Guillaume composed the *Repertorium* in parallel to the *Speculum*. It is a sort of inventory of the main issues dealt with in canon law, and is divided according to the order of *Liber Extra*, that is, into five books subdivided into sections. The issues do not receive a specific argumentative deepening, because Guillaume invites the reader to find the solution in some main texts of reference, primarily in the glosses on the *Decretum* and the *Liber Extra* and in the *lectura decretalium* of Innocent IV. He admittedly conceived the work as a compendium to compensate for the deficiencies of human memory, and he intended it to be useful to all those who, with different roles, have an interest in knowing the law.[21]

Not quite as satisfactory, in Guillaume's opinion, was the doctrinal panorama concerning the *iuris practica*. In the prologue of the *Speculum*, Guillaume enumerates a series of authors who, together with "many others," had written treatises that can be included in a broader sense in the typology of the *ordines iudiciarii*: Pillius, Bagarottus, Tancredus, Roffredus Beneventanus, Ubertus de Bobbio, Ubertus di Bonaccurso, Johannes de Deo, Gratia Aretinus, Bonaguida Aretinus, Jean de Blanot, ending with Egidius de Foscararis from Bologna. Unlike the *iuris theorica*, these writings had not handed down

[17] *Speculum*, prologue (I, p. 2a).
[18] Ibid. (I, p. 2b).
[19] Ibid. (I, p. 3b).
[20] See Lorenzo Sinisi, "Il *Repertorium aureum* di Guglielmo Durante: manoscritti ed edizioni," in press. I thank the author for having allowed me to share the results of his research.
[21] *Aureum Repertorium Guilelmi Duranti*... (Venetiis: per Paganinum de Paganinis Brixiensem, 1496), fol. 3ra.

the doctrine concerning the process "fully" (*ad plenum*).[22] The alleged incompleteness of this field of science and the importance of the matter, therefore, opened a space for the work of Guillaume Durand. Hence the idea of writing the *Speculum iudiciale* was born. The author explains the meaning of the title: in the *Speculum*, or "mirror," all the professional figures in a trial (judges, advocates and notaries, the parties, and the witnesses) can read how their respective tasks (*officia*) must be carried out duly (Latin *rite*) – that is, according to the rules of the process.

Although the thing reflected (in this case, the process and the judgment) is not in the mirror, the mirror nevertheless returns a faithful image of the shape of the mirrored thing.[23] The trope of the mirror was dear to Guillaume, and he uses it differently in his three main works. In the prologue to the *Repertorium*, Guillaume uses the theme of the mirror to signify the lability of memory (those who move away from the mirror forget the image they saw in it).[24] In the conclusion of the *Rationale divinorum officiorum*, Guillaume refers to the image of the mirror to define the features of his work, contrasting the insufficiency of human reason to the unfathomable greatness of the divine mysteries.[25] The passage contains a textual reference to the words of Saint Paul in the first letter to the Corinthians (13: 12): "At present we see indistinctly, as in a mirror, but then face to face." Moreover, *Speculum* is the title chosen for the great work on procedure. In this instance the author, with a good dose of pride and boldness, does not hesitate to boast of the merits for which the *Speculum* is destined to supersede all the procedural treatises of the jurists who preceded him: "let the volumes of the ancients on the process retreat before this mirror of clarity."[26] Guillaume recognizes the unique merit of his work in adhering to the practice of the courts, in the completeness of its treatment – while omitting all superfluous things – and in the synthesis of procedural material into a single volume, which relieves readers from resorting to many texts.[27]

The *Speculum iudiciale* is divided into four books or parts, each subdivided into *particulae* and titles. The first book concerns those involved in any judgment; the second describes the *ordo iudiciarius* in civil cases; the third deals with criminal procedure. The fourth book, divided into titles according to the rubrics of the *Liber Extra*, shows the forms of the libels (*libelli*, written complaints) and the examples of documents (*instrumenta*) that occur both in

[22] *Speculum*, prologue (I, p. 2b).
[23] Ibid. (I, p. 3a).
[24] *Aureum Repertorium*, fol. 3ra.
[25] *Rationale divinorum officiorum*, VIII, conclusion.
[26] *Speculum*, prologue (I, p. 3b).
[27] *Speculum, Conclusio operis* (II, p. 489b).

trials and in contractual practice. What for Guillaume was a source of pride – putting the models of practice, including those used in the Roman Curia, above the various and vacuous opinions of the masters[28] – is also one of features that current scholarship has underscored for appreciating the work: that is, the work documents a medieval procedural law that was constituted by the encounter between the schemes offered by Roman and canon law, the local laws, and the practices and styles of the courts. Historiography has nevertheless highlighted the technical and systematic defects of the *Speculum*, which remains a compilation built on the pyramid of the writings of previous jurists.

Guillaume's contemporaries had already noticed that he used his sources with great ease. A macroscopic case among many is the incorporation in the *Speculum* of the treatise *de summaria cognitione* by the Pisan jurist Johannes Faseolus (Fazioli), whom Guillaume mentions, but without the reader being able to understand that Fazioli is the author of the whole section.[29] The accusation of plagiarism was already formulated by Guillaume's contemporaries: *furtum* (theft) is the word that Johannes Andreae uses, significantly, in recording the places where Guillaume depends on other authors.[30] Yet Johannes Andreae himself increased the authority and circulation of the work with his precious *additiones* (completed in 1346), to which Baldus de Ubaldis (†1400) later added further. The authority that Guillaume's work acquired in a few years and maintained over the centuries is evidenced by the praise of the jurists who read it.[31] It seems that the *Speculum*, a work of jurisprudence as it was, acquired an authority similar to that of a normative source: in this sense, we could interpret a phrase by Albertus Gandinus, according to whom the *Speculum* "multum pro authentico habetur" [i.e., is considered highly authoritative].[32] Johannes Andreae, who had a taste for the history of the literary tradition of medieval law, recognized the singular usefulness of the *Speculum*, in that it contained testimonies of many dispersed works that otherwise would have been largely lost if Guillaume had not collected and

[28] *Speculum*, prologue (I, p. 3b).

[29] Johannes Andreae, *additio "Postremo"*, ad *Speculum*, I.1, *de officio omnium iudicum*, § *Postremo* (I, p. 145a–b) records other cases.

[30] For instance, Johannes Andreae, *additio "Dixit quoque"* ad *Speculum*, III.1, § *de notoriis criminibus* (II, p. 43b).

[31] Diplovatatius, *Liber*, 174–82.

[32] Hermann Kantorowicz, *Albertus Gandinus und das Strafrecht der Scholastik* (Berlin und Leipzig: Walter De Gruyer, 1926), II, 44.

reported them.[33] Johannes Andreae stated that "the exceptional usefulness of this work manifests itself in the facts: since we see that all the experts of both laws, when they face something new or doubtful, find refuge in it, looking for what they want according to the subject matters."[34]

The extraordinary and unquestionable diffusion of the *Speculum iudiciale* in the medieval and modern ages is attested by at least 130 manuscripts and by numerous printed editions, from the first, published in Strasbourg in 1473, to the last, published in Frankfurt in 1668.

MAJOR THEMES AND CONTRIBUTIONS

Although the title *Speculum iudiciale* refers specifically to the theme of the judicial process, the whole reality of law is reflected in the mirror of the process: it was not a coincidence that printed editions of the work often bore the title *Speculum iuris*. The jurisprudence of procedure, in fact, is inscribed in a conceptual framework deeply pervaded by the Christian conceptions of the origins of law (*ius*) and the value of laws (*leges*). This framework involved a reflection on the limits that the law poses to the action of the legislator (the "prince" – emperor, pope, or any other political authority): to what extent can the legislator regulate the process, which finds its fundamental rules in natural law? This conceptual framework required jurists to consider the way in which the *ordo iudiciarius* should be placed at the service of due process and the protection of some subjective situations that in our day we qualify as subjective (fundamental) rights.

IUS AND *LEX* IN THE HISTORY OF HUMANKIND AND THE ORIGIN OF THE PROCESS

Guillaume Durand places the exposition of procedural law into conceptual coordinates common to the jurists of his time. His starting point is the belief that life and human actions are regulated by both divine law (natural and positive) and human law, the latter being the law made by free human action in the spaces made available by divine authority. Divine law, in turn, is expressed both in the order that God established in creating humans as rational beings (*ius divinum naturale*) and through the commands that God, through the divine Word, has addressed to humankind by acting as "legislator"

[33] Johannes Andreae, *additio "Postremo"*, ad *Speculum*, I.1, *de officio omnium iudicum*, § *Postremo* I, p. 145a.

[34] Ibid., p. 145b.

(*ius divinum positivum*). The prologue to the *Speculum iudiciale* expresses these beliefs in an allegorical representation inspired by an image transmitted by the book of the Apocalypse: "From the throne of God come flashes of lightning, rumblings, and peals of thunder, and around it, night and day, the voices of the living creatures with six wings resound"(cf. Revelation 4: 1–8).[35] Guillaume interprets the allegory by explaining that the throne of God is the church, from which miracles (lightning), commandments, and persuasions (voices) arise, and from which the threats (thunders) resound. The living creatures with six wings are the doctors of the church (*ordo doctorum*) who, similarly to the cherub that God posed as guardian of Paradise, have the task of preserving the truth of the orthodox faith and guiding humankind to the salvation of eternal life: this role also belongs to lawyers, with the specificity of their calling.[36] The six wings of the living creatures represent the six laws that followed one another in the history of salvation. The first – in order of time and dignity, as Gratian had said – is the natural law (*lex naturalis*), which God granted to humanity at the moment of creation when breathing life into the first man, made in the image and likeness of God.[37] The Fall of humankind then made it necessary for God to indicate the right way with the *lex mosaica* and the *lex prophetica*. In the fullness of time and at the height of this process, God sent the Son as "legislator" to earth, so that Christ established the law of life and salvation with the *lex evangelica*.[38] From the Gospel law, for the needs of the times and the development of the church, the *lex apostolica* and the *lex canonica* sprang. The complex of these laws – on the one hand the direct or indirect work of the legislator God, and on the other hand the product of action by earthly authorities called to govern the people of God through history – offers solutions for every doubt concerning human conduct.[39] The complex of these *leges* therefore expresses a juridical order of the world that the *scientia iuris* has the task to understand, elaborate, and describe. The subject matter of the *Speculum iudiciale* is the science of the process: in the wake of Paucapalea, Gratian's ancient pupil, Guillaume Durand calls this science *placitandi scientia* [science of the process].This science is extremely necessary – says Guillaume – because unbridled greed, resulting from the corruption of the human condition after the Fall, is the generator of endless

[35] *Speculum*, prologue (I, p. 1b). An examination of the prologue is made by Beatrice Pasciuta, *Il diavolo in Paradiso. Diritto, teologia e letteratura nel Processus Satanae (sec. XIV)* (Roma: Viella, 2015), 141–50.

[36] *Speculum*, prologue (I, p. 1b).

[37] *Speculum*, prologue (I, p. 2a), and IV, *principium* (II, p. 53b).

[38] *Speculum*, prologue (I, p. 2a).

[39] Ibid. (I, p. 2a).

quarrels that mark the lives of people.[40] If litigiousness is a permanent condition of humankind after the Fall, the process and the fundamental rules that govern its development (*iudiciorum ordo et placitandi usus*) originated in Paradise. Here Guillaume proposes an acute intuition that Paucapalea formulated in the prologue to his *Summa Decretorum*,[41] which a few years later was developed by Stephen of Tournai (who seems to find the origins of the *ius divinum* in the origins of the process).[42] God, who knows everything, knew well that Adam and Eve had sinned by eating the forbidden fruit. Yet the Creator wanted to summon Adam ("where are you?" Genesis 3: 9ff.), to accuse him of his guilt. Adam, reproached for his disobedience, dumped on Eve the responsibility for his own actions, just as a defendant can propose an *exceptio*. In the reading of the jurists, therefore, the story recounted in Genesis represented the first process in the history of humanity. The procedures followed in Heaven formed the core of an *ordo iudiciarius* that – as Paucapalea had said already – was confirmed and developed in the Mosaic law when Moses ruled that a judicial fact was to be established only "on the testimony of two or three witnesses" (Deuteronomy 19: 15). If the *ordo iudiciarius* originates in divine law, it is the task of *scientia iuris* to define what the intangible core of this order is, that is, the nucleus that cannot be violated and changed by the human legislator.

Iudicium est actus trium personarum

"Judgment is an act of three persons."[43] This traditional formula – dating back to the time of Bulgarus at least[44] – summarizes the essential structure of the judicial process, based on the relationships among the plaintiff (*actor*), the defendant (*reus*), and the judge (*iudex*). The discussion concerning the parties in the process is a section of the *Speculum* that links issues of procedural and professional ethics with the definition of the rights and duties of the persons involved in the different roles. Although in the history of humanity the process was made necessary because of human litigiousness, Guillaume Durand reminds his readers that Christian ethics requires the faithful to be imitators of Christ in the spirit of peace. No one, therefore, should be inclined to fight:

40 Ibid. (I, p. 3a).
41 *Die Summa des Paucapalea über das Decretum Gratiani*, edn. Johann F. von Schulte (Giessen: E. Roth, 1890), 1.
42 *Die Summa des Stephanus Tornacensis über das Decretum Gratiani*, edn. Johann F. von Schulte (Giessen: E. Roth, 1891), 2.
43 *Speculum*, II.1, *de comparitione in termino*, n. 8 (I, p. 461a).
44 Pennington, "The Jurisprudence of Procedure," 130.

"therefore, in good faith we advise everyone to be more inclined to settle disputes rather than to contend."[45] The advocate plays an important role in achieving this goal.[46] As those who turn to an advocate have the duty to tell him the truth (as they would do with a confessor or a doctor),[47] so advocates must seek and know the truth of the facts and verify that the plaintiff or defendant has evidence to carry on their suit.[48] Moreover, advocates should not favor unjust or reckless causes with their patronage, nor give those causes a positive guise with their allegations, because "what is not supported by reason should not be defended." Guillaume notes, however, that advocates often do not act in this way; rather, they induce parties to sin by informing them that dubious causes can be won by cunning or fraud, through the ignorance of the opposing party, or even with an undue favor of the judge: "and yet this is harmful to the soul, which must be preferred to all things and all appearances."[49]

The role and powers of the judge have an incisiveness that corresponds to the very broad extension of his *officium*.[50] These powers are all the more extended where the law allows the judge to act according to equity, which falls halfway between the rigor of the law and mercy.[51] Guillaume considers with particular favor the judge who acts according to mercy, because this attitude makes the judge an imitator of God's benevolence towards humanity.[52] The extent of the functions of the judge (*officium iudicis*) proved to be particularly effective when it was necessary to find the right remedies in cases in which the Roman law system of *actiones* did not offer an adequate solution to those who demanded justice.[53] Medieval jurists identified contractual relations, the law of succession, and family relations as areas in which the *officium iudicis* could play a particularly effective role. The *officium iudicis* was an instrument that allowed the judge to consider the moral implications underlying the juridical relationships and to realize the *aequitas canonica*.[54] During the trial, the judge enjoys broad powers of substitution with respect to what has been omitted by

[45] *Speculum*, II.1, *de preparatoriis iudiciorum*, n. 9 (I, p. 334b).
[46] James A. Brundage, "The Practice of Canon Law," *The History of Courts and Procedure in Medieval Canon Law*, 51–73.
[47] *Speculum*, I.4, *de advocato*, § *Nunc tractemus*, n. 1 (I, p. 249b).
[48] *Speculum*, I.4, *de advocato*, § *Nunc tractemus*, nn. 3–4 (I, p. 250a).
[49] *Speculum*, I.4, *de advocato*, § *Nunc tractemus*, n. 5 (I, p. 250a).
[50] *Speculum*, I.4, *de officio omnium iudicum*, § I, nn. 2–3 (I, p. 133a).
[51] *Speculum*, I.1, *de dispensatione*, § I, n. 4 (I, p. 56a).
[52] *Speculum*, I.1, *de officio omnium iudicum*, § VI, n. 21 (I, p. 140b).
[53] *Speculum*, I.1, *de officio omnium iudicum*, § II (I, p. 133b).
[54] Charles Lefebvre, "Juge (recours à l'office du)," *Dictionnaire de droit canonique* VI (Paris: Letouzey et Ané: 1954), coll. 208–15.

the parties: if this is always true in matters of law, Guillaume admits that this power can sometimes be exercised also in matters of fact.[55] The function of the judge, however, remains structurally linked to a role of third party and guarantee, which cannot limit or cancel the right of the parties to defense: this role is a logical implication of the maxim *iudicium est actus trium personarum* [Judgment is an act of three persons], which reflects the concept of due process. Therefore Guillaume holds a sharply negative position on an issue that was hotly debated by jurists, namely, whether the judge can judge according to conscience, that is, on the basis of facts not in evidence in the process but personally known to him.[56] According to Guillaume Durand, both in civil and criminal cases the judge must judge according to the things alleged and the evidence presented in the trial (*secundum allegata et probata tantum*).[57]

THE *SUBSTANTIALIA IUDICII*, THE PRINCE, AND DUE PROCESS

Historiography has shown that the doctrine of medieval jurists on judicial procedure is closely intertwined with their conceptions of authority and power.[58] In fact, dealing with the trial meant considering a juridical institution that in their view had originated with the very creation of humankind and whose fundamental structure was governed by natural law. From this perspective, the formula *iudicium est actus trium personarum* acquires a powerful hermeneutical efficacy and expresses the sense of a realistic conception of the process. Thomas Aquinas, basing his conclusion on the authority of Isidore of Seville, had defined law (*ius*) as *ipsa res iusta* [the just thing itself].[59] Regardless of their awareness of this conception, jurists applied it to judicial procedure and thus conceived the trial as an institution intrinsically endowed with a dimension of justice, which manifests itself in its triadic articulation and in the relations of justice that exist among the necessary protagonists in the process (*actor, reus, iudex*).

[55] *Speculum*, II.2, *de disputationibus et allegationibus advocatorum*, § VI, nn. 4–5 (I, p. 705a–b).

[56] Knut W. Nörr, *Zur Stellung des Richters im gelehrten Prozeß der Frühzeit: Iudex secundum allegata non secundum conscientiam iudicat* (München: C. H. Beck'sche Verlagsbuchhandlung, 1967), 83–84.

[57] *Speculum*, II.2, *de disputationibus et allegationibus advocatorum*, § VI, n. 13 (I, p. 706b).

[58] Kenneth Pennington, "Due Process, Community, and the Prince in the Evolution of the Ordo iudiciarius," *Rivista Internazionale di Diritto Comune* 9 (1998): 9–47; idem, *The Prince and the Law, 1200–1600. Sovereignty and Rights in the Western Legal Tradition* (Berkeley: University of California Press, 1993).

[59] Thomas Aquinas, *Summa theologiae*, II^a–IIae q. 57 a. 1 ad 1.

Starting from this realistic conception of law, medieval jurists identified the "ontological foundation" of the process, which is revealed in the doctrine of *substantialia iudicii.*[60] These are the essential elements that define the "substance" of the process (*esse de substantia*):[61] their lack would cause the nullity of the trial and of the resulting sentence. Guillaume deals with this theme at the beginning of the second book of the *Speculum*. Not all the elements (*membra*) of the *ordo iudiciarius* belong to the substance of the process. Guillaume identifies as *substantialia iudicii* the summons (*citatio*), the presentation of the libel that introduces the suit (*libelli oblatio*); the *litis contestatio*, which is the "foundation of judgment," because it determines the matter of judgment; the oath *de calumnia* or *de veritate*; and, finally, the sentence. If any of these elements is omitted or is not performed according to the *ordo iudiciarius*, the sentence is void.[62] To explain the essential nature of these phases of the process, Guillaume proposes an analogy with the celebration of the Mass, in which only the words that consecrate the body and blood of Christ belong to the substance of the Eucharistic sacrifice; other words or formulas belong to the "solemnity" of the Mass, and therefore their omission would not cause the nonexistence of the Eucharistic sacrifice.

The theme of the *substantialia iudicii* not only concerns the autonomy and the different roles of the parties of the process, but also translates into the question of the limits of the power of the *princeps* on the process. In other words, jurists question the limits of human law (secular or ecclesiastical) inasmuch as it touches a substantial element of the process. The problem concerns, in particular, the right of the parties to defense. Guillaume shares with the jurists of his time the rhetoric of the *plenitudo potestatis*, which exalted the fullness of the power of the Roman pontiff with formulas that today appear undoubtedly hyperbolic. As a vicar of Christ, the pope has a "heavenly will" on earth; what pleases the pope has the force of law, and his will prevails over reason, provided his will does not violate Christian faith; no one can question the pope, because the pope cannot be judged by anyone.[63]

This rhetoric could confuse today's reader, but it did not affect the firm beliefs of medieval jurists.[64] They conceived the extent and depth of *plenitudo potestatis* within the limits of the mission that Christ entrusted to the church and in respect of natural and positive divine law. The limits of the *plenitudo*

[60] Nörr, *Romanisch-kanonisches Prozessrecht*, 48–52.

[61] Johannes Andreae, *Apparatus* in Clem. 5.11.2, v. *litis contestationem*.

[62] *Speculum*, II, *principium*, n. 1 (I, p. 333a–b).

[63] *Speculum*, I.1, *de legato* § VI, nn. 51–52 (I, p. 47a–b).

[64] Kenneth Pennington, *Pope and Bishops: The Papal Monarchy in the Twelfth and Thirteenth Centuries* (Philadelphia: University of Pennsylvania Press, 1984), 17–20.

potestatis are emblematically enunciated in the passages of the *Speculum* where Guillaume discusses the power of dispensation of the Roman pontiff. Although this discussion is not an example of a conceptual and systematic order, it clearly emerges that the pope can lawfully exercise the power of dispensation within the limits posed by natural and positive divine law and the constitution of the church (*status Ecclesiae*), and when there is a just cause (*iusta causa dispensationis*).[65] The problem remains as to how the church can react to an unjust act (law or dispensation) of the pope, since his position at the top of the ecclesiastical hierarchy does not allow him to be judged by any human authority (according to the ancient maxim *prima sedes a nemine iudicatur*). Guillaume does not seek solutions that go beyond this traditional principle: for him, the sanction arises on the moral level, because the unlawful act of the pope is a sin that will be judged by God.

How the powers of the *princeps* can affect the structure of the process is a problem that will arise concretely in the decades following the death of Guillaume. In his work the theme of due process is generally touched on with regard to the role of the judge and the right of defense in criminal trials. He strongly emphasizes the centrality of the right of defense in various parts of the *Speculum* where he relied on the teaching of the great decretalists of his time, in particular Innocent IV and Hostiensis. Guillaume is inspired by some decretals that recognized the right of excommunicated people to defend themselves in court. The legal basis for this is connected with the realistic conception of the process and with the legal ontologism that led jurists to talk about the "nature" of various institutes. For instance, "the nature of the right of defense" meant that no one brought to trial may be deprived of the right to defend themselves with *exceptiones* and *replicationes*, lest the innocent often be condemned. Indeed, "for the fact that I was granted the right of defense, as a result I have been granted all the things without which I could not defend myself."[66] In another famous passage of the *Speculum*, Guillaume deals with the problem of an abbot who promoted an inquisitorial process against a monk. Here Guillaume goes so far as to say that the abbot cannot deprive the accused of the right to defend himself, because this right should not be denied to an excommunicate or even to the Devil, if he were summoned to court.[67]

A particularly unusual situation arose with regard to notorious crimes, because the canonical tradition, consolidated in the law of decretals, affirmed that "manifest things do not need proof." Therefore, even Guillaume Durand

[65] *Speculum*, I.1, *de dispensatione*, § *de dispensatione domini Pape* (I, p. 80a–b).
[66] *Speculum*, II.1, *de exceptionibus et replicationibus*, § V, n. 5 (I, p. 500a).
[67] *Speculum*, III.1, *de inquisitione*, § *Ultimo nota*, n. 5 (II, p. 40a–b).

had to admit that, when a crime is notorious, "not observing the order established by law means proceeding according to the order established by law."[68] This situation, however, should not deprive the *reus* of his right to defend himself. Even in notorious crimes, the departure from the usual schemes of the *ordo iudiciarius* could not allow the omission of the summons: "in any case, however, it is required that the *reus* be summoned and, if present in court, hear the fact for which he is sued, and his defense is to be heard... Otherwise the sentence issued on a notorious crime is void."[69] In this context Guillaume does not hesitate to criticize the practice of his times, in which the discretion of the judge appeared to go beyond the limits allowed by the *ordo iudiciarius*. In practice – Guillaume states – judges restricted defendants' right of defense exceedingly, and often condemned people who had not been heard or had not been able to defend themselves: "but certainly, whatever is done, a legitimate defense should not be denied to anybody."[70]

In the first decades of the fourteenth century, some legislative interventions by the popes and emperors urged jurists to deepen the theme of due process. Jean Lemoyne's (†1313) gloss to the decretal *Rem non novam* of Boniface VIII is considered "the most sophisticated and complete summing up of juristic thinking about due process in the late thirteenth and early fourteenth centuries."[71] Lemoyne stated that the summons originates in natural law, so it would not be possible to convict a person who has not been summoned and has not had the opportunity to defend himself. In this context Lemoyne also formulated the conclusion that "everyone is presumed innocent until proven guilty" (*quilibet presumitur innocens nisi probetur nocens*):[72] as far as we know, this was the first statement of a principle that today is considered unquestionable in liberal societies.

The discussions of due process intensified during the conflict that opposed the emperor Henry VII and Robert of Anjou, sovereign of the Kingdom of Naples, in which a relevant part was assumed by Pope Clement V.[73]

[68] *Speculum*, III.1, *de notoriis criminibus* (edn. cit., II, p. 42b).
[69] *Speculum*, III.1, *de notoriis criminibus*, n. 8 (II, p. 43a).
[70] *Speculum*, III.1, *de notoriis criminibus*, n. 13 (II, p. 43b).
[71] Pennington, "Due Process," 34.
[72] Johannes Monachus, gloss to *Extravagantes communes*. 2.3.1, c. *Rem non novam*, v. *Non obstantibus aliquibus privilegiis* (Romae: in Aedibus Populi Romani, 1582). See Pennington, *The Prince*, 160–64; idem, "Due Process," 34–37.
[73] Pennington, *The Prince*, 165–201; Orazio Condorelli, "*Ius* e *lex* nel sistema del diritto comune (secoli XIV–XV)," in *Lex und Ius. Lex and Ius. Beiträge zur Begründung des Rechts in der Philosophie des Mittelalters und der Frühen Neuzeit*, edn. Alexander Fidora, Matthias Lutz-Bachmann, and Andreas Wagner (Stuttgart, Bad Cannstatt: Frommann-Holzboog, 2010), 27–88 (at 53–60).

The conflict reached its climax when Henry VII condemned Robert as a rebel of the empire (April 1313). The emperor had prepared the conditions for the sentence by publishing the constitutions *Ad reprimendum* and *Quoniam nuper*.[74] The former ordered the use of the summary procedure for the condemnation of the offenders of *lèse-majesté* and established that the sentence could also be pronounced against a defaulter (*in absentia*), provided that he had previously been sued according to the procedures provided for in the constitution. The second one defined the legal status of the *rebelles et infideles imperii*. Another protagonist of the story was the Apostolic See. Clement V reacted to the conviction of Robert (leader of the Guelph party in Italy) with the constitution *Pastoralis cura* (March 1314). Between 1312 and 1314 the constitution *Saepe contingit* was issued, which defined the features of the summary process.[75] Law schools inserted the two imperial constitutions in the fifth volume of the *Corpus Iuris Civilis*; the two papal constitutions found space in the *Clementinae*.[76] Important contributions on the theme of due process were developed in the effort to interpret these sources.

It is not possible to explore a debate in which the canonist Johannes Andreae and the civilian Bartolus de Saxoferrato were among the first protagonists. Suffice it to recall that jurists examined in depth the question of the limits of the authority of the prince, which are defined on the basis of the principles of natural law and the doctrine of *substantialia iudicii*, and in relation to the need for the *necessariae probationes* and *legitimae defensiones* to be guaranteed in the summary procedure.[77] In the background of the theoretical reconstructions of the jurists is the model of the trial originated in Paradise, which Paucapalea had imagined and Guillaume Durand had revived in the prologue of the *Speculum*.

CONCLUSION

It would be simplistic to talk about Guillaume Durand as one of the fathers of the science of European procedural law. His intellectual figure and his scientific personality were multifaceted, ranging from theology to liturgy and law. It is also true that the *Speculum iudiciale* is not just a treatise on procedural law, because the mirror of procedure can also return the image

[74] *Constitutiones et acta publica imperatorum et regum* IV.2, edn. Jakob Schwalm (MGH, Legum Sectio 4; Hannover, Leipzig: Hahn, 1911), respectively n. 929, pp. 965f.; n. 931, pp. 966f.

[75] Nörr, *Romanisch-kanonisches Prozessrecht*, 211–20.

[76] Clem. 2.11.2, c. *Pastoralis cura*; Clem. 5.11.2, c. *Saepe*.

[77] The two phrases are contained in the const. *Saepe*.

of the deep roots of medieval Christian conceptions of law. For Guillaume Durand, as for the jurists of his time, procedure is not a mere legal technique to reach the settlement of disputes. Trial is placed on the horizon of law and justice: judgment is called to realize justice, but it is itself a dimension of human experience in which justice is to be realized in the relations among the persons participating in the process. From here, problems arise that today we place in the background of due process and respect for fundamental human rights. The right to judicial protection of one's rights and the right to a fair trial are now listed in the catalogue of fundamental and inviolable human rights in the constitutions of democratic and liberal countries as well as in international conventions such as the *Universal Declaration of Human Rights* (1948) (Articles 8–11) and the *Convention for the Protection of Human Rights and Fundamental Freedoms* (1950) (Article 6). Nowadays, new rights emerge and go along with the traditionally estabilished rights. Today's observer tends to avoid the question concerning the foundation of human rights, including the right to a fair trial. When medieval and modern jurists discussed these issues, they did not hesitate to place their solutions in the background of a juridical order dominated by natural law as humankind's own law (*humanum genus*: Gratian, *dictum ante* D.1), founded on the dignity of the human person created as a rational being.

RECOMMENDED READING

Bertram, Martin. "Le commentaire de Guillaume Durand sur les constitutions du deuxième concile de Lyon." In Gy, *Guillaume Durand, evêque de Mende (v. 1230–1296). Canoniste, liturgiste et homme politique. Actes de la Table Ronde du C.N.R.S., Mende 24–27 mai 1990*, 95–104.

Colli, Vincenzo. "Lo 'Speculum iudiciale' di Guillaume Durand: codice d'autore ed edizione universitaria." In *Juristische Buchproduktion im Mittelalter*, edited by Vincenzo Colli, 517–66. Frankfurt am Main: Klostermann, 2002.

Diplovatatius, Thomas. *Liber de claris iuris consultis. Pars Posterior*, edited by Fritz Schultz, Hermann Kantorowicz, and Giuseppe Rabotti (= *Studia Gratiana* 10), 174–83. Bononia: Institutum Gratianum, 1968.

Falletti, Louis. "Guillaume Durand, ou Durant, souvent appelé le Speculateur." In *Dictionnaire de Droit Canonique*, edited by Raoul Naz, V, 1014–75. Paris: Letouzey et Ané, 1953.

Gaudemet, Jean. "Durand (Durant, Durante), Guillaume (Guglielmo), detto lo Speculatore." In *Dizionario Biografico degli Italiani* XLII, 82–87. Roma: Istituto della Enciclopedia Italiana, 1993.

Gy, Pierre-Marie. *Guillaume Durand, evêque de Mende (v. 1230–1296). Canoniste, liturgiste et homme politique. Actes de la Table Ronde du C.N.R.S., Mende 24–27 mai 1990*. Paris: Éditions du C.N.R.S., 1992.

Nörr, Knut W. "À propos du Speculum iudiciale de Guillaume Durand." In Gy, *Guillaume Durand, evêque de Mende (v. 1230–1296). Canoniste, liturgiste et homme politique. Actes de la Table Ronde du C.N.R.S., Mende 24–27 mai 1990*, 63–71.

Romanisch-kanonisches Prozessrecht. Erkenntnisverfahren erster Instanz in civilibus (Enzyklopädie der Rechts- und Staatswissenschaft, Abt. Rechtswissenschaft). Berlin, Heidelberg: Springer, 2012.

Pasciuta, Beatrice. "*Speculum iudiciale* (A *Mirror of Procedure*) 1271–1276/1296, edn. pr. 1473, Guilelmus Durantis (Guillaume Durand/Durant; William Durand, the Elder) (1230/1232–1296)." In *The Formation and Transmission of Western Legal Culture: 150 Books that Made the Law in the Age of Printing*, edited by Serge Dauchy, Georges Martyn, Anthony Musson, Heikki Pihlajamäki, and Alain Wijffels (Studies in the History of Law and Justice 7), 37–40. Cham: Springer, 2016.

Il diavolo in Paradiso. Diritto, teologia e letteratura nel Processus Satanae (sec. XIV). Roma: Viella, 2015.

Pennington, Kenneth. "The Jurisprudence of Procedure." In *The History of Courts and Procedure in Medieval Canon Law*, edited by Wilfried Hartmann and Kenneth Pennington (History of Medieval Canon Law), 125–59. Washington, DC: Catholic University of America Press, 2016.

"Due Process, Community, and the Prince in the Evolution of the Ordo iudiciarius." *Rivista internazionale di diritto comune* 9 (1998): 9–47.

The Prince and the Law, 1200–1600: Sovereignty and Rights in the Western Legal Tradition. Berkeley: University of California Press, 1993.

Roumy, Franck. "Durand (Durant, Durandi) Guillaume, l'Ancien, dit le Speculator, né vers 1230 à Puymisson (Hérault), mort vers le 1er novembre 1296 à Rome." In *Dictionnaire historique des juristes français XIIe–XXe siècle*, edited by Patrick Arabeyre, Jean-Louis Halpérin, and Jacques Krynen, 381–83. Paris: PUF, 2015.

Soetermeer, Frank P. W. "Wilhelm Durand, Gulielmus Duranti, Durantis (Guillaume Durand) (um 1230/31–1296)." In *Biographisch-bibliographisches Kirchenlexikon* 22 (Nordhausen: Traugott Bautz, 2003), 1527–39.

Viejo-Ximénez, José Miguel. "Guillermo Durando." *Juristas universales*, I, edited by Rafael Domingo, 472–74. Madrid, Barcelona: Marcial Pons, 2004.

4

Jacques de Revigny

(c. 1230–1296)

PAUL J. DU PLESSIS

BIOGRAPHICAL INTRODUCTION

Jacques de Revigny (Jacobus de Ravanis) is an important figure in the history of the development of legal doctrine in Europe.[1] Alongside Pierre de Belleperche (Petrus de Bellapertica), he is commonly described as one of the main representatives of the *Ultramontani* (the School of Orléans), a group of mainly French (but also some Italian) jurists who, during the thirteenth century, came to rival the Glossators of Bologna in their mastering of Roman-law texts. As such, Revigny's work and his influence represent important building blocks in the *translatio studii* from Rome to modernity via the European *ius commune*, since, as will be shown below, the scientific approach and scholarly output of these jurists had a lasting impact on their successors and, in turn, on the development of law in Europe.[2] As is well known, the *ius commune* – the amalgam of Roman, canon, and feudal law developed by successive generations of legal scholars during the late medieval period – came to act as the primordial ooze from which most of the national legal systems of Europe would develop during the early modern period. Although much used, this term is not without controversy. As Mayali observes:

> On the whole, medieval and early modern mentions of the *ius commune* . . . expressed belief in the existence of a common legal language. It exemplified

[1] For a full bibliography of works by and about this author up to 2007, see Hermann Lange and Maximiliane Kriechbaum, *Römisches Recht im Mittelalter Bd. II* (München: Beck, 2007), 518 (par. 57). To this should now be added Marguerite Duynstee, *L'enseignement du droit civil à l'Université d'Orléans du début de la Guerre de Cent Ans (1337) au siège de la ville (1428)* (Frankfurt am Main: Vittorio Klostermann, 2013). See also the entry by Frank Soetermeer on Jacques de Revigny in Patrick Arabeyre, et al. (eds.) *Dictionnaire historique des juristes français, XIIe–XXe siècle* (Paris: Quadrige, 2015), 663–65.

[2] Manlio Bellomo, *The Common Legal Past of Europe: 1000–1800* (Washington, DC: Catholic University of America Press, 1995), for a general survey of this development.

> a form of legal reasoning that governed the understanding of the purpose of law in a given society. The romanization of European legal traditions, from the middle ages to modern times, did not rest only on the strict adoption of rules and procedures that can be traced back to a particular section of Justinian's compilations.[3]

The latter part of this quotation is particularly worth noting. The success of the *ius commune* in the medieval period and of Roman law in the subsequent periods of European legal history cannot be attributed solely to the intellectual sophistication of the rules of law contained in the Justinianic *corpus*. The "culture" of the *ius commune*, reinforced by the idea of an unfolding Roman-law tradition across centuries, was equally important in reinforcing the notion of "legal families" in modernity.

For all Revigny's importance, however, much about his life remains unknown. His date of birth is uncertain, and, although Savigny in his magisterial *Geschichte* suggested a date around 1210/15, modern scholarship broadly supports a later date of 1230/40 based on more recent information regarding his teachers (and thus when he is likely to have attended university).[4] Not much is known about his place of birth, either. He may have been named after a small town in the Lorraine region of France, thus suggesting that either he was born there or his family hailed from there, but it has also been suggested that the Latin version of his name (de Ravanis) could refer to the Italian city of Ravenna.[5]

Even less is known about his life. We do not know, for example, where he undertook his primary education or when he began studying at university. Some information about his teachers (mainly Jean de Monchy, but also Guichard de Langres and Simon Parisiensis) is known, but the picture remains largely incomplete.[6] We know that at least during the first part of his life, he was professor at the University of Orléans. He seemingly also

[3] Laurent Mayali, "The Legacy of Roman Law," in David Johnston (ed.) *The Cambridge Companion to Roman Law* (Cambridge: Cambridge University Press, 2015), 379.

[4] Friedrich Karl von Savigny, *The History of the Roman Law during the Middle Ages: Translated from the Original German of Carl von Savigny* (Westport, CT: Hyperion Press, 1979), on Jacques de Revigny. For a discussion of the later date, see Deon Hurter van Zyl, *Geskiedenis van Die Romeins-Hollandse Reg* (Durban, South Africa: Butterworths, 1979), 116. For a full discussion, see Lange and Kriechbaum, *Römisches Recht im Mittelalter II*, 519.

[5] Anne Halley, "Arts, Law and Other Studies in Orléans in the Twelfth, Thirteenth and Fourteenth Centuries" (PhD thesis, City University of New York, 1979), 153 for an attribution to Lorraine. For other views, see Van Zyl, *Geskiedenis van Die Romeins-Hollandse Reg*, 116.

[6] Olivia Fiona Robinson, T. David Fergus, and William M. Gordon, *European Legal History: Sources and Institutions* (London: Butterworths, 1994), 61; Lange and Kriechbaum, *Römisches Recht im Mittelalter II*, 520.

practiced as a lawyer during this time.[7] In the latter years of his life, Revigny went into the service of the church, first as archdeacon of Toul and later as bishop of Verdun.[8] After retiring as bishop, he moved to Rome, where he died around 1296.[9] In a certain sense, although more contextual information would have been useful for the study of Revigny, the fact that the bare bones are known and that we have a large number of his writings still enables modern scholarship to assign him an important place in the development of law in Europe. Moreover, it is mainly his writings and their impact on subsequent generations of European legal scholars that are of interest to modern legal scholars.

Revigny's association with the church deserves specific comment. In the historiography of the development of law in medieval Europe, the University of Orléans has acquired somewhat of a reputation for producing clergy. This is not an unimportant point, for two reasons. First, it indicates an interaction between Roman and canon law at this law faculty that was different from the situation in Italy. Second, that most of the graduates of Orléans would move into the church bureaucracy suggests a relatively young faculty and student body. As Robinson, Fergus, and Gordon note:

> [N]orth of the Alps, students were almost invariably clerics who could expect to serve kings or princes in the administration of their territories, and to be paid for their services by clerical preferment. . . . This has the side effect, even more marked among teachers of canon law, of keeping down the average age of active scholars, since promotion usually took them away from their studies.[10]

THE SIGNIFICANCE OF THE ULTRAMONTANI

It is important to locate the Ultramontani within the broader context of an intellectual revival that had occurred from the twelfth century onwards in Europe. As Backman notes:

[7] Peter Weimar, "Jacobus de Ravanis (Jacques de Revigny 1230/40–1290)," in Michael Stolleis (ed.) *Juristen. Ein biographisches Lexikon. Von der Antike bis zum 20. Jahrhundert* (München: Verlag C. H. Beck, 1995 [2001]), 329, indicates that although he is said to have been a judge at the *Rota Romana*, there is no evidence to support this assertion.

[8] See Lange and Kriechbaum, *Römisches Recht im Mittelalter II*, 523 for a discussion of some of his problems with Revigny's feudal tenants during his term as bishop. On his term as archdeacon of Toul, see Kees Bezemer, *What Jacques Saw: Thirteenth Century France through the Eyes of Jacques de Revigny, Professor of Law at Orléans* (Frankfurt am Main: Vittorio Klostermann, 1997), 37.

[9] Lange and Kriechbaum, *Römisches Recht im Mittelalter II*, 520–22.

[10] Robinson, et al., *European Legal History: Sources and Institutions*, 61.

> By the end of the twelfth century, the intellectual revival of Europe was far advanced and clearly based on three essential texts: the Sentences for theology, the *Corpus* for secular law, and the *Decretum* for canon law. With these texts one could say that the medieval world had become in an important sense re-Romanized.[11]

The latter part of this quotation, concerning the renewed presence of Roman law as a force within legal studies, is well worth noting, as this presence laid the groundwork, through the *ius commune*, for almost a millennium of legal development. The reasons for the pervasive impact of Roman law upon the late medieval world are summarized by Mayali as follows:

> The success of Roman law was ... conditioned by its perceived historical prestige, but also heightened by its ability to provide suitable solutions to growing legal challenges. In doing so, it also projected a concept of legality that would in turn influence the perception of existing usages and social practices, thus contributing to their conversion into a newly defined customary law.[12]

The development had begun at the University of Bologna, where the first generation of legal scholars, collectively named the Glossators, began to teach Roman law from the newly discovered manuscript of the Justinianic compilation. As a group of scholars, the Glossators were predominantly known for their short notes (either interlinear or marginal) in which issues in the text were explained and supporting or contradictory texts elsewhere were pointed out. As Stein suggests:

> One of the aims of glossatorial scholarship was to discover general principles, or brocards, inherent in the *Corpus iuris*. Some of them were already assembled in the last title of the Digest, dedicated to maxims. Others were detached from their original context and were used as part of an argument on any matter to which they could be made relevant. Their function in litigation was to establish a presumption in favour of the party relying on them, but their exact scope was undefined and frequently they could be met by a counter-proposition, which put forward an opposing view. Collections of brocards appear in the last quarter of the twelfth century.[13]

[11] Clifford Backman, *The Worlds of Medieval Europe* (New York: Oxford University Press, 2015), 241.

[12] Mayali, "The Legacy of Roman Law," 376.

[13] Peter Stein, *Roman Law in European History* (New York: Cambridge University Press, 1999), 48.

The *Glossa Ordinaria*, compiled by Accursius around 1230, is the pinnacle of their intellectual achievement, as it sets out all the most important glosses on the medieval manuscript version of the *Corpus Iuris Civilis*. Although the Glossators continued to be active during the thirteenth century, there was a sense that things had moved on. As Lesaffer notes:

> The civilians who came after Accursius are known in historiography as the post-glossators or the commentators. The differences between the glossators and the commentators did not emerge all of a sudden. They were the result of a slow and gradual shift in the approach to Roman law that had already started with the later glossators.[14]

As the successors to the Glossators, the Ultramontani are commonly credited with having taken a new direction in the study of Roman-law texts. To that end, it is important to note that the Glossators, as a rule, approached Roman legal texts in a dogmatic fashion, without questioning either the order or the content of the texts as presented in the manuscript version of the *Corpus Iuris Civilis* to which they had access. In this sense, they were not interested in textual criticism as such. Backman opines:

> Irnerius [the first Glossator to have pupils] taught Roman law as a system, an organic whole, not merely as a compilation of various bits of legislation ... By glossing the text of the *Corpus* – explaining obscure words, relating various parts of the texts to one another, and showing how the system evolved over time – Irnerius emphasized that Roman law had an organic and inextricable relationship to the society that spawned it and that it, in turn, regulated. Law as represented by the *Corpus*, in short, is a constantly evolving social creation, not a static body of immutable customs.[15]

The method of exegesis of texts employed by the Glossators was primarily aimed at finding supporting and contradicting texts within the body of Roman-law texts. Thus, the Glossators were less interested in the reasoning visible in these texts or indeed in the order of the texts. The historical content visible in the texts was also of little interest to them.

The methods of the Glossators were based on dialectics and scholasticism. These methods were not unknown to other subjects forming part of the *trivium* or the *quadrivium* taught at medieval universities. In fact, there is much to be said for the similarity of method in legal and biblical exegesis in

[14] Randall Lesaffer, *European Legal History. A Cultural and Political Perspective* (Cambridge: Cambridge University Press, 2009), 257.

[15] Backman, *The Worlds of Medieval Europe*, 238.

the works of the Glossators. For the purposes of this discussion, it is important to focus on the meaning of these two terms, dialectics and scholasticism. Although difficult to summarize succinctly, the following two broad definitions will be used. According to the *Penguin History of Philosophy*, the term "dialectic" had its origins in Ancient Greece as "a kind of disputation undertaken as a game or exercise in which questions were asked and answers for the most part had to be 'yes' or 'no.' It resembled the formal cross-examination of a witness in a trial." Similarly, according to the same work, "scholasticism" was a mode of instruction used in medieval law schools: "One important feature that distinguished scholastic from monastic learning was the practice of disputations and the prevalence of learned disputes." These two concepts lay at the heart of law teaching in the Middle Ages.

Apart from these two basic concepts, however, the method of the Glossators contained further peculiarities. As van Caenegem states:

> The glossators had to devise methods and principles for assimilating and comprehending the *Corpus iuris*. Their main aim was like that of the scholastic theologians: just as the theologians aimed by the light of human reason to elucidate a Scripture whose authority was absolute, so the jurists attempted to understand the *Corpus iuris* with the aid of formal logic.[16]

The formal logic mentioned here was the logic derived from Greek philosophy through the use of dialectics. But the Glossators, as the first generation of legal scholars to "rediscover" the collection of Roman law compiled by order of the Emperor Justinian, approached the texts in a very specific way.[17] As any textbook of European legal history will reveal, the approach of the Ultramontani was somewhat different from the Glossatorial method. Peter Stein observes:

> They [the Ultramontani] did not introduce any particular novelty into the teaching of the civil law, but extended certain tendencies which were already observable in Bologna, particularly the use of dialectical reasoning. Instead of

[16] Raoul van Caenegem, *Legal History: A European Perspective* (London; Rio Grande, OH: Hambledon Press, 1991), 48–49.

[17] Franz Wieacker, *Privatrechtsgeschichte der Neuzeit, unter besonderer Berücksichtigung der deutschen Entwicklung* (Göttingen: Vandenhoeck [and] Ruprecht, 1967), 65–66, for a discussion of the peculiarities of their method compared to that of the Glossators. See also Stein, *Roman Law in European History*, 68–69. For a discussion of dialectics in Revigny's works and his use of Aristotelian philosophy, see Lange and Kriechbaum, *Römisches Recht im Mittelalter II*, 538–41. See also Eltjo Schrage and Harry Dondorp, *Utrumque ius: een inleiding tot de studie van de bronnen van het middeleeuwse geleerde recht* (Amsterdam: VU Uitgeverij, 1987), 60 and Donald Kelley, *The Writing of History and the Study of Law* (Aldershot, UK; Brookfield, VT: Variorum, 1987), xi–60.

> the ingenious citation of the texts, they adopted a freer approach, relying on logical argument and frequently extending the *ratio* of a text by analogy to what the Bolognese would have regarded as beyond the permissible limit.[18]

Any new approach to the texts was bound to be controversial, and there is evidence that the Glossators were not impressed with this new method.[19] Thus, according to Robinson, Fergus, and Gordon, some of the Glossators described the Ultramontani as: "airy-fairy philosophers and useless dialecticians, and [. . .] their arguments represented fantasy rather than reason."[20]

In fact, the intellectual contribution of the Ultramontani was far more substantial than this. As Robinson, Fergus, and Gordon observe:

> The willingness of the *Ultramontani* to argue independently of the texts may well owe something to the study of Aristotelian doctrine and to the work of St. Thomas Aquinas. Aquinas reconciled Aristotelian and Christian thought and gave a new importance to the creative role of reason in establishing legal rules where no definite guidance existed from divine or Natural law. He thus gave reason a more positive role than had been allowed to it by St. Augustine, whose approach had tended to dominate thinking up to the thirteenth century.[21]

Thus, as can be seen from these two quotations, the main innovations of the Ultramontani were, first, their ability to use analogy more extensively and to argue in favor of the *ratio* of the text; and, second, their critical approach to the nature and order of the texts in the manuscript editions of the *Corpus Iuris Civilis* available to the Glossators.

Although the relations between these two movements remained strained, there is evidence of eventual acceptance, since one of the great achievements of the Ultramontani is that their method influenced the subsequent generation of Italian legal scholars, the Commentators.[22] And as van Caenegem notes:

> [T]he School of Commentators differs from the glossators in that its authors took a greater interest in the law outside the *Corpus Iuris Civilis*, and in their scholarly work even paid attention to the social realities of the time. Thus

[18] Stein, *Roman Law in European History*, 67–68.

[19] Stein, ibid., 68–69, notes that the first generation of law teachers at Orléans was in fact Italian scholars dissatisfied with the methods of the Glossators. See also Schrage and Dondorp, *Utrumque ius*, 59.

[20] Robinson, et al., *European Legal History: Sources and Institutions*, 62.

[21] Ibid., 62–63.

[22] Ibid., 61.

commentators had firm views on the sources of non-learned law too, such as customs and ordinances.[23]

One cannot help but deduce that this method had its origins in the "real-world" problems faced by teachers of canon law in Orléans during the century before.

THE UNIVERSITY OF ORLÉANS

Not much can be said about the history of the university at which Revigny spent his career. It was a medieval university, in the sense of a fiercely independent community of scholars that operated largely according to its own conventions but with some state interference. The rise of the medieval university is an important aspect of the narrative of the growth of the *ius commune* in Europe during the late medieval period. As Curtius notes:

> With the universities, a new period of medieval legal education begins. In no sense are they, as one reads again and again, a continuation or a renewal of the antique schools of higher learning... Our universities are an original creation of the Middle Ages. Nowhere in the antique world were there any such associations, with their privileges, their established curriculum, their hierarchy of degrees ... The word "university" does not, as is generally believed, mean "the sum total of disciplines" ("universitas litterarum") but the corporation of students and teachers.[24]

French universities were, to a large extent, founded on the medieval Italian model, which as Grendler notes, operated as follows:

> A functioning, whole Italian university had two complementary parts. It possessed a papal or imperial charter authorizing it to confer license and doctoral degrees recognized throughout Christendom. A local college of doctors and the chancellor of the university, often the bishop or his representative, usually exercised the power bestowed by the charter. Possession of a papal or imperial charter permitted a commune to claim that a *studium generale* (university empowered to grant degrees) existed in the town. But this did not necessarily mean that it was a whole university. A university also had to offer advanced instruction in law, arts, medicine, and sometimes theology. A complete, if small, functioning Italian university had a minimum of six to eight professors teaching civil law, canon law, medicine, logic, natural

[23] Van Caenegem, *Legal History: A European Perspective*, 53.

[24] Ernst Robert Curtius, *European Literature and the Latin Middle Ages* (Princeton: Princeton University Press, 1953 [1990 paperback]), 54.

philosophy, and usually rhetoric, but not necessarily theology; in regular classes at an advanced level. Only the combination of charter and teaching made a university.[25]

When Revigny was called to the University of Orléans as professor, it was still a relatively young institution. Located in the north of France, it does not at first appear to have been a place where the teaching of Roman law would flourish. The reason for this, as many textbooks on medieval France will attest, is that the country was broadly divided into a southern part, closer to Italy, where written laws (i.e., Roman law) dominated, and a northern part, where unwritten laws (i.e., French custom) reigned supreme.[26] It must not be forgotten that the south of the country, owing to its proximity to the lands of the Holy Roman Empire, had a much greater cultural association with Roman law than the north. This, no doubt, contributed to a culture of Roman law pervading much of Southern Europe during the late medieval period. As Mundy writes:

> The north was slower to accept Roman law and even bridled at canon law. Not being as unified, France had no "common law" like England's but instead provincial laws. As a result, these "foreign laws" filled up the cracks.[27]

This is not an unimportant point, since it meant that in the north, Roman law was forced to confront a very powerful conception of customary law in a manner in which it was not called upon to do in Bologna or the other medieval Italian universities (with the possible exception of Pavia).

That the emergent French kings were wary of Roman law can be seen in the manner in which the teaching of the subject was curtailed under their influence. A papal bull of 1219 (*Super Speculam*), promulgated by Pope Honorius III, had led to the end of the teaching of Roman law at the University of Paris and had prohibited the teaching of Roman law in the north of France.[28] It has been suggested that the French kings, who drew their

[25] Paul F. Grendler, *The Universities of the Italian Renaissance* (Baltimore, London: Johns Hopkins University Press, 2002), 3–4.

[26] John H. Mundy, *Europe in the High Middle Ages: 1150–1300* (London. New York: Routledge, 2017), 280; Wieacker, *Privatrechtsgeschichte der Neuzeit*, 64. On French customs, see Kees Bezemer, "French Customs in the Commentaries of Jacques de Revigny," Brill Online, and Laurent Waelkens and Jacques de Revigny, *La Théorie de La Coutume Chez Jacques de Revigny: Édition et Analyse de Sa Répétition Sur La Loi De Quibus* (D.1,3,32)(Leiden: Brill, 1984).

[27] Mundy, *Europe in the High Middle Ages*, 280.

[28] Halley, "Arts, Law and Other Studies in Orléans in the Twelfth, Thirteenth and Fourteenth Centuries," 129; Mundy, *Europe in the High Middle Ages*, 292.

divine right to rule from French customary law, engineered this ban.[29] As will be shown below, Orléans, while in the north of the country, was seemingly exempt from this papal ban and thus benefited from the cessation of the teaching of Roman law in Paris.

That there was a difficult relationship between Roman law and the French monarchy can be seen from later evidence; for example:

> In 1312, when Philip the Fair reformed the study of law at the University of Orléans . . . he was careful to specify that the *Corpus iuris* possessed authority within his realm only because it constituted a customary form of law allowed its force by the king.[30]

There is evidence of teaching activities in what would become the University of Orléans as early as 1200. It was only around 1235, however, that Roman law came to be taught there, when the papal bull mentioned above was reinterpreted to exclude the University of Orléans.[31] From then on, both Roman and canon law were taught at Orléans, although not until 1305 did the university receive the right to award degrees and then, in 1306, to become a full-fledged medieval university.[32] Because of the teaching of canon law, Orléans soon gained a reputation as the center of study for future clergy.[33] It must not be forgotten that canon law, as a component of the medieval *ius commune*, had a close relationship with Roman law. As Helmholz observes:

> How and why it happened that the two laws became blended together to form the *ius commune* ... is only a little less difficult to estimate accurately ... That it happened is a fact. That it was a reflection of the medieval belief in the interdependence of the spiritual and secular sides of life is also a live possibility. That the two were the products of the same revival of legal study in the twelfth century furnishes an additional reason for the fusion that occurred. The two were taught side by side in most European

[29] Bezemer, *What Jacques Saw*, 97 on this point.

[30] Paolo Grossi and Laurence Hooper, *A History of European Law* (Chichester, UK; Malden, MA: Wiley-Blackwell, 2010), 45.

[31] Robinson, et al., *European Legal History: Sources and Institutions*, 61. For a discussion of the development of other French universities prior to the founding of the University of Orléans, see Wieacker, *Privatrechtsgeschichte der Neuzeit*, 65.

[32] Halley, "Arts, Law and Other Studies in Orléans in the Twelfth, Thirteenth and Fourteenth Centuries," 128–29.

[33] Robinson, et al., *European Legal History: Sources and Institutions*, 61. On the intellectual environment in Europe generally during this period, see Mundy, *Europe in the High Middle Ages*, 296; Edouard M. Meijers, "De Universiteit Van Orléans in de XIII EEUW," *Tijdschrift Voor Rechtsgeschiedenis/Legal History Review* 2 (1921/1920): 460–518; Robert Feenstra, *L'enseignement du droit a Orléans: état de recherches menée depuis Meijers* (Orléans: Société archéologique et historique de l'Orléanais, 1985).

universities and many aspiring lawyers studied both. This could of course be either a cause or an effect of their interdependence.[34]

REVIGNY'S WORKS

As a professor, Revigny was expect to give daily public lectures, which were free of charge, as well as more specialized lectures, for which students were charged extra. Many of these lectures survive, either as lecture notes by his students or as copies of his own annotations. More specifically, as Weimar has mentioned, his lectures on the *Digestum Vetus*, the *Digestum Novum*, the *Codex*, and the *Institutiones* survive.[35] Jacques de Revigny is known to have produced *lecturae* and *repetitiones* as well as, what Weimar describes as "the first legal dictionary," a *Dictionarium iuris*.[36] Although de Revigny's oeuvre is extensive, his work suffers from two major problems.[37] First, most of it remains only in manuscript form and is therefore accessible only to a small number of specialists who have access to these works and are versed in reading and transcribing medieval paleography. The second problem, exacerbated by the first, is that some of his works have been misattributed to other scholars of the period (e.g., Pierre de Belleperche and Bartolus de Saxoferrato). Anyone consulting his works should therefore consult Lange and Kriechbaum carefully when dealing with the manuscripts to avoid any pitfalls regarding editions or variations in reading.

REVIGNY'S CONTRIBUTION

Popular textbooks on European legal history maintain that the impact of the Ultramontani on the development of law in Europe was twofold. First, their works had a major impact on the Italian Commentators, the successors to the

[34] Richard Helmholz, "Canon Law and Roman Law," in David Johnston (ed.), *The Cambridge Companion to Roman Law* (Cambridge: Cambridge University Press, 2015,) 396–422, at 419.

[35] Weimar, "Jacobus de Ravanis (Jacques de Revigny 1230/40–1290)," 329.

[36] Ibid., 329. The author also notes that an edition of the *Summa feodorum*, sometimes ascribed to Jacobus de Ravanis, has been misattributed.

[37] Mundy, *Europe in the High Middle* Ages, 293–94 on the rise of academic treatises during this period, and 273–76 on a growing general culture of documentation and written pleadings. On Revigny's works, see Van Zyl, *Geskiedenis van Die Romeins-Hollandse Reg*, 116–17. See also Hans van de Wouw, "Quaestiones Aus Orléans Aus Der Zeit Vor Jacques De Revigny," *Tijdschrift Voor Rechtsgeschiedenis / Revue D'Histoire Du Droit / The Legal History Review* 48, no. 1 (1 January 1980): 43–56. For a full discussion, see Lange and Kriechbaum, *Römisches Recht im Mittelalter Bd. II*, 541–46; and Schrage and Dondorp, *Utrumque ius*, 60–64.

Glossators at Italian universities, in the fourteenth century. In turn, given the impact of the Commentators on the creation of the European *ius commune*, the Ultramontani and their ideas therefore had a lasting impact.[38] As Lesaffer noted: "The first law school to introduce a new style and method was that of Orléans in France ... The representatives of this school are not generally included among the commentators but they are regarded as their trail-blazers."[39] Second, and related to the first point, the works of the Ultramontani demonstrated that it was possible to take a different stance towards the authority of Roman-law texts. Unlike the Glossators, whose worldview and approach to these texts were influenced by their location as part of the Holy Roman Empire, the Ultramontani existed outside these boundaries. Thus, among the Ultramontani in northern France, Roman law fulfilled a different and more practical role (especially when studied in conjunction with directly applicable canon law). It is no doubt this approach to the texts, visible in the works of the Ultramontani, that would have such an impact on the Commentators during the fourteenth century.

According to Lange and Kriechbaum, de Revigny's lasting influence can be seen in three areas.[40] First, while familiar with the methods of the Glossators, he was also critical of them and was careful to note where he disagreed with them. Second, even though earlier scholarship maintained that he did not pay much attention to canon law, recent scholarship has shown that he was in fact quite knowledgeable about the subject and that his writings had an impact in the study of canon law as well. Finally, given the relationship between Roman law and customary law in his part of France, his writings are also important for our understanding of the nature of and interaction between learned law and customary during this period.

RECOMMENDED READING

Backman, Clifford R. *The Worlds of Medieval Europe*. New York: Oxford University Press, 2015.

Bellomo, Manlio. *The Common Legal Past of Europe: 1000–1800*. Washington, DC: Catholic University of America Press, 1995.

[38] Lange and Kriechbaum, *Römisches Recht im Mittelalter Bd. II*, 524–29 for a discussion of the various areas of substantive law upon which Jacques de Revigny's work had an impact.

[39] Lesaffer, *European Legal History*, 257.

[40] Lange and Kriechbaum, *Römisches Recht im Mittelalter Bd. II*, 524–25. For an assessment of his influence on specific legal doctrines and branches of law, see the chapters collected in John W. Cairns and Paul J. du Plessis (eds.) *The Creation of the Ius Commune: From Casus to Regula* (Edinburgh: Edinburgh University Press, 2010).

Bezemer, Kees. *What Jacques Saw: Thirteenth Century France through the Eyes of Jacques de Revigny, Professor of Law at Orléans*. Frankfurt am Main: Vittorio Klostermann, 1997.

"French Customs in the Commentaries of Jacques De Revigny." Brill Online. Accessed 20 February 2018. booksandjournals.brillonline.com.ezproxy.is.ed.ac.uk/content/journals/10.1163/157181994x00203?showFullText=pdf.

Caenegem, Raoul C. van. *Legal History: A European Perspective*. London, Rio Grande, OH: Hambledon Press, 1991.

Cairns, John W. and Du Plessis, Paul J. (eds.) *The Creation of the Ius Commune: From Casus to Regula*. Edinburgh: Edinburgh University Press, 2010.

Curtius, Ernst Robert. *European Literature and the Latin Middle Ages*. Princeton: Princeton University Press, 1953 [1990 paperback].

Duynstee, Marguerite. *L'enseignement du droit civil à l'Université d'Orléans du début de la Guerre de Cent Ans (1337) au siège de la ville (1428)*. Frankfurt am Main: Vittorio Klostermann, 2013.

Feenstra, Robert. *L'enseignement du droit à Orléans: état de recherches menée depuis Meijers*. Orléans: Société archéologique et historique de l'Orléanais, 1985.

Grendler, Paul F. *The Universities of the Italian Renaissance*. Baltimore, London: Johns Hopkins University Press, 2002.

Grossi, Paolo, and Laurence Hooper. *A History of European Law*. Chichester, UK; Malden, MA: Wiley-Blackwell, 2010.

Halley, Anne M. "Arts, Law and Other Studies in Orléans in the Twelfth, Thirteenth and Fourteenth Centuries." (PhD thesis, City University of New York, 1979).

Helmholz, Richard. "Canon Law and Roman Law." In Johnston, David (ed.) *The Cambridge Companion to Roman Law*. Cambridge: Cambridge University Press, 2015, 396–422.

Kelley, Donald R. *The Writing of History and the Study of Law*. Aldershot, UK; Brookfield, VT: Variorum, 1997.

Lange, Hermann, and Maximiliane Kriechbaum. *Römisches Recht im Mittelalter Bd. II*. München: C. H. Beck, 2007.

Lesaffer, Randall. *European Legal History. A Cultural and Political Perspective*. Cambridge: Cambridge University Press, 2009.

Mayali, Laurent. "The Legacy of Roman Law." In Johnston, David (ed.) *The Cambridge Companion to Roman Law*. Cambridge: Cambridge University Press, 2015, 374–95.

Meijers, Edouard M. "De Universiteit Van Orléans in de XIII EEUW." *Tijdschrift Voor Rechtsgeschiedenis/Legal History Review* 2 (1921 1920): 460–518.

Mundy, John H. *Europe in the High Middle Ages: 1150–1300*. London, New York: Routledge, 2017.

Robinson, Olivia Fiona, T. David Fergus, and William M. Gordon. *European Legal History: Sources and Institutions*. London: Butterworths, 1994.

Savigny, Friedrich Karl von. *The History of the Roman Law during the Middle Ages: Translated from the Original German of Carl von Savigny*. Westport, CT: Hyperion Press, 1979.

Schrage, Eltjo J. H., and Harry Dondorp. *Utrumque ius: een inleiding tot de studie van de bronnen van het middeleeuwse geleerde recht*. Amsterdam: VU Uitgeverij, 1987.

Soetermeer, Frank. "Jacques de Revigny." In Arabeyre, Patrick et al. (eds.) *Dictionnaire historique des juristes français: XIIe–XXe siècle*. Paris: Quadrige, 2015, 663–65.
Stein, Peter. *Roman Law in European History*. New York: Cambridge University Press, 1999.
Van Zyl, Deon Hurter. *Geskiedenis van Die Romeins-Hollandse Reg*. Durban, South Africa: Butterworths, 1979.
Waelkens, L., and Jacques de Revigny. *La Théorie de la coutume chez Jacques de Revigny: Édition et analyse de sa répétition wur la loi de quibus (D.1,3,32)*. Leiden: Brill, 1984.
Weimar, Peter. "Jacobus de Ravanis (Jacques de Revigny 1230/40–1290)." In Stolleis, Michael (ed.) *Juristen. Ein biographisches Lexikon. Von der Antike bis zum 20. Jahrhundert*. München: Verlag C. H. Beck, 1995 [2001], 329.
Wieacker, Franz. *Privatrechtsgeschichte der Neuzeit, unter besonderer Berücksichtigung der deutschen Entwicklung*. Göttingen: Vandenhoeck [and] Ruprecht, 1967.
Wouw, Hans Van De. "Quaestiones Aus Orléans Aus Der Zeit Vor Jacques De Revigny." *Tijdschrift Voor Rechtsgeschiedenis / Revue D'Histoire Du Droit / The Legal History Review* 48, no. 1 (1 January 1980): 43–56.

5

Pierre de Belleperche

(1247–1308)

YVES MAUSEN

BIOGRAPHICAL INTRODUCTION

Pierre de Belleperche was born in 1247 (according to a conjecture by Kees Bezemer) in the castle of Villars, near Lucenay-sur-Allier in the castellany of Belleperche, to a family of "middle-class" nobility. It was only after his studies in Orléans that he took the surname of his birthplace. Later still, as a royal official, Pierre de Belleperche became lord of Lucenay and had the castle of Villeneuve built, around which the village of Villeneuve-sur-Allier eventually developed.

He led a double life as a clergyman and as a confidant of the king of France.[1] As a cleric, he had a far-from-undistinguished career. He was successively canon of Auxerre, Bourges, and Chartres, and in 1305 Pope Benedict IX made him canon of Notre-Dame of Paris. Shortly after that, he became dean

[1] Little has been written about Pierre de Belleperche, and at the same time a lot has been said. Apart from earlier biographical works – among which need to be cited Félix Lajard's entry, "Pierre de Belleperche, Jurisconsulte," in *Histoire littéraire de la France. Quatorzième siècle*, vol. 25 (Paris: Firmin Didot, frères, fils et cie, 1869), 351–80 – the first decade of the twenty-first century brought forth two major works on our jurist. To these I am greatly indebted. If not indicated otherwise, the reader will find in these works any additional desired information on the aspects of Pierre de Belleperche's life and work highlighted in the present chapter. The first of these authoritative texts is a book by Kees Bezemer, *Pierre de Belleperche: Portrait of a Legal Puritan*, Studien zur europäischen Rechtsgeschichte, Veröffentlichungen des Max-Planck-Instituts für europäische Rechtsgeschichte Frankfurt am Main, vol. 194 (Frankfurt am Main: Vittorio Klostermann, 2005), centered on Belleperche's work and legal thinking. For his generosity in letting me utilize his research and for his helpful final remarks on this chapter, Kees Bezemer deserves my utmost gratitude. The second work comprises two papers by Alain Tardif: "Pierre de Belleperche, juriste et conseiller de Philippe le Bel," *Bulletin de la Société d'émulation du Bourbonnais* 74 (2008): 209–42; and "Recherches sur Pierre de Belleperche. Portrait d'un chancelier discret," *Tijdschrift voor Rechtsgeschiedenis* 77 (2009): 385–421. In November 2016 Alain Tardif unfortunately passed away. This chapter is dedicated to his memory.

of the canons of Paris. In 1306 he was nominated bishop of Auxerre by Pope Clement V at the request of the French king. But it was as a royal officer that he was able to use the best of his skills.

He first became a member of Parliament, and took part in 1298 and 1299 in the exchequer of Normandy, a court competent for cases related to revenue, and in 1302 in the Grands Jours of Troyes, i.e., extraordinary judicial sessions of the Paris Parliament for the Champagne region. In 1304 Belleperche was a member of the court of accounts (*chambre des comptes*), a central sovereign court competent for financial affairs. In 1306 he was named chancellor of France and keeper of the seals, a very high position as an officer of state responsible for the judiciary. A year later, he was replaced as keeper of the seals by Guillaume de Nogaret. This decision was taken at the precise moment when the king launched his attack against the Order of the Knights Templar. Thus, Belleperche did not have to get involved in this new political crusade of the king of France. A few months later, on January 17, 1308, Pierre de Belleperche died. He was probably buried in the choir of Notre-Dame.[2]

To a large extent, his professional abilities emerged from the legal wisdom he acquired as a student and later as a professor at the law school of Orléans. After Pope Honorius III banned Roman law from being taught in Paris, in 1219, so that the faculty of theology should not be drained of its students, civil lawyers gathered in Orléans to resume their studies. In 1235 Pope Gregory IX officially allowed this teaching to take place there, and in January 1306, Pope Clement V turned the law school into a university. From the beginning, Orléans was an important place for the study of Roman law where the gloss by Accursius on the Justinian Code was challenged and, eventually, virtually replaced by new commentaries. Together with Padua, Naples, and Toulouse, Orléans soon became a serious competitor for Bologna, which had been the centre for legal studies.[3] As far as France was concerned, the vast majority of royal officials and even church judges were trained in Orléans. The early students at Orléans included, for example, Yves Hélory de Kermartin, who would be canonized in 1347 and is better known to us as St Yves. Belleperche studied law in Orléans from about 1270 to 1280. His own teacher was Raoul d'Harcourt, a former student of Jacques de Revigny's. He was also following

[2] For a discussion of this fact, see François Pérot, "Esquisse biographique sur Pierre de Belleperche," *Bulletin de la Société Archéologique et Historique de l'Orléanais* 7 (1878–82): 510–14 [513f.].

[3] On the role of the University of Orléans, see Eduard Maurits Meijers, *Etudes d'histoire du droit*, vol. 3, *Le droit romain au moyen âge* (Leiden: Universitaire Pers Leiden, 1959), 108–24.

the lectures of Pierre de la Chapelle, Pierre de Mornay, and, for a short time, Revigny himself.

Belleperche became a professor in his own right around 1277. There was a time when some scholars thought he taught in Toulouse also, but this theory has to be abandoned.[4] Along with Jacques de Revigny's, his name has become indissociable from the fame of the Orléans law school. His first years as a teacher were far from easy, though, with the overpowering presence of Jacques de Revigny and his writings. Nonetheless, manuscripts of Belleperche's lessons are found in libraries all over Europe – in Florence, Naples, Madrid, Paris, Cambridge, Basel, Brussels, and Leiden, among others. Mostly, however, his work as an academic was to be passed on to future generations by one of the Italian students who had the opportunity to listen to him in Bologna: Cynus de Pistoia, about whom, more below.[5]

Belleperche resigned from teaching in 1296. Undoubtedly, he would have liked to stop even earlier, for he writes, *et si scivissem prima die qua veni ad civitatem istam, quod ita diu moratus fuissem ego non remansissem pro mille libris* ("And had I known the first day that I came to this city that I would stay here for that long, I would not have remained for a thousand pounds").[6] He resumed lecturing only once, at the University of Bologna, on the occasion of a diplomatic trip to Italy in 1300. From the end of the thirteenth century on, his public duties were to take up all of his time.

After his resignation in 1296, Belleperche became an adviser to the king of France, Philip IV, the Fair. Far from refusing to recognize Roman law and its merits, the king had always sensed that he could gain from an appropriate use of its juridical techniques and rules of public law, and he had surrounded himself with a team of jurists who had studied in Bologna, Montpellier, Orléans, and elsewhere. Certainly, they did not disappoint the royal expectations, for according to their common opinion, the king was to be considered equivalent to the emperor as far as the powers he was invested with and the independence he enjoyed were concerned. Among these lawyers, Belleperche undoubtedly was one of the most skilled. A telltale sign of the recognition of

4 For a discussion of this opinion, see Lajard, "Pierre de Belleperche, Jurisconsulte," 352f.

5 On Cynus de Pistoia, see Paola Maffei, "Cinus Sinibuldi da Pistoia (Pistoia, 1270 ca.–ivi, 24 dicembre 1336)," *Dizionario biografico dei giuristi italiani (XII–XX secolo)*, edn. Italo Birocchi, Ennio Cortese, Antonello Mattone, and Marco Nicola Miletti (Bologna: Il Mulino, 2013), vol. 1, 543–46. On the reliance of Cynus's work on Pierre de Belleperche's, see also William M. Gordon, "Cinus and Pierre de Belleperche," in his *Roman Law, Scots Law and Legal History: Selected Essays* (Edinburgh: Edinburgh University Press, 2007), 112–25.

6 From *lectura* ad Inst., proem., 8 (edn. Lyon, 1536), quoted by Meijers, *Études d'histoire du droit*, vol. 3, 97.

his talents is the fact that he was sometimes called *pater peritorum*, "father of the experts." As a matter of fact, others than the French king wanted to rely on his expertise concerning political matters. For example, in 1300 the city of Elbing (today Elblag in Poland, which at that time was under the power of Lübeck) sought Belleperche's advice concerning a privilege the Teutonic Order had granted them.[7] During his years in office, Belleperche mainly fulfilled diplomatic missions, notably concerning political conflicts in France during the reign of Philip IV. So, for example, in 1299 he helped to arrange the marriage between the daughter of Philip IV and the son of the emperor in order to heighten the peace to be concluded between France and the Holy Roman Empire. But Belleperche's main missions concerned English and Roman issues.

In 1296, he traveled to the provinces of Berry and Auvergne, which were possessions of the king of England. At the end of 1297, he was sent to the county of Barrois, which the French king wanted to prevent from turning into an ally of England. Once the truce had been agreed upon between France and England, Pierre de Belleperche and Pierre de Grez were sent to Arras in 1299 to decide the fate of Flanders. Eventually, the peace treaty remained silent on this point, even though Belleperche kept himself involved in its preparation: he helped to draft it in Montreuil-sur-mer and was part of the group of emissaries sailing to Canterbury to have it signed by King Edward I. When the war resumed in Flanders in 1300, Pierre de Belleperche and Pierre Flote, who was keeper of the seals at that time, were sent to prevent the French governor Jacques de Châtillon from causing bloodshed in fighting against the rebellious population of Bruges. The two emissaries calmed things down successfully. The final royal ordinance, from November 1301, which decided, among other things, the government of the city of Ghent, might have been inspired by Belleperche as well.[8] After the king's military successes in Flanders in 1304, Belleperche was mentioned again in connection with the peace treaty of Athis signed in 1305.

In 1297, with Pierre Flote, he went to see Pope Boniface VIII in Orvieto, from whom they obtained authorization for the king of France to collect taxes from the clergy. True enough, this success was not all Belleperche's, for the king had extorted the agreement from the pope by freezing the incomes of the

[7] Robert Feenstra, "L'école de droit d'Orléans au treizième siècle et son rayonnement dans l'Europe médiévale," *Revue d'histoire des facultés de droit et de la science juridique* 13 (1992): 23–42 [40].

[8] At least this is A. Tardif's guess, which I am inclined to follow (see "Recherches sur Pierre de Belleperche," 402 and 419).

church in France. Making a concession in turn, the king appointed Belleperche, who was canon of Auxerre at the time, as one of three jurists in charge of collecting money for the Holy Land.

In 1300 Belleperche, together with other clerics, accepted the pope's invitation to celebrate the Jubilee in Rome. He must have had at least the king's permission for this journey. It was on this occasion that he stopped in Bologna and gave a *repetitio* on damages, which Cynus de Pistoia attended. But, as was the case during his years in Orléans, the students showed little respect for his knowledge and interrupted his lesson when he started to criticize Franciscus, the son of Accursius. In 1301 Belleperche was back in Rome, this time in the company of Jean de Dijon, on a secret mission linked, undoubtedly, to the case of Bernard Saisset, bishop of Pamiers, whom the pope had sent to the king as an emissary, but whom the king had had arrested for high treason.

The dispute between Boniface VIII and Philip IV worsened further. Following the convocation of a council of the French bishops called to reform the kingdom of France and the letter *Ausculta fili*, when the pope claimed general superiority over kings, Belleperche was once again sent on a mission, with three French bishops, to Anagni in 1302. At the end of the year, after the pope had published the bull *Unam sanctam*, wherein he claimed his right to judge kings, it was also Belleperche, together with the king's own brother, who made the pope establish diplomatic contact with the king. The reforming ordinance from March 1303, calling for morally irreproachable behavior on the part of royal officials, bears the mark of Belleperche, even though the authorship remains anonymous.[9]

In any case, Belleperche was one of the four royal counselors invested with discretionary power to control and investigate the actions of territorial administrators. It is also very likely that he presented this ordinance to the pope during another mission the same year. After the unfortunate death of Boniface VIII, Belleperche and two other royal officials were sent to Rome to congratulate the new pope, Benedict XI, on his election in 1304. Benedict was anxious to make peace with his predecessor's enemy. He allowed the king again to collect taxes from the clergy and entrusted this task to Pierre de Belleperche and Pierre de Mornay. This is the political background to Belleperche's nomination by the pope as canon of Notre-Dame of Paris. When, in 1305, Philip IV succeeded in imposing his own candidate, Bertrand de Got, as Pope Clement V, he sent Belleperche to convince him to be crowned in Lyon. Clement agreed, and it was during his stay in 1306 that he granted privileges to

9 See Tardif, "Recherches sur Pierre de Belleperche," 407, also citing Méplain.

the school of law of Orléans, where he had been a student himself, and thus transformed it into a university. In fact, it is difficult to imagine that Belleperche did not prompt this decision.

It must be added that on the occasion of the pope's stay in Lyon, at his request and through the mediation of Belleperche, the king negotiated a treaty with the archibishop of Lyon. Already in 1297/98, Belleperche had gone to Lyon on behalf of the king to seek financial help from the local archbishop, who at the same time governed the city as a feudal lord. A few months earlier, Pope Boniface VIII had ordered the archbishop to serve the king's interests. The king's ultimate goal in 1297 – and still in 1305/07 – was to take sole control over the city, large parts of which still belonged to the empire. Not only was Belleperche responsible for the content of the treaty signed in 1305, but he also had to watch over the application of the privileges granted to the church of Lyon by the king in 1307.

During his years in Orléans, considering these two careers, the clerical and the secular one, Pierre de Belleperche did not hesitate to declare his penchant: *Non dubito: si bonum dignitatem secularem haberem, nunquam coronam acciperem* ("I am not in doubt: if I had a secular office, I would never accept the tonsure").[10] His involvement in the business of the church notwithstanding, at heart he was always a lawyer and a statesman. The unequivocal opinions he expressed in his work demonstrate this further.

THE WORK

We have a very incomplete picture of the works of Pierre de Belleperche, for not all of them are accessible through printed sources, and the works that are are not always easy to ascribe to him.[11] In particular, his most important work, the lecture on Justinian's Code, has never been printed (the lecture printed in Paris in 1519 under his name is in fact by Jacques de Revigny).

For the Middle Ages, *lecturae* are the truest possible reflection of a professor's lessons. They were usually written by a student performing the task of reporting. In the case of Belleperche, the reporter's name was William of Braundeston, an Englishman. As for the rest of Belleperche's work, fragments

[10] From *repetitio* on D. 12, 1, 40, v° *Lecta*, ms. Vatican Borghese 277, f° 90 rb, ms. Paris BN lat. 4488, f° 241 ra, quoted and translated by Bezemer, *Pierre de Belleperche*, 153.

[11] A useful survey of this matter is found in Frank Soetermeer, "Petrus de Bellapertica (Pierre de Belleperche), Legist, Gerichtsrat, Diplomat, Berater (ab 1296) und Kanzler (ab 1306) König Philipps IV. des Schönen, * im Dorf Lucenay-sur-Allier (Nivernois), † Januar 1308," *Biographisch-Bibliographisches Kirchenlexikon*, vol. 22 (Nordhausen: Traugott Bautz, 2003), col. 1071–78.

of his lecture on the New Digest were printed in Frankfurt in 1571 as part of a collection of *repetitiones*, and in 1512 an excerpt from his Paris lecture on the Institutes was published, which used a large part of Jacques de Revigny's teaching. In addition to these main lectures, a collection of *repetitiones* was printed first in Paris in 1515 and then again in Frankfurt in 1571, containing forty-nine special lectures on the Code and on the Old Digest, but mixed with texts by Jacques de Revigny. *Repetitiones*, that is, more or less detailed discussions of specific Roman law fragments, were an important feature of the teaching at the Orléans school and distinguished its method from the one followed in Bologna, for example.[12] Over two hundred *repetitiones* by Pierre de Belleperche have been preserved in manuscripts. Finally, a set of *quaestiones* and *distinctiones* was printed in Lyon in 1517, but with added texts by other authors. This editorial situation says much about the knowledge of the Orléans school during the Renaissance but very little about the importance of Belleperche's work in his own time. His teaching certainly was not to be mistaken for that of his rival, Revigny, and notwithstanding the small number of extant manuscripts, it was not overlooked either.

Quite the contrary is true, as is shown by the misattribution of Revigny's work to Belleperche. The success of the latter was such that scholars who do not see the need to bother with the two known manuscripts of his lecture on the Code are able to make up for this shortage by using Cynus de Pistoia's commentary on the same work (issued in print as early as c. 1475) because the Italian drew all too heavily on his teacher's lessons. Cynus's lecture certainly was a great success, with over thirty extant manuscripts. What is more, in its turn the teaching of Cynus was used by one of his own pupils, Bartolus de Saxoferrato. Another author of the same generation frequently expressed his admiration for Pierre de Belleperche: Iohannes Igneus, a professor in Orléans who became a senator of Milan and a frequent guest teacher at the University of Pavia. In these indirect ways, Belleperche's words and ideas were most widely spread and influenced later medieval common law. Nonetheless, Cynus left out numerous considerations that he deemed unnecessary outside the Orléanese context. Some of these considerations are of specific interest to this study, for they show the clerical background of the French law school or deal with questions related to church law, such as the extent of monastic poverty or the scope of immunity.

[12] See C. H. [Kees] Bezemer, *Les répétitions de Jacques de Revigny. Recherches sur la répétition comme forme d'enseignement juridique et comme genre littéraire, suivies d'un inventaire des textes*, (Leiden: Brill, 1987).

Belleperche appears to have been a most individual legal thinker. Not only did he address severe criticisms of Accursius's gloss in particular and the Italian school in general, as he undoubtedly should have, being an exponent of the Orléanese school, but inside his own academic family he either did not get along very well with his senior colleague Jacques de Revigny or did not always value Revigny's scientific methods and opinions very highly.

As a matter of fact, Belleperche's criticisms have their roots in his fundamental attitude towards the Roman-law texts. His approach was systematic, insisting on the internal coherence of the Code or the Digest. Through his use of distinctions and his demonstration of the connection between texts that are dedicated to the same subject matter, he consciously stresses and supplements the original coherence. The awareness of this essential unity ought to have prevented his students both from departing from the original meaning of the texts and from failing to understand their true meaning in the first place. The interpretation was made possible and at the same time limited by the individual context of the laws and the general order of the corpus. In other words, it should be neither too free nor too narrow-minded. Thus, the methods of the liberal arts – and above all dialectics and their exaggerated literalness – were to be avoided at all costs.

Yet an interpretation could never go against the law.[13] Belleperche was promoting a fidelity to the texts with a broader understanding, a fidelity both to their words and to their spirit. Thus, he often refers to the spirit of the law (*mens legis*) only to disprove an opinion, even if the opinion in question is concordant with the letter of a legal text: *Ista lectura veritatem habet et probatur infra de rerum permu, ex placito, tamen non est de mente legis.* ("This reading has truth in it and may be proven [. . .], but it is not about the spirit of the law.")[14] But within this framework, his preference clearly lies with strict interpretations, as he believes largely in the completeness of the *Corpus Iuris Civilis*. The spirit of the law should never claim to go against the written word. Quite the contrary is true, for spirit always has to rest on the letter: *Sed*

[13] See, e.g., in his *repetitio* on D. 16, 3, 32, published by Anne Lefebvre-Teillard, "Une *repetitio* de Pierre de Belleperche sur la 'loi' *Quod Nerva* [D. 16,3,32]," in *Meditationes de iure et historia: Essays in Honour of Laurens Winkel*, edited by Rena van den Bergh, Gardiol van Niekerk, Pascal Pichonnaz, Philip Thomas, Duard Kleyn, Francesco Lucrezi, and Jan Mutton (Pretoria: University of South Africa, 2014), vol. 2, 536–45 [542]: *ille Io. de Blanesco dicit contra [. . .], hoc est contra iura et ideo non tenetur.* ("John de Blano says the contrary [. . .], this is against the laws and therefore cannot hold."

[14] From *lectura* ad C. 2, 3, 27, v° *Petens*, ms. Cambridge, Peterhouse College 34, f° 44 rb, ms. Florence, Biblioteca Medicea-Laurentiana, Plut. 6 sin. 6, f° 73 ra, quoted by K. Bezemer, *Pierre de Belleperche*, 48, n. 25.

quomodo sciam ubi mens legis concurrat? Dico ubi penitus est eadem ratio in casu scripto. ("But how will I know where the spirit of the law concurs? I say where the same reason lies profoundly in the written case.")[15] Only through analogy or, to a lesser extent, by equity, was it conceivable to extend the number of rules beyond the body of law.

For all this severity, Belleperche was not contemptuous of other academic and cultural fields. His knowledge of Aristotle, for example, demonstrates that he participated in the Renaissance of the thirteenth century.[16] Nor was he oblivious of regional customary law. True enough, in the Middle Ages Justinian's *leges* never formed an ivory tower, and from the very first days when they were read in Bologna, they were always construed with regard to contemporary legal practice. However, the practical influence may have been significant mainly in the field of procedural law. Therefore, it is all the more noteworthy that Belleperche opened his own lectures to French customary rules even in matters of private law, although he does not welcome all institutions of French customary law, and his attitude may be more critical than Revigny's. In matters of customary law, too, Belleperche certainly favors a strict interpretation, but, at least in principle, in his view an established and rational custom or statute is no less just law and has no lesser authority than a law found in the *Corpus Iuris Civilis*.

His attitude towards the other body of law governing medieval life, canon law, is still more complicated to fully analyze. In the Middle Ages, the relationship between civil law and canon law was of course more intricate than the apparent symbiosis of *ius commune* would have it. Far from complementing one another, both often held antagonistic positions. It was all the more inevitable that their respective fields should be clearly separated. Belleperche is convinced that it is necessary to limit both the jurisdiction of ecclesiastical courts and the validity of canon law in order to secure Roman law and secular courts their specific areas. As an illustration of his position, he appeals to the image of the two luminaries, the sun and the moon, which is of course based on the Genesis creation narrative, and which Revigny had already employed: *Deus voluit ut iurisdictiones essent distincte. Hinc est quod fecit duo luminaria: unum quod preesset secularibus, aliud quod preesset spiritualibus, ut in aut. quomodo oportet ep., 6 i, coll. i. Item voluit quod unus*

15 From *lectura* ad Inst. 1, 1 (edn. Lyon, 1536), quoted by. Bezemer, *Pierre de Belleperche*, 51, n. 31.

16 See e.g., ibid., 539: *Philosophus dicit in primo libro celi et mundi [. . .]* ("The Philosopher says in the first book on Heaven and earth [. . .]." Lefebvre-Teillard stresses the fact that Pierre de Belleperche seems to have a more precise, so presumably firsthand, knowledge of this text than the other professors in Orléans.

non turbaret alium. ("God wanted the jurisdictions to be distinct. Therefore, he made two luminaries, one which should command the secular affairs, another which should command the spiritual ones [...]. In the same way, he wanted one not to disturb the other.")[17]

In a way, this theory is of course reminiscent of the classical doctrine of the Two Swords, if not for the fact that Belleperche constantly stresses the mutual equality and independence of both jurisdictional powers and of the rules they follow and apply. Concerning crimes, for example, only those committed in direct matters of faith should be assigned to the church courts: *quid tunc appellas crimen canonicum? Dico illud quod immediate respicit fidem catholicam [...] ut crimen hereseos. Istud est crimen canonicum de quo ecclesia habet iurisdictionem.* ("What shall you call a canonical crime? I say one that relates in an immediate way to the catholic faith [...] as for example the crime of heresy. That is a canonical crime over which the church has jurisdiction.")[18] What is more, the distribution of these powers is supposed to have been decided once and for all and cannot be changed by practice, custom, or law: *Sint diverse et separate iurisdictiones nec unus potest aliquid facere de iure pertinenti ad iurisdictionem alterius quod sit in sui preiudicium, set potest bene in sui favorem [...], maxime cum par in parem non habet imperium nec minor in maiorem.* ("May the jurisdictions be diverse and separate, and one cannot do anything concerning a right pertaining to the jurisdiction of the other which would be done to his prejudice, but he rightly can to his favor [...], above all because an equal has no power over another equal, nor does an inferior over a superior.")[19] Such an opinion was of course difficult to hold, especially in late thirteenth- and early fourteenth-century France, where even the academic minds had to come to terms with the policy of King Philip IV. Certainly, this was all the more true for someone who was to become the personal adviser to the monarch, and who already as a professor made no mystery of his allegiance by corroborating the imperial nature of French royal power. Given his personal career, the struggle between both laws might have stirred a twinge of conscience for Belleperche, but eventually he decided according to his loyalty to the French king. Thus, his alleged neutrality was doomed to be short-lived.

[17] From *repetitio* on auth. *Clericus* after C. 1, 3, 32, ms. Cambridge, Peterhouse College 34, f° 17 vb, ms. Florence, Biblioteca Medicea-Laurentiana, Plut. 6 sin. 6, f° 32 rb, quoted by Bezemer, *Pierre de Belleperche*, 101, n. 3.

[18] Ibid.

[19] From *repetitio* on C. 1, 26, 2, v° *Formam*, ms. Cambridge, Peterhouse College 34, f° 156 rb, ms. Douai, Bibliothèque municipale, 648, f° 7 rb, quoted by Bezemer, *Pierre de Belleperche*, 107, n. 16 (translation revised).

Even from a moral point of view, however, Belleperche shows his preference for Roman law. Concerning the law of appeal, for example, the large possibilities opened by canon law are considered unjust and inequitable because they prevent lawsuits from being finished quickly and efficiently. On other points, also, canon law is said to lack rationality compared to Roman law. In general, whenever Belleperche has to underline a contradiction between canon and Roman law, he systematically sides with the latter. Yet for all the criticisms he directs at canon law, the very fact that he discusses canon law at all distinguishes his commentaries from those of Jacques de Revigny. Arguably, this concern of his was linked to his personal status as a cleric, but mainly it allowed him to adress the issues his academic public had to face in everyday life, since most of his students were clerics themselves. As for the canonical literature, Belleperche cites few authors – principally Innocent IV, though even to his work, according to Kees Bezemer, Belleperche refers barely a dozen times in his lectures on the Code and in his *repetitiones*.[20] Even so, once again he does not refrain from criticism, especially when he has the feeling that a canonist does not interpret Roman law properly.

Without question, Pierre de Belleperche was a man of great diplomatic skills who earned the appreciation of the French king as well as of the different popes who came to know him. The least one could say of him as a cleric, however, is that he would not have lived up to the church's expectations – if there had been any! His nominations were largely honorary. Especially in the diocese of Auxerre, he did not leave a lasting impression, having been absent most of the time. But there is more to this than indifference towards the internal administrative business of the church. By reading his lessons, analyzing his legal opinions, and retracing his life as a diplomat, one clearly sees what his heart beats for. It is civil law and the secular power he is interested in, insofar as they ensure social and political order. If his religious convictions had any implications at all for his actions as a jurist, they would consist precisely of his efforts for promoting social peace by strengthening royal power. To this extent, he can possibly be seen as devoted to a certain Realpolitik.

RECOMMENDED READING

Bezemer, Kees. "Pierre de Belleperche: An Early Attempt to Make Public Law a Separate Branch of Legal Science." In *Science politique et droit public dans les facultés de droit européennes (XIIIe–XVIIIe siècles)*, edited by Jacques Krynen and

[20] Bezemer, *Pierre de Belleperche*, 118.

Michael Stolleis, 41–47. Studien zur europäischen Rechtsgeschichte, Veröffentlichungen des Max-Planck-Instituts für europäische Rechtsgeschichte Frankfurt am Main, vol. 229. Frankfurt am Main: Vittorio Klostermann, 2008.

Pierre de Belleperche: Portrait of a Legal Puritan. Studien zur europäischen Rechtsgeschichte, Veröffentlichungen des Max-Planck-Instituts für europäische Rechtsgeschichte Frankfurt am Main, 194. Frankfurt am Main: Vittorio Klostermann, 2005.

Feenstra, Robert. "L'école de droit d'Orléans au treizième siècle et son rayonnement dans l'Europe médiévale." *Revue d'histoire des facultés de droit et de la science juridique* 13 (1992): 23–42.

Gordon, William M. "Cinus and Pierre de Belleperche." In id., *Roman Law, Scots Law and Legal History: Selected Essays*, 112–25. Edinburgh: Edinburgh University Press, 2007.

Lajard, Félix. "Pierre de Belleperche, Jurisconsulte." In *Histoire littéraire de la France. Quatorzième siècle*, vol. 25, 351–80. Paris: Firmin Didot, frères, fils et cie, 1869.

Lefebvre-Teillard, Anne. "Une *repetitio* de Pierre de Belleperche sur la 'loi' *Quod Nerva* [D. 16,3,32]." In *Meditationes de iure et historia: Essays in Honour of Laurens Winkel*, Volume 2, edited by Rena van den Bergh, Gardiol van Niekerk, Pascal Pichonnaz, Philip Thomas, Duard Kleyn, Francesco Lucrezi, and Jan Mutton, 536–45. Pretoria: University of South Africa, 2014.

Meijers, Eduard Maurits. *Études d'histoire du droit*, 3: *Le droit romain au moyen âge*, 95–106. Leiden: Universitaire Pers Leiden, 1959.

Méplain, Ernest. *Les jurisconsultes de l'ancien Bourbonnais, sa législation et son administration judiciaire*, 31–71. Moulins, 1888.

Pérot, François. "Esquisse biographique sur Pierre de Belleperche." *Bulletin de la Société Archéologique et Historique de l'Orléanais* 7 (1878–82): 510–14.

Soetermeer, Frank. "Belleperche (*de Bellapertica*) Pierre de, né vers 1247 (?) à Lucenay-sur-Allier (Nivernais), mort au mois de janvier 1308." In *Dictionnaire historique des juristes français (XIIe–XXe sicèles)*, edited by P. Arabeyre, J.-L. Halpérin, and J. Krynen, 61–62. Paris: PUF, 2007.

"Petrus de Bellapertica (Pierre de Belleperche), Legist, Gerichtsrat, Diplomat, Berater (ab 1296) und Kanzler (ab 1306) König Philipps IV. des Schönen, * im Dorf Lucenay-sur-Allier (Nivernois), † Januar 1308." In *Biographisch-Bibliographisches Kirchenlexikon*, vol. 22, col. 1071–78. Nordhausen: Traugott Bautz, 2003.

Tardif, Alain. "Pierre de Belleperche, juriste et conseiller de Philippe le Bel." *Bulletin de la Société d'émulation du Bourbonnais* 74 (2008): 209–42.

"Recherches sur Pierre de Belleperche. Portrait d'un chancelier discret." *Tijdschrift voor Rechtsgeschiedenis* 77 (2009): 385–421.

6

Charles Dumoulin

(1500–1566)

WIM DECOCK

BIOGRAPHICAL INTRODUCTION

The vicissitudes of life as a legal practitioner and academic during the long period of religious upheaval that characterized early modern France can hardly be illustrated better than through the career of Charles Dumoulin (Lat. Carolus Molinaeus).[1] Born into a noble family of jurists in Paris in 1500, Dumoulin (sometimes spelled Du Moulin) was perhaps destined to become one of the most renowned legal scholars of his age, yet few would have expected him to make life so difficult for himself. By the end of his days, in 1566, Dumoulin had adhered to Catholicism, Lutheranism, and Calvinism, only to convert back to Lutheranism and, eventually, Catholicism on his deathbed. He had spent glorious years in his hometown as a lawyer at the Parlement of Paris, but had also been forced into exile after becoming involved in a diplomatic incident between the French crown and the Holy See concerning the privileges of the Gallican church and the legitimacy of the Council of Trent. And so it happened that, at the age of 52, he began an itinerant life for about five years. It saw him wandering from Basel to Geneva, Strasbourg, Marburg, Tübingen, Montbéliard, and Dole. But, then, Dumoulin was a typical Renaissance man, who preferred following his own convictions rather than obey authority or accept compromises. Perhaps no one has described his idiosyncratic character better than Dumoulin himself. He

[1] The factual information about dates and places in this article draws on Jean-Louis Thireau's unrivalled *Charles Du Moulin (1500–1566). Étude sur les sources, la méthode, les idées politiques et économiques d'un juriste de la Renaissance* (Genève: Droz, 1980) and his entry on Dumoulin in Patrick Arabeyre, Jean-Louis Halpérin, and Jacques Krynen (eds.) *Dictionnaire historique des juristes français (XIIe–XXe siècle)* (Paris: PUF, 2007), 276–78; where conflicting dates are mentioned, preference is given to the latter publication.

relished his independence, boasting that he did not yield to anyone and could not be taught by anyone (*ego qui nulli cedo et a nemine doceri possum*).[2]

Dumoulin may nevertheless have been impressed with the humanist tastes of Jean Pyrrhus d'Angleberme (*c.* 1470–*c.* 1521) and Pierre Taisant de L'Estoile (1480–1537), two law professors at the University of Orléans, where Dumoulin started his legal education at the age of 15.[3] Pyrrhus promoted Greek studies at Orléans, corresponded with Erasmus, and was one of the first commentators on the customary laws of Orléans.[4] Taisant de l'Estoile, also known as Petrus Stella of Orléans, combined traditional legal scholarship with a renewed sense of history and philology.[5] Besides Dumoulin, Stella also counted François Connan and John Calvin among his students. From Orléans, Dumoulin probably went on to study canon law at Poitiers, maybe in order to take specialist courses with Robert Irland (*c.* 1475–1561), but a great deal of uncertainty surrounds this period in his life. He later returned to Orléans to obtain his degree as a *doctor utriusque iuris* (doctorate in both civil and church law) and to lecture on the canon law of the impediments to marriage and the rules of consanguinity in civil and canon law.

From 1522 through 1535, Dumoulin practiced as a lawyer at the Parlement of Paris, although a speech disorder soon led him to concentrate on drafting written counsels rather than pleading before the court. He was hired as a legal adviser to the marshal of Montmorency, the duke of Nevers, and the queen of Navarre. Repeating a topos popular among scholastic jurists at least since the time of Baldus (1327–1400),[6] Dumoulin considered the tribunal as the true school in which to learn the law (*schola fori*), much more than the university. After thirteen years of legal practice, Dumoulin nevertheless chose to dedicate the majority of his time to writing.

Following a trend among French jurists in the first half of the sixteenth century, he started writing a commentary on the customary law of his hometown. Because of illness and financial problems, it took Dumoulin until

2 Franz Gamillscheg, *Der Einfluss Dumoulins auf die Entwicklung des Kollisionsrechts* (Berlin: de Gruyter, 1955), 9.

3 Thireau, *Charles Du Moulin (1500–1566)*, 28.

4 Michel Reulos and Peter G. Bietenholz, "Pierre and Jean Pyrrhus d'Angleberme," in Peter G. Bietenholz and Thomas B. Deutscher (eds.) *Contemporaries of Erasmus: A Biographical Register of the Renaissance and Reformation* (Toronto: University of Toronto Press, 1985), vol. 1, 57–58.

5 Steven W. Rowan, "Petrus Stella," in Bietenholz and Deutscher, *Contemporaries of Erasmus*, vol. 3, 284.

6 Wim Decock, "Elegant Scholastic Humanism? Arias Piñel's (1515–1563) Critical Revision of Laesio enormis," in Paul J. du Plessis and John W. Cairns (eds.) *Reassessing Legal Humanism and its Claims: Petere fontes?* (Edinburgh: Edinburgh University Press, 2016), 139.

1552 to finish this commentary (*Commentarii in consuetudines Parisienses*). In 1539, he managed to publish the first title on feudal law with the help of François Baudouin (1520–73), a student of the Louvain humanist jurist Gabriel Mudaeus. Baudouin, a life-long friend of Dumoulin, served as his secretary while editing the volume on feudal law.[7] The work established Dumoulin's reputation as a first-rank legal scholar.[8]

However, Dumoulin's increased exposure to the religious reform movement from around 1540 on,[9] combined with the need to address the dire state of his financial affairs, diverted his attention from his initial project of commenting on the customs of Paris. Instead, he prepared a commentary on the *Consilia* of the popular Italian jurist Alessandro Tartagni (1423/24–1477). Commentaries on the *Consilia* of Filippo Decio (1454–1536), another protagonist of the early modern *mos italicus*, would follow. Inspired by the new Protestant view on interest-taking, Dumoulin composed a treatise on commerce, contracts, rents, and money, the *Tractatus commerciorum, contractuum, redituumque pecunia constitutorum et monetarum* (1545). A French summary of the work (*Sommaire du Traité des usures*) appeared in 1547, and constituted not only one of the first juridical treatises in French but also an early symptom of the rise of vernacular humanism in the second half of the sixteenth century in France.[10] He complemented the *Tractatus commerciorum* with a treatise on damages and interests (*Tractatus de eo quod interest*, 1546). On the occasion of a lawsuit he brought against his brother Ferry in the late 1540s, Dumoulin prepared a treatise on donations in marriage contracts and another on inofficious testaments, gifts, and dowries. He continued during his life to revise these works, which appeared together as the *Tractatus duo analytici* in 1577.[11] In the dispute with his brother, the parliament ruled in favor of Charles Dumoulin, meaning that he finally found himself in a more comfortable financial position.

7 Michael Erbe, *François Bauduin (1520–1573). Biographie eines Humanisten* (Gütersloh: Mohn, 1978), 37.

8 Marie Seong-Hak Kim, "Charles Dumoulin, *Commentarii in consuetudines Parisienses*," in Serge Dauchy et al. (eds.) *The Formation and Transmission of Western Legal Culture: 150 Books that Made the Law in the Age of Printing* (Cham: Springer, 2016), 82–85.

9 See below, section on "Religious beliefs and political interests."

10 Donald R. Kelley, "France," in Roy Porter and Mikuláš Teich (eds.) *The Renaissance in National Context* (Cambridge: Cambridge University Press, 1992), 133.

11 Ferry had dilapidated the estate that Charles had donated to him in 1531 – a donation confirmed in Ferry's marriage contract in 1535. In 1551 the Parlement de Paris annulled the donation, considerably improving Charles Dumoulin's financial condition; see Thireau, *Charles Du Moulin (1500–1566)*, 26–27, nn. 37–39.

Dumoulin's antipapal attitude, roused by his exposure to Lutheran and Calvinist ideas, became apparent just a couple of years later in his critical annotations on Dino del Mugello's (*c.* 1253–1303) commentary on Pope Boniface VIII's rules of law (*Notae in commentarium Dini Muxellani in regulas iuris pontificii*, 1548) and in his commentary on the classical books of medieval canon law (*Annotationes ad ius pontificium*, 1550). Dumoulin's increasingly hostile engagement with canon law, which he designated as "popish law" (*ius pontificium*), soon turned against him, ushering in a period of hardship and vagrancy. When Dumoulin openly chose sides with Henry II in the French king's conflict with Pope Julius III over the validity of the Council of Trent, he came under fire from Catholic theologians at the Sorbonne. In fact, Dumoulin had published a pyrotechnical commentary on Henry II's edict from 1550 against the "little dates"[12] and abusive administration of benefices by the Roman Curia (*Commentarius ad edictum Henrici II contra parvas datas et abusus Curiae Romanae*, 1551), a commentary that turned into a hypercritical study of the history of the Catholic Church and a frontal attack on the pope.[13] Moreover, when Henry II abandoned the idea of establishing a French national church on the model of the Church of England, Dumoulin was sacrificed, politically speaking, as a sign of reconciliation. In May 1552, not only the theologians from the Sorbonne but also the

[12] The term "little dates" or "abbreviated dates" refers to a simplified way of dating administrative documents. It was practiced by bankers in Rome to date the requests for the conferral of benefices that they received from corresponding bankers in France. The Roman bankers received the requests first and dated them in a simplified way because it would have been too time-consuming to submit requests to the Datary, the papal office in charge of the administration of benefices. The practice of using "little dates" played an important role in one of the most abusive practices in the distribution of benefices, the so-called *resignatio in favorem* (see the critique by Pierre Rebuffi (1487–1557) in his *Praxis beneficiorum*, Lyon, 1579, part 3, 317). The incumbent of a benefice resigned in favor of a designated person while he was still alive, communicating this resignation to bankers in Rome who had the privilege of dating such requests. He also prepared a power of attorney for the resignation to be completed, but kept it with himself. Until the incumbent died, the power of attorney was kept with him and renewed every six months. Once the incumbent died, the power of attorney was sent to the bankers in Rome, so that the collation of the benefice could now be completed, but according to the old date; Denis Diderot, *Encyclopédie*, Paris, 1754, vol. 4, 635–36. The speed with which the request for collation of the benefice was made mattered, because otherwise there was a risk that the pope would fill the vacancy or that priority went to somebody else (*prior tempore, potior iure*); Charles L. Stinger, *The Renaissance in Rome* (Bloomington and Indianapolis: Indiana University Press, 1998), 125–27.

[13] Donald R. Kelley, "*Fides historiae*: Charles Dumoulin and the Gallican View of History," *Traditio* 22 (1966): 365–66.

parliament initiated proceedings against Dumoulin, who refused to abandon his heretical views. Parliament transferred the case to the king.[14]

Dumoulin found refuge in Basel, where he met Boniface Amerbach (1495–1562). He subsequently moved to Geneva, where he was welcomed by French Huguenots such as Theodore Beza (1519–1605) and François Hotman (1524–90). He became friends with John Calvin and Heinrich Bullinger (1504–75) but left Geneva in April 1553.[15] After brief stays in Lausanne, Strasbourg, and Marburg, Dumoulin was granted a chair at the university of Tübingen by Duke Christoph of Würtemberg in December 1553, thanks to diplomatic efforts by Bullinger.[16]

Dumoulin's lectures on parts of Justinian's Digest at Tübingen University would later form the basis of two treatises, his *Nova et analytica explanatio rubricae et l. 1 et l. 2 De verborum obligationibus* (1559), and the *Extricatio labyrinthi dividui et individui* (1561). Another influential juridical work dating to his time as a lecturer in Tübingen is his *Conclusiones de statutis et consuetudinibus*, dealing with issues in private international law.[17] It was part of a course on the first six books of the Code of Justinian. In Tübingen, Dumoulin even managed to indulge in his passion for history, drawing up a work on Roman public law.[18] It did not take long, however, before Dumoulin, then a staunch Calvinist, fell afoul of his colleagues. He openly offended their Lutheran convictions more than once. The strained relationship between Dumoulin and the University of Tübingen alarmed even John Calvin. He expressed fears that Dumoulin's "bad character was going to waste the good cause he took up to defend."[19]

Because of his uncompromising nature, Dumoulin was obliged to leave Tübingen after only one year. He sought refuge in Montbéliard, Dole, Besançon, and Troyes, but finally returned to Paris in January 1557, where

[14] Thireau, *Charles Du Moulin (1500–1566)*, 36–37.

[15] It deserves mentioning that Dumoulin's correspondence with Amerbach, Bullinger, and Calvin has been preserved. For an overview, see Thireau, *Charles Du Moulin (1500–1566)*, 437–40.

[16] Jean Carbonnier, "Du Moulin à Tubingue," *Revue générale du droit, de la législation et de la jurisprudence en France et à l'étranger* 40 (1936): 194–209.

[17] Gamillscheg, *Der Einfluss Dumoulins auf die Entwicklung des Kollisionsrechts*, 19–42; also discussed in Martin Gebauer, "Charles Dumoulin zum 450. Todestag," *Zeitschrift für europäisches Privatrecht* 24 (2016): 928–49 (at 930 and 944–46).

[18] Jean-Louis Thireau, "Une vision du droit public romain au XVIe siècle: le *Tractatus analyticus de dignitatibus, magistratibus et civibus romanis* de Charles Dumoulin," in Jacques Krynen and Michael Stolleis (eds.) *Science politique et droit public dans les facultés de droit* (Frankfurt am Main: Klostermann, 2008), 393–410.

[19] René Filhol, "Dumoulin, Charles," in Raoul Naz (ed.) *Dictionnaire de droit canonique* (Paris: Letouzey et Ané, 1953), vol. 5, cols. 41–67 (46).

he took up his work as a lawyer and scholar. A year later, his commentary on the second title of the customary law of Paris, about rent contracts, appeared. He also sent to press a collection of his counsels (*Consilia et responsa iuris*, 1560) and his programmatic treatise on the origin, progress, and excellence of the French kingdom and monarchy (*Traité de l'origine, progrès, excellence du Royaume et Monarchie des François et couronne de France*, 1561, translated into Latin in 1564). In fact, the latter work provided a new, extended edition of the historical part of his controversial commentary on Henry II's edict on the "little dates" and the abuses of the Roman Curia in attributing benefices – a clear sign that five years of exile had not changed Dumoulin's antipopish sentiments, but rather had strenghtened his commitment to French nationalism and the privileges of the Gallican church. In the meantime, Dumoulin had grown increasingly disillusioned with Calvinism, resenting the authoritarian way in which the Calvinist National Synod of Paris had imposed strict disciplinary rules in 1559. He spurned the servile reliance of the French Calvinists on the dictates coming from Geneva and repudiated their opposition to the French monarchy.[20]

At the outbreak of the religious wars in France (1562), the Catholics seized Paris and plundered Dumoulin's house, throwing his annotated copies of Philipp Melanchthon and Wolfgang Musculus into the toilets.[21] He had no choice but to flee to the Calvinist cities of Orléans and Lyon. Yet his overt criticism of Calvin's doctrines signalled the beginning of the end of his flirtations with Calvin's supporters. During his stay in Orléans, Dumoulin was called to account by the ministers for spreading heretical ideas. In Lyon, Calvinist ministers took offense at the publication of his Catechism (*Catéchisme ou sommaire de la doctrine chrétienne*, Latin and French, 1563). Moreover, Dumoulin was accused of publishing yet another controversial book that allegedly preached revolt against the king (*Défense civile et militaire des innocents et de l'Église de Christ*). Even if Dumoulin fiercely denied authorship of this work, he was no longer welcome among the Calvinists. He returned to Paris in January 1564, where more strained relationships were awaiting him, this time with the Catholics.[22] In his *Consultation de Paris pour la noblesse de Picardie* (1564), he advocated the election by the people of the most important prelates. He became fanatical about defending the privileges of the Gallican church, attacking the Jesuit order (*Consilium super commodis vel incommodis novae sectae seu factitiae religionis Jesuitarum*, 1564) and

[20] Thireau, *Charles Du Moulin (1500–1566)*, 46–47.

[21] Ibid., 47, n. 171.

[22] Ibid., 49–50.

opposing the reception of the decrees of the Council of Trent in France (*Conseil sur le fait du Concile de Trente*, 1564, translated into Latin in 1565). The fact that Dumoulin published his advice on the Council of Trent without royal permission stirred another controversy.[23] The Parlement ordered the imprisonment of Dumoulin – later revoked by the king – and forbade the sale of the *Conseil*.

Left on his own, Dumoulin resolutely continued to pursue his own ideas, publishing a work on the four Gospels (*Collatio et unio quatuor Evangelistarum*, 1565) that was condemned by both Catholics and Calvinists.[24] The book was burnt in Geneva and forbidden by the National Synod in Paris. Dumoulin stood up for himself and denounced the authoritarian tendencies of the Calvinists in a couple of apologies, whose publication was thwarted (*Copie des articles présentés par Maistre Charles Du Molin contre les Ministres de la Religion prétendue réformée*; *Deffense de Messire Charles Du Molin contre les calomnies des Calvinistes et Ministres de leurs sectes*).[25] On his deathbed, December 27, 1566, he converted back to Catholicism. His last work – the *Notae solemnes*, his notes on French customs – was included posthumously in *Le Grand Coutumier* (Paris, 1567), the first big collection of customs across France. Thus, his dream of a unified French customary law, already pronounced in his *Oration on the Harmony and Union of the Customs of France* (*Oratio de concordia et unione consuetudinum Franciae*, 1547; a French summary was added to the *Sommaire du Traité des usures*), was close to being realized. Even more than his epic struggle for a belief system that reconciled individual autonomy and national interests, he would be remembered for his lasting impact on the unification of French customary law.

MAJOR THEMES AND CONTRIBUTIONS

Religious beliefs and political interests

One of the most fascinating aspects of Dumoulin's life and work is his uncompromising quest for an interpretation of the Christian religion that could satisfy his spiritual needs and suit the interests of the French crown at the same time. Such a free spirit as his could not agree with the authoritarian

[23] Thomas I. Crimando, "Two French Views of the Council of Trent," *The Sixteenth Century Journal* 19 (1988): 169–86 (175–76).

[24] Thireau, *Charles Du Moulin (1500–1566)*, 52–53.

[25] M. Reulos, "Le jurisconsulte Charles Dumoulin en conflit avec les églises reformées de France," *Bulletin de la société de l'histoire du protestantisme français* 100 (1954): 1–12.

tendencies he perceived in both Catholic and Protestant circles. "I am neither Zwinglian nor Lutheran," he once wrote in a letter to Bullinger, "but Christian and an enemy of all faction."[26] What certainly would have attracted him to the Protestant reform movements was the rejection of papal authority, the denunciation of clerical abuse, and the creation of national churches. But he disagreed with Protestants on major dogmatic issues, such as the doctrine of predestination. Already in his *Commentarii in consuetudines Parisienses*, he explored the theological subject of predestination and free will, but still defended the more traditional views of Saint Augustine, Thomas Aquinas, and Erasmus against Martin Luther.[27] It was not until 1552 that Dumoulin encountered John Calvin and became one of his followers. As already noted, even Dumoulin's interest in Calvinism did not prevent him from cultivating an independent mind, and his affiliation with Calvinist circles was short-lived. He gave it up as soon as he realized that Geneva threatened the prerogatives of the French king.[28] In his *Deffense*, he denounced the fact that Calvinist ministers had gathered into a new clerical caste, often behaving in a more authoritarian and hypocritical manner than Catholic clergy. He cited the example of Theodore Beza, whom he despised.

Dumoulin's sympathy with the reform movement occurred relatively late in his life, in the early 1540s.[29] As Dumoulin recounts in a letter to Bullinger dated January 15, 1553, his conversion was triggered by reading Martin Luther's commentary on the book of Exodus. Subsequently, he started to delve into other Protestant works by Luther, Bullinger and, even more importantly, Melanchthon, whom he considered his spiritual father.[30] According to Jean-Louis Thireau, the conciliatory tone of the articles of the Augsburg Confession (*Confessio augustana*, 1530), which were greatly inspired by Melanchthon, come closest to expressing Dumoulin's views on religion.[31] The *Confessio augustana* emphasized not only justification by faith (art. 4 and 20) but also the limitations of ecclesiastical power (art. 28) and the sacred nature of temporal government (art. 16). In Dumoulin's eyes, the privileges of the Gallican church and the interests of the French crown were paramount. He dreamed of an autonomous national church in France, inspired by the

[26] Donald R. Kelley, *François Hotman: A Revolutionary's Ordeal* (Princeton: Princeton University Press, 1973), 70.
[27] Thireau, *Charles Du Moulin (1500–1566)*, 76.
[28] Ibid., 54 and 311.
[29] Ibid., 32.
[30] Ibid., 33.
[31] Ibid., 56.

Anglican model.[32] At the end of his life, Dumoulin became close to the circle around Catherine de Médici (1519–89) and Michel de l'Hôpital (1507–73) known as the "Politiques," whose primary interest was avoiding civil war by limiting the influence of religious authorities in temporal affairs.[33]

The political dimension of Dumoulin's approach to religious questions is apparent in his short advice against the introduction of the Jesuits in France. He delivered the *Consilium super commodis vel incommodis novae sectae seu factitiae religionis Jesuitarum* in March 1564 in the context of the Jesuits' attempt to gain permission by the Parlement of Paris for the establishment of a Jesuit college at the University of Paris. This *consilium* has received little attention in the secondary literature, but nonetheless contains some exemplary ideas.[34] According to Dumoulin, the Jesuits threatened the public interest (*bonum publicum*), because there were already too many religious orders and religious houses in France that exploited the people, especially women and the poor. Therefore, the establishment of the Jesuit order must be obstructed from the beginning. Dumoulin referred to the example of the Order of Minims, whose founder, Saint Francis of Paola (1416–1507), was called to Paris by the French king Louis X, only to stay at the royal court and oversee the rapid expansion of his order in France. Moreover, in Dumoulin's opinion, the public law (*ius publicum*) of both France and the Catholic Church did not allow for the foundation of new religious orders. He also played on xenophobic sentiments, repeating on several occasions that the Jesuits were suspect strangers from Italy and Spain. Because they were strangers, there was a grave risk for the French kingdom (*periculum regni*) that the Jesuits engaged in spying activities for foreign powers.

An argument from canon law advanced by Dumoulin in his advice against the Jesuit order was that they were a new religious order (*nova religio*). In his view, the old conciliar canons of the Church (*antiqui canones conciliares*), confirmed by the Fourth Lateran Council (1215), did not permit the founding of new religious orders. In addition, he referred to the alleged conclusions of a meeting of prelates convened by Pope Paul III in Nice in July 1538. According to Dumoulin, they had decided that one of the most efficient measures to stop the abuses in the Church was to forbid the entrance of new monks into existing orders. This measure had already been proposed by William of

[32] Kelley, "*Fides historiae*," 391; Thireau, *Charles Du Moulin (1500–1566)*, 56.

[33] Thireau, *Charles Du Moulin (1500–1566)*, 50 and 56.

[34] The Latin text accompanied by a French translation is available in *Annales de la Société des soi-disans Jésuites* (Paris, 1764), vol. 1, 23–28, available online at books.google.be/books?id=cnYPAAAAQAAJ&printsec=frontcover&hl=fr&source=gbs_ge_summary_r&cad=0#v=onepage&q&f=false (last consulted May 10, 2018).

Saint-Amour, a thirteenth-century scholastic "whom Jean Gerson held in high esteem," Dumoulin was keen to specify. His argumentation prompts three remarks. An obvious point is that Dumoulin knew canon law, even if he severely criticized the popes and did not accept that canon law was binding in France without prior approval by the king.[35] As Donald Kelley has observed, "canon law was Dumoulin's point of departure as well as his principal target."[36] Secondly, he lent great weight to the "old canons." As we will see, the reference to the old canons and, even more, to the primitive church, was typical of the Protestant movement and a recurring theme in Dumoulin's work. Thirdly, Dumoulin was convinced, like Gerson, that the main authority within the Church lay with the council, not with the pope. The pope is subject to the decisions of the general council and must respect the conciliar canons.

Eblematic of Dumoulin's conciliarist views is his commentary on the Decretals of Pope Gregory IX. He opposed the provisions in canon *Significasti* (X 1, 6, 4) that require an oath of obedience to the Apostolic See and loyalty to the unity of the Church. Dumoulin also rejected the argument in canon *Significasti*, which held that councils depended on the authority of the Roman Church. Instead, he argued that councils derived their authority directly from God and not from the Roman Church, certainly not from the pope, whom he considered as subject to the power of the general council.[37] Dumoulin adduced the authority of the Council of Constance (1414–18) and the tradition of the Gallican church. Indeed, conciliar supremacy had been confirmed in France by King Charles VII in the Pragmatic Sanction of Bourges (1438).[38] The Gallican endorsement of the principle of conciliar supremacy formed the basis of Dumoulin's attack on the Council of Trent in 1564.[39] He considered the Council invalid because it had been convened

35 Thireau, *Charles Du Moulin (1500–1566)*, 300; see also Mathias Schmoeckel, *Das Recht der Reformation. Die epistemologische Revolution der Wissenschaft und die Spaltung der Rechtsordnung in der Frühen Neuzeit* (Tübingen: Mohr Siebeck, 2014), 76.

36 Kelley, "*Fides historiae*," 371.

37 Charles Dumoulin, *Ad quinque libros Decretalium Gregorii IX*, in *Opera omnia* (Paris, 1612), vol. 3, col. 685, reader.digitale-sammlungen.de/de/fs1/object/display/bsb10495358_00839.html?zoom=0.6500000000000001 (last consulted May 11, 2018): "Tamen contrarium fuit determinatum in Concilio Generali Constantiensi in can. frequens, quod habet authoritatem immediate a Deo et non ab ecclesia Romana, et multo minus a Papa qui subest ecclesiae et Concilio Generali, a quo iudicari et deponi potest ut saepe factum fuit."

38 Crimando, "Two French Views of the Council of Trent," 171.

39 Thireau, *Charles Du Moulin (1500–1566)*, 49–50 and 313–14.

and run by the pope and not by the council, contrary to old custom (*mos antiquus*).[40] Moreover, in his advice on the Council of Trent, Dumoulin recalled not only the procedural requirements a valid council should meet but also the limited character of the competence of general councils. By virtue of the privileges granted to kings (*regale ius*), especially to the Gallican church, general councils had nothing to say about matters related to public policy. For example, Dumoulin did not accept the Tridentine decree stipulating that bishops should be competent for the education of poor children by using public funds.[41]

As Donald Kelley has demonstrated, historical criticism played a seminal role in Dumoulin's disdain for canon law and the Catholic Church.[42] For example, in his commentary on the *Decretum*, Dumoulin was eager to draw attention to Erasmus's discovery of the spurious nature of many of the sermons of Saint Augustine cited by Gratian. He also denounced the ubiquitous nature of fallacies in the *Decretum*, for instance regarding Saint Peter's alleged twenty-five-year residence in Rome or the biased theory that the primacy of the bishop of Rome went back to the third century. The historical foundations of his scathing critique of ecclesiastical abuse and papal power are also apparent in his commentary on Henry II's edict against the little dates. The "little dates" referred to abuses by the Roman chancery in awarding benefices, which damaged France's financial interests.[43] In this work, Dumoulin proposed a return to the primitive church (*vera ecclesia*), in which equality and collegiality, not ecclesiastical hierarchy, formed the basis of church government.[44] He offered historical examples of the supremacy of the kings and the obedience of bishops to the laws of the Frankish kings, even in ecclesiastical affairs.[45] He pleaded in favor of a renaissance of the caesaropapist

[40] Charles Dumoulin, *Consilium super actis concilii Tridentini* (Poitiers, 1565), 18, nr. 5, reader.digitale-sammlungen.de/de/fs1/object/display/bsb10174645_00018.html (last consulted May 11, 2018): "Ex his relinquitur, Tridentinum illud Concilium, quod praeter morem antiquum indictum fuit, solaque concitum, subnixumque romana auctoritate pontificia, nullum prorsus fuisse, nec eo teneri ullum quemquam hominem."

[41] Dumoulin, *Consilium super actis concilii Tridentini*, 64–65, nr. 44, reader.digitale-sammlungen.de/de/fs1/object/display/bsb10174645_00064.html (last consulted May 11, 2018): "Mitto quod de hac re constituere regalis semper habitum est iuris nec ad pontificia concilia attinet quicquam horum."

[42] Kelley, "*Fides historiae*," 372–73.

[43] See explanation above, footnote 12.

[44] Kelley, "*Fides historiae*," 378–79; Thireau, *Charles Du Moulin (1500–1566)*, 307.

[45] Charles Dumoulin, *Commentarius ad edictum Henrici II contra parvas datas* (Lyon, 1552), 2 [table of contents], nr. 20: "Legibus imperatorum et regum, etiam in rebus ecclesiasticis paruit non solum primitiva ecclesia sed etiam sub Justiniano Magno et Carolo Magno et

model promoted by Emperor Justinian and Charlemagne.[46] He also railed against popes such as Gregory VII and Innocent III.[47] The former he accused of denaturing the relationship between spiritual and temporal powers because he tried to abolish the regalian rights and created space for absolving subjects from their oath of allegiance to the king. The latter he blamed for introducing obligatory confession, the multplication of the number of monks and priests, and the establishment of the papal states.

Dumoulin saw a close connection between the restoration of primitive Christianity and the reformation of the church.[48] In a speech delivered at the University of Tübingen, he underlined the converging interests of the humanist jurists' quest for the original sources of Roman law and the reformed theologians' attempt to recover the ancient church (*Solemnis oratio de sacrae theologiae et legum imperialium dignitate, differentia, convenientia, corruptione et restitutione*). This oration also neatly sums up his views on the relationship between religion and politics. A bishop's or minister's task is to preach the word of God, to administer the sacraments, and to govern the church like a family through teaching the right doctrine and through good example. It belongs to the prince or Christian magistrate, however, to punish evil and to reward good behavior of his subjects, including the ministers of the church. Imposing rules and sanctions about human conduct, both within civil society and within the church, is in the hands of the temporal authorities, according to Dumoulin. The temporal authorities also have a unique mandate by God to interpret and protect the word of God and the power to legislate.[49] The prince is the guardian of all law (*custos totius legis*), even of the divine law. In fact, Dumoulin's oration started with a reflection on the divine nature of civil law and ended with an appeal to restore the original imperial laws, cleansed from the interpretations by the canon lawyers. Incidentally, he used the occasion to berate the theologians of the Sorbonne and

successoribus suis." reader.digitale-sammlungen.de/de/fs1/object/display/bsb10162559_00022.html (last consulted May 11, 2018).

46 Thireau, *Charles Du Moulin (1500–1566)*, 315; Kelley, "*Fides historiae*," 354.

47 Kelley, "*Fides historiae*," 374.

48 Ibid., 368–69.

49 Dumoulin, *Solemnis oratio*, [s.p.], nrs. 48–49, reader.digitale-sammlungen.de/de/fs1/object/display/bsb11072008_00038.html (last consulted May 11, 2018): "Principis autem vel magistratus Christiani officium est populo (in quo etiam ministri Ecclesiae continentur) praesse potestate eminenti et praecellenti ad vindictam quidem nocentium, laudem autem recte agentium, ad Rom. 13, 1, Pet. 2. Disciplinam omnem externam, sive civilem, sive Ecclesiasticam, servare et super omnia legem et verbum Dei legere, discere, custodire et custodiri facere, ut speciale mandatum et praeceptum habet a Deo, Deut. 17, Iosue, 1. (...) Est igitur voce Dei custos totius legis, etiam mere divinae, saltem quoad externa officia."

to criticize Gabriel Biel (d. 1495), one of Tübingen's most renowned scholastic theologians.[50]

Customary law, private law, and economic thought

Dumoulin's rejection of a universalist conception of the government of the church and his promotion of national churches finds a striking parallel in his seminal efforts to introduce a conceptual distinction between the universalist tradition of Roman law, on the one hand, and the particularist tradition of customary law, on the other. At the very outset of his commentary on the first part of the customs of Paris (*De feudis*, 1539), he insisted that the origins of feudal law did not reach back to Roman law but only to custom (*feudorum origo non a iure Romano sed a consuetudine*).[51] He expressly denied any genealogical connection between the feudal order and the Roman *clientela* system. Dumoulin claimed that this viewpoint had been adopted unanimously by all jurists, but, in fact, Guillaume Budé (1468–1540), the famous French jurist and philologist, had held the opposite opinion, as had Ulrich Zasius (1461–1535), the famous German humanist jurist.[52] Dumoulin's emphasis on the non-Roman roots of feudal law was later rejected by Jacques Cujas (1522–90), the great French humanist jurist, philologist, and historian.[53] Dumoulin nevertheless maintained that customary law was the only source of the feudal system. He did not just offer a historical explanation in doing so. It was a political statement that had an impact on the writing of the history of law in France and other European nations for centuries to come.[54]

[50] Ibid., [s.p.], nr. 28 and nr. 25, respectively.

[51] Charles Dumoulin, *Prima pars commentariorum in consuetudines Parisienses* (Paris, 1539), 2, nr. 2, books.google.be/books?id=3eVEAAAAcAAJ&printsec=frontcover&hl=nl&source=gbs_ViewAPI&redir_esc=y#v=onepage&q&f=false (last consulted May 11, 2018): "Et ego quidem diligenter excussi omnes tractatores feudorum, tam in summis, quam in lecturis et repetitionibus, quorum libri extant. (...) Omnes ubi de hoc tractant, concorditer tenere vasallos, feuda et eorum iura non esse de iure Romano, nec a Romanis legibus aut institutis fluxisse, sed solum ab illo iure consuetudinario, quod habetur in usibus feudorum originaliter processisse, ipsisque iurisconsultis et antiquis Romanorum imperatoribus penitus incognita et inusitata fuisse."

[52] Donald R. Kelley, "*De origine feudorum*: the beginnings of an historical problem," *Speculum* 39 (1964): 207–28 (219); Donald R. Kelley, "Legal Humanism and the Sense of History," *Studies in the Renaissance* 13 (1966): 184–99 (192).

[53] Xavier Prévost, *Jacques Cujas (1522–1590) jurisconsulte humaniste* (Geneva: Droz, 2015), 450.

[54] Ever since, European legal cultures have been said to rest on two pillars: the universalist pillar of Roman law (and its reception by the church, the universities, the pandectists, etc.) and the particularist pillar of the customary law, often called Germanic law because of developments in the early modern Holy Roman Empire and nineteenth-century German scholarship; see

The impact of Dumoulin's *Commentarii in consuetudines Parisienses* on the formation of a unified customary law for Paris and his contribution to the rise of a national French legal culture can hardly be overestimated.[55] The third and final section of this chapter, concerning the influence of Dumoulin's work, will briefly come back to this point. For reasons of space, the remainder of this section will be dedicated to a short overview of Dumoulin's contribution to substantive issues of private law and commercial law in his commentary on the customs of Paris and in other legal writings. Within the context of a volume that highlights the connection between religious beliefs and the development of legal thought, Dumoulin's engagement with the law of rents and moneylending, both in the context of his 1545 treatise on commerce and contracts and in the second part of his commentary on the customs of Paris (*De censive*, 1558), deserves special attention. Dumoulin is famous for allowing modest interest on loans as a matter of natural law, divine law, and civil law:[56] "it is necessary and useful that a certain practice of interest-taking is retained and tolerated." He immediately went on to warn, though, that the interest rate should be moderate.

Dumoulin's economic views offer a clear example of the impact of the new Protestant ideas about interest-taking on the legal tradition. Dumoulin accepted the charging of a moderate interest by relying on Johann Hoeck (also known as Johannes Aepinus, 1499–1553), a Lutheran theologian.[57] He was also inspired by Conrad Summenhart (*c.* 1455–1502), a Catholic scholastic from the University of Tübingen, who had already questioned the traditional arguments in favor of the prohibition on interest-taking in his *Septipertitum opus de contractibus*.[58] Both Lutheran and Catholic revisions of traditional conceptions of moneylending and interest, then, played a role in shaping Dumoulin's legal thought.

E. Conte, "Consuetudine, Coutume, Gewohnheit and Ius Commune. An Introduction," *Rechtsgeschichte – Legal History* 24 (2016): 234–43.

[55] Kim, "Charles Dumoulin, Commentarii in consuetudines Parisienses", 82–85.

[56] Charles Dumoulin, *Tractatus commerciorum et usurarum* (Paris, 1546), 239, nr. 535, reader.digitale-sammlungen.de/de/fs1/object/display/bsb10146331_00247.html (last consulted May 11, 2018): "Primum, et necesse et utile esse usum aliquem foenoris retineri et tolerari. Secundum, quod valde et quantum commode fieri potest, debet moderari et restringi (. . .). Tertium, quod hoc facto nedum iure humano, sed omni iure et divino et naturali licitus est."

[57] Rodolfo Savelli, "Diritto romano e teologia reformata. Du Moulin di fronte al problema dell'interesse del denaro," *Materiali per una storia della cultura giuridica* 23 (1993): 291–324.

[58] Thireau, *Charles Du Moulin (1500–1566)*, 353; Summenhart's attack on the traditional natural law arguments underpinning the interest prohibition is analyzed by John T. Noonan, *The Scholastic Analysis of Usury* (Cambridge, MA: Harvard University Press, 1957), 340–44.

Jean-Louis Thireau has convincingly shown that there is no evidence for the proposition that Dumoulin was directly influenced by Calvin or the other way around.[59] Similarities between Calvin's and Dumoulin's doctrines can be explained with reference to the use of common sources, especially the work of Aepinus. In his commentary on Psalm 15, Aepinus had argued in favor of the purchase and repurchase of annuities in the form of *Zinskauf*.[60] Aepinus had also "neutralized" the divine prohibition on lending at interest in the Gospel (Luke 6:35: *mutuum date nihil inde sperantes*) by giving it a very restrictive interpretation: it applied only in contracts between rich creditors and poor borrowers. That interpretation created the possibility for moneylending at interest in contracts with rich borrowers.[61] Dumoulin expressly adopted Aepinus's notion that there are three classes of Christians, namely, the poor, the rich, and those who are not entirely poor but can work.[62] Money loans at interest are allowed if the debtor belongs to the second category of people, whereas free loans are due to the last category and alms to the first.[63]

Apart from Dumoulin's influential reversal of the interest prohibition, a reversal that clearly bears the marks of his exposure to Lutheran moral theology, his major contributions to other issues in private law have been highlighted by many scholars.[64] His impact on the rule that donations can be revoked when the donator is suddenty confronted with the birth of a child has attracted much attention because Dumoulin's generalization of a provision from Justinian's Code to that effect was approved of by the Parlement of Paris and later included in Napoléon's Civil Code.[65] In the realm of feudal law, Dumoulin has been credited with shifting attention from the personal

[59] Thireau, *Charles Du Moulin (1500–1566)*, 356, refuting contrary conclusions, which are still widespread, submitted by Marcel Le Goff, *Du Moulin et le prêt à intérêt* (Bordeaux, 1905), 168–69.

[60] Paolo Astorri, *Lutheran Theology and Contract Law in Early Modern Germany (ca. 1520–1720)* (Leuven, 2018), unpublished doctoral dissertation, 50 and 298.

[61] Ibid., 287.

[62] Dumoulin, *Tractatus commerciorum et usurarum*, 38, n. 85, reader.digitale-sammlungen.de/de/fs1/object/display/bsb10146331_00046.html (last consulted May 11, 2018): "Dum haec ad excudendum recognoscerem, commodo venit in manus meas libellus elegantissimus eruditissimi viri Io. Aepini in Psal. 15, ubi tres facit hominum ordines, quos iuvare decet dissimili ratione et modo."

[63] Astorri, *Lutheran Theology and Contract Law in Early Modern Germany*, 290–94, 310, 324, and 428.

[64] Filhol, "Dumoulin, Charles," 54–55 and Gebauer, "Charles Dumoulin zum 450. Todestag."

[65] Frits Brandsma, "De Privy Council, Charles Du Moulin en Romeins recht," *Groninger Opmerkingen en Mededelingen* 33 (2016): 33–46 (39–42); see also Filhol, "Dumoulin, Charles," 54.

obligations between a lord and his vassal to the property relations, thereby strenghtening the legal position of the vassal.[66] In the field of matrimonial law, Dumoulin is said to have contributed to the weak legal position of married women, later taken up by Napoléon.[67] Attention has also been paid to Dumoulin's seminal contribution to the field of conflict of laws, where he is credited with granting more space to the autonomy of the will.[68] His nominalist doctrine in matters of debt repayments has been called "revolutionary."[69] Regarding contractual obligations, he advanced the thesis that the canon-law principle that all agreements were binding by virtue of mutual consent should be applied in civil courts as well.[70]

Dumoulin's contribution to private law and commercial law is not limited only to the technical refinement of doctrines. At the end of this overview, his impact on the deeper political–religious transformation of those fields of law merits attention. While canon lawyers and theologians in the early modern Catholic world continued to engage with the technical aspects of private and commercial law – as can be witnessed in the School of Salamanca[71] – Dumoulin contributed to the "secularization" of these fields of law by insisting that, henceforward, jurists and temporal authorities, not theologians or spiritual authorties, should provide the regulatory framework for private and commercial transactions.[72] In this sense, he contributed not only to the internal development of private and commercial law but also to a shift in the underlying doctrine of the sources of law and the constitutional background of legal technical rules that was typical of the Protestant revolution: theologians were supposed to keep quiet in affairs that now belonged to the exclusive competence of the jurists and the magistrates (*silete theologi in*

[66] Thireau, "Du Moulin," 277; Georges Boyer, "De la conception du fief chez Dumoulin et des principales conséquences qu'il en tire," in *Mélanges Georges Boyer* (Paris: Sirey, 1962), vol. 1, 37–56.

[67] Dumoulin, *Prima pars commentariorum in consuetudines Parisienses*, 247, nr. 3 (*nubens mulier capite minuitur*), reader.digitale-sammlungen.de/de/fs1/object/display/bsb10144799_00509.html (last consulted May 11, 2018).

[68] Gebauer, "Charles Dumoulin zum 450. Todestag," 944–46.

[69] Harry Dondorp, "The Effect of Debasements on Pre-existing Debts in Early Modern Jurisprudence," in David Fox and Wolfgang Ernst (eds.) *Money in the Western Legal Tradition: Middle Ages to Bretton Woods* (Oxford: Oxford University Press, 2016), 247–66.

[70] Jean Bart, "Pacte et contrat dans la pratique française (XVIe–XVIIIe siècles)," in John Barton (ed.) *Towards a General Law of Contract* (Berlin: Duncker and Humblot, 1990), 125–27.

[71] Wim Decock and Christiane Birr, *Recht und Moral in der Scholastik der Frühen Neuzeit 1500–1750* (Berlin: De Gruyter, 2016), 24.

[72] See his speech delivered in Tübingen (*Solemnis oratio*), discussed above.

munere alieno) – even if those jurists and magistrates had always to be mindful of Christian values and their own ultimately divine vocation.[73]

General Appraisal and Influence

In the 1658 edition of Dumoulin's *opera omnia*, the preface hailed the jurist from Paris as the summit, leader, and commander-in-chief of French law (*Gallici juris vertex, ille antistes et dictator*).[74] Furthermore, it praised the idiosyncratic nature of his views, claiming that Dumoulin was rightly proud of being stubborn and unteachable. This combination of nationalist convictions and a strong character has undoubtedly been a decisive factor in Dumoulin's continued popularity among French jurists over the last five centuries.

Dumoulin paved the way for the conception that not Roman law, but the local French customary law (*droit commun coutumier*), must be considered as the general law (*ius commune*) applicable within the French kingdom, thus contributing to the "de-romanization" of the notion of *ius commune*.[75] Similarly, he wanted to protect the Gallican church against the influence of Rome, radically rejecting the pope's interference in the organization of French ecclesiastical affairs. His distrust of foreign religious authority and his defense of French royal power even led him to abandon Calvinism when he saw that Geneva was about to become equally meddlesome and authoritarian as Rome. Like many of his contemporaries, he felt at ease neither in Rome nor in Geneva.[76] He dreamed of an autonomous legal and religious identity for France, centered on the French king in Paris. On that account, modern historians have called him an "arch-Gallican," a "royal champion," and a "national ideologist."[77] As Jean-Louis Thireau observed, Dumoulin "searched for a Henry VIII" in France.[78] He was attracted by the Anglican model of

[73] Christoph Strohm, "Silete theologi in munere alieno. Konfessionelle Aspekte im Werk Alberico Gentilis," in Heinrich de Wall (ed.) *Reformierte Staatslehre in der Frühen Neuzeit* (Berlin: Duncker and Humblot, 2014), 195–223.

[74] *Caroli Molinaei Franciae et Germaniae celeberrimi iurisconsulti et in supremo Parisiorum Senatu antiqui Advocati opera quae extant omnia* (Paris, 1658, [s.p.]) [typographus lectori]; available online at gallica.bnf.fr/ark:/12148/bpt6k97661182.r=molinaei%20opera%20omnia?rk=536483;2 (last consulted May 11, 2018).

[75] Nicolas Warembourg, "La notion de droit commun dans l'Ancienne France coutumière: point d'étape," *Glossae. European Journal of Legal History* 13 (2016): 4.

[76] Thierry Wanegffelen, *Ni Rome ni Genève. Des fidèles entre deux chaires en France au XVIe siècle* (Paris: Honoré Champion, 1997).

[77] Kelley, "*Fides historiae*," 350, 370, and 386.

[78] Thireau, *Charles Du Moulin (1500–1566)*, 330–31.

state–church relationships, which was popular among many "moyenneurs" in sixteenth-century France.[79]

Dumoulin's engagement with customary law and his Gallican convictions influenced major French jurists of the second half of the sixteenth century such as François Hotman (1524–90), the Calvinist author of the *Franco-Gallia*, and Guy Coquille (1523–1603), author of *Institution au droit des Français*, an introduction to the law of the French people, and of the *Traité des libertés de l'Église de France*, a treatise on the privileges of the Gallican church. In Dumoulin's footsteps, Louis le Caron (Charondas) (c. 1534–1613) promoted the notion of French law (*droit français*).[80] In the mid-eighteenth century, François Bourjon (d. 1751) took Dumoulin's commentary on the custom of Paris as the starting point for *Le droit commun de la France et la coutume de Paris* (1747), and Robert-Joseph Pothier (1699–1772) heavily drew on Dumoulin's work in developing his influential *Traité des obligations*. Both Pothier and Bourjon became a major source for the drafting commission of Napoléon's Civil Code, thus contributing to the continuation of Dumoulin's legacy.[81] It is not a surprise, then, that teleological narratives of French legal history in the nineteenth century have emphasized Dumoulin's seminal role in preparing the codification of a unified French law under Napoléon. As a matter of fact, French jurists in the nineteenth century heavily contributed to the nationalistic reading of sixteenth-century authors such as Dumoulin in the first place.[82] For example, Raymond-Théodore Troplong (1795–1869) considered Dumoulin the prince of the French jurists, citing him throughout *Le droit civil expliqué suivant l'ordre des articles du code*, his explanatory commentary on the French Civil Code.[83]

Dumoulin's idiosyncratic views, especially his anti-Roman sentiment, have not always met with sympathy. For example, his arguments about the

[79] Alain Tallon, "Gallicanism and Religious Pluralism in France in the Sixteenth Century," in Keith Cameron, Mark Greengrass, and Penny Roberts (eds.) *The Adventure of Religious Pluralism in Early Modern France* (Bern, 2000), 15–30.

[80] Guillaume Leyte, "Charondas et le droit français," *Droits* 39 (2004): 17–33.

[81] E.g., Jean-Louis Thireau, "Aux origines des articles 1217 à 1225 du Code civil: L'*Extricatio labyrinthi dividui et individui* de Charles du Moulin," *Tijdschrift voor Rechtsgeschiedenis* (1983): 51–109.

[82] David Deroussin, "Comment forger une identité nationale? La culture juridique française vue par la doctrine civiliste au tournant des XIXe et XXe siècles," *Clio@Themis* 5 (2012): 5.

[83] Géraldine Cazals, "*Molinaeus noster*. Charles Du Moulin (1500–1566), prince des juristes, praticien engagé et fondateur de l'école juridique française. Un modèle de jurisconsulte dans la France du XIXe siècle," in Anne Dobigny-Reverso, Xavier Prévost, and Nicolas Warembourg (eds.) *Mélanges en l'honneur de Jean-Louis Thireau* (Paris: Mare & Martin, 2019 forthcoming).

nonbinding nature of the decrees of the Council of Trent were refuted in 1583 by Pierre Grégoire of Toulouse (*c*. 1540–97), a law professor at the Jesuit university of Pont-à-Mousson and a member of the Catholic *Ligue*.[84] Among his contemporaries in Spain and the Southern Netherlands, Dumoulin was cited but also criticized. This is clear in the work of canon lawyers such as Diego de Covarrubias y Leyva (1512–77) and theologians such as Leonardus Lessius (1554–1623). The Portuguese jurist Arias Piñel rebuked Dumoulin for misinterpreting Roman imperial texts and misunderstanding the scholastic doctrine of *laesio enormis*.[85] Even French jurists in the nineteenth century who admired Dumoulin's work were sometimes irritated by his staunch anti-Roman views. For instance, Aubépin criticized the "demon of blasphemy," which Dumoulin had difficulties to contain, even if he went on to explain, quite respectfully, that "the interests of the king were always going to talk louder in Dumoulin's head than those of religion."[86] The Louvain canon lawyer Alphonse Van Hove (1872–1947) emphasized Dumoulin's arrogance and his hatred for the papacy.[87]

Differences of religious opinion and lack of sympathy have never prevented Dumoulin's reputation as an outstanding lawyer from spreading beyond the boundaries of the French kingdom. His works were considered not only as tokens of exceptional erudition but also as very useful instruments for legal practice.[88] For example, he ranks among the most frequently cited foreign authorities in practical legal literature in the Low Countries throughout the early modern period, from the Duchy of Brabant to the County of Namur and the Prince-Bishopric of Liège. Similar observations can be made with regard to the German area and regions in Southern Europe, such as Italy, where Dumoulin's work was put on the index of forbidden books by Pope Pius IV in 1559.[89] His ideas circulated regardless – for example, through the support of Italian jurists who published cleansed versions of Dumoulin's writings on interest-taking and his commentaries on canon law under their own name.[90]

[84] Crimando, "Two French Views of the Council of Trent," 176.

[85] Decock, "Elegant Scholastic Humanism?," 148–52.

[86] Cazals, "*Molinaeus noster*," forthcoming.

[87] Alphonse Van Hove, "Charles Dumoulin," *The Catholic Encyclopedia* (New York: Robert Appleton Company, 1909), vol. 5, www.newadvent.org/cathen/05190c.htm (last consulted February 11, 2019).

[88] Jean-Louis Thireau, "Charles Du Moulin avocat," *Revue de la société internationale de l'histoire de la profession d'avocat* 10 (1998): 9–27.

[89] Rodolfo Savelli, *Censori e giuristi. Storie di libri, di idee e di costumi (secoli 16.-17.)*, Per la storia del pensiero giuridico moderno 94 (Milan: Giuffrè, 2011), 93–148.

[90] Thireau, *Charles Du Moulin (1500–1566)*, 34, n. 94, citing Gaspare Cavallini (Caballinus, *c*. 1530–1589) and Nicola Antonio Gravazio (fl. 1560).

RECOMMENDED READING

Carbonnier, Jean. "Du Moulin à Tubingue." *Revue générale du droit, de la législation et de la jurisprudence en France et à l'étranger* 40 (1936): 194–209.

Cazals, Géraldine. "*Molinaeus noster.* Charles Du Moulin (1500–1566), prince des juristes, praticien engagé et fondateur de l'école juridique française. Un modèle de jurisconsulte dans la France du XIXe siècle." In *Mélanges en l'honneur de Jean-Louis Thireau,* edited by Anne Dobigny-Reverso, Xavier Prévost, and Nicolas Warembourg. Paris: Mare & Martin, 2019, forthcoming.

Filhol, René. "Dumoulin, Charles." In *Dictionnaire de droit canonique*, edited by Raoul Naz, vol. 5, cols. 41–67. Paris: Letouzey et Ané, 1953.

Gebauer, Martin. "Charles Dumoulin zum 450. Todestag." *Zeitschrift für europäisches Privatrecht* 24 (2016): 928–49.

Kelley, Donald R. "*Fides historiae*: Charles Dumoulin and the Gallican View of History." *Traditio* 22 (1966): 347–402.

Kim, Marie Seong-Hak. "Charles Dumoulin, *Commentarii in consuetudines Parisienses.*" In *The Formation and Transmission of Western Legal Culture: 150 Books that Made the Law in the Age of Printing*, edited by Serge Dauchy, et al., 82–85. Cham: Springer, 2016.

Savelli, Rodolfo. "Diritto romano e teologia reformata. Du Moulin di fronte al problema dell'interesse del denaro." *Materiali per una storia della cultura giuridica* 23 (1993): 291–324.

Thireau, Jean-Louis. *Charles Du Moulin (1500–1566). Étude sur les sources, la méthode, les idées politiques et économiques d'un juriste de la Renaissance*. Genève: Droz, 1980.

7

John Calvin

(1509–1564)

JOHN WITTE, JR.*

BIOGRAPHICAL INTRODUCTION

For all of his fame as a theologian and religious reformer of Geneva, John Calvin was also a major Christian jurist.[1] He studied law in Bourges, Orléans, and Paris and was steeped in legal humanism. He named his standard introduction to theology, the *Institutes of the Christian Religion* (1536), after the standard introduction to law, the *Institutes of Justinian*. His first major reforms in Geneva were new constitutional laws for church and state – the 1541 Ecclesiastical Ordinances, the 1542 Edict of the Lieutenant, and the 1543 Ordinances on Offices and Officers. He drafted some sixty ordinances thereafter on marriage, children, social welfare, public morality, education, and other topics. He left fragments of new laws on property, inheritance, and commerce, many of which were integrated into the lengthy 1568 Civil Edict of Geneva. He left fuller outlines of major new ordinances on civil and criminal procedure. He left some fifty formal legal opinions (*consilia*) on specific legal questions, and more than three hundred letters with leading jurists, judges, and lawyers discussing legal topics.[2] He sat as a judge in most of

* This chapter is drawn in part from John Witte, Jr., *The Reformation of Rights: Law, Religion, and Human Rights in Early Modern Calvinism* (Cambridge: Cambridge University Press, 2007), ch. 1 [hereafter RR], and John Witte, Jr. and Robert M. Kingdon, *Sex, Marriage, and Family in John Calvin's Geneva*, 2 vols. (Grand Rapids, MI: Eerdmans, 2005, 2019) [hereafter SMF 1 and 2].

1 Josef Bohatec, *Calvin und das Recht* (Graz: H. Böhlau, 1934); Basil Hall, "John Calvin, the Jurisconsults, and the *Ius Civile*," in *Studies in Church History*, edn. G. J. Cumming (Leiden: Brill, 1966), 202–16.

2 Most of these laws are collected in Emile Rivoire and Victor van Berchem, eds., *Les sources du droit du canton de Genève*, 4 vols. (Arau: H. R. Sauerländer, 1927–35) [hereafter SD] and in *Ioannis Calvini opera quae supersunt omnia*, edn. G. Baum, et al., 59 vols. (Brunswick: Schwetschke, 1863–1900), vol. 10/1 [hereafter CO].

the 300 to 550 cases per year that came before the Consistory of Geneva in the 1540s and 1550s, offering some lengthy opinions in cases raising complex legal issues.[3] He was a frequent legal and political adviser to the Genevan city council and other town councils. And Calvin dealt with many intricate legal issues in his theological writings and commentaries on the Torah and other biblical texts on law. Although he left no separate treatises on law, he showed full command of biblical and Talmudic law, Roman law and civilian jurisprudence, early church constitutions and medieval canon law, local urban and feudal laws, and classical and Christian natural-law theories.

While Calvin is best known for his work in Geneva, he was a lifelong Frenchman. He was born in 1509 in Noyon, France, into a devout, minor aristocratic Catholic family. His father, Gerard, served as a canon lawyer and secretary to the local bishop and cathedral chapter. Around 1521, Gerard sent young Calvin to a *collège* in Paris, where he followed a typical humanist curriculum. He then studied law at the Universities of Bourges and Orléans, working with such legal masters as Andreas Alciatus and Pierre L'Estoile. Calvin took his licentiate in law and then returned to Paris for further legal studies, now with the noted linguist and legal humanist Guillaume Budé. In 1531, Calvin's father died – as an excommunicant from the church, owing to an earlier dispute with the bishop. Calvin and his family tried in vain to have Gerard buried in a consecrated cemetery, precipitating an angry clash with local religious authorities that alienated Calvin from Catholicism. Sometime in the following year or two, Calvin "suddenly converted" to Protestantism.[4] In 1533, he and his friend Nicholas Cop, the rector of the University of Paris, had to flee Paris for expressing new Protestant sympathies.

Calvin remained an exile from France for the rest of his life. After intermittent stays in Basel, Geneva, and Strasbourg in the 1530s, he settled in Geneva in 1541 until his death in 1564. Even in exile, however, Calvin remained consummately French. He kept a prim French home, wardrobe, and diet. He preached and wrote in a simple and elegant French style. He helped prepare a French edition of the Bible and drafted several French catechisms and liturgies. He helped found the Geneva Academy, with principal instruction in French. Most of the seventy-plus volumes in his *œuvres* are in French, and they helped make Geneva one of the three biggest centers of the day for

[3] Robert M. Kingdon, ed., *Registres du Consistoire de Genève au Temps de Calvin*, 21 vols. (Geneva: Droz, 1996–).

[4] CO 31:22ff. See biographies: William J. Bouwsma, *John Calvin: A Sixteenth-Century Portrait* (New York/Oxford: Oxford University Press, 1988); Bernard Cottret, *Calvin: A Biography*, trans. M. Wallace McDonald (Grand Rapids, MI: Eerdmans, 2000).

publications in French.[5] Two of Calvin's closest coworkers in Geneva were French-trained jurists, Theodore Beza and Germain Colladon, and he collaborated with several other French jurists – including Hugo Donnellus, François Hotman, Charles Dumoulin, and Jacques Cujas, all of whom appear in this volume. Calvin also corresponded regularly with French aristocratic men and women who sought his counsel, and he welcomed many hundreds of French refugees into Geneva as religious tensions between and among Catholics and Protestants escalated.

Calvin led a top-to-bottom reformation of church, state, and society in Geneva, creating a model Protestant city emulated in hundreds of Calvinist towns in Europe, the British Isles, North America, and Southern Africa.[6] Alongside his ample legal and political reform work, Calvin was a busy pastor – preaching almost every Sunday and several days during the week, and performing hundreds of weddings, baptisms, and other pastoral calls. He was a prolific biblical commentator, leaving commentaries or lectures on almost every book of the Bible. He was a formidable polemicist, engaging in sharp and protracted debates with several Catholics, Libertines, Antitrinitarians, Antinomians, and Anabaptists. He also engaged in harsh polemics against detractors like Michael Servetus and Sebastian Castellio, and notoriously supported the Genevan authorities in their execution of Servetus.

This chapter samples Calvin's work on rights and liberties and on church and state. For Calvin, the church and state, separately and together, had the responsibility of protecting and promoting the law and liberty of a Godly Christian republic built on divine and natural law.

LIBERTIES AND RIGHTS

Liberties. Calvin opened his 1536 *Institutes of the Christian Religion* with a loud, Luther-like call for liberty. The book's lengthy dedication to King Francis I of France was, in reality, a cleverly drafted lawyer's brief on behalf of Protestants who were being persecuted by church and state authorities alike. Immediately after his glowing tribute to this "most mighty, illustrious and glorious" king, Calvin launched into his legal argument. He shrewdly singled out those abuses of Protestants that defied widely recognized rights and freedoms of his day,

5 CO has 59 vols.; others books are listed in W. de Greef, *The Writings of John Calvin*, trans. Lyle D. Bierma (Grand Rapids, MI: Baker Books, 1993).

6 Philip Benedict, *Christ's Church Purely Reformed: A Social History of Calvinism* (New Haven, CT: Yale University Press, 2002); John T. McNeill, *The History and Character of Calvinism* (New York: Oxford University Press, 1979).

particularly criminal procedural rights. Calvin protested the widespread and unchecked instances of "perjury," "lying slanders," "wicked accusations," and the "fury of evil men" that conspired to incite "public hatred" and "open violence" against believers. He argued that the case of the Protestants had "been handled with no order of law and with violent heat rather than judicial gravity." He railed against various forms of false imprisonment and abuses of prisoners: "Some of us are shackled with irons, some beaten with rods, some led about as laughing stocks, some proscribed, some most savagely tortured, some forced to flee." He protested the many procedural inequities: Protestants were "fraudulently and undeservedly charged with treason and villainy." They were convicted for capital offenses, "without confession or sure testimony." "Bloody sentences are meted out against this doctrine without a hearing." He objected to the bias of judges and the partiality of judicial proceedings: "Those who sit in judgment . . . pronounce as sentences the prejudices which they have brought from home." He lamented the intrusions on the church's freedoms of assembly and speech: "The poor little church has either been wasted with cruel slaughter or banished into exile, or so overwhelmed by threats and fears that it dare not even open its mouth." All these offenses stood diametrically opposed to basic political freedoms recognized at the time both in the Holy Roman Empire and in France. "A very great question is at stake," Calvin declared to King Francis: "how God's glory may be kept safe on earth, how God's truth may retain its place of honor, how Christ's kingdom may be kept in good repair among us."[7]

Later on, in this same title, Calvin called for the freedom not just of Protestants, but of all peaceable believers, including Catholics, Jews, and Muslims. He denounced the forced baptisms, inquisitions, crusades, and other forms of religious persecution practiced by the medieval church and state:

> We ought to strive by whatever means we can, whether by exhortation and teaching or by mercy and gentleness, or by our own prayers to God, that they may turn to a more virtuous life and may return to the society and unity of the church. And not only are excommunicants to be so treated, but also Turks and Saracens, and other enemies of religion. Far be it from us to approve those methods by which many until now have tried to force them to our faith, when they forbid them the use of fire and water and the common elements, when they deny them to all offices of humanity, when they pursue them with sword and arms.[8]

7 John Calvin, *Institutes of the Christian Religion*, trans. Ford Lewis Battles, rev. edn (Grand Rapids, MI: Eerdmans, 1986), dedicatory epistle [hereafter *Institutes* (1536)].

8 Ibid., 2.28.

Over the next twenty-five years, Calvin continued to build his case for freedom. His touchstone was the Bible, especially those many New Testament passages on freedom: "For freedom Christ has set us free"; "You were called to freedom"; "Where the Spirit of the Lord is, there is freedom"; "For the law of the Spirit of life in Christ Jesus has set [you] free from the law of sin and death"; "You will know the truth, and the truth will make you free"; "You will be free indeed"; You all have been given "the law of liberty" in Christ, "the glorious liberty of the children of God."[9] Calvin left scores of pages of sermons and commentaries on these passages. "There is nothing more desirable than liberty," he wrote. Liberty is "an inestimable good," "a singular benefit and treasure that cannot be prized enough," something worth "more than half of life." "How great a benefit liberty is, when God has bestowed it on someone." Calvin emphasized the importance of political suffrage and the franchise in the political community. The "right to vote," he once said, is the "best way to preserve liberty." "Let those whom God has given liberty and the franchise use it." "The reason why tyrannies have come into the world, why people everywhere have lost their liberty . . . is that people who had elections abused the privilege." "There is no kind of government more salutary than one in which liberty is properly exercised with becoming moderation and properly constituted on a durable basis."[10]

Rights. Drawing on his legal training, Calvin also discussed the subjective rights (*iura, droits*) of individuals alongside their liberties (*libertates, libertés*). Sometimes he used general phrases like "the common rights of mankind" (*iura commune hominum*), the "natural rights" (*iura naturali*) of persons, the "rights of a common nature" (*communis naturae iura*), and "the equal rights and liberties" (*pari iura et libertates*) of all.[11] Usually he referenced more specific subjective rights. He spoke, for example, about the "rights of Christian liberty," the "rights of citizenship" in the kingdom of God, the "right of adoption" that Christians enjoy as new sons and daughters of God and brothers and sisters in Christ. He referenced the right "to inhabit," "to dwell in," and "to claim the territory" that Yahweh gave to the chosen people of Israel. He mentioned "Paul's rights of Roman citizenship." He spoke

[9] Galatians 5: 1,13; 2 Corinthians 3: 17; Romans 8: 2; John 8: 32, 36; James 2: 12; Romans 8: 21 (RSV).

[10] John Calvin, *Institutes of the Christian Religion*, edn. John T. McNeill, trans. Ford Lewis Battles (Philadelphia: Westminster Press, 1960), 3.19.1–8, 14 [hereafter *Institutes* (1559)]; *Serm.*, Gen. 39: 11; *Serm.*, 1 Sam. 8, 17; *Comm.*, Harm. Law Deut. 15: 1–11; 17: 14–18; 24: 7; *Serm.*, Deut. 16: 18–19; 18: 14–18.

[11] *Comm.*, Gen. 4: 13; *Comm.*, Harm. Law Num. 3: 5–10, 18–22; Deut. 5: 19; *Comm.*, Ps. 7: 6–8; *Lect.*, Jer. 22: 1–3; 22: 13–14; *Lect.*, Ezek. 8: 17; *Comm.*, 1 Cor. 7: 37.

frequently, as a student of Roman law would, about property rights: the right to land and other property, "the right to enjoy and use what one possesses," the right "to recover" and "to have restored" lost or stolen property; the right to compensation for work; the right to sell, bequeath, and inherit property, particularly in accordance with the "natural rights of primogeniture." He spoke of the right to bury one's parents and other relatives. He also spoke frequently of the marital rights of husband and wife, and the "sacred," "natural," and "common" rights of parents over their children – in particular, the right and authority of a father to "name his child," "to raise the child," and to set the child up in marriage. He spoke in passing about the "sacred right of hospitality" of the sojourner, the "right of asylum" or of sanctuary for those in flight, the "right of redemption" for slaves, and the natural rights and "just rights" of the poor, needy, orphans, and widows.[12]

Subjective rights talk became increasingly common in Calvin's Geneva – and even more so in the next century, as Calvinists faced repression and genocide that were killing them by the tens of thousands and forcing others to rise up to vindicate their fundamental rights. It is telling that, by 1650, Calvinists on both sides of the Atlantic had defined, defended, and died for every one of the rights that would appear a century and a half later in the United States Bill of Rights of 1791 as well as most of the rights set out in the 1789 French Declaration of Rights of Man and Citizen.[13]

Natural Law Foundations. But Calvinist rights talk was always coupled with duties talk. The whole point of having rights and liberties, Calvin insisted, was to enable a person to discharge the duties and responsibilities of the faith. "We obtain liberty in order that we may more promptly and more readily obey God in all things" spiritual and temporal, he wrote.[14] Freedoms and commandments, rights and duties remained together in Calvin's formulation, balancing and bolstering each other. Subjective rights claims were grounded in an objective right order.

Calvin spent a great deal of time defining this right order. Sometimes he described it as a natural order, an order of nature, or an order of creation. Sometimes he used more anthropological language: our human conscience, the inner voice, our natural inclination or sense of right and wrong. More often, he described this order as a divine, spiritual, moral, or natural law. What this untidy gaggle of terms basically described was the set of norms that undergird and legitimize the positive laws of human authorities. God has

[12] Sources in *RR*, 57–58.
[13] Ibid., chaps. 2–5.
[14] *Comm.*, 1 Peter 2: 16; *Institutes* (1559), 3.17.1–2; 3.19.14–16; 4.10.5.

written this natural law on the hearts and consciences of all persons, rewritten it in the pages of scripture, and summarized it in the Decalogue.

Calvin often used the Decalogue as a crisp summary of the natural law, as well as a template of the natural rights and duties of each person. The First Table of the Decalogue, he said, prescribes natural duties that each person owes to God: the duty to honor God and God's name, to observe the Sabbath day of rest and holy worship, to avoid false gods and false swearing. The Second Table prescribes natural duties that each person owes to others: to honor one's parents and other authorities, not to kill, not to commit adultery, not to steal, not to bear false witness, not to covet. Each person's natural duties toward God in the First Table can be recast as that person's natural rights of religion: the right to honor God and God's name, the right to rest and worship on one's Sabbath, the right to be free from false gods and false oaths. Such religious rights are "inherent human rights," said Calvin, "part of our human nature," which church, state, and neighbor alike must respect. Such religious rights and duties are also extensions of God's divine rights: the "eternal right of God himself, to be properly worshipped and glorified," as Calvin put it. Each person's natural duties toward a neighbor in the Second Table, in turn, can be cast as a neighbor's natural rights to have those duties discharged. One person's duties not to kill, to commit adultery, to steal, to bear false witness, or to covet thus give rise to another person's rights to life, property, fidelity, reputation, and domestic privacy. Calvin outlined these themes in his many writings on the Decalogue. His followers, beginning with his Genevan successor, Theodore Beza, and Cambridge don Christopher Goodman, spun out elaborate Decalogue-based theories of "inherent" or "fundamental" rights.[15]

THE "USES" OF LAW

Beyond grounding each person's natural rights and liberties, the natural law, according to Calvin, had other uses in human lives and communities. The natural law may not be a pathway to salvation, Calvin argued, echoing the Protestant doctrine of justification by faith alone and not by works. But the natural law – and the positive laws built on its foundations – still remains "useful" in this earthly life. Combining earlier classical and Christian insights, Calvin distinguished "three uses of the law."[16]

First, the law has a *civil use* – to restrain the sinfulness of every person in the community, even those who have not been justified by faith in God's grace.

[15] Sources in *RR*, 121–41.
[16] *Institutes* (1536), 1.33.

"The law is like a halter to check the raging and otherwise limitlessly ranging lusts of the flesh... Hindered by fright or shame, sinners dare neither execute what they have conceived in their minds, nor openly breathe forth the rage of their lust." The law thus imposes upon them what Calvin variously called a "forced," "public," or "civil" righteousness. Although their consciences are "untouched by any care for what is just and right," the very threat of punishment compels sinners to obey the basic duties of the natural law – to fear God, to rest on the Sabbath, to avoid blasphemy, idolatry, and profanity, to obey authorities, to respect their neighbor's person, property, and domestic relationships, to remain sexually virtuous, to speak truthfully of themselves and their neighbors. God coerces sinful persons to adopt such civil righteousness in order to preserve a measure of order and liberty in the sin-ridden earthly kingdom. "Unless there is some restraint, the condition of wild beasts would be better and more desirable than ours." "Liberty would always bring ruin with it, if it were not bridled by the moderation" born of the natural and positive law, Calvin argued.[17]

Second, the law has a *theological use* – to condemn all persons in their consciences and to compel them to seek God's liberating grace. By setting forth a model of perfect righteousness, the law "warns, informs, convicts, and lastly condemns every man of his own unrighteousness." The law thereby punctures his vanity, diminishes his pride, and drives him to despair. Such despair, Calvin believed, is a necessary precondition for the sinner to seek God's help and to have faith in God's grace. "It is as if someone's face were all marked up so that everybody who saw him might laugh at him. Yet he himself is completely unaware of his condition. But if they bring him a mirror, he will be ashamed of himself, and will hide and wash himself when he sees how filthy he is." The law is that mirror. It drives persons to repent of their sin and seek the cleansing "spiritual liberty" available to them through faith in God's grace – the liberty of conscience from the condemnation of the moral law.[18]

Third, the law has an *educational use* – to teach believers, those who have accepted God's grace, the means and measures of sanctification. Even the most devout saints, though free from the condemnation of the law, still need to follow the commandments "to learn more thoroughly ... the Lord's will [and] to be aroused to obedience." The law teaches them not only the civil righteousness required of all persons, but also the spiritual righteousness that is becoming of sanctified Christians. As a teacher, the law not only coerces them against violence and violation but also cultivates in them charity and love.

[17] *Institutes* (1559), 2.7.10; *Lect.*, Jer. 30: 9.
[18] *Institutes* (1559), 2.7.6–9; 3.19.3–6; *Comm.*, Gal. 5: 13; *Comm.*, Gal. 3: 19; *Serm.*, Deut. 5: 23–27.

It not only punishes harmful acts of murder, theft, and adultery but also prohibits evil thoughts of hatred, covetousness, and lust. Such habits of spiritual righteousness are to pervade all aspects of the life of the believer – spiritual and temporal, ecclesiastical and political, private and public. Calvin stressed that redeemed Christians must take their faith and conscience directly into public life as "ambassadors and stewards of the treasure of salvation," whose exemplary lives not only glorify God but also induce others to seek God's grace.[19]

This formula of three uses of the law provided Calvin and his followers with another sturdy template to discuss the purposes of different types of law in different types of organized communities. For example, the deterrent, retributive, and rehabilitative purposes of criminal law and punishment matched closely the civil, theological, and educational uses of the law. Later Calvinists built intricate theories of criminal law and procedure on this basic tripartite formula.[20] Similarly, in discharging their authority, parents, teachers, masters, and employers had to balance the goals of restriction, instruction, and inspiration of their children, wards, and servants. Later Calvinists would build an elaborate industry of family laws, household manuals, and educational handbooks on this same three-uses formula.[21]

STATE AND CHURCH IN A GODLY REPUBLIC

Calvin also based his theory of church and state in part on the three uses of the law. The church and the state are separate legal entities, he argued. Each institution has its own forms of organization and order, its own norms of discipline and rule. Each must issue positive human laws on the basis of God's natural law and in protection of the people's natural rights and liberties. Each must play a distinct role in enforcing godly government and discipline in the community, and in fostering the uses of God's law. The state must focus on the civil use of the law – using coercive measures as needed to achieve a basic level of civil righteousness or public morality. The church must cater to all three uses of the law – using spiritual, noncoercive means alone to achieve not only civil but also spiritual righteousness or private morality.

[19] *Serm.*, Deut. 5: 4–7, 22; *Institutes* (1559), 2.7.12; 2.8.6; 2.8.51; 3.3.9; 3.6.1; 3.17.5–6; *Comm.*, 1 Peter 1: 14.

[20] John Witte, Jr., *God's Joust, God's Justice: Law and Religion in the Western Tradition* (Grand Rapids, MI: Eerdmans, 2006), 263–94.

[21] Samples in SMF 1 and 2; discussion in John Witte, Jr., *Church, State, and Family: Reconciling Traditional Teachings and Modern Liberties* (Cambridge: Cambridge University Press, 2019), ch. 4.

The Law and Structure of the State. Calvin described political rulers and laws in largely general and homiletic terms. God has appointed political rulers to be his vice-regents, vicars, and ministers in the earthly kingdom, he wrote. They are vested with God's authority and majesty. They are called to an office that is "not only holy and lawful before God, but also the most sacred and by far the most honorable of all callings in the whole life of mortal men." They are commanded to embrace and exemplify clemency, integrity, honesty, mercy, humanity, humility, continence, and other godly virtues.[22]

Political rulers must govern the earthly kingdom by written positive laws, not by personal fiat, Calvin insisted. These modern state laws must encompass the biblical principles of love of God and neighbor, including those set out in the Decalogue. But the modern magistrate must not embrace and enforce biblical laws per se, for those laws were the specific positive laws of the ancient Jewish people and the apostolic church, and are not binding, and sometimes not even relevant, for our day. Instead, "equity alone must be the goal and rule and limit of all laws," a term that Calvin used both in the classic Aristotelian sense of correcting defects in individual rules if they work injustice in a particular case, and in his own sense of adjusting each legal system to the changing circumstances and needs of the local community. Through such written, equitable laws, political rulers must promote peace and order in the earthly kingdom, punish crime and civil wrongdoing, protect persons in their lives and properties, and "ensure that men may carry on blameless intercourse among themselves" in the spirit of civil righteousness.[23]

The structure of the state must be constitutionally self-limiting, Calvin wrote, so that "rulers are checkmated by their own officers" and offices. Such inherent political restraints rarely exist in a monarchy, Calvin believed, for monarchs too often lack self-discipline and self-control, and too often betray little appetite for justice, prudence, and Christian virtue. Thus, "it is safer and more tolerable that government be in the hands of a number of persons who help each other," such as prevails in an aristocracy, or even better in "a [mixed] system comprised of aristocracy, tempered by democracy." What Calvin had in mind was rule by the best characters, by the spiritual and moral elite, who were elected to their offices by the people. Mere division of political authority, however, was an insufficient safeguard against political abuse or tyranny. Calvin thus encouraged all magistrates to govern through local officials and agents, to adhere to precedent and written rules, to divide their power among various self-checking branches and officials, to stand

[22] *Institutes* (1536), 6.33–35; 6.39.

[23] Ibid., 1.33; 6.36–37; 6.48–49; *Institutes* (1559), 4.20.

periodically for elections, to hold regular popular meetings in order to give account of themselves, and to give air to popular concerns.[24] Later Calvinist jurists, beginning with Johannes Althusius in his *Politics* (1603), wove these early insights into a strong argument for written constitutions that protected "the ultimate rule of laws (*leges*) and rights (*iura*) in human society."[25]

The purpose of the state, Calvin argued, is to help God achieve the civil use of the law – to cultivate civil restraint and civil righteousness in all persons, if necessary through coercion. Calvin described this function in various ways. Magistrates are "ordained protectors and vindicators of public innocence, modesty, decency, and tranquility; their sole endeavor should be to provide for the common safety and peace of all." Magistrates have as their appointed end "to adjust our life to the society of men, to form our social behavior to civil righteousness, to reconcile us one with another, and to promote general peace and tranquility."[26]

But Calvin called for further safeguards against political abuse and overreaching. First, he argued, magistrates were not to trespass or abridge the God-given rights and liberties of their subjects. To the contrary, said Calvin, "God empowered the magistrate to protect the rights of everyone" and called the magistrate to "pass uniform and consistent laws" to ensure that "no one suffered violations of his persons or property." Second, magistrates were to build on, but not violate, the laws of God, including notably the Decalogue. If magistrates violated any of the Ten Commandments, or presumed to define religious doctrine, liturgy, worship, or other aspects of spiritual life, their laws were null and void. "Earthly princes lay aside all their power when they rise up against God," Calvin wrote. "We ought rather to spit on their heads than to obey them when they are so restive and wish to rob God of his rights." Further, "When princes forbid the service and worship of God, when they command their subjects to pollute themselves with idolatry and want them to consent to and participate in all the abominations that are contrary to the service of God, they are not worthy to be regarded as princes or have to any authority attributed to them." For a Christian, in good conscience, "to resist tyrannical edicts and commandments which forbid us to give due honor to Christ and due worship to God" is not to be "rebellious against kings, for they be not so

[24] *Serm.*, 2 Sam. 1–4; *Serm.*, Job 10: 16–17; 19: 26–29; 34: 138; *Serm.*, Deut. 17: 16–20; 18: 14–18; *Institutes* (1559), 4.20.9–11, 31; *Comm.*, Rom. 13: 1–10.

[25] *Politica Johannes Althusius*, trans. F. S. Carney (Indianapolis: Liberty Fund, 1995), XVIII.94–95.

[26] *Institutes* (1559), 4.20.2, 9.

exalted, that they may go about like giants to pull God out of his seat and throne."[27]

But Calvin was no political revolutionary, even against manifest tyranny. He knew enough about the insurrection and rioting triggered by some Protestant radicals of his day and had read enough of classical history to know about the dangers of simply unleashing the crowd against tyrants. Given his penchant for orderliness and moderation, he wanted no part of this. He encouraged individual victims of political abuse and tyranny to disobey the law peaceably, if they could, or to flee to another land if they had to. And he called for a more structured collective response to a tyrant that depended on the lower magistrates to judge the case, to negotiate a better way if possible, and to organize the people's revolt if necessary. During the next 250 years, Calvin's followers greatly expanded on these early statements, developing robust theories of rights, resistance, revolution, and regicide that helped drive the democratic revolutions in the Netherlands, Scotland, England, America, and even Jacobin France.[28]

The Law and Structure of the Church. While the state held the coercive power of the sword, the church held the spiritual power of the Word, Calvin continued. And while the state used coercion to achieve the civil use of the law, the church used persuasion and inspiration to help achieve all three uses of the law.[29]

The church must have a distinct and independent ecclesiastical polity, Calvin asserted. Its powers and duties must be divided among self-checking church offices and officers. Ministers were to preach the Word and administer the sacraments. Doctors of the church were to catechize the young and to educate the parishioners. Elders were to maintain discipline and order and adjudicate disputes. Deacons were to control church finances and coordinate the church's care for the poor and needy. Each of these church officials was to be elected to office by communicant members of the congregation. Each was subject to the limitation of his own office and to the supervision and discipline of fellow church officers. Each was to participate in periodic congregational meetings that allowed church members to assess these officials' performance and to debate matters of doctrine and discipline. Each congregation was, at

[27] Sources and discussion in *RR*, 48–55, 114–17.

[28] Ibid. See Michael Walzer, *The Revolution of the Saints: A Study in the Origins of Radical Politics* (Cambridge, MA: Harvard University Press, 1965); John W. Sap, *Paving the Way for Revolution: Calvinism and the Struggle for a Democratic Constitutional State* (Amsterdam: VU Press, 2001); Dale K. van Kley, *The French Idea of Freedom: The Old Regime and the Declaration of Rights of 1789* (Stanford, CA: Stanford University Press, 1996).

[29] *Institutes* (1559), 4.1.1–17; *Serm.*, Deut. 5: 22.

heart, a democratic institution, later Calvinists insisted, with built-in checks and balances on spiritual power, and each was loosely "confederated" with others (from the Latin term *foedus* for covenant) in regional synods and councils.[30]

Collectively, church officials held three forms of legal power (*potestas*), said Calvin. First, the church held *doctrinal power* – the "authority to lay down articles of faith, and the authority to explain them." This authority included the power of the church to set forth its own confessions, creeds, catechisms, and other authoritative distillations of the Christian faith, and to expound them freely from the pulpit and the lectern. Second, the church held *legislative power* – the power to promulgate for itself "a well-ordered constitution" that ensured "proper order and organization" in daily church life and "proper decency" and "becoming dignity" in the church's worship, liturgy, and ritual. "When churches are deprived of . . . the laws that conduce to these things," said Calvin, "their very sinews disintegrate, and they are wholly deformed and scattered." Third, and "most importantly," said Calvin, the church held *jurisdictional power* – the power to enforce laws that helped maintain discipline and inspire piety among its members.[31]

The church's jurisdictional power was "wholly spiritual" in character, Calvin insisted. Its disciplinary rules had to be "founded upon God's authority, drawn from scripture, and, therefore, wholly divine." Its sanctions were limited to admonition, instruction, and, in severe cases, the ban and excommunication –with civil and criminal penalties left for the magistrate to consider and deliver. Its administration had to be "moderate and mild," and left "not to the decision of one man but to a lawful assembly" – ideally a consistory, with proper procedures and proper deference to the rule of law.[32]

The Genevan Consistory was a unique institution, first created by Calvin in his Ecclesiastical Ordinances of 1541. It was a hybrid of church–state authority, comprising two-dozen men who sat on two benches. On one bench sat all the ordained pastors of the city, headed by Calvin as their moderator. On the other sat twelve elected lay commissioners drawn from the city government. Initially, Calvin conceived of the Consistory's jurisdiction in rather modest terms, simply as a way of purging the church of manifest sin and sinners and of policing the purity of the Eucharist.[33] By the end of his life, however, he had given it far more sweeping jurisdiction.

30 *Institutes* (1559), 4.3; CO 10/1.15–30.
31 *Institutes* (1559), 4.1.5; 4.8.1; 4.10.27–38; 4.11.1; CO, 8.1–84.
32 *Institutes* (1559), 4.10.5, 30; 4.11.1–6; 4.12.1–4, 8–11; CO, 10/1.207–8, 210–11.
33 CO 10/1:15–30.

> The matters and cases which come most commonly before the consistories are cases of idolatry and other kinds of superstition, disrespect towards God, heresy, defiance of father and mother, or of the magistrate, sedition, mutiny, assault, adultery, fornication, larceny, avarice, abduction, rape, fraud, perjury, false witness, tavern-going, gambling, disorderly feasting, gambling, and other scandalous vices: and because the magistrate usually does not favor such gatherings, the consistory will use the ordinary reprimands, namely, brotherly admonition, as sharp and as vehement as the case demands, suspension from the Lord's Supper, deprivation of the Lord's Supper for a stated period of time; and persistent offenders will be publicly named, so that people will know who they are.[34]

Studies of Genevan life during Calvin's tenure show that the Genevan Consistory played an increasingly active role in the maintenance of spiritual and moral discipline for all Genevans. The Consistory worked hand-in-hand with the Genevan city council and served, effectively, as a grand jury, mediation center, and preliminary hearings court that created a factual record. In most cases that did not involve serious crimes, the Consistory would first call parties to their higher spiritual duties, backing its recommendations with (threats of) spiritual discipline in hopes that the parties would repent, reconcile, and return to the spiritual fold. If such spiritual counsel failed, the parties were referred to the Council to compel them, using civil and criminal sanctions, to honor at least their basic civil duties.[35]

Among most later Calvinists, the Genevan-style consistory was transformed into an elected body of pastors, elders, deacons, and teachers who governed each local church congregation, but often played a less structured political and legal role in the broader Christian commonwealth. Yet local clergy still had a strong role in advising magistrates on the positive law of the local community, and local churches and their consistories also generally enjoyed autonomy in administering their own doctrine, liturgy, charity, polity, and property and in administering spiritual discipline over their members without interference from the state courts.

Separation of Church and State. Outside of the hybrid structure of the Consistory, however, Calvin insisted on a basic separation of church and state. "There is a great difference and unlikeness between the ecclesiastical and civil power" of the church and state, said Calvin. "A distinction should always be observed between these two clearly distinct areas of responsibility, the civil and

[34] SD, vol. 3, no. 992.

[35] Samples in SMF 1 and 2; analysis in Bohatec, *Calvin und Recht*, 94–131; Josef Bohatec, *Calvins Lehre von Staat und Kirche* (Breslau: M. & H. Marcus, 1937).

the ecclesiastical." The church has no authority to punish crime, to remedy civil wrongs, to collect taxes, to make war, or to meddle in the internal affairs of the state. The state, in turn, has no authority to preach the Word, to administer the sacraments, to enforce spiritual discipline, to collect tithes, to interfere with church property, to appoint or remove clergy, to obstruct bans or excommunications, or to meddle in the internal affairs of a congregation. When church officials operate as members of civil society, they must submit to the civil and criminal law of the state; they cannot claim civil immunities, tax exemptions, or privileges of forum. When state officials operate as members of the church, they must submit to the constitution and discipline of the church: they cannot insist on political prerogatives or sovereign immunities. To permit any such interference or immunity between church and state, said Calvin, would "unwisely mingle these two [institutions] which have a completely different nature."[36]

Calvin's principle of separation of church and state bore little resemblance, however, to later American understandings of "a high and impregnable" wall between church and state, as the United States Supreme Court put it in 1947, let alone the modern French understanding of *laïcité*. Calvin ultimately did not contemplate a secular society with a plurality of absolutely separated religious and political officials within it. Nor did he contemplate a neutral state that shows no preference among competing concepts of the spiritual and moral good. For Calvin, each community, like Geneva, was to be a unitary Christian society, a miniature *corpus Christianum* under God's sovereignty and law. Within this unitary society, the church and the state had to stand as coordinate powers. Both were ordained by God to help achieve a godly order and discipline in the community. Such conjoined responsibilities inevitably require church and state, clergy and magistracy to aid and accommodate each other on a variety of levels. These institutions and officials, said Calvin, "are not contraries, like water and fire, but things conjoined." "The spiritual polity, though distinct from the civil polity, does not hinder or threaten it but rather greatly helps and furthers it." In turn, "the civil government has as its appointed end ... to cherish and protect the outward worship of God, to defend sound doctrine of piety and the position of the church ... and a public manifestation of religion."[37]

Law in a Godly Republic. To achieve this ideal of a godly republic, or miniature *corpus Christianum*, within each city, Calvin and his colleagues depended on sweeping new laws that reflected the wisdom of the *ius commune*

[36] *Institutes* (1559), 3.19.15; 4.11.3–16; 4.20.1–4; CO 10/1, 15–30, 215–17, 223–24.

[37] *Serm.*, 1 Sam. 11: 6–10; *Institutes* (1559), 4.11.1; 4.20.2–3.

but also embodied the new Protestant theology. New Calvinist *family* laws, for example, rejected traditional teachings of the marital sacrament and clerical celibacy and encouraged clergy and laity alike to marry. Treating marriage as a community covenant that should be freely available to all, these new family laws sharply reduced the impediments to marry but insisted on mutual, parental, and communal consent to the marriage and public liturgical celebration. They also strengthened the rights of wives and children within the household, introduced fault-based divorce, and insisted on the right of remarriage after divorce and death. And they placed a new premium on public and private sexual morality, with church and state cooperating closely in policing and punishing fornication of all sorts. New Calvinist *education* laws made primary education and catechesis mandatory and accessible for boys and girls alike in an effort to ensure that each person was literate enough to read the Bible and understand the sermons, and experienced enough to discover their talents and discern their distinctive Christian vocation in any walk of life.[38] New Calvinist *social welfare* laws rejected the spiritual value of mendicant poverty and monastic living, as well as the centrality of the church and its institutions in tending to the poor and needy. Instead, these laws instituted local, lay-run welfare systems administered by the local magistrate. These community funds at first comprised the church's monastic properties and endowments that had been confiscated during the early Reformation. They were eventually supplemented by local taxes and private donations. In these legal reforms, and in the reforms of many other areas of public, private, penal, and procedural law, Calvin and his fellow lawyers and theologians in Geneva were intensely active.[39]

Calvin's attention to both theology and law would become a trademark of early modern Calvinism. Theologians and jurists together formed the leadership of many later Calvinist communities. For every new Calvinist catechism, there were sundry Calvinist ordinances; for every fresh confession of faith, a new charter of rights or written constitution. Early modern Calvinists believed in law – as a deterrent against sin, an inducement to grace, a teacher of Christian virtue. Early modern Calvinists also believed in liberty – structuring their churches and states alike to minimize the sins of their rulers and to maximize the liberties of their subjects.

[38] SMF 1 and 2; Robert M. Kingdon, *Adultery and Divorce in Calvin's Geneva* (Cambridge, MA: Harvard University Press, 1995); Cornelia Seeger, *Nullité de mariage divorce et séparation de corps a Genève, au temps de Calvin: Fondements doctrinaux, loi et jurisprudence* (Lausanne: Société d'histoire de la Suisse romande, 1989).

[39] SMF 2; Jeannine E. Olson, *Calvin and Social Welfare* (London: Associated University Presses, 1988).

RECOMMENDED READING

Bohatec, Josef. *Calvin und das Recht*. Graz: H. Böhlau, 1934.
Calvins Lehre von Staat und Kirche. Breslau: M. & H. Marcus, 1937.
Doumergue, Emile. *Jean Calvin: les hommes et les choses de son temps*, 7 vols. Geneva: Slatkine Reprints, 1969.
Gamble, Richard C., edn. *Calvin's Thought on Economic and Social Issues, and the Relationship of Church and State*. New York: Garland Press, 1992.
Höpfl, Harro. *The Christian Polity of John Calvin*. Cambridge: Cambridge University Press, 1982.
Hesselink, John. *Calvin's Concept of the Law*. Allison Park, PA: Pickwick Publishing, 1992.
Hunt, George L., edn. *Calvinism and Political Order*. Philadelphia: Westminster Press, 1965.
Kingdon, Robert M. *Adultery and Divorce in Calvin's Geneva*. Cambridge, MA: Harvard University Press, 1995.
McKee, Elsie Anne. *The Pastoral Ministry and Worship in Calvin's Geneva*. Geneva: Droz, 2016.
Strohm, Christoph. *Calvinismus und Recht*. Tübingen: Mohr Siebeck, 2008.
Tuininga, Matthew J. *Calvin's Political Theology and the Public Engagement of the Church*. Cambridge: Cambridge University Press, 2017.
Witte, John, Jr. *The Reformation of Rights: Law, Religion, and Human Rights in Early Modern Calvinism*. Cambridge: Cambridge University Press, 2007.

8

Jacques Cujas

(1522–1590)

XAVIER PRÉVOST

INTRODUCTION

Jacques Cujas, one of the most famous French jurists, was a leading representative of legal humanism. His glory, forged during his lifetime through a rich career, has remained to this day. If the name of the man is still famous, the contribution of the jurisconsult is often unknown. His contribution integrated the main features of humanism into the study of law. A French humanist of the sixteenth century, Cujas lived in the midst of the civil wars that tore France apart. However, he seemed to want to stay away from the religious divide, which partially explained these conflicts. Cujas focused fundamentally on the humanistic analysis of legal sources, which deeply transformed the apprehension of law for the next centuries.

Medieval methods of teaching law were running out of steam in the course of the fifteenth century: the professors moved away from the explanation of civil and canonical compilations. At the same time, in Italy, then all over Europe, other areas of knowledge were experiencing an intense intellectual activity marked by the creation and rejection of the earlier period, then qualified as the Middle Ages. Some contemporaries described the previous centuries as a vast and dark period separated from Antiquity, which they wanted to revive. From this rebirth, the movement got its name, the Renaissance. Although it originally meant the renewal of the arts, the concept has received a broader meaning in historiography, which describes both a period and a civilization. The Renaissance took place first and foremost by the disruption of stale mental frameworks, a disruption brought about by a combination of ancient knowledge rediscovered and scientific and technological progress, notably the invention of the printing press, which favored the circulation of knowledge. As a result, the study of ancient languages and cultures resumed its place in the center of education. The humanist was then the one who privileges the *studia humanitatis* to give body to the Renaissance: human dignity was ensured by the work of reason, which was inseparable from the study of ancient letters. Although the trait should not be overstated, the humanists of the late Middle Ages often presaged a harsh judgment on previous scholarly techniques, including the study of law. Humanism, indeed, quickly spread to law during the *quattrocento*, owing largely to the works of Lorenzo Valla (1407–57). This field of humanism extended to France[1] at the beginning of the sixteenth century, notably thanks to Guillaume Budé (1468–1540) and Andrea Alciato (1492–1550).

The first important jurisconsult to extensively transpose humanist precepts to the study of law was the Milanese Andra Alciato. His relatively well-known work laid the foundations of legal humanism: a return to the ancient sources of legal, philosophical, and literary origin, the search for a purified language, and the desire for a theoretical and historical understanding of the law. Alciato did not break abruptly with the commentary of the Bartolists, but the innovative aspects of his method attracted to him a crowd of students, particularly during his teaching years in Bourges between 1527 and 1533.

At the same time, Guillaume Budé, trained in civil law in Orléans, also put his philological skills in the service of legal analysis of the sources and especially of the Digest. However, his *Annotations on the Pandects* were less the work of a jurist than the work of a historian who sought to rediscover the reality of ancient life. If the goals of Alciat and Budé partly diverged, their method relied on the same postulates of the return to the sources and the correction of medieval errors. In France, they had numerous followers, so much so that the new method was called *mos gallicus jura docendi* (French method of teaching law) in opposition to the *mos italicus*, which described the medieval commentaries of Roman and canon laws. Nevertheless, legal humanism was not a unified movement. If the upholders of the *mos gallicus* shared their main principles, such as the return to the sources, they were divided about their goals.

From the middle third of the sixteenth century – the peak of legal humanism and the period in which Cujas was active – two methods clashed,

[1] For an overview of French legal humanism, see especially Xavier Prévost, "*Mos gallicus jura docendi*, La réforme humaniste de la formation des jurists," *Revue historique de droit français et étranger* 89 (2011): 491–513; Jean-Louis Thireau, "Humaniste (Jurisprudence)," in *Dictionnaire de la culture juridique*, edn. Deni Alland and Stéphane Rials (Paris: Presses universitaires de France, 2003), 795–800; Donald R. Kelley, "Civil Science in the Renaissance: Jurisprudence in the French Manner," *History of European Ideas* 2 (1981): 261–76; Hans E. Troje, "Arbeitshypothesen zum Thema Humanistische Jurisprudenz," *Tijdschrift voor Rechtsgeschiedenis* 39 (1971): 519–55.

sometimes vehemently. On the one hand, the jurists described as systematists tried to discover the ancient system of Roman law. In their view, classical Roman law formed a coherent and rationalist system. Thus, François Connan (1508–51), Éguiner Baron (*c.* 1495–1550), François Le Douaren (1509–59), and, above all, Hugues Doneau (1527–91) designed an abstract and systematic idea of the law. The systematist jurists aimed to expound the law in a logical order according to a deductive approach, from general to specific. Far from rediscovering the ancient Roman law, however, they deeply transformed the European legal orders of modern times.[2]

On the other hand, the historicist jurists of legal humanism built their thought around the concept of evolution. Thanks to their knowledge of the ancient sources, they placed Justinian's compilations in their historical context. This approach represented one of the biggest breaks from medieval methods: the humanists thus removed the *Corpus iuris civilis* from its timelessness, underlining the different stages of the construction of the legal system. Cujas undoubtedly was the best representative of this historical method. Nowadays, both his emendations of the texts of the *Corpus iuris civilis* and his editions of sources are still references for Romanists.

CUJAS'S BIOGRAPHY

Jacques Cujas was born in 1522 in Toulouse, where his father was a sheep shearer. Little is known about the education received by the young Cujas before he entered the university of his hometown, where he earned his law degree. This part of his life was chiefly related by Cujas himself in a speech delivered at Bourges on September 22, 1556. He claimed to have followed the lessons of only one master: Arnaud Du Ferrier (1506–85). The student exalted his teacher's qualities both in this discourse and in later writings on Roman law. Ferrier was an innovator, who sought to integrate history and philology in the study of Roman law. When Cujas left the Faculty of Toulouse at the beginning of 1544, he imitated Ferrier.

Having spent time earning a law degree, he did not receive his doctorate until at least three years later. During this period, the young jurisconsult sought to deepen the aspirations raised by his teacher – aspirations that the

[2] Jean-Louis Thireau, "Hugues Doneau et les fondements de la codification modern," *Droits, Revue française de théorie, de philosophie et de culture juridiques* 26 (1997): 81–100; Vincenzo Piano Mortari, "La sistematica come ideale umanistico dell'opera di Francesco Connano," in *La Storia del diritto nel quadro delle scienze storiche. Atti primo congresso internazionale della Societa italiana di storia del diritto* (Florence: L. S. Olschki, 1966), 521–31.

legal curriculum did not seem to be able to fill. From 1544 to 1547, Cujas perfected his humanist culture without leaving law aside. He strengthened his knowledge of Latin literature and learned Greek, a symbol of his appetite for renewal. He gathered the sources: he did not just read them but studied them methodically so that he reused them throughout his work and his life. More mature, Jacques Cujas came back to the university, to become a teacher.

In 1547, Cujas was appointed lecturer in charge of Justinian's Institutes. This position earned him his first praise, but he did not manage to win a chair of Roman law in Toulouse. Thus, in 1554, he left for Cahors, where he succeeded Antonio de Goveia (1505–66) as professor. Less than a year later, Margaret of France (1523–74), Duchess of Berry, offered Cujas a chair at the renowned University of Bourges, which was then the center of the reform of legal studies. Cujas had to deal with the opposition of a part of the university: those who protested his appointment, led by François Le Douaren, wanted Hugues Doneau to have the chair. In this context, Cujas resigned himself to leave in 1557; however, after less than two years in the University of Valence, he returned to Bourges.

His return in November 1559 was very different from his initial experience at Bourges. He was no longer an unknown jurist: his first books had already begun to establish his reputation. In addition, he had multiplied publications during the seven years he spent in Berry. When Margaret of France, who had become Duchess of Savoy, called him to teach at Turin in 1566, he was already one of the most renowned jurisconsults in Europe. He stayed less than a year in Italy, where he was unable to refer to the Florentine manuscript of the Digest, despite a great deal of effort.

In September 1567, Cujas was back in Valence, covered with honor and wealth. Trying not to get involved in the wars of religion, he published widely, notably his famous *Paratitla* on the Digest and the books 9 to 14 of the *Observationes et emendationes*. Owing to a financial conflict, however, he accepted an offer from the University of Bourges. He returned to Berry in June 1575 after a few months in Paris, where the prohibition against teaching civil law had been suspended in his favor. Cujas ended his career at Bourges, where he died on October 4, 1590, celebrated as the greatest jurist of the time.

Ten folio volumes resulted from this long and brilliant career, which was devoted to the humanist reform of legal studies. Besides his positions at the university, Cujas was also counselor (1566–67) to Emmanuel Philibert, Duke of Savoy (1528–80), a member of the Parliament of Grenoble (1573–82), counselor (1576–84) to Francis, Duke of Anjou and Alençon (1555–84), and judge in the *présidial*, or provincial court, of Bourges (*c.* 1584).

Regarding his personal life, it was during his first stay in Valence that Cujas married Madeleine Du Roure, in 1558. About her background, we know only that she was the daughter of a doctor from Avignon or Valence, of Jewish origin. From this union was born, at the turn of the decade 1550–60 a son, also named Jacques, who died in 1581. Five years later, Madeleine also passed away, but shortly afterwards, in November 1586, Cujas married Gabrielle Hervé, daughter of Jacques Hervé and Anne Bochetel, but also a niece by marriage of a sister of Madeleine Du Roure. By this union, Cujas was related to illustrious families, many of whom held important positions in the court and in the church. From this second union was born in 1586 or 1587 a girl, Suzanne. Many rumors, often crude, circulated about the life of this girl, whose debauchery was criticized; however, the truth of these remains largely uncertain, as are the deep religious beliefs of Cujas.

THE RELIGIOUS BELIEFS OF CUJAS

Jacques Cujas was born shortly after the Lutheran break with Rome and lived in the heart of the civil wars that tore the kingdom of France between 1562 and 1598. Cujas sought to escape this division. An apothegm sums up his posture: to those who questioned him about religion, historiography says that he answered *Nihil hoc ad edictum prætoris* (it has nothing to do with the praetor's edict). Thanks to this rhetorical evasion, he tried to avoid the blows of the Catholic and Protestant camps, but in return, he gave rise to almost insoluble questions about his deep convictions. Indeed, some consider him the paragon of the pusillanimous Protestant, hiding his true ideas behind a fake Catholicism, while others believe he held an unfeigned orthodoxy. The existence of opposing arguments seems rather to indicate that Cujas was moving in another direction.

A real affinity with Protestantism, both personally and in terms of ideas, is evident in his life. It appears in his correspondence – for example, in a letter of 1561 to Antoine Dorsanne, the Reformed lieutenant general in Issoudun, and in a letter of 1568 sent to the father of his Reformed former pupil Claude Chifflet (1541–80). Some provisions of Cujas's will, written on the day of his death, seem similar to Huguenot views, such as the simplicity of the burial desired by the jurisconsult or the prohibition of the sale of his books to Jesuits. However, nothing is explicit in this text: the humanist moved masked across the religious ground; understanding him depends largely on the point of view of the interpreter. In his legal writings, Cujas does not hesitate to quote Reformed thinkers. The references to the German Lutheran reformer Philip Melanchthon (1497–1560) show his good knowledge of the work of Luther's disciple.

Apart from these textual elements, Cujas's network of relationships is also invoked in support of the Protestantism thesis. His entourage included many influential Reformers – for example, Antoine de Crussol (1528–73), Joseph Justus Scaliger (1540–1609), and Ennemond Bonnefoi (1536–74). All of this was in the context of the adherence of humanist jurists to the Reformation,[3] which some of them actively defended. François Hotman (1524–90) is the most famous among these, with his *Épître envoyée au Tigre de la France* (1560). Hugues Doneau was forced to flee from the kingdom after the St Bartholomew's Day massacre. More tragic was the fate of Jean de Coras (1515–72), who paid with his life for his attachment to the Reformation. However, not all humanist jurists adhered to these new ideas. Probing souls is complex, especially during this sixteenth century of rifts, reversals, and uncertainties.

Thus, equally convincing arguments can be made to support Cujas's Roman Catholic orthodoxy. Indeed, throughout his life, he never openly adhered to the Reformation; on the contrary, he tried to maintain an obvious Catholicism. The *super vita et moribus* investigation (compulsory review of "the good life and morals" for the reception of Cujas into the parliament of Grenoble) is one of the main arguments for the defenders of his Catholicism, since it demonstrates his orthodoxy through many certificates. Cujas also composed a defense of Jean de Monluc (1508–79), one of the alleged perpetrators of the St Bartholomew's Day massacre. Nevertheless, this is not a text in which Cujas dropped his religious reserve: rather, he sought to reject some outrageous attacks against his protector and friend. More particularly, he responded in this document to Doneau, who – under the pseudonym of Zacharias Furnesterus – had earlier violently attacked Jean de Monluc.[4]

Given these contradictory elements, some consider the French humanist an Erasmian Catholic. For my part, I think he had rather a "religious sensibility in-between," while applying to Cujas the thesis of Thierry

[3] An obvious sign of this trend was the adages that appeared then: *Omnis jurisconsultus male de religione sentit* (Each jurisconsult misjudges about religion), and *Bonus jurisconsultus, ergo malus christianus* (Great jurisconsult, therefore bad Christian).

[4] Hugues Doneau, *Epistola Ioannis Monlucii, Episcopis Valentini Regis Gallorum legati ad Poloniæ Ordines de Illustrissimo Andium Duce in Regnum Polonicum allegendo, Eiusdem Monlucii defensio pro Illustrissimo Andium Duce, adversus quorundam calumnias, Alia adversus huius ipsius defensionis calumnias, Zachariæ Furnesteri defensio pro iusto et innocente tot millium animarum sanguine in Gallia effuso* (Lausanne, 1574). In 1575, a response to the text of Cujas was published: *Pro Io. Monlucio, episcopo et comite Diensi præscriptio, adversus libellum Zachariæ Furnesteri, cui adiecta est eiusdem Zachariæ Furnesteri adversus eandem præscriptionem, defensio* (s.l., 1575).

Wanegffelen: confronted with the dissensions that tore France apart, some of the intellectual elite opted not to choose between Rome and Geneva.[5] Thus, the preceding elements show the proximity of our author with the Protestant circles, and certainly with some of their ideas, but they never prove a confessional choice of true adherence to the Reformation. The diligent reading of the Stoic philosophers (whom Cujas quoted very often in his writings) undoubtedly favored this intermediate religious conception. The Stoic precepts contain the keys to escape the conflicts of the second half of the sixteenth century. The sibylline formula *Nihil hoc ad edictum prætoris* could represent the distinction between the political and religious spheres resulting from Stoicism.[5] Cujas here fits a phenomenon common to a large part of the cultural elite of his century. Michel de Montaigne (1533–92) is the most famous of them: externally Catholic, he followed his stoic morality away from the dogmas of the Catholic Church.[6] After all, the few bits of evidence about Cujas's religious sentiments tend to prove that he refused to choose publicly in a definitive way. Nonetheless, he is buried in a Catholic church (Saint-Pierre-le-Guillard in Bourges), in a chapel that still bears his name, although no trace of his tomb remains.

MAJOR THEMES AND CONTRIBUTIONS

The work of Jacques Cujas ensured him a brilliant career and an international reputation. However, the books published during his lifetime form only a third of all his published writings. During his career, the humanist released about twenty books, or rather thirty, since the *Observationes et emendations* was published in eleven volumes (1556–95), and the *Ad Africanum Tractatus IX* was printed in two stages (1570–73). Many of these volumes were very successful, notably his *Paratitla* on the Digest (1570) and on the Justinianic Code (1579). They have been reedited several times and inserted in collections of complete works. Numerous *Opera omnia* were published posthumously in France, Germany, Switzerland, and later Italy, as the printing of unpublished texts, mostly taken from class notes.

5 Thierry Wanegffelen, *Ni Rome ni Genève: des fidèles entre deux chaires en France au* XVI*e siècle* (Paris: Honoré Champion, 1997), xv–xvi.

5 Regarding Stoicism in France during the religious wars, see Jean-Louis Thireau, "Stoïcisme moderne," in *Dictionnaire de philosophie politique*, edn. Philippe Raynaud et Stéphane Rials (Paris: Presses universitaires de France, 2003), 754.

6 Léontine Zanta, *La Renaissance du stoïcisme au XVIe siècle* (Paris: Librairie ancienne Honoré Champion, 1914, repr. Geneva, 1975), 25.

Although it is widely distributed in many libraries, Cujas's work is not easily accessible: in their reference version,[7] the *Opera omnia* are a patchwork of thirteen thousand columns in Latin comprising works of historical critique, course material, posthumous notes, publishing sources, and consultations. From a material point of view, it is rather difficult to find one's way through the *Opera omnia*, whose organization also varies according to edition. Moreover, understanding the goals of Cujas requires a very good knowledge of legal humanism, which broke with previous legal methods. Thus, the works of Cujas disconcert the regular reader of medieval jurisprudence, just as they can disturb the specialist of the sixteenth century by their lack of systematization. Indeed, Cujas's writings are varied: this diversity is reflected in both the sources he edited and his interpretative works, all still reprinted to the present.

Cujas's Publishing of Legal Sources

By the importance he gave to sources, Jacques Cujas fits fully into the intellectual renewal of the sixteenth century: the return to the source is the foundation of humanism. The *collatio* is indeed the first stage of the humanist's work, in order to be able to perform the *emendatio* and then the *interpretatio*. Humanist are interested in the original rather than the commentary or the translation. Before publishing a text, they looks for the manuscripts that transmitted it, they learn the original language, and they correct errors. Cujas fulfils all these criteria. Throughout his life, he was in search of new manuscripts. He knew Latin and Greek perfectly, and thus could restore the texts through his work as a philologist. From his period of personal study, he learned Greek and deepened his knowledge of Latin to be able to more easily analyze ancient texts, and he began to build an impressive library, symbolic of his frantic search.

Thus, Cujas was a great publisher of legal sources. In terms of volume and scholarly contribution, these editions are an important part of his work. Nevertheless, they remain more difficult to access, either because they have not been integrated into the *Opera omnia* or because they are presented as

[7] The reference edition was the work of Charles-Annibal Fabrot: Jacques Cujas, *Opera omnia, in decem tomos distributa, quibus continentur tam priora, sive quæ ipse superstes edi curavit, quam posteriora, sive quæ post obitum eius edita sunt vel nunc primum prodeunt. Editio nova emendatior et auctior cæteris omnibus quæ ante prodierunt, opera et cura Caroli Annibalis Fabroti IC.* (Paris, 1658). It was reprinted three times in Italy in the eighteenth century (Naples, 1722–27; Naples, 1758; Venice-Modena, 1758–83). I refer only to those editions. For a precise description of the composition of *Opera omnia*, see my thesis: Xavier Prévost, "Jacques Cujas (1522–1590), Jurisconsulte humaniste" (Geneva: Droz, 2015).

appendices of a larger work. However, they must not be put aside. Cujas rediscovered texts that still serve as references for Romanists. He contributed to the publication of writings of the postclassical period of Roman law, namely the *Collatio Legum Mosaicarum et Romanarum* (1573) and the *Consultatio veteris cuiusdam iurisconsulti* (1577).[8] His editions of the Theodosian Code (1566 and 1586)[9] are considered fundamental for the history of Roman law, as they are decisive for the knowledge of these texts. They go beyond the Theodosian Code, since Cujas added in his editions of this compilation many other pre-Justinian sources. The French humanist also published several Greek sources of Roman law: a manuscript about the legal conceptions of the time, titled *Περὶ χρονικῶν διατήματων ἀπὸ ροπῆς ἑὼς εκατὸν ετῶν* (1562), and a Latin translation of the last book of the *Basilika* (1566).

All these works are relatively raw editions, to which must be added the editions of sources with a well-developed critical apparatus. They present both an amended text and an explanation of the corrections, as well as an analysis of the main issues. These works show how the historicist interpretation is developed on a text that has itself been scrutinized philologically. Moreover, the diversity of these commentary editions shows that *mos gallicus* cannot be reduced to classical jurisprudence, since the sources studied by Cujas concern both pre-Justinian Roman law (*Tituli XXVIIII ex corpore Ulpiani, in eosdem titulos Notæ*, 1554; *Interpretationes in libros V. Receptarum Sententiarum Julii Pauli*, 1558) and the compilations elaborated by Tribonian (*Tres libri Codicis*, 1562; Justinian's Institutes, 1585), without neglecting the later texts. Indeed, one of the most important editions of sources made by Cujas concerns a medieval compilation of feudal law: in 1566, he published the first critical edition of the *Libri feudorum*, which is the basis of modern editions. Thanks to its methodological qualities, Cujas's work has thus crossed the centuries.

Cujas's Critique of Legal Sources

Affirming the primacy of the sources, the humanists questioned the principles of medieval scholasticism. They forged a new method that advocated abandoning the authorities and returning to the sources. Cujas was not the first to apply this method to law, but he brought substantial improvements to the techniques forged since the end of the fifteenth century. When he wrote his first works, legal humanism was a well-established movement, with marked

8 He edited the *Consultatio veteris cuiusdam iurisconsulti*, but the *Collatio Legum Mosaicarum et Romanarum* was published by his friend and pupil Pierre Pithou, with Cujas's help.

9 The edition of 1586 was made in collaboration with François Pithou, Pierre's brother.

differences from medieval jurisprudence but still undergoing internal debates. Humanistic methods were perfected, diversified, and truly empowered, and new fracture lines separated the members of the *scuola culta*. To the rejection of the previous doctrine were now added personal and scholarly clashes between the humanist jurists: thus, the place occupied by Cujas in this field with its blurred and multiple boundaries has to be determined.

Detailed study of his works reveals an undeniable principle of his method: the absence of dogmatism regarding the legal literature. As a true humanist, he rejected the authorities and asserted his freedom, especially the need for resorting to all available sources. If, for him, a particular doctrine had no value of intangible truth, it was not necessarily without any value. Cujas adopted this posture equally with regard to medieval jurisprudence and to his contemporaries. There are, of course, some exceptions. Taken by his argument, he sometimes rejected a gloss with virulence, just as, driven by the controversies of his time, he was led sometimes to sharp criticism of his adversaries. If these short sentences remain rather rare, considering the volume of his work, they must not be forgotten, just as they cannot be the only ones emphasized. Cujas's opinion concerning glossators and commentators appears much more nuanced than the traditional conception of *mos gallicus* suggests.

The references to the *Great Gloss* in the complete works of Cujas are countless. Cujas always quotes Accursius (*c.* 1182–*c.* 1260), especially in printed lectures. As surprising as it may seem, the *Glossa ordinaria* appears as the working basis for his lectures. In fact, the return to the sources proclaimed by the humanists meant also a return to the sources of jurisprudence. The commentary of Papinianus *D.* 18, 1, 72, Pr. illustrates the central place of the gloss for the cujacian method very well. After five columns concerning the distinction between pacts and contracts, Cujas notes expressly that he has to study the gloss in order to decide what he thinks is right or wrong.[10] He then devotes three columns to the *Great Gloss*. Cujas does not just list his agreements and disagreements, he develops his own explanations, especially when he disapproves Accursius. Certainly, Cujas considers the *Great Gloss* as the intellectual basis of his audience, and the French professor reveals his approach at the beginning of his commentary of *C.J.* 8, 13: "I will annotate just a little bit each constitution, unless the wealth of the subject requires it, and I will annotate so much those which Accursius did not observe, badly

[10] Jacques Cujas, "Commentarii in libros Quæstionum Papiniani," in *Opera omnia* (Venice-Modena, 1758–83), IV, 230.

observed, or insufficiently expounded."[11] He justifies the brevity of his comments by the soundness of some glosses and so refers the students to Accursius. Many other examples show that the *Great Gloss* forms the weft of Cujas's lectures on the *Corpus iuris civilis*: Accursius and the *Glossa ordinaria* appear in almost all the analyses. Therefore, it is not surprising that the French humanist defended regularly the works of the glossators. Cujas also made extensive use of the work of the commentators, especially the writings of Bartolus de Saxoferrato (1314–57).

Despite his interest in his predecessors, Cujas also recognized their shortcomings. While he pointed to convergences between his thinking and theirs, he did not hesitate to highlight his disagreements with medieval jurisprudence, especially with the Bartolists, but also with the glossators. These criticisms result essentially from methodological differences between the humanists and the medieval jurisconsults. Significantly, four main achievements characterized the great progress of the "second revival of Roman law": better command of the language and the search for a "classical" Latin; the consideration of Greek sources; the historical reading of legal texts; and finally, the discovery of interpolations and transcription errors.

The first of the humanistic requirements was the renovation of ancient languages. Thus, Cujas did not hesitate to denounce the errors of the earlier jurisprudence, which distorted the meaning of some texts out of ignorance of the subtleties of the language of the Roman jurists. For instance, in his lecture on the *Quæstiones Papiniani*, he enjoins his pupils to remove one of the glosses on Papinianus *D.* 35, 1, 73.[12] Indeed, Accursius has not understood the meaning of *exigere cautionem*. He assumes that the heir did not take all necessary precautions with regard to the *cautio Muciana* required in this case. Instead, the use of *exigere* by Papinianus means that the heir rightly ensured the protection of the heir's interests.

Knowledge of Greek was another break between legal humanism and medieval doctrine. Taking account of the Greek sources considerably

[11] His præmissis tempus est ut perveniamus ad constitutiones hujus tituli. In singulas pauca adnotabo, nisi si forte plura rei propositæ ubertas exigat, et ea tantum adnotabo, quæ vel Accurs. non observavit, vel male observavit vel non satis abunde exposuit. Cujas, "Commentarii in libros Codicis," in *Opera omnia*, IX, 1114.

[12] Accursius non intellexit hoc loco linguam Latinam, non intellexit, quid sit exigere cautionem, quam Papinianus ait, ab herede fuisse exactam sollicite. Plus est exigere quam agere: nam exigere est rem, sive cautionem extorquere et exprimere, satis accipere. Et Accursius contra manifesta verba legis ponit quasi certissimum, Titium heredi non cavisse cautionem Mucianam, qui error tolerari non potest, et delenda est Glossa ad verbum actiones. Cujas, "Commentarii in libros Quæstionum Papiniani," in *Opera omnia*, IV, 505.

modified the interpretation of Roman legal provisions. This novelty is illustrated by a double phenomenon. On the one hand, Cujas restored and examined the Greek texts of the Justinianic compilations, overlooked by medieval jurisprudence. On the other hand, he mastered the Byzantine jurisprudence that he could then confront with the Western writings. References to the Byzantine jurists are very numerous in Cujas's writings. Moreover, thanks to Greek sources, Cujas could know the destiny of the provisions of the *Corpus iuris civilis* during the centuries that followed its promulgation. Because of these advantages, in his writings the interpretations of the glossators and commentators did not always prevail.

Indeed, according to the humanist method, Cujas introduced taking account of history in the teaching of law. Thus, he broke radically with the medieval doctrine, to such an extent that he could be considered the first legal historian. Far from the timelessness of the Bartolist *ius commune*, Cujas sought the original scope of each fragment and each constitution. Roman law was no longer fixed in Justinianic marble but was the product of a historical evolution, which continued even beyond the sixth century. Historical criticism forms the matrix of Cujas's works. To this end, he developed new techniques and constantly improved textual analysis. The historical analysis of law is indeed one of the main contributions of legal humanism and in particular of Cujas's work. The clarity of the wording in his commentary of fragments *D.* 50, 16, 43 at 45 suggests the methodological revolution: "*Quod non intellexit Accursius propter ignorantiam juris antiqui* (What Accursius did not understand due to his ignorance of the ancient law)."[13] According to the French humanist, the title *De verborum significatione* is not just a legal lexicon. The difference with the exegetical approach of the glossators is obvious: unlike his predecessors, Cujas sought to put the fragments of this title in their original context. The method leads often to a very different interpretation from that common to the doctors. The formation of *ius commune* during the Middle Ages was the result of an ahistorical reading of the Justinianic compilations: the provisions they contain were considered by medieval jurisconsults as universal, applicable in any place and at any time.

The historical dimension of the humanist approach is also found in the desire to restore the texts to their original purity. Cujas was distinguishable from the previous jurists because his corrected text differed from the one they interpreted: their conclusions were often invalidated by the restored version of the text. In order to do that, the humanist resorted to both external criticism

[13] Cujas, "Commentarii in ceteros libros Digestorum," *Opera omnia*, VIII, 498.

and internal criticism of the provisions of the *Corpus iuris civilis*. He benefited from the numerous discoveries of manuscripts, the diffusion of the printing press, and the research of his predecessors. Thanks to his learning and his interest in the sources, the French jurisconsult managed to collate a multitude of Latin and Greek texts to find the different wordings of the provisions of Roman law. His main material was logically the *Corpus iuris civilis* itself, which he tirelessly compared with the different versions that came to his knowledge. Broadly, his method embraced all Roman and Byzantine legal sources (the importance of which is evident for this great publisher). More broadly, the breadth of knowledge of a humanist could not be limited to law. His criticism thus benefited from his erudite use of external literary sources. Once the collation of texts is complete, the provisions themselves must be analyzed. The internal critic ensures the restitution of the text, not by comparison with other sources but by the study of its contents. This content is twofold, both formal and material. To identify interpolations, Cujas studied both the language in the texts and the solutions they stated. His philological skills allowed him to detect changes in the provisions of the *Corpus iuris civilis* through the style of writing or the grammatical and orthographic forms. These modifications were also visible through the historical and logical analysis grids he used. In this respect, the cujacian writings appear to be the most representative of historicist humanism.

CONCLUSION

Locating the French professor Cujas within the thought of his time generally has led historiography to use superlatives and dithyrambic expressions insisting on his glory and the quality of his works. Thus, he has been described as "the prince of the Romanists"[14] or "the king of the jurists."[15] It is certain that he played a major role in the cultural history of the sixteenth century, while the jurisconsults probably represented the intellectual elite of the kingdom. They affirmed the centrality of legal science in the field of knowledge and the life of society. If they were above all jurists, they made use of the knowledge of the humanists. This dual competence conferred upon them a considerable influence, both intellectual and practical, since they participated directly in the government of the kingdom through administrative and judicial functions.

[14] Brigitte Basdevant-Gaudemet and Jean Gaudemet, *Introduction historique au droit, XIIIe–XXe siècles* (Paris: LGDJ, 2010), 167.

[15] Jules Périn, "Nouveaux documents biographiques sur Cujas et Roaldès," *Recueil de l'Académie de législation de Toulouse* 9 (1860): 502.

The university and judicial career of Jacques Cujas highlights the summits achieved by the French professor. However, we should not draw a hagiographic portrait of him. His aura in his lifetime, the glory he enjoyed after his death, and the great qualities of an immense work should not hide the limits of the man and of some of his analyses, as illustrated by the virulent oppositions with other figures of legal humanism that punctuated his career and his writings.

In the long run, too, the cujacian method showed its limits. Its purpose was to restore a reliable text to ensure a more reliable interpretation. On the contrary, the unbridled and often clumsy search for interpolations by Cujas's epigones has generated many uncertainties that have led to endless controversies. Likewise, the reinscription of Roman law in history contributed to weakening its universal reach. The *Corpus iuris civilis* then appeared as the product of a particular civilization at a given moment and no longer as an unalterable and valid whole at any time. The providential gave way to relativism. As a result of the work of the humanists, Roman law gradually lost its supremacy, leaving an ever-increasing place for national sources, which, however, still integrate large parts of Roman law.

The decline of Roman law in the legal order of the kingdom and the very historical dimension of Cujas's analyses are at the origin of a historiographic tradition denying his writings any practical scope. But they were not designed that way. The loss of influence of Roman law was only a mediate consequence of the historicism of the cujacian method. The French master did not voluntarily wish to question the authority of the *ius civile*. His work demonstrates the importance of Roman law, not only for legal science but also for legal practice itself. The *Opera omnia* – particularly his collection of consultations (1577) and his analysis of feudal law (1566) – show, indeed, Cujas's interest in the practice of law. The humanist then directly confronted the law in its most concrete aspect, while taking advantage of the contributions of his method. Indeed, Roman law renewed by humanism is perfectly applicable in most cases submitted to it, without prevailing in a systematic way. Beyond the content of Cujas's writings, their reception by the practice both during his lifetime and after his death demonstrates that their lack of concrete scope is a pure doctrinal construction. In any event, during the seventeenth and eighteenth centuries, Cujas was called "the jurisconsult *par excellence*,"[16] evidence that he has significantly marked the law and its history.

[16] *Biographie toulousaine ou Dictionnaire historique des personnages qui... se sont rendus célèbres dans la ville de Toulouse, ou qui ont contribué à son illustration...*, edn. É.-L. de Lamothe-Langon (Paris: L. G. Michaud, 1823), I, 148.

RECOMMENDED READING

Burns, James H. *The Cambridge History of Political Thought 1450–1700*. Cambridge: Cambridge University Press, 1991.

De Bruijn, Niels. "'No One is a Better Jurist than Accursius': Medieval Legal Scholarship as the Fountainhead of Inspiration for Jacques Cujas and Hugues Doneau?" *Tijdschrift voor Rechtsgeschiedenis* 82 (2014): 72–99.

Kelley, Donald R. "Civil Science in the Renaissance: Jurisprudence in the French Manner." *History of European Ideas* 2 (1981): 261–76.

MacDonell, John, and Edward Manson. *Great Jurists of the World*. Union, NJ: Lawbook Exchange, 1914, rep. 1997.

Mathieu, Martial. "Le professeur et les magistrats: la réception de Cujas au parlement de Dauphiné." *Revue d'histoire des facultés de droit et de la science juridique* 22 (2002): 7–32.

Prévost, Xavier. "La notion de norme ayant force de loi dans l'œuvre de Jacques Cujas." In *Normes et normativité, Études d'histoire du droit rassemblées en l'honneur d'Albert Rigaudière*, edited by Corinne Leveleux-Teixeira, Anne Rousselet-Pimont, Pierre Bonin, and Florent Garnier, 213–32. Paris: Economica, 2009.

"Jacques Cujas et les poètes de l'Antiquité tardive." *Cahiers de Recherches Médiévales et Humanistes* 24 (2012): 379–403; reprinted in *Miscellanea Juslittera* 2 (2016): 104–32, www.juslittera.com/wa_files/Article_20X__20Pre_CC_81vost.pdf.

"Cujas, Jacques." In *Encyclopedia of Renaissance Philosophy*, edited by Marco Sgarbi, www.springerreference.com, 2014.

Jacques Cujas (1522–1590), Jurisconsulte humaniste. Geneva: Droz, 2015.

"Reassessing the Influence of Medieval Jurisprudence on Jacques Cujas' (1522–1590) Method." In *Reassessing Legal Humanism and its Claims: Petere Fontes?*, edited by Paul J. Du Plessis and John W. Cairns, 88–107. Edinburgh: Edinburgh University Press, 2015.

"Cujas, Jacques (1522–1590)." In *Dictionnaires des réseaux intellectuels et culturels toulousains (1480–1780)*, edited by Fanny Nepote-Desmarres and Nathalie Dauvois, www.bibliotheca-tholosana.fr, 2015.

"*Observationum et emendationum libri XXVIII* (Jacques Cujas)." In *The Formation and Transmission of Western Legal Culture: 150 Books that Made the Law in the Age of Printing*, edited by Serge Dauchy, Georges Martyn, Anthony Musson, Heikki Pihlajamäki, and Alain Wijffels, 110–13. Cham: Springer, 2016.

"Notes sur les *Observationes et emendationes* (1565–1595) de Jacques Cujas." *Les Cahiers Portalis* 5 (2017): 103–09.

"Jacques Cujas (1522–1590)." In *Histoire littéraire de la France*, edited by the Académie des inscriptions et belles-lettres. Paris: De Boccard, 2018.

"Between practice and theory: Succession law according to Jacques Cujas (1522–1590)." In *Succession Law, Practice and Society in Europe across the Centuries*, edited by Maria Gigliola di Renzo Villata, 359–79. Cham: Springer, 2018.

Schmitt, Charles B., and Quentin Skinner. *The Cambridge History of Renaissance Philosophy*. Cambridge: Cambridge University Press, 1988.

Winkel, Laurens. "Cujas (*Cujacius*) Jacques." In *Dictionnaire historique des juristes français (XIIe–XXe siècle)*, edited by Patrick Arabeyre, Jean-Louis Halpérin, and Jacques Krynen, 291–93. Paris: Presses universitaires de France, 2015.

9

François Hotman

(1524–1590)

MATHIAS SCHMOECKEL

BIOGRAPHICAL INTRODUCTION

François Hotman was the eldest son of Pierre Hotman (1485–1554), an official of the Department of Woods and Forests.[1] By his marriage with Paule de Marle, Pierre became Seigneur de Villers-St-Paul and later the first marquis of this name. Pierre was the fifth son – out of fourteen children – of Lambert Hotman (1466–1514), of a Silesian family (Uthmann), who followed the Duke of Cleve when he became the sovereign duke of Nevers through marriage. Most of Lambert's descendants became lawyers, acquired noble titles, ascended to the French high nobility, and eventually mixed with the highest noblesse de robe. In 1544 Pierre was appointed as *conseiller* in the Parlement of Paris, the supreme court of central France.

François started his studies at the age of 14 at the University of Orléans, together with his lifelong friend Theodore Beza (1519–1605). After three years, Hotman obtained his *licence des droits*. Following the provisions of his father, in 1542 he started to work for the Parisian *parlement* under the famous lawyer Charles Dumoulin (1500–66), alongside François Baudouin (1520–73), from Arras.[2] (Throughout his life, Hotman became acquainted with the most

[1] For the most detailed analysis of Hotman's life, see the wonderful monograph by Donald R. Kelley, *François Hotman: A Revolutionary's Ordeal* (Princeton: Princeton University Press, 1973); and Étienne Blocaille, *Étude sur François Hotman: La Franco-Gallia* (Paris, 1902; repr. Genève: Slatkine Reprints, 1970).

[2] Thierry Wanegffelen, *Ni Rome ni Genève. Des fidèles entre deux chaires en France au XVIe siècle* (Paris: Honoré Champion, 1997), 103ff., for Boudouin's more irenic temperament; Mario Turchetti, *Concordia o tolleranza? François Bauduin (1520–1573) e i "Moyenneurs"* (Genève: Droz, 1984); Michael Erbe, *François Bauduin (1520–1573). Biographie eines Humanisten*, Quellen und Forschungen zur Reformationsgeschichte, XLVI (Gütersloh: Mohn, 1978); Donald R. Kelley, "Historia Integra: François Baudouin and his Conception of History," *Journal of the History of Ideas* 25, no. 1 (1964): 35–57.

interesting personalities of his time.) He chose to continue his studies in humanities and Roman law at Lyon. He was more interested in humanities and ancient Roman law than in lawsuits. Instead of following his father into the Parlement of Paris, he started to give law courses at the Parisian law faculty together with Baudouin in 1546. Hotman followed Baudouin's conversion to Calvinism and left Paris in 1547. He went to Lyon and approached Calvin via Pierre Viret, the vicar of Lausanne. Owing, however, to Hotman's accusations of plagiarism against Baudoin, their friendship slowly turned into lifelong competition.[3]

Calvin took over the role of a father, and in 1547 performed the marriage of Hotman to the French émigré Claudine Aubelin. The couple would go on to have four daughters and two sons (Jean, the eldest son and heir, became secretary to the duke of Leicester; Daniel[4] was disinherited). In 1553, François acquired the citizenship of Geneva. Pierre Hotman, for his part, in 1547 was appointed judge of the *Chambre ardente*, the French inquisition against Protestant heretics. For centuries, François Hotman remained the heretic outcast of this distinguished family.

Hotman served as Calvin's secretary and translator, and was rewarded with a professorship in classics at the University of Lausanne in 1550 and at Strasbourg in 1555. In 1558 he obtained his doctorate at the University of Basel. When the duke of Prussia offered Hotman a chair at the University of Königsberg in 1556, Hotman – once again following Baudouin – obtained his first law professorship, in Roman law, at Strasbourg. Thanks to his Calvinist connections, he received invitations in 1559 from Philipp Landgrave of Hesse to the University of Marburg, from the elector of Saxony to Leipzig or Wittenberg, and even from Queen Elizabeth to a chair at Oxford. But Hotman preferred to remain in Strasbourg, which facilitated contact with Protestant Germany.[5]

Hotman's position was interesting not only for Calvin but also for Henri de Bourbon, the Protestant king of Navarre and presumptive heir to the throne of France. Hotman could help Henri in his negotiations with German princes and often was sent as diplomat and representative of the French Huguenots. Later he even wrote a legal statement on Henri's right of succession to the

3 Kelley, *François Hotman*, 38.

4 For his ideas, cf. Wanegffelen, *Ni Rome ni Genève*, 456f.

5 Cf. Robert J. Knecht, *The French Wars of Religion 1559–1598*, 3rd edn (New York: Longman, 2010).

throne of France.[6] In spite of his descent and his numerous trips through Germany, Hotman never completely learned German. Henri rewarded him with the position of *maître des requêtes* in his court of Navarre; later Hotman received the same position for Prince Louis de Bourbon, duc de Condé. In 1560 Hotman published a political analysis against the Catholic opponents in France led by the dukes of Guise. In his famous libel *Épistre envoiée au tigre de la France*, he equated the Guise brothers with a brutal tiger longing to attack France.

Thanks to the Edict of Saint-Germaine in 1562, granting limited tolerance to French Protestants, Hotman could return to Orléans. Through the auspices of the bishop of Valence, Jean de Monluc, who favored the Huguenots, Hotman obtained a professorship at the University of Valence, near Grenoble, in 1563, once again following Baudouin. In 1567, however, a Catholic mob incinerated Hotman's home and library, and he had to flee to Bourges, the leading modern university of France – or even Europe – at this time. This ancient faculty of Le Douaren, Alciato, and Cujas now counted Hugues Doneau, Antoine le Conte – a relative of Calvin – and other famous lawyers among its members.[7]

After almost five months, however, Hotman was mobbed once again and fled to Paris. He found shelter in the house of Michel de l'Hôpital (1507–73), the chancellor of France and protector of the University of Bourges and of Hotman for many years. Thanks to l'Hôpital, the king appointed Hotman as his new court historian. This initiated his thinking about a new publication, which later became the *Francogallia*. In time, l'Hôpital helped Hotman to return to Bourges,[8] and in 1568 Hotman was sent to Blois to end a civil religious war as the representative of the Huguenot side. Afterwards, he was no longer tolerated in Bourges and had to move in 1569 to Sancerre University, where one of his children – and his wife, nearly – died during the third religious war in France. This experience induced him to write a theological commentary.[9] In 1571 Hotman was allowed to return to Bourges for a last time. When the butchery of the St Bartholomew's Day massacre started to spread through the kingdom, Hotman and his colleague Hugues Doneau very

6 Beatrice Reynolds, *Proponents of Limited Monarchy in Sixteenth Century France: Francis Hotman and Jean Bodin* (New York: Columbia University Press, 1931), 42 referring to Hotman's "De iure Successions" (1585).

7 Kelley, *François Hotman*, 203.

8 L'Hôpital helped Protestants deliberately in order to strengthen a new cohabitation between the confessions; cf. Henri Amphoux, *Michel de L'Hôpital et la liberté de conscience au XVIe siècle* (Paris: Fischbacher, 1900), 104.

9 For the "Consolatio e sacris Litteris," cf. Reynolds, *Proponents of Limited Monarchy*, 60.

narrowly escaped the city guards of Sancerre by feigning a simple stroll outside the town. Once again, he lost his possessions, although some manuscripts were returned to him a year later.

Hotman fled to Beza, in Geneva, where he taught until 1578. In 1579 he moved to Basel, where the law faculty accepted him as a full professor in 1584. He liked Basel so much that he even declined an invitation from Leiden University. But the plague compelled the family to move that same year to Mombéliard, where his wife died. Hotman looked for a safe house in Geneva with his sister-in-law and developed an interest in alchemy. In 1589 he moved back to Basel, where he died on February 12, 1590. He was buried in the cathedral of Basel.

The dire questions of the time, both theological and political, seem to have forced the lawyers to excel in their work. Hotman was surrounded by a number of the most famous lawyers of French history, and he was not the only one to become an exponent of the Calvinist party. Like his contemporaries, Hotman covered an astonishing number of subjects and fields. He was an expert in European history from ancient to modern times, and one of the most important French lawyers. His edition of Roman laws such as the "Twelve Tables" served as a new standard for some time.[10] He became known for his studies on Cicero and Caesar. With his *Consolatio* he even delivered a theological commentary. Fighting against recognition as a historian and philologist alone, Hotman concentrated more and more on the interpretation of Roman and feudal law.[11] But his most important works concentrate on questions of French public law. His major work on French law was his publication *De iure regni Galliae libri tres* (Basel, 1585). Hotman became known for his analytical skills but was able to systematize and synthesize law as well.[12] Hotman's elder son published his father's writings in 1599 in the three volumes of the *Opera*.[13] They display the thematic richness of his work, although the text occasionally was corrupted by the son.

Hotman was much more than just an erudite lawyer and a productive author. He helped Calvin and others to establish and defend their cause in France and Europe. He served the future Henri IV and others as a diplomat and still could be appointed as the court historian by the French king. He acted as an intermediary between the German princes and France, concluded

[10] Roderich von Stintzing, *Geschichte der Deutschen Rechtswissenschaft*, 1. Abtheilung (München/Leipzig 1880; reimpr. Aalen: Scientia, 1957), 399, 419.

[11] Ralph E. Giesey, *The Writings of François Hotman: Bibliography of the Works 1524–1590* (Iowa City, IA: n.p., 1971 [typography]).

[12] Cf. von Stintzing, *Geschichte der Deutschen Rechtswissenschaft*, 384.

[13] *Franc. Hotmani Iurisconsulti Operum*, vols. 1–3 (Geneva, 1599).

the peace treaty of Blois in 1568 for the Protestant side, and by his polemic writings tried to influence the public perception of political developments.

MAJOR WORKS

"The Tiger of France"

In 1560 Hotman anonymously published his first big success, *Épistre envoyée au tigre de France*. It is a pamphlet of fourteen pages and is directed against two brothers of the House of Guise – Henri, the Duke of Guise (1550–88), and particularly Charles, Cardinal of Lorraine (1524–74), who performed the marriage of their niece, Mary, Queen of Scots, to the French dauphin, who would briefly serve as King Francis II. As the leaders of the Catholic party, they used their influence to ally France with the pope. Contrary to their intent, however, they could not defend the Gallican freedom of the French church, particularly the French right to accept the papal legislation by free consent.[14]

Hotman accused the Guise brothers of taking advantage of the youth of the king. As the Guise family tended to work more for their own and family interests than for the French monarchy, this accusation could have some truth. The book claimed loyalty to the monarchy and advocated for the Huguenot party. Although it clearly was the position of a Protestant adversary, the argument helped to defend the legitimacy of its complaints and to unmask the Guise party as the true rebels. Only after the St Bartholomew's Day massacre, in 1572, when King Charles IX officially took responsibility for the butchery, could the argument be transferred to the monarchy. Hotman did not shy away from calling the dukes "enemies of virtue," thieves, monsters, barbarians, and headsmen. He accused them of abusing their power and disregarding the right of the legitimate princes, and he asked them to run away before they would receive their due sentence.

The book immediately caused an uproar, and some people who were found connected with it were sentenced to death, among them a poor book merchant. Nevertheless, Hotman continued to write pamphlets. Baudouin remarked that Hotman deserved less the title of "master of requests" than "master of libels."[15]

[14] Brigitte Basdevant Gaudemet, *Histoire du droit canonique et des institutions de l'Église latine, XVe–XXe siècle* (Paris: Economica, 2014), 480f, n.590f.

[15] Kelley, *François Hotman*, 115.

Antitribonian, *and the Necessity of a Modern French Jurisprudence*

Hotman presented his first major analysis of legal history with *Antitribonien ou discours d'un grand et renomme iurisconsulte de notre temps sur l'estude des loix. Fait par l'aduis de feu M. de l'Hospital*, written in 1567 but published only in 1603.[16] Hotman claimed that Michel de l'Hôpital asked him to write this book,[17] which responded to a new urgent question raised by humanism. The study of the Latin language and its history had shown that Roman law consisted of documents from more than a millennium before, and that they were contradictory in many parts. Which part of the venerated Roman law should now be respected most: admiration for the Twelve Tables legislation, for the classical period of Roman law, or for the sixth-century legislation by Emperor Justinian and his minister Tribonian? And what did this respect for Roman law imply for the French courts of Hotman's time? The Parisian court, the parlement, was divided on this question. One faction wanted to follow Roman law as the supreme law of Christianity, while others denied its application in favor of the autonomous French tradition. The president of the parlement, Christophe de Thou (1508–82), regarded French customary law as the true foundation of French law, whereas his predecessor, Pierre Lizet (1482–1554), considered Roman law as the true French common law.[18]

Hotman worked hard to become known as a specialist in Roman law. He had dedicated to Michel de l'Hôpital his studies on the Twelve Tables. But his *Antitribonian* – directed against Justinian's minister – displayed his mastery of legal history up to his century. Although Hotman did not cite his literature precisely, it is obvious that his knowledge – for example, of Irnerius (Werner), the medieval Italian jurist and glossator – exceeded that of later generations of historians. But this was not just the tract of an erudite historian. Unlike Baudouin, who used law to determine historical developments,[19] Hotman used his historical knowledge to develop a unique new perspective on the significance of Roman law.

After a first chapter on the value of law and of legal education for youth, in which Hotman follows Aristotle and Justinian, he points out the uselessness of education on issues that are out of date. He devotes the following chapters to

[16] Paris, 1603; reprint, St Etienne, 1980.

[17] Ralph E. Giesey, "When and Why Hotman Wrote the *Francogallia*," *Bibliothèque d'humanisme et Renaissance* 29 (1967): 581–611 (596).

[18] Reported by Guy Coquille, cf. Henri Duranton, "Introduction," in François Hotman, *Antitribonian [. . .]* (Paris, 1603; reimpr. St Etienne, 1980), III–XVII, IX.

[19] E. Fournol, "Sur quelques Traités de droit public du siècle," *RHDFE* 298 (1897): 298–323 (301).

the apparent differences between ancient Rome and the kingdom of France of his time. He compares the Roman republic to the French monarchy, the excessive personal right of the ancient *patres familias* over their family members to the modern rights of adult family members and the rights conferred by marriage. With respect to the ancient *res mancipi*, French property law also differed greatly from ancient law. The same was true, as Hotman could show, for the right of succession, as the European and French tradition still massively limited testamentary freedom. With respect to the *fideicommissum* and the general enforceability of contracts, he pointed to important modernizations of the law in his time. Of course, the tribunals and the procedural law of his time hardly resembled the ancient law. In order to teach the law, it would be better to acquaint students with judicial practice than with an almost forgotten system of the past.

The next chapters try to evaluate the work of Tribonian, collecting historical evaluations of his person and his work. Without denying the general worth of this codification,[20] Hotman pointed to different shortcomings, such as too-short, too-complicated proscriptions, lacunae, and deliberate choices made by Tribonian. For this reason, Hotman explained, medieval authors such as Irnerius and Gratian had to comment on the ancient law or collect other texts to ascertain a proper use of the law for their own era. The hints about medieval legal history prove the changing nature of the law and thus the necessity of a continuous new search to determine contemporary law. For Hotman, canon law, particularly after Gratian, led to a decline of all the law.[21] In the end, in spite of the historical value of Tribonian's work, Roman law could not be accepted as the law of France. The *Corpus iuris civilis* might be studied for the accomplishments of its time, but new times demand their own laws, he wrote. Representatives of the people should set up one or two volumes with the laws describing the actual order of the French *res publica* in a plain and understandable French language.[22] He reminds his readers that King Louis XI (1423–83) had already developed such plans for contemporary legislation. Such a *reformation de police* – deciding on the admission of free testaments, for instance – should establish equitable and just laws for France.

For Hotman, there was no such monument as Roman law. Famous laws were only relicts of history and remnants of antique cultures with little

[20] For Hotman, Tribonian did not fail – thus Giesey, "When and Why" (Rn. 394), 598f. – because he sees positive elements in his works.

[21] For this Protestant perspective, cf. Rodolphe Dareste, *Essai sur François Hotman* (Paris, 1850), 28f., 36 for an antipapal publication of Dumoulin.

[22] Hotman, *Antitribonian*, 154f.

importance for current times. Law in itself was a proof of change within history.[23] The historian, therefore, had to establish the differences between the past and the present, even though some parts of ancient culture could be regarded as models.

Hotman clearly argued for new legislation in the way of a national *coutumier*, or customary law, yet he does not mention the local customary laws of France.[24] Thus Hotman evaded the division of France into the southern territory under the Roman law tradition and the northern zone under customary law. In this respect, Hotman developed Michel de l'Hôpital's creed espousing the necessary unities of royal power, faith, and law (*un roi, une foi, une loi*).[25] But in contrast to the confusion of contemporary French law,[26] Hotman found universally recognized principles of civil law in Roman law. The new legislation, therefore, not only had to decide on the new structures of the state[27] but would have to combine Roman clarity with the demands of contemporary law.

There is certainly no general anti-Roman sentiment in *Francogallia*.[28] As a historian, Hotman points out the cultural differences, so that it becomes obvious that the law of the sixth century cannot be simply adopted a thousand years later. In this respect, his former employer, Charles Dumoulin, acted more like a lawyer than Hotman, when he used his famous commentaries on the *coutume de Paris* as a means to modernize contemporary law, whereas Hotman's studies on feudal law led him to comment on the political powers of France.[29] Here again, as in *Francogallia*, Hotman uses the historical

[23] George Huppert, *The Idea of Perfect History: Historical Erudition and Historical Philosophy in "Renaissance France"* (Urbana/Chicago/London: University of Illinois Press, 1970), 153; for the analogous thought of Luther, that the "Sachsenspiegel" ("Mirror of the Saxons" – the Saxon customary law) was for the Saxons, what the "Old Testament" had been for the Jews, cf. Mathias Schmoeckel, *Recht der Reformation. Die epistemologische Revolution der Wissenschaft und die Spaltung der Rechtsordnung in der Frühen Neuzeit* (Tübingen: Mohr Siebeck, 2014), 85.

[24] Giesey, "When and Why," 600, 602.

[25] Pierre Mesnard, "François Hotman (1524–1590) et le complexe de Tribonien," *Bulletin de la Société de l'Histoire du Protestantisme Français* (1957): 117–37 (123).

[26] Joseph van Kan, *Les efforts de codification en France. Etude historique et psychologique* (Paris: Rousseau, 1929), 47.

[27] Giesey, "When and Why," 601, 604.

[28] Julian H. Franklin, *Jean Bodin and the Sixteenth-Century Revolution in the Methodology of Law and History* (Westport, CT: Greenwood Press, 1963), 30; the imperfections of Roman law either arose from insufficient understanding of the time or were remedied by later research; see the German Roman Law expert Julius Baron, *Franz Hotmann's Antitribonian: ein Beitrag zu den Codificationsbestrebungen vom XVI. bis zum XVIII. Jahrhundert* (Bonn: Collini, 1888).

[29] Giesey, "When and Why," 606.

perspective as a weapon against royal aspirations of absolutism.[30] As Hotman equates the French kingdom with its past, it is no longer the present political will that counts but the historical predisposition.

Francogallia, *and the Distribution of Powers in France*

Francogallia essentially analyzes the origin and history of the French people and constitution. Hotman demonstrates a profound knowledge of ancient Greek and Roman authors in discussing the trustworthiness of Caesar's description. He seems to have used all the available writings of historians and lawyers from the establishment of the Roman province until the fifteenth century. It seems that this monograph was already partly written before 1568.[31] He used the term "Francogallia" for the French kingdom in previous works, and pamphlets in the late 1560s already implied analogous arguments. But unlike these tracts, *Francogallia* is the fruit of a most learned historical analysis. Most of the text was written from June 1571 to June 1572.[32] After Hotman lost his manuscripts and library at Bourges during the St Bartholomew's Day massacre, in 1572, some of his possessions were returned to him the following year. He finished his book early in the summer, and it was published a few months later.[33] The first Latin version was immediately followed by an almost identical French version, but subsequent Latin editions drew on the first version.[34]

Francogallia is dedicated to Frederick, the count Palatine, a major German protector of the Huguenots, and the dedication is dated August 21, 1573, almost exactly one year after the St Bartholomew's Day massacre.[35] This event, however, is not mentioned once in the work, not even in a veiled allusion.[36] The treatment of the massacre was reserved for Hotman's pamphlet *De furoribus gallicis*, published in 1573 along with its translations into German

[30] Saffo Testoni Binetti, *Il Pensiero Politico ugonotto dallo studio della storia all'Idea di contratto: 1572–1579* (Firenze: Centro editoriale toscano, 2002), 146.

[31] Henning Ottmann, *Geschichte des politischen Denkens. Die Neuzeit. Von Machiavelli bis zu den großen Revolutionen* (Stuttgart/Weimar: Metzler, 2006), 90.

[32] Giesey, "When and Why," 609.

[33] Ralph E. Giesey, "Introduction," *Francogallia*, edn. Giesey, translated by J. H. M. Salmon (Cambridge: Cambridge University Press, 1972), 38; Giesey, "When and Why," 591, 596.

[34] Julian H. Franklin, "Introduction," in *Constitutionalism and Resistance in the Sixteenth Century: Three Treatises* (Paris, 1969), 28: the third edition, in 1586, inserted a new chapter on fundamental laws and demanded the necessary approval of public council for royal decrees.

[35] Giesey, "When and Why," 581.

[36] Ibid., 583.

and French.[37] Yet *Francogallia* became Hotman's most famous publication.[38] Together with Theodore Beza's *De iure Magistrauum* (1574) and the *Vindiciae contra tyrannos* (1579), *Francogallia* forms the most notorious triumvirate of "monarchomach" scriptures. Once again, the strength of this book is its purely scientific approach, its antiquarian method, and the lack of any polemic.[39] *Francogallia* became Hotman's most famous text and had a lasting effect on French and European historical knowledge and political theory.[40]

The book starts with an analysis of ancient Gaul, which is characterized as a culturally conformed region unified by Caesar and distinct from the Germanic countries. The old Gauls, according to Caesar, had different territories and governments. This was a means to defend their original freedom. For Hotman this was the origin of basic freedom in French history.[41] The French language arose from the influences of not only ancient Roman and Gaulish languages but also Greek, all of which merged with the Frankish tradition.[42] Roman Gaul and the Frankish tradition formed the western Frankish kingdom, which Hotman calls Francogallia.[43] This approach allows him to draw on the Gaulish, Merovingian, and Carolingian traditions to define the nature of Francogallia.

Hotman could explain now why the kings of Francogallia in this tradition could be elected or, because of their faults, deposed.[44] Notwithstanding the diversity of the kings, the kingdom remained the same and could not lose its rights. Though Hotman used Roman-law arguments here to defend the unalienable rights of the monarchy, he referred to Salic law to describe individual particularities in French law.[45] As the royal power of Germanic kings had never been unlimited or free, this restricted authority also formed the lasting condition of Francogallia ("*regni Francogalliae constituendi forma*").[46] Though Hotman did not know the modern term "constitution,"

37 The French version has the title, "Discours veritable des rages exercées en France."

38 Walter Mönch, *Frankreichs Literatur im XVI. Jahrhundert. Eine nationalpolitische Geistesgeschichte der französischen Renaissance* (Berlin: W. de Gruyter, 1938), 185.

39 Thus Giesey, "When and Why," 586.

40 For its literary history, cf. Giesey, "When and Why," 587f., n.3; for the reactions on the side of the king and Queen Catherine, cf. Reynolds, *Proponents of Limited Monarchy*, 82f.; Binetti, *Il Pensiero Politico ugonotto*, 130; Mönch, *Frankreichs Literatur*, 189.

41 Paul Moussiegt, *Hotman et Du Plessis. Théories politiques des réformés au XVIe siècle* (Cahors: Coueslant, 1899), 28.

42 Hotman, *Francogallia*, 171.

43 Ibid., 187, 221ff.

44 Ibid., 221ff., c.7, 234.

45 Ibid., 250.

46 Ibid., c.12, 286.

this is exactly what he wanted to describe. The limited power of the *imperium Germanicum*, the German empire, seemed to be a good example for the right conclusion drawn from this history. Hotman even mentioned the *ephoroi* of ancient Sparta as examples of responsible magistrates to conserve the public order.[47]

Within Francogallia, history proved the existence of many institutions and forms which limited the royal power. Starting in the Merovingian era, Hotman found *placita*, the *curia regis*, and the origin of the *parlement* as forms by which the king accepted the cooperation of representatives of the people.[48] He regarded the *publicum concilium* as the institution that installed or deposed the king, decided on war and peace, and enacted public laws.[49] Within the ranks of the *praefecti*, Hotman names the *maiores domum* and the peers of France.[50] He clearly distinguishes between the king and other *curatores* of the kingdom.[51]

The kingdom cannot be equated, therefore, with the king, as the ship cannot be equated with its captain. The leader is appointed for the people and has to fulfill his duties.[52] *Francogallia* reveals an underlying basis of freedom in the French tradition. The reign was established upon this principle.[53] The powers of the kings of Francogallia therefore are limited by well-defined rights as well as by specified laws.[54] The Parlement of Paris is described less as a royal court than as the tribunal of the three estates of the realm.[55]

Hotman has often been connected with the beginnings of a debate about modern constitutionalism.[56] Of course, Luther had changed the status of Protestant princes considerably, and since his time the attribution of powers to the Protestant prince had been a major topic. Hotman did not yet use the term "constitution," so it can be argued that France in his day did not yet have a constitution.[57] Then again, England, without a written constitution even

47 Ibid., 302, 304.
48 Ibid., c.13, 323.
49 Ibid., c.14, 332.
50 Ibid., c.15, 350, c.17, 372.
51 E.g., ibid., c.23, 444.
52 Ibid., c.19, 398.
53 Ibid., c.23, 446.
54 Ibid., c.25, 458.
55 Ibid., c.27, 500.
56 Quentin Skinner, *The Foundations of Modern Political Thought*, vol. II: *The Age of Reformation* (Cambridge: Cambridge University Press, 1978), 195.
57 Nannerl O. Keohane, *Philosophy and the State in France: The Renaissance to the Enlightenment* (Princeton: Princeton University Press, 1980), 25.

today, may well have a constitutional history.[58] In this perspective, Hotman could be described as detecting the "ancient constitution" of Francogallia[59] "avant la lettre."[60] Hotman indeed assumed fundamental structures of the realm that over long periods of time would determine the distribution of power in the country. This might have helped to form the modern discourse on constitutions.[61] With regard to the creation of a firm law for all, Hotman once again carried out l'Hôpital's longing for a country united by law.[62]

More precisely, Hotman has been identified as the spokesman of a limited monarchy.[63] He certainly was not the first to have such a view of the French monarchy, as other authors like Claude de Seyssel (1450–1520) preceded him. Seyssel regarded the French monarchy as limited by the forces of religion, the judiciary, and administration. These moderations, however, were no sign of weakness for Seyssel, but instead reminded the king to rely on the forces of his realm.[64] This retraint was no moderation of power; rather, the monarchy was strengthened.[65] Hotman emphasized the cooperation of officials in the jurisdiction, administration, and legislation since Frankish times.[66] These officials were not just members of French nobility but specialists who accompanied the king in his royal duties. Hotman especially referred to the estates of France to link the institutions of the realm more with the representatives of the territory than with the royal power. The three estates in his work became *tria genera*, which combined the forces of the king, the *optimates*, and the people.[67]

[58] Cf. John G. A. Pocock, *The Ancient Constitution and the Feudal Law: A Study of English Historical Thought in the Seventeenth Century* (Cambridge: Cambridge University Press, 1987).

[59] Giesey, "When and Why," 608.

[60] Antoine Leca, "Introduction," in *François Hotman, Franco-Gallia* (Aix-en-Provence/ Marseille : Presses universitaires d'Aix-Marseille, 1991), ix.

[61] In this sense Keohane, *Philosophy and the State in France*, 316.

[62] Reynolds, *Proponents of Limited Monarchy*, 77.

[63] Cf., e.g., Domenico Taranto, *La miktè politéia tra antico e moderno. Dal "quartum genus" alla monarchia limitata* (Milano: Angeli, 2006), 92ff.; Charles Eisenmann, *La notion de régime mixte. Recueil d'études en hommage à Charles Eisenmann* (Paris: Éditions Cujas, 1977), 107; Isabelle Bouvignies, "Monarchie mixte et souveraineté des états chez les monarchomaques huguenots," in M. Gaille-Nikodimov, ed., *Le gouvernement mixte: de l'idéal politique au monstre constitutionnel* (Sainte-Étienne: Publications de l'université de Saint-Etienne, 2005), 117–38.

[64] Binetti, *Il Pensiero Politico ugonotto*, 45.

[65] Ibid., 35.

[66] Giesey, "When and Why," 597.

[67] Arlette Jouanna, *Le devoir de révolte. La noblesse française et la gestation de l'Etat moderne, 1559–1661* (Paris: Fayard 1989), 298; for the political chances for the Huguenot party connected with the Estates, cf. Reynolds, *Proponents of Limited Monarchy*, 42.

For one of the major three tracts of the monarchomachs, Hotman astonishingly does not treat the question of a right of resistance to the point of tyrannicide.[68] For some authors, Hotman even regressed in the discussion compared to achievements already obtained in this question.[69] His modernity lies rather in his emphasis on the officials as intermediate representatives of state power, which is not derived from royal permission but from the historical structure of the kingdom. In particular, his reference to ancient Sparta was utterly new at his time.[70] Once again, Hotman's strength lies in his historical analysis alone. He does not argue for new institutions to be introduced but displays preexisting structures which have to be kept to maintain public order, and his most pressing postulations are nothing more than the repetition of ancient ideas. He could even hide his plans of codification behind Louis XI.[71]

Ideas on political resistance, however, slowly died down in France with the increasing chance that Henri of Navarre would become king of France.[72] In 1584 Henri IV even told Hotman and Duplessis-Mornay to stop reflecting on the right of resistance and to concentrate more on cooperation and a balance between the confessions.[73] Regicide was not a solution for Hotman, as it would lead only to another monarch with identical problems. In this perspective, the modernity of a mixed government or the admission of magistrates invested with stately power of their own can be understood. For Hotman, only in this way could the freedom of the people and the observance of law be attained.

Hotman was not part of the group which slowly prevailed in France and forced Henri IV to adopt Catholicism. Hotman did not mix with the more irenic party,[74] nor did he share the belief of Étienne de la Boéthie (1530–63) that the realm needed the unity of confession at least for the public sphere.[75] Instead of limiting royal power, the tracts of the monarchomachs are

[68] Ottman, *Geschichte des politischen Denkens*, 90.

[69] Udo Bermbach, "Widerstandsrecht, Souveränität, Kirche und Staat," in I. Fetscher and H. Münkler, eds., *Pipers Handbuch der politischen Ideen*, vol. 3 (Munich: Piper, 1985–93), 101–62 (114).

[70] Maxime Rosso, *La renaissance des institutions de Sparte dans la pensée Française (XVIe–XVIIe siècle)* (Aix-en-Provence: Presses Univ. d'Aix-Marseille, 2005), 88f.

[71] Giesey, "When and Why," 605.

[72] Mathias Schmoeckel, "Gewissensfreiheit und Widerstandsrecht bei Charron und Montaigne," in Angela de Benedictis and Karl Heinz Lingens, eds., *Wissen, Gewissen und Wissenschaft im Widerstandsrecht (16.–18. Jh.)*, Studien zur europäischen Rechtsgeschichte, 165 (Frankfurt a. M.: Klostermann, 2003), 111–39.

[73] Jouanna, *Le devoir de révolte*, 351.

[74] Binetti, *Il Pensiero Politico ugonotto*, 130.

[75] Keohane, *Philosophy and the State in France*, 92.

considered rather to have caused the French movement towards absolutism.[76] But the participation of the people in the public sphere, based on (public) law, the separation of political duties, and the independence of the magistracy clearly point at the developments that led eventually to the establishment of modern European constitutions.[77] These ideas obviously had an impact on Rousseau, and this influence has been considered a Protestant source of the French Revolution,[78] for which Hotman might be regarded as its most famous lawyer.

CHRISTIAN INFLUENCE

The Power of the Magistracy

As is evident in Hotman's biography, he became one of the most well-known ardent followers of Calvin in the generation of his pupils and was indubitably one of the most prominent Calvinist lawyers in France in the second half of the sixteenth century. But how did this influence his writings? In his "Tiger of France," he attacked the Guise family, but in order to protect the king and the established order, not to introduce new concepts. His other major works, however, cannot be explained without the influence of Protestant Reformation.

Particularly *Francogallia*, with its new role for the magistrates, must be understood in this perspective. Calvin's influence in this matter has already been underscored.[79] The covenant between God and God's people created mutual rights and obligations for all men and women. They have to obey God and the divine will wherever they serve. Rendering justice is the main task of all public authorities.[80] This obligation lies not only on the prince but also on

[76] Isabelle Bouvignies, "La Francogallia de François Hotman (1524–1590) et l'historiographie française," *Bulletin de la Société de l'Histoire de Protestantisme Français* CLII (2006): 199–219 (200).

[77] Keohane, *Philosophy and the State in France*, 49, 95 for de la Boétie.

[78] Dale K. van Kley, *Les origines religieuses de la Révolution française* (Paris: Edn. du Seuil, 2002), 464 ; Keohane, *Philosophy and the State in France*, 95.

[79] Cf. Mathias Schmoeckel, "The Mystery of Power Verdicts Solved? Frederic II of Prussia and the Emerging Independence of Jurisdiction," in G. Martyn, A. Musson, and H. Pihlajamäki, eds., *From the Judge's Arbitrium to the Legality Principle* (Berlin: Duncker & Humblot, 2013), 119–43; more generally, Stefan Bildheim, *Calvinistische Staatstheorien. Historische Fallstudien zur Präsenz monarchomachischer Denkstrukturen im Mitteleuropa der Frühen Neuzeit* (Frankfurt a. M.: Peter Lang, 2001).

[80] This is not the occasion to present an in-depth analysis of Calvin's theory of state; cf. Gisbert Beyerhaus, *Studien zur Staatsanschauung Calvins* (Berlin: Trowitzsch & Sohn, 1910; reprint Aalen: Scientia, 1973); Josef Bohatec, *Calvins Lehre von Staat und Kirche mit besonderer*

his magistrates. Neither can achieve their duties if the people do not cooperate; therefore, this responsibility binds both rulers and subjects reciprocally.[81] Calvin speaks here not of *les supérieurs*, like Luther's *Obrigkeit*. To render justice is the office of the king and his magistrates, whereas the subjects have to obey them. Everything good in society depends on the execution of these duties. Public peace, security, honesty, and innocence are attained only when everybody respects his duties.[82]

When justice is denied, however, rulers and subjects risk the ire of God. The ruler is unjust when he disregards God's commandments; his disobedience to God makes him at the same time cruel and inhuman, as both qualities are understood as the opposite to justice.[83] These offenses against God – these sacrileges – will be punished by God with calamities and scourges against humanity such as war, plague, bad harvests, and floods.[84] Moreover, the social order established by justice is fundamental for preservation of life, especially of the poorer and weaker citizens, and it teaches citizens how to behave in order to fulfill the requirements of religion. For this reason, establishment of justice is also a precondition for eternal life.[85]

But preservation of justice is the duty not only of the prince but also of the magistrates. When Calvin talks of the magistrate, he sometimes means the monarch,[86] sometimes the judges or officials of the administration. Rendering justice is the office of the state and all its officers. For each of them, it is a personal duty to God. Thus, the magistrates have to act on their own, even when the prince fails to lead the way. As law needs to be exerted by a Christian government,[87] the prince and his officers fill the mute law with life. Both can therefore be called, according to Calvin, the living law.[88] The prince and judges together fulfill their duties as representatives of God when they

Berücksichtigung des Organismusgedankens (Breslau 1937; reimpr. Aalen: Scientia, 1968); Mathias Schmoeckel, "Die Gewährleistung der Freiheit des Einzelnen als Staatszweck nach Calvin," in H. de Wall, ed., *Reformierte Staatslehre in der Frühen Neuzeit* (Berlin: Duncker & Humbolt, 2014).

[81] Jean Calvin, *Institution de la religion chrestienne* (Paris, 1961), vol. 1, c.3, "le huitiesme commandement," 264.

[82] Ibid., vol. 4, c.16 : du gouvernement civil, 208: "Nous voyons donc que les Magistraz sont constituez protecteurs et conservateurs de la tranquilité, honnesteté, innocence, et modestie publique, lesquelz se doivent employer à maintenir le salut et la paix comune de tous."

[83] Calvin, *Institution*, vol. 4, c.16, 236.

[84] Ibid., vol. 4, c.16, 237 : "lesquelles, sons doubte, sont corrigées par telz fléaux [. . .]".

[85] Ibid., vol. 4, c.16, 200.

[86] Ibid., vol. 4, c.16, 210.

[87] Ibid., vol. 4, c.16, 201.

[88] Ibid., vol. 4, c.16, 216.

administer justice.[89] When magistrates disobey the commands of justice, their injustice can be as detrimental to society as the reign of tyrants. When the prince fails to act according to the norms of justice, it is the duty of the magistrates to preserve justice.[90] The magistrates have to resist the king when justice and the religion of the realm are endangered.

There is a noteworthy independence presupposed in this system. Everybody has to seek the fulfilment of justice in the realm. Even when a citizen fails, others must take over to prevent the worst. Therefore, the different members of the state have to act independently when one part of the body politic neglects its duties. Conversely, there is no real right of resistance. No government, according to Calvin, can last longer than three days without the will of God.[91] Whoever disobeys the government, even the unjust government, therefore, also disobeys God.

Hotman often emphasized the role of the magistrate. Magistrates are installed with the authority of the state (*imperium*) and with power to compel citizens to obey the law.[92] This distinguishes them from the *iurisconsultus*, who is just a powerless specialist of law. For Hotman, however, all these offices touching the state are reserved for lawyers. Those responsible for the education of lawyers must bear in mind, therefore, that they have to be taught the administration of the republic in three different ways: in the establishment of the law, in jurisprudence, and in the administration of military questions.[93]

The separation of powers between the king and the magistrates – even between legislation and jurisdiction and administration – was therefore well known already in the late sixteenth century. Charles-Louis de Secondat, Montesquieu (1689–1755), only introduced the generally acceptated and formative concept of three powers – legislative, judicial, and executive – in the eighteenth century.

[89] Ibid., vol. 4, c.16, 224.

[90] Ibid., vol. 4, c.16, 239.

[91] Ibid., vol. 4, c.16, 201 s.

[92] François Hotman, *Epitomatorum in pandectas libri XXII*, here: *De origine iuris* (D. 1.2), n.1, 6: "cui imperium potestásue publico consilio delata est, vt ciues iuri parere compellat"; n.5, 44.

[93] Franciscus Hotomanus, *Iurisconsultus, siue de Optimo genere Iuris interpretandi, libellus ab auctore recognitus, elementariae* (Geneva, 1589), 3. The division between the judiciary and the executive could not yet be established in France because many offices like the *intendants* held an office that – as representatives of the king in the provinces – combined these functions.

Immutable and Fundamental Rights

Another consequence of the covenant between God and God's people was the distribution of mutual obligations and duties between these parties. For God's conservation of the world, the people owed God obedience. With regard to the rights transferred by this covenant to the individual, these could not be denied or reduced by public legislation. This helped to introduce a class of intangible, undeniable rights. Whereas Calvin developed these notions primarily as a theologian, his pupils derived legal innovations from this perspective. Hotman is one of the first who understood its fundamental implications.

Scattered throughout his works we find positions and legal evaluations that he claims to be undeniable, unchangeable, and everlasting. Hotman was one of the first lawyers to adopt Melanchthon's view on contracts – contrary to Roman law – as the means of enabling a society of free and equal individuals.[94] For Hotman, everybody has an incontestable right to form his own society.[95] Similarly, for Hotman, the right to set up a last will was not subject to civil law, which the prince might change any day. Nor did Hotman consider the freedom of testation a part of the common consent of the peoples, which he – following Melanchthon[96] – equated with the ancient *ius gentium*. This classification would have helped to deny the royal prerogative to take away any individual right.[97] This particular standpoint became typical for

[94] Franciscus Hotomanus, *Partitiones iuris ciuilis elementariae* (Geneva, 1589), 133; for the evolution of the Protestant contract doctrine, cf. Mathias Schmoeckel, "Vertragsrecht," ZRG KA 2018, not yet published.

[95] François Hotman, *Commentarius in Quatuor Libros Institutionum iuris civilis*, 2nd edn (Lyon, 1567), 515 A; cf. Mathias Schmoeckel, "Die Geschichte der Vereinsfreiheit am Beispiel des Notariats," *Notar* 12 (2016): 403–13.

[96] Mathias Schmoeckel, "Ius belli ac pacis protestantium. Die Reformation als Grundlage des modernen Völkerrechts," papers.ssrn.com/sol3/papers.cfm?abstract_id=2639024 [last accessed 3.8.2015]; also in: M. Germann and W. Decock, eds., *Das Gewissen in den Rechtslehren der protestantischen und katholischen Reformationen* (Refo500) (Leipzig: Evangelische Verlaganstalt, 2017), 226–69. For the difference between the consented *ius gentium* and the natural law, cf. François Hotman, *Epitomatorum in pandectas libri* XXII, here: *De iustitia et iure* (D. 1.1), in *Operum volume primus*, n.12, 6, and *Commentaria* ad I.1.2, here: *Operum volumen secundus*, 27.

[97] Cf. Hotman, *Epitomatorum in pandectas* libri XXII, here: *De constitutionibus* (D. 1.4), n.3, 14: "Pragmatica sanctio est constitutio Principis non de priuatorum negocio, sed de corporum, collegiorum, ordinum iure vniuerso." For specific Calvinist opinions on expropriation, cf. Mathias Schmoeckel, "Omnia sunt regis: Vom allgemeinen Eigentum des Königs zur Enteignung des Bürgers. Ein Überblick zur Geschichte der Enteignung bis zum 18. Jahrhundert," in O. Depenheuer and F. Shirvani, eds., *Die Enteignung: historische, vergleichende, dogmatische und politische Perspektiven auf ein Rechtsinstitut* (Berlin: Springer, 2018), 3–23.

Calvinist authors.[98] In these ideas we find the first steps towards a theory of private, immutable rights, later called human rights.

In a broader perspective, Hotman added a chapter on fundamental rights in the third edition of his *Francogallia*, in 1586. This chapter, regarded by some as the origin of the fundamental rights theory,[99] describes the legal limitation of royal rights in France[100] and outlines several fundamental laws:

(1) The king cannot pass laws without the consent of the "public council," which refers to the Parlement of Paris.
(2) The other rights touch the succession of the king: e.g., the king is not allowed to adopt a son and to make him king, nor can he dispose of his office and territory by a testament.
(3) Instead, the realm in its integrity reverts to the eldest son. Consequently,
(4) No daughter is allowed to inherit the kingdom.
(5) Nobody is entitled to alienate a royal domain.
(6) Capital punishment cannot be remitted without the consent of the parlement.
(7) The king cannot dismiss a magistrate without examination and approval by the peers.

These fundamental laws limit the royal power and establish a legal framework for the French monarchy.

Compared to immutable individual rights, these fundamental laws are quite distinct in their nature. But both categories were invented to limit the central power of the state. Both help to understand the argument for Francogallia. It presupposes the stability of a Franco-Gaulish people, which in the course of history discerns its laws. The covenant between God and humankind is individualized for the French people. In spite of the progress of time and the change of laws, history helps to describe the lasting features of this society. Only in this perspective can immutable rights and fundamental laws claim stability. For these reasons, Calvin's covenant between God and God's people can be regarded as a foundation for Hotman's work.

[98] Mathias Schmoeckel, "Luther's Last Will and the Triumph of Testamentary Freedom," in Ole-Albert Rønning, Helle Vogt, and Helle Møller Sigh, eds., *Donations, Inheritance and Property in the Nordic and Western World from Late Antiquity until Today* (London/New York: Routledge, 2017), 179–212.

[99] Bouvignies, *La "Franco-Gallia" de Hotman*, 206.

[100] Hotman, *Francogallia*, c.25: Regem Francogalliae non infinitam in suo regno dominationem habere, sed certo iure certisque lgibus circumscriptam, 458ff.

Codification

We have to differentiate between political motives and religious influences on Hotman's plan of a uniform law code for France. Already during the estates of Orléans (1560) and Blois (1576), had plans for unification of the legally divided country been presented.[101] This concept was proposed even from more conservative sides.[102] Finally, l'Hôpital adopted the famous slogan of the necessary unity in the kingdom, the faith, and the law (*"un roi, une foi, une loi"*).

When Melanchthon started to read Aristotle, he learned about the regular education of youth in ancient Athens on the subject of Athenian law. Future citizens should be informed about their law. This history helped Melanchthon to develop a new, rather positive vision of law. Luther only saw the function of law (*usus legis*) in the list of interdictions (*usus civilis*), which nobody could attain perfectly in its complexity, so that human beings learned about their necessary perdition (*usus theologicus*). For Melanchthon, however, law could remind even those perfect Christians, already reborn in the faith, about their duties. Working on legislation was for him a device to determine God's will. Not only the discovery of divine and natural law but also the prolongation of such norms by new laws could help people to live in accordance with God's will. In the end, laws could serve as manuals to know and remember the duties of a citizen.[103]

Long after Melanchthon, Jeremy Bentham defined the conditions of a "codification." Certainly he did not derive this from English legal history but from his Protestant heritage. The particular term was created, therefore, long before its basic definition. To serve as a manual, law books for Melanchthon, as for Bentham, had to be short but comprehensive, in the language of the people, and systematically ordered so that the provisions could be easily found. There can be hardly a doubt that the Protestant countries of Saxony (1572), Denmark (1683), Norway (1687), Sweden (1734), and Prussia (1794) followed these criteria, whereas the great Bavarian legislation from 1751 until

[101] Joseph van Kan, *Les efforts de codification en France*, 49; Jacques Vanderlinden, "Le concept de code en Europe occidentale du XIIe au XIXe siècles. Essai de définition," *Études d'histoire et d'éthnologie juridiques* 33 (Bruxelles : Editions de l'Institut de Sociologie, 1967): sur Hotman, 330.

[102] For de Thou's plan, cf. Rene Filhol, *Le premier Président Christofle de Thou et la Reformation des Coutumes* (Paris: Recueil Sirey, 1937), 190f., 216f., with further references, e.g., on Loisel.

[103] Cf. Mathias Schmoeckel, "Leges et in carmina redigendae sunt. Die Erfindung der Kodifikation als Konzept durch Melanchthon und deren Rezeption in katholischen Staaten bis 1811," ZRG KA 126 (2009): 397–436; English version: "Education by Means of Law," in M. Welker and G. Etzelmüller, eds., *Concepts of Law in the Sciences, Legal Studies, and Theology*, Religion in Philosophy and Theology 72 (Tübingen: Mohr Siebeck, 2013), 239–49.

1756 clearly was not destined to be read by the people without a training in law.

In any case, François Hotman was one of the lawyers who promoted the idea of the new kind of legislation, which since Bentham we have been accustomed to calling codification. The basic question, however, remained how this unity of French law could be achieved. Melanchthon had differentiated between three legal methods:

(1) Melanchthon himself venerated ancient Roman law. He acknowledged the empirical value of history. The study of the Egyptian, Greek, and Roman history could teach about the prerequisites of stable empires and a just order.[104] Humanity now was able to learn through historiography. In France, François Baudouin was one of the first to follow these ideas. His approach has been characterized as the attempt to understand God as revealed in history.[105] But already Dumoulin's commentary in the *Coutume de Paris* can be understood as a first step in this direction. He used the historic text of the *coutume* and his knowledge of history and law to develop a modern interpretation of the actual law. Once again, we discover similarities and discrepancies between Baudouin and Hotman. Whereas Baudouin was mainly interested in understanding ancient sources and laws, Hotman used history to establish the rules of his time.

(2) Melanchthon also pointed at natural law as a source for understanding law. He did not explain, however, how natural law could be established. This led to a multitude of natural-law analyses, particularly in the seventeenth century, e.g., in the works of Grotius and Pufendorf.

(3) Finally, as early as his *Loci communes*, in 1521, Melanchthon used a rather systematic approach, which has since been labeled "topical". Established sentences of knowledge were used to determine the extent of their validity. In their totality, they were destined to depict the complete understanding of a certain subject.

This last approach, however, was not the only way to systematize erudition for epistemological interest. Pierre de la Ramée (1515–72), a victim of the St Bartholomew's Day massacre, became famous for his "geometrical" approach,

[104] Schmoeckel, "Das Recht der Reformation," 48; Jan Schröder, *Recht als Wissenschaft. Geschichte der juristischen Methodenlehre in der Neuzeit (1500–1933)*, 2nd edn (Munich: C. H. Beck, 2012), 88.

[105] Franklin, *Jean Bodin*, 116.

in which all facts and phenomena were combined on a map like a family tree.[106] The success of adding all knowledge in a map without contradictions was regarded as proof of its verity. Once again, the world was presupposed to be without contradictions. Another contemporary approach can be found in *Les trois notairs*, by Jean Papon (1505/7–90).[107] History and law had to be reconciled to determine the principles of current law. Papon presented different perspectives in three books destined to explain how law had to be rendered into words, following the three functions of public notaries as writers (*tabellio*), chancellors (*greffier*), and secretaries.

Yet another approach in this context was the attempt to derive an autochthonous legal system starting from Roman law. An early attempt in this direction was Jean Bodin's *Juris universi distributio*, published in 1578[108] – a rather short collection of definitions more in the style of Hotman's *Partitiones*. In this field, Hotman's *Partitiones iuris ciuilis elementariae*, printed in 1589,[109] first gives major definitions, then explains the status of free men and those who have to obey others. From the description of human relations, Hotman develops the major rules of family law. Afterwards, he treats things (*res*) and obligations before the short work concludes with litigation. Roughly, Hotman used the structure of Justinian's Institutes (*personae, res, actiones*). Another major work in this field was the commentary on civil law by Hugues Doneau (Hugo Donellus, 1527–91).[110] He has been considered the first to actually achieve a systematic description of the law.[111] With regard to the structure of Doneau's work, it seems like an enlarged version of Hotman's *Partitiones*.

Mos gallicus

The lawyers of the University of Bourges were mostly connected with a new method of studying law, the *mos gallicus*. As a particularly humanistic

[106] For literature on Ramus, cf. Schmoeckel, "Das Recht der Reformation," 113f.; for his understanding of method in 1555, cf. Cesare Vasoli, "Note su Jean Bodin e la 'juris universi distributio,'" *Quaderni Fiorentini per la storia del pensiero giuridico modern* 30, no. 1 (2001): 15–44 (20).

[107] Géraldine Cazals, "Jean Papon humaniste. La mise en ordre du droit et les enjeux du renouvellement de la pensée moderne," in M. Delmas-Marty, et al., eds., *Droit et humanisme. Autour de Jean Papon, juriste forézien* (Paris: Classiques Garnier, 2015), 15–39 (27); Laurent Pfister, "Les *trois notaires* de Jean Papon. Une systématisation du droit," in Delmas-Marty, *Droit et humanisme*, 65–113.

[108] Jean Bodin, *Exposé du droit universel* (French translation) (Paris: Pr. Univ. de France, 1985); cf. Vasoli, "Note su Jean Bodin e la 'juris universi distributio.'"

[109] Mesnard, *François Hotman*, 131.

[110] Hugo Donellus, *Commentarium de jure civili viginti octo, in quibus jus civile universum singulari artificatio atque doctrina explicatum continetur* (Frankfurt, 1595).

[111] Franklin, *Jean Bodin*, 30.

approach to law, emphasizing the prerequisite knowledge of history, ancient languages, philosophy, and other humanistic disciplines, the *mos gallicus* appears to have little connection at first sight to the Protestant Reformation.[112] Classically, the emergence of this new way of interpreting law is connected with two professors of Bourges, Alciati and Budé, and with Ulrich Zasius of Freiburg.[113] But already in 1529, Johann Oldendorp, an early follower of Luther, had summed up the rules of legal reasoning in a very modern way.[114] Nobody should follow the letter of the law, Oldendorp said. Instead, the judge must detect the true reasons for the case. A lawyer should read the whole of the law, not just one sentence. He should try to understand not only the wording but also the meaning and sense of a law (Celsus D. 1.3.17). Whoever wanted to apply a norm should ask for its historical conditions: who enacted the law, at what time, for which purpose? Did that purpose change in the course of time? The validity of a law should not be denied because the judge could not find an equivalent provision; he had to find out the true norm instead. All laws and customs should be applied according to God's will and human conscience. Even the judge should obey his conscience in his judgment, because the facts of a case would not simply dictate the sentence in an objective way.[115] Oldendorp used equity, therefore, to interpret, to ameliorate, and to contradict the law. Literal, systematic, historical, teleological, and equitable interpretation should be the means to determine the rule of a case. This seems essentially modern and close to the explication of Savigny developed in 1802.

Hotman himself emphasized the importance of this kind of education for young lawyers. They should study first the practice of *bonnes lettres et sciences humanes*, moral philosophy, until the age of 21. Thus, through a thorough basis in languages, they should develop eloquence, together with profound knowledge of history, philosophy, and theology. This period should be followed by a training in legal practice for two years in schools or universities. The students would be trained by famous legal experts (*iurisconsultes*) and by means of disputes to establish peace in their territory and to venerate God.[116]

[112] For the humanist influence, cf. Hans Erich Troje, *Humanistische Jurisprudenz*, Bibliotheca Eruditorum 6 (Goldbach: Kiep, 1993), 22* (= Wissenschaft und System in der Jurisprudenz des 16. Jahrhunderts, 66), for *mos gallicus*, cf. 143*ff ("Zur Humanistischen Jurisprudenz", 110ff.) and 276* ("'Verwissenschaftlichung' und 'humanistische Jurisprudenz,'" 62).

[113] Franklin, *Constitutionalism and Resistance in the Sixteenth Century*, 76.

[114] Johann Oldendorp, *Wat byllich unn recht* ys: eyne korte eklarung allen stenden (Rostock, 1529; repr. Frankfurt a. M., 1969), 48f.

[115] Ibid., 51f.

[116] Hotman, *Antitribonian*, 158f.

A thorough legal education, therefore, qualified its students in three basic ways: (1) as a grammarian, (2) as a dialectician, and (3) as a lawyer.[117] Since the time of Melanchthon and earlier, humanist lawyers excelled in plans for a new, more profound legal education. A huge number of "letters to young students" were printed to emphasize the necessity of philological, philosophical, theological, and other humanistic studies for future lawyers. This movement was of course connected with the humanist confidence that a better education would ameliorate humankind. So even Hotman could hope that the new legal schooling would form lawyers who understood the necessity of the Protestant Reformation.[118]

Catholics like Zasius could adopt the *mos gallicus*, although it denied the central authority of the pope in the definition of law and religion. For strict Roman Catholics, therefore, the method of Melchior Cano was inevitable, as it induced them to stick to the old *mos italicus*. Modernists, humanists, and Protestants used *mos gallicus*, which in this perspective was not exclusively connected with Protestantism.

CONCLUSION

Hotman is the most famous lawyer of Calvin's followers. His career led him to Basel and Strasbourg and even included an invitation to Königsberg, and the prestige of these appointments earned him positions at the court of the Roman Catholic king. His achievements demonstrate that political and religious frontiers at this time of religious wars could be overcome by brilliant minds. As the Protestant outcast of one of the most distinguished French Catholic families of the time, he created through his conversion a distance from his father and other members of his large family that cannot be overestimated.

Hotman fought fervently for Calvinism and a new society with more individual freedom and more limits on the central power of the king. It might be true that his controversial works at first were more beneficial to his opponents, the followers of absolutism. But in the long run, his influence on the ideas of human rights and a constitution based on the principle of separated powers prevailed. For this reason, his ideas – propagated by other Calvinists authors – had a considerable impact on other countries, where other Calvinists received and worked with his ideas, as in Germany (Althusius) and England as well as Scotland and North America. Hotman's impact on the legal ideas of the French Revolution cannot be denied.

[117] Kelley, *François Hotman*, 185.
[118] Mesnard, *François Hotman*, 133.

In a time of new theologies and the increase of individual thinking and public discussion, Hotman's work was not only influential for its specific statements and beliefs but also for its methodology. His mixture of history and law provided a model for the next generations as a means to develop a new order, which only followed and realized even better the pre-established major traditions of the land. The individuality of his approach becomes obvious particularly in comparison to those of his contemporary compatriots. It might be problematic to group the discussion into the two blocks of *mos italicus* and *mos gallicus*, because there were so many different individual approaches at his time. But as the modern methods increasingly neglected the old authorities, especially the authority of the pope and the church as mediators between God and humanity, the confessional perspective gave a sound reason to oppose such new approaches to medieval scholasticism.

The French discussion on the whole, without clearly admitting as much, owed a great deal to the new spirit of the Protestant Reformation. This is equally true for a number of other aspects of Hotman's writing. Mostly his legal innovations can be traced back to Melanchthon or Calvin. This is true for the proper power and obligations of the magistrates with their effect on a limited monarchy. Such ideas can equally be detected in the discussion of codification. As the position of humanity in society has been established by the covenant with God, all human rights and obligations finally assume an undeniable, everlasting character. Such underlying novelties had a great impact on Hotman's numerous works on law.

His most famous publication, however, remains his *Francogallia* and its remarkably well-informed description of French history. In spite of, or perhaps even because of, the religious wars and political tensions of his time, Hotman helped to shape a lasting perception of French history and identity. For this reason, Hotman was one of the great humanists of his century who helped to establish modern France.

10

Hugues Doneau

(1527–1591)

CHRISTIAN HATTENHAUER

LIFE AND WORK

Hugues Doneau (Hugo Donellus) was born on December 23, 1527, in Chalons sur Saône, to a family of *noblesse de robe*.[1] When he was 12, his sister converted him to Calvinism. He studied in Toulouse and Bourges, the latter being the main center of legal humanism (*mos gallicus*); there, Doneau completed his doctorate in 1551 and became a member of the faculty of law. He published his first writings and achieved great success as a teacher. His fame as a scholar recommended Bourges to many students throughout Europe, among them many Germans. He escaped the massacres of St Bartholomew's Day (August 26, 1572) by wearing a student's habit and slipping

[1] The term *noblesse de robe* signified a category of aristocrats in the *Ancien Régime* whose nobility derived from judicial or administrative offices. Regarding Doneau's vita, cf. Margreet J. A. M. Ahsmann, *Collegium und Kolleg: Der juristische Unterricht an der Universität Leiden 1575–1630 unter besonderer Berücksichtigung der Disputationen* (Frankfurt/Main: Klostermann, 2000), 343–78; Heinrich Buhl, "Donellus in Heidelberg (1573–1579)," in *Neue Heidelberger Jahrbücher* 2 (1892): 280–313; Aernout Philip Theodoor Eyssell, *Doneau, sa vie et ses ouvrages* (Dijon: Decailly/Lamarche, 1860); Scipio Gentilis, *Oratio habita in funere Hugonis Donelli* (Altorphii: Christophorus Lochnerus et Ioannes Hofmannus, 1591); Christian Hattenhauer, "Die Ehen des Monsieur d'Onneau? Eine biographische Anmerkung zu Hugo Donellus," *Zeitschrift für Rechtsgeschichte, Romanistische Abteilung* 130 (2013): 502–06; Ernst Holthöfer, "Hugo Donellus (1527–1591)," in *Fränkische Lebensbilder* 10 (1982): 157–78; Hans Liermann, "Donellus, Hugo," in *Neue Deutsche Biographie* 4 (1959), 70–71 [Online-Version], URL: www.deutsche-biographie.de/pnd11888395X.html#ndbcontent (16.3.2018); Caspar Paumgartner, *Anniversaria in honorem D. Hugonis Donelli* (Altorphii: Christophorus Lochnerus et Ioannes Hofmannus, 1592); Katrin Stapelfeldt and Jan Schröder, "Hugo Donellus," in Gerd Kleinheyer and Jan Schröder, eds., *Deutsche und Europäische Juristen aus neun Jahrhunderten*, 6th edn (Tübingen: Mohr Siebeck, 2017), 118–21; Roderich von Stintzing, *Hugo Donellus in Altdorf* (Erlangen: Eduard Besold, 1869); and Roderich von Stintzing, "Donellus, Hugo," in *Allgemeine Deutsche Biographie* 5 (1877), 331–32 [Online-Version], URL: www.deutsche-biographie.de/pnd11888395X.html#adbcontent (16.3.2018).

through the Bourges town gate surrounded by his German followers, eventually reaching the safety of Calvinistic Geneva.

In this time of distress, Doneau was offered the professorship of *Codex Justinianus* at the University of Heidelberg. This prospering and open-minded university town and electoral residency had a population of about six thousand by that time and, with elector Friedrich III having converted to Calvinism, had become a main center of Reformed piety. In Heidelberg, Doneau would be able to confess his faith; the Huguenots were allowed to worship in their own French language using a lecture hall of the university. Doneau accepted the offer immediately and thanked God for this unexpected blessing shortly after his salvation, as well as thanking the rector and senate of the university for their humanity and philanthropy.

In February 1573, Doneau arrived at Heidelberg, on the banks of the River Neckar. Soon he proved his extraordinary quality as a scholar and lecturer and succeeded in earning by far the highest wage at the university. He twice became dean of his faculty, was a member of the university's court, and eventually served as rector. He was fortunate in his private life, too: in 1575, Doneau married Suzanne Mondekens, from a Brabant family; two years later, their daughter was baptized.

Owing to the "re-Lutherizing" of the Electoral Palatinate by elector Ludwig VI, freedom of worship ended for the Reformed, and at the end of 1577, the elector dismissed the Reformed theological professors. At the urging of Doneau, the university protested against the dismissals, though in vain. In the meantime, the government interfered with various other matters of the university. In this tense situation, Doneau became rector in 1578. Breaking his promises, the elector did not ensure freedom of worship and continued violating the university's rights and privileges. All this led Doneau to resign his rector's office and accept a chair at the University of Leiden, in the Calvinistic Netherlands.

Doneau started lecturing in Leiden in October 1579. In 1585, he refused an offer to return to Heidelberg, which in the meantime had converted back to Calvinism. Only two years later, he lost his chair in Leiden owing to the conflict – both politically and religiously induced – between the States General of the Netherlands and Robert Dudley, the Earl of Leicester and governor general of the United Provinces. Leicester had the support of fundamentalist Calvinists, Doneau among them, who wanted to increase the influence of the church on the state (following the example of Geneva). Thus, they opposed the moderately reformed political line of the States General and, especially, of the ruling classes of the cities. Having caught Doneau distributing inflammatory pamphlets of fundamentalist Calvinistic parties and speaking against the States General in public, the municipal authorities and the curators of the University of Leiden dismissed him in April 1587.

In May 1588, Doneau moved to the academy of the free imperial city of Nuremberg, in Altdorf. The academy had attempted to hire him already in 1583. Moving to the Lutheran Altdorf was not a problem for the pugnacious Calvinist Doneau, as the confessional liberty of the Academy of Nuremberg made the differences between Lutheranism and Calvinism irrelevant. Famous and highly esteemed, Doneau died in Altdorf on May 4, 1591.

Doneau was at the head of the dogmatic school of legal humanism, which focused on the Roman law being applied at that time, a school he had joined under the influence of his academic mentor François Douaren. The dogmatic school was opposed to the antiquarian school, which dealt only with the ancient Roman-law sources and was directed by Doneau's scientific and personal adversary, Jacques Cujas.

Doneau's *Opera omnia* comprise eight thousand folio pages. Completing and crowning his *opus*, in Altdorf he published the first two volumes of his *Commentarii de iure civili* in 1589 (books 1–5) and 1590 (books 6–11). The third volume of the *Commentarii* was published posthumously in 1595 by his follower Scipione Gentili, to whom Doneau had left a completed and printable original. Gentili added volumes four (1595, books 17–22) and five (1596, books 23–28), including his own amendments from Doneau's literary estate.

Doneau presented his lectures in Bourges and Heidelberg in a conventional way, by treating individual parts of the *Corpus iuris civilis*.[2] In Leiden, he changed to a systematic approach toward lecturing, but he encountered resistance from the university administration. In Leiden, his "*maniere van doceren*," or style of teaching, was one of the reasons for justifying his dismissal. In Altdorf, the directors permitted him to lecture in the new systematic style but also wanted him to treat the texts of the *Corpus iuris civilis* in the traditional (exegetical) way.

[2] Regarding the following, cf. Robert Feenstra, "Hugues Doneau et les juristes néerlandais du XVIIe siècle: l'influence de son 'système' sur l'évolution du droit privé avant le Pandectisme," in Bruno Schmidlin and Alfred Dufour, eds., *Jacques Godefroy (1587–1652) et l'humanisme juridique à Genève. Actes du colloque Jacques Godefroy* (Basel: Helbing & Lichtenhahn, 1991), 231–43, at 234ff., and Christian Hattenhauer, "Ad totius iuris cognitionem. Zum Systemverständnis bei Hugo Donellus," in Arndt Kiehnle, Bernd Mertens, and Gottfried Schiemann, eds., *Festschrift für Jan Schröder zum 70. Geburtstag* (Tübingen: Mohr Siebeck, 2013), 51–67, at 53 with further references.

MAJOR THEMES AND CONTRIBUTIONS

Ad totius iuris cognitionem: *Doneau's* Commentarii de iure civili *as an* "ars iuris"

In his *Commentarii de iure civili*, Doneau newly systematized the Roman civil law that was being applied in his time; two hundred years later, the rational law and the pandectic school of law used the term "system" for this approach. Owing to the completeness of the *Commentarii* and its high level of dogmatic analysis, which had never been achieved before, this work outshone all other systematic treatments during the sixteenth and seventeenth centuries. Doneau's approach did not follow the legal order of the *Digests* (432 titles contained in fifty books), but the institutional composition (*personae, res, actiones*). In its first part (books 1 to 16), the *Commentarii* discussed as *ius nostrum* (our right) the substantive law of persons, of property, and of obligations (*personae, res*); the second part (books 17 to 28) covered as *ratio iuris nostri obtinendi* the procedural law (*actiones*).

In the nineteenth century, the German pandectists drew on Doneau as the principal supporter of their own understanding of "system." The German historical school of jurisprudence continued in the tradition of the *mos gallicus* by focusing on ancient sources and by systematizing the law. Friedrich Carl von Savigny, himself with Huguenot roots, considered the *Commentarii* the "best and almost only suitable piece of work"[3] of all preceding jurists. Based on the new concept of science (*Wissenschaft*) developed by Immanuel Kant, the system in that era was seen as a source of still-unknown legal concepts and terms. Roderich von Stintzing regarded Doneau's "method ... as the role model for the systematic jurisprudence of civil law for our century in Germany."[4]

Doneau himself, however, was not familiar with this understanding of system as a source of law.[5] Instead, his systematization of Roman law simply

[3] "Das beste und fast einzig brauchbare Werk," Friedrich Carl von Savigny, "Anleitung zu einem eignen Studium der Jurisprudenz nachgeschrieben im Winter 1802, vom 7. November 1802 bis 1. Merz 1803 [v. Jacob Grimm]," in Aldo Mazzacane, ed., *Friedrich Carl von Savigny, Vorlesungen über juristische Methodologie 1802–1842*, 2nd edn (Frankfurt/Main: Klostermann, 2004), 187.

[4] "Seine Methode ist das Vorbild der systematischen Civilistik unseres Jahrhunderts in Deutschland geworden": von Stintzing, "Donellus, Hugo," 331.

[5] Cf. with further references Hattenhauer, "Ad totius iuris cognitionem," 56ff. Recognizing a "productive system" at Doneau Avenarius, "'Neque id sine magna Servii laude...'. Historisierung der Rechtswissenschaft und Genese von System und Methode bei Donellus,"*Tijdschrift voor Rechtsgeschiedenis* 74 (2006), 61–93, at 70ff.

aimed to improve legal safeguards through easier perception and understanding of law to combat injustice and disorder. For him, the sole and highest aim of law is *iuste vivere* (to live righteously), while *iuste* just means "to give to each his own" (Comm. 2,1,2). Thus, among the three most important basic principles (precepts) of law – *honeste vivere, alterum non laedere, suum cuique tribuere* (to live honestly, to injure no one, to give to each his own), D. 1,1,10,1 [*Pseudo-Ulpian*] = I. 1,1,3) – Doneau considered the last one the highest. According to him, violation of the *suum cuique tribuere* leads to conflicts, wars, and riots resulting in the destruction of humankind. As a Huguenot refugee, Doneau had many painful experiences throughout his life. Thus, according to him, the state should be ruled by statute and law, which determine what is to be given to each as his or her own. For this purpose, he suggested that the Roman legal order would serve best because of its superiority to all other legal orders (Comm. praef. XXXIII and 1,16). But Justinian's large and cumbersome compilation of Roman law made it difficult to understand what was legal (Comm. praef. XXXVf.). Thus, aiming at a comprehensive understanding of the whole law (*ad totius iuris cognitionem*), already in teaching law (Comm. 1,1,12) Doneau presents his *ars iuris* (Comm. praef. XLIVf.).

Doneau shared with the other systematic approaches of his day this simple purpose of achieving a better order. On the other hand, the then-dominant method of Pierre de la Ramée, a Calvinist Parisian humanist and philosopher, was limited to the systematic presentation of assured knowledge.[6] The *methodus Ramea* was mainly followed by Reformed legal scholars, who highly esteemed La Ramée as a martyr of the St Bartholomew's Day massacre. As a dihairetic method, La Ramée's approach divided basic scientific terms further and further into increasingly subtle subtopics, classes, and species. Doneau did not explicitly base his *Commentarii* on this method, but following Cicero, he in fact acknowledged the dihairetic method. Not only in the missing work *De iure civili in artem redigendo* but also in *Brutus* (152–53) and in *De oratore* (1,42), Cicero postulated an *ars perfecta* – a perfect art, or in today's words a perfect system – by subtly dividing the Roman civil law into classes and subdivisions. To this aim, the *ius in artem redigendum*, Doneau refers at the very beginning of his *Commentarii* (Comm. praef. XIII and 1,1,1).

[6] About him, see Rafael Ramis Barceló, "Petrus Ramus on Law and Jurisprudence," *Journal on European History of Law* 4, no. 2 (2013): 107–17; and Walther J. Ong, *Ramus, Method, and the Decay of Dialogue* (Cambridge, MA: Harvard University Press, 1958).

Dogmatic Predominating Method: Rearranging the Rules on Warranty for Defects in Sales Law

Despite his close link to Cicero's program of *ars iuris*, rather than being a methodologist, Doneau was much more of a dogmatist. Not only in his explicitly systematic *Commentarii* but even in his early exegetical work, he intended to present a coherent dogmatic of civil law. After all, one can find systematic concepts in his early work as well as exegetical tendencies in his *Commentarii*.[7] As Doneau himself confirms, his systematizing thoughts reach far back (Comm. praef. XLV). We find a good example of this thinking in his systematization of liability for defects in sales law.[8] In 1558, still in Bourges, he succeeded in harmonizing the sales law bequeathed by Justinian in the *Digests* in an inconsistent way.

In ancient Roman law, the buyer could choose between various remedies in case of a defect of a purchased good. Using the *stipulatio*, the seller could guarantee that the good being sold was free of defects. In addition, the *aediles curules*, who were magistrates exercising jurisdiction over the markets, in their edict on the sale of slaves and draft animals granted legal actions for rescission and restitution (*actio redhibitoria*) and for price reduction (*actio quanti minoris*) regardless of any fault of the seller (Ulpian, D. 21,1,1 pr.-1). The possible exercise of *actio redhibitoria* expired after six months, and the *actio quanti minoris* after one year (Ulpian, D. 21,1,19,6).

In addition to these aedilitian actions of *ius honorarium*, the *ius civile* offered the sales action (*actio empti*) to the buyer. Primarily aiming at ensuring performance, the *actio empti* took on the function of a warranty. Originally, it applied only in cases of fraud, of assertions with no basis, and of guarantees that a purchased good was free from defects or had a special quality. In classic Roman law, the legal consequences of the *actio empti* regarding the compensation of damages were aligned with those of the aedilitian actions. If the buyer would have paid less for the good if he had known of the defect, he could claim a return of the difference (price reduction); if he had not bought the good at all, he could claim a full refund while returning the purchased item (rescission). Furthermore, according to Julian, even the upright seller was held liable for a price reduction, independently from having guaranteed

[7] Cf. Hans Erich Troje, "Die Literatur des gemeinen Rechts unter dem Einfluss des Humanismus," in Helmut Coing, ed., *Handbuch der Quellen und Literatur der neueren europäischen Privatrechtsgeschichte, vol. 1: Neuere Zeit (1500–1800). Das Zeitalter des gemeinen Rechts, part 1: Wissenschaft* (München: C. H. Beck, 1977), 615–795, at 763ff.

[8] Cf. Hattenhauer, "Ad totius iuris cognitionem," 62ff. with further references.

freedom from defects (Ulpian/Julian, D. 19,1,13 pr.-1). The *actio empti* would expire after the ordinary term of thirty years.

In the sixth century, Justinian extended the aedilitian remedies to all purchased goods in book 21 of the *Digests*, while in the first title of book 19 he nevertheless upheld the *actio empti* and its extensions. Consequently, from then on, the *actio empti* included the rescission and the price reduction as well as the liability of upright sellers, while the aedilitian actions were in fact rendered redundant. However, owing to his classicism, Justinian held on to the aedilitian actions.

This tradition of sources led to the question whether the warranty against defects is based on the aedilitian actions or on the *actio empti*.[9] The *actio empti*, which primarily ensures performance, assumes that a defect hinders full performance. The aedilitian remedies, which are not related to performance, determine that freedom from defect is not owed as part of performance; consequently, in case of defectiveness in the purchased good, the buyer cannot demand performance through remedy of the defect, but only his defect-related rights. If this is classification of a dogmatic nature, different prescription periods raise major practical questions: for instance, subsequent to the end of the period allowed for the aedilitian remedies, could a buyer pursue the same remedy by claiming the sales action for as long as thirty years after the conclusion of the contract?

Owing to its unclear tradition and unresolved fundamental issues, the sales law in the Roman sources challenged the systematic legal humanists to form a new, coherent concept not available in the traditional jurisprudence that followed the order of the Roman sources. Lawyers in the Middle Ages tended to focus on the sales action while regarding the aedilitian actions as special forms. Azo was the first to systematically harmonize the liability of edicts with the action for performance, while Accursius reverted to the self-standing warranty for defects. No convergence of these two approaches occurred, as can be seen by the way extremely different prescription periods continued to persist.

By distancing himself from the straitjacket imposed by the division of remedies in sales law in books 19 and 21 of the *Digests*, Doneau developed the first coherent, systematic, independent, and clearly structured warranty for defects. In his *Commentarius in titulum de aedilitio edicto* of 1558, he dealt in depth with the obligation of the seller to supply buyers with goods free from

[9] Regarding the following, cf. Walter Jürgen Klempt, *Die Grundlagen der Sachmängelhaftung des Verkäufers im Vernunftrecht und Usus modernus* (Köln, Stuttgart: Kohlhammer, 1967), 15ff.

defects (*incorrupta*):[10] the concurrence of both remedies resulted in absurd outcomes, when the buyer could proceed with a claim via the sales action despite the prescription of aedilitian action.

Using the historic reasoning of the *mos gallicus*, Doneau continues: prior to the edict, there was no general warranty for defects originated in sales contracts and, therewith, none besides the sales action. Since the *actio empti* as a contract claim comprises everything that usually needs to be performed by the seller, *a fortiori* it must include all that is based not on custom and habit but on special legal grounds, that is, the edict. The edict introduced a new sales action that is not adapted from the *ius civile* since the aediles stated it with tight time limitations. Here Doneau finds a solution: owing to its obligation for sellers to supply goods free of defects, the *actio empti* forms the foundation of the warranty for defects. Its substance, however, originates from the edict.

In his *Commentarii*, Doneau abstained from a methodical derivation but simply referred to his prior reasoning (Comm. 13,3,2) and determined these results (Comm. 13,3,10). A methodical derivation of these results apparently was not decisive for Doneau. His legal solutions are owed mainly to his attention to dogmatics, enhanced by his systematic approach.

Just one generation after Doneau, methods were an obviously greater issue to the German Calvinist jurist Johannes Althusius (Althaus). He developed Doneau's solution further and, by following the *methodus Ramea*, created a more coherent methodical version, which he also displayed on a Ramistic table.[11] This again illustrates Doneau's neglect of methodical issues. In the history of European jurisprudence, the *Commentarii* are a peak performance not in method but in dogmatics.[12]

[10] Hugo Donellus, *In titulum de usuris in Pandectis et sequentem commentarius [. . .] de usuris, et nautico foenere, de fructibus, causa et accessionibus, de mora nunc recens auctus et recognitus. Eiusdem in tres libros Pandectarum, vicesimum, vicesimum primum et vicesimum secundum commentarii [= de pignoribus et hypothecis, de aedilitio edicto, de evictione et duplae stipulatione, de probationibus, de fide instrumentorum, de testibus]* (Lugduni: Gulielmus Rovillius, 1558), 265–307, at 290ff.

[11] Johannes Althusius, *Dicaeologicae libri tres totum et universum ius, quo utimur, methodice complectens* (Herbornae Nassoviorum: Christophorus Corvinus, 1617), 1,74f. (including a Ramistic table on p. 218); cf. Christian Hattenhauer, "Johannes Althusius, Petrus Ramus und die Systematisierung der kaufrechtlichen Sachmängelhaftung," in Christoph Strohm and Heinrich de Wall, eds., *Konfessionalität und Jurisprudenz in der frühen Neuzeit* (Berlin: Duncker & Humblot, 2009), 239–61, at 250ff., and Hattenhauer, "Ad totius iuris cognitionem," 65ff.

[12] Jan Schröder, *Recht als Wissenschaft. Geschichte der juristischen Methodenlehre in der Neuzeit (1500–1933)*, 2nd edn (München: C. H. Beck, 2012), 88.

Suum cuique tribuere: *The Individualization of Private Law*

Doneau's central innovation consists in interpreting private law by taking the human being for its basis. Contrary to the *Institutes* of Gaius and Justinian, *persona* in Doneau's view is, on the one hand, no longer merely seen alongside *res* and *actiones*, but is the starting point of all legal consideration. On the other hand, and above all, the individual as legal entity forms the center of the entire private law. It is "our" law, which Doneau wants to secure according to the basic principle of *suum cuique tribuere*, i.e., the correct apprehension of law and justice by state authority. The *id quod nostrum est* (what is ours) Doneau divides into *quod nobis debetur* (what is owed to us) and *quod proprie nostrum est* (what is our own) – covering the relation of the person to outward things (*in rebus externis*) and to each individual (*in persona cuiusque*).

For the first time in civil-law literature, with regard to this phrase *quod proprie nostrum est in persona cuiusque*, Doneau enumerates a catalogue of individual legal interests given to each person by nature and God: *vita, incolumitas corporis, libertas*, and *existimatio* (life, physical integrity, freedom, and esteem, Comm. 2,8,3). With the exception of *vita*, for which he refers only to criminal law at this point, Doneau in the traditional way also deals with the legal protection of these objects in reference to the *actio iniuriarum* (action for a personal violation or injury, Comm. 15,25,2ff.). He interprets them further, however, as connected to the individual, and so he underlines their great significance not only by prepending and explicitly mentioning them but also by enumerating them in the preface (*vita, corpus, libertas et alia huius generis*, Comm., praef. XXX).

With his catalogue of individual legal interests, Doneau paved the way for the doctrine of the "right of personality." When Doneau describes life, integrity, freedom, and esteem as *suum in persona ipsa*, he does not lose sight of the civil-law context. So, for instance, he does not touch on the social and political significance of these rights and does not establish a catalogue of basic constitutional or human rights. Nevertheless, his mentioning of individual legal interests of course pioneered the later constitutional rights of the person with their basic principle of protecting the person through a focus on the state.

In the context of his emphasis on individual legal interests, Doneau uses the term *persona* for the first time as a legal concept.[13] While characteristics such as rational nature, individuality, and dignity already were attributed to the concept of persons in the philosophy and theology of the Middle Ages,

[13] Cf. Christian Hattenhauer, "'Der Mensch als solcher rechtsfähig' – Von der Person zur Rechtsperson," in Eckart Klein, ed., *Der Mensch als Person und Rechtsperson: Grundlage der*

persona had no technical meaning in common jurisprudence until the end of the sixteenth century. The reason for this lies in the tradition of the ancient Roman legal sources. Although Justinian's *Institutes* began consideration of law with the person (I. 1,2,12), this did not render the person a legal concept. In ancient times, *persona* in a nontechnical use meant simply "human"; for example, the *ius personarum* covered slaves as well as citizens. Originally connoting an actor's masks, and therefore the actor's roles, *persona* now meant the roles of humans within society. The starting point for law, however, was not *persona* but the civil-law *status* of respective groups of people – whether freedom, Roman citizenship, or one's position in the family. This corporately characterized triad of *status libertatis, civitatis*, and *familiae* defined civil law until the nineteenth century.

Doneau often equates *persona* with "human" but applies it in his *Commentarii* for the first time with a new technical legal meaning. Yet to create this "legal person," he was not inspired by the individual legal interests of *vita, incolumitas corporis, libertas* and *existimatio*; the equation of "human," "person," and "legal capacity" was not initiated by jurisprudence until the late eighteenth century under the influence of Kant. Instead, Doneau uses the classic Roman-law differentiation between *ius gentium*, as the right of all humans, and *ius civile*, as the right of a specific *civitas*. He allocates the four individual legal interests to the *ius gentium*, while restricting the *persona* in its legal meaning to the *ius civile*. Here, Doneau holds on to the traditional Roman doctrine of *status*: that the human becomes a legal person through the three statuses of Roman law (Comm. 2,9,1).

Thus, Doneau does not use the catalogue of individual interests to define the human as a person. Yet, because of the tendency to focus on the individual, he creates the new legal term "person": in a new technical legal meaning, *persona* becomes someone who has a positive *status libertatis, civitatis*, or *familiae* and thus participates in legal life. Still, full clarity is not yet reached. For instance, by treating individual legal interests pursuant to *ius gentium*, Doneau refers to the narrow term *persona* instead of the broader *homo*. A few years later, the German Calvinist jurist Hermann Vultejus captures the new legal term "person" in a strictly conceptual way:

> A person is a human having a civil status. . . . The word "human" derives from nature, the word "person" from civil law. Every person is a human, but not the other way around. Thus, we defined a "person" as a human, who had

Freiheit (Berlin: Berliner Wissenschaftsverlag, 2011), 37–66, at 39ff.; and Hattenhauer, "Ius suum tribuere," 14ff. with further references.

a civil status. ... But status is threefold – of liberty, citizenship, and family. Of these a slave has none, so a slave in law is not held to be a person.[14]

Because *(ius) suum cuique tribuere* plays a central role in his system, Doneau further assigns to the term *ius* the key role that it retains in today's civil law.[15] Following Paulus, D. 1,1,11, *ius* for Doneau means first of all an order of the natural, civil, or honorary law (the part of the Roman law developed by the high magistrates) or even the place of jurisdiction (Comm. 1,3,2 and 4). However, Doneau takes the definition of justice in D. 1,1,10 pr. as *constans et perpetua voluntas ius suum cuique tribuendi* (the constant and perpetual will to give to each his own) as a starting point to describe *ius* comprehensively as both what is given to each individual especially by law (*ea quae sunt cuiusque privatim iure tamen illi tributa*) and individual legal power (*facultas et potestas iure tributa*) (Comm. 1,3,3). The German pandectists took up Doneau's definition in the nineteenth century and complemented it: for Savigny, the subjective right is "the power justly appertaining to the individual person";[16] for Bernhard Windscheid, it is a "will-power or will-rule, granted by the legal order."[17] In combination with Rudolf von Ihering's definition of the subjective right as "legally protected interest,"[18] Doneau's approach thus imprints a central term of civil law up to the present day.

Oriented toward the *suum cuique tribuere* and the individual's right, Doneau helped civil law in general toward a new comprehension: he differentiates *ius privatum* from *ius publicum* in Ulpian, D. 1,1,1,2, pursuant to which the public law refers to the (Roman) state, and the civil law to the

[14] "Persona est homo habens caput civile. [...] Homo vocabulum est naturae, persona iuris civilis. Omnis persona est homo, sed non vicissim. Inde personam definiebamus hominem, qui caput haberet civile. [...] Sed caput civile triplex est, libertatis, civitatis & familiae. Horum servus nullum habet, ut servus in usu iuris pro persona non habeatur," Hermann Vultejus, *In institutiones iuris civilis a Iustiniano compositas commentarius* (Marpurgi: Paulus Egenolphus, 1598), ad I. 1,2,12.

[15] Helmut Coing, "Zur Geschichte des Begriffs 'Subjektives Recht,'" in Helmut Coing, ed., *Gesammelte Aufsätze zu Rechtsgeschichte, Rechtsphilosophie und Zivilrecht 1947–1975*, vol. 1 (Frankfurt/Main: Klostermann, 1982), 241–62, at 251f.

[16] Friedrich Carl von Savigny, *System of the Modern Roman Law*, trans. William Holloway, vol. 1 (Madras: J. Higginbotham, 1867), sect. IV, p. 6; "die der einzelnen Person zustehende Macht," Friedrich Carl von Savigny, *System des heutigen römischen Rechts*, vol. 1 (Berlin: Veit und Comp., 1840), § 4, p. 7.

[17] "Eine von der Rechtsordnung verliehene Willensmacht oder Willensherrschaft," Bernhard Windscheid, *Lehrbuch des Pandektenrechts*, vol. 1, 7th edn (Frankfurt/Main: Rütten & Loening, 1891), § 37, p. 88.

[18] "Rechtlich geschütztes Interesse," Rudolf von Ihering, *Geist des römischen Rechts auf den verschiedenen Stufen seiner Entwicklung*, 3rd edn (Leipzig: Breitkopf und Härtel, 1877), 3. Teil, 1. Abt., § 60, p. 327f.

interest of the individual (Comm. 2,7,2). By combining this definition with the *suum cuique tribuere*, or the definition of justice in D. 1,1,10 pr., Doneau describes civil law as the law giving to each his or her own: *Ad privatorum utilitatem recta pertinere ius intellegitur, quod privatis, et singulis, quod suum est, tribuit* (Comm. 2,7,3). Civil law now is a doctrine of several subjective rights.[19]

Orienting the restructuring of Roman law toward subjective rights, Doneau finally takes the decisive step away from a civil law characterized by legal actions to a substantive civil law. He thus came to a new comprehension of the relation between *ius* (right) und *actio* (claim). In the Roman sources, *actio* is the dominant term. That goes back to the idea of defining law as a "right of action" in classical Roman jurisprudence, deriving from the focus on praetorian legal protection and, thus, on the *actio* as the central concept. For legal protection, the existence of an *actio* was required. Surely, in civil law the concepts of property and other rights *in rem* as well as many questions about contract law are not to be found either in the words of the *formula actionis* or by interpreting it. Among practitioners, however, the question concerning the relevant *actio* was far more important than that concerning the underlying substantive legal relations. Although Justinian's codification of the revised *Institutes* of Gaius, mostly aligned to substantive law, pointed in the opposite direction, in his *Digests* the classicism of Justinian led right back to focusing on the right of action.

Medieval lawyers had already developed a system of subjective rights. They distinguished between the *actio* as the right to sue and the *ius* as the substantive subjective right, the latter being considered *mater* or *causa* of the *actio*.[20] Doneau took the decisive step forward: *De eo, quod nostrum est, sic dicemus: ut in singulis partibus iuris nostri adiungamus etiam remedia cuiusque partis propria, prodita iure ad unumquodque obtinendum* ("about that which is ours, we may say this: that in the individual parts concerning our subjective right we add also the special remedies of each part, which come out of the right to obtain each," Comm. 2,7,5). While the medieval glossators regarded *ius* and *actio* as on the same level, Doneau subordinates the *actio* as *remedium*, a mere remedy to the respective subjective right, which the *actio* serves as a legal protection. As a *facultas persequendi* (possibility to prosecute), the *actio* is a right in itself (Comm. 2,7,5). Doneau clarifies this further in his analysis of process law: *Actio est ius, id est potestas iure tributa* ("The action is the right, that is, a power given by law," Comm. 19,1,4). On the other hand, Doneau

[19] Coing, *Gesammelte Aufsätze*, I, 252.

[20] Cf. Azo, *Summa codicis et institutionum* (edn. Spirae: Petrus Drach, 1482), ad I. 4,6.

deals with the enforcement of law separately by opposing substantive law to procedural law (*ratio iuris nostri obtinendi* – the way to obtain our right) in the second part of the *Commentarii*, where, in books 19 to 22, he presents a separate consistent system of actions and exceptions for the *res in iudicium deductae* (things pending in court). In the nineteenth century, Savigny picked up Doneau's approaches: for Savigny, the *actio* coincides with the subjective right itself "in the state of defense."[21] Thus, Doneau left to the German historical school of jurisprudence "both systematic prioritization of the subjective right and consistent treatment of the right of actions."[22]

The Individualization of Private Law in Doneau's Work against the Background of Intellectual History and Religion

For the orientation of private law toward the human being in Doneau's work, several causes can be identified. Undoubtedly, his personal fate as a persecuted Huguenot refugee who barely managed to save his own life played a decisive role. This experience manifests itself in his focus on the central rule of the *suum cuique tribuere* in protecting the rights of the individual and, thus, peace itself.

In general, there was an underlying influence of the Renaissance and humanism, both of which were oriented toward the human being by recourse to ancient traditions, especially to the Stoic thought conveyed by Cicero.[23] Above all, Cicero's ethics, in *De officiis*, was widespread in countless editions in the sixteenth century. Neo-Stoicism had reached its peak in France and the Netherlands in the late sixteenth century. In these countries, which suffered under wars of religion and liberation, the Stoic focus on the individual striving for virtue and inner fulfilment independently from external circumstances was very attractive; compared with the ethics of Aristotle, which referred to the *polis* only, the Stoic individualist ethics was preferred.[24]

Doneau invokes Cicero at the central aspects concerning the individualization of private law: when outlining the correlations between the three basic

[21] "Im Zustand der Vertheidigung," Friedrich Carl von Savigny, *System des heutigen römischen Rechts*, vol. 5 (Berlin: Veit und Comp., 1841), § 204, p. 2f.

[22] Knut Wolfgang Nörr, "Aus dem Aktionenrecht der Historischen Schule, besonders bei Savigny," in Horst Heinrich Jakobs, Brigitte Knobbe-Keuk, Eduard Picker, and Jan Wilhelm, eds., *Festschrift für Werner Flume zum 70. Geburtstag* (Köln: Otto Schmidt, 1978), 191–98, at 191.

[23] Cf. Christoph Strohm, *Calvinismus und Recht* (Tübingen: Mohr Siebeck, 2008), 102ff.

[24] Cf. Christoph Strohm, "Neustoizismus," in *Theologische Realenzyklopädie* 32 (2000): 190–93, at 192.

principles of law (*honeste vivere, alterum non laedere, suum cuique tribuere*) he refers not only to *De officiis* 1,20f., but also to *Topica* 2,9 (Comm. 2,1,10ff.). According to Doneau the (*ius*) *suum cuique tribuere* comprises as *genus* the other two principles as *species* (Comm. 1,6,2; 2,1,6 and 9ff.). To support this thesis, Doneau quotes Cicero's definition of civil law in *Topica* 2,9 as *aequitas constituta eis qui eiusdem civitatis sunt ad res suas obtinendas* ("equity established among men who belong to the same city, for the purpose of insuring each man in the possession of his property and rights"); Doneau writes *ad res suas obtinendas*, which corresponds to *suum cuique tribuere* (Comm. 2,1,13).

With apparent deliberation, Doneau does not refer to *De officiis* 1,15: according to this passage, the second of the four elements of everything virtuous (*omne, quod est honestum*) lies in "protecting the human society and giving to each his own and in the reliability of contractual agreements" (*in hominum societate tuenda tribuendoque suum cuique et rerum contractarum fide*). Despite being pertinent *prima facie*, this passage does not fit into Doneau's concept, since he subordinates the *honeste vivere*, which is considered superior in the passage, to the *suum cuique tribuere*. Thus, he falls back on *Topica* 2,9. Eventually, Doneau also quotes this passage when defining private law (*ius privatum est, quod privatis, et singulis, quod suum est, tribuit* – private law is [that law] which gives to private individuals what is their own, Comm. 2,7,3).

In addition to neo-Stoicism, the biblical Christian idea of the personality and godlikeness of humanity has an impact on Doneau's work; however, any influence of John Calvin[25] on Doneau[26] cannot be identified easily.[27] On the one hand, the confessional peculiarity of Calvinism formed only in the second half of the sixteenth century; on the other, Calvinism itself was shaped significantly by humanist jurisprudence.

Specifically religious influences are rarely demonstrable in Doneau's work. Apart from the chapter about the distinction between *ius divinum* and *ius*

[25] All references to *Ioannis Calvini Opera quae supersunt omnia*, edn. Guilielmus Baum, Eduardus Cunitz, Eduardus Reuss, 59 vols. (Brunsvigae: C. A. Schwetschke, 1863–1900). The work will be cited in the text as "CO" with volume and page.

[26] This is the assumption of Volker Heise, *Der calvinistische Einfluss auf das humanistische Rechtsdenken. Exemplarisch dargestellt an den "Commentarii de iure civili" von Hugo Donellus (1527–1591)* (Göttingen: Vandenhoeck und Ruprecht, 2004) and "Die Betonung der Individualität im Recht als calvinistische Eigenart. Neue Entwicklungen in der Donellus-Forschung," in Andreas Bauer, Frank Theisen, and Karl H. L. Welker, eds., *Studien zur Rechts- und Zeitgeschichte. Liber discipulorum. Professor Dr. Wulf Eckart Voß zum 60. Geburtstag* (Göttingen: Universitätsverlag Osnabrück bei V&R unipress, 2005), 71–84.

[27] Cf. Strohm, *Calvinismus und Recht*, 79, n. 145 and 93ff.

humanum (Comm. 2,4), Doneau only touches upon the two biblical passages Psalm 96: 5 and Romans 2: 14f. (Comm. 2,6,3 and 1,7,2f. and 1,12,4) when dealing with fundamental questions about law itself. Even though he refers to Romans 2: 14ff. precisely during his description of his understanding of natural law, he only seems to base his theory significantly on the New Testament. When St Paul writes that the "requirements of the law are written on their [the pagans'] hearts" (*opus legis scriptum in cordibus suis*), he expresses in essence the Stoic ethics of attempting to recover the natural law within the individual conscience.[28] This Stoic tradition of a rational natural law focused on and limited to the individual human being had been promulgated principally by Cicero. Doneau preferred this Stoic concept to the derivation of natural law from the natural inclinations of all beings in the tradition of Aristotle, as expressed for instance by Ulpian in D.1,1,1,3. Equating the *naturalis ratio* with the immutable law of God in Romans 2: 14ff. via the Golden Rule, Doneau returns to the three basic principles of *honeste vivere, alterum non laedere, suum cuique tribuere* (Comm. 1,7,3).

At least certain parallels to Doneau's catalogue of individual legal interests can be found in the work of Calvin: for Calvin, too, the rights of one's own person (life, freedom) comprising the individual sphere of freedom are primeval and unimpeachable natural rights (CO 29, 554ff.; 24, 49 u. 628). In the same way that Doneau invokes the divine act of creation for the individual objects of legal protection, Calvin justifies the prohibition to kill in the Decalogue by reasoning that killing extinguishes the remnants of the divine image within the human being and therefore is a sacrilege. While according to Doneau one "rather does not have any life" without the three other individual legal interests *incolumitas corporis, libertas,* and *existimatio* (Comm. 2,8,3), for Calvin freedom is a gift from God (CO 29, 555f.) and more than half a life. To deprive a human of freedom is for Calvin almost the same as to kill (CO 24, 628). Despite limiting the objects of individual protection in his doctrine on subject matter to the *ius gentium* and constituting the legal entity upon the civil-law *status*, Doneau reasons in accordance with Calvin's doctrine: in the tradition of the New Testament, Calvin believes in the natural equality of all humans as creatures of God (CO 34, 658). However, in his conviction of the *ordo* he does not question whether the hierarchical structure of the society of his time was willed by God (CO 26, 321).

[28] Strohm, "Neustoizismus," 192.

Doneau's Influence on the Development of Civil Law

Doneau's fame already had faded a mere generation after his death.[29] Particularly in France, he remained ignored for a long time. There, ironically, Roman law lost its predominance at the very same time that Doneau developed his groundbreaking ideas about it. Over the course of the second half of the sixteenth century, France underwent a nationalization of its law, leading to an increasing dominance of judicial professionals over legal scholars. Initiated by judges and lawyers of the Parlement of Paris, based upon the amended *coutumes* (customary laws) and royal ordinances, a *droit commun de la France* arose. For this national law, Roman law became but one source of many. In his home country, there was no more need for Doneau's *opus*, which focused only on abstract and timeless Roman law and aimed at systematizing the complete European *ius commune*. In other countries of continental Europe that had kept a culture of academic law, Doneau's work remained familiar throughout the seventeenth and eighteenth centuries, especially in the Netherlands.[30]

However, the "*Donellus enucleatus*," an extract from the *Commentarii* supplemented by references from literature and dedicated to practical purposes, was preferred to Doneau's entire work.[31] The rediscovery of Doneau began during the new humanist period. In the second half of the eighteenth century, several editions of his *Opera omnia* were published in Italy (Lucca 1762–70, Rome/Macerata 1828–33, Florence 1840–47). Still, Doneau's work did not receive a comprehensive appreciation and recognition in German jurisprudence in the nineteenth century. By way of the German historical school of jurisprudence, Doneau's home country finally took note of him.[32]

As we have shown above, the modern doctrine of civil law has adopted Doneau's central thoughts, which are rooted in his systematization and individualization of civil law. Beyond that, Doneau's thoughts influenced German civil law at a central point: the abstract transfer of property by real agreement, which German law adopted under the influence of Savigny.

[29] Cf. Jean-Louis Thireau, "Hugues Doneau et les fondements de la codification moderne," *Droits* 26 (1998): 81–100, at 82ff.

[30] Feenstra, "Hugues Doneau," 236ff.

[31] Oswald Hilliger, *Donellus enucleatus sive Commentarii Hugonis Donelli de iure civili in Compendium ita redacti ut verum nucleum contineant, iurisq[ue] artem, quae amplo verborum cortice in illis tecta, apertius exhibeant*, 2 vols. (Jenae: Christophorus Lippoldus, 1610 and 1613).

[32] Eugène Lerminier, *Introduction générale à l'histoire du droit* (Paris: Alexandre Mesnier, 1829), 48f.

As Savigny himself relied on Doneau's thoughts,[33] the most typical characteristic of German law goes back to the Calvinist French jurist.

RECOMMENDED READING

Avenarius, Martin. "'Neque id sine magna Servii laude ...' Historisierung der Rechtswissenschaft und Genese von System und Methode bei Donellus." *Tijdschrift voor Rechtsgeschiedenis* 74 (2006): 61–93.

Buhl, Heinrich. "Donellus in Heidelberg (1573–1579)." *Neue Heidelberger Jahrbücher* 2 (1892): 280–313.

Cannata, Carlo Augusto. "Systématique et dogmatique dans les *Commentarii iuris civilis* de Hugo Donellus." In Schmidlin and Dufour, *Jacques Godefroy (1587–1652) et l'humanisme juridique à Genève*, 217–30.

Eyssell, Aernout Philip Theodoor. *Doneau, sa vie et ses ouvrages. L'École de Bourges; synthèse du Droit romain au XVIe siècle; son influence jusqu'à nos jours*. Dijon: Decailly/Lamarche, 1860.

Feenstra, Robert. "Hugues Doneau et les juristes néerlandais du XVIIe siècle: L'influence de son 'système' sur l'évolution du droit privé avant le Pandectisme." In Schmidlin and Dufour, *Jacques Godefroy (1587–1652) et l'humanisme juridique à Genève*, 231–43.

Hattenhauer, Christian. "Ad totius iuris cognitionem. Zum Systemverständnis bei Hugo Donellus." In *Festschrift für Jan Schröder zum 70. Geburtstag*, edited by Arndt Kiehnle, Bernd Mertens, and Gottfried Schiemann, 51–67. Tübingen: Mohr Siebeck, 2013.

"Ius suum cuique tribuere: Der Mensch als Fundament des Privatrechts bei Hugo Donellus." In *Heidelberger Thesen zu Recht und Gerechtigkeit. Ringvorlesung der Juristischen Fakultät der Ruprecht-Karls-Universität Heidelberg anlässlich ihres 625jährigen Jubiläums*, edited by Christian Baldus, Herbert Kronke, and Ute Mager, 1–25. Tübingen: Mohr Siebeck, 2013.

Heise, Volker. *Der calvinistische Einfluss auf das humanistische Rechtsdenken. Exemplarisch dargestellt an den "Commentarii de iure civili" von Hugo Donellus (1527–1591)*. Göttingen: Vandenhoeck und Ruprecht, 2004.

"Die Betonung der Individualität im Recht als calvinistische Eigenart. Neue Entwicklungen in der Donellus-Forschung." In *Studien zur Rechts- und Zeitgeschichte. Liber discipulorum. Professor Dr. Wulf Eckart Voß zum 60. Geburtstag*,

[33] Comm. 4,16,7ff.; Hugo Donellus, *Commentariorum sive Recitationum, Ad Librum Quartum Codicis Justinianei, Paralipomena* (Francofurti: Ionas Rhodius, 1602), ad C. 4,50,6, p. 396, n. 15; Friedrich Carl von Savigny, *System des heutigen römischen Rechts*, vol. 3 (Berlin: Veit und Comp., 1840), § 140, p. 312f. and *Das Obligationenrecht als Theil des heutigen römischen Rechts*, vol. 2 (Berlin: Veit und Comp., 1843), § 78, pp. 255ff; cf. Franz Hofmann, *Die Lehre von titulus und modus adquirendi und von der iusta causa traditionis* (Wien: G. J. Manz, 1873), 60ff. (treating the "Donellus–Savigny'sche Theorie"). Beyond that, in his famous doctrine of possession Savigny relied on Doneau: Comm. 5,6–13 and 15,32–38; Friedrich Carl von Savigny, *Das Recht des Besitzes. Eine civilistische Abhandlung* (Gießen: Heyer, 1803), XVII–XX, 29, 106f.; cf. Christoph Bergfeld, "Savigny und Donellus," *Ius Commune* 8 (1979): 24–35.

edited by Andreas Bauer, Frank Theisen, and Karl H. L. Welker, 71–84. Göttingen: Universitätsverlag Osnabrück bei V&R unipress, 2005.
Schmidlin, Bruno, and Alfred Dufour, eds. *Jacques Godefroy (1587–1652) et l'humanisme juridique à Genève. Actes du colloque Jacques Godefroy*. Basel: Helbing & Lichtenhahn, 1991.
Stapelfeldt, Katrin and Schröder, Jan. "Hugo Donellus." In *Deutsche und Europäische Juristen aus neun Jahrhunderten*, edited by Gerd Kleinheyer and Jan Schröder, 118–21. 6th edn. Tübingen: Mohr Siebeck, 2017.
Stintzing, Roderich von. *Hugo Donellus in Altdorf*. Erlangen: Eduard Besold, 1869.
Strohm, Christoph. *Calvinismus und Recht*. Tübingen: Siebeck Mohr, 2008.
Thireau, Jean-Louis. "Hugues Doneau et les fondements de la codification moderne." *Droits* 26 (1998): 81–100.

11

Jean Bodin

(c.1529/1530–1596)

DANIEL LEE

BIOGRAPHICAL INTRODUCTION

Jean Bodin was born in Angers, sometime around 1529/30. He entered the Carmelite order in his youth, around 1543, with the original intention of taking holy orders. With the support and patronage of the Angevin bishop, Gabriel Bouvery, Bodin was sent to Paris to receive his formal education in the Carmelite house in Paris under the tutelage of Guillaume Prévost, whose course of study would have introduced Bodin to Scholastic philosophy and theology. It is likely that, during his novitiate in Paris, Bodin also first encountered the humanist ideas of Pierre de la Ramée, whose ideas concerning method would shape Bodin's own analytical approach.[1]

Around 1550, Bodin, having been released from his monastic vows, turned from theology to law and began his studies at the University of Toulouse. Described as "the temple of jurisprudence," Toulouse was one of the major centers for legal education and scholarship in early modern France, rivaled in reputation only by Orléans and, especially, Bourges, the center of the new legal humanism championed by Andrea Alciato and his disciples.[2] The University of Toulouse, in its official curriculum in civil law, avoided the humanist fashion of Bourges and, despite the local presence of influential legal humanists such as Jacques Cujas, nevertheless remained a bastion of a more conservative approach to jurisprudence in France, an approach continuous with the method perfected by the Italian "princes of legal science"

[1] Kenneth McRae, "Ramist Tendencies in the Thought of Jean Bodin," *Journal of the History of Ideas* 16 (1955): 306; Howell Lloyd, *Jean Bodin, "This Pre-eminent Man of France": An Intellectual Biography* (Oxford: Oxford University Press, 2017), 12–14.

[2] Lloyd, *Jean Bodin*, 46; Donald Kelley, "Civil Science in the Renaissance: Jurisprudence in the French Manner," *History of European Ideas* 2 (1981): 261–76.

(as Bodin described them), such as Bartolus de Saxoferrato and Baldus de Ubaldis, the very targets of the French legal humanists.[3]

Among the skills that Bodin evidently acquired through his training was the specialized lawyerly ability to prepare *consilia*, or legal briefs, a genre of legal writing associated with the medieval "Bartolist" lawyers, a skill that Bodin deployed in later years both in his work as a practicing lawyer and in his theoretical writings.[4] During his time in Toulouse, Bodin also began to produce his own writing, some of which included nonlegal works such as a translation and commentary of Oppian's *Cynegetica*, a didactic Greek poem on hunting, and an *Oratio*, addressed to the Toulousan citizenry on the necessity of public education for a well-ordered state.[5] Bodin also prepared unpublished legal treatises on theoretical topics in legal theory such as the *legis actio*, the *officium iudicis*, and *imperium*, titles which suggest that Bodin originally intended to position his writings within an already well-defined genre of legal scholarship.[6] None of these short topical treatises survive: Bodin, while on his deathbed, ordered that they be burnt.

One legal text from Bodin's Toulouse period that did escape the flames, however, was the *Juris Universi Distributio*, an outline of general jurisprudence that Bodin would publish later in his life – first in a tabular form (1578) and then in a prose outline form (1580).[7] The *Distributio* is the first evidence indicating the humanist influence on Bodin's legal thought. Like his contemporary legal humanists attempting to apply philological techniques of textual analysis, Bodin criticized the privileged status traditionally enjoyed by the Justinianic compilations of Roman law, the *Corpus iuris civilis*, the single most important textual authority in Continental legal science. Roman law, as Bodin would later write, was merely the legal system of one ancient

[3] Kenneth McRae, "Bodin's Prefaces," *The Six Bookes of a Commonweale* (Cambridge, MA: Harvard University Press, 1962), A71.

[4] For example, see the discussion and marginalia in Bodin's *De Republica* (Paris: Jacques Du Puys, 1586), 59–63 [on French citizenship and immunity from the *droit d'aubain*]; 99–100 [on contractual obligations of sovereigns].

[5] Jean Bodin, *Oppiani de venatione libri IIII* (Paris: M. Vascosan, 1555); Jean Bodin, *Oratio de instituenda in republica juventute ad senatum populumque Tolosatem* (Toulouse: Petrus Puteus, 1559).

[6] Myron Piper Gilmore, *Argument from Roman Law in Political Thought* (Cambridge, MA: Harvard University Press, 1941), especially chapter 2, which cites numerous stand-alone treatises carrying such titles as Jean Gillot, *De iurisdictione et imperio libri duo* (Paris, 1538); Pierre Loriot, *Tractatus de imperio et iurisdictione* (Lyon, 1545); and Antoine de Govéa, *De iurisdictione omnium iudicum* (Toulouse, 1545). These are in addition to commentaries on the relevant passages, especially D.1.21.1, 2.1.3, and 2.1.5, in the *Digestum Vetus*.

[7] Jean Bodin, *Ivris vniversi Distribvtio* (Paris: Jacques Du Puys, 1578); Jean Bodin, *Ivris vniversi Distribvtio* (Cologne: Ioannes Gymnicus, 1580).

civilization. Given its antiquity, why should Roman law have any continuing authority in sixteenth-century Europe?

Bodin's answer is simple: it should not. But he acknowledges that Roman law historically served an important practical purpose. As the most complete legal system preserved in full, Roman law provided a textual foundation and an analytical vocabulary for a shared *ius commune*.

There is no good reason, however, why *Roman* law (as opposed to, say, Hebraic or Egyptian law) should enjoy this privilege, which is simply an accident of history. What Bodin attempts to do in the *Distributio*, therefore, is to move beyond Roman law and construct the fundamentals of a general theory of law – a sketch of what all independent legal systems, whether Roman or otherwise, would look like and what legal concepts they would have to include. While the *Distributio* clearly shows the influence of Bodin's civilian training, there are substantive differences, especially in the law of obligations, as well as previews of public-law doctrines to be developed fully in later works. Most important is Bodin's purpose, to create what he felt was a truly general legal vocabulary that would make possible a comparative legal science of all *gentes*, and not just those shaped by Roman law.

Bodin likely intended to pursue a career as a professor of civil law, but the highest position he attained on the academic career track was the status of *hallebardier*, a position similar to a graduate teaching assistant or untenured junior lecturer.[8] Having failed at securing a permanent academic post, Bodin turned instead to legal practice. He once again returned to Paris around 1560/61, this time to practice law as an *avocat* before the Parlement of Paris, the supreme appellate judicial body of *ancien régime* France.

Not much is known about Bodin's time as a legal practitioner in Paris, but we know from autobiographical notes in his later writings that the experience must have been transformative for him. It was in the Parlement, outside the academic ivory tower of Toulouse, that Bodin began to understand that "a real and solid knowledge of the law is found not in the dust of the [law] schools, but in the battleground of the forum; not in the quanitities of syllables, but in the scales of justice and equity."[9] But it seems that he lacked the personality, skill, and eloquence necessary for success as a litigator: one lawyer in Parlement observed that Bodin "never succeeded in pleading a case."[10]

[8] Lloyd, *Jean Bodin*, 23.

[9] McRae, "Bodin's Prefaces," A71.

[10] Lloyd, *Jean Bodin*, 52.

Consequently, Bodin's practice focused instead on providing consultation services in the form of *consilia* for litigants bringing suits before the Parlement.[11]

Given his access and proximity to the *chambres* of the Parlement, Bodin would likely have been familiar with recent cases brought and pleaded before the Parlement, particularly since he references such cases in later writings.[12] One such case, prominently discussed in Bodin's later work, concerned the validity of a sovereign king's pact concluded with subjects, a reference to the Contract of Poissy, which granted certain rights of worship to French Huguenots. Bodin's discussion is of interest, not only because it highlights one of Bodin's key doctrines of public law, that sovereigns are bound by their own contracts.[13] It also reveals a tendency, common throughout Bodin's writings, to misrepresent (as one commentator has argued) the facts of such cases in developing his own ideas.[14] This particular case, however, is especially noteworthy because it illustrates what was rapidly becoming the most urgent political issue in France – the contentious religious politics and violence of the Wars of Religion that would continue for the rest of Bodin's life.

Bodin's time in Paris also coincided with the publication of his first major work, the *Methodus ad facilem historiarum cognitionem* (1566, rev. 1572), a treatise concerning comparative methodology in historical writing and interpretation, inspired by the Renaissance genre of the *Ars historica*.[15] Organized as a critical study of methodology related to natural, human, and divine histories, it provided him the first opportunity to explore questions about law and state that he would develop in his later work.

As a young lawyer in Paris, Bodin enjoyed the patronage of a Toulousan nobleman, Guy du Faur, seigneur de Pibrac, who at this time served as the king's *avocat-général* in Parlement. Bodin's association with the

[11] Ibid., 93, references a *responsum* written by Bodin for Paul Scalich of Zagreb.

[12] One example of such case was the Cenamy case, concerning whether the escheat of foreigners' estates through the *droit d'aubain* can apply in the case of a French subject who had lived abroad in Venice for over a decade without explicitly renouncing citizenship. Bodin cites a proceeding from the Parlement of Paris dated June 14, 1554 at *Six livres de la république* (Paris: Jacques Du Puys, 1583), 92.

[13] This case is discussed in the *République* (1583), 152–53. The corresponding passage appears in the Latin *De republica* (Paris: Jacques Du Puys, 1586), 99. The Latin *De republica* uses the term *pacta conventa* for contracts, which is the same term used in reference to the "constitutional" conditions specified in the Polish offer of the crown to Henry. The coupling of *pactum conventum* appears earlier also in the *Distributio* $B_{s.v.}$ *Facta*.

[14] Richard Tuck, *The Sleeping Sovereign: The Invention of Modern Democracy* (Cambridge: Cambridge University Press, 2015), 39–40.

[15] Jean Bodin, *Methodus ad facilem historiarum cognitionem* (Paris: Martin le Ieune, 1566); Jean Bodin, *Methodus ad facilem historiarum cognitionem* (Paris: Martin le Ieune, 1572).

well-connected Pibrac made possible Bodin's initial entry into public life, and, for this reason, Pibrac would become the dedicatee of Bodin's most important work. It was through Pibrac's recommendation to the royal court and, especially, to the Toulouse-educated Chancellor of France, Michel de l'Hôpital, that Bodin attained his earliest appointments, including, in 1570, as a temporary royal commissioner tasked with administrative reforms of the forests of Normandy and, in 1571, as *maître des requêtes* for the king's youngest brother, François Duke of Alençon.

Bodin again entered royal service when Henry Duke of Anjou, the younger brother of King Charles IX and first in the line of royal succession, sought election to the vacant kingship of Poland in 1572, the same year of the notorious St Bartholomew's Day Massacre, of which Henry was a co-conspirator. Pibrac, acting as Henry's representative, recruited Bodin to assist in negotiations to prepare Henry's election and justify to a more toleration-minded Polish electorate Henry's actions leading to St Bartholomew. Bodin's first diplomatic experience came in this context, when he was ordered to join Pibrac and other senior French officials to receive a Polish delegation at Metz in 1573 and accept formally, on behalf of Henry, the offer of the Polish throne, an offer encumbered with numerous conditions of office [*pacta conventa*]. Bodin's role was to translate from Latin into French the public statement announcing Henry's election.

The sudden death of Charles IX in 1574, however, elevated the newly elected Polish king to the French throne. With Henry's accession, Bodin now found himself at the very center of royal politics during some of the most violent periods of the Wars of Religion. It was in this period that Bodin wrote and completed his most important work, the *Six livres de la république*, a comprehensive and systematic work on public law, the state, and political philosophy first published in 1576. It established Bodin's reputation as a modern Aristotle and proved to be an instant success in the later sixteenth-century book market. Bodin's *République* would be published eleven times during his lifetime, not including translations into Italian, German, Spanish, English, as well as a Latin version, *De Republica*, that Bodin would personally prepare and publish in 1586.

The *République* has been described as an "encyclopedia of political wisdom" in its scope and use of sources, drawing not only from textual authorities in Roman and canon law but also from classical history, philosophy, and scripture.[16] The work gave Bodin the opportunity to treat topics as

[16] J. H. M. Salmon, *French Religious Wars in English Political Thought* (Oxford: Clarendon Press, 1959), 22.

various as slavery, citizenship, feudal tenure, institutional design, constitutional history, the theory of justice, fiscal policy, money, and the influence of climate on political culture, all while engaging with writers as diverse as Aristotle, Polybius, Cicero, Bartolus, and Panormitanus. But probably its most important and lasting contribution was its analysis of sovereignty, which Bodin described as "the true foundation and pivot on which the state turns."[17]

Given his newfound fame as an expert on matters of state, Bodin became the quintessential scholar-statesman. For this reason, Bodin was elected not only as deputy to represent the *bailliage* of Vermandois in the Estates General of 1576 convening at Blois, but also as the presiding officer of the Third Estate. While at the Estates, Bodin was invited, through arrangements made by Pibrac, to dine occasionally with the king and to participate in private discussions on public affairs. But the royal favor that Bodin enjoyed proved to be short-lived, as a result of Bodin's stubborn posturing during sessions of the Third Estate, which he recorded in a journal.[18] One of Bodin's priorities concerned matters of fiscal policy, involving taxation and, especially, the proposed sale of lands attached to the royal domain as a potential source of revenue to pay off mounting debt. The legality of such sale and alienation was debatable, but Bodin had already taken a firm position in the *République*, in which he singled out the inalienability of the domain as one of two French "fundamental laws" that sovereigns cannot unilaterally alter or override (the other being royal succession according to Salic law). In Bodin's view, the royal domain belonged not to the king personally but to the people and the public fisc. Such lands formed no part of the king's private patrimony. The king, therefore, had no right to alienate the domain, since he was but a mere usufructuary or guardian holding in trust property belonging to another party – the *respublica* in an incapacitated condition of legal minority.[19] Any change in the domain would require the approval of its true owner – the people, as represented in the Third Estate. Such sentiments succeeded in alienating Bodin from court.

[17] Bodin, *République* (1583), 14.

[18] Bodin, *Recueil de tout ce qui s'est negotié en la compagnie du Tiers Estat de France en l'assemblée générale des trois estats, assignez par le roy en la ville de Blois au xv novembre* 1576 (1577).

[19] Especially striking is Bodin's use of the so-called minority thesis and the *auxiilium restitutionis* of C.2.54(53).4; 11.30.3 at *République* (1583), 158. On the minority thesis, see Walter Ullmann, "Juristic Obstacles to the Emergence of the Concept of the State in the Middle Ages," *Annali di Storia del Diritto* 12/13 (1968/1969): 43–64, and my "The State Is a Minor: Fiduciary Concepts of Government in the Roman Law of Guardianship," in *Fiduciary Government* (Cambridge: Cambridge University Press, 2018).

Perhaps the most urgent item on the Estates' agenda, however, concerned the limited policy of religious toleration established through Henry's Edict of Beaulieu, promulgated in May 1576, just months before the opening of the Estates in capitulation to Huguenot forces.[20] Generally aligned with the toleration-oriented *Politiques*, Bodin prioritized strengthening the policy of toleration for the sake of public concord. But in a *volte-face*, Henry revoked the edict in January 1577, abruptly ending the official policy of toleration after only eight months and declaring Catholicism the only legally permissible religion in France. In doing so, the king succumbed to overwhelming pressure and the existential political threat coming from the newly formed Catholic League, assembled under the leadership of the powerful Catholic Duke of Guise to combat Huguenots engaging in violence. By aligning himself with the Catholic League, the monarch rejected the *Politique* policy that Bodin had advocated.

Estranged from the royal court, Bodin settled in Laon – the home of his wife, Françoise Trouilliart, whom he married in 1576. It was likely during this period that Bodin prepared his third major work, devoted to the topic of demonology and witchcraft, the *Démonomanie des sorciers* (1580), a work that reveals Bodin's interest in the occult and the supernatural in the human world. Allegedly based on Bodin's firsthand experience in conducting a witch trial, the *Démonomanie* advised lawyers and judges on technical details of legal procedure and rules of evidence in prosecuting witches, procedural rules that implicitly criticize the rules used in Parlement.[21]

Meanwhile, Bodin found a new patron in François, the Catholic king's younger (and Huguenot) brother, now elevated to the title of Duke of Anjou. Through his association with François, Bodin traveled to England, joining the duke to deliver a proposal of marriage to Queen Elizabeth. He also participated in the duke's spectacular and costly failure to seize a princely title over Antwerp in 1582. François's death in 1584, however, signaled the end of Bodin's career in royal politics, and he returned to Laon, eventually to succeed in 1587 to the position of royal prosecutor in the *présidial* court previously held by his late brother-in-law.

Bodin's final years in Laon coincided with a bloody succession crisis. François's premature death not only meant that the childless and possibly homosexual King Henry III would be the last Valois sovereign but also that

[20] Owen Ulph, "Jean Bodin and the Estates-General of 1576," *Journal of Modern History* 19 (1947): 289–96.

[21] Jonathan Pearl, "Bodin's Advice to Judges in Witchcraft Cases," *Proceedings of the Annual Meeting of the Western Society for French History* 16 (1989): 95–102.

the heir presumptive to the throne by Salic law would be a Huguenot, the Bourbon king of Navarre, Henry. The assassination of Henry III in 1589, in retaliation for assassinating the Duke of Guise in the previous year, immediately introduced a power vacuum between two rival claimants to the throne, Henry of Navarre and Henry's Catholic uncle, Charles Cardinal de Bourbon, endorsed by the Catholic League. As a public official for the city of Laon, Bodin was forced to take a position, ultimately siding with the League for prudential reasons, outlined in an open letter of 1590.

With Laon under the control of the League, Bodin retreated from public life, inaugurating a remarkably productive retirement that yielded his two final major works – the *Universae Naturae Theatrum*, a treatise on natural philosophy published in 1596, and the *Colloquium Heptaplomeres*, a dialogue among representatives of major religious and philosophical traditions on the nature of religion, circulated anonymously in manuscript for centuries until its first publication in 1857. Although far removed from matters of law and state that characterized Bodin's career and earlier writings, the *Theatrum* and the *Colloquium* both show substantial points of continuity with his earlier work.

Bodin died of plague in 1596 and was interred, according to his will, as a Catholic in the Franciscan church of Laon.

MAJOR THEMES

Bodin's most important contribution is his theory of sovereignty – a concept rendered variously as *summum imperium*, *maiestas*, *suverenitas*, and, finally and most notably in French, *souveraineté*. Bodin famously defined sovereignty in the *République* as the "absolute and perpetual power of a state," a definition designed, at once, to distance him from classical authorities on the subject, such as Aristotle, Polybius, and Dionysius of Halicarnassus, while also positioning his theory within the parameters of the intricate Romano-canonical legal science of the *ius commune*.

Bodin first investigated sovereignty in his early theoretical writings, when he was most likely still attempting to pursue a career as a professor of civil law in Toulouse. The *Distributio*, for example, is notable in isolating *summum imperium* as a special kind of public authority within an independent legal system, to be distinguished from all inferior forms of public authority, such as the authority of magistrates and judges.[22] He specifies, within the same text, that the substance of this "supreme" or "sovereign" authority consists of the

[22] Bodin, *Juris Universi Distributio* E.

power "to uphold sacred matters, enact legislation, create magistrates, oversee deliberation concerning the state, declare and conclude war, impose criminal penalties and rewards, and carry out the execution of the laws."[23] Bodin expanded this investigation in the *Methodus*. The longest chapter of the work, *De Statu Rerumpublicarum*, which argues that states [*respublicae*] ought to be regarded as the chief unit of analysis in historical writing, raises the major theoretical question concerning the very concept of "statehood": what actually is a "state" [*respublica*]? He answers that it is "nothing more than an association of families and collegial bodies subjected under one and the same sovereign authority." Essential to this definition is sovereignty, which is to be distinguished from all other, lesser species of public authority (such as those of inferior judges or magistrates).

Bodin's analysis in the *République* and *De Republica* reveals a remarkable continuity with the basic architecture and structural elements of his theory of sovereignty. He continues to regard sovereignty as a form of public power whose primary function is to bind the many parts of the state (especially families) together as one unit. But there are important changes in his formulation and analysis of sovereignty. The *Methodus*, for example, identified only five prerogatives of sovereignty, the most important among them being the right of creating magistrates.[24] The *République* identifies no fewer than eight and introduces the controversial doctrine that all such sovereign rights are reducible to one indivisible and exclusive right, the *legislative* right to make and unmake laws.

Another important stylistic change is Bodin's invocation of the term "absolute power" [*puissance absolue*] to describe the scope of the state's sovereignty. Commentators have sometimes seen Bodin's description of sovereignty as absolute as if it were *prima facie* evidence of a supposed slide toward absolutism in Bodin's political thought.[25] If sovereign power were to be absolute in scope, then it must signal (according to these commentators) some commitment to absolutism. The worry is that, because sovereignty is "above the law," the bearer of sovereign authority is given license to rule without any legal limitation.

Bodin, however, explicitly rejects such a wide (and particularly English) interpretation of that term, which he crucially aligns, in the Latin *De*

[23] Bodin, *Juris Universi Distributio* $A_{s.v.}$ *Ius Publicum*.

[24] This list is most likely patterned on the analysis of Dionysius of Halicarnassus. The right of creating magistrates is positioned within a technical legal debate on how to interpret D.1.21.1 and 2.1.3, 2.1.5.

[25] The standard account of the absolutist interpretation is Julian Franklin, *Jean Bodin and the Rise of Absolutist Theory* (Cambridge: Cambridge University Press, 1973).

Republica, with the juridical term, *legibus solutus*, deriving ultimately from the *Digest* of Roman law (D.1.3.31). Following his civilian and canonistic predecessors, Bodin distinguishes the absolute *potestas legibus soluta* of the state from the "ordinary" or legally defined authority [*potestas legibus imminuta*] of public officials exercising some share of authority on behalf of the sovereign.[24] He does so to make the point that absolute power is necessary for a purpose – to make and unmake law.

Bodin specifies that the proper reading of *legibus solutus* means only that the sovereign authority is "immune," "free," or "exempt" [= *solutus*] from the binding force of *its own* legislation. It *does not* mean, however, that the sovereign authority is similarly immune, free, or exempt from *all* law, since not all law derives from voluntary, positive acts of sovereign legislation. The law of nations, for example, originates in the general consent and customary usages of all nations and, thus, is irreducible to any one single sovereign act. Even more important for Bodin are the equitable law of nature and the divine law of God, which, as Bodin puts it, derive as legislation from the *princeps naturae* and are universally binding on all humans, sovereign or not. No sovereign authority, therefore, may exempt or immunize itself from the legal duties activated by these higher laws, simply by invoking "absolute power." Sovereigns with absolute power are, as Bodin puts it, "debtors of justice," duty-bound to their divine creditor to do justice.

A crucial illustration of these limitations on absolute power concerns contracts [*pacta conventa*] – specifically, the theoretical question whether contractual obligations, such as treaties or pacts, are binding even on sovereigns with absolute power. Bodin's view is uncompromising: no sovereign can unilaterally dissolve or revoke valid contracts or exempt itself from performing its contractual obligations without the consent of other contractually bound parties.[25] This principle applies even in contracts concluded between sovereigns and subjects: such obligation is mutual; it obligates the two parties reciprocally, and one party cannot contravene it to the prejudice of the other

[24] On the background of D.1.3.31 and C.1.14.4, see Brian Tierney, "The Prince Is Not Bound by the Laws: Accursius and the Origins of the Modern State," *Comparative Studies in Society and History* 5 (1963): 378–400; Francis Oakley, "The Absolute and Ordinary Power of God in Sixteenth- and Seventeenth-Century Theology," *Journal of the History of Ideas* 59 (1998): 437–61; Ralph Giesey, "Medieval Jurisprudence in Bodin's Concept of Sovereignty," in *Verhandlungen der Internationalen Bodin Tagung in München*, edn. Horst Denzer (Munich: Verlag C. H. Beck, 1973).

[25] Bodin's use of the term *pacta conventa*, in Latin, signals not only the Roman law of obligations and his theory of contract in the *Distributio* but also the conditions, also designated the *pacta conventa*, stipulated to Henry upon his election to the Polish throne.

and without the other's consent [*sine mutuo consensu*]. In this case, the [sovereign] has no advantage over the subject.[26]

One explanation for Bodin's obduracy on this point is based on a technical, though vital, rule of Roman law: since all contractual obligations originate in consent or a "coming-together" [*conventio*], as at D.2.14.1, it follows that any later amendment or dissolution of the obligation must also be based on like consent.[27]

But the more important reason for Bodin's strict position is that valid contractual obligations of all kinds are ultimately governed by the law of nature, not the positive legislation authored by a sovereign legislator. What is remarkable about Bodin's position is its unorthodox quality with respect to the *opinio communis* in canon law, which was a vital source for prior discussions of princely authority. Writing of the papacy, medieval canonists argued that the pope's *potentia absoluta* included, *inter alia*, the power to dissolve contractual obligations at will. In the canonistic context, such absolute power was vital to explaining the nature of absolute power of temporal sovereign authorities. Jurists eager to expand the scope of temporal power thus borrowed from the canon law of contracts to stipulate that any sovereign with absolute power also has, like the pope, the power to dissolve contracts at will.[28] Bodin's analysis of absolute power in the *République*, whose presentation and use of legal authorities resembles a traditional *consilium*, resisted this canonistic trend by insisting on higher-law limitations on sovereignty with respect to contractual obligations: the sovereign

> is so strictly obligated by agreements [*civilibus pactis, ac stipulationibus arctius obligari*] that he makes with his subjects that he cannot impair them even by invoking his absolute power [*summa potestate*], as almost all the doctors of jurisprudence have agreed.[29]

Bodinian sovereignty thus has a double aspect: it is both bound [*ligatus*] by higher law (such as the natural-law rule requiring performance of contracts) and yet, at the same time, unbound or free [*solutus*] from its own positive

[26] *On Sovereignty*, 15.

[27] D.50.17.35.

[28] In general, see Kenneth Pennington, *The Prince and the Law, 1200–1600: Sovereignty and Rights in the Western Legal Tradition* (Berkeley: University of California Press, 1993); Wim Decock, *Theologians and Contract Law: The Moral Transformation of the Ius Commune, ca.1500–1650* (Leiden: Martinus Nijhoff Publishers, 2013).

[29] Bodin, *République* (1583), 153; *De republica*, 100. I have used Franklin's translation from *On Sovereignty*, 35–36. Among the "doctors" Bodin has in mind are Baldus on D.1.3.31, Paul de Castro, and Philip Decius.

legislation. One important question emerging from this double aspect concerns the sovereign's status as *legibus solutus*. Why must a sovereign authority be free from the binding force of its own positive enacted legislation [*lois, leges*]? After all, couldn't a sovereign authority simply decide to bind or subject itself voluntarily to its own legislation, through some act of legislative entrenchment or precommitment, such as an oath or promise to keep the laws as they are?

Bodin's reply is that such acts of sovereign self-binding or self-obliging are conceptually incoherent. This is because all legislation [*loi, lex*], in Bodin's theory, is ultimately a form of command, as opposed to contract.[30] Indeed, this is an important moment in the history of jurisprudence. Early modern jurists began to take up the question that would become the starting point of modern philosophy of law: what counts as valid law? One popular theory answered the question in terms of common consent: all valid legislation ultimately derives from an act of common consent, so that legal validity requires the approbation of the political community at large: *Quod omnes tangit ab omnibus approbetur*. But since consent was the cornerstone of all contractual relations, jurists speculatively concluded that legislation should be regarded as a species of contract, a form of analysis that became especially commonplace among Calvinist lawyers such as François Hotman and Theodore Beza investigating the permissibility of popular resistance.

Bodin, however, thinks this analysis involves a basic category error, one that involves mistakenly confounding *legislation* for *contract*, as he believes some jurists have tended to do in suggesting that laws can be crafted through popular consent. Legislation, according to Bodin, is unlike contract because it is modeled on command. And what makes command (and, thus, legislation) distinctive is precisely that it does not require anybody's consent for it to be valid. That does not, of course, preclude an expression of consent: in fact, consent might be a nice additive to legislation, for practical reasons. Bodin's point, however, is that common consent is inessential for legislative activity of the sovereign.

Thus, when a sovereign enacts legislation, what it is really doing is *commanding* those persons subject to its authority to perform some specific act, by binding them under a generalized undifferentiated duty of legal obedience.[31] By treating legislation as commands, Bodin concludes that it must be

[30] The contrast between legislation and contract is highlighted at *République* (1583), 135, with reference to C.1.14.5 and D.50.16.19.

[31] In this respect, Bodin may be regarded as the first theorist of the so-called command theory of law that is often attributed to Hobbes, Bentham, and Austin.

impossible to give a law unto oneself, for the same reason that it is impossible to give a command unto oneself.[32] Both scenarios create the absurd situation where one is allegedly bound under an obligation owed to oneself – which is to say that it is no obligation at all.

To demonstrate his point, Bodin appeals to a well-known rule in the law of obligations: *Nulla obligatio consistere potest, quae a voluntate promittentis statum capit.*[33] The point of this important text is to illustrate the absurdity of self-binding or self-obliging acts. It would be absurd to think that one can make (or break) a promise to oneself, or to owe (or default on) a debt payable to oneself. One could, of course, certainly try to comply with one's own legislation. It may even be good politics to do so. But this is all supererogatory. Javolenus's (and Bodin's) point is that none of these self-legislated rules can be truly binding upon oneself. This is why there is no consequence or sanction if one breaks one's own New Year's resolution or cheats on a self-imposed diet, just as there is no consequence if one breaks a supposed promise to oneself or fails to repay a debt to oneself.

This doctrine raises another related interpretive question. Why insist that sovereigns must be absolute in this technically specific way? It is *not* because (as many commentators have assumed) Bodin adhered to some vague notion of absolutism (incidentally, a term that was invented by French liberal historians in the aftermath of the French Revolution, some two centuries after Bodin's death).

Rather, the absolute character of sovereignty was intended in large part as a remedy to what Bodin saw as the inevitable imperfection, and even injustice, bound to emerge in any legal system, a problem especially devastating in democracies. Indeed, because positive legislation is the product of a sovereign authority with limited human reason and foresight, every independent legal system must have an inbuilt procedure for such sovereigns to change and remedy inequitable laws. Amending and even "overriding" [*deroger*] ordinary legislation – what Bodin, citing the lawyer-pope Innocent IV, regarded as the very essence of a sovereign's absolute power – embodied the moral purposes of sovereignty, which was to serve as an agent of justice by continuously

[32] Cf. D.4.8.51. The incoherence of sovereign autolimitation in Bodin's theory places him in opposition to modern neo-Kantian theorists of *Selbstverfplichtung* such as Georg Jellinek. On this theme, see Diego Quaglioni, *I limiti della sovranita: Il pensiero di Jean Bodin nella cultura politica e giuridica dell'eta moderna* (Padova: CEDAM, 1992).

[33] Bodin, at *République* (1583), 132; and *De republica* 85, cite D.45.1.108.1 (which deals specifically with promises) and 32.1.22.pr.

engineering a system of legislation thought to be in harmony with the higher law of equity.[34]

Once having established the doctrine of sovereignty and its function in binding the many elements of the state together as one whole, Bodin is able to investigate the practical details concerning how a sovereign state might be effectively governed.[35] Needless to say, the possibilities are numerous, and Bodin presents the question of government more as an open-ended constitutional choice to be decided by the sovereign authority. A sovereign prince, for example, may choose, as is his right of sovereignty, to govern through magistrates, appointed to permanent and legally defined offices. But it is as much the sovereign's right to choose to govern through "commissioners" – Bodin's generic term for private cronies who are personally loyal to their sovereign master or lord [*seigneur*, *dominus*] – serving at the pleasure [*suffrance*; *arbitrio*] of the prince, a form of government that Bodin routinely compares to the "seigneurial" or "despotic" governing style of Turkish and Muscovite princes.

Bodin's catalogue of the numerous possibilities of government, whether through commissioners, or through proper magistrates holding a proper office, or through some hybrid of these basic forms of delegated authority, reveals details of Bodin's normative political theory, which favors *droit gouvernement* and the rule of law over the arbitrary *seigneurial* rule of despots.

What makes this distinction between sovereignty and government possible is the concept of delegation, which joins the two together as participants locked together in a principal–agent relationship. For Bodin, anybody exercising some share of public authority, of whatever degree, rank, or magnitude, on behalf of a sovereign authority, is an agent. On this analysis, then, both the lowliest clerk and the highest public official can be seen equally as subordinate agents of the sovereign (though agents of different rank).

One may object at this point, however, that by stipulating a capacity for sovereigns to govern vicariously, by way of delegation and agency through others, Bodin seems to be violating a fundamental axiom of sovereignty, concerning its alleged *indivisibility*. What makes sovereign authority distinctive is that it is exclusive, and the powers constitutive of such sovereignty cannot be shared between the sovereign and anyone else: "For if they were shared, there would be no sovereign" at all.[36] On this objection, then,

[34] Bodin, *République* (1583), 133, citing Innocent IV on the *Liber Extra* 1.6.20.

[35] Bodin introduces the distinction between *de l'etat, & du gouvernement* at *République* (1583), 272.

[36] Julian Franklin, ed., *On Sovereignty* (Cambridge: Cambridge University Press, 1992), 46.

delegation of any kind would not be permissible since it ostensibly involves undermining that basic principle of sovereign indivisibility.

Bodin, however, anticipated this objection and developed his reply by stressing the critical difference between *dividing* sovereignty and *delegating* sovereignty. Delegating the exercise of sovereignty to an agent, of which Bodin supplies numerous illustrations in his work – most famously the Roman dictatorship – never impairs or diminishes the sovereign's right in any way. Even when, in moments of constitutional emergency, a state suspends the ordinary institutions of government and temporarily delegates absolute power to a dictator, sovereignty has not been divided or lost in any way. Indeed, what makes delegation different from an alienation or transfer of sovereignty is that the sovereign retains something like a title or right of ownership in the powers being delegated, so that "he never gives so much that he does not hold back even more."[37]

Most striking, and even ingenious, in Bodin's analysis is the use of the Roman law of obligations in specifying the particulars of principal–agent relations created in different forms of government. We can see this in Bodin's habit of describing government officials as "lessees," "depositaries," and "pledgors" of sovereignty, and even suggesting, at one point, that tenure of government office is not simply a "trust," but also a kind of "lease" [*commodatum*] on someone else's property.

Here, Bodin is deliberately deploying the model of Roman real contracts, such as the *commodatum*, the *depositum*, and the *pignus* to model principal–agent relations.[38] In doing so, he is making several points at once. One is the simple, but central, point that a government agent does not own the powers attached to his office, but is merely holding power in trust, as a fiduciary or placeholder, on the expectation that the power will be returned to its proper owner at some later specified time. Because the agent is a fiduciary in this way, Bodin feels justified in saying that the agent is duty-bound under something like a contractual obligation.

But the obligation goes both ways, which is the second point. Roman real contracts, such as lease and deposit, are bilateral in structure, a feature that Bodin acknowledges in his more systematic treatment in the *Distributio*. As bilateral contracts, they bind mutually and reciprocally, such that both parties (whether lessor and lessee, or depositor and depositary) are duty-bound to each

[37] This is Julian Franklin's rendering at *On Sovereignty*, 2, of the corresponding passage at *République* (1583), 123, which invokes, among other Romano-canonical sources, D.41.3.33.4, 41.2.18, and VI.3.4.14.

[38] In the *Distributio*, Bodin reclassifies such contracts as "mixed transactions" involving credit.

other. The upshot, then, is that sovereigns and agents must also be locked into a mutually binding obligation, so long as the latter holds an office of public trust. The agent, even the most senior magistrate entrusted with the sovereign's authority, is nevertheless duty-bound, burdened by obligation to return power to its proper owner at the end of the specified term of office. But what is crucial to observe is that the sovereign is *also* duty-bound, under a reciprocal obligation *not* to interfere or intermeddle in affairs of state while it is entrusted, as a lease or deposit of public authority, to someone else's care.

Not all appointments and delegation of public authority, however, involve such bilateral or reciprocal obligations. A seigneurial prince who chooses to govern through commissioned cronies serving only at the sovereign's pleasure creates one-sided obligations comparable (according to Bodin) to *precaria* in private law – temporary grants or tenancies that an owner is entitled to cancel or revoke arbitrarily at any time without giving notice or justifying a cause. Such a seigneurial or despotic style of government, while technically lawful under the *ius gentium*, creates a politics of dependence more appropriate for primitive peoples prior to the invention of law.[39]

States whose sovereigns govern through the law [*droit*], rather than by naked arbitrary will [*seigneuriale*], emerge as the normative ideal driving Bodin's theory of state. Undergirding that theory, however, is the basic axiom that even sovereigns, though immune from the force of their own laws, nevertheless remain duty-bound to perform obligations defined by higher laws – the law of nations, of nature, and of God. One purpose for such higher laws is to reinforce sovereign duties owed to other sovereigns in the context of international relations such as treaty obligations and compliance with rules of war.

But the more important reason for the oblique references to such higher laws is to position Bodin's theory of state sovereignty within a broader juridical theology, which pictures the whole of nature as a harmonious law-governed order ruled by one divine sovereign. For Bodin, God is that sovereign whose *respublica* is the whole cosmos, and God governs this cosmic *respublica* through divine and natural laws of God's own making. What is noteworthy is that divine sovereignty is patterned on the same legislative analysis introduced in Bodin's earlier legal and political texts. Just as the sovereign *princeps* is *legibus solutus*, so that the *princeps* can make and unmake *lex*, so, too, is God *legibus solutus* – specifically, *naturae legibus solutus* ("exempt from the

[39] The conquering party in a lawful war acquires not only a right and title of sovereignty but also the right to govern as a *seigneur*. Since states begin through war and conquest, the general history of the world is a progression from *seigneurial* government to *droit* government. Cf. *République* (1583), 393.

laws of nature") precisely so that God can make and, if God so wills, unmake laws of nature [*voluntate arbitrioque suo interdum mutat*].[40] Because of God's role as a legislator, Bodin feels justified in referring to God as a *princeps* – specifically, the *princeps naturae*, the great "prince of nature," whose sovereignty extends over all of creation. It also means that there are certain implied limitations built into even God's divine sovereignty.[41]

Perhaps most striking in this presentation is the postulation of a radical divine voluntarism, a conclusion entailed by Bodin's thesis that the law of nature – rendered in Latin notably as *lex naturae*, rather than the more conventional *ius naturale*, as at D.1.1.1.3 – is a voluntary creation of divine will. Like the whole of created nature itself, the law that governs nature is also a divine *creatio ex nihilo*. It can be made, and, in principle, it can be unmade.[42] In adopting this view, Bodin immediately positions his divine voluntarist theory of natural law against Stoic and Thomist views of natural law as *recta ratio* or intellect and aligns himself with nominalists such as Duns Scotus and Maimonides.[43]

Bodin's God, however, was not simply a creative *primum movens* who, once having created the world, retreats out to an extracosmic void, detached from created nature. As Howell Lloyd put it, the prince of nature "was no disconnected entity but actively directed human affairs."[44] Bodin's was an interventionist God, whose medium of intervention, as Bodin intimates in the *Démonomanie*, could be angels as well as demons.

What about Christ? Most striking about Bodin's juridical theology is that, despite his outward profession of the Catholic faith throughout his life, often required for professional advancement, his understanding of the divine is only superficially Christian, and it is for this reason that Bodin was repeatedly accused of heresy throughout his life. This fact raises vital interpretive questions: what kind of a God is Bodin's God? Is it even a *Christian* God, let alone a Catholic or a Reformed God? And what role does Christ or the Trinity play in that juridical theology? Bodin's reputation as a "Judaizer" and his apparent Neoplatonist sympathies, emerging in the *Theatrum* and *Colloquium*, only

40 Lloyd, *Jean Bodin*, 74.

41 For example, God cannot create another God, a doctrine that Bodin explains with an Aristotelian analysis, *Rep.* 1.10.

42 Daniel Lee, "Unmaking Law: Jean Bodin on Law, Equity and Legal Change," *History of Political Thought* 39, no. 2 (2018): 269–96.

43 In *Methodus*, Bodin uses Duns Scotus's language of divine-command theory in describing the authority of sovereigns and magistrates, exercising their discretionary *officia iudicis*, to act *praeter legem et contra legem*.

44 Lloyd, *Jean Bodin*, 74.

complicate the different routes one might take in navigating through these difficult questions.[45] Even more uncertain is Bodin's provocative treatment of Christ, described in one document in quasi-Promethean terms as "most holy... bringer of fire."[46] Missing from Bodin's theology, however, are principled statements on the major theological problems of the day – justification by faith, the Trinity, the Eucharist.

Given the interpenetrative quality of Bodin's grand system of thought, it is worth closing with one final, though no less important, point regarding method. What unites Bodin's thought as one coherent whole is the method of analysis that he applies without exception across the various subjects covered in his major treatises. It is a method that demands strict definition, so as to segregate universals from particulars of a subject matter and allow for proper comparison across context. In applying this methodological outlook to the study of human history and institutions, Bodin may be regarded not only as an early modern progenitor of the comparative social sciences but also as a serious student of language and meaning.

RECOMMENDED READING

Becker, Anna. "Jean Bodin on Oeconomics and Politics." *History of European Ideas* 40 (2014): 135–54.

Blair, Ann. *Theater of Nature*. Princeton: Princeton University Press, 1997.

Denzer, Horst, edn. *Jean Bodin: Verhandlungen der Internationalen Bodin Tagung in München*. Munich: Verlag C. H. Beck, 1973.

Franklin, Julian. *Jean Bodin and the Rise of Absolutist Theory*. Cambridge, New York: Cambridge University Press, 1973.

Giesey, Ralph. "Medieval Jurisprudence in Bodin's Concept of Sovereignty." In Denzer, *Jean Bodin: Verhandlungen der Internationalen Bodin Tagung in München*, 167–86.

Kelley, Donald. "The Development and Context of Bodin's *Method*." In Denzer, *Jean Bodin: Verhandlungen der Internationalen Bodin Tagung in München*, 123–50.

Lee, Daniel. *Popular Sovereignty in Early Modern Constitutional Thought*. Oxford: Oxford University Press, 2016.

"Unmaking Law: Jean Bodin on Law, Equity, and Legal Change." *History of Political Thought* 39, no. 2 (2018): 269–96.

Lloyd, Howell. *Jean Bodin, "This Pre-eminent Man of France": An Intellectual Biography*. Oxford: Oxford University Press, 2017.

edn. *The Reception of Bodin*. Leiden: Brill, 2013.

[45] Paul Lawrence Rose, *Bodin and the Great God of Nature: The Moral and Religious Universe of a Judaiser* (Geneva: Droz, 1980).

[46] Lloyd, *Jean Bodin*, 65–66.

McCuaig, William. *Carlo Sigonio: The Changing World of the Late Renaissance.* Princeton: Princeton University Press, 1989/2016.

Parker, David. "Law, Society and the State in the Thought of Jean Bodin." *History of Political Thought* 2 (1981): 253–85.

Rose, Paul Lawrence. *Jean Bodin and the Great God of Nature: The Moral and Religious Universe of a Judaiser.* Geneva: Librairie Droz, 1980.

Salmon, J. H. M. "The Legacy of Jean Bodin: Absolutism, Populism or Constitutionalism." *History of Political Thought* 17 (1996): 500–22.

Tuck, Richard. *The Sleeping Sovereign: The Invention of Modern Democracy.* Cambridge: Cambridge University Press, 2016.

12

Jean Domat

(1625–1696)

DAVID GILLES

Trained at the Collège de Clermont by the Jesuits, Jean Domat, a magistrate and practitioner, studied law in Bourges and started in the late 1670s to draft what would become *The Civil Law*. The "Jurisconsult of Port-Royal,"[1] pensioned by Louis XIV, continued this work from 1682 until his death on March 16, 1696. *The Civil Law in Its Natural Order* (hereafter CL),[2] with a preface titled A *Treatise of Laws* (hereafter TL), was first published from 1689 to 1694; the work was posthumously completed by *The Public Law, Following the Civil Law in Its Natural Order* (hereafter PL) in 1697.

Defender of a natural law that is more classic than modern, Domat is outside the school of *ius naturale* and *ius gentium*, even if, like Grotius, he bases natural law on human reason and the clear and obvious principles it illustrates. He refuses, however, to remove God[3] while laying down a rational systematization of the law.[4] He remains faithful to the Christian conception of an objective order responding to Creation: he starts from God and from the primordial foundations of the order God has established for the life of humanity. The legal science of the civil law is for Domat primordial because it proceeds from the analysis of human behavior in society and of humanity's divine destination:

1 P. Nourrisson, *Un ami de Pascal: Jean Domat* (Paris: Recueil Sirey, 1939), 50.

2 J. Domat, *Les Lois Civiles dans leur ordre naturel*, 1st edn (Paris: J.-B. Coignard, 1689–94), and *Le Droit Public, suite des Lois Civiles dans leur ordre naturel*, 2 vols. (Paris: J.-B. Coignard, 1697).

3 We search in vain under the pen of the jurisconsult for the equivalent of the words of Grotius allowing one to consider a legal system without God; H. Grotius, *Le Droit de la guerre et de la paix*, trad. J. Barbeyrac, 2 vols. (Amsterdam: Pierre de Coup, 1724; reimpr., Caen, 1984), vol. 2, p. 40.

4 M. Villey, *La formation de la pensée juridique romaine* (Paris: PUF, Léviathan, 2003), 555–58.

> All the matters of civil law have among themselves a simple and a natural order, which forms them into one body, in which it is easy to see them all, and to perceive with one view in what part everyone hath its rank.[5]

Domat wants the double law of love of the sovereign good (love of God) and love of neighbor to reign over these matters. He deduces from this divine order a plan of exposition that breaks with the legal tradition. In *The Civil Law*, he then states and puts commitments on one side and inheritance on the other. He sets the tone for his work in introductory observations under *A Treatise of Laws*. He then moves to the main portion of his treatise and discusses the various rules and principles under *The Civil Law*. This presentation falls into parts, books, titles, and sections, with the various units prefaced by headers, introductions, and summaries. Roman numerals, annotated in the margins by key words, and accompanied by references to Roman law in footnote format, separate the actual narratives. He is therefore carrying out a refounding and restructuring, in order to establish the links among the natural rules. This must be done according to a very strict program:

> The design therefore proposed in this book, is to set the Roman laws in their true order: to distinguish the matters of the law, and to place them according to the rank which they have in the body which they naturally compose: to divide each matter according to its parts.[6]

Jansenist, Gallican, and libertarian, Domat's originality lies in the reconciliation of the seeming paradox of building a legal corpus between Christian thought and modern rationalism. This surprising combination that he builds – between the weight of the divine foundation of his legal system, on the one hand, and the will to establish a purified, jusnaturalist, rational, and geometric law on the other hand – characterizes his work. This ambition seems natural to him, as a man of the Great Century nourished both by the scriptures and by the Cartesian *cogito*.

FROM PLAN OF SALVATION TO LEGAL ORDER

It is the search for a foundation that guides Domat.[7] He places himself more in the legal tradition of the sixteenth century than in the modernity of the emerging Enlightenment. The burden lies on him to abandon the plan of

[5] TL, Ch. XIV, 1 and 2, p. liii.
[6] J. Domat, author's preface, cl.
[7] TL, 9, 6.

Justinian compilations.[8] But he does not intend to follow only a modern way of uncovering foundations, based on *mos geometricus*,[9] to bring out natural and Christian principles in a law of pagan origin. The order of nature and religion is here confronted with the darkness of fallen humanity. For Domat,

> although these principles are known to us only by the light of religion, yet it points them out to us in our very nature, with so much clearness, that we see plainly that man is ignorant of them only because he does not know himself; and therefore that nothing is more astonishing than the blindness that hinders him from seeing them.[10]

There is therefore a natural law that finds its expression in Roman law, in which, however, the great principles underlying the rules of natural law are lost. It is therefore necessary to find these natural and Christian principles by resorting to reason. This is why Domat is building a new, exhaustive legal system with the help of a refined Roman law, cleansed of its ancient remnants and enlightened by the Christian religion. If natural laws allow humanity to live in harmony with divine precepts, there must be a coercive force capable of bringing every member of the community back toward these laws. This force, this power desired by God, must also act in accordance with divine precepts. The principles of natural law thus extend from *The Civil Law* to *Public Law*.

Domat intends to force humanity, by law, to respect the divine order. If the soul and reason of human beings are partly obscured, then human law is also plunged into the darkness of incoherence. This is why we must return to the first precepts of scripture to morally create a body of law capable of embracing the entirety of human society based on the two main laws of love. To constitute a law capable of satisfying the goals that Domat sets for any legal system, meaning to bring humanity back to God, it was necessary to reveal in a striking way the first truths that everyone must know naturally by a deductive system. The true foundation of the law, therefore, can only be religious and Christian. For Domat, in frontal opposition to Hobbes, there is no state of nature where all would be at war against all others.[11] There is no social contract between individuals; humanity has remained in the hands of God despite the Fall, and if human beings are led to bind themselves to others, it is

[8] TL, Ch. 1.

[9] M.-F. Renoux-Zagamé, "Domat, le salut et le droit," *RHFD* 8 (1989): 70–111, at 103.

[10] TL, Ch. I.

[11] T. Hobbes, *Le Léviathan* (Paris: Sirey, 1971), Ch. 13, pp. 122–24.

by virtue of the law of love for one another.[12] Otherwise, "we know," according to Domat, that God only allowed evil and self-love to happen "because he foresaw that by his almighty Power and infinite Wisdom he should be able to draw Good out of it."[13] If the first principles of law and the detail of the essential rules that are its consequences and extensions have a "character of truth"[14] also affecting the mind and the heart, the light of religion participates in the knowledge of these legal principles. If human beings ignore these principles, it is because they do not know themselves.

THE FIRST TWO LAWS OF LOVE

The first two laws are a reflection of the divine pattern. Pushing each person to commitments, the law of love of neighbor naturally influences legal commitments by instilling the spirit of the Christian religion:

> The first is that of the natural powers, which respect natural engagement; such as the power which marriage gives to the husband over the wife, and that which birth gives to parents over their childern.[15]

The first law, which is the spirit of religion and commands the search and love of the sovereign good, largely eludes the legal sphere, even if it constitutes its objective purpose. On the other hand, the law of love for one another, which flows from the first law, naturally has almost infinite legal consequences:

> For this law, which is the foundation and first principle of all the others. For this law, which commands man to search after and to love the sovereign good, being common to all mankind, implies a second law, which obliges them to unity among themselves, and to the love of one another; because being destined to be united in the possession of one only good, which is to make their common happiness, and to be united in it so closely, that it is said that they shall be but one; they cannot be worthy of that union in the possession of their common end, if they do not begin their union, by linking themselves together by the tie of mutual love in the way that leads them to it.[16]

Domat can see the power of self-esteem over the souls of men and women, so it is essential to build a body of law that abides by the first two laws, because

[12] TL, Ch. II, 1 and 2.
[13] TL, Ch. IX, 3.
[14] TL, Ch. I, 2.
[15] TL, Ch. IX, 7, p. xxi.
[16] TL, Ch. I, 7, p. iv.

the realization of the finality of human beings and their salvation is conditioned by the conjunction of these two laws. The challenge of the work is therefore to translate this metaphysical love for God and God's creatures into applicable and effective legal precepts. The law of love for one another and the principle of love that results from it can be translated into general principles, such as the prohibition of usury or the prohibition of violence in contracts, but also into moral precepts that unite society differently. From this destination to "sovereign Good,"

> we shall also discover in it his destination to Society, and the several Ties which engage him to it from all parts; and that these Ties, which are Consequences of the Destination of man to the exercise of the first two Laws, are at the same time the Foundation of the particular Rules of all his duties, and the Foundation of all laws.[17]

Domat sets Christian values as cardinal values. This is true of family values,[18] of the *humanitas* and the *caritas*[19] that inform rules like the prohibition against contractual violence aimed at the weakest, or the prohibition against usury. The Roman notion of *humanitas* strengthens natural equity, as Domat does regarding people's legal incapacity to inherit. Similarly, *caritas* expresses itself in help given to the poor, in application of the second law of love.[20] From Exodus, Deuteronomy, and the first Book of Kings,[21] Domat draws a rule of natural law, an "indispensable law," which establishes the right of each to obtain from his or her neighbor the help necessary for survival.[22] But the spirit of charity is not always subject to legal sanction. This is true, for instance, in the case of acquisitive prescription, when possession in bad faith over a long term can be validated by law under the principle of continuous possession by legitimate owners.[23] Then conscience comes into play and, failing that, canon law, which alone can overturn the acquisitive prescription.[24] The law of love of neighbor is therefore not always exactly translated into the body of positive law, as in the case of acquisitive prescription[25] or establishment of fair prices, which is part of the validity of a convention.

[17] TL, Ch. I, 8, p. iv.
[18] PL, L.I, T.IX, S.II, preamble.
[19] PL, L.I, T.XVIII, preamble.
[20] Domat quotes the Theodosian Code in PL, L.I, T.XVIII, preamble.
[21] Exod. 23: 10–11, Deut. 15: 7–8, and I Kings 2 and 7.
[22] PL, L.I, T.XVIII, preamble.
[23] CL, L.III, T.VII, S.IV, 14.
[24] CL, L.III, T.VII, S.IV, 18.
[25] Ibid.

Domat, however, refuses the principle of a rescission of rights in case of sale at an excessive price. By the same logic, he prohibits usury and undue enrichment because they violate *caritas* and thus the law of love of the neighbor;[26] he wishes to "open everyone's eyes" to the divine light. Both types of loans – for value or for no consideration – are a consequence of the natural law of love of the neighbor. Money loans with interest not only violate the law of love of neighbor but also constitute a contract that by its nature is unbalanced for the benefit of the creditor. This inequality is the basis for the prohibition of usury by divine law, natural law, and royal ordinances without legitimate exception.

BIBLICAL SOURCES AS THE FOUNDATION OF A RATIONALIZED RIGHT

The Christian matrix in which Domat's thought takes place is relatively classic for a man and a jurist of the seventeenth century. Like the sixteenth-century jurists – the authors of the second scholasticism[27] or the French humanists – he refers largely to biblical texts, thus extending the phenomenon of sacralization of the law.[28] Suffused with an Augustinianism that reigns supreme over classical thought – and is even more striking in Jansenist circles – Domat owes a lot to the Bishop of Hippo and St Thomas Aquinas. He maintains a close link between law, evangelical morality, and theology.[29] Rich in various influences, he does not show in his legal work a particularly sustained knowledge of the various theological debates that agitated his time. He relies little on canon law and does not stand out from the common science of the magistrates of the time. On the contrary, his evocation of the scriptures is rich, but the use he makes of them is more moral than legal. His use of evangelical texts shows that he did not envision creating a legal order or revealing his vision of humanity in society without referring to the theological foundations of Christian thought, in line with medieval jurists and canonists.

Domat thus appears as a conservative author of a certain legal tradition. His *Treatise of Laws* is organized almost entirely on maxims derived from

[26] CL, L.I, T.VI, S.I, preamble.

[27] See Luisa Brunori's brilliant study, "*Societas quid sit*": *La société commerciale dans l'élaboration de la Seconde Scolastique. Personnes et capitaux entre le XVIe et le XVIIe siècle* (Paris: Mare & Marin, 2015), 37–58.

[28] J.-L. Thireau, "Préceptes divins et normes juridiques dans la doctrine française du XVIe siècle," in J.-L. Thireau, ed., *Le droit entre laïcisation et néo-sacralisation* (Paris: PUF, 1997), 109–43, esp. 113–27.

[29] J.-L. Halpérin, *L'impossible Code Civil* (Paris: PUF, 1992), 65.

scriptures. In a canonical tradition, he wishes, on the basis of the teachings of patristics, to bring closer and sometimes mix natural law and divine law. This idea that God alone determines the meaning and content of justice, that it gives humanity finality, and that God's word constitutes a source of law goes back to St Augustine. Domat therefore seeks to verify the conformity of positive laws with divine law and thus enlighten the jurist and the Christian in the quest for justice.[30]

In general, Domat multiplies recourses to the authority of the scriptures in *A Treatise of Laws*, in public law and in civil law. Even in very technical developments, Domat does not hesitate to refer to scriptural texts, references that must not make us forget or neglect the natural law itself or the arbitrary laws. There must be convergence and compatibility between the divine precepts, natural rules, and positive laws. It is not a true union of theology and jurisprudence but an intimate collaboration, made necessary by the interpenetration of divine, natural, and human elements in law. The jurist must then resort to sacred texts because he cannot conceive justice independently of the word of God and the higher principles that it enacts without characterizing their legal value. For example, concerning usury, Domat asserts that the divine law – in this case the moral precepts of divine law – is self-sufficient, and he then provides efficient norms without transposition by positive law,[31] even if he quotes the royal ordinances to show the compatibility between divine principles and arbitrary laws.

However, in most uses of the principles derived from the divine law in *The Civil Law*, the latter do not seem to represent true, directly applicable legal norms. There is no longer the traditional distinction between *judicalia* – positive laws of the Jewish people, incontestable legal rules – and *moralia* – immutable general principles found in the scriptures – that could be seen in Dumoulin,[32] even if Domat seems to mention this distinction only exceptionally in succession matters. In *A Treatise of Laws*, he points out that even God abrogated divine laws, which are therefore not immutable to God but remain immutable to humanity.[33] In general, one can identify strong lines in his use of scriptures, even if it is heterogeneous. First of all, he does not draw on all the holy texts. His references are essentially limited to the Old Testament.

Quotations of the scriptures in *Public Law* are found primarily in the first titles – "Government," "Power," "Prince's Counsel," and "Use of Forces

[30] CL, L.II, T.IX, S.II, 1.
[31] CL, L.I, T.VI, preamble.
[32] CL, Second part, L.IV, preamble, VII.
[33] TL, Ch. XI, 33.

Necessary to Maintain a State" – strengthening the divine foundation of power. The model of the virtues of princes is found in his eyes in Deuteronomy and Ecclesiastes.[34] When it comes to more technical issues, such as state funding, he comes back to the "royal ordinances." In matters of clergy, scriptural texts are used equally with canonical decrees and royal ordinances. Domat still makes many references to the Tridentine decrees to establish the organization of the clergy.[35] He borrows examples and images from the scriptures to educate his readers and engage them in the way of salvation. He uses the example of King David to emphasize the attachment of every subject to the prince and the attachment of the prince to subjects. If Roman law no longer responds to the needs of his time, Domat nevertheless sees the spirit of the divine law that endures and transcends the uses of the church, calling for a return to the rigor of the church of Justinian, even of the early church.[36] As a Jansenist, he recalls the natural truths that must reign over the heart of each of us. This leads him to use the scriptures to establish the foundation of the great principles of civil law found in *A Treatise of Laws* and then in *The Civil Law*.

This is how the scriptures enable him to establish the husband's authority over his wife, "which is natural and divine law,"[37] and the legal consequences that flow from that authority. He also invokes the Old Testament in support of paternal power[38]or the distinction between illegitimate and legitimate children.[39] Likewise, the natural order of successions *ab intestat* is "so just and so natural that it has been established as such by the divine law which has confirmed its use."[40] In the matter of commitment following a loan,[41] he again quotes divine law to legitimize the absence of responsibility in case of loss of the thing lent.[42] Scripture also establishes the general principle of exoneration of liability following an accident. It is the same for the repair of damage resulting from such an accident.[43] Scriptural sources, however, do not give him the foundations of his entire body of work. Thus, if Domat still invokes divine law in matters of deposit and sequestration or dower,[44]

[34] Deut. 20: 1 and Eccles. 8: 8, PL, L.I, T.X, S.II, 4.
[35] PL, T.X, S.II, 14.
[36] PL, L.I, T.X, S.II, 15.
[37] Domat quotes Gen. 3: 16., Ephes. 5: 23, 1 Cor. 11: 3, I Pet.; CL. Preliminary book, T.II, S.I, 1.
[38] Domat quotes Exod. 20: 12, Eccles. 7: 30, and Eccles. 3: 8.
[39] Domat quotes Deut. 23: 2.
[40] CL., Second part, L.IV, preamble, VII.
[41] CL., preliminary book, T.II, S.I, 2.
[42] CL L. I, T.V, S.II, 6.
[43] CL, L. I, T.VII, S.III, 4. Exod. 22: 10 and Exod. 22: 12.
[44] CL, L. I, T.IX, S.II, 1.

it disappears in matters of society, *inter vivos* donations, usufruct, servitudes, transactions, compromises, powers of attorney, mandates, and commissions.

A remark must be made, however, about the use of scriptures in *The Civil Law*. Domat uses them most often in the preambles of his developments or in articles giving the definition of a domain or laying down a general rule, which marks the divine foundation of his corpus. This is the case in his discussion about dowry, where he cites the scriptures only in the preamble to the title (with the biblical example of Tobit's marriage)[45] and in the first article of section 2.[46] It is in the same manner that he suggests the scriptural texts concerning the "vices of conventions." The biblical prohibition of the use of force provides justification for establishing a general principle invalidating any convention established by force, as deemed without cause.[47]

This use of scriptural rules has a double interest for Domat's system. It gives an undeniable foundation to his solutions. On the other hand, it allows him to back up the rule prohibiting conventions inspired by the first two laws that Domat has laid down as fundamental principles. For example, he makes it clear that anyone who uses a form of violence in a contract violates the divine principle of Leviticus and thereby despises God. Thus, the natural order extends or expresses the first two laws, without necessarily finding a direct invocation of the divine word as it is transcribed in the biblical texts. Wishing to create a system that conforms to the divine law, Domat acts, reasons, and builds as a jurist and not as a theologian. Domat must convert the moral aspirations that animate him into a natural legal system.

THE QUEST FOR A CHRISTIAN NATURAL ORDER

This quest takes place in a context marked by Domat's belonging to the first Jansenism.[48] Italian historiography has dwelt for a long time on the relations

45 Tob. 7: 15. CL, L. I, T.IX, preamble.

46 Exod. 22: 17, 34: 16; Deut. 7: 3; CL, L. I, T.IX, S.II, 1.

47 CL, L. I, T. XVIII, S.II, preamble.

48 See M. Cottret, *Jansénisme et Lumières: pour un autre XVIIIe siècle* (Paris: Albin Michel, 1998); C. Maire, *De la cause de Dieu à la cause de la Nation* (Paris: Gallimard, 1998); D. Van Kley, *The French Idea of Freedom: The Old Regime and the Declaration of Right of* 1789 (Stanford, CA: Stanford University Press, 1994), and R. Tavenaux, "Jansénisme," in *Dictionnaire du Grand Siècle*, edn. F. Bluche (Paris: Fayard, 1990), 778–83. F. di Donato analyzes legal issues more profitably; see essentially *L'ideologia dei robins nella Francia dei lumi. Costituzionalismo e assolutismo nell'esperienza politico-istituzionale della magistratura di antico regime* (1715–1788) (Napoli: ESI, 2003); Jag Tans, "Les idées politiques des jansénistes," *Néophilologicus* 40, edn. J. B. Wolters (Groningen/Djakarta, 1956), 1–18, at 7.

that Domat maintained with Port-Royal.[49] One would seek in vain for the dogma of predestination or effective grace in the juridical work of Domat. Some Jansenists, such as Domat, Pierre Nicole,[50] or, later, Joseph Duguet will seek, through the bits of divinity that maintain the link between the fallen creature and God, to consider the world as an undoubtedly imperfect order. This imperfect state, where the adequacy between divine and human will is possible and even desirable, is, however, wanted by God. Domat's jusnaturalist vision is in opposition with that of Pascal, who prefers custom.[51]

By following St Augustine and Cornelius Jansen in their reading of Genesis, the Jansenists agree that the sin of Adam and Eve is the cause of the corruption of human nature. The consequences they derive from this sin vary, however. According to Pascal, reason itself is corrupt. For Domat, on the contrary, if humankind is corrupt, reason remains the only share of divinity preserved in this world. The Christian who is Domat therefore places himself in a rather ambiguous position. As Carmine Ventimiglia has shown, Domat and the Port-Royalist doctrine – taken in its diversity – embrace a world where fallen humanity must unite to find God.[52]

Domat adheres to the fundamental axioms of Jansenism: corruption of the soul and ignorance of the designs of God.[53] But if he believes in immanent grace, he intends, nevertheless, to build on Christian principles a morality and a legal system capable of bringing Christians back to God.[54] Unlike Nicole, who believes that the political order is an "admirable invention,"[55] Domat perceives more than a simple element of peace in the social order.

Legally and religiously for him,

> all the different ideas that can be conceived of the various kinds of laws which are expressed by the names of divine and human laws, natural and positive, of

[49] F. Todescan, *Le radici teologiche del giusnaturalismo laico II. Il problema della seccolarizzazione nel pensiero giuridico di Jean Domat* (Milano: Giuffrè Editore, 1987); C. Ventimiglia, *Societa, politica, diritto: Il cristiano e il mondo* de *Pascal e Domat* (Parma: Edn. Zara, 1983). See N. Mateucci, *Jean Domat, un magistrato giansenista* (Bologne: il Mulino, 1959), 14–39.

[50] E. D. James, *Pierre Nicole, Jansenist and Humanist: A Study of His Thought* (The Hague: Nijhoff, 1972).

[51] B. Pascal, *Pensées*, in *Oeuvres complètes*, edn. Jacques Chevalier (Paris: Bibliothèque de la Pléiade, 1962), B. 294, p. 1163.

[52] Ventimiglia, *Societa, politica, diritto*, 20–32.

[53] See L. Goldmann, *Le Dieu caché: essai sur la vision tragique dans les Pensées de Pascal et le théâtre de Racine* (Paris: Gallimard, 1955), 182–96.

[54] See G. Rodis-Lewis, "Augustinisme et cartésianisme à Port-Royal," *Descartes et le cartésianisme hollandais, Études et Documents* (Paris: PUF, 1950), 131–82.

[55] R. Tavenaux, *Jansénisme et politique* (Paris: Armand Colin, 1965), 92.

> religion and the police of the law of nations, civil law . . . are reduced to two species, which include all laws of any kind: one, laws that are immutable, and the other, laws that are arbitrary.[56]

Very classically, Domat posits the ends of divine law as limits of the civil law guaranteeing the social order. The ultimate foundation of natural law is God, while its next foundation is the nature of humankind. The juridical system, which recalls in its rigor and its binary classification the geometric classic French gardens, is built around a mathematical method, clear structure, and succinct articles. Starting from the two laws of love, the system is structured by a *summa divisio* between immutable natural laws, on the one hand, and arbitrary human laws on the other. The distinction between eternal and transient law preoccupied lawyers and theologians on the Continent and in England.[57] In choosing the natural-law framework found in the *ratio scripta* of Roman law, Domat, although a fervent Jansenist, departs from the legal posture of Pascal, for example, by constituting a singular voice within this movement.

IMMUTABLE LAWS, ARBITRARY LAWS

In *The Civil Law*, Domat defines natural laws as "those which God himself has established, and which he teaches to men by the light of reason";[58] these "are natural and so just always and everywhere, that no authority can change them or abolish them."[59] These are the direct consequences of the first two principles from which the set of norms in a society must flow.[60] Yet Domat does not claim to logically deduce the natural laws from human nature; rather, natural laws are gradually revealed by human reason. The law of nature, for Domat as for the Christian tradition from St Augustine to Aquinas, has an ethical end consistent with human nature. Its principle, the light of natural reason, becomes the supreme condition of morality because natural reason is able to determine what corresponds to human nature and what does not.[61] Among these immutable laws are the great principles of contractualism, which derive directly from the two laws of love,[62] but also

56 TL, Ch. XI, 1.

57 Richard J. Ross, "Distinguishing Eternal from Transient Law: Natural Law and the Judicial Laws of Moses," *Past & Present* 217, no. 1 (2012): 79–115.

58 CL, preliminary book., T.I, S.I, 2.

59 TL, Ch. XI, 1.

60 Ibid.

61 See A. Dufour, "Droit naturel, droit positif," *A.P.D.* 35 (1990): 59–79.

62 TL, Ch. XI, 4.

certain operating principles of the public authority, the rejection of all unjust enrichment, avarice, usury, and so on. According to Domat, there are natural matters, that is to say, materials that are so natural and so essential to the most frequent needs, "that they have always been in use in all places; exchange, lease, deposit, loan for use, and several other conventions."[63]

But natural laws are not limited to these great principles and are found in certain rules that Domat wishes to make universal, such as the law that a possessor should not be disturbed in the enjoyment of his property, or that the state should not take advantage of a taxpayer's doubt in the case of an unfounded tax claim. It is because it is rooted in human reason – symbolic of the link with God – that natural law applies to all humanity, in a Christian theological tradition. For Domat, if natural laws cannot be modified,[64] there nevertheless can be exceptions. Expressions of the divine order, natural laws can be restricted by exemptions or exceptions or by temperaments, even while it is necessary to abide by the first two laws of love. These laws, however, "do not fail to be immutable."[65] The immutable rules with regard to which no exceptions can be made are, for example, those supporting good faith and loyalty, and those prohibiting deceit, fraud, and surprise. Others, such as the natural law that prohibits all swearing, find exception, for instance, in cases of swearing an oath of justice. Domat then sets up a web of norms, both natural and arbitrary, that limit each other to the point of creating a complete body of law,[66] filling the entire legal sphere.

By basing his work on a very moralistic view of the law, like Joseph Le Caron or Hugues Doneau before him, Domat does not intend to devalue positive law. Not all people have pure enough reason to recognize the justice of the laws or have a right enough heart to obey them. It is then the police who "give these laws another empire independent of the approval of humanity, by the authority of the temporal powers who keep them."[67] In the end, these natural rules, whatever they may be, despite their "natural authority over our reason," do not always make it possible to answer all legal questions and must be limited or extended by arbitrary laws. Obvious legal principles, they nevertheless need to be extended by positive norms.

The humanity envisaged by Domat is a fallen humanity but destined for God.[68] In a society perverted by both original sin and self-esteem, civil law

[63] TL, Ch. XI, 1.
[64] TL, Ch. XI, 20, and CL, preliminary book, T.I, S.I, 8.
[65] TL, Ch. XI, 20.
[66] Ibid.
[67] Ibid.
[68] TL, Ch. I and IX.

must be constructed while "God himself made men"[69] for God himself. The perspective, however, is that of eudaemonism, the end of humanity being the happiness found only in the sovereign good and the salvation completing Domat's *visio Dei*. To understand the law, one must understand human beings as they are, their true nature[70] and their end. Human beings are naturally pushed toward each other[71] and toward God. Domat wishes to restore the Augustinian order[72] through the convergence between the natural order and the divine order. It is nothing but the natural law, itself a transcription of the law of God engraved in the hearts of men and women. Disorder, however, does not call into question the very existence of society.[73]

There must therefore be, on the one hand, the maintenance of divine order on earth and, on the other, a struggle against the sources of disturbances of self-esteem and its consequences – trials, crimes, and wars. To bring back order, religion and law come together. Justice is the measure of acceptability of any politico-legal order. The idea that sin lies at the origin of the state, the political institution being at once the result and the remedy for sin, evokes Jansenist thought. Domat is also faithful to Thomist thinking by his invocation of human reason as revealing natural law. It is necessary for him to bring to light the foundation of natural law. He joins Cicero in this way of thinking.[74] There is the conjunction of the teaching of religion and the feeling of reason.[75] For him the foundation of law is, by its theological essence, a theology that associates, as active principles, faith and reason. The question arises, therefore, whether law is the result of reason or will. For Domat, following Aquinas, reason is the driving principle of legal revelation,[76] which makes the law apparent, and it is in reason that justice resides.[77] Domat wishes to use reason to raise humanity toward God.

The foundation of the law according to Domat derives from an extension of the idea of natural law to the whole legal field, natural law reflecting the divine nature. Natural law – given the doctrine of original sin and fallen humanity – can only be an imperfect image of the *lex aeterna*, but accessible to humanity by the exercise of speculative reason. The arbitrary law of Domat

[69] TL., Ch. I, p. 2. See St Augustine, *The City of God*, XIV, IV, 1.
[70] TL, Ch. I.
[71] Ibid.
[72] Augustine, *City of God*, XIX, XII, 2.
[73] TL, Ch. IX.
[74] Cicero, *De Legibus*, L.XII, 33.
[75] TL, Ch. IX. See Rom. 2: 14.
[76] St Thomas Aquinas, *Summa theologiae*, Ia, IIae, Qu. 93, art. 1.
[77] Ibid., Qu. 58, art. 4.

is a resumption of the *lex humana* of Aquinas, as human reason elaborates the practical rules of individual and social life. It establishes the idea of a relationship between three legal strata: the two first principles, natural laws, and finally arbitrary laws. It is a legal structure leading to an ante-Kelsenian relationship, necessary and decreasing between the norms. According to the Scholastic tradition, human and arbitrary law must be to the natural law what the natural law is to the divine law and the first principles. The reason of the Scholastics ensures the unity of the system. Domat thus departs from the Thomist inheritance on two essential points: the value of the first principles[78] and the legal structure operating a normative reduction in a *summa divisio* natural law and arbitrary law.

Contrary to the eternal Augustinian law, the two first principles – the law of love of the sovereign good and the law of love of one's neighbor – are not distinguished by their nature from the rest of natural laws. The rest of natural laws only depart from the two first principles because of their place in the tree structure. This set – to which is added the arbitrary laws involving a part or an application of a natural law – forms the natural law. Through his reading and reflection, Domat is also close to the second scholastics. In his search for the perfect foundation of his legal system, Domat draws on the same sources in order to establish the internal legal order of a state.

The distinction between natural and positive law derives from Christian thought.[79] For Domat, as for Suarez,[80] it is a matter of elaborating or recalling just laws as applying the principles contained in natural law. The crux of the problem lies in the links between positive law and natural law.[81] Positive law is engendered by reason and will. Reason is exercised differently in these two types of law. Concerning natural law, reason acts as an immediate active principle, the natural law is then known by intuition, and its imperatives immediately appear. Positive law, on the other hand, is elaborated by reasoning; it is a construction of reason and not a consequence of the action of reason.

Domat believes that if laws are right, if laws conform to the divine order, then they can participate in the salvation of humanity.[82] The relationships between reason and will, which partly forms the basis of the passage from

[78] Ibid., Ia, IIae, Qu. 95, art. 2.

[79] See A. Vincent, "La notion moderne de droit naturel et le volontarisme (de Vitoria et Suarez à Rousseau)," *A.P.D.* 13 (1963): 237–59, at 238.

[80] Edward J. Capestany, "Four Dimensions of Natural Law in Suarez: Objectivity – Knowledge – Essence – and Obligation," *Catholic Lawyer* 16, no. 1 (2017): 58–77.

[81] See F. De Vitoria, *Leçon sur le pouvoir politique* (Paris: Vrin, 1980), 65.

[82] Suarez, *Des lois et du Dieu législateur,* L.I, C.XIII, 4, 273.

classical jusnaturalism to modern jusnaturalism, are thus reflected in his writings. The discovery of laws proceeds from reason, which acts as revealing; the act of will is incidental to the exercise of reason. By establishing a direct relation in his system between natural principles, natural laws, and the laws that follow from them, Domat follows Suarez as to the purpose of the law. If Domat participates in the evolution toward a greater force of will in the face of pure reason – a voluntarism that will really break out in the school of modern natural law – he places this voluntarist action in a scheme where God cannot be forgotten. Domat's voluntarism stops at the contract, an expression of the law of love of neighbor.

The necessity of regulating the difficulties arising from the application of the immutable laws legitimates for Domat a large part of the arbitrary laws that must either apply natural laws or limit them. Arbitrary laws, by their prescriptions, then mediate for humanity the order of divine creation. He distinguishes in these arbitrary laws two characters constituting appropriate norms between natural norms and arbitrary norms in the strict sense, which "make two laws into one."[83] There is then in these arbitrary laws a part – director – belonging to natural law and another part – mediator – that is arbitrary. This is the case of the law making children legitimate, which contains two provisions. We can then speak of complementary rules to the natural laws, which come to regulate the detail of what immutable laws ignore or cannot govern. Hierarchically subordinate to divine law, and necessarily subject to the directives of natural law, positive law thus appears as its indispensable complement for two reasons. On the one hand, divine and natural principles, while fundamental, cannot suffice to govern society in all its complexity. On the other hand, fallen humanity must have practical and effective rules to return it to the right path. Human beings cannot be content with moral or natural legal precepts if their reason does not enlighten them. By this logic, Domat wishes to bring arbitrary laws into conformity with natural laws.

The point on which Domat most resorts to the dialectic of arbitrary laws as a consequence of natural laws is the question of the limits of natural law. While he seeks to affirm and illuminate immutable principles, he is aware that natural rules inevitably have limits. Sometimes a conflict arises from several natural norms, such as *intestat succession*.[84] "La légitime" is then an arbitrary rule that prolongs two immutable laws while confining them and making them effective, or more exactly applicable. As such, it finds its place in the legal system described by Domat. Arbitrary laws also establish the

[83] TL, Ch. XI, 11.
[84] TL, Ch. XI, 7.

requirements for the possession of property,[85] the age of majority,[86] the setting of amounts for causes of action regarding lesion.[87] By leaving humanity with the possibility of establishing the legal rule appropriate to their needs, he is getting closer to Protestant jurists.[88] But the arbitrary rules, for Domat, do not simply frame or limit immutable laws. According to him, there are subjects over which arbitrary laws are the rule, even if natural law is not definitively excluded from them.

CONCLUSION

In the end, Domat cannot be clearly affiliated in a Manichean way to one or the other stream of Christian thought, but he is infused with the Christian Catholic reflection of his time. This natural law resides in a juridical order of divine origin, perceptible only to the light of natural Christian reason, which alone allows the clear perception of this law. Revelation and tradition make this perception easier for the Christian. Domat does not appear – or does not want to appear – to be involved in doctrinal or theological debates. Legally, he is at the hinge of classical and modern jusnaturalism without taking a decisive step. Politically, Domat rejects the neo-Thomist tradition,[89] a source of protest, in favor of a vision of the state and society close to that of Bossuet, supporting a solid state. Finally, from a religious point of view, he links Augustinianism and Thomism in a perspective that partly marks the thought of the Port-Royalists.

On the level of law, one must ask the question of the existence of a legal Jansenism that would have nourished the thought of the eighteenth century and the Civil Code. These ideas are sometimes seen as mistakenly linked.[90] The specific legal works of Domat, Pothier,[91] or the Civil Code can be analyzed as a consequence of a moralist and rationalist current within the law. This does not make these works the legal extension of Jansenist thought.

[85] LT., Ch. XI, 8.

[86] TL, Ch. XI, 9.

[87] TL, Ch. XI, 10.

[88] See J. Gordley, *The Philosophical Origins of Modern Contract Doctrine* (Oxford: Clarendon Press, 1991), 130–32.

[89] See F. Daguet, "Saint Thomas et les deux pouvoirs," *Revue Thomiste* (oct.-déc. 2002): 531–69.

[90] J. Carbonnier, "L'importance de d'Aguesseau pour son temps et pour le nôtre," *Le chancelier Henri-François d'Aguesseau: Limoges 1668–Fresnes 1751* (Limoges: Desvilles, 1953), 36–58. See also D. Gilles, "De la plume d'un avocat du roi à celle d'un Chancelier: Henri-François d'Aguesseau, lecteur de Jean Domat," *Cahiers Poitevins d'histoire du droit* 3 (2011): 163–83.

[91] É. Gojosso and D. Gilles, "Sur Pothier et le Code civil," in *Étude d'histoire du droit privé en souvenir de Maryse Carlin*, edn. O. Vernier (Paris: Mémoire du droit, 2008), 403–17.

It is by wishing to put humanity on the path of salvation that Domat engages in the search for a unique source of law responding to Christian precepts. But in doing so, his jusnaturalism is more conservative than that of the school of modern natural law. His attachment to the Christian tradition and the Gospels certainly means for him the misery of humanity without God. Moreover, the truth of humanity and human laws cannot exist without God. Domat's entire work therefore tends to express the consciousness of spirituality that must animate the positive legal apparatus of humanity. This is why he must build a legal system combining natural laws and positive laws, fulfilling the divine purpose and the needs of positive human law. The construction of a streamlined, structured civil law will be Domat's major legacy in the eighteenth century, and later in the great codifications of the early nineteenth century.

Unfortunately for him, it is the legal structure and solutions that will go on to know a widespread use in the French civil code, in the Louisianan codes, and in the civil code of Lower Canada in particular. The Christian foundations and the desire to bring humanity back to God through law will be abandoned by the codifiers, depriving Domat's work of his Christian soul for the benefit of his legal thought.[92] Still today, in many works throughout the world, and in particular in the United States, the evocation of Domat's thought is made when we talk about the law of obligations, usufruct, arbitration, prescription, the origins of Louisiana, Canadian law, or the various realms of civil-law tradition around the world. Salvation and God are then far from this globalized heritage.

RECOMMENDED READING

Church, William F. "The Decline of the French Jurists as Political Theorists, 1660–1789." *French Historical Studies* 5, no. 1 (1967): 1–40.

Clark, David S. "Comparative Law in Colonial British America." *The American Journal of Comparative Law*, 59, no. 3 (2011): 637–67.

Gilles, David. "*La pensée juridique de Jean Domat, Du Grand siècle aux Codifications*" (Doctoral Thesis, Aix-Marseille University, 2004).

"Les *Lois civiles* de Jean Domat, prémices des Codifications? Du Code Napoléon au Code civil du Bas Canada." *Revue juridique Thémis*, 43, no. 1 (2009): 2–49.

"Jean Domat et les fondements du droit public." *Revue d'Histoire des Facultés de droit et de la science juridique*, 25–26 (2006): 93–119.

"Jean Domat et l'esprit de la codification. Du Grand siècle au Code civil." *Passé et présent du droit* 5 (2008): 101–65.

[92] See, as an example, Roscoe Pound, "Classification of Law," *Harvard Law Review* 37, no. 8 (1924): 1–37.

"Jean Domat, avocat du roi et jurisconsulte auvergnat." *Passé et présent du droit* 7 (2009): 129–78.

Gordley, James. "The State's Private Law and Legal Academia." *The American Journal of Comparative Law* 56, no. 3 (2008): 639–52.

Goyard-Fabre, Simone. "La philosophie du droit de Jean Domat ou la convergence de l'ordre naturel et de l'ordre rationnel." In *Justice et Force: Politiques au temps de Pascal*, edited by G. Ferreyrolles, 187–207. Paris: Klincksieck, 1996.

"César a besoin de Dieu ou la loi naturelle selon Jean Domat." In *L'État classique*. Henri Méchoulan and Joël Cornette (dir.), 149–60. Paris: Vrin, 1996.

Greenberger, Gerald A. "Lawyers Confront Centralized Government: Political Thought of Lawyers during the Reign of Louis XIV." *The American Journal of Legal History* 23, no. 2 (1979): 144–81.

Parker, David. "Sovereignty, Absolutism and the Function of the Law in Seventeenth-Century France." *Past & Present* 122 (1989): 36–74.

Renoux-Zagamé, Marie-France. "Domat, le salut et le droit." *Revue d'histoire des facultés de droit et de la culture juridiques (RHFD)* 8 (1989): 70–111.

"Domat: du jugement de Dieu à l'esprit des lois." *Débat* (1993): 54–68.

Stein, Peter. "The Attraction of Civil Law in Post-Revolutionary America." *Virginia Law Review* 52, no. 3 (1966): 406–07.

13

Henri François d'Aguesseau

(1688–1751)

ISABELLE BRANCOURT

Many decades before French people had in mind a national "Pantheon" to honor the memory of their nation's most esteemed personalities, the French Enlightenment, flourishing in the intellectual salons of the second half of the eighteenth century, already celebrated Henri François d'Aguesseau as a great man. But was the Age of Enlightenment, when he flourished, really Christian in its ideas? Voltaire's invectives against what he called "*L'Infâme*" (that is, the "vile" church), the promotion of skepticism by Pierre Bayle, and the ascension of aggressive materialism and militant atheism by famous philosophers such as Diderot, La Mettrie, d'Holbach, and Helvétius, marked the first major rupture in Western thought with the traditional Christian ideal that had prevailed until then. Here lies one of the many difficulties about the reception of Chancellor d'Aguesseau's ideas after his death.

Nothing is more instructive than reading the forewords introducing each of the thirteen volumes of the first edition of the *Œuvres de M. le chancelier d'Aguesseau*, published between 1759 and 1789, and appreciating the tone and words chosen to describe him. Our "Hero of the Fatherland," this "great orator and true philosopher,"[1] is indeed crowned with all the secular virtues of his time: reason, eloquence, attachment to his native land, and dedication to the state and its laws (foreword to volume 1). "This prodigy of erudition and science" is gifted at the highest level with human qualities so dearly asserted by his contemporaries: a good memory, an abundance of imagination, pristine style, a methodical and critical mind, "rare sagacity," and so on (volume 7). However, in the following years, d'Aguesseau is celebrated insistently more for his attachment to "Religion," an expression so typical of the Enlightenment vocabulary, but also, in a personal capacity, for his humble Christian virtues

[1] Henri François d'Aguesseau, *Œuvres de M. le chancelier d'Aguesseau*, 13 vols. (Paris: Les Libraires Associés, 1759–89; hereafter *Œuvres*), vol. 1, "Avertissement."

(volume 12), his love for his wife and children, his honesty and equity, and his unshakable faith in God, church, and king (volume 13).

In short, d'Aguesseau is considered the embodiment of conservative values, such as love of country, religion, family, and order. The Bourbon restoration, a period during which d'Aguesseau's work was republished,[2] finds in his person an opportunity to "renew the chains of time,"[3] thus erasing the memory of former civil conflicts, especially the Terror and the idea of a "blank slate" promoted by the revolutionaries. Indeed, the Restoration involved restoring a tradition of enlightenment and intelligence which, reasonably and rationally, would also have been perfectly Christian, in a process of repairing the tie between faith and reason.

BIOGRAPHICAL INTRODUCTION

Henri François, born in Limoges on November 27, 1668, was the first-born son of Henri d'Aguesseau and Claire le Picard de Périgny. By both his paternal and maternal ancestry, he descended from a respected lineage of magistrates, of whom he would later become the most distinguished. His family, recently ennobled by the crown, included notably François d'Aguesseau, presiding magistrate of the parlement of Bordeaux, and Henri François's father, Henri, who first was a councillor in the parlement of Metz, then master of requests of the *hôtel* (acting as the king's *intendant* in the Limousin province), and finally appointed state councilor, an office in which he gained unanimous acclaim. From his mother's side, Henri François received a renowned inheritance from Omer and Denis Talon, whose exceptional talents as prosecuting attorneys were especially noticed within the parlement of Paris during the Fronde and in the first thirty years of the reign of King Louis XIV.

From this particularly good beginning, Henri François d'Aguesseau, after many years of study, provided mainly by his father, entered the legal profession at the age of 21. He was appointed king's counsel for the *Châtelet* of Paris in 1690; he joined the public prosecutor's office of the parliament, first as a

[2] It is in the era of the Pardessus edition (from the name of the law professor Jean Marie Pardessus at the reestablished University of Paris) of the *Complete Works of d'Aguesseau* (1819, in 8vo, 16 vols.) to which the very conservative D.-B. Rives contributes in 1823 by providing the two previous collections (that in 4to of the Associated Booksellers, of the eighteenth century, and that in 8vo of Pardessus) the volumes (one in 4to and two in 8vo) of private correspondence between the chancellor and his wife, his children, and some friends, which were thought more revealing of his character, his goodness, his intelligence – in short, his all-Christian virtue.

[3] Cf. Alain Blondy, *Nouvelle histoire des idées* (Paris: Perrin, 2016): "renouer la chaîne des temps."

prosecuting attorney from 1691 to 1700, then as the king's general prosecutor from 1700 to 1717. Appointed chancellor of France by the regent on February 2, 1717, d'Aguesseau was promoted to the first office of the monarchy, thus becoming one of the closest advisers of King Louis XV. However, his field of competence remained limited to the management of interior affairs because of an unpleasant period of being repeatedly in and out of office as keeper of the seals.[4] D'Aguesseau mostly dealt with legislation and the control of judicial authorities. His faithful, self-effacing manner, especially with regard to political scheming, earned him the trust and friendship of the king, who made him one of the longest-serving chancellors in the history of France.

In 1750, d'Aguesseau's sons, who had assisted their father for many years, encouraged him to retire from office to find rest and cope with the infirmities of old age. When he retired on November 27, 1750, Henri François d'Aguesseau had only seventy-four days to live. He passed away at the hotel of the Chancellery, in Paris, on February 9, 1751, leaving only three surviving children, of the twelve he had fathered, to carry on his legacy (Henri François-de-Paule, Jean-Baptiste Paulin, and Claire Thérèse de Chastellux).[5]

BETWEEN LEGAL REASON AND ENLIGHTENMENT REASON, *IN MEDIO STAT* D'AGUESSEAU

The first question that arises concerning d'Aguesseau is about his status as a jurist. In the language of the eighteenth century, the chancellor was undeniably one of the most eminent jurisconsults of his time, even "the most consummate." Henri François d'Aguesseau perfected his legal science in the parlement of Paris at the cost of incessant labor "in this inexhaustible source of wisdom and prudence,"[6] the precious mine of the records of the kingdom's highest court.[7] There is no doubt that, like most of the great names of his generation (e.g., Lamoignon, Portal, Harlay), including ministers of his time (e.g., Colbert, Pontchartrain), d'Aguesseau drew without restraint from the source of these "sacred" registers, even if justice at that time in France – unlike in England – was not based simply on case law, in the contemporary sense of

[4] Disgraced from January 1718 to June 1720, then from February 1722 to August 1727, he was denied the title of keeper of the seals during those periods. He then returned to favor, but without the seals until 1737.

[5] In the list of monographs, the writings of two descendants – Marie Judith, Marchioness of La Tournelle, and Louis-Philippe, Earl of Segur – are the most symbolic of this family legacy.

[6] *Œuvres*, vol. VII, *Requêtes et Mémoires* (Paris, 1772), Avertissement, p. I, p. xxxix.

[7] Cf. Isabelle Brancourt, *Un Gilbert méconnu. Magistrature et quotidien du Parlement de Paris dans le premier XVIII*[e] *siècle* (Paris: SFEDS, 2016).

the term. In politics, as in law, he had respect for history and a sense of the value of precedent. Like his colleagues and friends Joly de Fleury, Gilbert de Voisins, and others, d'Aguesseau was in contact with the officers and clerks of the registry – such as Nicolas Dongois and his secretary, Jean Gilbert de L'Isle, the most faithful and most intelligent of his office – who no doubt spent most of their time researching the registers in the service of the judiciary and justice. In short, our magistrate was a hard-working and proven professional, served by an excellent and faithful memory, which left even the most cautious critics in admiration. From his first intervention as general counsel, the famous Denis Talon exclaimed that he "would like to finish as this young man had begun."[8]

D'Aguesseau thus quickly acquired a reputation as the "Eagle of Parlement,"[9] which explains his prestige, the speed of his ascent, and the interest we have in him. One of his first biographers concludes: "Each year multiplied the successes of d'Aguesseau and developed in him the features for which the true jurisconsult is recognised. This rare title was conferred on him during his lifetime."[10] Indeed, d'Aguesseau's title of jurisconsult, which he held after 1717[11] despite having never published a treatise of law, is only analogical and reflects the influence he practiced in the judiciary from the time of his first duties. At the moment of his elevation to the chancellery, the speeches of the leading lights of the Paris bar – Tartarin, Terrasson, and Cochin – were filled with the praises best supported by the "science" of *cet esprit de premier ordre*, bringing together all the "qualities necessary for those who perform such an important function" in his office at the first parliament. One of the forewords presenting the first volume of d'Aguesseau's collected works gives a summary of his qualities:

> eloquence equal to the greatest subjects, but proportionate to the simplest one; an erudition sufficiently large and reserved enough to present itself only as much as necessity requires; lucidity to unravel the most thorny affairs; wisdom and knowledge to draw the truth from the abysses or from obscurities that surround it; a depth of reasoning which, by sweet and useful violence, shakes and sets all votes.[12]

8 Words reported more than once; among others, by Morlhon, *Œuvres*, vol. I, xcix.

9 Duc de Saint-Simon, *Mémoires*, edn. Arthur André Gabriel Michel de Boislisle, et al., 22 vols. (Paris: Hachette, 1873–86), vol. 3, 92.

10 A.-A. Boullée, *Histoire de la vie et des ouvrages du chancelier d'Aguesseau* (Paris: Desenne, 1835), vol. 1, 146.

11 *Œuvres*, vol. I, *Discours* [. . .] *le 2 juin 1717*, lxxx.

12 Ibid., lxi–lxii.

Reading this monumental work immediately persuades the reader of d'Aguesseau's amazing "soundness," as his son remarked in 1761.[13] His speeches and instructions "included beautiful ideas and excellent recommendations." All these qualities have been confirmed, in the light of the most accomplished study of law, by analysts and commentators who have recognized d'Aguesseau's real power of legal conception in the light of contemporary questioning of the premises of modern law. This power consists of the great vigor of his *legicentrism* and unquestionable strictness and rigor in leaning on "the spirit of law." He innovates in structuring the sources of law, natural reason, the rights of nature and people, and customary and royal law, which together were called French law, a rubric under which these subjects were taught after 1679. Finally, d'Aguesseau demonstrated a real ability to foresee, not without prudence, the evolution that would lead to the conceptual legal breakup of the Revolution.[14]

D'Aguesseau was, in fact, immediately recognized as a grand magistrate, a remarkable practitioner of the law in every respect, unanimously claimed by many friends and enjoying great reputation. He is therefore not a jurist in the sense of a legal theorist. When he wrote letters, dissertations, or projects (every day in his role as public prosecutor), his aim was always pragmatic. It was the improvement of the distribution of justice, "serving public interest."[15] On the other hand, he had, like most of the high magistracy of his time, a very high idea of justice, a real judicial "doctrine" – reasoned, thoughtful, and firm – especially in the criminal field, which was "such an important matter."[16] He maintains that crime is crime and should not go unpunished:

> I have been hearing for a long time and from all sides that the prosecution of crimes is more neglected than ever [. . .], that a large number of crimes, and very serious crimes, remain unprosecuted or at least pursued so weakly that it

[13] Letter to F.-X. Chiflet, councillor in the parliament of Besançon, Municipal Library of Besançon, Chiflet's collection, 193, fol. 255.

[14] Apart from the study of d'Aguesseau's "Cartesianism" by Francisque Bouillier in the nineteenth century, Henri Regnault (1883–1948) initiated a series of works in legal history and legal studies concerning d'Aguesseau: Paule Combe in 1928, Alain de Féron in 1933, Marthe Folain-Le Bras in 1941, and Jean Portemer in 1957. The most recent research is by Christophe Blanquie, based on archival documents, in 2004. Marie-France Renoux-Zagamé (2001 and 2007) published an innovative rereading of the general counsel's pleadings. And since 2012, Emilie Leromain has been studying little-known surveys, investigations, and archives.

[15] Municipal Library of Besançon, Chiflet's collection, 193, fol. 255.

[16] Chancellor's Circular letter of October 9, 1733, quoted by Emilie Leromain, "Monarchie administrative et justice criminelle en France au XVIIIe siècle" (unpublished doctoral thesis, Université de Strasbourg, 2017), vol. 2, 7.

> is rare to see examples of them, and the greatest excesses multiply by the hope of impunity.

This point of view is entirely traditional. Only his method is modern – Cartesian – and, according to the expression he himself claimed with force, *more geometric*, rejecting a false and easy pretension to equity that would abstain from the rigor of the letter, the stringent respect of forms.[17]

The originality of d'Aguesseau, compared to that of his eminent contemporaries (foremost of whom was one of his models and most intimate correspondents, Chancellor Pontchartrain),[18] lies in the fact that an *œuvre* was published that served him much better than his epitaph as a pedestal. This work became, in the form of a doctrinal corpus, a sort of political and legal testament that explains his reputation. Friedrich-Melchior Grimm writes:

> We have collected in two volumes . . . the speeches and other writings of Mr. Daguesseau, Chancellor of France, who died four or five years ago. It is a very imperfect collection compared to what would remain to be printed if we wanted to make it complete. You will find the life of this illustrious magistrate at the head of the first volume. Mr. Daguesseau enjoyed a great reputation. He was learned, profound in his part, I will even say eloquent.[19]

Grimm was speaking about a sort of unauthorized edition, to which the deceased chancellor's family had not given its approval and whose source was, in many ways, faulty. "This collection," warns the jurist's son and state counsellor Henri François-de-Paule d'Aguesseau,

> was published without anyone having seen the originals of the documents it contains. Copies may have been found, made formerly by a secretary who my father sometimes got to tidy up his speeches. This secretary had kept secret the copies he had kept for himself. His heirs had other views, but they did not dare to deal with them during the chancellor's life. . . . the collection is neither complete nor free from clerical mistakes.[20]

Around 1757, Associated Publishers approached d'Aguesseau's two sons,[21] who subsequently entrusted the chancellor's last librarian with the task of

[17] *Œuvres*, vol. 7, xxii.

[18] Cf. Erwan Barraud, "Le chancelier de Pontchartrain et la magistrature (1699–1714)" (thesis, Université de Panthéon-Assas-Paris II, 2005).

[19] Friedrich-Melchior Grimm, *Correspondance littéraire, philosophique et critique*, edn. M. Tourneux (Paris, 1878), vol. 3, 222.

[20] Municipal Library of Besançon, Chiflet's collection, 193, fol. 217.

[21] "You know that booksellers have undertaken to give to the public the work of an author whose memory seems to you worthy of being dear. His family is just consenting" (ibid., fol. 252).

collecting and publishing all his writings, speeches, pleadings, diatribes, essays, memoirs, instructions, meditations, and letters, even though many of them were unfinished pieces, sometimes scraps or drafts. The entire collection forms thirteen volumes, leaving only d'Aguesseau's family correspondence to a later time (1823). The chancellor's "religion" precisely explains editing delays that occurred: indeed, he had set as a rule of principle, which he kept his whole life, that he was writing only for the utility of his profession. At best, he increased the scope of this mission to the few people – his children, mostly – whom he considered to have a duty of transmission, thus following his own father's example. When, in 1718, while writing his *Address to my children about my father's life, death, character, and moral habits*,[22] d'Aguesseau mentions this book in a letter: "I didn't myself complete copying the essay you're asking for. . . But this is a book which cannot be read outside *the private circle of the family to which it refers*."[23] This last feature adds to his natural reserve, a modesty that comes close to self-effacement. In one of his letters to Valincour, he writes, "[I don't] have the itching desire to become an author, nor to acquire a reputation of erudition. [I consider myself] to be unworthy."[24] Flattery, even the most sincere, did not impress him: "Fortunately, or perhaps unfortunately, for me, I only need a moment with myself to find a definitive antidote to your praises."[25] He even displays a certain humor within his modesty, calling himself a "countryside tutor" with regard to his children, laughing at his own lack of Latin, at the monotonous parts in his own writings.

Of course, as soon as he had some free time, even against his own will, d'Aguesseau had a strong liking for writing. Furthermore, he admits to the infinite pleasure he finds in this activity, "going back to the Republic of Letters just like [my] childhood universe." He passes time by writing. His goal is not to diffuse "his" doctrine, but to clarify his own ideas. His will to write can thus be interpreted as purely for himself: "I'm only talking to myself here," as he asserts at the beginning of his *Metaphysical Meditations*.[26] At the end of this work, he affirms the restricted diffusion of "these Meditations, in which I only speak to myself and to a few friends of mine." In this, d'Aguesseau is the antithesis of Montesquieu and strictly forbids his work to be published, as proven by several testimonies taken from his correspondence. On April 18, 1743, for example,

[22] Municipal Library of Limoges, ms. 142, eighteenth century, paper, 136 sheets, 318 x 205 mm.
[23] *Œuvres complètes*, edn. Jean-Marie Pardessus (Paris: Fantin and associates, 1819; hereafter *Œuvres complètes*), vol. 16, 298. My emphasis.
[24] Ibid., 65.
[25] Ibid., 303.
[26] *Méditations métaphysiques. . .*, *Œuvres complètes*, vol. 14, 2.

d'Aguesseau writes: "I beg you to remember the promise you made to me to not publish this manuscript nor to make any copy of it."[27] On September 23, 1756, his eldest son asserts that, during the chancellor's life, "there were only two of his speeches which were printed in the country, and he gave orders so prompt and vigorous that the edition was returned to him. He then ordered the copies to be burnt in his presence."[28]

None of his professional successes could even incite him to abandon either his sincere humility or his absolute and strict sense of dedication to the common good; this involved renouncing his personal interests and potential leisure activities. The chancellor's Christian asceticism is the unquestioned origin of this rule of discretion he followed until his death, a rule his family finally broke after many years. At the time of the publication of the first volume of the *Œuvres*, state counsellor Henri François-de-Paule writes: "You know the booksellers took the initiative to give the public the work of an author whose memory seems worthy of your attention. His family did nothing but give its consent."[29] In this, d'Aguesseau was a statesman at a time when secrecy was the first quality of a good government, not because it conceals but because it protects. What results, in the edition of the *Œuvres*, is a systematic policy of suppression of people's proper names, reproduced, in the absence of the original filing, in the collection of 1819. This is the main difficulty of interpreting the *Œuvres* and the importance of using archives, despite their being scattered all over France and abroad.

In spite of these difficulties, the *Œuvres* sufficiently demonstrates the monumental character of d'Aguesseau's contribution as an eminent lawyer. Joined to legal and administrative archival resources and to those of contemporary, epistolary testimonies or memories, d'Aguesseau's work assembled in the published collections represents a mine for jurists. His contribution to the construction of law cannot be denied. That his sons were certain of it does not speak to family hagiography or the blindness of filial love. Thus, on July 19, 1761, Henri François-de-Paule entrusts to his friend Chiflet volumes 2 to 4 of the edition byAassociated Booksellers:

> I believe that they all will be useful... We have assembled in the first volume what should please everyone, and indeed what has been produced from several oratorical speeches, instructions, the beginning of a work on public law, which contain beautiful ideas and excellent opinions... We have

[27] Departmental archives of Seine-et-Marne, 134 F 174, from Versailles, to Mr Radet (possibly Elie Radet, lawyer in the Parliament of Paris).

[28] Municipal Library of Besançon, Chiflet's collection 193, fol. 217.

[29] Ibid., fol. 252.

> undertaken a collection of his pleas [as general counsel]. There remains enough to form, according to appearances, four volumes of the same size as that which is in your cabinet. There are a number where he adopts the highest tone, and if we provided those only, I believe that there would be parity between the first volume and those where they [the pleas] would be, albeit in a different genre. But it was more useful not to omit those pleadings where he tackles, in not very famous causes, issues of fact and law with great solidity. On the one hand, they make known the nature of, and reason for the judgments delivered, which could be badly quoted, and which were already very little quoted in a volume of the *Journal of the Audiences of the Parliament of Paris*. On the other hand, it will be a model for those who have to work in this genre. And finally, as he wished to tackle everything, there are a number of laws, maxims, jurisprudence, and opinions of authors that are applied, which constitute a store of principles and could be of great use to [young] magistrates, the bar, and parties and in relevant affairs. Sometimes, there are only notes, but in which we can immediately see principles and authorities that very clearly outline a handsome and erudite discourse. We have made the decision to print them as they were only putting into French the words he wrote in Latin because he found it a more concise language, and we have left several of these [Latin words] when they are expressions drawn in substance from jurisconsults.

The legal contribution of d'Aguesseau therefore involves, first, his rare ability to clarify and simplify legal standards in light of a renewed interpretation of the sources of law. For example, d'Aguesseau brings remarkable wisdom to questions and evidence of the status of individuals, to inheritance and to domain property or crown matters. He holds a critical, prudent, and extremely innovative view of French law. Always pragmatic, he attacks, after others no doubt but more than anyone else, what he considers a scandal, that is, the diversity and especially the conflicts of court jurisprudence. Following the approach of Jean Domat, d'Aguesseau indeed always sought compliance of civil law with the principles of natural justice. He states, "The laws of nature form the substance and are the real and essential strength of civil laws."[30] The laws were endowed with a more or less great internal value according to their proximity to natural law: thus, private law was of capital interest because it "embraced an infinity of ideas, reflections, and reasoning even on the first principles of equity and natural justice." In d'Aguesseau's view, "This right is

[30] All the quotations that follow are taken from *Œuvres complètes*, either from the *Essai d'une institution au droit public* (vol. 15), the *Mémoire sur les vues générales... pour la reformation de la justice* (vol. 13), the *Méditations métaphysiques* (vol. 14), finally certain *Discours* (vol. 1), or official correspondence and legislative texts themselves (vol. 12).

perceived… as a type of common right because it effectively contains these first concepts of justice, which are common to all people." Moreover, the essence of d'Aguesseau's legislative activity related to this part of French law.

On the other hand, any positive law, the fruit of a ruler's arbitrary will, which would be contrary to natural law, "would resist the very nature of humanity." Such positive law contrary to natural law had to be rejected. As a result of these principles, d'Aguesseau was led generally to interrogate all of traditional French law. To him, customary law did not seem to arise directly from natural law: it was therefore indispensable "to build up oneself the judgement in some way from customs, and attempt to discover what the principle is that should be preferred." Roman law, on the contrary, had in his eyes the immense superiority of teaching the first principles: it was "jurisprudence that [was] the basis of all others. Its principles are drawn from the purest source, that is, from the law, or natural equity."

This general critique of ancient law was to be carried out following the only criterion possible: reason. The law was, according to d'Aguesseau, "the reason of those who do not have any." Indeed, its goal was to "direct the conduct of an intelligent being that does not live at random, and to whom reason has been given as his first law." Civil laws must therefore be, in the first instance, in line with strict reason. Moreover, they had to be in agreement with the rational nature of human beings: such laws necessarily bore in themselves that character of uniformity and equality that d'Aguesseau remarked in humanity. The preamble of the *Ordonnance sur les donations* (1731), composed by the chancellor, clearly outlined this principle:

> Justice should be as uniform in its judgments as the act is one in its provision, and does not depend on the difference of time and place as it prides itself on ignoring that of individuals; … there is no law which does not contain the vow of perpetuity and uniformity.

Justice consisted of giving every one his due: in presupposing the natural equality of human beings, d'Aguesseau considered justice the equitable enforcement of a unique, general, and uniform rule for all to whom equal dignity granted the same rights. Regardless of the form of society, justice should always consider individuals in their natural state, that is, in "this perfect equality that nature had put in them, and that they still have in the eyes of justice."

As a result, the diversity of laws appeared as a serious breach of the nature of human beings. D'Aguesseau writes to Machault d'Arnouville: "It is an abuse that resists the nature of justice, one of the main characters of which is to be uniform, without any distinction of time and place." The multiplicity and diversity of the laws of his time seemed to d'Aguesseau a true scourge, a disastrous consequence of human weakness and sin. He laments:

> Every nation, every province has its laws, and, if we dare say, its justice. The mountains and rivers that divide empires and kingdoms have also become terminals that separate the just from the unjust. The difference of laws forms multiple states into one. It seems that, to cut down human pride, God took pleasure in spreading the same confusion in their laws as in their languages; and the law which, like the word, is given to humanity only to bring it together, has become, like the word, the sign and often the subject of its divisions.

An unexpected consequence of the Tower of Babel: d'Aguesseau tirelessly revisited this theme. He thought the diversity of legislation was a major cause of the misapplication of the laws, because the magistrate himself had legitimate reluctance "to strain himself every day more and more in this immense sea of old and new laws whose multitude has always been seen by wise men as proof of the republic's corruption." Customary law flanked this quasi-rationalist criticism: "By their diversity, and often by their conflict, [customs] form rules of justice so dissimilar to each other that what falls short of a stream is beyond unjust." It sounds like the echo of Voltaire's taunts,[31] but also Pascal's. Like a refrain, d'Aguesseau took up the idea of the need for uniformity in law:

> It seems very strange... that in the same kingdom, there are almost as many different laws as there are cities or bailiwicks, and it was long ago that great magistrates designed the plan to reduce all customs to a single one, which would be the general law of all the provinces governed by what is called French law.

Such was the ambition of d'Aguesseau. It can be understood that he is one of the recognized ancestors of the Civil Code.

AGAINST THE BACKDROP OF THE JANSENIST CRISIS, THE DOCTRINAL AMBIVALENCES OF A PUZZLED CATHOLIC

The day after his birth, in the parish of Saint-Pierre-du-Queyroix, Limoges, Henri François was baptized in accordance with the formula, "in the Catholic, apostolic, and Roman religion." As early as September 30, 1742, less than ten years before his death, the chancellor signed his will to "put himself in a

[31] *Dictionnaire philosophique*, vol. 18, art. customs.

state of no longer fearing the surprises of death, or the weakness and disorder of disease." Thus, he writes at the beginning:

> after recommending my soul, for time and for eternity, to the infinite mercy of God my Creator, of Jesus Christ his only Son, my Redeemer, and of the Holy Spirit the Comforter, after having implored for the remission of the countless sins that I committed, the help and the intercession of the Blessed Virgin Mary Mother of God, of my holy Guardian Angel, of my patron saints, of all the saints in general and especially my father, my mother, and the other holy souls that I had the good fortune to have in my family, I declare that I want to be buried in the cemetery of the parish of Auteuil at the feet of the holy woman that God had given me and of whom I was not worthy, happy if, by His extreme Kindness, He will grant me the grace of being placed near her in the abode of eternal bliss.

Faith, hope, love – of God, of his ancestors, of his wife – and humility in contrition. Everything is said, in the purest religious tradition of the post-Tridentine West and, on the other hand, against the current of the wave of questioning, of contestations, skepticism, and religious libertinism that d'Aguesseau had denounced on entering the chancellery in his position as chief censor: it must be remembered that he denied, in 1721, the anonymous *Persian Letters* the privilege of publication, mainly for their relativistic irony,[32] and refusing moreover the same privilege, in 1748, to *De l'Esprit des lois*, to the great displeasure of its author.

His religion is continually reflected in his work. D'Aguesseau demonstrated his unwavering attachment to Christianity and to the church of Jesus Christ. Not only did he undertake to write *Reflections on Jesus Christ*, but he encouraged many fellow, often ecclesiastical, authors to produce apologetics works. Thus, a letter from Father Bonardy to President Bouhier refers to a book of Dom Prudent Maran on the divinity of Jesus Christ "composed by chancellor's order."[33] In the same way, d'Aguesseau congratulates Father Joly on his criticism of Bayle: "I highly praise the zeal that inspired in you the courage to attack a book as dangerous as the Bayle *Dictionary*"; it was

[32] How could he, for example, allow this famous passage to pass: "There is another magician more powerful still, who is master of the king's mind, as absolutely as the king is master of the minds of his subjects. This magician is called the pope. Sometimes he makes the king believe that three are no more than one; that the bread which he eats is not bread; the wine which he drinks not wine; and a thousand things of a like nature" (Montesquieu, *Lettres persanes*, Letter 24, text established by André Lefèvre (Paris: A. Lemerre, 1873), 51–55).

[33] *Correspondance littéraire du président Bouhier*, edn. Henri Duranton (Saint-Etienne: Publications de l'Université de Saint-Etienne, 1976–82), vol. 5, 109.

necessary, at all costs, to fight against "a spirit of irreligion, which unfortunately has been only too widespread for some time in this country," and to undertake to "discredit a work so contrary to religion and good habits."[34] Seen together with his profession as jurist and magistrate, which is at the heart of our interest in d'Aguesseau, his Christianity prompts three distinct questions.

The first one is the contradiction, or at least the paradox, which puts side by side an undeniable rationalist temptation and his Christian fidelity. This paradox is perhaps the best explanation for the incompleteness of many works, especially his *Metaphysical Meditations on the True and False Ideas of Justice*. With his attachment to a Cartesianism mixed with Malebranchism, d'Aguesseau attempts to build an unstoppable and mathematical doctrine of what he calls justice. On the basis of a renewed demonstration of the existence of the "Supreme Being," he elaborates, step by step and not without hesitation, a natural right fully accessible to reason. This puts him on the same level as those who claim to teach natural law.[35]

This is obviously his method in his *Essay on an Institution in Public Law*, also left unfinished. We cannot help but compare his approach to the analytical and systematic drive of J.-J. Burlamaqui in his *Principles of Natural Law* (1748):

> By natural law is meant a law that God imposes upon all people, and that they can discover and know by the light of reason alone, by carefully considering their nature and their state. Natural law is the system, the assembly, or the body of these same laws. Finally, natural jurisprudence will be the art of getting to know the laws of nature, to develop them, and to apply them to human actions.

In short, society and the general law that governs it appear to d'Aguesseau's eyes as natural phenomena, but only insofar as human nature is *reason*.

It is therefore impossible to be astonished by the major sources of d'Aguesseau's thought. On the one hand, he was influenced by the great authors of ancient Stoicism (Cicero, Marcus Aurelius), who had already been reviewed and interpreted since the beginning of the seventeenth century. On the other hand, he is marked by a real fascination with Grotius and his heirs, mainly Pufendorf. But at the center of his thought remains St Augustine, whom he quotes consistently, even in the form of adages. D'Aguesseau thus demonstrates an original type of Christian rationalism. Despite the affirmation of a contrary intent, d'Aguesseau's philosophy – stopped in full flight, let us

[34] National Library of France, Cabinet des Manuscrits, Nouv. Acq. fr. 767, fol. 1 and 3.
[35] In 1771, at the Royal College, a chair of natural law was founded.

remember – was to end by dechristianizing natural law, removing the law from divinity, the world organizer, and in the long run (although he never took this step) removing transcendence from the *res publica*: "divinity will look at the law in its attributes only to the extent that it will be nothing but reason."[36]

D'Aguesseau is thus, perhaps reluctantly, one of the relayers – and the most credible! – of modern natural law, the most obvious consequence of which is the secularization of natural law. Thus, he is the bearer of an egalitarian vision of human nature and consequently of civil law and society, the holder of a state of individual freedom, and, finally, the promoter of a political contractualism that d'Aguesseau, like Hobbes, whom he nevertheless hates, associates with the uniqueness, indissolubility, and infallibility of sovereignty, which he fully acknowledges for the king. We detect the ingredients of Christian democracy in the style of an author like Lamennais. In the contradictions and conceptual fluctuations after the revolutionary break, the nineteenth century was to converge all these data into legal "conservatism"[37] based on a natural right that the end of the century would integrate into what is called "the social doctrine of the [Catholic] Church."

The second question concerns the point of view of magistrate d'Aguesseau toward other religions – Judaism, for example, or Christian heterodoxies – that presented a real problem to the Catholic hierarchy and French Catholics of his time. I wish to talk about the Protestants, on the one hand, and the Jansenists, on the other.

D'Aguesseau never departed from a perfectly determined position: "whatever the judgment about the privileges" [of which they may be in possession], all religions "are subject to the laws of the kingdom and subject to police regulations, which concern the respect due to the [Catholic] religion, as to all others." Consequently, Jews must be contained within the limits of "the protection that the favor of commerce has caused them to grant"; otherwise, they can have – and d'Aguesseau remains inflexible – neither the right to assemble in improvised synagogues, nor rabbis and preachers. Moreover, they must exercise the same public respect for the Eucharist "by kneeling like Catholics" in the streets during processions or the passage of priests carrying the Blessed Sacrament – or retire home discreetly. The chancellor, if he incites local authorities to negotiate, justifies by law and by law alone "the

[36] Paul Hazard, *La pensée européenne au XVIIIème siècle* (Paris: Boivin, 1946), vol. 1, 197.

[37] Cf. Jean-Philippe Vincent, *Qu'est-ce que le conservatisme? Histoire intellectuelle d'une idée politique* (Paris: Les Belles Lettres, 2016), 272.

severity" he recommends, outside of any violence.[38] He belongs in no way to the next generation, that of Pierre Gilbert de Voisins or Malesherbes, who, with regard to Jews and Protestants, seriously consider and eventually adopt in favor of Protestants a change in royal legislation and their legal place in the kingdom.

Concerning the Protestants, d'Aguesseau clearly expressed himself in his *Discours on the life and Death of Mr. d'Aguesseau, State Councillor* [his father]: the father had transmitted to the son his hostility to all pressures or violence that immediately preceded the revocation of the Edict of Nantes, and indeed to the revocation itself, even though in Languedoc, where he was intendant until 1683, he fought the illegal assemblies in the Cevennes and the insubordination movements led by the Huguenots. Although the d'Aguesseaus were unconditional supporters of a Catholic apostolic conversion by persuasion and teaching, the same principle of application to the rigor of the law provided a Huguenot anti-proselytism by maintaining a restrictive legal framework for the exercise of the *Religion Prétendue Réformée*, according to the termes of the time.

Finally, with regard to the Jansenists, d'Aguesseau's position is all the more difficult to determine because, from one end of his life to the other, the question aroused, both in the court and the city of Paris as well as in the dioceses of the provinces, an unending stream of gossip, slander, denunciation, and rumors. We know the poison these cases of Jansenism and the constitution Unigenitus (1713) were for the political climate during the reign of Louis XV. We will not once again investigate the file on d'Aguesseau's alleged or possible Jansenism or of his eventual turnaround that Cornelius Jansen's most ardent partisans denounced as treason (1720). It remains perfectly clear that the chancellor kept, against the Jansenists, defending the rule of law as it resulted from the main Declarations (of accommodation, mainly), which punctuated his ministry management, after that one of August 1720 recorded in parliament on December 4 of that year.

The third and greatest question about d'Aguesseau's religion and its impact on the legal discipline concerns his view of the relationship between spiritual and temporal powers – that is, on the one hand, his idea about the place of religious authority and jurisdiction over the state, and on the other, the conception he shared with the entire higher magistracy about the weight and nature of authority that Rome could apply to national churches, including, obviously, the Gallican church. His reputation as a Jansenist arose

[38] *Œuvres*, vol. 10, pp. 266–69.

principally from his opinionated defense of Gallican liberties on the occasion of "blunders" in the pope's and Louis XIV's attitude in the Jansenist affairs at the beginning of the century. Moreover, he made no secret of his wholehearted adherence to Gallican treatises, even the most radical ones. This was without doubt his keenest political attitude as chancellor, the most assertive in his work.

While arising from the traditional distinction of the temporal and spiritual, this conception, both religious and political, not only illuminates his actions in the parlement of Paris but also completes his conception of the role of the parlement in the state. The chancellor belonged to this trend, later named Gallicanism, of which officers of the courts made itself the champions from the beginning of the seventeenth century. Indeed, he believed that temporal power possessed two essential characteristics: it was both universal and independent, thus fully self-sufficient. He thus claimed for it absolute divine right. He writes: "When [kings] are unfaithful, they are still ministers of God." In erecting the absolute divine right of the prince, d'Aguesseau secularized him and, finally, denatured him: he speaks of the divine right of the state, no longer a divine right of the kings of France linked to the baptism of Clovis I at Reims and the mystical conception of royalty that had prevailed at least until the fifteenth century. This marked the collapse of the doctrine of the royal ministry.

Thus, nothing is less surprising than that d'Aguesseau considered the theory of the "power of popes over kings" abominable. Logically, he was an ardent and constant defender of the *Déclaration des Quatres Articles* approved by the Assembly of the Clergy in 1682. When he wrote, of course, the idea of papal intervention in major state affairs had been, for a long time, rejected almost unanimously in France. Constantly reignited, the Gallican feud was livelier than ever, and on a strictly religious level it questioned the structure of the church itself. Combining an episcopal Gallicanism with a radical political Gallicanism, d'Aguesseau – prepared to be more royalist than the king and more episcopalian than the bishops, if circumstances permitted – was the sum of parliamentary Gallicanism: Catholic, indeed, but not very Roman.

Finally, the work of d'Aguesseau, as we can see, was a "constructed" homage, which, from "complete" or partial republications to complementary editions, responded to a certain vision of the man to be magnified: that of a great classic figure, politically rejected for brief moments because of his moderation and prudence, a man of the middle ground between absolute power and liberty, an enlightened mind and a remarkable administrator, but a loyal servant of the monarchy for the sake of the state and public service, and, ultimately, the model of a great Christian.

RECOMMENDED READING

D'Aguesseau, Henri François. *Œuvres de M. le chancelier d'Aguesseau*. 13 vols. Paris: Les Libraires Associés, 1759–89.

Œuvres complètes de d'Aguesseau. Edited by Jean Marie Pardessus. 16 vols. Paris: Fantin and Associates, 1819.

Le chancelier Henri François d'Aguesseau. Limoges 1668–Fresnes 1751: journées d'études tenue à Limoges à l'occasion du bicentenaire de sa mort. Limoges: Desvilles, 1953.

"D'Aguesseau." *Corpus*, no. 52. Edited and introduced by Isabelle Storez-Brancourt, with the collaboration of Christophe Blanquie, Louis de Carbonnières, Laurent Fedi, Françoise Hildesheimer, Patrick Latour, Claude Polin, Agnès Ravel-Cordonnier. Chronological note and bibliography by I. Storez-Brancourt. Paris: CNL and the University of Paris X-Nanterre, July 2007.

Storez, Isabelle. *Le chancelier Henri François d'Aguesseau (1668–1751), Monarchiste et libéral*. Paris: Publisud, 1996.

14

Robert-Joseph Pothier

(1699–1772)

OLIVIER DESCAMPS

BIOGRAPHICAL INTRODUCTION

Oracle of Orléans,[1] one of the "fathers of the French Civil Code,"[2] and probably one of the most important jurists in French history, Robert-Joseph Pothier was born in Orléans on January 6, 1699. He was the son of a judge of the presidial court in Orléans but was eight years old when his father died.[3] Pothier studied at the Jesuit college, where he showed skills in humanities and mathematics. He continued his studies at the University of Orléans, which had enjoyed a great reputation since the Middle Ages. In fact, after the prohibition of teaching Roman law in Paris, Orléans became the main place for studying the *leges*. He began to work on legal matters with an analysis of the *Institutes*, one of the major pillars of Justinian compilations, dating from the sixth century and rediscovered in the mid-eleventh century. He found valuable help in books by Arnold Vinnen (Vinnius, d. 1657), a famous professor at University of Leiden, who wrote an extensive commentary on the *Institutes*.[4]

Pothier developed a great interest in religion and would have liked to become a priest, but he had such a significant attachment to his mother that he renounced the priesthood to stay with her. In 1720, he began his career as a judge at the presidial court of Orléans, following in the footsteps of his father and grandfather. He was only 21 years old. Normally, he would not have been

1 Jean-Louis Sourioux, "Pothier ou le sphinx d'Orléans," *Droits* 39 (2004): 69.

2 Joël Monéger, Jean-Louis Sourioux, and Aline Terrasson de Fougères, *Robert-Joseph Pothier, d'hier et d'aujourd'hui* (Paris: Economica, 2001), 11.

3 Auguste-Frédéric-Mathilde Frémont, *Recherches historiques et biographiques sur Pothier* (Orléans: Gatineau, 1859), 12.

4 Arnoldus Vinnius, *In quatuor libros institutionum imperialium commentarius academicus et forensis*, (Amstelodami: L. Elzevirium, 1652).

able to take part in judicial decisions until the legal age of 25. But an exception was granted to judges who prepared reports about cases and could assess them.[5] The extent of Pothier's knowledge, the quality of his analyses, and his spirit of equity led the president of the presidial court to entrust him with the most sensitive cases. Moreover, Pothier always excelled with his clarity and precision of concepts. This situation could have generated jealousy because Pothier earned much money with the French system of *épices* (the salary of the judges was too low and they received supplement by the litigants, either in kind or in cash). But money did not interest him, as he had a personal fortune.

When he was not working at the court, Pothier studied law with such an intensive rhythm so that he earned the nickname of "Benedictine of Law." In 1749, the chair of French law at Orléans became vacant after the death of Michel Prévost de la Jannès. The following June, King Louis XV appointed Pothier as royal professor of French law at the university where he had studied.[6] His nomination was the result of the particular interest that French Chancellor Henri François d'Aguesseau had for Pothier's work. Pothier proposed to give his remuneration to Pierre-Jean-Jacques Guyot, the other candidate for the position. Guyot refused and was appointed instead to the chair of Roman law.

Pothier taught a new subject, French law, including customs, royal legislation, jurisprudence, and doctrine, with the goal of proposing the unification of the law. He also tried to improve teaching methods. In fact, because the University of Orléans had progressively lost its esteemed reputation, he applied punctilious clarity when he was teaching lessons and courses. Moreover, he decided to foster competiton among students by giving funds to prepare gold and silver medals for the best in each class. When he was not at court or teaching, Pothier stayed at home to receive students and others who wanted to consult him about legal issues.

His skills and capacity to combine opposing legal positions led him to be appointed as an arbitrator. To avoid a lawsuit, he would gather both parties and try to resolve the conflict. These same skills justified his frequent presiding over court hearings in the absence of the president. Pothier often shortened hearings or trials because of his knowledge of the forthcoming arguments of each litigant.

5 Olivier de Bouillane de Lacoste, "Pothier juge, vu par les magistrats des XVIIIe et XIXe siècles," in Monéger, et al., *Robert-Joseph Pothier*, 56.

6 Jean-Louis Sourioux, "Aperçu de la vie de Robert-Joseph Pothier," in Monéger, et al., *Robert-Joseph Pothier*, 19.

While Pothier was a judge and a professor, he was also a public administrator. In 1746, the citizens of Orléans elected him as an alderman for three years. He gave much advice to the municipal administration and found a problem in the city's finances before offering solutions to it. On his death, in 1772, several authors wrote eulogies.[7]

POTHIER'S WORK

Pothier wrote a vast number of books, and we can say that he was the first jurist to analyze so many different legal topics during the Old Regime. He began with *Paratitles*, that is to say, a short book about Roman law. The lack of organization of Roman law had become evident, and Pothier decided to put the *Digest* in order. The preparation took a long time. At first, he hesitated to bring out his work; both the failure of Nikolaus Vigel (d. 1600) and his own modesty led him to be cautious. Indeed, Vigel had proposed to put the *leges* in order, but without success. But Pothier knew that other authors had tried to pursue this goal with more positive results. This was the case of Jean Domat (d. 1696), whose famous *Les Loix civiles dans leur ordre naturel* was published in 1689. Domat had aimed to present Roman law by subject with a rational method. Pothier wanted to continue this method of conceiving the *Digest*, eliminating inconsistencies and contradictions.

The first outpourings of Pothier's work were sent to Chancellor d'Aguesseau by Michel Prévost de la Jannès, minister of Louis XV, who was enthusiastic about the project and encouraged Pothier to go on. On September 24, 1736, d'Aguesseau sent a report with several observations. After twelve years of preparation, the first volume appeared in 1748 under the title *Pandectae Justinianae in novum ordinem digestae*. Two more volumes followed, in 1749 and 1752. At first glance, it seemed that nothing had been changed from the original version of the *Digest*. But, in fact, while Pothier kept the traditional division, every title constituted a specific treatise on the topic under discussion. This major enterprise of Pothier earned him the nickname of *Pandectae restitutor felicissimus* ("very happy restorer of Pandectae"). The success of this book led to a second edition in 1762. Criticism of the work by German jurists gave birth to controversial discussions about it, as German

[7] Daniel Jousse (d. 1781), a famous jurist and, with Pothier, author of commentaries on Orléans customs, was the first to write a eulogy. Other eulogists included Leconte de Bièvre, the king's prosecutor in Romorantin; Breton de Montramier, professor at Orléans College; and Guillaume-François Le Trosne, the king's advocate at the presidial court of Orléans, a very close friend of Pothier.

scholars defended the *Usus modernus Pandectarum* (that is to say, the reception of Roman law as a common law of the Holy Roman Empire) and sought to conceive a system of law based on Roman law.[8]

When Pothier was working on the *Pandectae Justinianae*, he was invited in 1740 by Daniel Jousse and Prévost de la Jannès to prepare an extensive commentary on the customs of Orléans.[9] He chose to deal with the following topics: fief, quitrent property transfer tax, joint estate, dowry, and action for possession. In this work, one of Pothier's main goals was to present general concepts. The book was popular and quickly went out of print. When the editor asked Pothier to prepare a second edition to be published in 1760, he decided to modify the structure of the commentary and to write a general introduction to the customs of Orléans. It was really an introduction to the ancient laws of France with a specific study of the notion of custom.

Pothier's work on the *Digest* had prepared him to write a long series of treatises on specific topics with a historical perspective. In 1761, he began with the law of obligations. The great success of this book led to a second edition in 1764. Then Pothier decided to analyze special contracts. He started with sale (1762) and continued with a treatise about the law of rent (1763). His interests were eclectic, and in the same year (1763), he produced a book on exchange, bill of exchange, and other negotiable instruments. His interest in special contracts led him to study rental agreements and rent (1764), partnership contracts, and leasing of cattle (1765). In this kind of contractual mapping, Pothier continued with treatises on the laws of benficence, hire, and consumer loan (1766). His analysis focused on the topics of contract of deposit, mandate contract, pledge, insurance contract, and aleatory contract (1767). Posthumously, other books by Pothier were published on the law of obligations, on loan contract, and on bottomry loan (1777).

Pothier wrote numerous treatises on the law of obligations, but he did not overlook the importance of family law and persons. In 1768, he authored a book on persons and the marriage contract. In the course of the next year, he brought out an analysis on the matrimonial regimen of community and followed that with a study on dowry in 1770. He continued with a treatise covering developments about the right of occupation, donations between spouses, and the manual act of donation. In this same field, others books

[8] Léopold Thézard, *De l'influence des travaux de Pothier et du Chancelier d'Aguesseau sur le droit civil moderne* (Paris: Durand, 1866), 55.

[9] David Deroussin, "Pothier, la coutume (d'Orléans) et le droit coutumier," in *Les décisionnaires et la coutume: contribution à la fabrication de la norme*, Études d'histoire du droit et des idées politiques, no. 23 (Toulouse: PUT, 2017), 413.

appeared after his death in 1772. One concerned successions and wills (1777), and another donations *inter vivos* (1778). Pothier was also interested in property law. In 1772, his study on possession was published, followed four years later by a treatise on fiefs and taxes in connection with property. But, the extraordinary production of the famous magistrate also dealt with other fields of law, including civil and criminal procedure (1778).

Since the eighteenth century, Pothier's treatises have been gathered into complete works. But it was particularly in the nineteenth century that several editions of his complete works appeared. Between 1805 and 1862, four editors assembled all of his studies. To construct his analysis, Pothier built up a very extensive library of books by medieval authors (Bartole, d. 1357) and modern French jurists (Dumoulin, d. 1566; Cujas, d. 1590). It is however, odd that Pothier quoted Domat only rarely, whose works he knew well, and who was above all a Christian jurist with a specific conception of law.[10] Pothier also had an extensive collection of foreign books from the school of modern natural law. He did not hesitate to use German and Dutch books, and asserted his admiration of Hugo Grotius (d. 1645) and quoted Samuel von Pufendorf (d. 1694) and Christian Wolff (d. 1754). He knew well all the doctrines of the authors of *Usus modernus Pandectarum* (for instance, Gerhard Noodt, d. 1745).

Despite Pothier's learning and influence, his reputation faded during the French Revolution, and he was scarcely quoted.[11] François-Régis Cambacérès (d. 1770), author of three drafts of the civil code between 1793 and 1796, referred to him only in the third version of his work. But Pothier was mentioned by drafters of the French civil code because his work could make a link between ancient law and laws enacted between 1789 and 1799.[12] It was above all under the Bourbon restoration (1814–15 and 1815–30) that his name was specifically mentioned. The reason for this revival was an appreciation of the main features of his works. The conservative society of this period liked the way Pothier intertwined different materials, particularly Roman law and ancient law. Moreover, he sought consensus, so that liberal philosophers and publicists also appreciated his moderation and prudence. Nevertheless, he received many indirect criticisms from Friedrich Carl von Savigny (d. 1861), who asserted that the drafters of the French civil code had a slavish

[10] See, in this volume, Chapter 12, David Gilles on Domat.

[11] Jean-Louis Halpérin, "La lecture de Pothier par la doctrine du XIXe siècle," in Monéger, et al., *Robert-Joseph Pothier*, 65.

[12] David Gilles and Éric Gojosso, "Sur Pothier et le Code civil," in Olivier Vernier, et al., eds., *Études d'histoire du droit privé en souvenir de Maryse Carlin* (Paris: La Mémoire du Droit, 2008), 403–17.

devotion to his treatises. On the other hand, German pandectists recognized his great value because Pothier wanted to regard Roman law as positive law. His thought did not fit with the evolution of technical society, and his work led the interpretation of the civil code toward an old conception of law.

POTHIER'S CONCEPTION OF LAW

Unlike Domat, Pothier did not write a treatise about his own conception of law. Reading the *Pandectae Justinianae* is a disappointment because Pothier did not change the order of the *Digest*. He only modified the order of titles within the known fifty books of this corpus. However, book 50, title 17, *de diversis regulis iuris antiqui* ("about different ancient rules of law"), which gathered numerous rules, provided the occasion for Pothier to formulate general principles and, above all, gave a glimpse of a new treatise.[13] Without the intervention of Chancellor d'Aguesseau, Pothier likely would have conceived this treatise as a specific book. But the minister of Louis XV convinced him to keep it in *Pandectae Justinianae*.

This work consists of five parts. The first brings together general rules of natural law and civil law. The second deals with persons, the third with property, the fourth actions and procedure, and the fifth public law. This was also, in fact, the structure of the *Institutes*. Pothier was among those who followed the plan of Gaïus's book but utilizing the contribution of modern rationalist thought. He asserted that there were two categories of *res*: *res in commercio*, i.e. subject to private ownership or acquisition and *res extra commercium*, i.e. not subject to private ownership or acquisition). In the first category, he made a distinction between *res corporales* (corporeal thing) and *res incorporales* (incorporeal thing). *Res corporales* included *proprietas* (ownership) and *possessio* (possession) leading to *ius in re* (a real right or a right in property enforceable by a real action). *Res incorporales* contained different rights as easements and, above all, *ius creditum* (claim), that is to say a debt claim, which illustrated *ius ad rem* (a right to a thing, that is, a personal right over an article of property that usually arises from a contractual obligation). This presentation showed the individualist aspect of Pothier's conception of law.

Like other modern authors, Pothier was keenly interested in sources of law. Because of his birth, he belonged to the part of France where customary laws were applied. In his important *Introduction générale aux coutumes d'Orléans*,

[13] André-Jean Arnaud, *Les origines doctrinales du Code civil français* (Paris: LGDJ, 1969), 164.

which he inserted in the second edition of *Customs of Orléans*, he analyzed the notion of custom. For him, this notion constituted the municipal law of the province. This definition led him to find general principles that could be applied for all the customs in the northern part of France. It also permitted a comparison of customs with Roman law.[14]

As a professor of French law, a discipline officially taught at universities since 1679, he knew the famous dispute about the place and the role of Roman law in France. Between the independence of French law and the function of common law assumed by Roman law, he chose the first doctrine.[15] This choice led him to argue that a legal gap in the customary legislation should be filled by a reference to customs of Paris and not to Roman law. For instance, there was the issue regarding the important question of *legitime* (reserved portion of an estate for children). Many customs did not state the ratio of a reserved portion of estate that should be given to children. There were specific provisions in Justinian's Novel 18, in which the emperor conceived a variation between a third to a half of the estate in relation to the number of children. Pothier chose to refer to the custom of Paris, and it was a dogmatic position. His doctrine maintained the position of famous predecessors like Dumoulin and Coquille (d. 1603), among others. All these jurists defended the idea that Roman law was applied in the southern part of France on the basis of royal license. In fact, however, it was just a custom to follow Roman law there. In the northern part of France, Roman law could be used only if it received an official validation, either by royal legislation or by decision of the courts. The other provisions had only doctrinal value. Under these circumstances, Roman rules had only an argumentative significance – in other words, not *ratione imperii* (on the basis of power) but *imperio rationis* (by force of reason). This doctrine considered Roman law as *ratio scripta* (written reason).

While Pothier did not develop a general conception of law, he nevertheless did consider law of obligations as the matrix of the regulation of specific contracts, including contracts of marriage.[16] He made the law of obligations the central substratum of private law, and was the first author to deal with law

[14] Jean-Louis Halpérin, "Pothier Robert-Joseph, Traités sur différentes matières de droit civil, Paris-Orléans, 1773–1774," 4 vol.; Œuvres par Bugnet, Paris, 1861, 10 vol., in *Dictionnaire des grandes œuvres juridiques*, edn. Olivier Cayla and Jean-Louis Halpérin (Paris: Dalloz, 2008), 460.

[15] Jean-Louis Thireau, "Pothier, le droit romain et le droit naturel," in *Les Grands juristes. Actes des journées internatonales de la Société d'Histoire du Droit. Aix-en-Provence, 22–25 mai 2003* (Aix-en-Provence: PUAM, 2006), 116.

[16] Jean-Louis Halpérin, "Préface," in *Traité des obligations* (Paris: Dalloz, 2011).

of obligations in a specific treatise. His conception of obligations was original and different from Domat's. For Pothier, there were two kinds of obligation. The first were imperfect obligations, by which we are answerable to God. It is impossible to get a judgment about these before courts of justice. The second kind comprised perfect obligations, which could be censured by the courts.

Pothier wrote treatises on specific topics, taking either a customary approach or one based on Roman law. His method allowed him to present a general overview of legal rules in application in France. But he did not take this opportunity to propose a draft for the unification of French law. Pothier knew how to take into account the contribution of his predecessors. For instance, regarding property, he combined Bartole's approach and a natural-law approach. There was a connection between the *ius disponendi* (right of disposal of property) and the subjectivist conception of property. Pothier's definition was the following: the right to use something at discretion without harming others or contravening law.

Pothier used Roman law as a means to understand French law. He did not hesitate to recognize what French law owed to Roman rules. For example, consensualism was preferred to formalism, and was a direct outgrowth of Roman and canon law. But he also said that the French system did not retain the Roman subtleties. Pothier distinguished Roman provisions reflecting positive law that customary law and French law could not reproduce because they were the expression of an era. But there were Roman laws that represented the expression of general principles or natural law. These timeless rules could be transplanted into the French legal system because their force did not rely on specific political authority so much as on their conformity to human nature. Thus, Pothier developed an individualist natural law that identifies itself with human reason. Nevertheless, he was not able to separate clearly natural law and the law of nations, as he used both expressions interchangeably. His conception of natural law was equated with fundamental principles, and these rules were more in relation to social morality than law. Legal standards had to reproduce these principles.

This process was exactly in concordance with one of the goals conceived by the school of natural law, namely the moralization of law. Pothier made a connection between the law of obligations and natural principles: always keeping our promises, not changing our minds to avoid harming others, and compensating for damages caused by faults. Pothier recognized in the natural law a causal force imposing on us respect for our words and the need to make good damages to others. He believed that natural law includes institutions, which are a common legal heritage of humanity. Among these institutions we can include property, accession, occupation, and legal transfer.

These notions arising from natural law were in contradiction to those developed in civil law. For instance, Pothier said that formalism, with its specific conditions, was an issue in relation to civil law, whereas consensualism was inherent to natural law. Within natural law, a distinction separated two kinds of laws. The first was a law imposing an order that positive law should respect. The second was a law giving authorization or power that positive law could modify. Pothier retained the idea that Roman law had value and utility, but only for general principles with the aim of finding general solutions.

A JANSENIST JURIST?

Deeply religious, Pothier inherited his faith from his mother, who instilled in him a profound devotion. After studying at university, he wanted to become a canon regular like his uncle, who was a follower of Jansenism. But Pothier's will to please his mother led him to change his choice of career. Studying law and jurisprudence was a key vehicle toward equity and fairness that he endeavored to apply each day in his work and social life. He also attended mass with great fervor. For ten years, between the ages of 20 and 30, he studied religious topics to enlighten and deepen his faith. In his work, he combined theology, ethics, and law. This association was reflected in many treatises whose subtitles included the phrase "according to the internal forum [the conscience] and the external one." Features in connection with the conscience were often described by references to canon law or evangelical morality.[17] During the nineteenth century, different authors criticized this distinction between the internal and the external. Raymond-Theodore Troplong (d. 1869), president of the French Court of Cassation (France's highest court) and author of commentaries on the French civil code, considered Pothier too much of a casuist, like the church fathers.[18] Jean-Jacques Bugnet, who reedited all the Pothier's works, asserted that drawing parallels between conscience and law was dangerous and useless. He added that the distinction was false and antisocial.[19]

We may question Pothier's supposed attachment to Jansenism. This doctrine gave great importance to original sin, denounced human depravity, and preached the necessity of divine grace. It is true that Pothier was interested in

[17] Aimé Rodière, "Pothier," in *Les grands jurisconsultes* (Toulouse: Privat, 1874), 377.

[18] Raymond-Théodore Troplong, *De la vente ou commentaire du titre VI du livre III du Code civil* (Paris: Hingray, 1834), vii.

[19] Jean-Jacques Bugnet, *Œuvres de Pothier*, vol. II (Paris: Plon, 1862), lxxi.

the works of Augustine of Hippo, often quoted by Jansenists. Moreover, he read books by Pierre Nicole (d. 1695), one of the leading French Jansenists. But the influence of Jansenism in his treatises or others works calls for some nuance. Surely, he found in Jansenist doctrine a moral discipline and elevation. This thought was largely widespread among magistrates in the eighteenth century. The opposition between Jansenists and Jesuits regarding the place of divine grace, among others issues, sharpened during this period. Pothier did take part in this struggle when he had to carry out a sentence from the parliament in Paris against the Jesuits. Their expulsion was enacted, and Pothier did not oppose the decision, although he did not justify *a posteriori* the Jansenist doctrine.

His religious sensitivity justified his refusal to deal with criminal cases in which torture could be used during the procedure. His Christian spirit and deep sense of morality led him to compensate a widow to whom he had given bad advice.[20] Pothier was a man of great charity toward others.

His work was clearly influenced by Christianity, but it is risky to draw conclusions about his Jansenism in numerous treatises. Pothier often quoted the Old Testament and New Testament, the church fathers, and canon law collections. He also referred to the Spanish theologian-jurists, such as Tomas Sanchez,[21] a Jesuit. But he also quoted Jansenist authors and often referrred to Augustine of Hippo, an important influence of Jansenist doctrine. In fact, Pothier did not hesitate to support theses in contradiction to Jansenist precepts. For instance, he defended the idea that gambling was not in opposition to natural law. In his view, gambling relied on the freedom of an adult to dispose of his or her property. It answered to human needs for relaxation and the search for legitimate gain without dispossessing others. Normally, time and chance belong to God, and human beings could not play with it. Authors examined the issue under the question of remuneration or return. Some took the position that gambling was inherently unfair, so that winners should give back their winnings. On the other hand, many authors made a distinction between an unfair reward and the winnings when the gambling contract did not contain any injustice. For Pothier, it was important that the contract be fair and that players gamble with their own possessions freely. He added that

[20] M. de la Place de Montevray, "Robert-Joseph Pothier," in *Biographie universelle ancienne et moderne*, edn. T. Michaud, Vol. XXXIV (Paris: Desplaces, 1843), 187.

[21] On this Jesuit author, see Rafael Domingo, "Thomas Sanchez," in John Witte and Gary S. Hauk (eds.), *Christianity and Family Law: An Introduction* (Cambridge: Cambridge University Press, 2017), 245–58; and Rafael Domingo, "Tomás Sánchez," in Rafael Domingo and Javier Martinez-Torron, eds., *Great Christian Jurists in Spanish History* (Cambridge: Cambridge University Press, 2018), 225–39.

players should have equal contractual position. For him, gambling entailed only a bad goal, namely, the search for gain. If gambling were prohibited, he proposed that the prohibition should be based on the sin of benefiting monetarily, and he urged paying back winnings or making charitable donations with them.

In fact, Pothier was above all a Gallican jurist. This doctrine was based on the affirmation of secular independence from the Catholic Church. It led to a movement of secularization that progressed in France from the sixteenth century onward. In France, the phenomenon of Gallicanism started at the beginning of the fourteenth century but experienced a significant expansion during the sixteenth and seventeenth centuries. One question at the core of disputes regarding the relationship between state and church concerned the doctrine of marriage.

From a religious point of view, Pothier developed his arguments in following other French authors who upheld the authority of secular jurisdiction over marriage. In fact, he wrote, marriage has a double nature. It is a contract and a sacrament. The contractual aspect, defined by scholars in the Middle Ages, led to the affirmation of secular power over marriage. Thus, it is subject to the authority of princes, who can legislate on the marriages of their subjects. Pothier invoked theologians who tried to use the contract qualification to justify ecclesiastical authority over this fundamental institution. They affirmed the existence of two kinds of marriage contract. The first one pertained to the *ius gentium*, or natural law, and was shared by all peoples. The second one came from the *ius civile* and was particular to each nation. These theologians argued that Jesus Christ intended the marriage sacrament not for a specific state but for all nations. These theologians concluded that if the content of marriage did not contradict the *ius gentium* (law thought to be held in common by all peoples) but did contradict the *ius civile* (law reserved to Roman citizen), the matrimonial link was still valid.

Pothier contested this analysis and considered that some conditions were required by the *ius gentium* and some by the *ius civile*. Those required by natural law were required everywhere and for all peoples. Those demanded by *ius civile* were only enforced by the state where those particular laws were implemented. Above all, Pothier criticized the possible validity of a contract pertaining to the *ius gentium* if it was in opposition to *ius civile*. If the marriage was invalid in the civil order, it was also unenforceable by natural law.

Pothier thought that secular princes also could remove obstacles to marriage and regulate its formalities. That was the reason why marriages of minors contracted without the consent of their parents were declared null and void. Moreover, all matters of marriage, including separation, divorce, or nullification, pertained to secular tribunals. Pothier clearly defended this doctrine in his treatise about marriage contract. He reasserted the double nature of marriage as both sacramental and legal but stressed the contractual characteristic, saying that this feature made the institution part of the political order. Pothier recalled that God instituted the secular power to safeguard an eternal order. He concluded that marriage, being a contract dealing with the right order of society, should be subject to secular legislation. Pothier did not hesitate to defend a clear position on the consequences of the contractual aspect of marriage. The Church could be the right jurisdiction only for the sacrament. Therefore, all obstacles to marriage established by the Church could concern only the sacrament and not the civil contract. The enforcement of obstacles should be accepted by princes as their responsibility for integrating marriage into the secular legal order.

CONCLUSION

Pothier enjoyed a great reputation during his lifetime. His works were repeatedly reprinted. Many abstracts were prepared, like the *Pothier des notaires*,[22] in which his main volumes were summarized. But his fame continued because the fathers of the French civil code used many of his conceptions, doctrines, and legal elaborations. That is the reason why all his works had been reedited during the nineteenth century, not only in France but also in Italy, in the Netherlands, in Poland, and in the Iberian Peninsula. The Napoleonic conquests explain this movement in part, but it was above all the quality of his conceptions that justified such a success. The influence of the French civil code throughout the world led to the prolongation of his authority in the codification movement. For instance, in 1825 the writers of the Louisianian civil code used most of the doctrines of Pothier.[23] He had become an authority, a reference to explain civil codification.

RECOMMENDED READING

Primary Sources

Pothier, R.-J. *Pandectae Justinianae in novum ordinem digestae*. 3 vols. Orléans: 1748, 1749, 1752.

Traité des obligations selon les règles tant du for de la conscience que du for extérieur. Paris: Debure l'aîné, 1761, 1764; reprinted, 2011.

[22] M. Ledru, *Le Pothier des notaires ou abrégés de ses divers traités* (Paris: Veuve Dabo, 1823).

[23] Sylvain Soleil, *Le modèle juridique français dans le monde. Une ambition, une expansion (XVIe–XIXe siècle)* (Paris: IRJS éditions, 2014), 381.

Traité des retraits pour servir d'appendice au traité du contrat de vente par l'auteur du traité des obligations. Paris: Debure l'aîné, 1762.
Traité du domaine de propriété, auquel on a joint deux traités de la possession et de la prescription. Paris: Debure l'aîné, 1762.
Traité du contrat de constitution de rente, par l'auteur du traité des obligations. Paris: Debure l'aîné, 1763.
Traité du contrat de change, de la négociation qui se fait par la lettre de change et autres billets de commerce. Paris: Debure l'aîné, 1763.
Traité du contrat de bail à rente, par l'auteur du traité des obligations. Paris: Debure l'aîné, 1764.
Traité du contrat de société, selon les règles tant du for de la conscience que du for extérieur, par l'auteur du traité des obligations. Paris: Debure l'aîné, 1764.
Traité du contrat de louage, selon les règles tant du for de la conscience que du for extérieur. Paris: Debure l'aîné, 1764.
Traité des cheptels, selon les règles, tant du for de la conscience, que du for extérieur, par l'auteur du traité des obligations. Paris: Debure l'aîné, 1765.
Traité des contrats de bienfaisance, selon les règles tant du for de la conscience que du for extérieur. Paris: Debure l'aîné, 1766.
Traité du contrat de mariage, par l'auteur du traité des obligations. Paris: Débure l'aîné, 1768.
Traité de la communauté, auquel on a joint un traité de la puissance du mari sur la personne et les biens de la femme, par l'auteur du Traité des obligations. Paris: Debure l'aîné, 1770.
Traité du douaire, par l'auteur du traité des obligations. Paris: Debure père, 1770.
Traité du droit d'habitation, pour servir d'appendice au traité du douaire. Traité des donations entre mari et femme, et du don manuel, par l'auteur du traité des obligations. Paris: Debure père, 1771.
Traité du domaine et de propriété, par l'auteur du traité des obligations. Vol. 1 ; *Traité de la possession et de la prescription*, Vol. II. Paris: Debure père, 1772.
Traité sur différentes matières de droit civil. Paris: Debure, 1773–74.
Œuvres pothumes de M. Pothier. Edited by Pierre-Jean-Jacques-Guillaume. Guyot, Paris: J. J. Massot, 1776–78.
Traité des fiefs, avec un titre sur les cens. Orléans: Veuve Rouzeau, 1776.
Œuvres de Pothier. 13 vols. Paris: Beaucé, 1817–20.
Œuvres de Pothier contenant les traités du droit français. Nouvelle édition mise en ordre et publiée par les soins de M. Dupin. 11 vols. Paris: Béchet, 1824–25.
Œuvres complètes, annotées et mises en corrélation avec le Code civil et la législation actuelle par M. Bugnet. Paris: Cosse et Delamotte, 1845–48.
R.-J. Pothier, D. Jousse, and M. Prévost de la Jannès. *Coutumes d'Orléans avec des observations nouvelles*. Orléans, 1740.

Secondary Sources

Arnaud, A.-J. *Les origines doctrinales du Code civil français*. Paris: LGDJ, 1969.
Batiza, R. *Domat, Pothier and the Code Napoléon: Some Observations Concerning the Actual Sources of the French Civil Code*. n.p., 1973.

Boudinhon, A. "Robert-Joseph Pothier." In *Catholic Encyclopedia*, vol. 12, 1913, available at en.wikisource.org/wiki/Catholic_Encyclopedia_(1913)/Robert_Joseph_Pothier

Deroussin, D. "Pothier, la coutume (d'Orléans) et le droit coutumier." In *Les décisionnaires et la coutume: contribution à la fabrication de la norme*, 413–47. *Études d'histoire du droit et des idées politiques*, no. 23. Toulouse: PUT, 2017.

Dupin, M. *Dissertation sur la vie et les ouvrages de Pothier*. Paris, 1825.

Frémont, A.-F.-M. *Recherche historiques et biographiques sur Pothier*. Orléans: Gatineau, 1859.

Gilles, D., and É. Gojosso. "Sur Pothier et le Code civil." In *Études d'histoire du droit privé en souvenir de Maryse Carlin*, edited by O. Vernier, et al., 403–17. Paris: La Mémoire du Droit, 2008.

Halpérin, J.-L. "Pothier Robert, Joseph, *Traités sur différentes matières de droit civil*, Paris/Orléans, 1773–74, 4 vols. *Œuvres* par Bugnet, Paris, 1861, 10 vol." In *Dictionnaire des grandes œuvres juridiques*, edited by Olivier Cayla and Jean-Louis Halpérin, 460–62. Paris: Dalloz, 2008.

"Préface."*Traité des obligations*. Paris: Dalloz, 2011.

Monéger, J., J.-L. Sourioux, and A. Terrasson de Fougères. *Robert-Joseph Pothier, d'hier et d'aujourd'hui*. Paris: Economica, 2001.

Naz, R. "Pothier." In *Dictionnaire de droit canonique*, vol. 7, cols. 70–71. Paris: Letouzey, 1965.

Place de Montevray, M. de la. "Robert-Joseph Pothier." In *Biographie universelle ancienne et moderne*, edited by T. Michaud. Vol. XXXIV. Paris: Desplaces, 1843.

Rodière, A. "Pothier." In *Les grands jurisconsultes*, 374–78. Toulouse: Privat, 1874.

Sourioux, J.-L. "Pothier ou le sphinx d'Orléans." *Droits* 39 (2004): 69–75.

Thézard, L. *De l'influence des travaux de Pothier et du Chancelier d'Aguesseau sur le droit civil moderne*. Paris: Durand, 1866.

Thireau, J.-L. "Pothier et la doctrine française des XVIe et XVIIe siècles." In Monéger, et al., *Robert-Joseph Pothier, d'hier et d'aujourd'hui*, 35–54.

"Pothier, le droit romain et le droit naturel." In *Les Grands juristes. Actes des journées internationales de la Société d'Histoire du Droit. Aix-en-Provence, 22–25 mai 2003*, 113–28. Aix-en-Provence: PUAM, 2006.

"Pothier Robert-Joseph." In *Dictionnaire historique des juristes français*, edited by P. Arabeyre, J.-L. Halpérin, and J. Krynen, 636–38. Paris: PUF, 2015.

15

Jean-Étienne-Marie Portalis

(1746–1807)

NICOLAS LAURENT-BONNE

BIOGRAPHICAL INTRODUCTION

Jean-Étienne-Marie Portalis, also known as Portalis the Elder, was born on April 1, 1746, in Beausset. This is a small village in the *département* of the Var, where the Portalis family, originally from Italy, had resided since the end of the fifteenth century. His father, Étienne Portalis, held the office of royal notary.[1] As a child, Portalis was cared for by his maternal grandparents, the David family, at the nearby La Cadière estate. When he was seven, Portalis began his education with the Oratorians of Toulon, who taught him as much about Enlightenment texts as they did about theology. The future legislator and imperial minister was an assiduous reader of Montesquieu (1689–1755), Rousseau (1712–78), Grotius (1623–62), Bossuet (1627–1704), and Fénelon (1651–1715). According to his son, Jean-Étienne-Marie Portalis's eclectic education protected him against "the spirit of irreligion which prevailed in the world"[2] and nourished his liberal Christian faith and the political Gallicanism that followed him through his career, from the bar at Aix to his service as minister of religion.

[1] The acts are housed in the departmental archives of the Var, under reference numbers 3 E 25 77 to 92.

[2] Joseph-Marie Portalis, *Souvenirs manuscrits*, p. 30, cited by Joël-Benoît d'Onorio, *Portalis l'esprit des siècles* (Paris: Dalloz, 2005), 47. Besides the important monograph by d'Onorio, and among the abundant literature relating to Portalis, see: Auguste-Aymé Boullée, *Essai sur la vie, le caractère et les ouvrages de J.-É.-M. Portalis* (Paris: Didier et Cie, 1859); Joseph-Casimir Frégier, *Portalis, philosophe chrétien* (Paris: Challamel Ainé, 1861); Louis Lallement, *Éloge de Jean-Étienne-Marie Portalis* (Paris: A. Durand, 1861); René Lavollée, *Portalis. Sa vie et ses œuvres* (Paris: Didier et Cie, 1869); Lydie Adolphe, *Portalis et son temps. Le bon génie de Napoléon* (Paris: Sirey, 1936); Jean-Luc Chartier, *Portalis: le père du Code civil* (Paris: Fayard, 2004); and Joël-Benoît d'Onorio, ed., *Portalis le Juste* (Aix-en-Provence: Presses universitaires d'Aix-Marseille, 2004). Finally, see the entry by Catherine Delplanque in *Dictionnaire historique des juristes français, XIIe–XXe siècle* (Paris: PUF, 2015), 634–36.

In 1762, at the age of 17, Portalis returned to Aix, where he began his law degree. He studied civil law under Jean-Joseph Julien (1704–89), who was prosecutor of Provence from 1747 to 1753[3] and the author of *Élémen[t]s de jurisprudence selon les loix romaines et celles du royaume*.[4] Portalis also studied canon law under the tutelage of Joseph-Sextius Siméon (1717–88), whose daughter, Marguerite Françoise, Portalis would marry on August 8, 1775.[5] After qualifying in both canon and civil law, he was called to the Aix bar in 1765. As a lawyer, he would oppose Beaumarchais (1732–99) and Mirabeau (1749–91) in defense of the latter's wife, Émilie de Marignane, during their separation proceedings. He intervened in cases covering a multiplicity of subjects: personal and family law, commercial law, tax law, and penal law were all bread and butter for Portalis. The lawyer from Aix was reputed for the elegance of his pleas and the modesty of his fees.[6] On top of his judicial duties, he performed active consultancy work. The most renowned of his clients was Louis XV's minister, the Duke of Choiseul, with regard to the validity of Protestant marriages.

At this time Portalis joined the Freemasons.[7] He was elected in 1768 to the office of Venerable Master in a Scottish Rite lodge. He frequented the homes of fellow Masons for the remainder of his life – notably, Jean-Jacques-Régis de Cambacérès (1753–1824), to whom he probably owed his favorable business affairs under the Consulate. It is safe to assume that, without turning away from his Catholic faith, Portalis gained from his Masonic experiences the opportunity to discuss his favored philosophical subjects, for which he had been fêted since his youth.

Between 1765 and 1790, Portalis was called to elective office, both municipal and provincial. First, he was elected as a councillor at Aix in 1776 before becoming an assessor for the town and for the prosecutor of Provence in 1778. The latter post had been held by both his supervisor, Jean-Joseph Julien, and his father-in-law and professor of canonical law, Joseph-Sextius Siméon. In 1782, Portalis was sent to Paris to defend provincial interests. He would have the chance to support his hometown once again, in a report commissioned by

[3] Laurent Reverso, "Julien Jean-Joseph," in *Dictionnaire historique des juristes français*, 565–66.

[4] Jean-Joseph Julien, *Élémens de jurisprudence selon les loix romaines et celles du royaume* (Aix, 1785).

[5] D'Onorio, *Portalis l'esprit des siècles*, 58–63.

[6] Ibid., 76–97; Lavollée, *Portalis. Sa vie et ses œuvres*, 6; and Jean-Louis Gazzaniga, "Portalis avocat," in d'Onorio, *Portalis le Juste*, 43–61.

[7] In the nineteenth century, this element was missing from the biographies of Portalis, notably those of Boullée, Frégier, Lallement, and Lavollée.

the government in 1787 concerning the former states of Provence, which had not been united since 1639.[8]

During the French Revolution, Portalis definitively abandoned his legal career and entered politics. In September 1795, he was elected as deputy to the Veterans' Council, before becoming their secretary on November 23, 1795 (2 Frimaire, Year II), then president on June 19, 1796 (1 Messidor, Year IV). The coup d'état of September 4, 1797 (18 Fructidor, Year V), led by the Directory against the Council, resulted in Portalis being exiled. He spent his period in the political wilderness with his son Joseph-Marie (1778–1858), beginning in Switzerland in October 1797 and finishing in Holstein, at the château of Emkendorf, where they were welcomed by the Count and Countess von Reventlow. During this time, he wrote the philosophical work *On the Usage and Abuse of the Philosophical Spirit during the Eighteenth Century*, published posthumously by his son in 1820.[9] After the coup d'état of 18 Brumaire, Portalis and his son were recalled from exile on December 27, 1799 (5 Nivôse, Year 8). Benefitting from the protection of the consul, Cambacérès, and fully adhering to the new regime, Portalis became a member of the State Council on September 22, 1800, and was appointed to the civil and criminal legislative section. On August 12, 1800, he was selected as one of the four members of the governmental commission tasked with the Civil Code project, alongside the former advocate of Louis XVI, François-Denis Tronchet (1745–1825), Jacques de Maleville (1741–1824), and Félix-Julien-Jean Bigot de Préameneu (1747–1825). It was Portalis who delivered the famous *Preliminary Speech*,[10] given in the name of the four members of the governmental commission, on the principles that had inspired the Civil Code's creation. The very symbol of the wisdom and moderation of the code is the spirit of transaction, which is, in Halpérin's words, a "balancing act."[11] Under the influence of Montesquieu, Burke, and the new philosophy of history, whose development he presumably saw during his German stay,

[8] D'Onorio, *Portalis l'esprit des siècles*, 103–15; Lavollée, *Portalis. Sa vie et ses œuvres*, 17–25 and 31, n. 1; Lallement, *Éloge de Jean-Étienne-Marie Portalis*, 18–19; Boullée, *Essai sur la vie, le caractère et les ouvrages de J.-É.-M. Portalis*, 11–12; and Éric Gasparini, "Portalis, archétype de l'administrateur provençal de la fin du siècle des Lumières," in d'Onorio, *Portalis le Juste*, 63–76.

[9] Jean-Étienne-Marie Portalis, *De l'usage et de l'abus de l'esprit philosophique durant le XVIIIe siècle* (Paris, 1834; reprint, Paris: Dalloz, 2007).

[10] *Discours préliminaire sur le projet de Code civil présenté le 1er pluviôse an IX* in *Discours, rapports et travaux inédits sur le Code civil, par Jean-Étienne-Marie Portalis*, edn. Frédéric Portalis (1844), 1–62; a modern edition is *Le discours et le Code. Portalis, deux siècles après le Code Napoléon* (Paris: LITEC, 2004), xxi–lvii.

[11] Jean-Louis Halpérin, *L'impossible Code civil* (Paris: PUF, 1992), 286.

Portalis was no stranger to the transactional spirit that flowed through the new codification, torn as it was between reaction and revolution.

The father of the Civil Code was equally tasked with presenting the Concordat and the Organic Articles to the State Council, before taking them to the legislative body on April 5, 1802 (15 Germinal, Year X). As the state councillor for any issues concerning religion, Portalis became the great defender of religious peace. On July 10, 1804, he was named minister for religion, probably owing to his unshakable constitutional support for Napoléon: having defended the Consulate before the State Council on May 10, 1802, he mounted the Senate rostrum on May 16, 1804, to present the organic Senate-Consulate project relating to the establishment of hereditary, imperial government, which was proclaimed on May 18, 1805. Portalis died on August 25, 1807, at the age of 61. He was still minister for religion, and the interim management of the post was left to his son, Joseph-Marie, until the nomination of Bigot de Préameneu on January 1, 1808.

As a Christian, Portalis was like the majority of his contemporaries. His biographers reveal that he was "sincerely and profoundly Christian."[12] However, this affirmation risks bending his legal-philosophical thought somewhat, for he never affirmed the divine foundations of natural law, for instance. Some, including Louis Lallement, the author of a biography published in 1861, defended the Aixan orator against those who sought to attack Portalis "for not going quite far enough in the support of Catholicism."[13] While clearly Catholic, Portalis was nonetheless Gallican and liberal, as shown by his writings and his statesmanlike actions under the Consulate and the Empire. His clear Gallicanism, his political and religious liberalism, his incessant references to the school of modern natural law and the philosophy of Hume and Locke, his defense of Protestants and religious liberties as well as the philosophical spirit and reason, and his stigmatizing of unjust privileges invite the drawing of a more nuanced image of an Enlightenment man. This is best reflected in the works of his youth, the preparation of the Civil Code, and the implementation of the Concordat.

THE PHILOSOPHICAL AND GALLICAN JURIST

During his law studies in Aix, Portalis was lauded for his writing. In 1763 he published, under the title *Observations on the Work Entitled Émile or On*

[12] D'Onorio, *Portalis l'esprit des siècles*, 206; also see Boullée, *Essai sur la vie, le caractère et les ouvrages de J.-É.-M. Portalis*, 124.

[13] Lallement, *Éloge de Jean-Étienne-Marie Portalis*, 90.

Education, a lively critique of Rousseau's philosophy, "where pride and irreligion play a greater role than love of truth."[14] He believed he could recognize in the Genevan philosopher's thinking a type of atheism that tended to be "less about educating than about destroying Christianity and the wise."[15] In this youthful work, Portalis offered particular developments to natural law, which Rousseau described as "chimeric,"[16] or even a religious fanaticism that he compared to atheism. Portalis claimed that he was neither "a theologian nor a devotee."[17] In Rousseau's writing, however, he discovered a philosophy without religion, tearing natural law from the heart of the moral and the virtuous. The Provençal student still referred to the fanatic and the atheist who both divide the citizenry and undermine the interests of the state.[18] Developed in an incisive manner, these themes foreshadowed the later positions of Portalis, the craftsman of natural law and defender of religious freedom and toleration.[19]

Taking advantage of a dispute between the clergy and the magistracy of Aix, Portalis published, in 1765, a pamphlet titled *Principles on the Distinction of the Two Powers – Spiritual and Temporal*, in which he supported royal Gallicanism. From the first page of this work, he pointed out that spiritual power and temporal power, which derive from the same principle, have, nevertheless, different objectives and purposes: while the first "is established to make justice and the truth in hearts," the second is used "to preserve order and tranquillity in the state."[20] Drawing on a famous letter of Pope Gelasius I, Portalis hastily deduced that "the church had only one authority, and that kings, on the contrary, had real power";[21] in other words, he said, the first invites and convinces, the second strikes and subjugates. From this theoretical postulate, Portalis drew consequences relative to the means that could be used by the two powers: the government of the church acts upon souls alone, whereas the temporal government "behaves in the mortal way of public authority and the severity of temporal punishment." In this brochure, written in a judicial manner, the young Gallican describes the king as "the protector

[14] Jean-Étienne-Marie Portalis, *Observations sur un ouvrage intitulé Émile ou De l'éducation* (Avignon: 1763), 6.

[15] Ibid., 7.

[16] Ibid., 38–44.

[17] Ibid., 43.

[18] Ibid., 13–18.

[19] Portalis attacked Rousseau's philosophy in a second work, titled *Prejudices*, published probably in 1763 (Jean-Étienne-Marie Portalis, *Des préjugés*, s.l., n.d.).

[20] Jean-Étienne-Marie Portalis, *Principes sur la distinction des deux puissance spirituelle et temporelle* (Avignon, 1765), 1.

[21] Ibid., 2.

of religion"[22] and "the canons of the church" as a hindrance to executing the decisions of the ecclesiastical authorities, "which would be contrary to the older canons and to the true spirit of the Church."[23] While this Gallican thesis was severely denounced from the pulpit by Pierre-François-Xavier de Reboul de Lambert (1704–91), bishop of Saint-Paul-Trois-Châteaux, Portalis needed to justify himself while reiterating his fidelity to religion.[24] This work, written in his youth, announced the point of view that he would develop in the coming decades, notably when, as minister for religion, he was tasked with ensuring the execution of the Concordat on April 5, 1802 (15 Germinal, Year X), once it was signed with the Holy See.

Among Portalis's early works, the *Consultation on the Validity of Protestant Marriage* merits closer inspection, insofar as it shows the dual influences of the Enlightenment and Gallicanism on the young lawyer's thinking. Pushed by Voltaire (1694–1778), the Duke of Choiseul (1719–85), who was principal minister of Louis XV, decided to create a city of religious tolerance. The town plan, which was perfectly octagonal, was approved by Louis XV in 1773. It preceded the construction of a Catholic church and its Protestant counterpart, which were erected on opposite sides of the town square. The ambition was to allow Catholics and Protestants to live side by side in the same town, while rivalling the economic power of Geneva.

Prior to beginning this work, in 1770, Choiseul consulted the young Portalis, aged 24, on the validity of Protestant marriage, which would be celebrated in the Swiss municipality of Versoix.[25] In France, the difficulties arising from the marriage of Protestant couples had previously been recognized under the pacification edicts as a means to try to end the religious wars at the end of the sixteenth century. The famous Edict of Nantes, issued by Henri IV on April 30, 1598, had recognized the validity of unions officiated by a Protestant pastor. Protestant marriage had to respect the canonical rules of matrimonial discipline, including the publishing of banns, the competence of witnesses, and the age of majority.[26] These requirements ostensibly guaranteed freedom of conscience for Protestant subjects of the kingdom, according to the legislator. However, on October 15, 1685, Louis XIV revoked the

[22] Ibid., 7 and 19.

[23] Ibid., 8.

[24] D'Onorio, *Portalis l'esprit des siècles*, 72.

[25] The context of the consultation is recalled by Joseph-Marie Portalis, in his *Souvenirs manuscrits*, 9–10.

[26] *Édit de pacification* (Nantes, 30 avril 1598), art. 23, in *Recueil général des anciennes lois françaises, depuis l'an 420, jusqu'à la Révolution de 1789*, Vol. 15, edn. Isambert, Taillandier, and Decrusy (Paris, 1829), 178.

Edict of Nantes, using a recall edict recorded on October 22. The revocation of the pacification edict occurred in the wake of a series of suppressive measures taken since 1679: an edict in November 1680 forbade Catholics to marry Reformed Christians;[27] another, enacted in August 1684, forbade Protestant ministers from holding office for longer than three years in the same place.[28] Moreover, the destruction of Protestant churches was authorized by local parliaments, where specific prohibitions existed against certain professions and trades. "If God keeps the king," wrote Madame de Maintenon in 1681, "there will not be another Huguenot for twenty years."[29] The edict of Fontainebleau, issued in October 1685 and written by Le Tellier (1641–91),[30] forbade the celebration of Protestant ceremonies.[31] Pastors were exiled if they did not convert to Catholicism within fifteen days.[32] Protestant schools were obliged to close their doors[33] as they left the kingdom.[34] Children were required to be raised in the Catholic faith.[35] Protestant churches, which had thus far escaped destruction, were razed.[36] Moreover, after the revocation of the Edict of Nantes, Protestants no longer had the opportunity to marry under the authority of a pastor. To the revoking edict of 1685, a declaration was added, published on December 13, 1685, which, in matters pertaining to marriage, enjoined the Protestant subjects of the king of France to observe "the solemnities prescribed by the holy canons."[37] An edict issued at Versailles in March 1697 created a single, national form of marriage, which presupposed the presence of a parish priest. Article 1 of this edict prescribed the obligation to celebrate marriages, regardless of the confession of the spouses involved, "in

[27] *Édit portant que les catholiques ne pourront contracter mariage avec les religionnaires, et que les enfans qui en proviendront seront illégitimes et incapables de succéder à leurs pères et mères* (Versailles, novembre 1680), in *Recueil général des anciennes lois françaises*, Vol. 19, 257–58.

[28] *Édit portant que les ministres protestans ne pourront exercer leurs fonctions plus de trois ans dans le même lieu* (Versailles, août 1684), in *Recueil général des anciennes lois françaises*, Vol. 19, 454–55.

[29] Cited by Émile-Guillaume Léonard, *Histoire générale du protestantisme*, Vol. 2, *L'établissement (1564–1700)* (Paris: PUF, 1961), 365.

[30] *Édit portant révocation de l'édit de Nantes* (Fontainebleau, octobre 1685), in *Recueil général des anciennes lois françaises*, Vol. 19, 530–34.

[31] Art. 2–3 (ibid., 532).

[32] Art. 4 (ibid., 532).

[33] Art. 6 (ibid., 533).

[34] Art. 10 (ibid., 533).

[35] Art. 8 (ibid., 533).

[36] Art. 1 (ibid., 532).

[37] *Déclaration sur l'édit de 1685, contenant règlement pour l'instruction des nouveaux convertis et de leurs enfans* (Versailles, 13 décembre 1685), art. 7 (*Recueil général des anciennes lois françaises*, Vol. 20, 316).

the presence of the priest contracted to them," in accordance with canon law.[38] A declaration made in 1724 at Versailles solemnly recalled the dispositions of this edict issued in 1697.[39] This legislative policy, begun under the reign of Louis XIV and continued by Louis XV, was obviously not without difficulties for Protestant couples. Failing to observe the forms prescribed by royal law and canon law, Protestant marriages, celebrated "in the desert," were null and void. In such cases, couples were deemed concubinary and their children declared illegitimate bastards.

For an answer to this crisis, the minister-philosopher Choiseul turned to Portalis for his services. Written with exemplary speed, the manuscript of the consultation on the validity of Protestant marriage was sent to Voltaire through the Geneva publisher Moultou. The patriarch of Ferney is full of praise for the works of the "philosopher" Portalis, particularly in view of the courageous positions Portalis took on the legislative policy on marriage since the reign of Louis XIV and, still more, vis-à-vis the revoking edict.[40] In response to Choiseul's question, Portalis responded in the following manner: on the one hand, he believed that, in the state under positive law, Protestants could not be obliged to observe the formalities of canonical marriage, and therefore their marriages could be valid without the sacrament; on the other hand, he asserted that the good faith of the spouses sufficed to legitimize Protestant marriages in France, where the state was simply the protector of the Protestants of France and not of a sacrament.[41] In other words, Portalis proposed to

[38] *Édit portant règlement pour les formalités des mariages* (Versailles, mars 1697), art. 1, in *Recueil général des anciennes lois françaises*, Vol. 20, 288–89.

[39] *Déclaration concernant la religion* (Versailles, 14 mai 1724), art. 15, in *Recueil général des anciennes lois françaises*, Vol. 21, 268.

[40] As well as the copious annotations in the margins, see Voltaire's letter adressed to Portalis and conserved in the Library of the Cour de cassation, ms. 501, p. 558: "Si les avocats sont assez courageux pour signer cette dissertation qui n'est pas assurément une consultation, si les juges sont assez sages et assez hardis pour faire une loi nouvelle, je me fais porter en litière tout mourant que je suis et je vais les remercier je leur dirai *nunc dimittis servum tuum domine*. Mon cher philosophe ne vous permettez vous pas des espérances trop flatteuses? Les hommes seraient-ils devenus raisonnables? Mr Dalembert sera bientôt en Provence. Il pourrait beaucoup servir. Par Dieu, je voudrais bien voir la sotte révocation de l'édit de Nantes bernée. Bonsoir mon très cher philosophe." [*If lawyers are brave enough to sign this dissertation, which is certainly not a consultation, if judges are wise and bold enough to make a new law, then I am going to be carried in my bed, dying as I am, and I will thank them, whilst saying that nunc dimittis servum tuum domine. My dear philosopher, do you not allow yourself hopes that are too flattering? Have men become reasonable? Mr. Dalembert will soon be in Provence. He could be of great help. God-willing, I would like to see that the stupid revocation of the Edict of Nantes be hoodwinked. Good night, my dear philosopher*]

[41] Jean-Étienne-Marie Portalis, *Consultation sur la validité des mariages des protestants de France* (Paris: 1771), 16.

leave to Protestants the natural freedom "to marry without any legal form"[42] whenever they had, in good faith, respected "virtue and morals."[43] To support such a position, Portalis essentially relied on the doctrine of Gallican jurists, including Charles Févret (1583–1661),[44] Jean-Pierre Gibert (1592–1671),[45] and Pierre Le Ridant (1700–68).[46] By quoting these men, Portalis unsurprisingly sided with the canonists who considered marriage primarily a civil contract. He agreed with the thesis that, by instituting matrimonial union, Jesus Christ made no change to the nature of the civil contract, governed by the secular power, much as pagan pre-Christian societies had already experienced themselves.[47]

In addition to the Gallican theses, there is clear influence of the school of modern natural law, to which Portalis adhered, and which dominated his century. Among the materials collected to draft the consultation, Portalis transcribed the developments of Grotius[48] and Pufendof (1632–94)[49] in the translation of Jean Barbeyrac (1674–1744), a refugee Protestant jurist in Lausanne. The consultation bears the marks of the school of modern natural law and its "new scholastic marriage,"[50] which awarded a decisive place to the concept of a contract. In his consultation, Portalis thus defended the validity of unions celebrated "in the desert," making the intrinsic value of marriage under natural law prevail regardless of its sacramental dimension. In addition to legal materials, the intellectual influence of the Enlightenment was

[42] Ibid., 88.

[43] Ibid., 100.

[44] He retranscribed in his rough notes (Bibliothèque de la Cour de cassation, ms. 501, p. 380) fragments of Févret's treatise *De l'autorité du clergé et du pouvoir du magistrat politique, sur l'exercice des fonctions du ministère ecclésiastique* (Amsterdam, 1767). For Févret, see the entry of Brigitte Basdevant-Gaudemet in *Dictionnaire historique des juristes français*, 428–29.

[45] He equally retranscribed, in his rough notes (Bibliothèque de la Cour de cassation, ms. 501, p. 509 and p. 531) fragments of Gibert's *Institutions ecclésiastiques et bénéficiales* and his *Consultations canoniques sur le sacrement de mariage*. For Gibert, see the entry of Brigitte Basdevant-Gaudemet, in *Dictionnaire historique des juristes français*, 476–77.

[46] He cited, apart from *Code matrimonial ou recueil complet des loix canoniques et civiles sur les questions de mariage*, a *Mémoire théologique et politique au sujet des mariages clandestins des protestans de France*. For Le Ridant, see the entry of Brigitte Basdevant-Gaudemet, in *Dictionnaire historique des juristes français*, 649–50.

[47] Brigitte Basdevant-Gaudemet, "Les doctrines canoniques sur le sacrement du mariage aux XVIIe et XVIIIe siècles," *Revue de droit canonique* (1992): 298–307.

[48] Bibliothèque de la Cour de cassation, ms. 501, 65–79 and 479.

[49] Ibid., 35–37 and 265–66.

[50] Jeanne-Marie Tuffery-Andrieu, "Le droit canonique, source du code civil de 1804 en matière de mariage?"*Revue de droit canonique* 60, no. 1/2 (2010) [*Liturgie. Droit. Institutions. Hommage à Marcel Meztger*]: 224.

present. In fact, Portalis gathered philosophical fragments from the work of Montesquieu,[51] Rousseau,[52] and even Voltaire, whose treatise on tolerance occupies a central place in the drafts of the consultation.[53] This subtle equilibrium testifies more broadly to the philosophical spirit of the Enlightenment applied to matters of legislation and public administration – a spirit that Portalis acquired during his period of revolutionary exile.[54] This pamphlet, written in a more legal than philosophical style, still appeared, precociously, as a plea for religious freedom of conscience. It prefigured, with surprising modernity, the edict of tolerance adopted in 1787 under the impetus of Malesherbes (1721–94).

From the Oratorians of Toulon to the Aix bar, Portalis refined his position as a liberal Catholic and a Gallican, torn as he was between the philosophical spirit of the Enlightenment and Christian spiritualism, yet marked by a certain traditionalism. Once again, it is this spirit that suffuses two imperishable works of which he was the artisan: the Civil Code and the Concordat.

THE PREPARATION OF THE CIVIL CODE

Appointed by Napoléon Bonaparte to the State Council, Portalis received a new charge even before heading to the Palais des Tuileries, where the State Council was sitting. He was designated as one of the four members of the governmental commission charged with presenting a draft civil code, through an order dated August 12, 1800 (24 Thermidor, Year VIII). Joining him on this commission were a Parisian, François-Denis Tronchet; a Breton, Félix-Julien-Jean Bigot de Préameneu; and a Périgourdin, Jacques de Maleville. Educated under the *Ancien Régime*, all the members of the commission were former lawyers and represented the different traditions of old French law. Similar to the partisans of the constitutional monarchy during the Revolution, they did not adhere to the civil egalitarian laws of Year II. According to most of his biographers, however, Portalis was the most brilliant and probably the most cultured of the four.[55] Undoubtedly an excellent speaker, he was one of the main architects of the codification and had been carefully chosen to carry out

[51] From his rough notes, fragments of *Esprit des lois* on divorce, polygamy, or the relationship between civil law and theological law (Bibliothèque de la Cour de cassation, ms. 501, 211–25).
[52] He transcribed the passages of *Contrat social* (Bibliothèque de la Cour de cassation, ms. 501, 35–37 and 31–32).
[53] Notably, Bibliothèque de la Cour de cassation, ms. 501, 11–30.
[54] See Portalis, *De l'usage et de l'abus de l'esprit philosophique durant le XVIIIe siècle*, Vol. 2, 226.
[55] D'Onorio, *Portalis l'esprit des siècles*, 194.

the project of Bonaparte. If not truly a "father of the Civil Code,"[56] Portalis appeared in many ways to be the soul of the new codification and to have controlled the entirety of its content.

On January 21, 1801 (1 Pluviose, Year IX), the commission submitted the draft Civil Code to the State Council. The copy was also accompanied by a long report titled *Preliminary Speech*, signed by all four commissioners but in fact essentially written by Portalis. This text comprised an assemblage of discourses that he had delivered to the Council of Elders [*Conseil des Anciens*], along with extracts of his study on *The Use and Abuse of the Philosophical Spirit during the Eighteenth Century*, which was published posthumously. It is the spirit of new codification which Portalis wanted to set in stone and which has become one of the most famous texts in the history of French law.

If one believes the future minister of the Empire, the Civil Code was intended to be a work of compromise, "a transaction between the written law and customs."[57] By borrowing in a balanced way from Roman law, canon law, customary law, and even royal legislation, the Civil Code would put an end to quarrels between lawyers from the north and south of France, thus fostering national unity through the abandonment of local idiosyncrasies. Moreover, Portalis suggested that the Civil Code was halfway between old law and revolutionary legislation, thereby retaining only the best traditions of Old France and the achievements brought about by the Revolution. Basically, the codifiers, and Portalis in particular, refused to carry out a regeneration of humanity, as the revolutionaries had dreamed of doing in the past;[58] hence, the commissioners preferred proven solutions and traditional models to the politics of *tabula rasa*.

This official presentation, which borrowed much from the moderating spirit so dear to Montesquieu, carries some truth. Roman law was one of the intellectual sources of the new law of obligations, while the new matrimonial law was largely inspired by canon law. In the customs of Paris and customary common law, the drafters of the Code notably adopted the system of communal property between spouses, largely reusing D'Aguesseau's ordinances on donations and wills, promulgated in 1731 and 1735. Furthermore, the Code draws on doctrinal materials, such as those of Domat and Pothier for French doctrine and, in a more diffuse way, those of the theoreticians of the school of

[56] Chartier, *Portalis: père du Code civil*.
[57] *Discours préliminaire*, 20.
[58] Jean-Louis Halpérin, "Le droit privé de la Révolution. Héritage législatif et héritage idéologique," *Annales historiques de la Révolution française* 2 (2002): 135–51.

modern natural law, such as Grotius and Pufendorf. The four commissioners undertook a selective sorting of the revolutionary legislation: it was also the case with property, described as "inviolable and sacred"; the equality of legitimate inheritances; civil marriage and, to a lesser extent, divorce.

Although it presents a partial truth, the *Preliminary Speech* remains, nonetheless, a "masterpiece of Napoleonic propaganda," in the words of Jean-Louis Halpérin.[59] The usual concern for balance and neutrality that Portalis displayed seems to clash with some of his frankly counterrevolutionary statements. After almost losing his life twice during the Terror, the lawyer from Aix severely criticized the revolutionary disorder that overthrew traditional political principles. He looked askance at "the frightful" Revolutionary Government, which he considered even more awful "than an invasion of the barbarians could ever have been."[60] Even in the *Preliminary Speech*, Portalis looked suspiciously at the laws that overthrew fathers' power, flouted marital authority, and erected a new class of landlords. Without being truly hostile to all reforms carried out under the Revolution, Portalis was, nevertheless, a firm believer in the traditional order, of which the return to previous law was one of the most eminent marks.

Portalis was conservative and heir to legal traditions, and thus attempted to introduce the "philosophical spirit" to his work. This he defined as having been born "of scientific culture, from the habit of closely observing the continual practice of a sound dialectic, based on the sound principles of enlightened metaphysics."[61] An assiduous reader of Montesquieu, whom he describes as a "great man," Portalis is full of praise for *The Spirit of the Laws*, which "preaches tolerance," "proscribes slavery," "classifies crimes," "graduates punishments," "encourages the people," and "compares governments." From the castle of Emkendorf, where he wrote his treatise *On the Use and Abuse of the Philosophical Spirit during the Eighteenth Century*, Portalis drew his first conclusions of the application of Enlightenment philosophy on matters of legislation and politics: notably the opening of marriage to Protestant couples, by Malesherbes; the destruction "of the remains of real servitude" by Necker (1732–1804); freedom to trade; suppression of the corvée; and making the distinction between interest-bearing loans and usury.[62] Using examples drawn from European legislation, Portalis attempted to prove the benefits of the Enlightenment: freedom of the press in Denmark, introduced

[59] Jean-Louis Halpérin, *Histoire du droit privé français depuis 1804* (Paris: PUF, 2012), 14.
[60] Portalis, *De l'usage et de l'abus de l'esprit philosophique durant le XVIIIe siècle*, Vol. 2, 389.
[61] Ibid., Vol. 1, 125–26.
[62] Ibid., Vol. 2, 224.

in 1770 by Christian VII, to whom Voltaire had dedicated an *Epistle*; drafting of a Prussian civil code under the reign of Frederick the Great in 1749; and the intellectual influence of the work of Beccaria on the penal legislation of Grand Duke Leopold of Tuscany. Portalis's philosophical spirit, however, was clearly hostile to materialism and atheism. This was shown by the striking manner of the accusation he made in 1763 of Rousseau's *Emile*. Empirical and radically unfavorable to the spirit of the Rousseau's system, Portalis attacks the "abuses of the philosophical spirit" when it stands in opposition to Christian faith.

In the field of legal thought, this eclecticism is reflected in a complex and protean thought, which is often elusive to a secular reader. Jean-François Niort argued that Portalis was both "a man of the Enlightenment and a traditionalist; a conservative and an empiricist; a moralizer and a sociologist,"[63] who was inspired by Montesquieu's pragmatic realism.

Portalis's position on marriage is particularly interesting in this respect. Faithful to the teachings of the school of natural law, he asserted that marriage is neither "a civil act, nor a religious act, but a natural act,"[64] regulated by civil law and "sanctified by religion."[65] In this formula, passed down to posterity, the Gallican jurist seeks a middle way between the theological and legal conceptions of marriage, which he repeatedly sees as "the holiest of contracts,"[66] probably in order to underline its singularity. Writing with a legislator's pen, Portalis sees marriage as, indeed, an indissoluble contract both in nature and in its assigned aim of perpetuating the species.[67] By moderately rallying to the contractual nature of the matrimonial union, Portalis favored the consecration of certain revolutionary legal principles, such as the secularization of marriage, and even the possibility of divorce, in spite of his personal convictions. To the philosophical spirit of the Enlightenment he had grafted

[63] Jean-François Niort, "Retour sur 'l'esprit' du Code civil des Français," *Histoire de la justice* 19, no. 1 (2009) [*Les penseurs du Code civil*]: 137. See also, by the same author, "Les Portalis et l'esprit du XIXe siècle," *Droits* 42, no. 2 (2005): 93–118.

[64] *Discours préliminaire*, 22.

[65] It was also the position taken in his *Rapport* of 29 Prairial, Year V, to the Conseil des Anciens, during the debates on divorce (cited by d'Onorio, *Portalis l'esprit des siècles*, 155–56). See Joël-Benoît d'Onorio, "L'esprit du Code civil selon Portalis. D'un siècle à l'autre…," *Droits* 42, no. 2 (2005): 75–92.

[66] Notably in Conseil des Anciens, 27 Thermidor, Year V, *Rapport fait par Portalis sur la résolution du 29 prairial an V*, 27, and in his *Preliminary Speech* (p. 31). He reuses this expression by Rousseau; see the fragment of *Émile* that Portalis transcribed in the notes of his *Consultation sur la validité du mariage des protestants* (Bibliothèque de la Cour de cassation, ms. 501, 199).

[67] Sylvain Bloquet, "Le mariage, un 'contrat perpétuel par sa destination' (Portalis)," *Napoléonica. La Revue* 14, no. 2 (2012): 74–110.

his liberal Gallican Catholicism. In his *Preliminary Speech*, Portalis explained that divorce is a consequence of a political regime that admitted freedom of worship and freedom of religious conscience, for which he had pleaded for so long, notably in his *Consultation on the Validity of Protestant Marriage*. Since "we need laws for all," he rationalizes, "we have therefore believed that we should not prohibit divorce to ourselves." On this point, Portalis's general philosophy is marked by sociologism and moderation: maintaining divorce is justified by the new social, political, and religious configuration of France at the dawn of the nineteenth century.

If a moderating spirit permeates the legislator's reflection and the texts of his marriage project, Portalis emphasizes points of divergence with revolutionary legislation. Having abandoned all desire to regenerate humanity, he decries the revolutionary legislation of 1789 that dissolved the very fabric of society through the relaxation of marriage bonds and the breaking of old customs.[68] In a break with the Revolution, the Code bears the unavoidable mark of a return to order within the broader Bonapartist political project. Portalis was, of course, aware of this return to the traditional model of social regulation, which thus announced the forthcoming moral order of the nineteenth century. On March 19, 1804 (28 Ventose, Year XII), in front of the legislature, he saluted the work of the lawmaker who "laid down wise rules for the government of families," "restored the magistracy of fathers," and "reiterated the means that guaranteed the submission of children."[69] Regarding divorce, Portalis was very unfavorable to the introduction of "incompatibility of mood" or "mutual consent" as valid causes, as he had already had the opportunity to express from the rostrum of the Council of Elders in 1797.[70] It is a question of preventing "the holiest of contracts from becoming the play thing of caprice, inconstancy, or even the object of all the shameful speculations of a low avidity."[71]

The debates on marriage highlight Portalis's complex and apparently variegated thoughts. He was a man of the Enlightenment and yet a traditionalist,

[68] Pierre-Antoine Fenet, *Recueil complet des travaux préparatoire du Code civil* (Paris, 1836), Vol. 1, xcix.

[69] Ibid., cii–ciii.

[70] Éric Gasparini, "Regards de Portalis sur le droit révolutionnaire: la quête du juste milieu," *Révolutionnaire française* 328 (2002): 121–33.

[71] *Discours préliminaire*, 31. If the project of Year X rejected these causes for divorce, judged too voluntarist and revolutionary, divorce by mutual consent was, however, restored by the intervention of Bonaparte at the State Council, preferring the "light of reason" over "religious prejudice" (Antoine-Claire Thibaudeau, *Mémoires sur le Consulat, 1799 à 1804* [Paris, 1827], 448).

too – both a conservative and a sociologist. The lawyer from Aix demonstrated a liberal Catholicism, deeply anchored in the traditions of *Ancien Régime* France while, at the same time, turned towards the progress of a changing society. It is this spirit that marks the preparation of the Organic Articles and the implementation of the Concordat.

THE IMPLEMENTATION OF THE CONCORDAT

Although Portalis's name is attached to the Concordat, he was neither its negotiator nor its editor. The responsibility for religion was entrusted to the Aix lawyer only three months after the signing of the treaty with the Holy See on July 15, 1801 (26 Messidor, Year IX).[72] His biographers, such as Joel Benoît d'Onorio,[73] however, suggest that Portalis participated unofficially in the negotiations for this treaty, whose ambition was to restore religious peace and ensure the support of the Holy See and Catholic France for the future emperor. On the other hand, Portalis was given the task of drafting the Organic Articles and presenting the provisions of the Cocordat before the State Council and, again, before the Legislative Body, on April 5, 1802 (15 Germinal, Year X).

At the head of the General Directorate of Religion, Portalis worked directly with the consuls to whom he needed to present all the bills, regulations, orders, and decisions in matters of worship. The appointment decree of October 8, 1801 (15 Vendémiaire, Year X) also proposed the appointment of the first consul and decided who would be considered apt to occupy the position of minister within various denominations; Portalis examined all the rescripts, bulls, and writs of the Court of Rome before their publication in France. Immediately, Portalis strove to draft the Organic Articles, which unilaterally complemented the Concordat negotiated between France and the Holy See. In the absence of any negotiations with the pope, these Organic Articles appeared a real coup, aimed at exercising control over the affairs of the Church. Under these 77 additional articles, government authorization was now required for the mere receipt, publication, and execution of any document or appointment from Rome.[74] Like any official, the bishops also had to reside in their diocese. Their movements were further restricted, as they could

[72] Franck Bouscau, "Portalis et les cultes," in d'Onorio, *Portalis le Juste*, 123–48. The activity of Portalis is equally documented by an edition of Frédéric Portalis of *Discours, rapports et travaux inédits sur le Concordat de 1801* (Paris, 1845).

[73] D'Onorio, *Portalis l'esprit des siècles*, 243.

[74] Art. 1.

no longer leave their diocese without the express permission of the first consul.[75] In addition, parish priests had to take an oath of loyalty to the new regime before the prefect of their department, who exercised control over the diocesan clergy.[76] Even the priests were obliged to pray and have the parishioners pray for "the prosperity of the French republic and for the consuls."[77] With these additional articles, the State Council was firmly established as arbiter of ecclesiastical disputes.[78]

Written under the leadership of Portalis, these provisions clearly reveal the instrumentalization of Catholic worship in favor of the emerging Napoleonic regime. Moreover, the Organic Articles appear as concrete translations of Gallican positions previously held by Portalis. This policing regulation is, in fact, only the translation of the Gallicanism he expressed earlier, especially in the booklet published in 1765 titled *Principles on the Distinction of the Two Powers – Spiritual and Temporal.*

Faced with a *fait accompli,* and in the absence of any negotiations, the pope did not fail to express his disapproval, in a consistory address followed by a detailed note of protest handed to Portalis and Talleyrand (1754–1838), the Minister of Foreign Relations. Though Gallican, the state councillor tasked with religion was nevertheless Catholic and remained faithful to the pope. He tried to calm the discord and minimize the importance of the Organic Articles in a diplomatic response sent on January 6, 1804 (15 Nivôse, Year XII) to Cardinal Caprara.[79]

This attachment to the Christian faith and the Church Portalis expressed again in his famous speech on the organization of denominations, delivered during the presentation of the Concordat to the Legislative Body.[80] Were he a supporter of freedom of worship, he certainly would not intend to favor atheism, which he compared to "barbarism."[81] He sought to fight sects and irreligiosity during his ministry, both out of personal conviction and in his role as statesman: the spirit of irreligion, which he once believed to be in Rousseau's writings, he indeed saw as a threat to both morals and the social order.

75 Art. 20.
76 Art. 27.
77 Art. 51.
78 Art. 6–8.
79 D'Onorio, *Portalis l'esprit des siècles*, 248.
80 Speech published in 1802: *Organisation des cultes. Discours du Citoyen Portalis, orateur du Gouvernement, au Corps législatif* (s.l., 1802). This speech is critically commented upon by Chartier, *Portalis: le père du Code civil*, 261–68 as well as by d'Onorio, *Portalis l'esprit des siècles*, 249–56.
81 *Organisation des cultes*, 17.

A virulent detractor of atheism, Portalis nevertheless preached a spirit of tolerance and moderation when referring to the atheist and the fanatic. "Religious tolerance is a duty," he said, "a human virtue" which, legally, supposes "the respect of government for the conscience of citizens, and for their objects of veneration."[82] Reviewing the provisions of the Concordat, he finally employed an openly Gallican interpretation of the treaty, ensuring the preponderance of civil power over the Holy See. This speech, delivered by the man who would become minister of religion, on July 18, 1804, is a masterpiece of balance, mixing the Christian faith of the author, Gallicanism, and tolerance.

Portalis's decision to ensure religious peace is clearly not trivial. The choice of this liberal Catholic, torn between the philosophical spirit of the Enlightenment and a respect for tradition, made it possible to "console misfortunes," to "suppress malice," to "rally all hearts," and to reconcile "the revolution with heaven."[83] Carried off by illness in 1807, Portalis had little time to benefit from the national harmony that he thought he had achieved with the Civil Code and the Concordat.

RECOMMENDED READING

Beaubrun, Marcel, et al., eds. *Le discours et le Code. Portalis, deux siècles après le Code Napoléon*. Paris: LITEC, 2004.

Bloquet, Sylvain. "Le mariage, un 'contrat perpétuel par sa destination' (Portalis)," *Napoléonica. La Revue* 14, no. 2 (2012): 74–110.

Chartier, Jean-Luc. *Portalis: le père du Code civil*. Paris: Fayard, 2004.

D'Onorio, Joël-Benoît. "L'esprit du Code civil selon Portalis. D'un siècle à l'autre...," *Droits* 42, no. 2 (2005): 75–92.

Portalis l'esprit des siècles. Paris: Dalloz, 2005.

Portalis le Juste. Aix-en-Provence: Presses universitaires d'Aix-Marseille, 2004.

Gasparini, Éric. "Regards de Portalis sur le droit révolutionnaire: la quête du juste milieu," *Révolutionnaire française* 328 (2002): 121–33.

Niort, Jean-François. "Les Portalis et l'esprit du XIXe siècle," *Droits* 42, no. 2 (2005): 93–118.

"Portalis, père du Code civil?," *Revue de la recherche juridique-Droit prospectif* 1 (2005): 479–490.

"Retour sur 'l'esprit' du Code civil des Français," *Histoire de la justice* 19, no. 1 (2009) [*Les penseurs du Code civil*]: 137.

82 Ibid., 28.

83 Ibid., 62.

16

Alexis de Tocqueville

(1805–1859)

MARY ANN GLENDON

BIOGRAPHICAL INTRODUCTION

Although Alexis de Tocqueville was both a Christian and a jurist, the literature on his life and work has paid relatively little attention to his religious beliefs or his legal formation. Some might be surprised, therefore, to see him listed as a French Christian jurist. Yet if one should ask what accounts for the stunning insights of this great social theorist, or what enabled him to see so clearly into the roots and trajectories of the political transformations of his time, it would be hard to discount the role of a keen legal mind and a deep religious sensibility.

Alexis de Tocqueville was born into an aristocratic family in 1805, one year after Napoléon Bonaparte initiated the codification of the French legal system with his famous Civil Code. Among Tocqueville's noble ancestors were many eminent jurists, including Chrétien de Malesherbes, a man of the Enlightenment and an early advocate for the civil rights of Protestants and Jews. Malesherbes was renowned for his courage and independence. In 1787, on principle, he resigned his position as Louis XVI's minister of state after the ill-fated monarch failed to make what he regarded as necessary liberalizing reforms. Yet when the king was charged with treason, Malesherbes came out of retirement to defend him. In the Reign of Terror, Malesherbes paid the ultimate price for that decision. He himself ended up on the guillotine, along with several relatives. Tocqueville's parents narrowly escaped the same fate thanks to the fall of Robespierre a few days before they were slated to be executed. One might say that Tocqueville himself was born with one foot in a world that was fast passing away and the other on the threshold of a new world whose outlines were just beginning to become visible.

After the French Revolution, two decades had to elapse before members of royalist families like the Tocquevilles again had opportunities to render high public service. But with the restoration of the Bourbon monarchy in 1814, Tocqueville's father was welcomed into the administration of Louis XVIII, and in 1823, with an eye toward a political future, Alexis de Tocqueville chose to study law. Although his career as a lawyer was to be short-lived, the influence of a legal education based on the Napoleonic codifications is evident in the writings that made him famous.

Napoléon's far-reaching legal reforms had both consolidated the French Revolutionaries' rejection of the country's feudal past and laid the foundation for an economy based on freedom of contract and protection of private property. His five codes, especially the civil code popularly known as the Code Napoléon, were widely admired for having brought legal uniformity to a country where the local laws were so diverse that Voltaire once quipped that a traveler changed his law as often as he changed his horses. For Tocqueville, however, the legal legacy of Napoléon provided an early occasion to ponder the pros and cons of centrally imposed legal uniformity and its relation to the concentration of political power.

On completing his legal studies, Tocqueville took a position as a junior magistrate from which, in the normal course of events, he would have risen within the judiciary. But the times were anything but normal. He was barely three years into his job when the Revolution of 1830 toppled the Bourbon regime and replaced it with the constitutional monarchy of Louis-Philippe, whose supporters among the rising entrepreneurial class looked with suspicion on persons with family ties to the old monarchy.

Under the circumstances, the apprentice judge decided that the best way to pursue his political aspirations would be to take a study trip abroad and to write reports that would gain him public recognition. Accordingly, he and his similarly situated friend Gustav de Beaumont embarked in 1831 on a nine-month journey that took them to most parts of the United States, ostensibly to examine its prison system.

On their return, the two travelers dutifully prepared their report on American penitentiaries.[1] Tocqueville then turned all his energies to writing the first volume of the book that would become his major work, *Democracy in America*. By that time, he was convinced that the advance of some form of democracy was inevitable, that it was driven primarily by a passion for equality, and that the only question was what kind of society it would bring into being. He concluded that the most pressing political challenge of the times was to do all one could to assure that the establishment of democratic regimes would

[1] Gustave de Beaumont and Alexis de Tocqueville, *On the Penitentiary System in the United States and its Application in France* (Carbondale: Southern Illinois University Press, 1979).

promote "equality in freedom rather than equality in servitude" (a phrase he would use repeatedly in his works). To that end, he supplemented his firsthand observations with a program of reading, research, and interviews so extensive that he referred to it as his second trip. In that process, he consulted frequently with American lawyers and relied heavily on *The Federalist Papers*, James Kent's *Commentaries on American Law*, and Joseph Story's *Commentaries on the Constitution of the United States*. The result was an instant bestseller that made its author a celebrity on its publication in 1835.

In the book's introduction, Tocqueville described the impulse that was to guide much of his work as a scholar and statesperson in the years ahead. "To me, the Christian nations of our day present an alarming spectacle; the movement which carries them along is already too strong to be halted, but it is not yet so swift that we must despair of directing it; our fate is in our hands, but soon it may pass beyond control" (*DA*, 12).[2] With a predominantly French audience in mind, he wrote that "a kind of religious dread" had impelled him to urge his countrymen not to reach back toward the past, but to seek to derive from democracy all the benefits it might bring, furthering its noblest aims and restraining its dangerous tendencies (*DA*, 12, 245).

Four years later, Tocqueville achieved his goal of election to France's Chamber of Deputies. There he served for twelve years, but without achieving the distinction for which he had yearned. It is likely that his lack of success was due in large part to an independent personality that prevented him from aligning himself with any established political party. By his own lights, however, he acquitted himself honorably, devoting most of his energies to extending the right to vote, abolishing slavery in the colonies, and improving the condition of the working classes and the poor. His literary renown, meanwhile, continued to grow with the publication of the second volume of *Democracy in America* in 1840. Although less acclaimed than its predecessor, it consolidated his reputation as a public intellectual.

That reputation helped him to gain appointment to the drafting commission for a new constitution after the Revolution of 1848, which led to the installation of Napoléon Bonaparte's nephew, Louis Napoléon, as head of state. In 1849, Tocqueveille was appointed minister of foreign affairs, the highest public post he ever attained, only to lose it five months later, when

[2] Except where indicated, all references to *Democracy in America* are from Alexis de Tocqueville, *Democracy in America*, 2 vols., trans. George Lawrence, edn. J. P. Mayer (Garden City, NY: Doubleday Anchor, 1969). The work will be cited in the text as *DA* with the page number.

Louis Napoléon became dissatisfied with the cabinet and dismissed all its members. Tocqueville's fall from favor was complete when he was arrested and briefly imprisoned after joining several other deputies in denouncing the president's increasing arrogation of power.

Disillusioned with politics and experiencing early symptoms of the pulmonary illness that would cause his death in 1859 at the age of 53, Tocqueville withdrew from public life and resumed the work that had first brought him recognition. Although he died before he could finish his history of the French Revolution, he lived to see its first volume, *The Old Regime and the French Revolution*, become a commercial and critical success.

MAJOR THEMES AND CONTRIBUTIONS

The writings that gained lasting recognition for Tocqueville arose from his preoccupation with the inexorable advance of democracy, by which he meant not only a form of government but a new kind of society where equality would be a leading principle. The fact that his aristocratic upbringing had provided him with knowledge of an entirely different way of life helped him to see more clearly than most of his contemporaries what advantages democracy might bring, and what might be lost when aristocratic civilization gave way to democratic habits and attitudes. Stoutly rejecting nostalgia for the *Ancien Régime*, he made it his project to figure out what made democracy work, what hidden forces drove it on, and, above all, what needed to be done to keep it from leading to some new form of despotism. Although convinced that there was no turning back the democratic tide, he firmly believed that human beings to some extent could influence the direction democracy would take.

The democratic experiment underway in the United States was encouraging in his view because it indicated that a free, egalitarian republic was possible. He was careful, however, to avoid any suggestion that America's example could be copied. Each country would have to chart its own course within the context of its own history and circumstances, "but the Americans have shown that we need not despair of regulating democracy by means of laws and mores" (*DA*, 311). The challenges facing all emerging democracies were so novel and formidable that "a new political science" would be needed to maximize the benefits of the new regimes while steering clear of the pitfalls (*DA*, 12).

Tocqueville's contributions to that new science were considerable, as John Stuart Mill was probably the first to realize. On reading his review copy of the first volume of *Democracy in America*, Mill wrote the author to say, "You have changed the face of political philosophy."[3] Tocqueville, like his forerunner Montesquieu, possessed a restless intellect that led him far beyond law into history, political theory, and culture in search of the deep springs and indirect consequences of social phenomena.[4] He is particularly noted for his insistence on the roles of law and culture in maintaining a free, democratic society; his emphasis on the importance of the mediating institutions in which civic character and competence are formed; and his profound but tragic insight that democracy not only depends on certain conditions but helps to shape those conditions, sometimes in ways that threaten the very habits, attitudes, and institutions on which its health depends.

THE PRIORITY OF MORES AMONG THE CONDITIONS THAT FAVOR DEMOCRACY

Of the three factors that Tocqueville saw as having the most decisive influence on a democratic republic's chances for success – its physical circumstances, its laws, and its mores – he accorded paramount importance to the mores (*les moeurs*), a word he used often and by which he meant all the habits, opinions, and attitudes that make up the moral and intellectual state of a people (*DA*, 287). As a lawyer himself, he was keenly aware that even the best legal arrangements are unsteady unless they are supported by the practices and opinions of law-abiding citizens and statespersons. To leave no doubt on the subject, he stated that "one mother thought" had guided all his work. All his studies and experiences, he said, had constantly brought him back to the key role of the mores:

> I find it occupies the central position in my thoughts; all my ideas come back to it in the end ... If in the course of this book I have not succeeded in making the reader feel the importance I attribute to the practical experience of Americans, their habits, their opinions, and, in a word, their mores, in maintaining their laws, I have failed in the main object of my work. (*DA*, 308)

Although mores had first place in his thoughts, law was not far behind. Tocqueville took a deep interest in America's distinctive legal arrangements, both for their role in maintaining democracy and for the great influence law

[3] Hugh Brogan, *Alexis de Tocqueville: A Life* (New Haven, CT: Yale University Press, 2006), 370.

[4] Montesquieu, Rousseau, and Pascal were the three writers with whom Tocqueville said that he "lived a little every day." Alexis de Tocqueville, *Selected Letters on Politics and Society*, trans. James Toupin and Roger Boesche (Berkeley: University of California Press, 1985), 5.

seemed to have exerted on American culture. Having observed the growing centralization of power in France, he looked at the American constitutional design with something like awe, calling it "one of the great discoveries of political science in our age" (*DA*, 156). The framers of the Constitution had managed to create a central government without centralizing every aspect of administration. They gave the national government enough power to reduce the risks of instability and ineffectiveness that had afflicted the new nation under its Articles of Confederation, but they reserved enough power to the states and the people to avoid regulatory reach into every corner of society. In his view, this ingenious system was well suited not only to counter the dangers of majority rule but to foster the development of the skills of self-government.

To fully understand his fascination with details that most Americans took for granted at the time, one must bear in mind that Tocqueville had lived his entire life in a country where centralization of power was as deeply rooted as township government was in the United States. In France, administrative centralization had already begun under the *Ancien Régime*. The French Revolutionaries accelerated the process by abolishing associations they saw as competitors for loyalty with the state, establishing a central registration of civil status, imposing a national identification system, and transferring much of the power of local communes to the national government. The movement to the center continued apace under Napoléon, who, in Tocqueville's words, "surrounded France with a web of centralization which smothered all individual effort and all collective and individual resistance."[5]

It is hardly surprising, therefore, that the French observer marveled at America's independent townships and its multitude of political, social, and religious associations. Besides buffering the power of the state, they served as seedbeds for the formation of the civic competence and character that a self-governing regime would require. Lamenting that not a single European country had understood communal liberty, he warned: "[I]f you take power and independence from a municipality, you may have docile subjects, but you will not have citizens" (*DA*, 62, 68–69).

Tocqueville's admiration for local governments in America was largely based on New England towns, whose small size afforded citizens many opportunities to have a role in government, and whose open town meetings enabled the townsfolk to have a say in setting the conditions under which they lived, worked, and raised their children. Since most people do not come

[5] Quoted in the editors' introduction to Alexis de Tocqueville, *The Old Regime and the Revolution*, trans. Alan Kahan, edn. François Furet and Françoise Mélonio (Chicago: University of Chicago Press, 1998), 55.

naturally to an appreciation of procedure and regularity, he likened these towns to little schools where citizens could acquire the skills needed for the responsible use of freedom, a clear sense of their rights and duties, and a taste for order. Another such free public school was the common experience of jury duty. To Tocqueville, the American jury was much more than an element of the court system. It was an educational setting where citizens received practical lessons about their civil and criminal laws under the tutelage of a black-robed instructor (*DA*, 275).

What he found especially intriguing was the way in which a legalistic spirit had not only presided over the American founding but had penetrated the whole society. He attributed that curious phenomenon in part to the first English settlers, who established forms of self-government in the colonies. To be sure, the settlements of the Pilgrims were far from being exemplary democratic societies. Tocqueville knew that the religious dissenters who came to America seeking freedom to worship God in their own way often persecuted other Christians who worshipped in a manner different from their own. But he discerned in the political organization of these communities "the fertile germ of free institutions" and the origins of "that local independence which is still the mainspring and lifeblood of American freedom" (*DA*, 33, 44).

By the time of Tocqueville's visit, the New England model had spread to many other parts of the country, to the point where he likened that region's townships to "beacons on mountain peaks whose warmth is first felt close by but whose light shines to the farthest limits of the horizon" (*DA*, 35). Even the colonists' eventual revolt against English rule had been fueled by "a mature and thoughtful taste for freedom ... No disorderly passions drove it on; on the contrary, it proceeded hand in hand with a love of order and legality" (*DA*, 72). The Americans had thrown off the English yoke but retained many of England's laws.

The influence of the new nation's large legal profession was another factor that impressed Tocqueville as likely to temper the potential excesses of egalitarianism and majority rule. He observed that the country's legislatures and public offices were teeming with lawyers, most of whom, by training and the nature of their work, had acquired "habits of order, something of a taste for formalities, and an instinctive love for a regular concatenation of ideas" (*DA*, 264). Although a goodly number of lawyers, then as now, were vigorous agents of change, he thought the majority had so much in common that they amounted to something like an aristocracy, a social body that would be a useful counterforce to the unreflective passions of democracy. All in all, it seemed to the French visitor that the American people had acquired "some of the ways and tastes of a magistrate," and that it was not a bad thing for the republic that a legalistic spirit had found its way into the speech and mentalities of the whole society (*DA*, 270).

SEEDBEDS OF COMPETENCE AND CHARACTER

Having insisted on the priority of mores over law, Tocqueville had to deal with the question of how emerging democracies could be assured of an adequate supply of citizens and statespersons who would possess the requisite qualities of character, as well as a degree of competence in the civic arts of deliberation, compromise, consensus-building, civility, and reason-giving.

Tocqueville's treatment of that question made him the first modern writer to elaborate on the political importance of what he called "secondary bodies," the structures of civil society that stand between the individual and the state. In all likelihood, it was the experience of having lived in a country where such bodies had been intentionally marginalized that enabled him to appreciate the value of what Americans simply took for granted. Surely it was France he had in mind when he wrote in a famous passage that "there are countries in Europe" where:

> the inhabitant feels like some sort of farm laborer indifferent to the fate of the place where he dwells. The greatest changes may take place in his country without his concurrence; he does not even know precisely what has happened ... Worse still, the condition of his village, the policing of his road, and the repair of his church and parsonage do not concern him; he thinks that all those things have nothing to do with him at all, but belong to a powerful stranger called the government. (*DA*, 93–94)

When a people has come to that point, he warned, "either they must modify both laws and mores or they will perish, for the fount of public virtues has run dry; there are subjects still but no citizens" (*DA*, 94). Democracies, he argued, would have to come to terms with the likelihood that their very survival depends on the vitality of groups that centralized governments have often regarded as dangerous competitors for their citizens' loyalty.

The most promising seedbeds for the development of the knowledge and skills useful to active citizenship were, in his view, associations and local governments. Those varied settings enabled great numbers of Americans to learn how to keep order among members of a group and to work together toward common goals. At the same time, they promoted freedom by countervailing the power of large, impersonal public and private organizations. As an attentive reader of Rousseau, Tocqueville understood that "partial societies" could pose a threat to good government, but he held that freedom in democracies depended on preserving their autonomy as much as possible.

He also knew that good government required more than civic skills. A healthy democracy would also need a critical mass of citizens who possessed certain qualities of mind and heart. Thus, some of the most insightful passages of *Democracy in America* deal with the political importance of the family and religion – the family as an institution that fosters habits of self-restraint and cooperation, and religion as an institution that helps to counter tendencies toward self-absorption, present-mindedness, and undue preoccupation with material comfort. In particular, he highlighted the roles of women as the main teachers of children: "There have never been free societies without mores, and . . . it is woman who shapes these mores. Therefore everything which has a bearing on the status of women, their habits, and their thoughts is, in my view, of great political importance" (*DA*, 590).

By dwelling on religion as one of the chief supports of free political institutions, Tocqueville was directly challenging the common belief among his French contemporaries that religion was an impediment to the development of free societies. His thinking was quite close, in fact, to that of George Washington, who wrote in his 1796 Farewell Address that

> Of all the dispositions and habits which lead to political prosperity, religion and morality are indispensable supports. In vain would that man claim the tribute of patriotism who should labor to subvert these great pillars of human happiness, these firmest props of the duties of man and citizen.

Tocqueville himself had struggled with religious doubts from the age of 16, when he came across writings in his father's library that shook his childhood faith. It is not known which authors had that effect on him, but decades later, he wrote to a friend that doubt had "hurtled in with an incredible violence," and that from time to time those feelings "take possession of me again . . . and I am lost and bewildered in this universal motion that upsets and shakes all the truths on which I base my beliefs and my actions."[6] From accounts in the two most thorough biographies, it appears that those doubts related more to aspects of Catholic teachings than to the existence of God.[7] Nevertheless, Tocqueville regularly described himself as a practicing Catholic (*DA*, 295).

[6] Letter dated February 26, 1857, quoted in André Jardin, *Tocqueville: A Biography*, trans. Lydia Davis with Robert Hemenway (Baltimore, MD: Johns Hopkins University Press, 1998), 61.

[7] Brogan, *Alexis de Tocqueville*, 625; and the account of Tocqueville's last days by Beaumont, *On the Penitentiary System*, quoted in Jardin, *Tocqueville* at 529.

There is some controversy about his entry into full communion with the Catholic Church in the last months of his life – not about the fact of reconciliation, but about its significance. Biographers André Jardin and Hugh Brogan take a rather dismissive view, with Jardin seeming to believe that doubt is incompatible with faith, and Brogan concluding that since Tocqueville "had always believed in a recognizably Christian God, it was natural that he now found comfort in a ritual which had been an essential part of his happy childhood."[8] It does not seem to have occurred to either biographer that struggle with doubt is a normal feature of Christian life, famously afflicting even the Apostles.[9] As Pascal, one of Tocqueville's favorite writers, put it, "To deny, to believe, and to doubt well are to a man what the race is to a horse."[10]

Regarding the notion that religion could be a mainstay of democracy, Tocqueville had no doubts at all. The hostility to religion common among his fellow heirs of the Enlightenment was, in his view, an unexamined leftover from the old regime, when religious leaders had undermined their own credibility by becoming too closely entwined with government. In *The Old Regime and the Revolution*, he wrote that it was far less as a religious faith than as a political institution that Christianity became an object of revolutionary hatred:

> The priests were not hated because they claimed to regulate the affairs of the other world, but because they were landowners, lords, tithe collectors, and administrators in this one.[11]

In the coming democratic era, he wrote,

> partisans of freedom ... should hasten to call religion to their aid, for they must know that one cannot establish the reign of liberty without that of mores, and mores cannot be firmly founded without beliefs. (*DA*, 17)

The United States, he said, was proof that the spirit of religion and the spirit of liberty could be mutually reinforcing:

[8] Brogan, ibid.; Jardin, *Tocqueville*, 528–32. For excellent discussions of what is known about Tocqueville's religious views and his struggles with faith and doubts, see John Lukacs, "The Last Days of Alexis de Tocqueville," *Catholic Historical Review* 50 (1964): 155–70; and Nolan, *What They Saw in America*, 50–52.

[9] See, e.g., Joseph Ratzinger, *Introduction to Christianity* (San Francisco: Ignatius Press, 1990), 45: "[W]e have already recognized that the believer does not live immune to doubt but is always threatened by the plunge into the void"; see also Ratzinger as Pope Benedict XVI, referring to Peter's "troubled faith," *Angelus* (August 7, 2011).

[10] Blaise Pascal, *Pensées* (New York: Dutton, 1958), 76.

[11] Tocqueville, *The Old Regime and the Revolution*, 97.

> Freedom sees religion as the companion of its struggles and triumphs, the cradle of its infancy, and the divine source of its rights. Religion is considered as the guardian of mores, and mores are regarded as the guardian of the laws and pledge for the maintenance of freedom itself. (*DA*, 47)

Later, he goes so far as to say that religion is "needed in democratic republics most of all" (*DA*, 294). "How," he asks, "could society escape destruction if, when political ties are relaxed, moral ties are not tightened? And what can be done with a people master of itself if is not subject to God?"

DEMOCRACY'S INFLUENCE ON CULTURE

After placing so much emphasis on the role of mores in the maintenance of a free democratic regime, Tocqueville had to confront a central dilemma of democracy: it not only depends on the mores but also helps to shape them, sometimes in ways that endanger its own survival. From Rousseau he had gained a keen sense of how change in the social order can give rise to new feelings and ideas, to the point where a person who lived in one age would be nearly unrecognizable to a person who lived in another.[12] Pondering the advent of democracy in that light, he was particularly uneasy about the potential effects of degraded forms of equality and individualism combined with growing love of material comforts. Certain habits that form in freedom, he warned, could one day become fatal to that freedom (*DA*, 254).

Still drawing on Rousseau, he foresaw that the equality principle would affect nearly every aspect of society, including the character of the citizens. The idea of equality, he wrote, "extends far beyond political mores and laws, exercising dominion over civil society as much as over government; it creates opinions, gives birth to feelings, suggests customs, and modifies whatever it does not create" (*DA*, 9). While applauding the "manly and legitimate passion for equality which rouses in all men a desire to be strong and respected," he warned that "the human heart also nourishes a debased taste for equality, which leads the weak to want to drag the strong down to their level and which induces men to prefer equality in servitude to inequality in freedom" (*DA*, 57). "Every central power," he wrote, "instinctively worships uniformity and loves the passion for equality that resents every distinction it sees" (*DA*, 673).

[12] Jean-Jacques Rousseau, Second Discourse, in *The Social Contract and Discourses*, trans. G. D. H. Cole (New York: Dutton, 1973), 104.

Similarly, where individualism was concerned, Tocqueville noted with concern the growth of a kind of individualism that he distinguished both from ordinary selfishness and from the independence of mind that he greatly admired. The individualism he feared consisted of a tendency to withdraw into one's own small sphere of family and friends, focusing on one's private concerns, leaving society at large to itself. That sort of individualism, he saw, would engender indifference to public affairs, which in turn could easily lead to the loss of freedom.

What, he wondered, would be the effect of the combined forces of debased egalitarianism, narrow individualism, and another tendency that democracy seemed to foster: the kind of materialism that gives rise to desires that can never be satisfied? As an attentive reader of Montesquieu, Tocqueville knew that despotic regimes thrive on whatever keeps their subjects separated from one another. Thus, he foresaw that a polity where people were inclined to focus exclusively on their own interests would be susceptible to new and insidious forms of tyranny.

SOFT TYRANNY

In the years between the first and second volumes of *Democracy in America*, Tocqueville became increasingly convinced that tendencies within democracy could lead to a kind of domination that would be different from the despotisms of the past. In the first book, he had been concerned primarily with the well-known dangers of majority rule, and with the way majority power could be exerted subtly through the force of public opinion to the point where people could lose their independence of mind and will. By the time he wrote volume two, his apprehension that freedom could be lost by imperceptible degrees had intensified and merged with his longstanding fears about excessive centralization.

He saw that the passion for equality, together with growing individualism and materialism, could lead to political apathy, which in turn could lead, not to tyranny of the majority, but to some all-encompassing form of dictatorship in which the power of the state would exceed that of ancient tyrants. This new despotism would be milder than the old because people would have lost much of their independence of mind and spirit. That he had a specific case in mind is evident from notes he later made about Napoléon:

> I would like to show... with what incomparable art [Napoléon] discerned in the most demagogic aspects of the Revolution all that was useful for despotism ... I want to contemplate the exertions of that almost divine

> intelligence, grossly employed in shackling human liberty; that perfected, scientific organization of power ... so that intelligence slowed, the human spirit languished, souls shrank, great men no longer emerged.[13]

All over Europe, and in contrast to the United States at the time, Tocqueville saw charitable associations coming under government control, and education being concentrated in the hands of the state. Like John Stuart Mill, with whom he was in contact, he found the state's control over education especially alarming.[14]

> The state receives ... the child from its mother's arms to hand it over to functionaries; it takes the responsibility for forming the feelings and shaping the ideas of each generation. Uniformity prevails in schoolwork as in everything else; diversity, as well as freedom, is daily vanishing. (*DA*, 681)

In the somber vision that pervades much of the second volume of *Democracy in America*, some of the appearance of freedom could be maintained even as real political liberty gradually slipped away. Thus, what the ancients called license, as distinguished from liberty, might actually serve the interests of despots or oligarchs. What could be more convenient for enemies of democracy than a people "so engrossed in a cowardly love of immediate pleasures that ... they will prefer tamely to submit to a strong central power that will attempt to regulate everyone and everything according to a uniform central plan" (*DA*, 645, 670). Men and women preoccupied with personal concerns, small pleasures, and material goods would come willingly under a form of domination quite different from the tyrannies of the past. Imagining what the new, milder tyranny might look like, he wrote that the state's regulatory power "would degrade men rather than torment them":

> I see an innumerable multitude of men, alike and equal, constantly circling around in pursuit of the petty and banal pleasures with which they glut their souls. Each one of them withdrawn into himself, is almost unaware of the fate of the rest ... Over this kind of men stands an immense, protective power which is alone responsible for securing their enjoyment and watching over their fate. That power is absolute, thoughtful of detail, orderly, provident, and gentle. (*DA*, 691–92)

[13] Quoted in Brogan, *Alexis de Tocqueville*, 96–97. See also Tocqueville, *The Old Regime and the Revolution*, 85.

[14] John Stuart Mill, *On Liberty* (Indianapolis, IN: Bobbs-Merrill, 1956), 129.

Anticipating Nietzsche's soulless "last men," who seek only comfort and security, as well as C. S. Lewis's "men without chests," who behave like animals, Tocqueville added that such a government "would, in the end, strip each man there of several of the chief attributes of humanity" (*DA*, 695). Every so often, the subjects would arise, "just long enough to exercise the right to vote for their masters."

Tocqueville's stern and invariable prescription for averting the loss of freedom in democracy was the *practice* of freedom. Tendencies toward debased forms of liberty and equality would have to be countered by habits of political participation and association. That would require wise laws, decentralized administration, local governments, independent judges, political and social associations, a free press, and, above all, habits and attitudes formed first in families and furthered by religion, "the guardian of the mores." Religion (by which he nearly always meant Christianity) would help to take people out of themselves and to work toward distant goals. Associations would keep people aware that they live in a society. And an enlightened view of self-interest would make an individual understand that he or she benefits from considering others, respecting their rights, helping persons in need, and giving time to public service.

Though sometimes criticized for his description of self-interest as "the only stable point in the human heart" (*DA*, 239), Tocqueville did not go so far as Machiavelli to dismiss the idea of virtue. Rather, he is close to Aristotle's *Ethics* when he says that self-interest rightly understood

> cannot make a man virtuous, but its discipline shapes a lot of orderly, temperate, moderate, careful and self-controlled citizens. If it does not lead the will directly to virtue, it establishes habits which unconsciously turn it that way. (*DA*, 527)

Tocqueville's unpublished notes shed further light on his thinking about enlightened self-interest and its relation to Christianity:

> There is, finally, a doctrine infinitely purer, more elevated, less material, according to which the basis of actions is duty. Man penetrates divine thought with his intelligence. He sees that the purpose of God is order, and he freely associates himself as much as he is able with this great design ... Thus Christianity at one end touches the doctrine of interest well understood and at the other the doctrine that I developed afterward and that I could call with Christianity itself, the doctrine of the love of God. In sum, a religion very superior in terms of loftiness to the doctrine of interest well understood because it places interest in the other world and draws us out of this cesspool of human and material interests. The doctrine of [self-interest]

> well understood can make men honest. But it is only that of the love of God that makes men virtuous. The one teaches how to live, the other teaches how to die, and how can you make men who do not want to die live well for long?[15]

GENERAL APPRAISAL AND INFLUENCE

Tocqueville's profound understanding of democracy's strengths and weaknesses, his gift for predictions,[16] and his graceful writing style have earned him generations of readers, and his works a lasting place among the landmarks of Western political and social thought. Those works defy conventional classification, for the independent spirit that proved such an obstacle to Tocqueville's political career led him to range far and wide among legal, historical, political, philosophical, and what we would now call sociological materials. Today he is quoted and claimed as a kindred soul by men and women across the political spectrum. Sociologists, political theorists, and historians regard him as one of their own.

His masterpiece, the two-volume *Democracy in America*, has become a classic, as predicted by John Stuart Mill, who in his review of the first volume called it, "the beginning of a new era in the science of politics."[17] Tocqueville's posthumously published memoir, *Recollections*, is regarded by many as the best account of the Revolution of 1848. Although *The Old Regime and the Revolution* was only the first part of a projected work, it is a major contribution to the understanding of the causes and consequences of the French Revolution (which he defined as a continuous process extending from 1789 through the Napoleonic regime).

Tocqueville's work has influenced and continues to influence the human sciences in major respects. His love of liberty and his reflections on the power of public opinion found an early and appreciative audience in Mill, who drew deeply from *Democracy in America* when he wrote his famous essay *On Liberty*. Tocqueville's analysis of the dangers of excessive centralization is an important tributary to the literature on what today would be called the theory

[15] Tocqueville, *Democracy in America*, vol. 3, trans. James Schleifer, edn. Eduardo Nolla (Indianapolis: Liberty Fund, 2010), 924–25.

[16] Often noted, although not entirely original with Tocqueville, is his prediction that the United States and Russia would be the two nations where the drama of emerging democracy would be played out, one trending toward equality in freedom, the other toward equality in servitude under a despotic regime (*DA*, 413).

[17] Brogan, *Alexis de Tocqueville*, 371.

of subsidiarity, an approach to the distribution of powers among levels of government and to the allocation of social tasks between governmental and private entities.[18] His analyses of the roles of local governments and the mediating groups of civil society in promoting freedom have inspired a voluminous literature on the political importance of families, local communities, and all sorts of associations.[19]

No writer has probed the dilemmas of democracy more deeply than Tocqueville. Yet the central themes of his work deal less with democracy as such than with the relation of equality to freedom; indeed, he often used the words equality and democracy interchangeably. One of the most important lessons he wished to impart was that freedom takes work. The benefits of equality are readily apparent, while the advantages of political liberty are seen only over time. Thus, the spirit of liberty is always in danger of being overwhelmed by the passion for equality, and democracies are always vulnerable to degenerating into forms of tyranny:

> A great deal of intelligence, knowledge, and skill are required in these circumstances to organize and maintain secondary powers and to create among individually weak citizens, free associations which can resist tyranny without destroying public order. (*DA*, 676)

Tocqueville is sometimes called a melancholy liberal because his great love of liberty coexisted with a tragic sensibility. He had a keen sense of the perils lurking in every advance, of the obverse side of many virtues, and of the flaws in human nature. He understood that many of democracy's defects are so tied to its merits that they can be moderated but not cured. But he never wavered in his insistence on the ability of human beings in society to affect the course of events. His closing words to readers of *Democracy in America* were a call to action:

> The nations of our day cannot prevent conditions of equality from spreading in their midst. But it depends upon themselves whether equality is to lead to servitude or freedom, knowledge or barbarism, prosperity or wretchedness. (*DA*, 705)

[18] Subsidiarity is based on the notion that, in general, social tasks should be handled at the lowest level that can deal with them adequately, thus giving people the maximum opportunity to have a say in setting the conditions under which they live.

[19] E.g., Robert A. Nisbet, *The Quest for Community* (Oxford: Oxford University Press, 1969); Robert N. Bellah, et al., *Habits of the Heart* (Berkeley: University of California Press, 1985); Robert Putnam, *Bowling Alone* (New York: Simon & Schuster, 2000).

RECOMMENDED READING

Aron, Raymond. "Tocqueville." In *Main Currents in Sociological Thought*. Vol. 1, 237–302. Garden City, NY: Doubleday Anchor, 1968.

Brogan, Hugh. *Alexis de Tocqueville: A Life*. New Haven, CT: Yale University Press, 2006.

Damrosch, Leopold. *Tocqueville's Discovery of America*. New York: Farrar, Straus, and Giroux, 2010.

Fortin, Ernest. "A Tocquevillean Perspective on Religion and the American Regime." In *Ever Ancient, Ever New: Ruminations on the City, the Soul, and the Church*, edited by Michael Foley, 147–62. Lanham, MD: Rowman & Littlefield, 2007.

Glendon, Mary Ann. "Tocqueville the Politician." In her *The Forum and the Tower*. New York: Oxford University Press, 2011.

Jardin, André. *Tocqueville: A Biography*. Translated by Lydia Davis with Robert Hemenway. Baltimore, MD: Johns Hopkins University Press, 1998.

Manent, Pierre. *Tocqueville and the Nature of Democracy*. Translated by John Waggoner. Lanham, MD: Rowman & Littlefield, 1996.

Mansfield, Harvey. *Tocqueville*. New York: Oxford University Press, 2010.

Mansfield, Harvey, and Delba Winthrop. "Editors' Introduction." In *Alexis de Tocqueville, Democracy in America*, translated by Mansfield and Winthrop, xvii–lxxxvi. Chicago: University of Chicago Press, 2000.

Nolan, James L., Jr. *What They Saw in America: Alexis de Tocqueville, Max Weber, G. K. Chesterton, and Sayyid Qutb*. New York: Cambridge University Press, 2016.

Tocqueville, Alexis de. *Democracy in America*. 2 vols. Translated by George Lawrence, edited by J. P. Mayer. Garden City, NY: Doubleday Anchor, 1969.

The Old Regime and the Revolution. Translated by Alan Kahan, edited by François Furet and Françoise Mélonio. Chicago: University of Chicago Press, 1998.

Recollections. Translated by George Lawrence. Garden City, NY: Doubleday Anchor, 1971.

Selected Letters on Politics and Society. Translated by James Toupin and Roger Boesche. Berkeley: University of California Press, 1985.

Zetterbaum, Marvin. "Tocqueville." In *History of Political Philosophy*, edited by Leo Strauss and Joseph Cropsey, 761–82. 3rd edn. Chicago: University of Chicago Press, 1987.

17

Paul Viollet

(1840–1914)

ANNE-SOPHIE CHAMBOST

BIOGRAPHICAL INTRODUCTION

Born in Tours on October 24, 1840, Paul Viollet passed away in his apartment at the Paris Law Faculty on November 22, 1914, aged 74. Chief librarian of the Paris Law Faculty since 1876, he came from a traditional background. A father of seven children, he was seemingly an archetype of French petty bourgeoisie, but under a classical appearance, and evolving in the environment of the Paris Law Faculty, this intellectual Catholic and legal historian scholar was committed to some of the many fights that divided French society at the end of the century.

Paul Viollet's family origins immerse us in the youth of a Legitimist, or Royalist, Catholic of the French provinces during the second half of the nineteenth century. The childhood education of this son of a director of a silk factory was overseen by Abbot Eugène-Jean Viot, a former faculty member (he was a professor of Latin, and author of two books on this subject, published in 1857). The decision for Viollet to study at the École des Chartes was not made *a priori* to emancipate the young man from his surroundings among the French Catholic lower-middle class. The school was founded by order of Louis XVIII in 1821, during the Restoration, and reorganized in 1846 during the July Monarchy by a government ordinance of François Guizot. After the disruption of the French Revolution, the school was intended to renew French historiography through the study of archival files and manuscripts, many of which had been confiscated during the Revolution; more prosaically, it would also train young scholars in historical work, to be recruited later as curators and archivists.

Paul Viollet graduated as valedictorian with the bachelor of law degree from the École des Chartes in 1862. After a brief period as secretary-archivist in his hometown of Tours (1863–66), he became an archivist at the Library of the

Archives of the Empire (predecessor of *Archives Nationales*) before applying for and receiving an appointment as chief librarian of the Paris Law Faculty in 1876 (he would also be appointed archivist in 1878). His founding membership in the Société de l'histoire de Paris and his other scholarly activities allowed Viollet to join the Académie des inscriptions et belles lettres in 1887. At first glance, this is nothing but a classic scholar's biography.

Although he was appointed professor of legal history at the École des Chartes (1890), the atypical character of Viollet led him to retain simultaneously his (modest) librarian's position at the Paris Law Faculty. This unusual combination had its coherence, however: as we shall see, for this tireless worker the activities of librarian, archivist, and legal historian fed into each other. Above all, behind a very conventional appearance, Viollet in fact had a complex profile: in his commitments, this liberal Catholic did not hesitate to go against his surroundings.

PROFESSOR AND (LEGAL) HISTORIAN

His dual institutional positioning led Paul Viollet into a potentially ambiguous situation: he worked every day in the Paris Law Library, where some professors considered him as one of their own – even though he was neither a doctor of law nor a qualified teacher of law (a fact that barred him from applying for professorships in law faculties[1]); it was an unlikely situation, because law professors tended rather to consider librarians as merely guardians of book collections! Owing to his obligations in the law library, he usually spent time only in passing at the École des Chartes, where he was recruited in 1890, after having filled in for Adolphe Tardif in 1881–82.

Viollet immediately associated teaching with educational writing: since the curriculum of the École des Chartes involved scientific and vocational training, the textbooks he wrote for his students at the École were faithful to this double vocation. In 1884 he published the first part of his *Précis de l'histoire du droit français, accompagné de notions de droit canonique* (1884–86, reprinted in 1893 and 1905); in 1890, at the time of his recruitment with permanent tenure to the chair of civil law and canon law, he published *Histoire des institutions politiques et administratives de la France* (completed in 1898 and 1903). To harmonize the two works after the publication of this second textbook, Viollet changed the title of the *Précis* to *Histoire du droit privé*. But this medievalist also dedicated research to the period of the *Ancien*

[1] Contra Paul Fournier, who defended two doctoral thesis, one at the Paris Law School and the other one at the École des chartres; see Chapter 18 on Paul Fournier.

Régime (*Le Roi et ses ministres pendant les trois derniers siècles de la Monarchie*, published in 1912) as well as to the French Revolution: the foreword of his translation of Adolphe Schmidt's four-volume *Paris pendant la révolution* (published in 1880, 1885, and 1890) is republished in the chapter "French Law in the Age of the Revolution," a contribution of Paul Viollet to the *Cambridge Modern History*, edited by Lord Acton, Stanley Mortaund Leathes, Adolphus William Ward, and George Walter Prothero (1904).[2]

Viollet did not clarify his method, but the preliminary chapter of his handwritten thesis for École des Chartes offers an interesting statement that justifies recourse to legal history for understanding and analyzing society and its development (*Étude sur la cour du Vicomte, ou juridiction bourgeoise en Orient au temps des croisades*, January 25, 1862[3]). Taking an opposite tack, Raoul Grand, his successor at the École des Chartes, would distinguish in his inaugural lecture the method of a professor of legal history from the method of his former master:

> one studies old French law as a simple introduction to current law, which is his real object . . . One's other purpose is to teach you the direction of private institutions of old France, its genesis and its evolutions, to allow you to understand old texts in their spirit and in their expression.[4]

In French Law Schools, a course in the general history of public and private French law (*histoire générale du droit français public et privé*) was established by a decree of December 28, 1880; Adhémar Esmein embodied this new discipline, on which he imposed his republican vision to make legal history a history of institutions. For that first generation of professors, legal history was not only a reservoir of patterns, useful for the understanding of substantive law: it was *the* scientific approach for the study of law. With his textbooks, Paul

[2] Adolphe Schmidt, *Paris pendant la Révolution d'après les rapports de la police secrète, 1789–1800*, translation and foreword by Paul Viollet (Paris: Champion librairie, 1880 [vol. 1], 1885 [vol. 2], 1890 [vol. 3]. See the interesting warning by Viollet about the complexity of the analysis of the French Revolution: "if the historian is focused on the pathetic history of men and on events, if he follows the short-lived fate of constitutions, there is a risk he misses excellent results in civil or even in political order; with an excessive, complacent, emphasis on the 'victories of 1789', there is a threat of neglecting to bring the lector's attention on political inexperience of this great drama's actors, on one's faults and on other's crimes ; the historian risks to give the Revolution an original and creative power, largely overstated: one should not forget that the greatest transformations realized in 1789 had been matured by the slow effect of times, they were necessary benefits, from an historical necessity."

[3] See expo-paulviollet.univ-paris1.fr/galerie-le-professeur/

[4] Roger Grand, *L'histoire du droit français. Ses règles, sa méthode, son utilité. Leçon d'ouverture du cours d'histoire du droit professé à l'Ecole des Chartes (3 novembre 1919)*, 1920.

Viollet was an agent in the development of French legal history. Elsewhere I have pointed out how the textbooks of Paul Viollet differed in style and content from those of Adhémar Esmein, Ernest Glasson, and Paul Brissaud, law professors who also published some of the first textbooks in legal history.[5] Moreover, Viollet conceived legal history

> as a collective work to which a crowd of workers contributes, from any language and any nation, personally unknown to each other, but collaborating from a distance, each providing their own contribution to the common building.

Viollet perfectly illustrated this concept, for instance, in his own textbook of private legal history while stressing significant progress in the study of Roman law at the end of the nineteenth century.[6]

There does not seem to have been a significant difference between Viollet's textbook on the history of private law and the course he offered at the École des Chartes.[7] But Viollet's writings reflect as much the work of the librarian as that of the archivist: his textbooks are distinguished both by the mass of bibliographic references and by numerous references in footnotes to his work in archives, which was the basis of his professional practice. It is also striking that Viollet never imposed in his books a *discourse of authority*: on the contrary, his scientific discourse was always based on *his* working hypotheses, *his* doubts, and *his* refutations. He mostly discussed interpretations of manuscripts, both in the main body of his text and in his numerous footnotes; he confronted sources to counter certain studies and make further proposals.[8] Finally, there is the very rich bibliography of his textbooks, which should be put into perspective with the monitoring of legal literature he organized at the Paris Law Library, where one of the most important activities of his team consisted precisely in keeping updated bibliometric forms, which were very useful for researchers.[9]

[5] Anne-Sophie Chambost, "A propos des manuels d'histoire du droit de Paul Viollet," *Colloque Paul Viollet*, Ecole des Chartes, septembre 2015 forthcoming.

[6] Paul Viollet, *Droit privé et sources. Histoire du droit civil français* (Paris: Larose, 1893), VII: 27–28.

[7] Henri-François Delaborde, "Notice sur la vie et les travaux de M. Paul Viollet," *Bibliothèque de l'Ecole des Chartes* (1918): 147–75.

[8] For instance, see Viollet, *Droit privé et sources*, 181–82 (about the anteriority of the book of *Jostice et Plet* compared with the *Etablissements de Saint Louis*).

[9] Anne-Sophie Chambost, "Un lieu de conservation, de diffusion et d'élaboration des manuels. La bibliothèque de la Faculté de droit de Paris à l'époque de Paul Viollet (1876–1914)," in *Histoire des manuels de droit*, edited by Anne-Sophie Chambost (Paris: Lextenso-LGDJ, 2014), 35–50.

But Paul Viollet also related to the works of nonjurist historians. Besides his scholarly works for the Académie des sciences morales et politiques and the *Bibliothèque de l'École des Chartes* (*BEC*, the review published by École des Chartes, to which he contributed many articles and reports[10]), Viollet was distinguished by his critical edition of the *Établissements de Saint Louis* (four volumes published between 1881 and 1886). A Catholic historian, he was also the author of a digest titled *Œuvres chrétiennes des familles royales en France*, a set of prayers and kings' religious fragments. All of these areas of study enabled him to discuss the underlying subject of relations between church and state, crucial for this Catholic who favored reunification of French Catholics with the State, and who dedicated his life to the reconciliation of French Catholics with their national history. He supported the *Revue critique d'histoire et de littérature* (1866), launched by Paul Meyer and Gaston Paris, two of his classmates at the École des Chartes.

But Viollet was finally, and above all, the contemporary of the *école méthodique* (methodical school), which emancipated historical research from any philosophical speculations; the symbolic media of this school of thought were the *Revue Historique* of Gabriel Monod (1876, to which Viollet sent book reviews) and Langlois and Seignobos's *Introduction aux études historiques* (*Introduction to Historical Studies*, 1898). For those who defended this method, to make history a science presupposed work on documents (preserving, inventorying, and classifying them), which required not only an internal criticism of a document's content but also an external analysis of the work (elaboration of index and forms, and listing of the work's sources, nature, creators, and date and place of creation); after that, it was possible for the historian to achieve synthetic operations: comparison (which allows one to establish facts) and grouping of documents in large frameworks, from which, by deduction and analogy, the historian could fill in the gaps of his documentation. Paul Viollet's textbooks offer an interesting implementation of this method.

A bachelor of law with a diploma from the École des Chartes, where he taught legal history, Viollet prompts the question whether he was in the final analysis a jurist or a historian. In 1890, Eugène de Rozière offered an opinion to the Council of Improvement of the École des Chartes, which met to nominate the future chair holder in private legal history: Viollet was considered more of a historian, while his competitor, Adolphe Tardif's son, would

[10] *BEC* is one of the oldest French scientific journals, created in 1839 for the diffusion of Chartistes' scholarly works.

have "a more jurisconsult nature."[11] Yet Viollet's scholarly productions are without doubt those of a legal historian, and they contributed unquestionably to the institutionalization of that academic discipline.[12] Adhémar Esmein's *Cours élémentaire d'histoire du droit français*, published in 1892, overrode other competitors in public legal history, explaining why Viollet's *History of Public Law* textbook failed to be republished, compared to his *History of Private Law* textbook (published three times). It must also be remembered that Viollet's textbooks were among the reference books (*usuels*) of the Paris Law Library, on the same level as those of jurist professors. This was not due only to his status as chief librarian, however, as lecturers in law recommended his books in the bibliographies of their own textbooks. (Viollet indicated, moreover, that Esmein and Henri Monnier, professor in Caen, had reviewed his manuscripts.)

In contrast to those of his fellow law professors, Paul Viollet's textbooks demonstrate the importance of sources for novice archivists, for whom the professor indicates the stakes in the hierarchization of sources in historic research. But above and beyond legal texts, he also drew attention to the necessity of popular heritage, which composed an essential common fund.[13] Offering the reverse of a view of history centered only on ideas or abstract understandings of formalism and a contemporary trend for dogmatism, Viollet developed a realistic conception of legal history, in which a critical analysis of texts, centered on facts, should inform the legal reality of each era. For him (as well as for his colleague Jean-Baptiste Brissaud), history could strive for conformity with science only if it produced general laws – otherwise it would be only "a directory, an inventory of political and social fragments." That is how, for instance, in describing a society in tension between innovative and conservative forces, he developed his textbook of historical public law around both the law of division of labor and functions and the law of progressive centralization.[14] But Viollet also shared his contemporaries' faith in the laws of evolution, which filled the "spirit of French law" with a shape of *continuism*.[15] He played so much on this trope that it sometimes even gives his speech

[11] See Patrick Arabeyre and Frédéric Audren, *Paul Viollet (1840–1914), bibliothécaire, professeur et historien du droit, "Un grand savant assoiffé de justice"* : expo-paulviollet.univ-paris1.fr.

[12] Chambost, "Un lieu de conservation, de diffusion et d'élaboration des manuels."

[13] Paul Viollet, *Droit public* (Paris: Larose, 1898), 15 ("I repeat it: the history of science has to take into account not only political and legal history but also this contribution of the vulgar, which plays a very big role").

[14] Ibid., introduction.

[15] Ibid., 16 and 17 note ("Evolution in the physical order is a pure hypothesis. Evolution in the social and political order is a fact, an undeniable fact.").

the character of a narrative: his textbooks confirm the idea of an evolving trajectory of law, made from progress and *regrès* (an expression of Elisée Reclus).[16]

Michel de Certeau has since underscored that "a reading of the past, even though it is based on documents, is always led by a reading of the present"[17] (that is, current considerations); Paul Viollet's textbooks confirm this analysis. He did not openly express any political commitment. Unlike Esmein's republican involvement, he did not reveal any political partisanship; his writings show a political mix of liberal and conservative. Nevertheless, very strong social convictions emerge from his textbooks – in the criticism of the exploitation of both colonized peoples and workers and women in modern capitalist society.[18] These convictions are especially clear in his resolute struggle against any form of anticlericalism, which appears to be the counterpart of his struggle against anti-Semitism at the time of the Dreyfus Affair (see below). This ideological aspect of Paul Viollet's textbooks, which is never prescribed or imposed from above but appears in the course of his illustrations, gives his textbooks a political value that makes them interesting testimonies of the times in which they were written; it also highlights the many personal commitments of their author.

THE CHALLENGES OF AN INVOLVED CHRISTIAN CITIZEN DURING THE THIRD REPUBLIC

Paul Viollet was a proponent of natural law theory: his conception of law was based on values and principles superior to substantive or positive law, which should deal with those principles. That being said, however, his thoughts did not enlist him in the ranks of conservatives and even less in those of counterrevolutionaries. Although a Catholic, Paul Viollet was a republican – even while the republican never forgot in turn that he was a Catholic! He illustrated, in sum, what Émile Littré called "Catholicism according to universal suffrage."[19] Yet such a positioning is not straightforward, and it placed Viollet in opposition to the upholders of clericalism (in French, the word had been used since the 1850s). Clericalists denied the separation between the

[16] E.g., ibid., 19.
[17] Michel de Certeau, *L'écriture de l'histoire* (Paris: Gallimard, 1975).
[18] Viollet, *Droit privé et sources*, 292–94, 380–81.
[19] Jean-Louis, Clément, "Un canoniste mis à l'Index en 1906: Paul Viollet (1840–1914)," *Revista critica de Derecho Canonico Pluriconfessional* (2014/1): 81–96.

spiritual and the temporal and followed the line drawn by Pope Pius IX in the Encyclical *Quanta Cura* (December 8, 1864), which condemned the "monstruous errors" of the nineteenth century (among others, naturalism, secularism, and anticlericalism). But one also should never forget, by contrast, the persistent suspicion with which the Third Republic regarded clerics, who were targeted in many purges. Education in religious congregations was particularly intended for reform, with the aim of a "*républicanisation*" of the elites (an intention still active until after World War I), which proposed to substitute secular education for congregational schools. With mixed feelings, Paul Viollet sought to reconcile his understanding of law and justice with his Catholic convictions.

Within the framework of the Dreyfusard struggle, he was one of the founding members of the Human Rights League, whose statutes he helped write in 1898. The following year, he became the president of the Committee for Protection and Defense of Natives (created in 1893), and he created the Catholic Committee for the Defense of Rights. The study of each of these commitments in turn will highlight the way in which the struggles of the private man help to understand the knowledge of the legal historian, since his historical studies overlapped with contemporary issues.

THE DREYFUS AFFAIR[20] AND THE HUMAN RIGHTS LEAGUE

As a Catholic and jurist, Paul Viollet confounded expectations by not reverting to *anti-Dreyfusisme*. He admitted to having been convinced of the innocence of the Jewish captain after a close study of Dreyfus's handwriting; his commitment in the case did not depend only on this, obviously, but it seems quite symptomatic that the professor at École des Chartes stressed his knowledge of palaeography – at a time when historians were beginning to be sought as experts before the courts. From then on, Viollet would engage in an

[20] The Dreyfus Affair begun in 1894 with treason charges against Captain Alfred Dreyfus, a member of the staff of the Ministry of War (he was alleged to have delivered secret documents to the German Empire). While proclaiming his innocence, Dreyfus was demoted and condemned to hard labor for life and sent to the penal colony of Guyana (Devil's Island). Involving judicial plot and espionage, the affair occurred in a context of tensions within a French army weakened after the defeat of 1870 by Prussia, anti-Semitism, and hostility bred by nationalism and hegemonic rivalry with the German Empire. The affair revealed the deep cleavages of French society, durably divided between supporters and opponents of Dreyfus. The press played a major role in the evolution of French public opinion. In 1906, Dreyfus was finally discharged by the Court of Cassation.

attempt to convince the Catholic world to abandon the anti-Dreyfusard cause, applying to this end the modalities of action he would display in his other struggles: mobilization through press coverage and petitions, meetings with political and ecclesiastical officials, and, above all else, the structuring of the struggle through a framework of associations.

This commitment forced Viollet to go against expectations, by denouncing the trend of Catholic anti-Semitism. But it also illustrates the ambiguity of his institutional position. Law Schools and their fellow members did not engage in the Dreyfus Affair – one consequence of this disengagement is that law professors have given way to *intellectuals* (a term used from that time) as main actors in shaping public opinion. On the other hand, the life of École des Chartes was very seriously disturbed by internal division between pro- and anti-Dreyfusards. Yet, while he would come to the École only for his weekly classes, through his daily presence in the Law Library Viollet more frequently would meet the jurists of the Faculty of Law. Nevertheless, it was at the École des Chartes that this right-wing man found the main support for his commitment to Dreyfus, alongside his left-wing fellow *Chartistes* (Paul Meyer, Arthur Giry, and Auguste Molinier). Still, it is important to note that Viollet's investment in the Dreyfus Affair was not only a matter of the injustice against the captain (an archetype of miscarriage of justice, doubled by a series of illegalities); his engagement with it is understandable above all by the more general cause of the defense of human rights.[21] Viollet was one of the founding members of the Human Rights League, whose statutes he wrote (the founding manifesto was edited on June 14, 1898). The Catholic *jusnaturaliste* assumed the rationalist legacy of the Enlightenment and the defense of the natural, sacred, and inalienable rights of all.

He soon distanced himself from the League, however, after colliding with a refusal of the board of that association to spread the struggle for recognition and application of ordinary law to the priests of congregations in the same way as to Jews. Since the worship Viollet devoted to liberties should necessarily extend to freedom of religion, he justified his resignation from the League by invoking the sixth article of the *Declaration of the Rights of Man and of the Citizen* (1789): law being the expression of the general will

> has to be the same for all, whether it protects or whether it punishes. All the citizens being equal before it are also eligible to any dignities, places, and public employments, according to their capacity, and without other distinction than that of their virtues and of their talents.

[21] Jean-Marie Mayeur, "Les catholiques dreyfusards," *Revue Historique* 261, no. 2 (1979): 336–61.

FIGHTING ABUSES IN FRENCH COLONIES

Paul Viollet was led by a sense of justice long before the beginning of the Dreyfus Affair, as evidenced by the fact that he was already member of the Committee for Protection and Defense of Natives, created in 1893. In 1899 he became president of the committee, succeeding Alexandre Isaac, senator of Guadeloupe, a man of color whose lone presence in the committee contradicted any underlying racial intention in the idea of protection of natives.[22] The inspiration for this committee arose in reaction to the massacres committed in the kingdom of Dahomey by French troops in the autumn of 1892. The committee was quite small, with a maximum of about forty members (there were only nine in 1899); members would be recruited by unanimous election – hence the presence of Chartistes, historians, and, to a lesser extent, jurists: in other words, three of Viollet's networks. Alongside Abbé Jules-Auguste Lemire, the committee included Chartistes like Arthur Giry and Auguste Molinier, as well as Charles Gide, a fellow professor in the Paris Faculty of Law – all of whom Viollet met within the ranks of *LDH (Ligue des Droits de l'Homme, Human Rights League)*. The purpose of the committee was to denounce all violence against colonized peoples.[23]

Without direct access of its members to colonies or colonized peoples, the Committee for Protection and Defense of Natives was quite properly described as a "documentation center," created to record the frequent illegal practices perpetrated in the colonies with complete impunity. If most of the committee members had an indirect but indeed precise knowledge of the colonies, they did not, however, claim to be experts on the colonial reality; they all presented themselves as attentive citizens, concerned about exercising a right to survey the republican administration of the colonial empire. The committee thus collected and was engaged in a critical review of all information available about colonization and the colonies. This legal monitoring appears, moreover, as an extension of the daily work of Paul Viollet in his library, where he had organized the monitoring of legal literature.

[22] Emmanuelle Saada, "Penser le fait colonial à travers le droit en 1900," *Mil Neuf Cent* 27, no. 1 (2009): 103–16; Emmanuelle Sibeud, "Une libre pensée impériale? Le comité de protection et de défense des indigènes (ca. 1892–1914)," *Mil Neuf Cent* 27, no. 1 (2009): 57–74.

[23] Viollet, *Droit privé et sources*, 335: in his textbook of private law, it apears that the developments about slavery give Viollet an occasion to denounce "the subjection of the weak peoples by the so called civilized peoples"; see also Viollet, *Droit public*, 25–26: the author rejects the argument of the need to civilize colonized peoples: "can uniformity, regardless of any circumstance, be considered as a benefit? I am afraid that it implies, if not in pure theory, at least in fact, an impoverishment, a reduction."

The committee's actions essentially consisted of requests for pardon (letters to the cabinet and to members of parliament), circulation of public petitions, publishing of articles in the press (the newspaper *Le Temps* was an active supporter of colonial policy), or the writing of brochures. Thus, between 1901 and 1911, the committee edited five brochures – about land despoilment against Kanaks in New Caledonia (1901); about hard labor under slave-like conditions in the Comoros (1904); about the situation in the Congo (1905); about financial abuses in colonies (1907); and against compulsory collective civil downgrading of the inhabitants of Sainte-Marie (an island of Madagascar), who were considered subjects rather than citizens by the colonial administration (1911). The entry registers of books in the Paris Law Library indicate that some of these brochures were given to the library by Paul Viollet himself. The purpose of all these initiatives was to impose the application of *droit des gens* rules for colonized peoples as well as for independent nations. As specified by Emmanuelle Sibeud, if the committee was not anticolonialist, it nevertheless denounced all the injustices ensuing from colonialism, and it challenged the principle of a "mission to civilize" used to justify colonization.[24]

Viollet also challenged the Code of Indigenous Status,[25] the heart of French colonial law, which transfererd to the agents of colonial administration a power of repression linked to a state of war. The Committee for Protection and Defense of Natives expressed that "the laws of justice and fundamental rules of *droit des gens* are common to all peoples; the weakness and barbarism of a people do not exclude it from *droit des gens*." Colonial wars being wars against a nation's own, the war against Madagascar (1895) offered the committee an occasion to remember that the Geneva Convention (1864) guaranteed the Malagasy the protection of the rules of war (in the Madagascar case, the protection of wounded soldiers on the battlefield). In 1907, during the 16th Universal Peace Congress in Munich, Viollet still pleaded for colonized populations to be considered as civilian populations in wartime, benefiting, as such, from the protective measures of The Hague Convention, signed in 1899 (Louis Renault, international lecturer in the Paris Faculty of Law and a future Nobel Peace Prize laureate, was an active participant in the adoption of this text). In 1907, during the second Hague Convention, the committee repeated that both civilized nations and aboriginal peoples fell within the

[24] See contributions of Emmanuelle Sideud on Paul Viollet's virtual exhibition: expo-paulviollet .univ-paris1.fr

[25] *Code de l'indigénat*, 18 June 1881; from 1887 on, this status, initially planned for Algeria, was gradually extended to all French colonies in Africa.

sphere of *droit des gens*; therefore, international law had to be applied to colonized peoples. But Emmanuelle Sideud also reminds us that Viollet's realism led him to plead for arms sales to assaulted peoples (the Catholic was not a pacifist, even though he had misgivings about this policy proposal).

Linked with his struggle for the cause of Dreyfus, the involvment of Paul Viollet against abuses of colonization demonstrates the coherence of his commitment. He was faithful to what he thought to be the image of modern Catholicism united to the Republic, according to Pope Leo XIII's encyclical *Rerum novarum* (1891), a text based on the autonomy of the individual and the duty of solidarity for Christians. But the Catholic scholar was also very active in promoting the imperatives of justice and truth, bonded to republican ideals.

FROM CONGREGATIONAL ADVOCACY ... TO OSTRACISM (*MISE À L'INDEX*)

There is probably no better evidence of the pattern of a Catholic going against his camp than the blacklisting of one of his books. *The Pope's Infallibility and the Syllabus: Historic and Theological Study* is a short text, published by Paul Viollet in 1904 under the auspices of the Catholic Committee for the Defense of Rights. This committee, of which Viollet was one of the founders, was created in 1899 to challenge measures that undermined Catholic education of congregations, and to denounce republican anticleralism, which contravened the principles of tolerance and the guarantee of liberty inherited from French Revolution. For Vincent Duclert, it was not a question of "denominational, but of loyalty to the liberal and democratic values which established the Dreyfusard struggle."[26] If the committee joined the struggle against anti-Semitism in the Dreyfus Affair, its establishment was a reaction to the reluctance of the Human Rights League to commit to defending the priests involved in congregational education, a reluctance that Viollet denounced as a form of anti-Christianity. These tensions must be viewed within the debate that had been dividing French society for approximately twenty-five years, about the place of the church and Catholics in civil society – a debate that led to the separation of church and state in the law of December 9, 1905. Viollet's critical Catholicism united, then, with his liberal political convictions to denounce a violation of personal freedom and noncompliance with

[26] Vincent Duclert, "Un défi à la République? Paul Viollet et le comité catholique de protection et de défense des indigènes," in Silvia Marton, Anca Oroveanu, and Florin Turcanu (eds.) *L'Etat en France et en Roumanie aux XIXe et XXe siècles* (Bucharest: New Europe College, 2011): 359–84, at 380.

the *Declaration of the Rights of Man and of the Citizen* (Article 6 guarantees the equal eligibility of citizens to "dignities, places, and public employments according to their capacity and without other distinction than that of their virtues and of their talents").

The advocacy of congregational education has a close link with Paul Viollet's other struggles: to ensure that the republic is in compliance with its principles, Catholics should receive the same protections as those recognized for other citizens. He did not hesitate to claim this also in his textbooks, where one can guess the convictions of the author: thus, about the fact that every French adult should enjoy the same civil and political rights, Viollet wrote:

> [I]t is, anyway, what I wrote in 1883; but, since then, the right to teach in public schools was suspended for anyone who is not laic. French citizens, in a too large number, were struck by that special incapacity; it is obviously contrary to every principle of modern society. Just look at the law of October 30–31, 1886, article 17. It is obvious that neither our customs nor public opinion admitted the entry into certain public employments of the priests and members of a religious order. If a legislator who does not worry much about the letter of modern principles would promulgate certain political incapacities in this spirit (e.g., Switzerland, federal constitution of 1874, article 75) he would simply put into practice, probably without suspecting it, the old canonical axiom: *nemo militans Deo implicetur negotiis saecularibus*. But neither modern opinion nor tradition classifies education among these *negotia saecularia*.[27]

This combination of faith and freedom is the purpose of Paul Viollet's interpretation of the *Syllabus*, a catalog of eighty proposals settled by Pope Pius IX, which accompanied the encyclical *Quanta Cura* (1864). The liberal Catholic was also a canonist, of whom Jean-Louis Clément notes that he aspired "to bound strictly the spring of papal infallibility, to perpetuate the principle of a free church in a free state."[28] Viollet refused the dogma of papal infallibility, about which, he asserted, the *Syllabus* mentioned nothing. In January 1905, a review of Viollet's book was published by Jesuit priest Pierre Bouvier in *Études*, the monthly review of the Society of Jesus. Bouvier denounced historical mistakes about the origins of papal infallibility, as well as misinterpretations of some of the proposals of the catalogue (e.g., on proposal 67, about indissolubility of marriage, which Viollet set against Naquet's law of July 27, 1884; Viollet considered that this law, which

[27] Viollet, *Droit privé et sources*, 244 (footnote 1).
[28] Clément, "Un canoniste mis à l'Index en 1906," 81–96.

authorized divorce in France, did not break natural law[29]). Thus attacked, Viollet responded by republishing his study during the spring of 1905 (*Infallibility and Syllabus, Answer to Les Etudes*), to which he added a methodological analysis, which can be read as a position in a debate that also had shaken Law Schools since the end of the nineteenth century: as a legal historian, he denounced the formalism that allowed one to deduce a series of logical consequences from an abstract principle considered inviolable, without any concern for social and historical context. Added to the social and political commitments of Viollet and his strong defense of a compatibility of Catholicism with the spirit of the French Revolution, this criticism of the dogma of infallibility was treated as too much of a transgression: in March 1906, his book was blacklisted (put on the *Index Librorum*).

In exploring the path of Paul Viollet through his work, both academic and activist, we hope to have demonstrated that in his many commitments as a Catholic, as much as in his scholarly works as a legal historian, Viollet always challenged every border: disciplinary, professional, religious, and political. In this way, he endorsed throughout his life what he considered to be the function of an intellectual in the French Republic, fully conscious that democratic progress, still vulnerable, had to be firmly protected.

RECOMMENDED READING

Viollet, Paul. *Précis de l'histoire du droit français, accompagné de notions de droit canonique et d'indications bibliographiques*. Paris: Larose et Forcel, 1885; republished as *Droit privé et sources. Histoire du droit civil français*. Paris: Larose, 1893 (2nd edn) and 1905 (3rd edn).

Droit public. Histoire des institutions politiques et administratives de la France. Paris: Larose et Forcel, 1890 (vol. 1), 1898 (vol. 2), and 1903 (vol. 3).

"French Law in the Age of the French Revolution." In *Cambridge Modern History*, vol. 8, chapt. 24. Cambridge: Cambridge University Press, 1904.

L'infaillibilité du Pape et le syllabus; étude historique et théologique. Besançon. Paris: Lethielleux, 1904.

Infaillibilité et Syllabus. Réponse aux "Etudes." Besançon, Paris: Roget et Chernoviz, 1905.

Histoire des institutions politiques et administratives de la France. Le roi et ses ministres pendant les trois derniers siècles de la monarchie. Paris: Larose et Tenin, 1911.

"Foreword." In Adolphe Schmidt, *Paris pendant la Révolution d'après les rapports de la police secrète, 1789–1800*. Translated by Paul Viollet. Paris: Champion librairie, 1880 (vol. 1), 1885 (vol. 2), 1890 (vol. 3).

[29] Viollet, *Droit privé et sources*, 443, 449.

Arabeyre, Patrick, Frédéric Audren, and Alexandra Gottely. *Paul Viollet (1840–1914), bibliothécaire, professeur et historien du droit, "Un grand savant assoiffé de justice."* Exhibition organized by Cujas Library, Ecole nationale des Chartes, Sciences Po Paris Law School, 2015: expo-paulviollet.univ-paris1.fr . This virtual exhibition offers a complete overview of Paul Viollet's publishing output and of his beliefs. See especially the contributions of Frédéric Audren, Patrick Arabeyre, Anne-Sophie Chambost, Jean-Louis Clément, and Emmanuelle Sibeud.

Audren, Frédéric. "Viollet Paul." In *Dictionnaire historique des juristes français*, edited by Patrick Arabeyre, Jean-Louis Halpérin, and Jacques Krynen, 774–75. Paris: Presses Universitaires de France, 2007.

Cabanel, Patrick. "La République contre les catholiques?" In *Serviteurs de l'Etat*, edited by Baruch Marc-Olivier, et al., 167–80. Paris: La Découverte, 2000.

Chambost, Anne-Sophie. "Un lieu de conservation, de diffusion et d'élaboration des manuels. La bibliothèque de la Faculté de droit de Paris à l'époque de Paul Viollet (1876–1914)." In *Histoire des manuels de droit*, edited by Anne-Sophie Chambost, 35–50. Paris: Lextenso-LGDJ, 2014.

"A propos des manuels d'histoire du droit de Paul Viollet." *Actes du colloque Paul Viollet*. Paris: École des Chartes, septembre 2015.

Chatelain, Emile, and Henri Stein. "Éloges funèbres Paul Viollet." *Bibliothèque de l'Ecole des Chartes* (1914): 442–48.

Clément, Jean-Louis. "Un canoniste mis à l'Index en 1906: Paul Viollet (1840–1914)." *Revista critica de Derecho Canonico Pluriconfessional* (2014/1): 81–96.

de Certeau, Michel. *L'écriture de l'histoire*. Paris: Gallimard, 1975.

de Cock, Laurence, and Emmanuelle Picard. *La fabrique scolaire de l'histoire, illusions et désillusions du roman national*. Marseille: Agone, 2009.

Delaborde, Henri-François. "Notice sur la vie et les travaux de M. Paul Viollet," *Bibliothèque de l'Ecole des Chartes* (1918): 147–75.

Duclert, Vincent. "Raison démocratique et catholicisme critique au début du XXe siècle. A la recherche des influences de Paul Viollet." In *Charles de Gaulle. La jeunesse et la guerre*, 1890–1920, edited by J. Foyer and Pierre Mauroy, 107–8. Fondation Charles de Gaulle. Paris: Plon, 2001.

"Un défi à la République? Paul Viollet et le comité catholique de protection et de défense des indigènes." In *L'Etat en France et en Roumanie aux XIXe et XXe siècles*, edited by Silvia Marton, Anca Oroveanu, and Florin Turcanu, 359–84. Bucharest: New Europe College, 2011.

Fournier, Paul. Chronique "Paul Viollet." *Nouvelle Revue Historique de Droit Français et Etranger* 38 (1914): 816–25.

Grand, Roger. *L'histoire du droit français. Ses règles, sa méthode, son utilité. Leçon d'ouverture du cours d'histoire du droit professé à l'Ecole des Chartes (3 novembre 1919)*, 1920.

Guyon, Gérard. "Paul Viollet." In *Juristas Universales. Vol. 3: Juristas del siglo XIX: de Savigny a Kelsen*, edited by Rafael Domingo, 476–78. Madrid: Marcia Pons ediciones juridicas y sociales, 2004.

Guyotjeannin, Olivier. "Paul Viollet." In *Dictionnaire biographique des historiens français et francophones*, 320–21. Paris: Indes savantes, 2004.

Mayeur, Jean-Marie. "Les catholiques dreyfusards." *Revue Historique* 261, no. 2(1979): 336–61.

"Paul Viollet: pour 'les libertés.'" *Mil Neuf Cent* 11 (1993): 38–44.

Naquet, Emmanuel. "L'Autre dans la réflexion théorique et la mise en pratique juridique en France et dans les années 1890–1930 à travers l'exemple de la Ligue des Droits de l'Homme." In *La République et son droit (1870–1930)*, edited by Frédéric Audren, Jean-Louis Halpérin, and Stora-Lamarre Annie, 201–19. Besançon: Presses universitaires de France-Comté, 2011.

Naz, Raoul, "Paul Viollet." In *Dictionnaire de droit canonique*, 7: 1510–12. Paris: Letouzey et Ané, 1965.

Ribémont, Thomas. "Les historiens chartistes au cœur de l'affaire Dreyfus." *Raisons politiques* 18 (2005): 97–116.

Saada, Emmanuelle. "Penser le fait colonial à travers le droit en 1900." *Mil Neuf Cent* 27, no. 1 (2009): 103–16.

Sibeud, Emmanuelle. "Une libre pensée impériale? Le comité de protection et de défense des indigènes (ca. 1892–1914)." *Mil Neuf Cent* 27, no. 1 (2009): 57–74.

18

Paul Fournier

(1853–1935)

BRIGITTE BASDEVANT-GAUDEMET AND RAFAEL DOMINGO

BIOGRAPHICAL INTRODUCTION

One of the greatest historians of medieval canon law of the last two centuries, Paul Fournier was an indefatigable, prolific, and meticulous scholar. He opened new paths in research to new generations in a time when French jurists paid little attention to canon law.[1] Fournier's academic mission would precisely cover that important intellectual gap, giving new life and light to the study of canon law in French public universities.

Descended from a family of sailors and merchants, Paul-Eugène-Louis Fournier was born in Calais on November 26, 1853.[2] After receiving a refined classical and Christian education at the Institution Libre de Marcq-en-Baroeul,[3] Fournier went to Paris at the end of 1871 to enroll in law school. After graduation, attracted by history more than by legal codes, Fournier enrolled in the École Nationale des Chartes in 1875, where he was a pupil of Adolphe Tardif (1824–90). This *grande école* was a well-known higher-education research center specializing in historical study. There, Fournier learned Latin and French paleography, archaeology, medieval Latin, and history, among other subjects, and in 1879 he graduated with highest honors and became an archivist-paleographer. He synchronized his studies in the

[1] The canon-law historian Ernest Joseph Tardif (1855–1923) complained that for a century France had produced only a few textbooks of canon law, which were of no scholarly value. See Ernest-Joseph Tardif, "*Les officialités au Moyen Âge… par Paul Fornier,*" in *Bibliothèque de l'École des chartres* 42 (1881): 52–56, at 52.

[2] The best account on the life of Fournier is provided by Gabriel Le Bras, "Paul Fournier, sa carrière, son œuvre, son esprit," in *Revue historique de droit français et étranger* 15 (1936): 1–54.

[3] Information about this school is available at www.marcq-institution.com/

École with the elaboration and defense of his law school doctoral thesis on Roman law (1878),[4] a discipline that Fournier taught for decades, but to which he devoted only occasional research.

In January 1879, he defended a second doctoral thesis at the École des Chartes – an essay on the organization, jurisdiction, and procedures of the episcopal courts from 1180 to 1328, published a year later under the title *Les officialités au Moyen Âge*.[5] The work remains indispensable for any researcher interested in ecclesiastical justice in the Middle Ages. In May 1880, Fournier was appointed professor of Roman law at the Grenoble Law School, where he also served as dean for ten years (1904–14). In 1884, he married Marie Chrétien, sister of one of his colleagues. The couple had a daughter. In 1890–91, Fournier spent a sabbatical at the French School of Rome,[6] where he had the fortunate opportunity to consult many manuscripts for his research on canonical collections.

In 1914, Fournier was appointed professor of Roman law at the University of Paris to replace the distinguished historian and legal scholar Adhémar Esmein (1848–1913). The First World War took most of Fournier's students from class, but in 1920, the university created for him a chair in the history of canon law. Courses on canon law had completely disappeared from French law schools since the French Revolution. The new chair would not reestablish canon law itself as a subject in the public university, but only the history of canon law, as a branch of the history of law. Innovation, therefore, remained limited. Before the endowment of this new chair, courses in canon law were taught only at the École des Chartres and at the École Pratique des Hautes Études. Robert Génestal would succeed Fournier as the chaired professor of the history of canon law at the University of Paris, and later Gabriel Le Bras, one of the most loyal and brilliant students of Fournier, replaced Génestal.

Fournier helped found the Society of Legal History (Société d'Histoire du Droit), which he chaired for fifteen years. He was a member of the executive

[4] Paul Fournier, *Des collèges industriels dans l'Empire romain; et Des droits du mari et de la femme sur la fortune mobilière propre à la femme mariée en dehors du régime dotal* (Paris: Malverge et Dubourg, 1878). These are two entirely different works submitted in order to obtain the title of doctor: one related to the private corporations during the Roman Empire, and another on the legal regime of the dowry.

[5] Paul Fournier, *Les officialités au Moyen Âge: étude sur l'organisation, la compétence et la procédure des tribunaux ecclésiastiques ordinaires en France, de 1180 à 1328* (Paris: E. Plon 1880; reprint Aalen: Scientia Verlag, 1984). The book is available at: archive.org/details/lesofficialitsaoofourgoog

[6] Founded in 1875, the École Française de Rome is a public scientific, cultural, and professional institution under the supervision of the Ministry of National Education, Higher Education, and Research. See information at: www.efrome.it/

committee of the *Revue historique du droit français et étranger* and held the position of vice president of the Société d'Histoire de l'Église de France. Honored often, Paul Fournier was elected a member of the Académie des Inscriptions et Belles-Lettres and an officer of the Legion d'honneur, among others. His renown surpassed the boundaries of France. He was a member of the Bavarian Academy of Sciences in Munich, the Lincei Academy in Rome, and the Medieval Academy of America in Cambridge, Massachusetts. He received honorary doctorates from Oxford University, the University of Vilnius, and the University of Leuven.

Paul Fournier died in Paris on May 14, 1935, at 82, after a long illness. His funeral, celebrated in his parish, St Francis Xavier's Church, was presided over by Monsignor Alfred Henri Baudrillar, president of the Catholic Institute of Paris and months later a cardinal of the Catholic Church.

SCHOLARLY CONTRIBUTION

Paul Fournier was a creative and fruitful scholar. A list of all his academic publications was published by Gabriel Le Bras[7] in the *Mélanges*, with which the Society of the History of Law honored Fournier in 1929.[8] The list attests to the breadth and diversity of Fournier's research. Certainly, the history of canon law and the history of ecclesiastical law and institutions occupied a prominent position, but studies on foreign law, modern law, and the philosophy of law also have their place there. This list was updated and completed by Le Bras in 1936 in a tribute to Paul Fournier after his death.[9]

Fournier's first important contribution to the history of canon law was his pioneering research on the organization, competences, and procedures of medieval ecclesiastical courts, titled *Les officialités au Moyen Âge*.[10] The volume is in many ways unmatched and unsurpassed, and probably will remain fundamental for a long time.[11] The creation of medieval episcopal courts corresponded to the period when the powers of the bishop, the head of

[7] On this French legal historian, see Chapter 25.

[8] Société d'histoire du droit, *Mélanges Paul Fournier* (Paris: Sirey, 1929): xxxix–lxiv. The volume contains essays by fifty-seven contributors, preceded by "Allocutions prononcées à l'occasion du jubilé de m. Paul Fournier. Journées d'histoire du droit, 6 juin 1929," the list of contributors, and a bibliography of the works of Fournier, compiled by Gabriel Le Bras.

[9] Gabriel Le Bras, "Paul Fournier," 1–54, at 53–54.

[10] Paul Fournier, *Les officialités au Moyen Âge*.

[11] In the same vein, Charles Donahue, Jr. and Sara McDougall, "France and Adjoining Areas," in Wilfried Hartmann and Kenneth Pennington (eds.), *The History of Courts and Procedures in Medieval Canon Law* (Washington, DC: Catholic University of America Press, 2016), 300–43, at 301.

the diocese, were increasingly challenged by those of his chapter, on the one hand, and the pretensions of the archdeacons, on the other. The will to fight against the abuses of those who were in principle subordinate to the bishop was undoubtedly no small part of the process leading to the establishment of episcopal court officials. These officials were legal experts freely appointed and dismissed by the bishop, to whom the bishop delegated most of his judicial duties. The court officials provided justice at no cost and received only a salary paid by the bishop. The institution of officials served as a model for the secular jurisdictions of later centuries, and in many respects for modern laws. The superiority of the canonical legislation over the uses and rules followed by the secular courts attracted a great number of cases even beyond their jurisdiction. Recurrent litigants, especially traders, even sought to secure clerical privileges in order to fall under ecclesiastical jurisdiction, and the pope had to take pains to limit these abuses.

Fournier's study is also very useful in establishing the distinction between the prerogatives of ecclesiastical judges and those of secular judges. Certain medieval scholars accused the officials of being pure legal technicians without taking into consideration pastoral concerns in their decisions. Fournier did not ignore these criticisms, but he demonstrated how the ecclesiastical courts were, on the contrary, a great mechanism for the development of the law of the Church that even inspired secular legal reform.

Some points of Fournier's volume were contested, notably by Édouard Fournier (1873–1954, no relation to Paul). Nevertheless, Paul Fournier's observations regarding the places and dates of reforms or improvements of the courts have rarely been questioned since. During Paul Fournier's life, further research led by Robert Génestal provided new important information on jurisdictional issues. This probably explains why, at the end of his life, Paul Fournier planned a new edition of this book on medieval ecclesiastical courts, taking into account the new research as well as discovery of new treatises on procedure, called *ordines judiciarii*. He never finished the projected edition, however.

After researching medieval ecclesiastical courts, Fournier planned to examine the history of religious institutions by going back a little in time and focusing mainly on the Carolingian period. The personality of Hincmar (806–82), archbishop of Reims and adviser to Charles the Bald (823–77), particularly caught Fournier's attention. He was soon persuaded that institutions could not be deeply studied until all the relevant sources had been clearly identified and related. In this work of clarification, simplification, and explanation, the German historian Friedrich Maassen (1823–1900) had made important contributions, but the scope of his research took him only to the end of the ninth century.[12] However, the period from the *False Decretals* (the ninth century) to Gratian's *Decretum* (about 1140) was almost unknown to the small community of canon-law historians. Fournier decided to devote himself intensely to the study of this period and, especially to studying the canonical collections.

The canonical collections were the first source of the law of the church in the early Middle Ages. The authors drew indifferently on various sources of canon law, the main ones being scripture, patristic or other later doctrinal writings, and texts for the most part without normative value but capable of acquiring the authority of a legal ruling by their inclusion in a canonical collection. Canonical collections consisted also of canons of general or provincial councils, as well as extracts of papal decretals, the fundamental sources of canon law. The compilers often had recourse to secular law – Carolingian capitularies or Roman law – used mainly from the second half of the twelfth century, when Justinian's compilation was discovered in the West.[13] Canonical collections could also contain apocryphal texts – spurious works made up of bits and pieces to bolster the thesis of an author and pseudonymously produced under the authority of a distinguished person in the church (e.g., the group of Pseudo-Isidorian decretals composed in the ninth century and falsely attributed to the popes of the first centuries). Moreover, the compilers made various interpolations, often deliberately, sometimes resulting from a predecessor's error that they faithfully copied. Once incorporated in a collection, all the texts, whatever their origin, author, or date of production, acquired the general value of the whole collection. The value of a collection – generally compiled privately – depended on the moral or doctrinal authority of its author, usually a bishop or abbot. Sometimes, however, the authors were popes who ordered the elaboration of some collections or who confirmed some existing collections by promulgating them. These papally sanctioned collections, therefore, acquired official value, and they were required to be put into practice throughout the Latin church. The elaboration of collections transformed canon law by adapting it to new circumstances and necessities of society.

[12] Friedrich Maassen, *Geschichte der Quellen und Literatur des canonischen Rechts im Abendland I. Die Rechtssammlungen bis zur Mitte des 9. Jahrhunderts* (Graz: Leuschner & Lubensky, 1870; reprinted Graz Akademische Druck- und Verlagsanstalt, 1956).

[13] For an overview of the canonical collections, see Briguitte Basdevant-Gaudemet, "Canonical Collections," in André Vauchez (ed.), *Encyclopedia of the Middle Ages* (Oxford, New York: Oxford University Press, 2005), online. See also, Jean Gaudemet, *Les sources du droit canonique VIIIe–XXe siècles* (Paris: Cerf, 1993).

The research method inaugurated and implemented so brilliantly by Fournier had a decisive influence on his successors and especially on Jean Gaudemet,[14] who was also concerned about the modalities of the collections, and the way each of them gave an account of the realities of the church, society, and canonical law of a particular time. The study of the collections, far from being enclosed in a study of texts that could have been as tedious as it was barren, became the study of the church itself.

Fournier dealt with the canon-law collections elaborated throughout the entire West, including the Anglo-Saxon islands, the Iberian Peninsula, and Rome. But he undoubtedly attached particular importance to those collections of the Frankish kingdom, while constantly insisting on the role of the papacy in preserving unity against local particularisms, which, he said, would have damaged the unity of Christendom. For each of these collections, Fournier tried, more than Maassen did, to specify the sources used, the milieu of the author, and the context and circumstances of the drafting. In doing so, Fournier indicated the orientation of each collection – for instance, not only the contribution of the Pseudo-Isidorian decretals to the doctrines of the Roman primacy over the emperor, but also the subsequent use by Gregorian canonists of ancient texts, particularly the writings of the church fathers.

The collections reveal that the Gregorian reform (*c.* 1050–80) was "Roman" and already preoccupied with asserting pontifical power over imperial power to avoid imperial interventionism. This objective continued to grow during the following decades and led to the idea that the supreme ruler (*dominus mundi*) of a unitary world should be not the emperor but the pope, even if this political power was ephemeral. The emperor was the secular ruler to whom God had entrusted the physical protection of the papacy.[15] Thus, through the history of the sources appears the history of the church, its evolution, and the development of doctrines. Le Bras emphasized that, for Fournier, the plotting of collections is therefore the plotting of history. Canonical collections were born in a concrete environment, with precise ends and aims. Each compiler was able to choose the texts, to modify them or to orient them, and thus human freedom and the necessity of time have altered most authentic texts. Paul Fournier worked on the history of the transmission of general ideas by the transmission of masses of texts. Consequently, the study of canonical

[14] On Jean Gaudemet, see pp. 422, 424 and 431.

[15] For an overview on this topic, see Kenneth Pennington, *The Prince and the Law, 1200–1600: Sovereignty and Rights in the Western Legal Tradition* (Berkeley: University of California Press, 1993); and James Muldoon, *Empire and Order: The Concept of Empire 800–1800* (London: Macmillan; New York: St Martin's Press, 1999), esp. 64–100.

collections was, in his view, the necessary preparation for the study of canonical institutions.[16]

Describing the spirit peculiar to each collection, Fournier indicates, beyond that, the spirit of the Gregorian reformers, namely their tendency toward Roman centralization and the triumph of the papacy over the emperor; condemnation of investiture of ecclesiastics by laymen, including kings;[17] condemnation of simony; imposition of the rule of continence on ordained clerics in major orders; description of relations between Rome and the empire; and consolidation of episcopal prerogatives. Fournier did not himself prepare a critical edition of the manuscripts. He certainly had the required expertise to do so, but he was more interested in analyzing the substance of each of these works. He wanted, as Jean Gaudemet pointed out, to provide "the critical apparatus of an edition which he refuses to do."[18]

Fournier's excellent paleographic skills gave him access to the most difficult documents and manuscripts.[19] Between 1887 and 1930, he published more than thirty articles on these collections of canons. In the aftermath of the First World War, Fournier had gathered almost all the materials necessary for the elaboration of a major book, which he published in collaboration with Gabriel Le Bras: *Histoire des collections canoniques en Occident depuis les Fausses Décrétales jusqu'au Décret de Gratien* [The History of the Canonical Collections in the West from the False Decretals until the *Decretum* of Gratian].[20] This two-volume work, which has lost none of its importance, was possible thanks to the numerous ad hoc studies he carried out on these collections throughout his career. It is a sort of synthesis, sometimes a summary, of his works retracing the evolution of the preoccupations of the medieval canonists.

Fournier became in his lifetime and remains today a universally recognized specialist of the canonical collections. His research and the hypotheses he

[16] Le Bras, Gabriel, "Paul Fournier": 33, 37, 38, 39.

[17] For an overview of this medieval controversy, see Uta-Renate Blumenthal, *The Investiture Controversy: Church and Monarchy from the Ninth to the Twelfth Century* (Philadelphia: University of Pennsylvania Press, 1988).

[18] Jean Gaudemet, "Avant Propos," in *Paul Fournier, Mélanges de droit canonique*, vol. I, edn. Theo Kölzer (Aalen: Scientia Verlag, 1983), 5–11, at 7.

[19] For a bibliographical guide to the manuscript and literature of the canonical collections, see Lotte Kéry, *Canonical Collections of the Early Middle Âges (ca. 400–1140)* (Washington, DC: Catholic University of America Press, 1999).

[20] Paul Fournier, in collaboration with Gabriel Le Bras, *Histoire des collections canoniques en Occident depuis les Fausses Décrétales jusqu'au Décret de Gratien*, vol. I, *De la Réforme carolingienne à la Réforme grégorienne* (Paris: Sirey, 1931), and vol. II, *De la Réforme grégorienne au Décret de Gratien* (Paris: Sirey, 1932).

formulated have had a decisive influence on canonical studies, even though some current scholars question some of his assertions. The nuanced conclusions he drew on the value of the *Penitentials*[21]or on the *Decretum* of Burchard of Worms (*c.* 965–1025),[22] for example, have endured for a century.

Fournier made special contributions[23] on the collections attributed to Ivo of Chartres:[24] the *Tripartita*, the *Decretum*, and the *Panormia*. Using a new and exemplary method of analysis, for the most part still valid in our day,[25] Fournier was undoubtedly the first to emphasize the contribution of Ivo of Chartres to the emergence of canon law as a legal science in its own right. In particular, Fournier saw this birth of canon law in the *Prologus*, a text whose relevance Fournier always fully recognized.[26] According to Fournier, the *Prologus* was a sort of introduction to *Panormia*, but this is no longer the dominant view. Peter Landau was the first to see in the *Prologus* a treaty in its own right and not merely the introduction of another treaty.[27] Landau's argument was confirmed by Bruce Brasington[28] and by Jean Werckmeister,[29] who contested Fournier's opinion on this point.[30]

Scholars also questioned Fournier's hypotheses about the chronological sequence of the three major canon-law collections of Ivo of Chartres (*Tripartita*, *Decretum*, *Panormia*). He considered that all three formed a

[21] Penitentials were books containing instructions for confessors, including lists of sins with a set of penances attending the quality of the sin.

[22] A voluminous canonical collection on twenty books predating the Gregorian reform. Master Gratian made numerous borrowings made from it when he composed the *Decretum*. See Fournier and Le Bras, *Histoire des collections canoniques*, 364–421.

[23] Paul Fournier, "Les collections canoniques attribuées à Yves de Chartres," in Paul Fournier, *Mélanges de droit canonique*, vol. I, 451–678.

[24] See Chapter 1 on Ivo of Chartres.

[25] Christof Rolker, *Canon Law and the Letters of Ivo of Chartres* (Cambridge, New York: Cambridge University Press, 2010).

[26] See Jean Werckmeister, "Le premier canoniste: Yves de Chartres," *Revue de droit canonique* 47 (1997): 53–70.

[27] Peter Landau, "Die Rubriken und Inskriptionen von Ivos Panormie," *Bulletin of Medieval Canon Law* 12 (1982): 31–49; and "Ivo von Chartres," *Theologische Realenzyclopadie* 16 (1987): 323–37.

[28] Bruce Brasington, "The Prologue of Ivo de Chartres: a Fresh Consideration from the Manuscripts," in Stanley Chodorow (ed.) *Proceedings of the Eighth International Congress of Medieval Canon Law* (Monumenta Iuris Canonici, Subsidia 9, Vatican City: Biblioteca Apostolica Vaticana, 1992), 3–23.

[29] Yves de Chartres, *Prologue* (traduction, introduction, et notes par Jean Werckmeister; Paris: Cerf, 1997).

[30] For an overview of Fournier's contribution and critique, see Rolker, *Canon Law and the Letters of Ivo of Chartres*, 41–46.

comprehensive work, drafted in a very short time. Some scholars,[31] however, have put forward a convincing critical argument: *Decretum* and *Panormia* reflect different preoccupations than those expressed in *Tripartita*, and these two collections were composed a few years after the *Tripartita*, not before 1096. Although this new thesis invalidated some of Fournier's conclusions, it does not affect the substantial value of his contribution to the knowledge and scope of the work of Ivo of Chartres.

In addition to the canonical collections, Fournier dealt with a great variety of topics related to the history of the church: the pontifical government of Gregory VII leading the centralist reform of the church in favor of Roman authority; the registers of the popes of the thirteenth and fourteenth centuries; and the crisis of the fourteenth century arising from the schismatic struggles between pretenders to the papacy. On all these topics and many others, Fournier published numerous detailed book reviews. He did not merely point out the issues addressed in each volume, but he carried out a thorough critical analysis, bringing in new elements and in some ways completing the book submitted to him. In doing this, he often appealed to Roman law, scholastic philosophy, theology, or liturgy, which he refused to separate from the history of canon law. In 1983, Theo Kölzer edited and published a two-volume selection of Fournier's twenty-five most relevant articles on the history of canon law.[32]

Fournier also made relevant contributions to the encyclopedic history of French literature called *Histoire littéraire de la France*.[33] He began his regular collaboration with this project in 1915, replacing the famous French historians Paul Viollet (1840–1914)[34] and Noël Valois (1855–1915). Fournier's mastery of medieval sources, particularly scholastic theology and Aristotelian commentaries, enabled him to fully ground the canonical and theological entries. His contributions to volumes 15, 16, and 17 were considerable. They included studies on Jesselin de Cassagnes, Guillaume de Montlauzun, Jean Faure,

[31] Martin Brett, "Urban II and the Collections Attributed to Ivo of Chartres," in Chodorow (ed.), *Proceedings of the Eighth International Congress of Medieval Canon Law*, 27–46; and Rolker, *Canon Law and the Letters of Ivo of Chartres*, 41–46.

[32] Paul Fournier, *Mélanges de droit canonique*, 2 vols. (edn. Theo Kölzer, Aalen: Scientia Verlag, 1983).

[33] *L'Histoire littéraire de la France* is a monumental history of French literature begun in 1733 by the Benedictines of the Congregation of Saint-Maur at the initiative of Dom Antoine Rivet of La Grange. Since 1814, the work has been led by the Academy of Inscriptions and Belles-Lettres, which still underwrites its publication. By 2016, forty-five volumes had been published. Information about this relevant project is available at: www.aibl.fr/publications/collections/histoire-litteraire-de-la-france/article/histoire-litteraire-de-la-france-646?lang=fr

[34] See Chapter 17 on Paul Viollet.

Pierre Jame d'Aurillac, Guillaume de Cun, the theologian Gui Terré, Henri Bohic, and Guillaume de Breuil, but also entries on Jacques Fournier (Pope Benedict XII), Pierre Roger (Pope Clement VI), and many other ecclesiastical dignitaries and masters of theology, canon law, and civil law. Studying each of these characters, Fournier was animated by the same concerns as when he considered the authors of canonical collections, endeavoring to scrutinize the substance of each of the formulated doctrines. All these studies showed the profound thought of a canon-law scholar who wished to grasp the ideas, motivations, and inspirations of the Christian society of the time.

Fournier was also interested in local history. In this field, his main work was *The Kingdom of Arles and Vienne (1138–1378)*, which is clearly defined by the subtitle: "Study on the Territorial Formation of France in the East and South-East."[35] Largely devoted to imperial power, this volume is the fruit of research carried out over nearly ten years. It especially analyzes the processes that enabled the French monarchy to take precedence over Germanic authority, starting from the Great Interregnum (1250–73), which permanently weakened the Holy Roman empire. The research earned Fournier the Gobert Prize of the Academy of Inscriptions and Belles Lettres in 1891. Another important contribution in the field of local history is his *History of the Seigneury of Chaligny*.[36] This work resulted from research he undertook while on vacation, surrounded by his family, in his house at Meurthe-et-Moselle in the Lorraine. For Fournier, research was not an activity, but a style of life.

Regarding French institutions – whether churches, schools, or other public or private organizations – Fournier wrote numerous reports and book reviews but few specific articles. Nevertheless, these critical accounts constituted an important substantive contribution to French institutional history. For instance, he disagreed with the German legal historian Ulrich Stutz (1868–1938), who regarded the private church regime as a purely Germanic system. Fournier, however, demonstrates a much broader geographic dispersion of the regime growing out of the legal realities of the late Roman Empire.

CHRISTIAN SCIENTIFIC SPIRIT

Paul Fournier lived in conformity with his Christian beliefs, feelings, and ideals. His students and colleagues emphasized his deep spiritual life, his sense of duty and work, the clarity and lucidity of his mind, his common sense, his

[35] Paul Fournier, *Le Royaume d'Arles et de Vienne* (1138–1378) (Paris: Picard, 1891).

[36] Paul Fournier, *Chaligny. Ses seigneurs et son comté. Histoire d'une seigneurie lorraine* (Nancy: Crépin-Leblond, 1907).

horror of preconceived ideas, and his profound understanding of the variety of rhythms in the evolution of institutions. He was a passionate defender of his own opinions but at the same time very respectful of the opinions of others. His career as a researcher took place during the convulsive time of the French Third Republic (1870–1940). His political action was discreet but real and always at the service of both France and the universal church, a conjunction of two objectives which at that time were not always easy.[37]

"The religious history of Paul Fournier is the history of the difficult adaptation of a Christian from the *ancien régime* to the new social conditions," writes Gabriel Le Bras.[38] In fact, Fournier's family and his education in classical religious institutions had made him a nostalgic legitimist of the old ways of France and an advocate of traditional Catholicism. Like many French Catholics, the young Paul Fournier called with zeal for a monarchical restoration, which he thought would again assure the irreducible prevalent position of the Catholic Church. But he changed his mind, especially after a trip to England in which he learned of the Oxford Movement and read the *Grammar of Assent* (1870) by John Henry Newman.[39] Cardinal Newman's original genius captivated Fournier. Remaining in absolute fidelity to the Roman Catholic Church, Fournier sought after this trip to reconcile Catholicism with the important changes of the moment, whether scientific, political, or social.

The historical context was tumultuous. From the 1880s, the republicans in power implemented a severe and often aggressive anticlerical policy. During this period of the "two Frances,"[40] the majority of Catholics, persuaded that the Church could survive only with the return of a monarchical regime, strongly opposed the republicans, who in turn were convinced that the survival of the new regime depended on the anticlerical struggle. The opposition between these two approaches had gradually developed since the French Revolution, but it had grown to a stark divide during the decades of the 1870s and 1880s, when France was ruled by a republican regime, a majority of whose deputies were monarchists. Consistent with his convictions, Fournier disapproved the constant bullying by the republicans against the Church and criticized the secularization laws of the end of the nineteenth century.

[37] See Gabriel Le Bras, "Paul Fournier et l'histoire de l'Église de France," in *Revue d'histoire de l'Église de France* 21, no. 93 (1935): 535–36.

[38] Ibid., 535.

[39] John Henry Newman, *An Essay in Aid of a Grammar of Assent* (South Bend, IN: University of Notre Dame Press, 1992).

[40] See the expression coined by Émile Poulat, *Liberté, laïcité. La guerre des deux France et le principe de la modernité* (Paris: Cerf and Cujas, 1987).

However, he also denounced the intransigence and even the provocations of certain monarchical Catholics. Committed to Catholicism, and without completely denying his monarchist opinions, Fournier knew how to use his moral authority to try to find means of conciliation. Faced with what may have seemed to be a retreat from Catholicism in France, Fournier wanted to ensure the continuity of the Catholic Church in nineteenth-century French society through his intellectual work on the history of the Church. This concern for pacification appeared several times during these years of politico-religious struggle, but it was not always successful.

Fournier was somewhat confused by the celebrated "Toast of Algiers," on November 12, 1890, in which Cardinal Lavigerie, at the request of Pope Leo XIII, encouraged French Catholics to adhere unreservedly to the republican form of government. Fournier also was troubled when the pope himself later called on French Catholics to rally in support of (*ralliement*) the new political regime in France.[41] Nevertheless, Fournier followed the invitation of the pope to accept the republic and submit to it, and he reproached the persistent intransigence of Catholics monarchists.

The promulgation of the law of 1905, which introduced the separation of churches and the state in France,[42] was another source of misgivings. Fournier, however, agreed to believe in the possibility of a new organization of the Church within this new framework, and, before the condemnation of the law by Rome,[43] he sought to establish religious associations allowed by the new law of separation. To this end, he spoke with several French bishops, and in Rome he met several cardinals, notably Rafael Merry del Val and Mariano Rampolla. His commitment to the religious associations ceased after the encyclical *Vehementer nos* of Pius X (February 11, 1906), in which the pope firmly condemned the French law of separation as a breakdown of the concordat between the French state and the Holy See. Soon after, in 1907, the publication of the encyclical *Pascendi* by Pius X, condemning modernism, constituted a new source of anguish. True, Fournier approved the pontifical condemnation. But his desire for peace and his open-mindedness led him to fear, on the one hand, strong reactions in anticlerical circles and,

[41] The Ralliement refers to the attitude of a part of the French Catholics who, following the advice of Pope Leo XIII and his encyclical *Inter sollicitudines* (February 20, 1892), joined the Republic. However, that did not mean the acceptance of legislation hostile to Catholicism, but merely a rallying to republican institutions, which Catholics now endeavored to support with all their might.

[42] See introduction to this volume, 13–14.

[43] See encyclical letter *Vehementer nos* of Pius X (February 11, 1906), available at: w2.vatican.va/content/pius-x/en/encyclicals/documents/hf_p-x_enc_11021906_vehementer-nos.html

on the other hand, as Gabriel Le Bras noted, an even greater concern that scholarly activity among clerics and freedom in scientific research in general might cease.[44]

In the aftermath of the Great War, Fournier was the first president of the Catholic Union of International Studies. In this capacity, and in view of Fournier's moral authority, Prime Minister Georges Clémenceau charged him with drafting the texts relating to the appointment of the bishops of Metz and Strasbourg. In 1918, France once again exercised sovereignty over Alsace and the Moselle, and thus over the dioceses of Strasbourg and Metz. At the time, these dioceses were governed by the system of public-law religious corporations established by Napoléon in 1802, a system somewhat modified by German legislation after 1871. The 1905 French law of separation did not apply in these districts, which were under German control until 1918. After the First World War, the question arose whether to maintain the existing regime or to impose the republican legislation promulgated for the rest of France between 1871 and 1918. The issue was delicate. The solution adopted was that of preserving a "local right," which still exists in the twenty-first century, with certain adjustments.[45] It was in this context that Fournier had to advise the government, since the head of the French state was empowered to "nominate" candidates for these two episcopal chairs. The Holy See did not accept the first proposals of the republican government. On all these points, and on others, Fournier's opinion was often not taken into account. Yet he always attempted to reconcile his fidelity to the Catholic Church with his loyalty to the political regime.

CONCLUSION

A leading figure and restorer of the history of canon law in France, Paul Fournier became in his lifetime, and remains today, a worldwide distinguished historian of medieval canon law. Many of his writings, especially those dealing with medieval ecclesiastical courts and those referring to canonical collections, have held up under the scrutiny of time. His academic

[44] See Le Bras, "Paul Fournier et l'histoire de l'Église de France," 542.

[45] Established in 1919 after the end of the First World War, this local law is applied in the French departments of Bas-Rhin, Haut-Rhin and Moselle, grouped under the generic name of Alsace-Moselle, which is now in the region Grand East. For an explanation of this local law, see Chapter 24 on Robert Schuman, pp. 408–409, note 14. For an overview of the local law in Alsace and Moselle, see Institut du Droit Local Alsacien-Mosellan (ed.), *Le guide du droit local: Le droit applicable en Alsace et en Moselle de A à Z* (4th edn, Strasbourg: Institut du Droit Local Alsacien-Mosellan 2015).

footprint has continued through the work of great students and students of students, such as Gabriel Le Bras[46] and Jean Gaudemet.[47] As a supporting actor in the religious events related to the French Third Republic, Fournier was able to accommodate his traditional Catholicism to the new social trends and to sow peace in a turbulent moment in the relations between the Church and the French state. The influence he exercised over the general ideas of his time, both in the legal field and in philosophical and moral terms, cannot be minimized. Men like Fournier enabled the Church to reconcile itself with the state and with science.

RECOMMENDED READING

Basdevant-Gaudemet, Brigitte. "Fournier, Paul-Eugène-Louis." In *Dictionnaire historique des juristes français, XIIe–XXe siècle*. Edited by Patrick Arabeyre, Jean-Louis Halpérin, and Jacques Krynen, 343. Paris: PUF, 2007.

Brundage, James A. *Medieval Canon Law*. London, New York: Longman, 1995.

Coville, Alfred. "Éloge funèbre de M. Paul Fournier, membre de l'Académie." *Comptes rendus des séances de l'Académie des Inscriptions et Belles-Lettres* 79 (1935): 189–94.

Fournier, Paul. *Les officialités au Moyen Âge: étude sur l'organisation, la compétence et la procédure des tribunaux ecclésiastiques ordinaires en France, de 1180 à 1328*. Paris: E. Plon 1880; reprint Aalen: Scientia Verlag 1984.

Mélanges de droit canonique. 2 vols. Edited by Theo Kölzer. Aalen: Scientia Verlag, 1983.

in collaboration with Gabriel Le Bras. *Histoire des collections canoniques en Occident depuis les Fausses Décrétales jusqu'au Décret de Gratien*, Vol. I, *De la Réforme carolingienne à la Réforme grégorienne* [Paris: Sirey, 1931]; Vol. II, *De la Réforme grégorienne au Décret de Gratien* [Paris: Sirey, 1932].

Gaudemet, Jean. "Avant-Propos." In *Paul Fournier, Mélanges de droit canonique*, Vol. I. Edited by Theo Kölzer, 5–11. Aalen: Scientia Verlag, 1983.

Grand, Roger. "Paul Fournier." *Bibliothèque de l'École des chartes* 97 (1936): 228–32.

Guyon, Gérard. "Paul Fournier." In *Juristas universales* III: *Juristas del siglo XIX*. Edited by Rafael Domingo, 642–44. Madrid, Barcelona: Marcial Pons: 2004.

Hartmann, Wilfried, and Kenneth Pennington, eds. *The History of Courts and Procedure in Medieval Canon Law*. Washington, DC: Catholic University of America Press, 2016.

Le Bras, Gabriel. "Paul Fournier et l'histoire de l'Église de France." *Revue d'histoire de l'Église de France* 21, no. 93 (1935): 532–49.

"Paul Fournier, sa carrière, son œuvre, son esprit." *Revue historique de droit français et étranger* 15 (1936): 1–54.

[46] See Chapter 25.

[47] See pp. 422, 424 and 431.

Maassen, Friedrich. *Geschichte der Quellen und Literatur des canonischen Rechts im Abendland I. Die Rechtssammlungen bis zur Mitte des 9. Jahrhunderts*. Graz: Leuschner & Lubensky, 1870; reprinted Graz Akademische Druck- und Verlagsanstalt, 1956.
Poulat, Émile. *Liberté, laïcité. La guerre des deux France et le principe de la modernité*. Paris: Editions du Cerf and Editions Cujas, 1987.
Rolker, Christof. *Canon Law and the Letters of Ivo of Chartres*. Cambridge, New York: Cambridge University Press, 2010.
Société d'Histoire du Droit. *Mélanges Paul Fournier*. Paris: Sirey, 1929.

19

Raymond Saleilles

(1855–1912)

MARCO SABBIONETI

BIOGRAPHICAL INTRODUCTION

One of the most distinguished jurists of the *fin de siècle*, Raymond Saleilles was born on January 14, 1855, in Gigny-par-Beaune, a small village in the heart of Burgundy. Attending secondary school in his hometown, in 1873 he became a *bachelier ès-lettres* and *bachelier ès-sciences*. In the same year, he received the *prix Marchand*, the highest recognition given by the school in Beaune. He completed his studies in jurisprudence at the Institut Catholique of Paris, earning his law degree [*licence en droit*] in 1879. During those years, he attended the Place du Panthéon school, where he was intellectually engaged in courses taught by Charles Beudant, Paul Gide, Émile Labbé, and Charles Bufnoir (his eventual father-in-law, after his marriage to Marguerite Bufnoir).

On April 5, 1883, Saleilles defended two theses: one in civil law and the other in Roman law.[1] On May 12 of the following year, he came in fifth in the competition for *agrégation*. That same month, he was assigned to the Faculty of Grenoble, where, starting on September 30, he began teaching a class on the history of law. On October 17, 1885, he transferred to the Faculty of Law of Dijon, assigned with teaching history of law and, starting in 1892, constitutional law.[2] During his time in Dijon, he began to develop an interest in

[1] *De la possession des meubles en doit romain. De l'aliénation des valeurs mobilières par les administrateurs du patrimoine d'autrui en droit français*. Paris, 1883.

[2] On this subject, some of the most important publications include: "Development of the Present Constitution of France," in *The Annals of Political and Social Science* (Philadelphia, 1895): 1–78; "La représentation proportionnelle," in *Revue du droit public* 9 (1898): 215–34; *Rapport d'ensemble résumant les rapports divers présentés au Congrès international de droit comparé de 1900 sur la question du parlementarisme, Procès-verbaux des séances et documents*, vol. 1 (Paris, 1905), 69–85.

comparative law, which would soon take on a key role in his general understanding of legal science, closely following the preparatory work for Germany's civil code (BGB).[3] On April 17, 1895, Saleilles moved to Paris, where, in September of that year, he taught a course on penal law,[4] replacing Léveillé. Lastly, with a decree dated November 28, 1898, he was appointed professor of civil law at the university in the French capital, replacing Bufnoir, who had passed away two years earlier.

Saleilles's time in Paris undoubtedly marked a coming into his own, with his research becoming richer and more complex. Among other achievements worth noting are the organization of the International Conference of Comparative Law (coinciding with the Universal Exposition of 1900), the creation of the *Revue trimestrielle de droit civil*, and the founding of the *Société d'études législatives*,[5] in addition to his translation of the general section (*Allgemeiner teil*) of the German Civil Code (BGB) and articles related to the general theory of contract law. These were the years when Saleilles, working closely with his friend François Gény, fully developed his proposed methodology, laying down the foundations for a radical renewal of French legal science. This period also was marked by interest in theological and scriptural debate, made livelier and more complicated by the contemporary Modernist crisis, which Saleilles reflected in his essay on the *Méthode historique et la Bible* and in his translation of some of Newman's texts,[6] as well as in his participation as the *cardinal vert*[7] in France's separation crisis, taking the side of acceptance of the law of 1905.[8]

Saleilles passed away in Paris on the morning of March 3, 1912, symbolically completing his life on earth almost exactly at the end of the Belle Époque, which was interrupted in the most traumatic way shortly after by the catastrophe of war.

[3] For publications on this subject in those years, see: *Étude sur les sources de l'obligation dans le projet de code civil allemand* (Paris, 1889); *Étude sur la théorie générale des obligations dans la seconde rédaction du projet du code civil pour l'empire d'Allemagne* (Paris, 1895); *Note sur l'acquisition de la personnalité civile dans le code civil allemand* (Paris, 1899).

[4] His most important scientific work arising from this penal parenthesis was the essay titled *L'individualisation de la peine: étude de criminalité sociale* (Paris: F. Alcan, 1898).

[5] In relation to that organization, Saleilles dealt with crucial topics, such as the foundation of private law, collective bargaining contracts (via trade unions), abuse of rights, and laws concerning married women.

[6] *La foi et la raison. Six discours empruntés aux discours universitaires d'Oxford* (Paris, 1905); *Le Chrétien. Choix de discours extraits des sermons de Newman* (Paris: P. Lethielleux, 1906).

[7] This term was used to indicate a group of French intellectuals favorable to the law of 1905.

[8] *Le régime juridique de la séparation* (Paris: A. Pedone, 1907).

SCHOLARLY CONTRIBUTION

Saleilles's entire scientific oeuvre emerges as the expression of a uniform blueprint inspired by a clear strategy: redefine the coordinates of republican citizenship to provide a juridical role suited to the new political–legal landscape of the late 1800s, a period characterized by the transition from revolution-derived democracy to social democracy. In short, that blueprint consisted of an imposing epistemological reestablishment effort, with immediate political repercussions. In it the three main components of the human/scholarly personality of the Burgundian jurist converged, further nourishing it: Germanophilia, Modernism, and a complex Catholic sensibility.

Over the second half of the nineteenth century, in a rapidly evolving sociopolitical context and at the height of the so-called "crise allemande" of French culture, the foundations were laid for the definitive abandonment of *Exégèse*, or the exegetical method. This was a specific jurisprudential mentality developed after the start of the codification that required substantial identification between law and right, and aspired to complete the juridical phenomenon within the narrow confines of the Civil Code. In the 1850s, *Exégèse* was at its peak. The exegetical method took hold, reaching complete maturity and silencing the few *frondeurs* of the *Thémis*.[9].In 1855, Alexandre Duranton's *Cours de droit français suivant le Code Civil* ([Course of French law according to the Civil Code], published in 1837 and reissued multiple times) was already a classic for those who wanted to dedicate themselves to an orthodox study of civil law. Charles Aubry was about to publish the third edition of his *Cours de droit civil français* [Course of French Civil Law], and in 1851, amid honors and admiration, he became the dean of the Faculty of Law at the University of Strasbourg. Two years later, Jean Charles Florent Demolombe, then working on the ninth volume of his *Cours de Code Civil*, was dean of the faculty of Caen. In the meantime, while the restless Victor-Napoléon Marcadé, a liberal Catholic theorist, was writing the fifth edition of the *Explication théorique et pratique du Code Napoléon* [Theoretical and practical explanation of the Code Napoléon], Raymond Théodore Troplong was working on the *Commentaire de la loi du 23 mars 1855 sur la transcription en matière hypothécaire* [Commentary of the law of March 23, 1855, on the transcription in mortgage matters]. But 1855 was also the year in which Edouard de Laboulaye published the prophetically titled article in the *Revue historique du droit français et étranger* that closed the brief parenthesis of the

[9] The *Thémis* was a legal journal accommodating jurists who did not accept the legal methodology of *Exégèse*.

historic French school, brimming with a sense of legacy: "la méthode historique en jurisprudence et son avenir" [historical method in jurisprudence and its future].

When the young Saleilles landed at the school of the Place du Panthéon at the end of the 1870s (after a short sojourn at the Institut Catholique), the dominant cultural paradigm was still the one created by the jurists of the first half of the century. The Code remained wrapped in a mythical halo, occupying the entire horizon of juridical culture on its own. Teaching rigorously followed the canons of the *Exégèse*. However, the apex of a school often coincides with the beginning of its end. The exegetical model, solidly rooted in the university, was on its last legs. The tumultuous evolution that French society encountered during the nineteenth century, foreseen by Pellegrino Rossi, ended up exposing the inadequacy of the *Exégèse* and, with it, its scientific impracticality and, ultimately, the growing futility of the commentary. Legal positivism, which seemed to be the end point of the French juridical sequence of events, proved to be increasingly useless. It was precisely at this time, as a reaction to the distaste provoked by the sort of codistic indoctrination found in the lecture halls of the Sorbonne, that Saleilles blindly accepted Laboulaye's invitation, sensing that if French legal science were to have a future, it had to be reestablished. Thus began an engaging scholarly journey, mostly carried out in the solitude of a Parisian studio, the result of which was a titanic, behemoth work, rich with infinite suggestions, which progressively took on the connotations of a true "blueprint."

Saleilles quickly realized that reestablishing legal science in an antiformalistic, antilegalistic sense presupposes overcoming the Revolution's political–juridical paradigm: the legalistic paradigm, characterized by the centrality of the *loi* (understood in the Rousseauvian sense) on the one hand, and the individualistic paradigm, characterized by the centrality of the individual (understood as a sovereign and solitary subject, exclusive protagonist of the juridical landscape governed by the Code) on the other. With this in mind, methodological reflection took on a central role, inasmuch as it is clear that renewal presupposes a radical revision of the well-established method. It is no coincidence that Saleilles's blueprint begins with a reflection on methodology, while the entire piece, in its complexity, proves to be a coherent application of a clear methodological direction, its fundamental link. The reestablishment of legal science through methodological reform did not take place through the elaboration of a complete method discourse (*discours de la méthode*), but was rather the result, in a dogmatic context, of the application of a few, clear methodological directives first instituted in the 1890s. In other words, Saleilles redesigned French juridical culture from within, as a technocrat of the law, a civilist immersed in the tumultuous trenches of jurisprudence at the end of the nineteenth century. For this very reason, the updated method was revealed and clarified much more through its immediate dogmatic translations than through the crafting of complete summae of general theory.

Saleilles's investigation started with a rationalist critique of natural law and of certain profiles of Savignyan historicism. It eventually came to define an experimental method based on the observation of facts, on history and comparison, and on the ongoing quest for cohesion between juridical forms and the social dimension. Saleilles considered law a living force, a representation of social life; reality, with its ever-changing needs, took precedence over the abstractions that resulted from juridical systems, even if they never seemed to completely lose their allure. Thus, the historical method (*méthode historique*) was born, undoubtedly the most precious "creature" from Raymond Saleilles, his main contribution to the renewal of juridical epistemology and to the theory of interpretation.

But if overcoming the exegetical paradigm, consubstantial with the liberal legal model, was simultaneously the starting point and one of the essential elements of the blueprint, it was so much more as well. In other words, Saleilles's response was the adoption of a sociologically oriented method, based on observation and experimentation. This method was inserted into the historical era and into the concreteness of social relationships, founded on the category of the conflict, à la Rudolf von Jhering. It was also Saleilles's way to grapple with the imposing question of rationalization pressing on the realm of law from the outside. In this context, civil law became the equivalent of public law, taking on immediate, direct constitutional value in view of democracy sensitized to the plurality of objectives and identity demands of the groups it comprises. For this reason, if we want to properly understand the "Saleilles blueprint," placing it within the right perspective, it is important to remember that overcoming the exegetical model was not simply the result of an intradisciplinary requirement, a mere reaction to the exegetical *sécheresse* or desiccation. Rather, the new blueprint resulted from the creation of a type of private law of welfare able to juridically translate and establish the transition from political democracy (the result of the revolutionary event) to social democracy (understood as the definitive fulfilment of the promises of 1789). In other words, the blueprint was a decisive prerequisite to the creation of the social extension of revolutionary *citoyenneté*, inevitable given the socio-political context of France in the late 1800s.

Saleilles's blueprint, in short, can be interpreted as a radical work to reestablish legal science, carried out first via the historical method, whose goal is the creation of a private law of social welfare that is functional to the technical–juridical construction of social democracy. As such, the *méthode historique* is the fundamental element in a complex strategy of "saving" the *République*, consisting of containing and organizing conflict through the tool of juridical rationality.

Indeed, over the last twenty years of the nineteenth century, legal science was called upon to save a fragile republican structure. The work of jurists took on an intrinsically political quality, insofar as the Republic turned to law and to a renewed juridical rationality as a tool to redefine and consolidate the identity of the Republic and as a means to identify the conditions for lasting sociopolitical equilibrium. In this sense, therefore, the "Saleilles blueprint" can be interpreted as the basis for a plan for the Republic, for the fate of what would become "la plus longue des Républiques" was linked to legal science's ability to renew itself. We undoubtedly are dealing with a jurist perfectly aware of the strategic role of law and of the intrinsically political value taken on by juridical reflection in that specific historical context. The renewed method made it possible to bring a never-before-seen social law (*droit social*) to life, created by reinterpreting (but not denying) the essential principles of the legal system starting from the notion of solidarity (*solidarité*), a keyword in the political–legal culture at the end of the century, encapsulating the meaning of the republican compromise.

However, creating a social democracy did not mean simply using the law to address the challenges posed by the so-called Fourth Estate bursting on to the political scene. Rather, it meant digging much deeper and redesigning the entirety of an institutional model that appeared to be stiffened by and prone to multiple contradictions. If the *République* did indeed call upon new jurists (*jurisconsultes*) to strengthen its fragile foundations and to define its identity, if it appeared parched and especially in need of law, it was because law was at the center of a consensus-building strategy. The law was the idea-force that made a more concrete basis of the consensus possible, as it was mainly through law that, in specific "crossroads institutions," the union of the moral elites of the "non-partisan country" could come into fruition.

The absolutely central role of legal science at the time cannot be fully grasped unless the crisis enveloping the newly formed Republic is properly taken into account. It can be defined, in essence, as a serious identity crisis. The French Third Republic, the result of a difficult compromise between a monarchical and a republican regime, seems to have been plagued by multiple contradictions from the start. It has been noted how the choice to establish the Republic based on popular suffrage and not on the Paris insurrection of 1870 resulted in the end of the Revolution, transforming the

Republic into a national institution founded on the legal, democratic consensus of citizens. However, the planning aspect and the anxiety about regeneration that characterized the Revolution of 1789 would not simply cease to have an influence and would eventually contribute to tearing apart and destabilizing the political–institutional fabric of a republic founded on conservative consensus. This destabilization resulted (despite the institutionalization of the principles of 1789) in a deep schism in public opinion, corresponding to a breakup of the consensus following the French Revolution. It is no coincidence that the first years of the new government were marked by an extremely bitter face-off between "républicains" and "réactionnaires," between advocates of the Revolution and political forces or pressure groups (Legitimists, Orléanists, Bonapartists) opposed to the republican form of the country. This turmoil was aggravated by the tendency to use religion as an instrument of political struggle.

It should be no surprise that, starting from the 1880s, the regime already seemed to be in crisis, "*à bout de souffle*" – out of breath. Its future, which was suddenly uncertain, depended on the ability of the ruling class to properly manage the unprecedented problems faced by a country in the grips of radical changes to its socioeconomic fabric. In short, the regime depended on the ability to reinterpret and completely overhaul the republican ideas on which it was founded. The individualist philosophy at the core of the republican tradition at this point seemed unable to sustain its institutions in the face of the social imbalances generated by rapid, chaotic industrialization. In view of such a grave institutional crisis, the common thread of political–legal reflection would thus become a "quest for new sources of harmony in a society that could no longer be reduced to a mere aggregation of individuals" ["*recherche de nouvelles sources d'harmonie au sein d'une société qui ne pouvait plus se réduire à un simple agrégat d'individus.*"][10]

The main challenge that the ruling class of the French Third Republic had to grapple with was the need to metabolize universal suffrage, that is, the need to rethink the institutional context given changes of historical importance, simultaneously managing the imbalances and conflicts emerging from the rapidly changing socioeconomic fabric. The introduction of universal suffrage, in this perspective, was much more than symbolic: from this point on, the people ceased to be just an undifferentiated, threatening mass and became a politically relevant group. The bursting of the masses on to the scene, the sudden importance of the crowd in the political arena, determined a

[10] Cf. Christophe Jamin, "Dix-neuf cent," in Denis Alland and Stéphane Rials, eds., *Dictionnaire de la culture juridique* (Paris: Presses Universitaires de France, 2003), 380f.

painstaking revision (at least in this specific French context) of political culture and consolidated institutional structures, whose purpose was to stabilize the Republic through the combination of democracy, fraternity, and individualism, and the identification of a valid alternative to the traditional model of the gendarmerie-state. The novelty of universal suffrage would inevitably help make the social question even more tangible and promote policies of state intervention to deal with the most fragile segments of the population and to encourage their integration. This development spurred an even further distancing from traditional revolutionary universalism and a progressive "compromise," moving closer to a welfare state. The characteristics of the welfare state (*État-Providence*) began to take shape little by little, the social policies of which would be divided among three pillars: work, insurance, and assistance.

The result of this deep-seated transformation of the socioeconomic context, marked by the emergence of the crowd as a relevant political subject, was the progressive crisis of the bourgeois legal model and of the individualist paradigm that was its premise (with its corollaries: free will, freedom of contract, and the dematerialization of property, considered a mere projection of the owner's power). That model hinges on the transformation of the individual into a citizen, understood to be an elemental, isolated monad that helps shape the political body to the extent that it is inserted into it. Consequently, the state will become the exclusive agent of the constitution and of social bonds, resulting in a deep-seated depoliticization of the primary memberships. This depoliticization, derived from a vacuum of sociability, leads to a withdrawal of the subject to the private sphere. On the legal side, such a construct ensures that it is possible to create legal rules starting from the theoretical figure of an abstract individual, disconnected from any historic context, regardless of the concrete reality that surrounds and conditions him. In other words, the law can be established *ex nihilo*, regardless of history and society, thereby claiming to free itself from the constraints of reality.

The Modernist project thus develops in clear opposition to this model, understood as artificial, despotic, and sterilizing, trying to recover and juridically translate what, in the eyes of a "juriste de combat," seems to be a lost intricacy. Saleilles's entire scientific reflection is indeed aimed at encouraging the overthrow of that model, complicating the linear yet simplistic horizon typical of the Napoleonic legal conception. The latter started from the representation of a timeless person endowed with inalienable, equal rights, and from a reverence for law, which, in its generality and abstraction, has the pretext of resolving the extreme variety of the juridical dimension on its own.

From Saleilles's point of view, that model can be overcome through the creation of private law of social welfare (made possible through the implementation of renewed methodology), that is, by constructing private law that strives to translate the principles of the general welfare doctrine in technical terms. Solidarity and solidarism, as terms that condense the meaning of a fragile, precious compromise, become the key words to understanding the mentality of politicians and engaged intellectuals of the Belle Epoque. Their main concern was the search for an effective synthesis of liberty, equality, fraternity (*liberté*, *égalité*, and *fraternité*), attempted by thinking of fraternity no longer as a mystic synthesis but rather as an "exigence de solidarité, sans laquelle ni la liberté ni l'égalité n'ont de sens."[11]

That doctrine, which quickly rose to the rank of official philosophy of the French Third Republic, was the result of the painstaking quest for a possible compromise between individualism and collectivism. It was the opportune instrument that made it possible to temper individualism without slipping into socialism, and that presented itself as the ideal formula for a gradual, painless transition from the gendarmerie-state to the welfare state. It is no coincidence that a wide range of political and social forces of the time, from social Catholicism to radical socialism, converge at this very point. The clear connection that links Saleilles's work to welfare allows us to get an even clearer understanding of the "orthopedic" function of his work in relation to fragile republican institutions. *Droit social* and Modernism appear, in this perspective, as attempts to create the social welfare compromise that would make the fate of the *République* juridically plausible. Likewise, this connection would explain the inevitably "compromising" nature of that juridical blueprint, which proposes to renew legal science from within, while not entirely sacrificing the individualist premise – that is, starting from a juridical-centric option far removed from the idea of collective law founded on relationships of force and antagonism between opposing social classes.

The goal, in other words, was that of rationalizing the conflict, juridicizing it, bringing social excess and political excess within ordered categories (even in an updated version) of legal science, identifying technical instruments through which to generate a satisfying reading of the social – often in light of technical responses, but always "médiatisée par des concepts juridiques."[12]

[11] "A requirement of solidarity, without which freedom and equality are meaningless." Cf. M. Ozouf, "La Révolution française et l'idée de fraternité," in *Atti della "Natio Francorum"* (Bologna, October 5–7, 1989): 365ff.

[12] "Mediated by legal concepts." Cf. Christophe Jamin and Pierre-Yves Verkindt, "Droit civil et droit social: l'invention du style néo-classique chez les juristes français au début du XXe siècle," in Nicholas Kasirer, ed., *Le droit civil, avant tout un style?* (Montréal: Thémis, 2003), 110.

Saleilles's blueprint therefore represents a systematic attempt to intellectually reestablish the Republic on the basis of a type of sociology that highlights the characteristics of the individual's social existence. This sociology rests, therefore, on the premise of the individual's naturally belonging to entities, groups, and associations that form the basis of social reality. With that scope, the technical–legal element was destined to play a central role. Since the opening to the social must happen via law, it must pass through the essential medium of juridical rationality, and thus through jurisprudence, whose identity is reinforced by way of encounter with sociology.

The solidaristic approach therefore makes it possible to overcome the impasses of revolutionary law founded on the notion of social and political contracts, of a typically individualistic imprint, unable to harmonize the founding premises of the democratic regime – freedom and equality. As we have seen already, solidarism requires abandoning the cultural paradigm of the *Exégèse* and, in particular, the tendency to reduce the essence of law to positive law. In the new democracy founded on social citizenship (*citoyenneté*), there is no longer room for a rigidly mechanical and voluntarist understanding of the law or for a one-dimensional concept of it. The political–legal landscape can no longer be resolved in a simplistic tête-à-tête between state and individual. For that reason, the generation of private law of welfare is the indispensable premise to completing the revolutionary parable, as a decisive tool to make the passage to social democracy juridically plausible (with that passage understood as the final landing place and the realization of an only partially completed political process).

The Saleilles blueprint, however, is destined to remain unappreciated unless the religious dimension, which pervades it and from which it draws constant nourishment, is duly considered. It is no coincidence that such a reflection is accompanied by his lively interest in the theological debate of the day. The study of biblical hermeneutics undoubtedly captivated Saleilles and has evident repercussions in the theory of juridical interpretation, in that it favors generating a methodological historicism that makes evolutionary interpretation a decisive expedient for enlivening the judicial system, overcoming the rigidity produced by a hierarchical system of sources of rights. The *méthode historique*, undoubtedly Saleilles's most precious bequest to European jurists of the twentieth century, is a historical–evolutionary hermeneutical canon, within which the law loses the original nature of command, voluntaristically connoted, to take on the nature of living organism (*organisme vivant*). The law is a living cell independent of the legal order; it is understood organically, and thus can evolve according to changed historical–social contingencies. The old exegetical mentality was banished, thanks to a methodological reflection that, while it rejected the law (*loi*) understood in the Rousseauvian sense, also made it the place par excellence of legality, within which the law, transfigured, constituted the basis and the essential point of reference for a work of legal science that was once again aware of its own autonomy and its own creative role.

The resulting theory of interpretation was premised on an understanding of law as the place of legal development [*milieu du développement juridique*], as a consequence of replacing eighteenth-century juridical voluntarism with an objective and organicist–finalistic understanding of the law and the legal system. The new theory rejected the view of interpretation as a search for the legislators' intention [*voluntas legis*], as a way of giving law a meaning corresponding to the presumed will of its author, independent of the time span that separates its promulgation and its application. Instead, interpretation should be understood as a progressive activity, aimed at "harmonizing texts with the law of the land as a whole, hence with the set of principles that govern it and direct its development as soon as one has to apply it." The law thus ceases to be considered an act of will, comparable to a testament, but becomes a "principle of social order," a "procedure for regulating organic life," emanated by the legislator like a "principle that must be sufficient in itself." Viewed thus, law has, as its subject, not only the satisfaction of the needs of the moment (which determine its promulgation), but the satisfaction of the permanent needs of the collectivity, insofar as they are connected to the subject that it describes and regulates. Thus, law is not an isolated, self-sufficient source, but rather part of a legal mechanism that it fits into like a gear necessary for the general functioning of the whole. This conception of law creates one fundamental consequence: interpretation is essentially adaptation and evolution, as the law-organism changes incessantly to ensure the proper functioning of the overall system of which it is part.

Saleilles's organicism arose from the realization that interpretation in the field of law cannot have the purpose of reconstructing a will, that the claim to reveal the will of the legislator is in vain, impossible, purely fiction, as it would amount to chasing down the will of all voters and carving out, from the average of them, the general will of the majority. It would be a useless operation (as well as impossible), as the legislator issues a law not as an act of will but as a principle of social order, an organism, a living entity, destined to enter into a relationship with society and to advance and evolve with it. This is the equivalent of saying that the will is "consumed" without leaving a trace as soon as the law is approved. It follows that the nature of the law changes radically, as it becomes a regulating principle of social life, having an organic nature. It is thus subject to development independent of the will that brought it into being. Located at the center of a complex legal fabric, the law is captured in its objective dimension, where what counts is the network of nexuses of which that text is an opportunity every time the community welcomes it and relives it. The shift of attention from the moment the measure is issued to its life in time and space, and thus to the moment of application, ensures that the debate on method transforms into a debate about interpretation: the hub of the regulation moves from an immobilized, idealized text to its interpretation, understood as an intermediary between text and subsequent circumstances. The hermeneutic operation is thus the result of two mirrored activities, entrusted to the interpreter: the *assouplissement*, that is, the evolutionary, relativizing interpretation of the legal text, which is bent to fit the changing contents of realities proposed by different historical contingencies; and the *encadrement*, or the reconciliation of those contingencies, of events, in the packaging that has been made flexible by the legal text, considered the *couvert nécessaire* of hermeneutic operation.

Interpretation is thus the outcome of a dialectic relationship between the juridical dimension and factual reality, whose correct articulation is shifted to the judge. Proceeding by *assouplissements* and subsequent *encadrements*, the judge ensures a solution that meets social expectations, an expression of the vitality of the juridical organism as a whole. Given this context, legal scholarship has a crucial task: it is called on to establish the objective bases of evolutionary interpretation, starting from the assumption that the inspiring principles of juridical hermeneutics must be sought not so much in the texts as in the large currents of opinion that influence institutions. Since these objective principles are predetermined on a doctrinal level, there is no risk of coming up against subjectivistic deviations or of reproducing the whims and *a priori* assumptions typical of the old school of natural law.

CHRISTIAN SCIENTIFIC SPIRIT

The human and scientific parable of Raymond Saleilles is entirely enclosed within the temporal horizon of the French Third Republic. Consequently, his Catholicism was the faithful reflection of a notably complex, rich era, characterized by the arrival of a new political–constitutional regime, compromising by nature, which struggled to take root in a country torn apart by apparently insurmountable tensions. The young republic, emerging from the defeat of Sedan, suffered the backlash of the violent political and social tensions that rattled France in the late nineteenth century, in a setting in which the religious question took on absolute centrality. For a long time, before the policy of acceptance of the Republic (*ralliement*) promoted by Pope Leo XIII, an insuperable wall separated French Catholics from the republican state, considered hostile and unacceptable, before which they appeared like a potentially subversive foreign body.

From the start of his path, Saleilles chose to belong to the most "uncomfortable" and unquestionably smallest minority in the French Catholic church, that is, the tiny circle of *catholiques libéraux*. This did not stop him, however, from developing a marked sensitivity to topics dear to social Catholicism over time, as he himself demonstrated in an account published in *La Croix* on September 14, 1906. There, in addition to the definition of the salient points of a genuinely Catholic political program, we find him proudly laying claim to the merits of French Catholicism. He considered it one of the avant-garde movements in social reform because the slow, patient pressure exerted by Catholic reformism had allowed for the spread of requests for reform even among classes traditionally hostile to social action. The complexity of Saleilles's Catholicism is undoubtedly "genetic" and can be traced back to the early years of his spiritual training as an adult, when, as a university student, he began to attend the Conférence Olivaint, a student society founded to prepare its members for public life. Within this institution Raymond Saleilles perfected his own form of Catholicism, developing a lively interest in the rich theological and scriptural debate of the era.

The Conférence was a place of recruitment for young people coming from noble or bourgeois families, and thus had a markedly elitist nature. Its scope was Catholic training and placement, according to the specific modalities of Ignatian spirituality, of the country's future ruling class. In a certain sense, the Conférence Olivaint faithfully reflected the complexity of French Catholicism in the specific sociopolitical context of the French Third Republic. If, on the one hand, the Conférence from its beginning made up a "stronghold of most resolute opposition to the republican regime," it also acted as a fundamental meeting point between the various sensibilities of the Catholic world. Within it, the hottest topics of the era were debated (the *ralliement*, the separation crisis, the condemnation of the *Action française*), with the result that it became a valuable place of discussion and even conflict between positions and sensibilities that at times were considerably far apart.

The development of Saleilles's Catholicism began with this initial experience, tapping into three fundamental sources of inspiration. The first, and certainly the highest, was that of John Henry Newman, one of the greatest theologians of the nineteenth century. Saleilles dedicated himself to Newman on different occasions, even taking on the translation of his discourses.

The second inspiration was Marc Sangnier, founder and soul of Le Sillon (The Furrow), a movement with which Saleilles shared an essential theoretical hypothesis, namely, that democracy has religious value; that such a system of government is the only form of social organization able to elevate the civic consciousness of citizens to the highest levels; and that democracy ultimately derives from the insertion of religious values into the modern world.

The third source of inspiration was the priest and social reformer Jules Lemire, one of the most famous *abbés-démocrates*, and leader of the Christian Democratic movement. Lemire was a key figure in the republican, progressive Catholicism that, in a climate of frontal opposition, tried to find the path to durable coexistence with institutions, in line with the strategy outlined by Pope Leo XIII. Lemire can therefore be considered a prominent representative of that sort of hybrid social coalition that characters of different political cultures belonged to, whose aim was to promote and support the solidarist pact. An analysis of Lemire's work and personality can help us understand, by reflection, a large part of Saleilles's human and scientific actions.

There are quite a few similarities between Lemire's political and social activities and the legal topics that the jurist from Beaune pondered on multiple occasions. The topics that Lemire pondered in his sociopolitical reflections coincide with a few of the large topics debated within the Christian Democratic movement: the political development of public assistance and an obligatory social security system; the gradual disappearance of the proletariat through the development of the cooperative movement; the development of smallholdings as a central element of citizenship and the tendency to highlight the social function of that right; the reform of the electoral system – to reestablish the social bond (*lien social*) and integrate the masses following the novelty of universal suffrage – through the introduction of proportional representation, family vote (*vote familial*), and professional representation; and, in particular, the introduction of the right of association as an engine of the new social democracy, in the conviction that the foundation of an authentic democracy is made up of a differentiated society in which the associative phenomenon and the reappearance of new intermediary bodies make it possible to overcome rigid revolutionary individualism.

The admiration and esteem shown toward Lemire help us focus on the peculiar characteristics of Saleilles's piety. In years marked by bitter theological debate and continuous attempts to exploit religion in the name of politics, Lemire set to reconciling the truths of Catholic beliefs with the freedom and dignity of believers. The *Lettre à Lemire*, which served as the introduction to Saleilles's translation of Newman's sermons, contains a sort of defense of the mayor of Hazebrouck. Saleilles considered Lemire the model of priesthood prefigured by the great English theologian, the defining element of which is the presence of a "*forte individualité de libre chrétien*," that is, the ability to embody the evangelical message beyond confessional struggles, resisting any attempt at political exploitation. In this context, the meditation on the margin of freedom left open to believers was central. Saleilles clarified it on the basis of reflections that echo Charles Péguy's distinction between an authoritarian dimension and a mystical dimension of Christianity (a distinction that coincides with the traditional and merely apparent conflict between divine grace and the institution). Saleilles's reflection turns Protestantism into a providential presence and, paradoxically, an enlivening element for Catholicism. The reference to "*inspiration personnelle*," embodied in the Pauline teaching, of which Lemire seems to be a champion, was decisive in Saleilles's eyes, as it made it possible to trace the path for believers who wanted to constructively face the challenges posed by modernity.

In the wake of Sangnier and Lemire, Saleilles presented himself as a prophet of progressive, socially oriented Catholicism and, over the years, developed an analysis whose essential thematic poles were the problem of the relationship between state and church and the complex relationship between faith and reason, rendered urgent by the observation of rampant religious indifference. In this perspective, he became the promoter of a strategic line divided into two levels, distinguished according to their final objectives. First, to bring the masses back to Catholicism, it seemed necessary to avoid validating the existence of a link between politics and religion through disastrous initiatives, such as the idea of starting a Catholic-inspired political party. Second, to bring the elites back within the fold of religion, it would be necessary to overcome the intellectual crisis that resulted from the apparent incompatibility between theological thought and more recent conquests of technical–scientific progress.

The conviction about the singularity of the religious experience, of its difficult-to-convey character, made the idea of a confessional state or a state religion intolerable in his eyes, as he viewed such a state as the mixture of areas that should remain strictly separate. This particular view of religion allows us to understand the role carried out by Saleilles in the inflamed sociopolitical climate of the early 1900s, in particular his position on the 1905 law and his participation in the role of "green cardinal" in Brunetière's letter to the French bishops. As a jurist and a consultant to broad sectors of the French episcopate, Saleilles spoke out in favor of accepting the law of 1905, clearly grasping its positive elements: faced with the loss of a preferential juridical regime and the institutional visibility that it had enjoyed for centuries, the church had the chance to gain never-before-seen independence and freedom in its actions regarding political power. That gain seemed decisive in the context of a conception that made the future destiny of Christianity depend on reawakening the consciences of individuals, on a renewed spiritual impulse, and not on the transformation of religion into a tool for political struggle.

The other central element in Saleilles's thought concerned the relationship between Catholicism and modernity. Saleilles developed his thinking by paying close attention to the Modernist crisis, toward which he showed interest and even sympathy without, however, adhering to the most extreme and dissolving conclusions of that stream of thought. Building upon the work of Harnack, Delitzsch, Lagrange, König, Loisy, and, of course, Newman, Saleilles postulated the compatibility between evolutionism and the dogmatic structure of Catholicism. This compatibility is possible by distinguishing, in the dogma, the *fond*, the "essence" – the essential nucleus, the reflection of a "*vérité objective transcendante*" – from the external elements, from the inevitably changeable, contingent, historical manifestations of the church's teaching. It follows that the truth of the dogma presumes a focus on the essential elements of revelation and is the result of a work of collective interpretation, entrusted to a community of particularly authoritative interpreters, whose interpretation gains value and credibility in the degree to which it is organic in nature and inserted into a dynamic process of evolution and adaptation.

RECOMMENDED READING

Alland, Denis, and Stéphane Rials, editors. *Dictionnaire de la culture juridique*. Paris: Presses Universitaires de France, 2003.

Arabeyre, Patrick, Jean-Louis Halpérin, and Jacques Krynen, editors. *Dictionnaire historique des juristes français, XIIe–XXe siècle*, 694–96. Paris: Presses Universitaires de France, 2007.

Arnaud, André-Jean. *Da giureconsulti a tecnocrati: diritto e società in Francia dalla codificazione ai nostri giorni*. Naples: Jovene, 1993.

Les juristes face à la société du XIXe siècle à nos jours. Paris: Presses Universitaires de France, 1975.

"Une doctrine de l'état tranquillisante: le solidarisme juridique." *Archives de philosophie du droit* (1976): 131ff.

Atias, Christian. "Premières réflexions sur la doctrine française de droit privé (1900–1930)." *Revue de la recherche juridique* (1981/82): 189–201.

Audren, Frédéric, and Christian Chêne, editors. *Raymond Saleilles et au-delà*. Paris: Dalloz, 2013.

Beaud, Olivier. "Doctrine." In Alland and Rials, *Dictionnaire de la culture juridique*, 384–88.

Bonnecase, Julien. *L'École de l'exégèse en droit civil: les traits distinctifs de sa doctrine et de ses méthodes d'après la profession de foi de ses plus illustres représentants*. Paris: E. de Boccard, 1924.

Bureau, D. "Les regards doctrinaux sur le Code civil." In Lequette and Leveneur, *1804–2004: Le Code civil: un passé, un présent, un avenir*, 171–210.
Cachard, Olivier, and François-Xavier Licari, editors. *La pensée de François Gény*. Paris: Dalloz, 2013.
Digeon, Claude. *La crise allemande de la pensée française 1870–1914*. Paris: Presses Universitaires de France, 1992.
Ewald, François. *L'État Providence*. Paris: B. Grasset, 1986.
Gaudemet, Eugène. "Raymond Saleilles." *Revue bourguignonne de l'Université de Dijon* 22 (1912): 161–263.
Grynbaum, Luc, and Marc Nicod, editors. *Le solidarisme contractuel*. Paris: Economica, 2004.
Gutmann, D. "La fonction sociale de la doctrine juridique-Brèves réflexions à partir d'un ouvrage collectif sur 'Méthode d'interprétation et sources en droit privé positif.'" *Revue trimestrielle de droit civil* (2002): 455ff.
Halpérin, Jean-Louis. *Histoire du droit privé français depuis 1804*. Paris: Presses Universitaires de France, 1996. See especially 171ff.
Imbart De La Tour, Pierre. "Raymond Saleilles." *Le bulletin de la semaine* (22 May 1912): 241–42.
Jamin, Christophe. "Dix-neuf cent." In Alland and Rialos, *Dictionnaire de la culture juridique*, 380–84.
"François Gény d'un siècle à l'autre." In *François Gény, mythe et réalités. 1899–1999 Centenaire de Méthode d'interprétation et sources en droit privé positif, essai critique*, 3–33. Québec: Blais , 2000.
"L'oubli et la science. Regard partiel sur l'évolution de la doctrine privatiste à la charnière des XIXe et XXe siècle." *Revue trimestrielle de droit civil* (1994): 815–27.
Jamin, Christophe, Frédéric Audren, and Sylvain Bloquet, editors. *Lettres de François Gény à Raymond Saleilles: une trajectoire intellectuelle, 1892–1912*. Paris: LGDJ, 2015.
Jestaz, Philippe, and Christophe Jamin. "En relisant Eugène Gaudemet." In *L'interprétation du Code civil en France depuis 1804*, edited by Eugène Gaudemet, et al. Paris: La mémoire du droit, 2002.
Lazar, Marc. "La République à l'épreuve du social." In *La démocratie en France*, edited by Marc Sadoun, 309–406. Paris: Gallimard, 2000.
Lequette, Yves, and Laurent Leveneur, editors. *1804–2004: Le Code civil: un passé, un présent, un avenir*. Paris: Université Panthéon-Assas, 2004.
Matthey, N. "Le Code civil et le développement du droit vus par Raymond Saleilles." In Lequette and Leveneur, *1804–2004: Le Code civil: un passé, un présent, un avenir*, 211ff.
Mazet, P. "Le courant solidariste." In Grynbaum and Nicod, *Le solidarisme contractuel*, 13ff.
Nicolet, Claude *L'idée républicaine en France*. Paris: Gallimard, 1982.
Niort, Jean-François. *Homo civilis: contribution à l'histoire du Code civil français, 1804–1965*. Aix-en-Provence: Presses Université d'Aix-Marseille, 2004. See especially volume II, 371ff. and 417ff.
Remy, P. "La genèse du solidarisme." In Grynbaum and Nicod, *Le solidarisme contractuel*, 11ff.

Rosanvallon, Pierre. "La République du suffrage universel." In *Le siècle de l'avènement républicain*, edited by François Furet, Mona Ozouf, Keith Baker, et al., 371ff. Paris: Gallimard, 1993.

Saleilles, Raymond. *L'œuvre juridique de Raymond Saleilles*. Edited by Robert Beudant. Paris: Arthur Rousseau, 1914.

Stora-Lamarre, Annie. *La République des faibles*. Paris: Armand Colin, 2005.

Tellier, F. "Le droit à l'épreuve de la société. Raymond Saleilles et l'idée du droit social." *Revue d'histoire du droit et de la science juridique* 20 (1999): 147–77

20

Maurice Hauriou

(1856–1929)

JULIEN BARROCHE

BIOGRAPHICAL INTRODUCTION

If the Christian inspiration of Maurice Hauriou's thought cannot be doubted, that fact does not detract from the profound originality of an author uninclined to be locked into an intellectual system, even that of Thomas Aquinas. A man of deep faith, the master of Toulouse nevertheless was always reluctant to engage in public debate as a Catholic.[1] The great jurist, whose name is definitively associated with the Faculty of Law of Toulouse, was a man of his time, a conservative defender of a certain moral order, but this rigor of temperament was connected to a very strong independence of mind and a heterodox intellectual approach. The man was classical, the thinker resolutely atypical, even iconoclastic: unusual in his interests, in his methods of work, but also in his methods of teaching.[2] Hauriou, an intellectual nomad, nourished himself with the whole spectrum of scientific knowledge available without worrying *a priori* about disciplinary boundaries, ranging from philosophy to history, not to mention sociology and the physical sciences.

It is no exaggeration of his intellectual legacy to recall his indelible imprint on French public law. Perhaps he did not acquire a following, but Maurice Hauriou bequeathed a considerable work that inspired many, even in his lifetime, and spread far beyond the French borders.[3] Primarily known for his

[1] Unlike a Raymond Saleilles or a Louis Le Fur. Let us note, for example, that Hauriou never participated in *Semaines sociales*, an annual meeting of Catholic intellectuals.

[2] Contrary to the sometimes-rigid form of legal teachings, Hauriou innovated by creating the first meeting room for public law conferences at the Faculty of Toulouse. Moreover, it was on his initiative that, in 1894, a free course of social science was opened, of which he took charge.

[3] See *La Pensée de Maurice Hauriou et son influence* (Paris: Pedone, 1969). Let us mention the influence of Hauriou on some of Carl Schmitt's writings, even though the German jurist strongly distorted the thought of someone he may have considered an "elder brother." Moreover, the same observation of misinterpretation applies to the putative heirs of Hauriou,

career as an administrativist and an *arrêtiste* (a jurist who comments on decisions by a supreme court – here, the French Conseil d'État), Hauriou was nonetheless always a jurist, always eager to comprehensively apprehend his various research objects. He was part of a generation who understood law as a general subject, grouping together all dimensions of social life – from civil law to public law and nascent constitutional law.[4] In terms of intellectual itinerary, retrospective reconstructions are often misleading; they are so in this case because nothing predestined Hauriou to become the great administrativist we know. It was the contingencies of the university career that led the jurist, first a Romanist and law historian, to specialize in administrative law,[5] until he received the title, fully justified, of the founder of the discipline.

Born in 1856, Maurice Hauriou grew up Catholic in the rural southwest of France. While his family was based in Ladiville, a small commune of Charente, the young Hauriou graduated from high school in Angoulême and then studied law at Bordeaux. He defended his thesis (*Du terme en droit romain et en droit français* [Study on completion in Roman law and French law]) in 1876 and then his doctoral thesis on the notion of *Condictio* three years later (*Étude sur la* condictio. *Les contrats à titre onéreux entre époux*, [Study on Condictio. Contracts for valuable consideration between spouses]). After two unsuccessful attempts, he passed his law *agrégation* in 1882. His rank of major allowed him to be appointed the following year to the law faculty of Toulouse, the second in France after Paris. He was first in charge of the course on general history of law, then, from 1887, the course on administrative law. While his first wish, expressed as early as 1883, was to join the faculty in Paris,[6] Hauriou became gradually anchored in Toulouse. He was tenured as professor in a chair of administrative law in 1888, and in 1906 was elected dean of the faculty, where he spent the remainder of his career (he was constantly reelected dean until his retirement in 1926). A new period began when, in

who, with the exception of Achille Mestre and André Hauriou, did not embrace the whole body of the work but only some of its dimensions (Georges Renard, Georges Burdeau, Jean Rivero, Georges Vedel, for example).

[4] Only international law does not seem to have sustained his attention. The reflection of Maurice Hauriou is essentially limited to the internal dimension of the law.

[5] Throughout the 1880s, Hauriou continued to publish articles on the history of law and Roman law.

[6] Between 1883 and 1899, the young professor sought several times to be recruited by the University of Paris, but his atypicality (his propensity to go beyond the field of law *stricto sensu*) was a key obstacle. Let us add that he had to wait until 1919 to sit on the public law *agrégation* board and until 1920 to accede to the presidency of the jury.

the aftermath of the First World War, Hauriou, then nearly 65 years old, left his chair in administrative law to occupy the chair of constitutional law during the last six years of his career (1920–26) – without quitting, however, his tireless activity as an *arrêtiste* or abandoning the regular updating of his doctrinal reflections in administrative matters. He died in 1929 at the age of 72, only a few months after the man who was his eternal interlocutor and opponent, Léon Duguit.

Spread over forty years, Hauriou's publications logically followed the rhythm of his main teachings. We can cite three major works, which have not all had the same editorial success and the same lasting impact. His most famous legal work is the *Précis de droit administratif*, a tome of more than seven hundred pages first published in 1892 and revised ten times at regular intervals until 1927.[7] His least understood book, the *Principes de droit public*, which condenses a real theory of the state, had two successive editions, in 1910 and 1916. Finally, his most mature work, the *Précis de droit constitutionnel*, represents the last stage of his intellectual journey as a dean. The two versions of the second *Précis* (1923 and 1929) chronologically straddle the writing of an important text that condenses the essence of Hauriou's philosophy of law: "The Theory of the Institution and the Foundation" (1925).[8] To this seminal text and to the three great works and numerous articles (including those published in the *Recueil de législation de Toulouse*, which develop or amplify specific points of the larger works), it is necessary to add more than 350 comments of judgments (1892–1928) and the sociological writings of the 1890s – *La Science sociale traditionnelle* (1896) in particular – which decisively guided the jurist's scientific research.

Without wanting to homogenize it retrospectively, one can say that his body of work shows a great unity. Beyond the necessary inflections of a perpetually searching mind that always refused fidelity to a system, the intellectual itinerary of the Toulouse jurist shows striking coherence. From his earliest writings, the outlines of his thought are, so to speak, fixed: a broad vision of the science of law, a naturalist and finalist definition of the law, a concomitant defense of the authority of the state and rights of the individual, a very sharp distinction between public and private law, an affirmed criticism of the sanctification of the law, and an affirmed criticism of parliamentary sovereignty.

[7] Not to mention the posthumous edition of 1933, coordinated by his son André.

[8] Hauriou considered the theory of the institution as "the great work of his life." Although his final formulation appeared in 1925, his lineaments were set nearly twenty years earlier, even in sociological writings (see below). With the *Principes*, the theory of the institution provides the theoretical framework for the dean's constitutional thinking.

INDIVIDUALISM AND CATHOLIC NATURAL-LAW THEORY

Hauriou's philosophy of law is rooted in the highest spheres of theology, but this Catholic anchoring of the jurist does not make him an antimodernist thinker. For Hauriou, power, far from being the fruit of any human convention, is conceived first as a natural phenomenon that ultimately finds its origin in God. Law, meanwhile, does not derive from the rationality of a human legislator; rather, as a social phenomenon, product of the sociality of man, it is observed in the nature of things.[9] Humanity's first vocation is to constitute a pole of moral resistance in the face of evil, to contain the evil present in every human being. For Hauriou, the law cannot be understood outside of a deep anthropological pessimism inherited from awareness of the Fall; in such a frame, power in general and the state in particular play the role of institutional figures of redemption. However, Hauriou's conservatism may refer to the nature of things, which is dynamic; he remained always attentive to the work of time and "creative developments" so dear to Henri Bergson. Along with the philosopher of intuition, the jurist of the institution shares the same feeling of an unpredictable evolution of the world in perpetual reinvention.[10] Consequently, the natural order does not proceed without continual correction, which improves the order but in a "slow and uniform movement."[11]

A Catholic who rallied to the Republic and committed to the fundamental values of the traditional right, Hauriou is conservative but also liberal. His thinking is symptomatic of a particular context, that of the modernist crisis of French Catholicism, the product of the meeting of the Catholic world with the liberal and individualistic world.[12] Certainly, Hauriou draws on the thought of Thomas Aquinas, but this intellectual reinvestment is unique in that it takes place in a moment of historical rupture, the precise moment when

[9] Society has an objective existence, right is not created by the state (see below). It is this "faithful mirror of society" that the jurist devotes himself to deciphering by considering it not as a conceptual abstraction but an unprompted reality. (Maurice Hauriou, "De la personnalité comme élément de la réalité sociale," *Revue générale du droit, de la législation et de la jurisprudence en France et à l'étranger* 1 [1898]: 5–23, 2 [1898]: 119–40.)

[10] The jurist's biographers often rightly point out Bergson's influence on Hauriou. It should also be noted that Hauriou did not wait for the publication of *L'Évolution créatrice* (1907) to express his positions on social dynamics. Having read Bergson, he referred to *L'Évolution* regularly. His intellectual companionship with philosopher Jacques Chevalier attests to this Bergsonian sensitivity.

[11] Maurice Hauriou, *Principes de droit public*, 1st edn (Paris: Sirey, 1910): 7; *Précis de droit constitutionnel*, 2nd edn (Paris: Sirey, 1929): 76.

[12] Hauriou was close to Monsignor Battifol, a great figure of the modernist current within the Catholic Church.

the Catholic Church, under the impetus of Leo XIII, the pope of Thomist revival, organizes its strategic rallying to modernity. Of course, the depth of Hauriou's analysis cannot be reduced to simple expression of a context. It remains that the historical configuration of the late nineteenth century and the beginning of the twentieth largely determines the formulation and articulation of the main thesis of Hauriou's analysis. Hauriou defends what he calls the "individualistic social order" and adheres, without complaining, to the liberal regime of separations, including the separation of church and state.[13] However, he rejects the dimensions of liberal ideology that are incompatible with faith: moral relativism, materialism, and subjectivist voluntarism.

Thus becomes clear the sociological investment of Maurice Hauriou. His detour through sociology is a means of doing justice to his fundamental metaphysical options by translating them into the modern language of the social sciences. Hauriou will eventually seek external support for the modern definition of law to revigorate Christian morality and revive, in his own way, the classical doctrine of natural law. The social science he promotes is "traditional"; he considers it in the service of law.[14] Charged to carry the message of a tradition shaken by modernity, it wants to break with the utilitarianism and amoralism of nascent sociology.[15] Therefore, as in traditional Catholic doctrine, positive norms ultimately receive their validity not from being posited by the human will, but from their divine origin and vocation to develop conclusions virtually contained in natural law. Hauriou also rejects, as contrary to the nature of things, the modern dogma of equality. He emphasizes the beneficial character of inequalities and, in the vein of a Saint-Simon or an Auguste Comte, insists on the role of elites – not in the aristocratic sense but in the functional understanding of competence. His hierarchical representation of the social order makes it possible to understand the limits he constantly put on the democratic principle and the options he defended in terms of constitutional organization of powers. If he unambiguously accepted universal suffrage as an unavoidable reality in the evolution of Western societies, Hauriou remained deeply suspicious of the egalitarian philosophy in which it was rooted.

[13] Without engaging in public debate, Hauriou defended the liberal spirit of the 1905 law.

[14] This can be seen as a response to the claim of sociology to become the mother of scientific disciplines. See Frédéric Audren and Marc Milet, "Maurice Hauriou sociologue. Entre sociologie catholique et physique sociale," Preface to Maurice Hauriou, *Écrits sociologiques* (Paris: Dalloz, 2008).

[15] Maurice Hauriou, *La Science sociale traditionnelle* (1896), in *Écrits sociologiques* (Paris: Dalloz, 2008).

Hauriou's sociological tooling is coupled with a metaphysical realism that prevents him from any kind of nominalism (ideas and collective beings exist in the same way as things and individuals) and clearly expresses itself in his theory of the institution. From a schema that symbolically echoes the dogma of the Trinity, the jurist identifies the three elements of the definition of the institution: first, at the source of the institutional formation, "an idea of work"; second, an organization that perpetuates itself over time; finally, a personification by adhesion and consent, making institutional realities the very source of the rules of law.[16]

From there, he developed an original synthesis of scientific positivism, partly inherited from Auguste Comte, and Christian metaphysics, drawn particularly from St Thomas. Hauriou was indebted to the father of French sociology, Émile Durkheim, and much more to Gabriel Tarde (*Les Lois de l'imitation*, 1890), even though Hauriou's Catholicism protected him from Tarde's psychologically based individualism. Carried to moderation, Hauriou's Catholicism also protected him from the reactionary thinking of a Frédéric Le Play as well as *L'Action française*. Hauriou operated a kind of synthesis integrating traditional themes of nineteenth-century Catholicism to a liberal conservatism compatible with the Republic.[17]

Among Hauriou's fundamental options, the reference to natural law obviously calls for specific development. On this point, as on many others, the lawyer should not so much be identified with a specific school as considered a thinker creating his own path. The Thomist inspiration for Hauriou is undeniable, and he clearly claimed it. However, in the light of disparate influences, it would be wrong to confine the jurist to the classical doctrine of Catholic natural-law theory. Against St Thomas, or the dominant interpretation of the thought of the Angelic Doctor (think of Michel Villey), Hauriou also defended an immutable natural right, but it ultimately aimed at the idea of justice (the idea of justice is eternal, and the human order is directed to its realization).[18] Beyond a certain latency in vocabulary, the jurist relied clearly on a Thomistic definition of the law and a Thomistic view of right order. His criticisms of the generality of the law as well as of the valorization of the prudence of the law recall Aristotle: justice does not find expression so much

[16] Maurice Hauriou, "La théorie de l'institution et de la fondation. Essai de vitalisme social," *Cahiers de la Nouvelle Journée* 4 (1925): 1–45.

[17] There were also liberal Catholics at the tip of the Christian Democratic movement, such as Paul Archambault and Marcel Prélot, who worked to publicize the work of the Toulouse lawyer beyond academic circles, in the *Cahiers de la Nouvelle Journée* or the review *Politique*.

[18] See Olivier Beaud, "Hauriou et le droit naturel," *Revue d'histoire des Facultés de droit de la science juridique* 6 (1988): 123–38.

in general laws, one understands, as in specific decisions – be they judicial or administrative decisions.

More than realistic (in the old sense), the Haurioutist philosophy is finalist: it is in striving towards their end that beings and things express their true essence and their ultimate meaning. The law is teleological; it is directed towards an end, that of justice and the common good, of order and morality. It might be confused with simple fact if it were separated from morality, but, polarized by the distinction between good and evil, it is, as it should be, ordered to the Christian idea of truth.[19]

For the rest, Maurice Hauriou's individualist bias necessarily distanced him from classical natural law. Positive law has the fundamental vocation of becoming increasingly compliant with natural law, which is interpreted in the light of the realization of the "individualistic social order." Hauriou put his Aristotelian–Thomist conception of politics at the service of individualist liberalism, but he defended a certain conception of liberalism and individualism.

THE COLLECTIVE POINT OF VIEW OF PUBLIC LAW

Hauriou sometimes suffers from an unjust reputation: that of advocating an authoritarian thought unconditionally defending the verticality of public power. This distorted image is the result of an aspect, ultimately isolated and unrepresentative, of his dialogue with Léon Duguit, in the version that was bequeathed to posterity: the Toulouse school of public power (*puissance publique*) against the Bordeaux school of public service (*service public*).[20] Hauriou's vehement opposition to the strike of civil servants,[21] his notion of "enforceable decision" (*décision exécutoire)*, or his postwar defense of administrative centralization may have fueled this reputation, which was as erroneous as it was persistent.[22] It is enough to attentively revisit writings of the master of

[19] Suffice it to mention the very strict remarks of Hauriou on the consumption of alcohol (note on CE, 1915, Delmotte), his final judgment on the licentious character of theatrical activity (note on CE, 1916, Astruc), or his condemnation of prostitution (note on CE, 1919, Dames Dol et Laurent) to understand his uncompromising defense of a certain moral order.

[20] Titled "La puissance publique et le service public" (Public Power and Public Service), the preface to the eleventh edition of the *Précis de droit administratif* (1927) can be read as an answer to Gaston Jèze, even more than to Léon Duguit.

[21] Maurice Hauriou, *Précis de droit administratif*, 10th edn (Paris: Sirey, 1921): 577–78.

[22] In the ninth edition of the *Précis* (1919), Hauriou presented administrative centralization as an imperative in the face of internal and external threats in a climate of weakening national peace and as a condition of freedom in the face of plurality of interests at work in society. In the eleventh edition, Hauriou distinguished the notion of enforceable decision (*décision*

Toulouse to find that he was the first French jurist to have legally consecrated the notion of public service and that he refused to oppose the terms public service (that is, the administrative state in a functional sense) and public power (that is, the specific means used by the administrative state). What has been wrongly interpreted as authoritarian thought ultimately reveals itself as a thought of the collective, of collective action, which would be expressed in particular in the theory of the institution and, more generally, in the Haurioutist definition of public law. Here lies the great contribution of Maurice Hauriou: by upgrading the social fact in relation to the human will, he sought to identify an object specific to public law, to enhance its collective demands, and to emphasize the separation of the public and private spheres – marks of the liberal state.

The major pillars of his administrative doctrine were established as early as 1892 in the first edition of the *Précis de droit administratif*, which paved the way to a veritable doctrinal turn. The book contrasts with existing publications, if only because of its ambition to embrace all fields and all objects of administrative law. Above all, it offers a reflection on public law that integrates social facts without simply listing or compiling applicable rules of law. At the heart of a clear distinction between private acts and acts of public authority, the concept of public service is for the first time advanced in the third edition, published in 1897, then two years later in *La Gestion administrative*.[23] This short but dense and deeply innovative text received a more-than-skeptical reception. It was too innovative, probably. Hauriou overrode the usual distinction – notably systematized by Édouard Laferrière (*Traité de la juridiction administrative*, 1887) – between acts of authority and acts of management,[24] and thus upset established habits and some intellectual laziness, while affirming that acts of management can also bring into play prerogatives of public power. Anxious to consolidate the jurisdiction of the administrative judge by not limiting it to acts of authority, Hauriou intended to distinguish, among acts of management, between those calling for ordinary means

exécutoire) from the category of unilateral act to emphasize the objective specificity from the collective point of view. It was the objective necessity of the execution of the act in the interest of the collective that justified his denomination of enforceable decision, where the unilateral act remained mainly defined by its intersubjective logic (will of the author of the act).

[23] Maurice Hauriou, *La Gestion administrative. Étude théorique de droit administratif* (Paris: Larose, 1899).

[24] It should be noted that Hauriou had just published *La Science sociale traditionnelle* (1896) and was preparing to publish his *Leçons sur le mouvement social* – a second book that would be less welcome than the first, in which he mobilized mechanics and thermodynamics to grasp the movement of the social order (Maurice Hauriou, *Leçons sur le mouvement social* (1899), in *Écrits sociologiques* (Paris: Dalloz, 2008)).

(hypothesis of private management) and those calling for means derogatory to common law (hypothesis of public management). The jurist's interest is obviously in this second category, which refers to the most common acts and concerns essentially the management of public services. On the one hand, the administrative act of management ultimately finds its criterion of identification, if not of definition, in the purpose it pursues, and not in the means it uses. On the other hand, the public management act in question is subjected to trial in the administrative court.

Hauriou sought ultimately to show that the jurisdiction of the administrative judge covers full litigation (*plein contentieux*) rather than being confined to litigation concerning excess of power (he did not accept that the judicial judge arrogates the entire litigation with full jurisdiction). The jurisdiction of the administrative judge is not solely limited to administrative acts of authority. Administrative management acts, wrongly deemed empty of public authority, must, in his view, also lie with the administrative court. Hauriou here introduced a subject for future jurisprudence (CE, 1903, Terrier), but, as a good defender of the liberal state, he would not refrain from later criticism by refusing to absolutize the finalist teleologico-functionalist criterion of public service.[25] If, at the turn of the nineteenth and twentieth centuries, the coincidence was almost perfect between public service and public management, between the field of public service and the procedure derogating from common law, it was soon broken. A product of the birth of modern administrative law, the equation was no longer workable, since the execution of public services would, for the most part, follow the path of private management.

From the sixth edition of the *Précis*, published in 1907, we observe a rise in power of the institutionalist theme from the jurist's pen.[26] The state is now called the "institution of institutions,"[27] and Hauriou makes the institution the seminal place of his theoretical reflections, which culminate in the famous text of 1925. This inflection in Hauriou's thought marks the ambition to keep at a distance both from the subjectivism of the dominant legal doctrine and from the objectivism of Duguit. If Hauriou clearly leans towards objectivism, he refuses the complete objectivism of his Bordeaux counterpart, which leads

[25] Jean Rivero, "Hauriou et l'avènement de la notion de service public," in *Mélanges Achille Mestre* (Paris: Sirey, 1956): 461–71.

[26] As always, his *Précis* is the receptacle and catalyst of more general reflections that found their expression in articles. Let us cite, in particular, two great texts: Maurice Hauriou, "L'institution et le droit statutaire," *Recueil de législation de Toulouse* 2 (1906): 134–82; and "Le point de vue de l'ordre et de l'équilibre," *Recueil de législation de Toulouse* 5 (1909): 1–86.

[27] Maurice Hauriou, *Précis de droit administratif*, 6th edn (Paris: Larose, 1907), VII.

Duguit to deny both the existence of individual subjective rights and the legal personality of the state. Hauriou's rejection of subjectivism is justified by a very simple reason: it prevents the state from properly thinking in terms of public law. Against the German legal tradition (Gerber, Laband, Jellinek) but also against French sanctification of the law (Esmein, Carré de Malberg), Hauriou argues that one cannot subsume the concept of state under the category of a legal person – doing so would impoverish its meaning. The prevailing doctrine, he notes, bases the law on the sole will of the subject (whether the individual or the state) without considering the objective order of institutional aim, social purpose, and function. In such a scheme, he reminds us, the public law of the state is more or less reduced to the subjectivist model of private law, which makes it impossible to justify its own identity. Of course, the jurist did not dispute the relevance of a reading in terms of legal personality but strongly contested the idea that this category can exhaust the question of the state[28] – as that of the individual elsewhere.

This bias in favor of the specificity of public law does not prevent Hauriou from thinking of the necessary – liberal – limitation of the state. Quite the contrary: in a context of profound change in the role of the state, the jurist puts himself in a position to think about the two mutually supportive dimensions of the same political issue: to clear the state's field of action and to ensure the protection of citizens before an ever more interventionist public power. His concern for the collective is permanently tempered by a fierce defense of private property and by his attentive distinction between public and collective interest, between the political and socioeconomic order. Suffice it to recall that, literally haunted by the specter of collectivism,[29] Hauriou strongly opposed the so-called practice of municipal socialism.

The most attentive readers of the great jurist insist that the theory of the institution provides the key to reading the whole of the Haurioutist doctrine and provides the basis of its structure.[30] It allows us to understand this tension between concern for collective action and defense of individual freedom.

[28] The definition of the state as a juridical person is not sufficient in itself, but in international law it entails the right of exchange and relation *par excellence*. Hence, Hauriou's lack of interest in this discipline.

[29] So much so that the denunciation of collectivism is a *leitmotiv* of his thought. For Hauriou, private property is a political institution absolutely necessary to social life, and not merely an economic institution peculiar to the commercial sphere. He sees nothing less than "le grand exutoire des passions individuelles" (the great outlet of individual passions): Maurice Hauriou, "Le régime d'État," *La Revue socialiste* 293 (1904): 564–81.

[30] See Jean-Arnaud Mazères, "La théorie de l'institution de Maurice Hauriou ou l'oscillation entre l'instituant et l'institué," in *Mélanges Jacques Mourgeon* (Bruxelles: Bruylant, 1998): 239–93.

The institution, in fact, and principally the state, is a whole irreducible to the sum of its members; it only appears where communion in an idea brings people together and gives rise to a group oriented towards action.

A POLITICAL THEORY OF THE LIBERAL STATE

The strength of the state in Haurioutist theory is based on its broad conception of law. One can even say that his theory of the state is not properly legal but much more political. Nevertheless, that would be defining the law too strictly. The fact remains that, for Hauriou, the state is first and foremost a political reality, even a moral idea, which must be institutionalized politically. We summarize here the thesis developed in the *Principes de droit public* (1910, 1916[31]) and structured around two main notions: that of state regime (*régime d'État*), advanced in 1904, and that of social constitution, then turned to account in the *Précis de droit constitutionnel*.

The concept of state regime embraces not only the state but also all social institutions within the nation. The state regime is not only a certain political and legal regime but also a form of society whose main characteristic is based on separation of public and private life. The state regime is first defined as a "civil regime" based on private property and exchange; it is also civil in the sense that it subordinates military power. Finally, it is a secular system in which the state subordinates the power of churches and a social system in which the state guarantees enjoyment of individual rights and the benefit of public services.

The state regime is therefore not the state, although it includes and gives rise to the state. Reasoning from the national framework, Hauriou seeks to demonstrate how the nation, a product of a certain Western historical tradition, is changing into a state regime to allow the emergence of the state in the classical sense of legal person. However, there is some ambiguity in the relationship between state and the state regime. On the one hand, the state regime appears as the condition of possibility of the state. On the other hand, the relationship sometimes seems to be reversed to the point of making the state regime a product of state action. In this dialectical oscillation, it seems that the two notions ultimately revolve around the idea of the process of

[31] Compared to the first edition, that of 1916 is more heavily influenced by war and contains a much sharper criticism of the German publicist doctrine (but note that Hauriou never reached the level of virulence of a Duguit); the expression of religious beliefs is also more explicit.

statehood, the state regime thus contributing to the thinking of the state in its historical movement, and emphasizing the intimate link that unites state, nation, and capitalist economy.

The notion of social constitution, on the other hand, recalls the irreducibility of society and the right to the state. The state, in fact, does not contain all social life; it is based on a political constitution that organizes it as an "institution of institutions" but provides for a life proper to the social constitution, namely all individual rights, public liberties, and spontaneous social institutions. This is the social constitution of a state that defines the criteria for constitutional legitimacy. In his various positions in favor of the exception of unconstitutionality before the ordinary judge, Hauriou is constantly committed to recall that the submission of the state to the law goes not only through the classical constitutional mechanisms but also by the constitution, a source of true objective self-limitation of the state.[32]

Here, too, it is important to dispel a contradiction that finds itself resolved in the theological and Catholic substratum of Hauriou's thought. On the one hand, the jurist insists on the primacy of the social constitution over the political constitution. On the other, he emphasizes the passivity of society. The social is superior to politics, but the social is eminently passive. Indeed, the social order is reputed to be powerless to arrange itself spontaneously; its ordering requires a mediating authority, that of the state. In short, society precedes the state; it naturally has its constitution. At the top of institutions, the state is its political protector; it is not superior to the social body itself, it is superior only to serve it.

In coherence with his theory of the state regime and the social constitution, the dean of Toulouse finally deploys a broad and material conception of the separation of powers. Under his pen, the separation of powers is not limited to the classical trilogy, or a balanced articulation of constitutional forms (legislative power, executive power, judiciary power); rather, it takes into account the social organization as a whole: political parties, military power, economic powers, the church, and other institutions are thus integrated into his analysis. With little concern for disciplinary boundaries, the lawyer does not hesitate to become a sociologist to consider the fundamental balances at work in society "between political and economic forces, between military power and civil power, between public life and private life, between public property and private property, between the activity of the public administration and private activity."[33]

[32] By this, Hauriou stigmatizes all theories of subjective self-restraint of the state brandished by opponents of the control of constitutionality of laws.

[33] Hauriou, *Principes de droit public*, 11.

For the rest, Hauriou proposes a new tripartition of constitutional powers: executive power, deliberative power, and the "power of suffrage" (*pouvoir de suffrage*). Its originality lies less in the vocabulary than in the hierarchy it implies: supremacy is indeed reserved for the "minority power" (*pouvoir minoritaire*), the executive power that cannot be reduced to the sole function of law enforcement because its role, properly political, includes initiative and direction.[34] Backed by the administrative state elite, which includes both the government and the higher administration, it embodies the "commanding national will," that is, the unity of the state in action. The "majority power" (*pouvoir majoritaire*) resides with the people, who have, for their part, a simple faculty of assent that consists of a "sovereignty of subjection" (*souveraineté de sujétion*)[35] – namely, power to acquiesce to obedience by suffrage and "manifestations of communion." In other words, the citizens are sovereign to the extent that, willing to accept the idea of being subject to the power of the rulers, they can grant or deny their trust.

For its part, the role of the parliament must be limited to deliberation and control. If Hauriou's mistrust towards universal suffrage led him to value the role of the referendum, it is also essentially to counter parliament's claim to sovereignty.[36] In the general scheme of his constitutional thinking, the power of suffrage must allow the executive to be reaffirmed in the face of parliamentary sovereignty as it was established under the Third Republic. As evidenced by his theory of the constitutional cycles of French political history since 1789, Hauriou is thus the architect of a parliamentary regime that reserves the institutional primacy to the executive – both the government and the head of state – which must cover the right of dissolution and draw its legitimacy directly from the people.

It must be understood that Hauriou's schema is the reverse of the French constitutional orthodoxy of the time. In his thinking, the executive is not a submissive power. On the contrary, it has its own autonomy. Its primacy ultimately originates in the necessity – in its naturalness, one might say – of power within any human community. To consider the history (Hauriou refers to the king of the Old Regime), power first took the form of executive power then underwent a gradual nationalization process, ultimately leading to the advent of national sovereignty.

[34] Hauriou, *Précis de droit constitutionnel*, 383.

[35] Hauriou, "La souveraineté nationale," *Recueil de législation de Toulouse* 8 (1912): 1–154; *Précis de droit constitutionnel*, 89. Significantly, Hauriou speaks of power of suffrage by defining it less as an individual right than as an individually exercised social function.

[36] As evidenced by his refusal of any popular initiative referendum.

Beyond the usual categories of legislative and executive powers, it is the modern idea of representation that Hauriou reworks from end to end in his schema. To the extent that power exists in itself, and to the extent that it does not come from the people or the nation, the rulers exercise it without delegation; they are simply invested. By breaking with the ideology of parliamentary sovereignty, especially embodied by Adhémar Esmein, who puts the source of all power in the nation, Hauriou breaks a taboo from the French Revolution and refuses to identify representatives to the represented. Not only does parliament not express the general will, but its appointment by election cannot confer on it a higher title of representation. Much more than coming from election, representation lies in competence and the capacity to work for justice: to act for the state and not "to want for the nation" (*vouloir pour la nation*), one could say by borrowing the famous formula of Antoine Barnave.

Finally, we will note the absence of judges in Hauriou's trilogy of powers. This absence does not signify a devaluation of their role. On the contrary, by a politicization of the jurisdictional function Hauriou grants judges a greater autonomy by detaching the political and legal registers. The dean of Toulouse, who never hesitates to refer to Montesquieu, emphasizes the change of context compared to the time when the philosopher wrote *De l'esprit des lois*. The judges no longer endorse a political power in good and due form, they now exercise a properly legal power, which has no less dignity but is on a different plane. It is precisely this legal character of the judges' power that makes it possible to understand why they are not integrated into the theory of the separation of powers proposed by Hauriou. Regarding their role, it is highly valued by the jurist, if only by the centrality given to customary and jurisprudential sources of law. Moreover, Hauriou does not fail to insist on the office of the judiciary, because the ordinary judge is responsible for ensuring the constitutionality of the laws, not only in terms of the political constitution but also in the arena of the social constitution.[37]

While breaking with the constitutional law resulting from the Revolution (the cult of the law, the ideology of national sovereignty, the mystique of parliamentary representation, the devaluation of the judicial authority), the Toulouse master is no less representative of the French culture of the state, which motivates both its liberalism and its Catholicism. Hauriou's attachment to the state, and particularly to the administrative state, is symptomatic of a properly hexagonal idiosyncrasy, still persistent today. Considering the long train of political history, as well as the influence of Haurioutist thought, one

[37] By this, Hauriou defends a form of control of supraconstitutionality entirely in phase with natural-law theory.

can say that liberalism and Catholicism have powerfully fueled the French culture of the state, while keeping it in check.

RECOMMENDED READING

Joseph Barthélemy et al., *Mélanges Maurice Hauriou*. Paris: Sirey, 1929.
Gabriel Marty et al., *La Pensée de Maurice Hauriou et son influence*. Paris: Pedone, 1969.
Alonso, Christophe, Arnaud Duranthon, and Julia Schmitz, eds. *La Pensée du doyen Hauriou à l'épreuve du temps: quel(s) héritage(s)?* Aix-en-Provence: Presses universitaires d'Aix-Marseille, 2015.
Audren, Frédéric, and Marc Milet. "Maurice Hauriou sociologue. Entre sociologie catholique et physique sociale." Preface to Maurice Hauriou. *Écrits sociologiques*. Paris: Dalloz, 2008.
Barroche, Julien. "Maurice Hauriou, juriste catholique ou libéral?" *Revue française d'histoire des idées politiques* 28 (2008): 307–36.
Beaud, Olivier. "Hauriou et le droit naturel." *Revue d'histoire des Facultés de droit de la science juridique* 6 (1988): 123–38.
Blanquer, Jean-Michel, and Marc Milet. *L'Invention de l'État. Léon Duguit, Maurice Hauriou et la naissance du droit public moderne*. Paris: Odile Jacob, 2015.
Broderick, Albert, edn. *The French Institutionalists. Maurice Hauriou, Georges Renard, Joseph T. Delos*. Cambridge, MA: Harvard University Press, 1970.
Dufour, Alfred. "La conception de la personnalité morale dans la pensée de Maurice Hauriou et ses fondements philosophiques." *Quaderni Fiorentini* 11–12 (1982–83): 685–719.
Eisenmann, Charles. "Deux théoriciens du droit: Duguit et Hauriou" (1930). In *Écrits de théorie politique, de droit constitutionnel et d'idées politiques*. Edited by Charles Leben, 13–47. Paris: Éditions Panthéon-Assas, 2002.
Foulquier, Norbert. "Maurice Hauriou, constitutionnaliste." In *Le Renouveau de la doctrine française*. Edited by Nader Hakim and Fabrice Melleray, 281–306. Paris: Dalloz, 2009.
Gray, Christopher B. *The Methodology of Maurice Hauriou*. Amsterdam, New York: Rodopi, 2010.
Gurvitch, Georges. "Les idées maîtresses de Maurice Hauriou." *Archives de philosophie du droit* 1 (1931): 155–94.
Hauriou, Maurice. *Écrits sociologiques* (1893–99). Edited by Frédéric Audren and Marc Milet, Paris: Dalloz, 2008.
Précis de droit administratif. Paris: Larose, 1933 (12th edn). Republished Paris: Dalloz, 2002.
Principes de droit public. Paris: Sirey, 1910 (1st edn). Republished Paris: Dalloz, 2010.
"La théorie de l'institution et de la fondation. Essai de vitalisme social." *Cahiers de la Nouvelle Journée* 4 (1925): 1–45.
Précis de droit constitutionnel. Paris: Sirey, 1929 (2nd edn). Republished Paris: Dalloz, 2015.
Notes d'arrêts sur décisions du Conseil d'État et du Tribunal des conflits (1892–1929). Paris: La Mémoire du droit, 2000, 3 vols.

Hummel, Jacky. "De la fondation de la liberté politique par les institutions constitutionnelles." Presentation to Maurice Hauriou. *Précis de droit constitutionnel.* Paris: Dalloz, 2015.

Maulin, Éric. "Hauriou, Maurice." In *Dictionnaire des grandes œuvres juridiques.* Edited by Olivier Cayla and Jean-Louis Halperin, 246–54. Paris: Dalloz, 2010.

Mazères, Jean-Arnaud. "La théorie de l'institution de Maurice Hauriou ou l'oscillation entre l'instituant et l'institué." In *Mélanges Jacques Mourgeon*, 239–93. Bruxelles: Bruylant, 1998.

"Réflexions sur une réédition: les *Principes de droit public* de Maurice Hauriou." *Jus Politicum* 6 (2011): 1–25.

Melleray, Fabrice. "Remarques sur l'école de Toulouse." In *Mélanges Jean-Arnaud Mazères*, 533–53. Paris: Litec, 2009.

Millard, Éric. "Hauriou et la théorie de l'institution." *Droit et Société* 30–31 (1995): 381–412.

Rivero, Jean. "Hauriou et l'avènement de la notion de service public." In *Mélanges Achille Mestre*, 461–71. Paris: Sirey, 1956.

Schmitz, Julia. *La Théorie de l'institution du doyen Maurice Hauriou.* Paris: L'Harmattan, 2013.

Sfez, Lucien. *Essai sur la contribution du doyen Hauriou au droit administratif français.* Paris: Librairie générale de droit et de jurisprudence, 1966.

21

Léon Duguit

(1859–1928)

M. C. MIROW

BIOGRAPHICAL INTRODUCTION

French jurist Léon Duguit was a theorist of the modern state and its relationship to law. His work on the nature of property and ownership, defining them as social functions, was an important step towards dismantling the conceptual wall between public and private law. Thus, his work resounds in two areas – political theory and our understanding of the state on the one hand, and social limitations on property and indeed other aspects of traditional private law on the other. Duguit belonged to the group of French antiformalists who rejected the prevalent approach to law as an autonomous discipline best understood through an internal deductive science.[1] He sought to apply sociological and scientific analysis to his study of law and the state.

Duguit noted that Roman Catholicism was deeply embedded in French culture, and his work demonstrates intellectual sensitivity to this fact.[2] While little of his work expressly invokes Christianity, his move towards solidarity and public service in the area of public law and his development of the social function of property in the area of private law reveal a level of concordance with Christianity and particularly Roman Catholic thought in late nineteenth- and early twentieth-century France and Europe. Although grounded in secular analysis and goals, his theories logically led to practical repercussions in accord with the recent surge of Catholic social doctrine. Thus, different aspects of Duguit's thought and their logical implementation might be easily accepted by adherents of neo-Thomism and Catholic social teaching on the

[1] Mauricio García-Villegas, "Comparative Sociology of Law: Legal Fields, Legal Scholarship, and Social Sciences in Europe and the United States," *Law & Social Inquiry* 31 (2006): 349–56.

[2] Léon Duguit, *Le Régime du Culte Catholique antérior à la loi de séparation et les causes juridiques de la séparation* (Paris: Librairie de la Société du Recueil J.-B. Sirey, 1907), 36–37.

state, labor, and property.[3] For example, the very idea of solidarity, a pivotal concept in contemporary French sociology, shared such lay and Roman Catholic lineage.[4] This harmony of goals permitted a much wider acceptance of his theories into modern constitutionalism in Europe and Latin America than might otherwise have been expected.

Duguit spent his early years in the city of his birth, Libourne, France, about twenty miles northeast of Bordeaux. He studied law at the University of Bordeaux, an institution central to his academic life.[5] A talented student, he rose quickly in the academic world of nineteenth-century France. Although Duguit's greatest contributions were to the fields of constitutional and public law, he was trained in private law and wrote theses on stipulations in Roman law and on civil acts in French law.[6] By 1880, he held a doctorate in law through competition and, in light of his young age, was granted permission to prepare for the *agrégation* he obtained in 1882. His first teaching post was at the University of Caen, where he taught legal history. With economist Edmond Villey, Duguit founded the *Revue d'economie politique*, a scholarly journal that continues today. A few years later, in 1886, he returned to the University of Bordeaux, where he would teach and write for the next forty years.[7] He became dean of the faculty of law in 1919 and served in this position until his death.[8] A proponent of scientific and sociological methods in studying law and political institutions, Duguit advocated the introduction of sociology into law faculties.[9]

Bordeaux was Duguit's academic, social, and political home. He was admired as a thoughtful, dedicated, and engaging teacher whose time with

[3] M. C. Mirow, "Léon Duguit and the Social Function of Property in Argentina," in Paul Babie and Jessica Viven-Wilksch, eds., *Léon Duguit and the Social Obligation Norm of Property: A Translation and Global Exploration* (Cham: Springer, 2019); M. C. Mirow, "*Rerum Novarum*: New Things and Recent Paradigms of Property Law," *The University of the Pacific Law Review* 47 (2016): 188–91; M. C. Mirow, "Origins of the Social Function of Property in Chile," *Fordham Law Review* 80 (2011): 1196.

[4] J. E. S. Hayward, "Solidarity: The Social History of an Idea in Nineteenth Century France," *International Review of Social History* 4 (1959): 274–75, 280–82; José Luis Monereo Pérez and José Calvo González, "Léon Duguit (1859–1928): jurista de una sociedad en transformación," *Revista de derecho constitucional europea* 4 (2005): 540.

[5] M. Milet, "Duguit, Léon," in Patrick Arabeyre, et al., eds., *Dictionnaire historique de juristes français (XIIe–XXe siècle)* (Paris: Presses Universitaires de France, 2007), 271–72.

[6] Nader Hakim, "Duguit et les privatistes," in Fabrice Melleray, ed., *Autour de Léon Duguit* (Bruxelles: Bruylant, 2011), 82.

[7] Milet, "Duguit, Léon," 271–72.

[8] Monereo Pérez and Calvo González, "Léon Duguit (1859–1928)," 483.

[9] Milet, "Duguit, Léon," 271–72.

students in and out of the classroom informed the style and content of his scholarship.[10] He was also a member of a national group of productive legal scholars who enjoyed warm professional and social relations.[11] Meeting regularly with academic friends who helped to shape his thought, Duguit served as a professor of constitutional law and published consistently on the topic. His two volumes on the state, *L'Etat, le droit objectif et la loi positive* (1901) and *L'Etat, les gouvernants et les agents* (1903), gave him a national reputation in the field and established frameworks for his future work.[12] For the next twenty-five years, Duguit taught, published, and visited law faculties throughout the world, but always as a representative of Bordeaux and its school of legal study.[13] He lectured at the University of Coimbra, the University of Cairo, the École des Hautes Études Sociales, the University of Buenos Aires, Columbia University, and the University of Bucharest.[14] In 1910, he was made a knight of the Legion of Honor.[15] In 1911, he published his *Traité de droit constitutionnel* in two volumes, which were substantially expanded into five volumes published between 1921 and 1925. Although not his most extensive work, *Le droit social, le droit individuel et la tranformation de l'Etat* (1908; second edition 1911; third edition 1922) has been recognized as a sound précis of his thought, covering the highlights of ideas explored more fully in his other works. *Le droit social* is of particular importance in the international dissemination of Duguit's ideas. It was translated into Russian (1909), Spanish (1919), Greek (1923), and (notably by Frida and Harold Laski) English (*Law and the Modern State*, 1919).[16]

Duguit was an administrator in the army and ran a military hospital during the First World War, in which he lost one of his two sons. In 1926, with Austrian legal theorists Hans Kelsen and Franz Weyr, he founded an international journal on legal theory, the *Revue internationale de théorie du droit.*

[10] Marcel Laborde-Lacoste, "La vie et la personnalité de Léon Duguit," *Revue juridique et économique du Sud-Ouest, série juridique* 10 (1959): 99–100.

[11] Frédéric Audren and Jean-Louis Halpérin, *La culture juridique français: entre mythes et réalités XIX*[e]*–XX*[e] *siècles* (Paris: CNRS Éditions, 2013), 125.

[12] Léon Duguit, *L'Etat, le droit objectif et la loi positive* (Paris: A. Fontemoing, 1901); Léon Duguit, *L'Etat, les gouvernants et les agents* (Paris: A. Fontemoing, 1903).

[13] Audren and Halpérin, *La culture*, 129.

[14] Milet, "Duguit, Léon," 271–72.

[15] Jean-Michel Blanquer and Marc Milet, *L'Invention de l'État: Léon Duguit, Maurice Hauriou et la naissance du droit public moderne* (Paris: Odile Jacob, 2015), 206.

[16] Bruno Debaenst, "Le droit social, le droit individuel et la tranformation de l'État," in Serge Dauchy, et al., eds., *The Formation and Transmission of Western Legal Culture: 150 Books that Made the Law in the Age of Printing* (Cham: Springer, 2016), 430.

The year before his death, he assisted in founding the International Institute for Public Law. In addition to his academic activities, Duguit was involved in various local causes and societies, including the Union for the Truth (a group supporting Dreyfus) and the *Cercle Voltaire*. In 1908, he served on the municipal council, but when other elective positions eluded him, his interest in public office declined. He died in Bordeaux in 1928.[17]

Despite Duguit's lack of engagement with the church's teachings in his scientific exploration of the state and law, his relationship to Catholicism remains difficult to determine. It appears that on the personal level, the church was more than a societal entity. Duguit's mother was admired for her piety and social action resulting from her faith.[18] Duguit received religious instruction as a child and demonstrated great aptitude in this field as in others.[19] Indeed, Duguit admitted that throughout his life, he was drawn to theological questions and analysis, and his library contained volumes on theology and religion, including the works of Thomas Aquinas and a collection of papal encyclicals.[20] Nonetheless, Duguit was reported as saying that if he could hold on to just one book in his library, it would be *Candide*.[21]

His friend and colleague the neo-Thomist Henry Vizioz would most likely have discussed questions of Christianity and faith with Duguit.[22] One of Duguit's biographers surmises that Vizioz aided Duguit when he turned to religious studies after World War I and the loss of his son.[23] Other scholars demonstrate that Duguit had been familiar with the writings of Aquinas since at least his early twenties.[24] In any event, Duguit made it quite clear that he did not mock or denigrate religion, and he expressed his tolerance and deep respect for sincere religious beliefs. Duguit's challenge was to reconcile such beliefs with his unremitting search for a positive truth.[25] For example, shortly after assuming the deanship of the faculty at Bordeaux, Duguit proposed

[17] Milet, "Duguit, Léon," 271–72.

[18] Laborde-Lacoste, "La vie," 96.

[19] Jean-Michel Blanquer and Marc Milet, "Les idées politiques de Léon Duguit: un prisme contextuel et biographique," in Fabrice Melleray, ed., *Autour de Léon Duguit* (Bruxelles: Bruylant, 2011), 12.

[20] Ibid., 2–13; A.-J. Boyé, "Souvenirs personnels sur Léon Duguit," *Revue juridique et économique du Sud-Ouest, série juridique* 10 (1959): 119–20.

[21] Boyé, "Souvenirs," 120.

[22] Ibid., 124; Laborde-Lacoste, "La vie," 94, 96.

[23] Laborde-Lacoste, "La vie," 102.

[24] Blanquer and Milet, *L'Invention*, 281.

[25] Boyé, "Souvenirs," 117; Laborde-Lacoste, "La vie," 102.

public lectures from the faculty to the community on topics of general concern within the expertise of the faculty. The first series was on the topic of religious liberty and Roman Catholicism.[26] Considering this mix of influences and Duguit's comments or actions in favor of the church, recent scholars have rejected a simplistic narrative of Duguit, the great lay jurist, in direct and constant intellectual combat with Maurice Hauriou, the great Catholic jurist of the time.[27]

CONSTITUTIONAL THEORY AND THE STATE

Duguit's method of legal analysis stressed scientific approaches, particularly the flourishing methodologies of sociology, to describe and critique law. As Bruno Debaenst aptly summed up Duguit:

> He only recognized "scientific problems," problems that could be observed by experience. Everything outside these experiences was metaphysical and could not be known. Therefore, he opposed French revolutionary concepts, such as "social contract," "national sovereignty," and "natural individual rights." These concepts were inherited from Roman jurists and medieval scholastics and simply passed on through the French Revolution.[28]

Although the product of several schools of thought, Duguit's core methodology was built upon scientific empiricism and sociological modes of analyzing law and the state.[29]

His major contributions examined the relationship between the state and law and asserted that the difference between the governed and the governing was one of function rather than substance. Greatly influenced by his sociologist friend Émile Durkheim, also on the faculty of the University of Bordeaux, Duguit put forth the idea of a social state of the rule of law tied to notions of solidarity and social interdependence.[30] This approach differed greatly from established theories, and Duguit's work engaged and challenged the works of German jurist Rudolf von Jhering and German and Austrian jurist Georg

[26] Blanquer and Milet, *L'Invention*, 268–69.

[27] Ibid., 13. On Hauriou, see Chapter 20 in the present volume.

[28] Debaenst, "Le droit social," 430.

[29] Roger Bonnard, "Léon Duguit: ses oeuvres, sa doctrine," *Revue du droit public et de la science politique en France a l'étranger* 46 (1929): 5, 16–17.

[30] Debaenst, "Le droit social," 430; Jaime Orlando Santofimio Gamboa, "León Duguit y su doctrina realista, objetiva y positiva del Derecho en las bases del concepto de servicio público," *Revista digital de derecho administrativo* 5 (2011): 60–68.

Jellinek.[31] His debates with his countryman Maurice Hauriou are best known.[32]

Following the work of Durkheim, Duguit uncovered functions of law and the state that reflected social rules and social interdependence, or solidarity. These social aims were the foundation of legitimate government and state.[33] The notions of social interdependence and social solidarity grew from the work of many European theorists of the state and society, including Auguste Comte, Émile Durkheim, Charles Secrétan, and Charles Gide.[34] Duguit's work flowed from these and similar authors as he adopted and reacted to their approaches to the state.

With this conception of the state, Duguit focused on the idea of public service (*service public*) as a central aspect of the modern state in which the state's social function performed service to the collective.[35] Thus, using empirical methods and sociological approaches, Duguit critiqued existing theories of the law and the state, and entered deeply into the European literature on these topics.[36] Based on the fundamental principles of social solidarity and social interdependence, the state for Duguit was a social function in which the distinction between governed and governing disappeared.[37] In this characterization of the state, individual rights had to give way to the social function, law and government were limited by the social function, and sovereignty was replaced by concrete public services in their social function.[38] Understood this way, the state for Duguit "is not a power to command, a sovereign; it is the cooperation of public services organized and controlled by the governed."[39] The state became a state of public service, and social solidarity limited state action.[40] All subsidiary functions of the state, such as law, were similarly viewed in light of human solidarity and social

[31] Milet, "Duguit, Léon," 271–72.

[32] Blanquer and Milet, *L'Invention*; Monereo Pérez and Calvo González, "Léon Duguit (1859–1928)," 505–08.

[33] Monereo Pérez and Calvo González, "Léon Duguit (1859–1928)," 509–10, 534–45.

[34] M. C. Mirow, "The Social-Obligation Norm of Property: Duguit, Hayem, and Others," *Florida Journal of International Law* 22 (2010): 201–03.

[35] Léon Duguit, "The Concept of Public Service," *Yale Law Journal* 32 (1923): 425–35; Cécile Laborde, "Pluralism, Syndicalism and Corporatism: Léon Duguit and the Crisis of the State (1900–25)," *History of European Ideas* 22 (1996): 233–34; Milet, "Duguit, Léon," 272–73.

[36] Bonnard, "Léon Duguit," 13–19, 24–32, 42.

[37] Monereo Pérez and Calvo González, "Léon Duguit (1859–1928)," 511–15; Santofimio Gamboa, "León Duguit," 59.

[38] Santofimio Gamboa, "León Duguit," 65–75.

[39] Monereo Pérez and Calvo González, "Léon Duguit (1859–1928)," 497–98.

[40] Laborde, "Pluralism," 229–31; Monereo Pérez and Calvo González, "Léon Duguit (1859–1928)," 499–502.

interdependence. Subjective rights were a mere chimera.[41] This appeal to social solidarity and limitation by social function has led some scholars to connect Duguit's theories to natural law.[42]

Duguit's first major study of the state, his two volumes titled *l'État* (1901 and 1903), addressed the properties and will of government, the will of legislative bodies, the creation and effect of positive law, nations, sovereignty, representation in government, parliaments and legislative bodies, heads of state, agents and delegation in governmental functions, and decentralization of government. Throughout the discussion of these general facets of government and the state, Duguit wove essential aspects of his critiques of earlier attempts to describe these elements: the failure of subjective rights, limitations properly placed on law and rights when observed through a lens of social solidarity, and the underlying social function of government, subdivisions of government, and law.[43]

CHURCH AND STATE

The Roman Catholic Church and its relationship to the state, particularly the French state, could not be ignored when considering this subject. The most significant piece of French legislation establishing the separation of church and state, and a foundational document of French secularism (*laïcité*), was enacted at the end of 1905. From the final decades of the nineteenth century, the Republic had removed the Roman Catholic Church from the position of religious, social, and political dominance it held under the Concordat of 1801. Building on these small changes, the law of 1905 established a complete separation between the Roman Catholic Church (and all religions) and the secular French state. This change led to the break in diplomatic relations between France and the Holy See until 1926.[44] As a student of the state, and having just completed two volumes on the topic, Duguit gave a series of lectures, subsequently published, on this dramatic change in historical and theoretical perspective. This work was perhaps the fullest description of Duguit's thought on the church and the place of Christianity in the state.[45]

[41] Monereo Pérez and Calvo González, "Léon Duguit (1859–1928)," 486–97, 504–05, 516–24.

[42] Philippe Raynaud, "Léon Duguit et le droit naturel," *Revue d'historie des facultés de droit et de la science juridique* 4 (1987): 169–80.

[43] Duguit, *L'Etat, le droit objectif*; Duguit, *L'Etat, les gouvernants*.

[44] *Loi du 9 décembre 1905 concernant la séparation des Églises et de l'État*; Blanquer and Milet, *L'Invention*, 161–69.

[45] Duguit, *Le Régime*, 36–37.

In favor of this change, Duguit explained that the rupture between church and state was inevitable owing to the fundamental inconsistency between the modern state and the Roman Catholic Church as the church gained greater control over national expressions of Roman Catholicism. Duguit's analysis examined the historical underpinnings of the Concordat of 1801 and closely broke down its three central constituent principles:

> (1) The Catholic religion was the official religion of the French state; (2) The French Catholic Church, while remaining united to the universal Catholic Church, whose head is the Roman pontiff, formed a national church, the governance of which was directly tied to the civil authority; and (3) The Catholic religion was a public service of the French state.[46]

Duguit explored each aspect as it unfolded between the Concordat and the present. For our purposes, his characterization of the Roman Catholic Church as a public service of the French state was particularly important because of the centrality of the notion of public service in his overall understanding of the modern state. Duguit noted three ways in which the French church was a public service.

First, the church was a state obligation through its juridical commitments and as desired by the general conscience. The Concordat resolved pressing questions of the Holy See's recognition of the French revolutionary expropriation of ecclesiastical property and France's payment of religious pensions. These were essential aspects of constructing a new relationship between France and the Holy See.[47]

Second, the French church accomplished this mission by its absorption into the state through agents who were subject to the hierarchy and discipline of the state. In this sense, the religious in the French church from the Concordat until the law of 1905 were, according to Duguit, properly "state functionaries" (*fonctionnaires*) with all the implications of that term within French political and legal culture.[48] In Duguit's words, Pope Pius VII accepted that "the ministers of the Catholic religion became functionaries of the French government."[49] Clergy submitted to political oaths and swore to uphold the constitution of the French Republic. Bishops, too, were functionaries of the French state, and papal communications were subject to French diplomatic means of transmission. Excessive exercises of religious authority

46 Ibid., 3.
47 Ibid., 22–24.
48 Ibid., 23.
49 Ibid., 24.

were subject to challenges of abuse (*recour pour abus*) brought in the French parliament.[50]

Third, the French church's status as a public service guaranteed allocation of public funds and financial support to continue its mission. The French state provided funds for clergy and their expenses, recruitment, and training. State-sanctioned groups of individuals under civil authority guided the maintenance of buildings, grounds, and other property.[51]

For Duguit, these central aspects of the Concordat were intractably at odds with both the modern state and the Roman Catholic Church. Duguit proposed that religious neutrality was a condition so tied to the modern state that it was beyond debate. Similarly, recent developments in the growth of the Roman Catholic Church as a universal church, and particularly the recognition of papal infallibility in 1870, meant that the church could no longer serve as a national church or a national public service. Indeed, the proclamation of infallibility reflected for Duguit a new and certain form of government of the Roman Catholic Church that rejected a federation of national churches in favor of a centralized large monarchy.[52] Duguit noted the incongruity of a national church and the church as a public service with Bellarmine's observation that "[t]he pope has a full, universal, ordinary, and immediate jurisdiction over all dioceses."[53] With these observations, Duguit opined that the Concordat could not be reestablished, and he concluded on this topic:

> Whether we like it or not, the establishment of the Roman Catholic Church has been a capital event in the history of humanity; and again today with its dogmas, discipline, and hierarchy, the Catholic Church occupies a place of first order in the world; it counts everywhere and particularly in France millions of faithful and, if I can speak this way, France has been *steeped* in Catholicism. These are the facts that a man of state, worthy of the name, may not ignore or fail to recognize. Does the French legislature understand this? Has it sown the seed with the Law of 1905 of a future organization, assuring the free exercise of their religion and giving religious peace to the country? A grave question that my colleague and friend Saleilles will study in the next conference.[54]

The kind mention of Saleilles is worth noting here. Duguit's relationship with Saleilles may have provided a significant intellectual bridge between Duguit's

[50] Ibid., 24–27.
[51] Ibid., 23, 28–31.
[52] Ibid., 32–35.
[53] Ibid., 35.
[54] Ibid., 36 (Duguit's emphasis).

sociological and empirical methods and Saleilles's work on a similar topic from his own Catholic perspectives. Saleilles was an open and ardent Roman Catholic well versed in both theology and the social teachings of the church.[55] Saleilles brought these perspectives to his work, and his work was an important influence on Duguit.[56]

THE SOCIAL FUNCTION OF PROPERTY

For two months in 1911, Duguit delivered a course of lectures in Buenos Aires, Argentina. These lectures studied changes to the civil law since the French Civil Code of 1804. The six lectures were subsequently published in 1912, translated into several languages, and later republished in French.[57] The sixth lecture was on property, and Duguit famously asserted his new formulation, "property is not a right; it is a social function."[58] Duguit described the central point of this lecture this way: "[i]n the sixth lecture, I have developed the idea that capitalist property, and particularly real property, is increasingly less of a subjective individual right and more of a social function."[59] And again, in slightly different terminology, "[p]roperty is no longer the subjective right of the owner; it is the social function of the possessor or wealth."[60]

This new perspective on property was informed by Duguit's overall observations of the modern state. If the state had a social function of collective service, then each constituent institution of the state, such as legal obligations or property, should also serve this general function. Thus, Duguit's reconceptualization of property was consistent with the work he had been doing on the nature of the state.[61]

The idea that property should be limited or bounded by social responsibility contrasted starkly with the accepted and established notions of property as an absolute right through which the owner has complete dominion over the property. This liberal notion of property as a right was firmly entrenched in legal literature and thought, and found expression in both the common law

[55] Jean-Louis Halpérin, "Saleilles, Raymond," in Patrick Arbeyre, et al., eds., *Dictionnaire historique de juristes français (XIIe–XXe siècle)* (Paris: Presses Universitaires de France, 2007), 695. On Saleilles, see Chapter 19 in the present volume.

[56] Mirow, "The Social-Obligation Norm," 213–14.

[57] Duguit, *Les transformations générales du droit privé depuis le Code Napoléon* (Paris: F. Alcan, 1912).

[58] Duguit, *Les transformations générales du droit privé depuis le Code Napoléon*, 2nd edn (Paris: Félix Alcan, 1920), 21.

[59] Ibid., iv.

[60] Ibid., v.

[61] Mirow, "The Social-Obligation Norm," 200.

and civil law. Duguit's reconceptualization of property was highly influential throughout the world, particularly in Europe and Latin America, and found adherents in the United Kingdom and the United States.[62]

Duguit's six lectures in Buenos Aires in 1911 addressed the following topics: (1) the recent transformation of law and its methodology; (2) liberty and its relationship to social interdependence and social solidarity, with particular regard to property, contract, and individual responsibility for fault; (3) the autonomy-of-will theory of law and its relationship to juridical acts; (4) contract; (5) torts, civil responsibility, and negligence; and (6) property.[63] Following the groundwork in the first five lectures, Duguit asserted in the sixth that property had become socialized. This meant that property was no longer an individual right and that aggregate collectives of wealth protected by law were on the rise.[64]

Duguit began his lecture on property with the historical primacy of private property as an absolute subjective right that provided the owner's complete and unfettered dominion over the property. He observed this characterization of property in Roman law, the Declaration of Rights of 1789, the French Civil Code, and, appropriate for his audience, the Argentine Civil Code. Looking to France as an example, Duguit noted that not much legislation recognized the social function of property. France had no laws that required farmers to farm their land, or owners of houses to maintain them, or to make capital productive. Duguit, however, observed the movement towards the social function of property in France in some judicial decisions. By the second edition of the lectures, published in 1920, Duguit could point to several legislative instances of these developments in addition to the judicial recognition of these phenomena.[65]

For our consideration of Duguit as a Christian jurist, his final example of the growing social function of property is of particular interest. As the final example of his last lecture in Argentina, Duguit presented the nature and control of church property, which had been confiscated by the state in France, as a recent example of the distinction between his formulation of property and property as a subjective right. Duguit began with the law of 1905 and its transfer of ecclesiastical property to state property with a usage for ecclesiastical purposes under "cultural associations" to administer the property. In response to these seizures and as part of the general breakdown in relations

[62] Ibid., 192–96.
[63] Duguit, *Les transformations* (1920); Mirow, "The Social-Obligation Norm," 203–07.
[64] Duguit, *Les transformations* (1920), 149.
[65] Ibid., vii–viii, 152, 162, 165.

between France and the Holy See, papal prohibitions of clerics and lay Catholics from participation in these associations quickly followed.[66] In response, the Briand Law of January 2, 1907, provided that where there was no cultural association, the property would continue to be left to the disposition of the "faithful and of the ministers of religion to practice their religion."[67] Battles between bishops and mayors ensued, with local civil officials at times seeking to nominate schismatic clergy. The Council of State stepped in to resolve these disputes in favor of the clergy proposed by ecclesiastical authorities.[68] Duguit noted that the property interests held by the faithful and the clergy under these circumstances was nothing more than an "affectation" successfully asserted against the actual owner of the property. In this instance, property had become "an affectation that was energetically protected as it was, without one being able to find a subject of the right or a subjective right."[69] Thus, Duguit's final example was drawn from the complex situation of the relationship between church and state recently introduced in France by the law of 1905. Here was another example of law abandoning a subjective right to property and imposing on property limitations arising from its social function.

Duguit had grappled with the extent of property and its social function for many years before the lectures and the publication of *Les Transformations* in 1912. In the first volume of *l'État* (1901), Duguit noted that functionaries of the French state – such as judges, professors, officers, ministers of state, and notaries – held something akin to a property right in their positions, something like a subjective right.[70] Furthermore, Duguit had earlier characterized the church as a public service and priests as functionaries under the Concordat of 1801.[71] Perhaps it was in the arena of public servants and state functionaries that Duguit first began to observe the link between property and a social function.

CONCLUSION

Léon Duguit's fundamental work on the nature and function of the state, government, constitutional law, and property transformed accepted understandings of these fields. Applying empirical approaches and sociological methods, Duguit purported to disclose more accurately the subjects of his study. His observations led him to conclude that social solidarity and human

66 Ibid., 170–71.
67 Ibid., 172.
68 Ibid., 172–75.
69 Ibid., 175.
70 Duguit, *L'Etat, le droit objectif*, 581–82.
71 Duguit, *Le Régime*, 23.

interdependence served as the basis of the state. Therefore, the state and all its constituent elements were best understood as social functions. This meant that sovereignty, subjective rights, the distinction between governed and governing, and the distinction between public and private law were illusory. Duguit reframed the discussion of these essential aspects of state, government, law, and property.

Léon Duguit was a secular jurist who operated in the milieu of a Catholic country and Christian continent. His sociological approaches to the state, law, labor, and property led him to observations and solutions to problems that were remarkably in accord with the rapidly developing doctrines of the Roman Catholic Church's social teachings. Faith and reason led to the same results. This meant that politicians and policymakers could easily appropriate ideas and solutions that had radically different theoretical substructures.

When Duguit engaged directly with Christianity in his writings, he addressed the church in its historical and institutional role. It is on this worldly level for Duguit that the church functioned in the modern world of his modern states. The church and Christianity presented themselves to Duguit as social and political phenomena to be recognized, respected, observed, and theorized. Their salvific role in human and divine history was not part of Duguit's intellectual project. Nonetheless, it appears that in the later years of Duguit's life, he turned to Augustine and Thomas Aquinas to reexamine their place in his work.[72] As one colleague recounted, when he found Duguit with a copy of the *Summa*, Duguit remarked, "I would have saved ten years of research if I had known this earlier."[73] Perhaps Duguit made the comment in jest. It is more likely, however, that the event illustrates Duguit's constant consideration of Christianity's place in French and modern culture. It was something a good lay sociologist of law could not ignore, and it was apparently something Duguit respectfully considered throughout his life.

RECOMMENDED READING

Audren, Frédéric, and Jean-Louis Halpérin. *La culture juridique français: entre mythes et réalités XIXe–XXe siècles*. Paris: CNRS Éditions, 2013.

Blanquer, Jean-Michel, and Marc Milet. *L'Invention de l'État: Léon Duguit, Maurice Hauriou et la naissance du droit public moderne*. Paris: Odile Jacob, 2015.

"Les idées politiques de Léon Duguit: un prisme contextuel et biographique." In *Autour de Léon Duguit*, edited by Fabrice Melleray, 3–28. Bruxelles: Bruylant, 2011.

[72] Boyé, "Souvenirs," 124–25.

[73] Ibid., 124.

Bonnard, Roger. “Léon Duguit: ses oeuvres, sa doctrine.” *Revue du droit public et de la science politique en France à l'étranger* 46 (1929): 5–51.
Boyé, A.-J. “Souvenirs personnels sur Léon Duguit.” *Revue juridique et économique du Sud-Ouest, série juridique* 10 (1959): 115–28.
Debaenst, Bruno. “Le droit social, le droit individuel et la tranformation de l'État.” In *The Formation and Transmission of Western Legal Culture: 150 Books that Made the Law in the Age of Printing*, edited by Serge Dauchy, Georges Martyn, Anthony Musson, Heikki Pihlajamäki, and Alain Wijffels, 429–31. Cham: Springer, 2016.
Duguit, Léon. *Le Régime du Culte Catholique antérior à la loi de séparation et les causes juridiques de la séparation*. Paris: Librairie de la Société du Recueil J.-B. Sirey, 1907.
Les transformations générales du droit privé depuis le Code Napoléon. Paris: Félix Alcan, 1912; 2nd edn, Paris: Félix Alcan, 1920.
“The Concept of Public Service.” *Yale Law Journal* 32 (1923): 425–35.
García-Villegas, Mauricio. “Comparative Sociology of Law: Legal Fields, Legal Scholarship, and Social Sciences in Europe and the United States.” *Law & Social Inquiry* 31 (2006): 343–82.
Hakim, Nader. “Duguit et les privatistes.” In *Autour de Léon Duguit*, edited by Fabrice Melleray, 81–114. Bruxelles: Bruylant, 2011.
Halpérin, Jean-Louis. “Saleilles, Raymond.” In *Dictionnaire historique de juristes français (XIIe–XXe siècle)*, edited by Patrick Arabeyre, Jean-Louis Halpérin, and Jacques Krynen, 694–96. Paris: Presses Universitaires de France, 2007.
Hayward, J. E. S. “Solidarity: The Social History of an Idea in Nineteenth Century France.” *International Review of Social History* 4 (1959): 261–84.
Laborde, Cécile. “Pluralism, Syndicalism and Corporatism: Léon Duguit and the Crisis of the State (1900–25).” *History of European Ideas* 22 (1996): 227–44.
Laborde-Lacoste, Marcel. “La vie et la personnalité de Léon Duguit.” *Revue juridique et économique du Sud-Ouest, série juridique* 10 (1959): 93–114.
Milet, M. “Duguit, Léon.” In *Dictionnaire historique de juristes français (XIIe–XXe siècle)*, edited by Patrick Arabeyre, Jean-Louis Halpérin, and Jacques Krynen, 271–73. Paris: Presses Universitaires de France, 2007.
Mirow, M. C. “The Social-Obligation Norm of Property: Duguit, Hayem, and Others.” *Florida Journal of International Law* 22 (2010): 191–226.
“Léon Duguit and the Social Function of Property in Argentina.” In *Léon Duguit and the Social Obligation Norm of Property: A Translation and Global Exploration*, edited by Paul Babie and Jessica Viven-Wilksch. Cham: Springer, 2019.
“Origins of the Social Function of Property in Chile.” *Fordham Law Review* 80 (2011): 1196.
“*Rerum Novarum*: New Things and Recent Paradigms of Property Law.” *The University of the Pacific Law Review* 47 (2016): 183–97.
Pérez, Monereo, José Luis, and José Calvo González. “Léon Duguit (1859–1928): jurista de una sociedad en transformación.” *Revista de derecho constitucional europea* 4 (2005): 483–547.
Raynaud, Philippe. “Léon Duguit et le droit naturel.” *Revue d'historie des facultés de droit et de la science juridique* 4 (1987): 169–80.
Santofimio Gamboa, and Jaime Orlando. “León Duguit y su doctrina realista, objetiva y positiva del Derecho en las bases del concepto de servicio público.” *Revista digital de derecho administrativo* 5 (2011): 43–86.

22

Georges Ripert

(1880–1958)

FRÉDÉRIC AUDREN

BIOGRAPHICAL INTRODUCTION

Georges Ripert is one of the most important and influential French jurists of the twentieth century. A respected civil lawyer, dean of the Paris Law Faculty, continuator of Marcel Planiol's work, and author of several essays on contemporary transformations of the law, he joined the Vichy regime and served for a few months as secretary of state for public instruction and youth. This political commitment has long tarnished his reputation as a law professor. Politically conservative, Ripert distinguished himself by taking original and vigorous legal positions in a series of highly acclaimed essays. A resolute opponent of natural law, he nevertheless defended the influence of Catholic morality on the law. He was a fine connoisseur of social and human sciences and firmly promoted the specificity and autonomy of the legal discipline.

Georges Ripert was born on April 22, 1880, in La Ciotat (Bouche-du-Rhône). He belonged to the Provençal petty bourgeoisie. His grandfather, a small rural landowner, wanted his children to benefit from a solid education. In turn, Georges's father, Joseph, a solicitor at the court of appeal of Aix-en-Provence, took care of the education of his sons who entered higher education (Georges and Émile) and the *Conseil d'État*, or Council of State (Henri, who died prematurely). Georges studied at the Collège de Draguignan and the Lycée Mignet of Aix-en-Provence and graduated in 1896 before completing his brilliant education at the faculty of law in Aix-en-Provence. He obtained a law degree (1899) and was immediately called to the bar. He also received two doctorates, the first in legal sciences (with the thesis *De l'exercice du droit de propriété dans ses rapports avec les propriétés voisines*, 1902), and the second in political and economic sciences (with the thesis *Des plus-values indirectes résultant de l'exécution des travaux publics*, published as a book in 1904). Admitted to the *agrégation de droit privé* in the first position (1906), he was appointed to the Faculty of Law of Aix-en-Provence (as Ripert recalls years later, this city which "lived entirely for the law, or at least for and by jurists"), where he taught until 1918.

Initially responsible for teaching both European and American political institutions as well as public and administrative law, he became professor of civil law in 1910. During World War I, Ripert was transferred, despite his request for suspension, to the army's ancillary services, where he exercised duties within the War Council, the Marseille Revision Council, and the Economic Action Council. After being discharged from his military obligations, he joined the Faculty of Law in Paris, where he taught commercial and maritime law before taking up civil law classes. In 1933, he was transferred from the chair of civil law to that of commercial law and comparative commercial legislation. At the same time, he gave courses at the École des Hautes études commerciales, the École coloniale and the École libre de Sciences Politiques (where he took over Charles Lyon-Caen's course).

Academic authorities have emphasized that, throughout his career, Ripert's pedagogical qualities and the depth of his knowledge attracted many students to him. He was also very involved in academic life and governance: a member of the Conseil supérieur de l'Instruction publique, president of the Association des Professeurs des Facultés de Droit, assessor to the dean of the Paris faculty, and dean of the Paris faculty, a position he was elected to in 1938 and held until his suspension in 1944. This suspension was the consequence of his appointment, under the Vichy regime, as secretary of state for public education and youth (September 6 to December 13, 1940). He was notably responsible for implementing the "francization of the civil service" in universities and for enforcing the first Jewish status law in higher education (although Ripert did not seem particularly favorable to this law). Under his authority, Freemasons, civil servants of foreign origin, and Jews were immediately dismissed. At the same time, he increased the subsidies granted to Catholic education and called for the reintroduction of "duties towards God" in public schools.[1] He also chaired the Legislation Committee of the General Secretariat for the Presidency of the Council (whose role was to examine the draft laws of the various ministerial departments before their presentation to the Council of Ministers) and sat on the National Council, an advisory body created in January 1941 with limited influence to compensate for the disappearance of representative institutions.

[1] Claude Singer, *Vichy, l'Université et les juifs* (Paris: Les Belles Lettres, 1992), 60–64, 91–95.

An avowed conservative, attached to the traditional values of the French bourgeoisie and landowners, nostalgic for an idealized national past, he had nevertheless expressed, during the 1930s, his concerns about the murders of Czech students and German anti-Semitism. He then encouraged students to welcome their fellow refugees from across the Rhine.[2] Like other members of the Democratic Alliance of Pierre-Étienne Blandin (the leader of the liberal right, to whom he was close), Georges Ripert rallied to Pétain and his National Revolution because Ripert detested the Front Populaire and parliamentary democracy, and feared the decline of the West and the "Bolshevization" of the law. His colleague René Cassin, personally affected by anti-Semitic legislation and stripped of French nationality, was particularly severe towards the defeatism of his dean.[3] Ripert gave up his position at the Secretariat of State in favor of its former secretary general, the philosopher Jacques Chevalier. This departure from the government did not, however, constitute a move away from Vichy policy: in December 1941, Dean Ripert was delighted, addressing the students and his colleagues, to be able to find "the true figure of France in misfortune." He added, "We are now between the French. May the communion of thought give to each of us the most ardent desire to see the homeland come alive again." At the end of the war, he was suspended from his duties as dean and professor because of his involvement in the Vichy government. Arrested at home and imprisoned, he was eventually placed on probation. In May 1947, the High Court of Justice dismissed the case against him and even acknowledged his participation in the resistance. At the end of this episode, Ripert claimed his pension rights (January 1948). He left the university with bitterness, despite the collective tribute paid by his colleagues, who offered him voluminous "mélanges" (*Le droit privé français au milieu du XXe siècle. Études offertes à Georges Ripert*, 2 volumes [Paris, 1950]). In his last writings, he prophesied the "decline of the law" and the destruction of individual rights. Ripert died suddenly on July 4, 1958.

Despite Vichy's shadow on his path, Ripert has been showered with honors and marks of recognition, illustrating the respect and admiration he still enjoys in academic circles in France and abroad. Appointed as a member of the Académie des Sciences Morales et Politiques of the Institut de France in 1937 (under the patronage of Henri Capitant), he was also a correspondent of the Royal Academy of Madrid (1953), a member of the Royal Academy of

[2] Simon Epstein, *Un paradoxe français. Antiracistes dans la Collaboration, antisémites dans la Résistance* (Paris: Albin Michel, 2008), 38–39.

[3] Antoine Prost and Jay Winter, *René Cassin et les droits de l'homme: le projet d'une génération* (Paris: Fayard, 2011), 73 and 138.

Romania (1937), of the Pontifical Academy of Rome (1949), and of the Royal Dutch Academy (1950). Several universities awarded him an honorary doctorate: Université Libre de Bruxelles (1934), and the Universities of Cluj (1938), Iasi (1938), Montréal (1939), Liège (1939), and Louvain (1954). He was also made an officer of the Legion of Honor, of the Black Star of Benin, of the Order of Leopold of Belgium, and of the Crown of Italy. He was elevated to the rank of Grand Officer of the Crown of Romania, Commander of the Order of the Oak of Luxembourg, and of the Order of Saint Sava of Serbia.

MAJOR THEMES AND CONTRIBUTIONS

The Vices of Modern Society: The Power of Money, Democratic Mmysticism, and the Destruction of Traditions

Georges Ripert was a remarkable analyst of his time. He was fascinated (and, at the same time, frightened) by the social, economic, and political upheavals taking place before his eyes. This was a characteristic and one of the strengths of his work: it was resolutely contemporary, written with a sense of urgency, seeking to diagnose the evils from which France and its legal tradition were suffering. In five essays (his "tetralogy," as his colleague René Morel curiously calls it[4]), but also in his various treatises and articles, he always claimed to start from the "reality" of society as it was, from the conflicts and crises that were pervading it, and from the reforms that this society was trying to implement in order to remedy these tensions. Ripert thus faced the acceleration of history, which saw an intensification of sociotechnical progress, an increase in demands for social regulation and state intervention, as well as an intensification of exchanges between people and goods. By taste, he concentrated his attention on areas of law that were in direct contact with these developments affecting Western civilization. Thus, the jurist showed a keen and early interest in the modernization of means of transport, inseparable from scientific progress and the shrinking of the space-world. On the advice of his mentor Edmond Thaller, in 1913 he wrote a two-volume treatise on maritime law that went through four reprints and, several years later, a *Précis de droit maritime*

[4] "Discours de René Morel," *Discours prononcés pour la remise du livre "Le Droit privé français au milieu du XXe siècle" offert au professeur Georges Ripert par les professeurs des facultés de droit le 21 octobre* 1950 (Paris: LGDJ, 1950), 20. This "tetralogy" consists of *La règle morale dans les obligations civiles* (1925), *Le régime démocratique et le droit civil moderne* (1936), *Aspects juridiques du capitalisme moderne* (1946), *Le déclin du droit* (1949), and *Les forces créatrices du droit* (1955).

(1939), published by Dalloz. He endeavored to describe the evolutions of merchant marine and maritime exploitation: "Today, the large steamer has eliminated the modest sailboat. For it, the ports have expanded, new routes have opened. Traffic has increased in proportions that no one expected. Maritime trade has become one of the conditions of national life."[5] In publication after publication, he contributed to identifying not only the particularism of maritime law but also the effects on this law from the major transformation undergone by ships, personnel, or goods. Ripert's expertise in this field was recognized and sought after: he took part in the activities of the International Labour Office in relation to the international status of seamen (1923), in the Diplomatic Conference for the Unification of River Law within the framework of the League of Nations (1930), and in some fifteen maritime law conferences throughout Europe, in particular in Antwerp, Brussels, and Amsterdam. A member of the French Maritime Academy, he served as the honorary president of the French Association of Maritime Law and became a member of the permanent committee of the International Maritime Committee. His competence was also sought in matters of air law (a discipline on which, however, he wrote less), and participated in several international legal conferences on aviation and international diplomatic conferences on air law.

From transport law to commercial law was only a short step. Holder of the Parisian chair of commercial law as of 1933, Ripert endeavored to explore a field that he had until then only occasionally touched upon. He brought his thoughts together in his *Traité élémentaire de droit commercial* (1948), which, going beyond a simple analysis of the Commercial Code's provisions, offered a synthesized overview of merchants, commercial companies, legal operations, commercial contracts, and bankruptcy. More than ever, Ripert took the economic situation of French society seriously. As a great legal expert, he assumed the position of an intellectual in the polis. For instance, in his book *Aspects juridiques du capitalisme moderne* (1946), he diagnosed a "commercialisation of law"; even more, he revealed the grip of industrial and financial capitalism on all aspects of social life.[6] "When all members of society are imbued with this spirit [of capitalism], the supreme goal of life becomes for all

[5] Georges Ripert, "La législation maritime française de 1870 à 1920," in *Les transformations du droit dans les principaux pays depuis cinquante ans (1869–1919). Livre du cinquantenaire de la Société de législation comparée*, vol. 2 (Paris: LGDJ, 1923), 46 [our translation].

[6] For a discussion of this book, see Jean-Pascal Chazal, "Georges Ripert, *Aspects juridiques du capitalisme moderne*, Paris LGDJ, 1e éd. 1946; 2e éd. 1951,"*Revue trimestrielle de droit civil* (2013): 712.

the acquisition of wealth. The power of money dominates society as a whole."[7] This spirit was a "new mysticism."[8] Such an exclusive consideration of wealth concerned all social strata and ultimately would destroy solidarity and traditional hierarchies. Despite the attacks it faced, capitalism (whether state or private) was far from disappearing.

The tyranny of enrichment was inseparable from the democratization of societies. With a certain Tocquevillian emphasis, Ripert wished to highlight the fact that freedom was now being sacrificed to equality, that "rights–debts" (*droits–créances*) prevailed over "rights–freedoms" (*droits–libertés*), that the action of the state replaced individual initiatives, and that social levelling and the desire for revenge of the weakest intensifed the war against the strongest. And in a society that imposed equality, where "birth, class, intelligence, employment count for nothing, or not much, wealth becomes the only means of superiority. The luxury of material life in modern society is a manifestation of this need for distinction that men have."[9] The power of money (that is, the spirit of capitalism) and the power of numbers (that is, democratic mysticism) were two sides of the same movement leading towards the dislocation of the "Christian West" and its values.

In *Le régime démocratique et le droit civil moderne*, a book marked by the coming into office of the Front Populaire and by the specter of socialism, Ripert fulminated against this "modern France [which] is a democracy, where universal suffrage makes the force of numbers reign." He describes at length how this major evolution radically transformed the way of governing, the relationships between individuals, the conception of living together, and the moral foundations of social life. Echoing a certain counter-revolutionary ideology, he underlined on page after page how the democratic Leviathan disrupted the order of families (he has long discourses on gender equality, the role of the father, and marriage and divorce), redistributed power and entrusted it to a mass that used the ballot as a weapon, and broke the thread of (a Christian and liberal) national history in the name of progress, secularism, and equality.

Raymond Aron said of Ripert that he was the "most antidemocratic" professor of the faculty. There is no doubt that nostalgia is everywhere in Ripert's words, but, strictly speaking, there is no dream of a restoration of an

[7] Georges Ripert, *Aspects juridiques du capitalisme moderne* (Paris: LGDJ, 1946), 340 [our translation].

[8] Ibid., 346.

[9] Georges Ripert, *Le régime démocratique et le droit civil moderne* (Paris: LGDJ, 1936), 192 [our translation].

ancient order. Rather, he was driven by the ambition (which, arguably, is even more provocative) of a "conservative revolution" that would end the hullabaloo of modern society. Underneath the jurist, master of his knowledge, there always was an angry moralist loathing triumphant modernity.

Legal Policy: The Jurist, a Guardian of Individual Rights and Freedoms

Georges Ripert's ambition was to examine the influence of the capitalist system and the democratic regime on French civil law, and to shed light on how modernity has shaken the pillars of private law (individual property, contractual freedom, and tort liability). Recognized as an uncontested authority of the discipline, heir of Planiol, Henri Capitant, Étienne Bartin, and a few others, Ripert left a decisive academic contribution: in addition to the revival and recasting of Planiol's *Traité*, he was the initiator and editor of the *Traité pratique de droit civil français* (a fourteen-volume collective enterprise) but also a subtle and feared critic in doctrinal controversies (he vigorously attacked Emmanuel Lévy's "legal socialism," François Gény's conceptions on natural law, and Louis Josserand's positions on the abuse of rights).

It would be wrong to claim that Ripert relegated the legal profession to a technical activity. Rather, he denounced the tendency to "take refuge in the study of technique": "An entire generation, mine, has been amused and abused by the study of technique."[10] In his view, jurists must be involved in the "legal policy" of the nation; they should be viewed as engineers who co-construct law and society, and guide, through legal instruments, the conduct of citizens and the evolution of the nation. In any legal debate, neutrality is neither possible nor desirable, and the jurist must be a politically committed actor. It is not a question of seeking a foundation superior to the law (Ripert claimed to adhere to positivism; a "pseudo-positivism," some said) but to think of its construction and its application *en context*.[11] The specific task of jurists, in his words, "is to know why the law is as it is and why it changes."Ripert adopted a resolutely realistic posture. To understand the law adequately, one must understand the social forces (public opinion, electorate, trade unions, political parties, etc.) and the competing interests that contribute to its formation and evolution.[12] In this regard, his latest work, *Les forces créatrices du droit*

[10] Ibid., 8–9 [our translation]. Ripert considered this book a "work of legal policy"; ibid., 13.

[11] Christophe Jamin, "Le rendez-vous manqué des civilistes français avec le réalisme juridique: un exercice de lecture comparée," *Droits* 1, no. 51 (2010): 137–59.

[12] Georges Ripert, *Les forces créatrices du droit* (Paris: LGDJ, 1955), 71–134; "Le bilan d'un demi-siècle de vie juridique,"*Recueil Dalloz* (1950), 1–4.

(1955), prefigured much subsequent research on interest groups and legislative drafting. Thanks to his sociological sensitivity, his entire "tetralogy" places him in a stream of legislative realism that brings him closer to authors like Jean Cruet and Maxime Leroy (although they remain ideologically very distant). In any case, Ripert noted that the life of law was now trapped by the demands of the proletariat, by an ideology of social equality, and by the myth of progress. This democratic and capitalistic atmosphere led to reforms which, at an accelerated pace, disrupted the legal order by attacking individual property and the freedom of contract, by introducing "social rights" (or even "class rights"), or by granting excessive protection to the weakest.[13]

Among the sources of the law, Ripert paid particular attention to legislation, not because it is the expression of a will (whether popular or general) but because it illustrates unambiguously this "struggle for the law" – an example of numerous references to Rudolf von Jhering – this conflict between categorical interests. Dominated by social passions, anxious to seduce a captive electorate, parliament ends up adopting laws dictated by circumstances, pressures, and trade-offs (not to say compromises). In his darkest book, *Le déclin du droit* (1949), Ripert noted that this legal disorder was accentuated after the Liberation of France by accumulating poorly drafted laws, despising subjective rights more than ever, and abandoning traditional legal principles. Reacting against all these legal innovations, he entrusted the lawyers, those trained by the faculty, with the task of maintaining French law, "formed on Roman data by the Christian civilization, ordained during centuries of work and peace, perfected by the clear reason of jurists."[14] It is *ius* rather than *lex*; Rome (though too pagan) rather than Athens. Only lawyers, *ontologically conservative* (that is, dominated by a spirit of order, moderation, and tradition[15]), were in a position to ensure a measured evolution of the law, to implement its practice (and not to revolutionize it), that is, to support a progress of the law achieved "in the ever stricter observance of what constitutes the very essence of the law: order based on justice"[16] – and, one could add, in the respect of its conceptual tools. The stability (or "stagnation") of the law and its forms was not synonymous with the inertia of legal life. This stability never prohibited

[13] Jean-Pascal Chazal, "Georges Ripert et le déclin du contrat," *Revue des contrats* 2 (2004): 244–56.

[14] "Discours de René Morel," in *Discours prononcés pour la remise du livre Le Droit privé français au milieu du XXe siècle*, 47 [our translation].

[15] On the conservatism of jurists, see Ripert, *Les forces créatrices du droit*, 1–30.

[16] "Discours de René Morel," in *Discours prononcés pour la remise du livre Le Droit privé français au milieu du XXe siècle*, 49 [our translation].

continuous transformations of the law; they were, however, carried out in the *memory* of its normative dimension. Ripert described himself as the "mainteneur" (a Provençal expression) of the French legal culture.

If the law is the result of a transaction between competing social forces, it is formally created by the will of the "Power." Despite his detestation of parliamentary politics, Ripert's struggle was neither the destruction of legicentrism nor the toppling of the law from its pedestal: rather, he assumed his positivism and did not imagine that judges could replace the legislator. The judge, he reiterated, does not have the power to create legal rules. Still, Ripert entrusted lawyers, judges, and other legal professionals with the task of sometimes stating "to what extent a reform can be achieved without compromising the stability of existing law,"[17] and sometimes saying and applying the law with prudence and concern for the long term, while respecting its own forms.

Ripert was therefore a vigilant observer of civil case law and, as a professor of law, did not hesitate to point out certain abuses of judges, which he considered worrying (for example, in the field of liability or of the law of obligations[18]). Jurists, he thought, should be in the front line in the fight for a certain idea of the law but also for "the maintenance of our civilization through law." On the basis of major principles, respect for the human person and a sense of justice must be defended against the "ideological conception of indefinite progress and social equality achieved by an all-powerful state." Concerning the legal field, strictly speaking, it was subjective rights (in particular, property rights) and individual freedoms (for example, contractual freedom) that must be protected, while also ensuring that the invasion of private law by public law remained limited. Similarly, Ripert considered as an absolute necessity the slowing down and the supervision of the movement towards the socialization of goods and the extension of "rights to reparation" linked to increase of risks. What makes the action of jurists so important and indispensable was that it is based on a *sens pratique*, which, by articulating reality and dogma, could to a large extent protect them from the modernist ideology. By clearly assessing the forces at work that make and break the law, jurists, placing themselves at the level of the social world, would be able to shape and reasonably institute the flow of demands and struggles that animate society. All of Ripert's work is nourished by this paradox: the legal dogmatic finds in the approach of realism the grounds for its effectiveness and deepening, and vice versa.

[17] Ripert, *Les forces créatrices du droit*, 32 [our translation].

[18] André Rouast, "L'œuvre civiliste de Georges Ripert," *Revue trimestrielle de droit civil* 57 (1959): 1–9.

Christian Morality: Law as Moral Science and Practice

How, Georges Ripert asked himself, can we prevent the barbarity that is becoming more and more apparent every day? How can we save, if still possible, the traditional values of the West and fight against the collapse of its legal civilization? How, in short, can we ensure that legal developments are guided by a sense of justice and respect for individual rights? This task could no longer be entrusted to the legislator who, working under pressure from opposing forces, had lost his bearings. One could only ask for the least bad laws possible and respect the major legal principles as much as possible. It was, in reality, up to the judge (and the law professor) to ensure that the law progresses well and is properly applied. It is the judge who, tested by the concrete realities and private interests of individuals, draws the line between the lawful and the unlawful. As for the law professor, under penalty of treason, he had to be a censor of the public mind and of the legislative movement. Nevertheless, how could one make a *good judgment*, that is, without sinking into progressivism, socialism, or relativism? Every lawyer undoubtedly ought to be conservative and realistic, but this was not enough to ensure a proper use of legal tools. By what must he adjust his judgment of the law so that it would not be distorted by the illusions of modernity? To this last question, Ripert gave an original answer in French scholarship (*doctrine*): *Christian morality*. A somewhat surprising answer from this character who, unlike many of his colleagues, was not known for his commitment to defending religion (although a practicing Catholic, he was said to be rather anticlerical).

In his most celebrated work, *La règle morale dans les obligations civiles* (1925), Ripert argued that the technicality and abstraction of the "law of obligations" (for example, contract law, tort law) must not obscure the fact that it is almost entirely based on moral precepts. The jurist must "strive to bring his moral ideal into law" and revive obligations by "a continuous rise of moral sap." When he especially pointed out a moral duty, Ripert answered, on the same occasion, the German jurists who, at that time, saw in civil obligation a relation not between two persons but between two patrimonies.[19] Unquestionably, his work as a whole is a "struggle for the moral ideal," an ideal embodied in Christian morality:

[19] Ripert's hostility toward Germany and its law clearly manifested itself during the First World War; see Georges Ripert, "L'idée de droit en Allemagne et la guerre actuelle," *Revue internationale de l'enseignement* 69 (1915): 169–83.

> The jurist cannot forget that the law must apply to a society based on Christian morality. This morality, by its particular conception of the ends of humanity in this world, imposes a series of rules that tend not only to ensure respect for others but also to perfect the soul. It is a very precise code of human duties towards God, towards others, and towards oneself. Civilization increases to the extent that [these moral rules] triumph.[20]

One must not be mistaken, however, about the meaning of such a proposal: Ripert did not dream of imposing religious legislation or placing French law under the authority of the church. Unlike many of his colleagues in Catholic faculties,[21] he did not aspire to the restoration of a divine law. Ripert fully acknowledged the secularization of legal institutions and rules: the principle of secularism required the elimination of religious forces in the creation of law and the exclusion of religion from the legislator's concerns: "No rule of law can be adopted because it is claimed by religious morality; none can be condemned solely because it would be rejected by that morality."[22] Ripert repeatedly highlighted the fact that there was indeed a *technical distinction* between law and morality (Catholic or not), and that this distinction had been favorable to the political freedom of the French. From a positivist point of view, the law, as an act of political will, does not need morality to be valid, legitimate, and applicable. Perhaps it even draws its effectiveness from this *amoralism*, which does not expose it to suspicion and endless discussion. This does not mean, however, that law is independent of morality: in Ripert's view, a rule of law is nothing more than an embodiment, a formalization – thanks to technical tools – of a moral idea. The law is nourished by moral life, which refracts and crystallizes in the positive legal order. In family law, how many provisions reflect moral concerns?

This defense of morality *in* law is not a promotion of natural law. On the contrary, Ripert sought to liquidate the classical theory of natural law and was particularly tough on its supporters (among them, François Gény, Raymond Saleilles, and Joseph Charmont).[23] Natural law, falsely universalist, without any real consistency, was of no help in seriously establishing a rule or a legal

[20] Georges Ripert, *La règle morale dans les obligations civiles*, 4th edn (Paris: LGDJ, 1949), 27 [our translation].

[21] On French Catholic jurists, see Frédéric Audren, "La Belle époque des juristes catholiques (1880–1914)," *Revue française d'histoire des idées politiques* 28, no. 2 (2008): 233–71.

[22] Ripert, *Les forces créatrices du droit*, 147 [our translation].

[23] Anne Simonin, "La morale juridique de Georges Ripert," in *La République et son droit (1870–1930)*, edited by Annie Stora-Lamarre, Jean-Louis Halpérin, and Frédéric Audren (Besançon: Presses Universitaires de Franche-Comté, 2011), 359–79.

decision. Worse, it was a dangerous instrument in the hands of revolutionaries and tyrants, sometimes justifying the most complete submission, sometimes justifying radical upheavals in the name of the higher interests of justice.[24] Nor was Ripert's defense of morality in law an affirmation of social morality. Ripert noted the success of the idea of conscience or social justice in legal circles influenced by sociology. He was equally implacable against this *new look* to morality that made the collective interest and social solidarity the foundation of the rule of law. It was indeed *Christian* morality (also called *traditional morality*) that constituted the instrument *par excellence* of the reasonable legal policy he called for.

But what is this Christian morality? Those who would seek a precise definition in his writings will be disappointed. From a substantial point of view, developments were meager and evasive. For example, Ripert wrote on the protection of women and children, the limitation or elimination of abusive private powers, the improvement of the condition of children born out of wedlock, the assistance granted to large families, and the promotion of education. He preferred to point out the influence of this morality in matters of standards of behavior (*bonne mœurs*), good faith, repression of fraud, the obligation to compensate for damage, and so on. "Our law of contracts and obligations remains bathed in traditional morality."[25]

If the content and contours of this Christian morality are vague, there is no doubt that it is neither confused with Catholic morality (Ripert approved more than once of legal orientations that clearly contravene the positions taken by the Catholic Church) nor refers to a constituted normative corpus. This Christian morality appears above all as a common ground of values and prescriptions, a culture that has stood the test of time and is shared by all or part of French society. This conception poses more historical and sociological problems than it solves, but that was irrelevant for Ripert: his focus was not to rebuild the legal order on specific texts or more solid, higher principles. Positivism (despite all its infirmities) seemed to him sufficient: the law is what power wants, and power, through the monopoly of coercion, is best able to enforce laws. There was no need to look outside the positive order for a basis of law and the decisions it imposes. The search for new rules in morality was vain and useless. Ripert's goal was quite different, radically the opposite: to bring about or maintain traditional morality in law, to *moralize* law.

[24] Georges Ripert, *Droit naturel et positivisme juridique*, commenté par Philippe Jestaz, Tiré à Part 8 (Paris: Dalloz, collection, 2013).

[25] Ripert, *Les forces créatrices du droit*, 154 [our translation].

From this point of view, it is not a question of legal *theory* but a question of legal and judicial *practice* – not to establish the rule of law but to think morally about the role of a jurist. To try to succeed in such a gambit, Ripert adopted two distinct and complementary strategies. The first was to *naturalize* this morality in legal circles. Since such morality has dominated and inspired the law for centuries for the greater benefit of civilization, jurists must perpetuate this vision indefinitely. In *La règle morale dans les obligations civiles*, he devotes himself entirely to demonstrating how, even in modern times, legal relationships were immersed in updated traditional morality. Law schools and practitioners had an important role to play in instilling and renewing such traditional solutions – in short, to train young jurists in this moral atmosphere, to constantly bring legal professionals back to this culture against all opposing forces.

The second strategy, which strangely brings Ripert closer to the pragmatism of William James, was to conceive the moral rule as a *rule of action* (and not a legal rule). By relying on this understanding, it becomes possible for the judge and the practitioner faced with a legal problem to take its measure and to adjudicate with justice and accuracy. For the judge and the practitioner, the question of the ultimate basis of a rule is a false problem, but, conversely, they need (good) reasons to judge one way or the other. What can be done about the removal of healthy organs from the human body, about experiments on a condemned patient, about the euthanasia of an incurable person? These and other examples were raised by Ripert.[26] By naturalizing Christian morality, we make it an active rule *within us*, an intelligent *habit* according to which we will act when the opportunity presents itself. The attachment to morality is therefore not the sign of any idealism (law governed from the "World of Ideas") but, on the contrary, the capacity of the jurist to move in the realm of the concrete, to follow moral intuition, to be led by this intuition to an adequate decision. Certainly, the jurist has, in principle, the choice of ideas, of morals. Pluralism is, in fact, inescapable in society and among jurists themselves: social morality, republican morality, natural law, amoralism, and so on. But Ripert's conviction never changed: in a society threatened with dissolution, faced with the worrying progress of scientific or socialist morals, jurists had every reason to rely on Christian morality to fulfil their mission as guardians of civilization. Moved by his obsessions and fears, Ripert did not shrink from the temptation to elevate Christian morality as the only

[26] Ibid., 156.

legitimate and tolerable morality. Behind the moralist lay an authoritarian lawyer prone to denounce the enemies of French legal culture.

Much thought has been given to how to classify Ripert, who seems to bring together, in his person, all the opposites: pseudo-positivism, spiritualist positivism, moralist positivism. He was undoubtedly a paradox: a positivist (by reason) and a realist (by conviction). He was doubly realistic: in his analysis of the forces that make and break the law, but also in his proposal to monitor the *moral* activity of lawyers, that is, the impossibility for them to act without reason. All of this constituted a strange modernity (not to say modernism) for a jurist who, to this day, still incarnates reactionism.

RECOMMENDED READING

Allinne, Jean-Pierre. "Georges Ripert, un positiviste spiritualiste." In *Les facultés de droit de province au XIXe siècle*, edited by Philippe Nélidoff, 257–80. Études d'histoire du droit et des idées politiques 15. Toulouse: Presses Universitaires de Toulouse 1 Capitole, 2011.

André, Christophe. "Justice contractuelle et utilité sociale dans les œuvres de Georges Ripert." Thesis, Université Paris I Panthéon Sorbonne. Paris: 1994.

Chazal, Jean-Pascal. "Georges Ripert et le déclin du contrat." *Revue des contrats* 2 (2004): 244–56.

Centenaire de Georges Ripert (1880–1958). Laval: Imprimerie Barnéoud, 1980.

Discours prononcés pour la remise du livre "Le droit privé français au milieu du XXe siècle" offert au Professeur Georges Ripert par les professeurs des facultés de droit le 21 octobre 1950. Paris: LGDJ, 1950.

Georges, Julien. *Les passions politiques de la doctrine juridique. Le droit de propriété aux XIXe et XXe siècles*. Doctoral thesis, Université de Toulouse 1 Capitole. Toulouse: 2008.

Halpérin, Jean-Louis. "Ripert, Georges." *Dictionnaire historique des juristes français. XIIe–XXe siècle*, edited by Patrick Arabeyre, Jean-Louis Halpérin, and Jacques Krynen, 876–77. 2nd edn. Paris: Dalloz, 2015.

Jamin, Christophe. "Le rendez-vous manqué des civilistes français avec le réalisme juridique un exercice de lecture comparé." *Droits* 51, no. 1 (2010): 137–59.

Planiol, Marcel, and Georges Ripert. *Traité élémentaire de droit civil conforme au programme officiel des facultés de droit*. 10th edn. Paris: R. Pichon et R. Durand-Auzias, 1925–27.

Ripert, Georges. *La règle morale dans les obligations civiles*. [1925] 4th edn. Paris: LGDJ, 1949.

Le régime démocratique et le droit civil moderne. [1936] 2nd edn. Paris: LGDJ, 1948.

Aspects juridiques du capitalisme moderne. [1946] 2nd edn. Paris: LGDJ, 1951.

Le déclin du droit. Paris: LGDJ, 1949.

Les forces créatrices du droit. [1951] 2nd edn. Paris: LGDJ, 1955.

Traité général théorique et pratique de droit commercial. IV. Droit maritime. [1914] 4th edn. Paris: Rousseau, 1950.

Précis de droit maritime. Paris: Dalloz, 1939.
Droit naturel et positivisme juridique. Commenté par Philippe Jestaz. Paris: Dalloz, 2013.
Rouast, André. "L'œuvre civiliste de Georges Ripert." *Revue trimestrielle de droit civil* 57 (1959): 1–9.
Rousselet, Marcel. "Notice sur la vie et les travaux de Georges Ripert (1880–1958)." *Académie des sciences morales et politiques: lue dans la séance du 25 janvier 1960*. Paris: Institut de France, 1960.
Simonin, Anne. "La morale juridique de Georges Ripert." In *La République et son droit (1870–1930)*, edited by Annie Stora-Lamarre, Jean-Louis Halpérin, and Frédéric Audren, Besançon, 359–79. Besançon: Presses Universitaires de Franche-Comté, 2011.
Singer, Claude. *Vichy, l'Université et les juifs*. Paris: Les Belles lettres, 1992.

23

Jacques Maritain

(1882–1973)

WILLIAM SWEET

BIOGRAPHICAL INTRODUCTION

Jacques Maritain was born on November 18, 1882, in Paris. He was the son of Paul Maritain, a prominent lawyer, and Geneviève Favre, daughter of the French statesman Jules Favre. Maritain was baptized in the Lutheran church, raised by his mother in a secular home, and, as a young man, had socialist sympathies.

Maritain attended the Sorbonne, obtaining a *licence* in philosophy (1901) and in the natural sciences (1902). In 1901, he met Raïssa Oumansoff, a fellow student in the natural sciences. Both were struck by the materialism and positivism of their professors, and they made a vow to commit suicide within a year should they not find some answer to the apparent meaninglessness of life. On the advice of a friend, Charles Péguy, Maritain attended Henri Bergson's lectures at the Collège de France, which challenged the dominant positivism and allowed room for questions of purpose and meaning. This sufficed to lead Jacques and Raïssa to give up their thoughts of suicide, and they married in 1904. Soon thereafter, through the influence of the writer Léon Bloy, the Maritains were received into the Roman Catholic Church (1906).

Maritain received his *agrégation* in philosophy in 1905. After a two-year stay in Heidelberg, the Maritains moved to Versailles, where Jacques busied himself with popular writing and where, in late 1910, on the encouragement of Raïssa, he began an intensive study of the writings of Thomas Aquinas. In 1912, Maritain became professor of philosophy at the Lycée Stanislaus, and in 1914 was appointed assistant professor of modern philosophy at the Institut Catholique; he became full professor in 1921 and in 1928 was appointed to the chair of logic and cosmology.

In his earliest philosophical work, Maritain sought to defend Thomistic philosophy from its secular opponents. His interests soon expanded to include aesthetics (for instance, *Art et scholastique*, 1921; 2nd edn 1927) and social issues (*Primauté du spirituel*, 1927), studies of religion and culture, the philosophy of science, and epistemology (for example, *Distinguer pour unir ou les degrés du savoir*, 1932; 8th edn 1963). Friendships with the Russian philosopher Nicholas Berdiaev (beginning in 1925) and Emmanuel Mounier (from 1928) also influenced his work. By the mid-1930s, Maritain began to produce a number of texts that articulated a personalist humanism and a defense of human rights, culminating in *Humanisme intégral* (*Integral Humanism*, published in 1936, though based on a series of lectures given at the Universidad Internacional de Verano de Santander in 1934).

By this time, Maritain was an established figure in Catholic thought. In January 1933, he delivered a course of lectures at the Institute of Mediaeval Studies in Toronto, Canada, and in 1936 gave a number of lectures in Argentina and Brazil. Largely as a result of the "liberal" character of his political philosophy, he increasingly came under attack from both the left and the right, in France and abroad. Maritain returned to lecture in Toronto and in the United States in 1938 and again in January 1940. With the German invasion of France in June 1940, the Maritains decided to remain in North America. During the Second World War, they lived in the United States, where Maritain taught at Princeton University (1941–42) and Columbia University (1940–44), and where he was active in the war effort (recording broadcasts destined for occupied France and contributing to the Voice of America). Maritain lectured and published on a wide range of subjects, but among his most influential texts were studies in aesthetics, political philosophy, and the philosophy of natural law, including *De la justice politique* (1940), *Les droits de l'homme et la loi naturelle* (1942), *Christianisme et démocratie* (1943), and *Principes d'une politique humaniste* (1944). After France was liberated by summer's end in 1944, General Charles De Gaulle named Maritain French ambassador to the Holy See, where he served until 1948.

While ambassador, Maritain also served as head of the French delegation to UNESCO and, in late 1947, delivered the opening address at the second general conference of UNESCO, in Mexico City, where he gave an impassioned defence of the work of the United Nations and UNESCO, emphasizing that "one of the most important tasks undertaken by the United Nations is the new declaration of the rights of man, which Unesco is helping to draft."[1] Although Maritain was not involved directly in the development of the Universal Declaration of Human Rights (1948), his work was, arguably, significantly influential in it.

[1] Jacques Maritain, "The Possibilities for Cooperation in a Divided World," in *The Range of Reason* (New York: Scribner's, 1952), 172–84, at 182.

In the spring of 1948, Maritain was appointed professor of philosophy at Princeton to teach Aquinas's moral philosophy; upon retirement in 1952, he became professor emeritus. Maritain used his time in the United States to lecture at a number of American and Canadian universities, particularly at the University of Notre Dame and the University of Chicago, although he returned to France in the summers, sometimes to give short courses in philosophy, notably at "L'Eau Vive," at Soisy-sur-Seine, near Paris. During this time, Maritain continued writing on a wide range of topics but frequently returned to fundamental questions of moral and political philosophy and the foundations of human rights – *Man and the State*, based on lectures given in 1949 but published in 1951; the posthumously published (1986) *La loi naturelle ou loi non écrite*, lectures delivered in August 1950; as well as *Neuf leçons sur les notions premières de la philosophie morale* (1951), *Le philosophe dans la cité* (1960), and *La philosophie morale* (1960).

Maritain and his wife returned to France to live in June 1960. Raïssa, whose health was always frail, died in November, and the next year Maritain moved to Toulouse, where he lived with and eventually joined a religious order, Les Petits Frères de Jésus. Maritain continued to write essays and books on spiritual topics before dying on April 28, 1973. He is buried alongside Raïssa in Kolbsheim (Alsace), France.

MAJOR THEMES AND CONTRIBUTIONS

The Philosophy of Law

Maritain's work in the philosophy of law focused on the origin, nature, purpose, and limits of law and on the rights that followed from or correlated with law. To understand this work properly, however, one needs to recognize that it is situated within Maritain's interpretation of Aristotelian–Thomistic epistemology, metaphysics, and the conception of the human person.

For Maritain, law is a "practical" science, that is, a systematic discipline concerned with action and correct conduct. Although the practical sciences may draw on speculative principles, they are not speculative activities, that is, activities engaged in for their own sake. As a practical science, law has as its end the direction of human action, and because of this it is part of the sphere of moral philosophy. In fact, for Maritain, concepts such as "law," "right," and "the just" are fundamentally moral concepts prior to their use in the juridical order.[2]

[2] Vittorio Possenti, "Philosophie du droit et loi naturelle selon Jacques Maritain," *Revue Thomiste* 83 (1983): 598–608, at 600.

In addition, since law concerns the direction of human action, it rests on a knowledge of what human beings are, and why and how they act.

Maritain's turn to the analysis of law and to the philosophy of law had two principal objectives. The first was to elaborate and develop his Christian personalist philosophy, explained at length in *Humanisme intégral*, which emphasized the role and intrinsic value of the human person and the importance of human freedom. The second objective, related to the first, was Maritain's interest in providing a critique and an alternative to the dominant, primarily positivist views of the time – for example, those of Hans Kelsen and Raymond Carré de Malberg – but also to what he called rationalist and empiricist theories of law.

Law in general. Maritain's account of law follows, in large part, that provided by St Thomas Aquinas. For Aquinas – and for Maritain – law as such is, first, "an ordinance of reason for the common good, made by him who has care of the community, and promulgated."[3] Law is an ordinance or a command, although it is not simply a command – as Maritain believed positivists held. (He regarded them as largely voluntarists, i.e., maintaining that law is simply an expression of sovereign will.) The commands of law must be reasonable. Thus, Maritain writes, the divine law derives from "the reasonable will of God, and the human law from the human will ruled by reason."[4] Second, law does not aim at a private good, such as the private good of the sovereign or lawmaker, but at a common good. Third, such commands cannot be made by anyone; only the person or body that has "care for the community" can, strictly, make law. Finally, since the objective of law is to direct human conduct within a community, it must be known and must, therefore, be promulgated. For example, it is unreasonable to expect members of a society to obey a statute that they do not or cannot know. This definition of law, inherited from Aquinas, shows the essential connection between law and morality. Because of the relation of the law to reason and to the common good, Maritain insists that "as a general rule, moral rules are not exterior to the laws of the state, [and] the juridical order itself is essentially pervaded by morality."[5]

For Maritain, as for Aquinas, the aim of law is the perfecting of the human person – to help to make people good and develop in them a life of virtue,[6]

[3] *Summa Theologiae*, I–II, 90 4 resp.

[4] Maritain, "La philosophie du droit," in *The King's Good Servant: Papers read to the Thomas More Society of London*, edn. Richard O'Sullivan (Oxford: Basil Blackwell, 1948), 40–48, at 46. All translations of this text are my own.

[5] Ibid., 48.

[6] Ibid., 41.

not, as in some positivist thinkers, simply to ensure social control. More specifically, the aim of law is to guide the human person to complete liberty. (Maritain notes that law, however, is not sufficient for obedience; there is also a need for divine grace to enable one to commit oneself to following the law.[7]) While this aim may seem rather broad, it reminds the reader that law is primarily, and inherently, a moral rule. This also reflects Maritain's personalism – that is, the theory that emphasizes the fundamental value of the human person and that holds that persons are not ultimately subordinate to the community; that maintains that freedom is essential to being a person; and that challenges the impersonal character of materialist and collectivist views such as Marxism.

Kinds of law. Maritain holds that there are four kinds of law: natural law, eternal law, the common law of civilizations, and positive law.

To begin with, since the aim of law is to enable human beings to become good, there is a law that applies specifically to human beings – a "natural law" – comprising a set of fundamental principles of right and wrong, based on human nature, and prescriptive on human beings. This law is natural, first and most obviously, because it is found in the nature of human beings and is reflected in their natural inclination to seek certain ends and goals. The basic human end of happiness, common to all human beings, provides a standard of what is good. Human beings, therefore, have both a natural tendency and (because they are free and have the power to go against this good) a moral obligation to seek this end. Thus, the law is natural in that it is rooted in human nature – it has an ontological foundation – and describes the way human beings *should* (that is, naturally do) seek this happiness. The ontological, not moral, character of this "should" putatively avoids the objection of inferring an "ought" from an "is."

Second – and this is something that Maritain emphasizes in a way that Aquinas does not – this natural law is natural in the sense that it is or can be known naturally. By a process of *synderesis*, human beings can come to know, connaturally, basic principles of morality, that is, the precepts of the natural law, such as that human beings must seek the good and avoid evil. Once people also know what nature and human nature are – a knowledge achieved largely through experience and reflection on it – they can know specifically what they should and should not do. Thus, the natural law exists *virtually* in persons.

Maritain adds or emphasizes one other feature of the natural law that Aquinas did not: that the natural law has a historical dimension. Knowledge

[7] Ibid., 41–42.

of the natural law grows and develops, as indeed knowledge of human nature and human inclinations grows and develops, and this has an impact on morality and on law. Maritain writes that the contemporary understanding of natural law emerged only gradually, and, he adds, "very likely it [this understanding] will continue to develop and to become more refined as long as humanity exists."[8]

Key questions are, where does the natural law come from, and what makes this natural law obligatory? Some natural-law theories hold that the source of the obligation is, simply, in human nature. This, however, is not Maritain's view, for if human nature were to change, then the natural law could vary or change. While the natural law is "in" human beings, it does not have its obligatory force from the human person or from human nature. Since human existence and human nature are not self-explanatory and must have come from somewhere, there must have been a source of that existence and nature, and this is the source of the natural law. Moreover, since human reason is, by itself, fallible, and thus insufficiently authoritative to establish law, there must be some greater reason underlying law. Consequently, the ultimate source of this natural law is what Maritain calls the eternal law; this is a second kind of law. The eternal law is "the ideal plan, *ratio*, of the governance of things in the divine mind."[9] This is, however, a philosophical, not a theological, matter. Maritain holds that every law is a work of reason.

Natural law expresses what is obligatory for human beings as such. Since human beings are essentially social beings – that is, beings who naturally live in community – Maritain identifies a third kind of law that applies to all human beings insofar as they are members of any political society. These laws have their root in what is natural but suppose certain conditions of fact, such as "the state of civil society or the relationship between peoples."[10] These laws ought to be present in every society, although their precise formulation may vary according to their specific instantiation; for example, there are laws concerning the possession of property, but the particular conditions for acquisition or transfer may vary. Maritain calls this kind of law the *ius gentium* or "common law of civilizations," and as such it provides not only a core of law for political society but also principles of international law or standards of international justice.

8 *The Rights of Man and Natural Law* [*Les droits de l'homme et la loi naturelle (1942)*] (London: Geoffrey Bles, 1944), 37.

9 Aquinas, *Summa theologiae*, I–II, q 91, a 1; cf. Maritain, "La philosophie du droit," 42.

10 Maritain, *The Natural Law and Human Rights* (Windsor, ON: The Christian Culture Press/ Assumption College, 1942), 17.

Finally, again following Aquinas, there is what Maritain calls the positive law. Human positive law, or law posited by human authorities, follows from the first principles of natural law. Positive laws are "conclusions virtually contained in the precepts of the natural law," but are determined by "the reason and the will of man" when they are dealing with the specific regulations or customary practices characteristic of a particular community.[11] Thus, the many statutes necessary to ensure social order and stability in a particular community, such as those in civic bylaws, are posited by local authorities. These statutes are, so to speak, an extension of the natural law into a particular place, and, as they, too, are rational, are rooted in the natural law, and aim at a common good and at human wellbeing, they also have a moral character. Maritain holds that there is a divine positive law as well – a law known only by revelation. Examples of pure divine positive law are the dietary and ceremonial laws of the Jews (e.g., the laws pertaining to animal sacrifice), and the sacraments and rites that Christ gave his Church (for example, concerning the sacrifice of the Mass, confession, and so on).

These four kinds of law, then, provide a guide for human beings as they develop their virtues and seek to achieve genuine freedom. What may not be clear from the above, however, is how exactly law applies to human beings, and what the limits of law are. Maritain is able to address such concerns given his account of the nature of the human person. This account of the human person also bears on Maritain's account of human rights.

The human being as person and as individual. While Maritain follows Aquinas in holding that the natural law is rooted in human nature, he develops Aquinas's views by emphasizing certain elements that Aquinas did not, and by providing a more sophisticated account of the human person.

Maritain's account of human nature reflects the general Thomistic understanding of nature. For Aquinas, following Aristotle, the nature of a thing is not merely what it is at a particular moment in time, but what it has in itself to become. Thus, human nature includes the ends humans naturally seek and their natural inclinations towards these ends; and it is knowledge of these ends that enables one to have a robust understanding of human nature. Moreover, for Maritain, as for Aquinas, the human being is a substantial unity of soul (or form) and body (or matter). As material beings, humans have material needs, such as food and shelter. Yet human beings are more than material beings; they are rational and free, have an urge to communicate knowledge and love, and are capable of a supreme good. Human beings are also social and political

[11] Maritain, "La philosophie du droit," 43.

beings. Social life is necessary to the development of reason, language, moral character, and virtue. Finally, human beings have an end or a purpose, specifically, an ordination to the divine.

In his work of the late 1930s and early 1940s, Maritain makes an important distinction – rarely noted by others – between the human being as a member of, and ordered to, society (the individual), and the human being as having a supernatural destiny and ordered to the divine (the person). Here, Maritain notes that human beings, as material and social beings, are individuals and part of political society. As an individual, then, a human being is dependent on and related at a fundamental level to others, and so has duties towards them. Thus, the individual must, as a part of the social whole, serve the common good. Society can therefore impose restraints upon individuals and, for example, even oblige citizens to risk their lives in a just war. Similarly, for the sake of the well-being of the community, human beings may be required to renounce engaging in activities that may be noble in themselves.

But human beings are also persons, that is, beings of an intellectual, rational, and free nature who possess a spiritual soul. Since the human being is made by God for eternal life – this, before society exists – a person's end is an end "superior to all temporal societies."[12] A person, then, is a relatively independent whole,[13] "possessing a right to its own existence," and tending towards realization and completion while transcending self and the community.[14] While human persons are connected to other persons – for Maritain, the person "tends to communion"[15] – they are particularly "ordained to the absolute and ... summoned to a destiny that is beyond time."[16] Thus, given that the soul has an eternal destiny, society exists for the person and is subordinate to it. This does not conflict with one's character as an individual. When human beings are willing to sacrifice themselves for the community, this contributes to their spiritual growth. In short, human beings need political society and have obligations to it, but there are limits on to what the state can expect of its members and, by extension, there are limits on the law. Law must

[12] Maritain, *The Person and the Common Good* [*La personne et le bien commun*] (Notre Dame, IN: University of Notre Dame Press, 1947), 61. This text appeared first in the *Revue Thomiste* (mai–août 1946): 237–78, based on lectures from 1939 ("The Person and the Individual") and 1945 ("The Human Person in Society"). It appeared, almost simultaneously in English, in *The Review of Politics*. In 1947, it was published in book form with some minor revisions.

[13] Maritain, *The Person and the Common Good*, 30.

[14] Ibid., 67.

[15] Ibid., 37.

[16] Ibid., 61.

always treat the human being as a person – as a whole, not just as a part – and recognize that political society is subordinate to the perfection of the person, and that there are fundamental limits on the demands that society can place on human beings.

Maritain's emphasis on the person, found initially in *Integral Humanism*, was opposed by some fellow Catholic thinkers, such as Julio Meinvielle (1905–73) and Charles De Koninck (1906–65). In *De la primauté du bien commun contre les personnalistes* (1943),[17] De Koninck argued that personalists (such as Emmanuel Mounier and – though he did not refer to him by name, many suspected – Maritain) placed too much emphasis on the priority of the person, and De Koninck particularly rejected the view that persons had a priority over the common good. The debate continued: Maritain's friend Yves Simon (1903–61) argued that the view attacked by De Koninck was not Maritain's, and the Dominican scholar I. Theodore Eschmann (1898–1968) maintained that it was Maritain's view, and that Maritain was correct. Maritain attempted to address De Koninck's criticisms himself, albeit indirectly, in *The Person and the Common Good*, which appeared in 1946.

Challenges to contemporary theories of law. Maritain saw his theory of law – in particular, his natural-law theory – as offering an alternative to the then-contemporary discussion of law. Maritain noted that, in the years following Aquinas's death, other natural-law theories had claimed that natural law had its source in human nature, and had removed all reference to eternal law. Later, positivist theories had attempted to base law simply on the desire or will of the sovereign,[18] or to make it a product of a social contract. Maritain challenged both approaches.

Maritain considered and rejected the modern "rationalist" view of natural law – a view that he associated with Hugo Grotius and Samuel Pufendorf. On this view, nature is an order that can be thought of as self-subsistent and necessary. It is an absolute; it is the ground of, but is not exhausted in,

[17] Charles De Koninck, *De la primauté du bien commun contre les personnalistes. Le principe de l'ordre nouveau* (Montréal: Éditions Fides, 1943).

[18] Maritain argued that the notion of sovereignty was connected with that of political absolutism and, by extension, unaccountability – and must be "scrapped." If the state or the law were genuinely sovereign, "Law did not need to be just to have force of law. Sovereignty had a right to be obeyed, whatever it might command. Sovereignty was above moral law." See Maritain, *Man and the State* (Chicago: University of Chicago Press, 1951), 48, 53. Patrick McKinley Brennan uses Maritain's view to challenge the claims to the sovereignty of the state and the courts in the United States; see his "Sovereign States? The State of the Question from a Catholic Perspective," in *Faith and Law: How Religious Traditions from Calvinism to Islam View American Law*, edn. Robert F. Cochran (New York: NYU Press, 2007), 176–94.

experience and has something almost inerrant about it.[19] Nature has normative force intrinsically (that is, not by virtue of divine reason or of eternal law), and human beings can come to know this law by a kind of deductive procedure, independent of experience. Maritain argues, however, that this view misunderstands how law is known and that it does not address the fact that, without an objective ground, natural law could, in principle, change.

Maritain rejected positivist theories of law because they ignore the moral, objective, and rational character of law and, moreover, do not provide a sufficient account for its normative force. While some classical positivists – here, Maritain has in mind the empiricist philosophers Hobbes, Locke, and Hume – continue to employ the term "natural law," they use it in a radically different way from the rationalist or Maritain's own view. On the empiricist view, there is no necessity in nature, and there is no genuine universality of any law. Thus, strictly speaking, there is no natural law. For Maritain, law, on a positivist account, depends only on desire or will – it has no objective basis in nature. For example, Maritain writes that in Hobbes, the natural law is reduced to – or is a product of – the axiom that "contracts must be kept," and while Locke appears to place a greater emphasis on natural law, Maritain claims that Locke's understanding of natural law is that it is "a simple dictate of the common sense."[20]

Maritain also challenged more recent positivist theories, such as those of Max von Seydel (1846–1901), Georg Jellinek (1851–1911), and Raymond Carré de Malberg (1861–1935) as fundamentally voluntaristic. Maritain noted that Carré de Malberg, for example, viewed law and right as emanating from the state, not from morality or natural law, and that Jellinek considered international agreements as just only so far as they reflect the free will of the contracting parties.[21] While some of these authors allowed that there are moral rules that bear on law, these rules lie outside the juridical order. In short, for Maritain, positivist views ignore the place of reason and morality in the law.

Maritain noted, however, that some recent approaches, such as the "sociological positivism" of Léon Duguit (1859–1928), seemed to allow for a kind of nonmetaphysical natural law rooted in the needs, natures, and characters of human beings as social beings, which "one may consider as the atrium or

[19] Maritain, *La loi naturelle ou loi non écrite*. Texte inédit, établi par Georges Brazzola (Fribourg: Éditions universitaires, 1986), 87. An English edition, *Lectures on Natural Law*, trans. William Sweet, is in preparation for University of Notre Dame Press.

[20] Ibid., 92.

[21] Maritain, "La philosophie du droit," 43.

vestibule of the natural law."[22] (Duguit is criticized on this point, however, by Alf Ross in *On Law and Justice*.[23])

HUMAN RIGHTS

Given this anthropology and account of natural law, the recognition of human rights was, for Maritain, obvious. Maritain held that, "[i]f man is morally bound to the things which are necessary to the fulfilment of his destiny, obviously, then, he has the right to fulfill his destiny; and if he has the right to fulfill his destiny he has the right to the things necessary for this purpose." Moreover, Maritain adds, "the natural law [. . .] recognize[s] rights, in particular, rights linked to the very nature of man" as a morally free and rational being, and "[t]he notion of right [. . .] [is] founded on the freedom proper to spiritual agents."[24] All human beings, therefore, have natural, human rights.

Maritain's account of human rights developed principally in the late 1930s and early 1940s. It was a product of his personalist views, but it also reflected the shift within the Catholic Church that emphasized human freedom in the face of the totalitarianism spreading through much of Europe and beyond. In *Humanisme intégral*, for example, we see the beginnings of Maritain's discussion of rights. For Maritain, the "earthly city" must be so ordered as to "*recognize* the right to existence, to work, and to the growth of their life as persons."[25] (The key word here is "recognize," as it is not a matter of these rights being a product of a political community.) Whatever was necessary to "life as persons," however, Maritain left undeveloped.

In later essays in 1939[26] and 1940[27] (based on lectures given in 1938), we see a more elaborate statement of what these human rights are. They include "the right to live, to bodily integrity, to the necessary means of existence; the right of man to tend towards his ultimate goal in the path marked out for him by God; the right of association and the right to possess and use property"[28] – and

[22] Maritain, *La loi naturelle ou loi non écrite*, 116.

[23] Alf Ross, *On Law and Justice* (Berkeley: University of California Press, 1959), 256.

[24] Maritain, *The Rights of Man and Natural Law*, 37.

[25] Maritain, *Integral Humanism; Temporal and Spiritual Problems of a New Christendom* [*Humanisme intégral*], trans. Joseph W. Evans (Notre Dame, IN: University of Notre Dame Press, 1973), 137, emphasis mine.

[26] Maritain, "Integral Humanism and the Crisis of Modern Times," *The Review of Politics* 1 (1939): 1–17.

[27] Maritain, *Scholasticism and Politics* (New York: Macmillan, 1940).

[28] Ibid., 111.

here, Maritain is referring specifically to rights enumerated by Pope Pius XI in his 1937 encyclical *Divini redemptoris*.

By early 1942, however, Maritain's list of rights had become even more robust. In *Les droits de l'homme et la loi naturelle*, Maritain enumerates and explains some twenty-seven rights in three categories: rights of the human person as such (eleven), rights of the civic person (seven), and rights of the social – particularly the working – person (nine). (Maritain acknowledged later that many of these rights, specifically the rights of the social person, *go beyond* those found in most understandings of human rights.[29]) One might think that these three categories of rights correspond to the different kinds of human law – natural law, the *droit des gens*, and the positive law. Yet Maritain's account in *Les droits de l'homme* does not consistently line up with this division.

For rights of the human person, first Maritain lists rights ascribed to human beings simply because they are human beings: "from the simple fact that man is man, nothing else being taken into account." These rights are "[m]an's right to existence, to personal freedom and to the pursuit of the perfection of moral life." Maritain, however, adds other rights, such as "the right to the private ownership of material goods," "[f]reedom of every person to worship God in his own way" (or "freedom of conscience"), and "[f]reedom of speech and expression"[30] – which Maritain says later is better understood as "freedom of investigation [...] to seek the truth."[31] Maritain does not, however, call these latter rights natural rights, for he says that they fall within the *droit des gens* or *ius gentium*. Unlike the first three rights enumerated above, these latter "follow from the first principle [of natural law] in a *necessary* manner,[32] but [as we saw earlier...] supposing certain conditions of fact, as for instance the state of civil society or the relationship between peoples" – that is, they "concretize" natural rights. While such rights are not natural, strictly speaking,

[29] Maritain, "Communication with regard to the Draft World Declaration on the Rights of Man," letter of 18 June 1947, 3, section 5. See unesdoc.unesco.org/images/0012/001243/124341eb.pdf . See also his "On the Philosophy of Human Rights," *Human Rights: Comments and Interpretations* (London: Allan and Wingate, 1949), 72–77, at 74.

[30] Maritain, *The Rights of Man and Natural Law*, 39–41. See also Maritain, *Natural Law: Reflections on Theory and Practice*, edn. William Sweet (South Bend, IN: St Augustine's Press, 2001), 96–98.

[31] Maritain, *The Rights of Man and Natural Law*, 49.

[32] It is, admittedly, not entirely clear how other rights follow in a "necessary manner" from these three basic rights, unless one assumes (a) that they could be deduced from them in a system of moral philosophy or (b) that knowledge by inclination would arrive at, or recognize, these as the "concretions" or fruits of "the first principle" of the natural law – i.e., that which gives rise to basic human rights.

they are practically "universal, at least insofar as these conditions of fact are universal data of civilized life."[33]

Rights of the civic person – "of the human individual as a citizen" – include political equality within the state, equality before the law, and equal admission of all citizens to public employment according to their capacities. Maritain states that these rights "spring directly from positive law and from the fundamental constitution of the political community." Yet it seems as though one could argue that some of these rights are *natural*. Since human beings are "naturally made to live in society" and "naturally" "lead a political life and . . . participate actively in the life of the political community," it seems as though possessing these freedoms and rights is not subject entirely to the positive law or to civil authority.[34]

Maritain also refers to the rights of the "social person, more particularly of the working person." Such rights are the right to work, the right to a just wage, the freedom to organize (in trade unions), and the right to strike.[35] These rights may seem to be a product simply of positive law, as they seem to depend on contingent factors, such as the level of economic development and the presence of a certain level of technology.[36] Yet Maritain affirms that human beings possess these rights "*as such*," and in virtue of "the dignity of the human person" in his or her social, economic, and cultural functions. Maritain notes that "[g]enerally speaking, a new age of civilization will be called upon *to recognize* and define the rights of the human being in his social, economic and cultural functions," and that "[h]uman law will doubtless *acknowledge* other rights to labour as the economic system becomes transformed."[37] This suggests that such rights are recognized, not created, although the time when these rights are recognized depends on the material conditions present in the society. Again, since the basis for these freedoms and rights is objective, it is clear that they are not rights that civil authorities could simply choose to respect or not.

[33] Maritain, *The Rights of Man and Natural Law*, 39–40. It should be noted that these rights of the human person include the right to conscience – "droit à la poursuite de la vie eternelle selon la voie que la conscience a reconnue comme voie tracé par Dieu" (see English translation, p. 46) – which is a right that goes far beyond "freedom of worship" or freedom of religion as classically understood. Such a right to conscience was rarely heard of at that time and was, and is still, contested.

[34] Ibid., 46–49.

[35] Ibid., 51–53.

[36] Maritain, *La loi naturelle ou loi non écrite*, 190.

[37] Ibid., 51–52, emphases mine.

Maritain does not seem concerned whether the rights of the human person, the civic person, and the social person are natural rights, but he does insist that they are human rights. One might well ask why Maritain prefers the term human rights. Often, the extent to which many of the above rights are recognized and can be acted upon depends on the state of the economic and political structure and on the resources available in society. Thus, they may seem contingent and variable. Yet because these rights consistently reflect something about human nature and are not simply a matter of the will of the public authority, and because they are knowable naturally, they accrue to all human beings, regardless of whether they are natural rights as such.

Although Maritain sketched out these rights by early 1942, one may note a number of similarities between them and the rights enumerated in the 1948 Universal Declaration of Human Rights (UDHR). As noted earlier, Maritain has sometimes been described as being involved in the drafting of the UDHR, but this is strictly speaking incorrect. Maritain was not a member of the United Nations Economic and Social Council (ECOSOC), or of the UN Commission on Human Rights, or of the subcommittee that drafted the Declaration. *Les droits de l'homme et la loi naturelle* was, however, read by members of the drafting committee;[38] Maritain's political philosophy had a significant influence of the views of Charles Malik, one of the four members of the drafting committee and the chair of the Commission on Human Rights; and Maritain was actively involved with UNESCO committees that worked concurrently with the Commission on Human Rights. There were other influences as well.

One of Maritain's concerns with the UDHR was that no philosophical foundation was given for the rights it enumerated. UNESCO had anticipated the question whether there were shared common values that could serve as a basis for the UDHR, and in early 1947, it recruited a number of leading thinkers for the Committee on the Theoretical Bases of Human Rights. Maritain became involved in this committee, and he wrote the Introduction to its principal report, a volume titled *Human Rights: Comments and Interpretations* (1948/1949).[39] Maritain noted that the work of the Commission on

[38] Marc Agi, *René Cassin, prix Nobel de la paix, 1887–1976, père de la 'Declaration universelle des droits de l'homme'* (Paris: Perrin, 1998), 212. See also J. M. Winter and Antoine Prost, *René Cassin and Human Rights: From the Great War to the Universal Declaration* (Cambridge: Cambridge University Press, 2013), 164.

[39] *Human Rights: Comments and Interpretations; A Symposium*, edited by UNESCO, July 25, 1948 / A Collective approach to the problems of human rights; original contributions by Mahatma Gandhi, Salvador de Madariaga, Harold Laski, Benedetto Croce, Aldous Huxley, E. H. Carr, R. P. McKeon, F. S. C. Northrop, etc., with an introduction by Jacques Maritain

Human Rights and the UNESCO committee showed that there could be practical agreement on the existence of human rights, but no theoretical agreement; he wrote, "we agree about the rights, *but on condition that no one asks us why*."[40] Maritain nevertheless held repeatedly that the rights of the UDHR – and any account of human rights – required a philosophical foundation in human nature, and specifically in natural law.

In short, Maritain saw human rights as an essential part of a genuine humanism but also as the product of a natural-law theory. Human rights were not just important to human beings as individuals and as persons. They were also part of the common good and necessary to the peace and development of cultures and societies. Yet Maritain also recognized the fact of pluralism – that many modern societies are not monolithic and obviously do not share a conception of the common good – and that agreement on the foundations of human rights was impossible. Nevertheless, given his view that "rights [are] linked to the very nature of man,"[41] all those who understood human nature could recognize at least some basic human rights, and Maritain was ready to emphasize that there could be a practical agreement on human rights.

Maritain was a major advocate for the UDHR, both during its drafting and afterwards. Yet he was also unceasing in his insistence that at the basis of any coherent account of human rights was a doctrine of natural law. He continued to write and lecture on natural law and natural rights through the 1950s, but after 1960 his work turned to more spiritual subjects.

GENERAL APPRAISAL AND INFLUENCE

Through much of the twentieth century, Maritain was likely the best-known living Catholic philosopher in the world. Moreover, in his time, Maritain's work had a strong influence in those countries where Catholicism and, particularly, Thomistic philosophy had its place. His writings on natural law and natural rights, for example, had an influence not just on some of those involved in drafting the Universal Declaration but on others behind various international and national declarations of rights in Latin America and Canada, and on the preamble to the Constitution of the Fourth Republic in France (1946). The Christian democratic movement in Italy (for instance,

(provisional manuscript). unesdoc.unesco.org/images/0015/001550/155041eb.pdf 15 June 1948. This was republished as *Human Rights: Comments and Interpretations* (London: Allan and Wingate, 1949).

[40] Maritain, *Human rights: Comments and Interpretations* (1948), I, emphasis mine.

[41] *The Natural Law and Human Rights*, 14.

Aldo Moro and Alcide De Gasperi), Belgium (Wilfried Martens), and Chile (Eduardo Frei and Jaime Castillo), was indebted to Maritain's personalism and his social and political philosophy.[42] Maritain's writings also had an influence on the social teaching of the Catholic Church. Pope Paul VI was an intellectual disciple of Maritain[43] and, at the conclusion of the Second Vatican Council, chose him to receive the conciliar "Message to Men of Thought and Science" on behalf of the intellectual community. Maritain's writings have also influenced Pope John Paul II, and Maritain's integral humanism has been argued to have influenced Pope Francis's "integral ecology."

Today, some of Maritain's writings seem overly polemical and too rooted in debates of his time. Moreover, because Maritain wrote so much, often for very general audiences, some of his writing from the 1940s and 1950s shows signs of being hasty and undeveloped. Maritain's legacy is also paradoxical. He has been regarded as a person of the political left, but also of the political right. In his time, Maritain's integral humanism, personalism, and defense of human rights were very controversial and led to accusations by Luis Arturo Pérez in Chile and Julio Meinvielle in Argentina that his work was communist.[44] At the same time, some consider Maritain's personalist humanism and natural-law theory – midway between "liberal individualism" and "collective communitarianism" – as insufficiently progressive.[45]

Nevertheless, interest in Maritain's philosophy, particularly his political philosophy and natural-law theory, endures. There are international and

[42] On Maritain's influence in Europe and beyond, see Mary Anne Perkins, *Christendom and European Identity: The Legacy of a Grand Narrative since 1789* (Berlin: de Gruyter, 2004), 71–72. See also Paul Sigmund, "The Transformation of Christian Democratic Ideology: Transcending Left or Right or Whatever Happened to the Third Way?," in *Christian Democracy in Latin America: Electoral Competition and Regime Conflicts*, edn. Scott Mainwaring and Timothy R. Scully (Stanford, CA: Stanford University Press, 2003), especially 67–68. There was a similar influence in Mexico in the 1940s; see Soledad Loaeza, "The National Action Party (PAN): From the Fringes of the Political System to the Heart of Change," in *Christian Democracy in Latin America*, 197–245, at 205.

[43] Montini translated one of Maritain's books in the late 1920s, wrote an introduction to the Italian translation of *Humanisme intégral*, and dined with Maritain frequently when he was ambassador to the Holy See. This relationship is detailed in Philippe Chenaux, *Paul VI et Maritain: Les rapports du 'montinianisme' et du 'maritainisme'* (Brescia: Istitutio Paulo VI, 1994).

[44] See, for example, Julio Meinveille, *De Lamennais à Maritain* (Buenos Aires: Edn. Nuestro Tiempo, 1945) and *Critica de la Concepción de Maritain sobre la Persona Humana* (Buenos Aires: Edn. Nuestro Tiempo, 1948); and Luis Arturo Perez, *Estudio de filiosofia politicosocial* (Santiago de Chile, 1948); see also Olivier Compagnon, *Jacques Maritain et l'Amérique du Sud. Le modèle malgré lui* (Villeneuve-d'Ascq: Presses universitaires du Septentrion, 2003), 165–70.

[45] See John Hellman, "The Opening of the Left in French Catholicism: The Role of the Personalists," *Journal of the History of Ideas* 34 (1973): 381–90, at 385.

national associations devoted to Maritain's work in some sixteen countries, research centers on Maritain's thought at Notre Dame, Strasbourg, and Rome, and several philosophical journals and book series dedicated to his philosophy. Maritain's philosophy of law and political philosophy continue to be of interest to philosophers, historians, and jurists alike.

RECOMMENDED READING

Barré, Jean-Luc. *Jacques et Raïssa Maritain, les mendiants du ciel.* Paris: Stock, 1996. English translation: *Jacques & Raïssa Maritain: Beggars for Heaven.* Translated by Bernard E. Doering. Notre Dame, IN: University of Notre Dame Press, 2005.

Brennan, Patrick McKinley. "Jacques Maritain: Philosopher of Law, Politics, and All That Is." In *The Teachings of Modern Christianity on Law, Politics, and Human Nature*, edited by John Witte, Jr. and Frank Alexander, vol. 2, 34–67. New York: Columbia University Press, 2006.

Charette, Léon. "Le droit naturel et le droit des gens d'après Jacques Maritain." *Maritain Studies/Etudes Maritainiennes* 5 (1989): 41–62.

De Koninck, Charles. *De la primauté du bien commun contre les personnalistes. Le principe de l'ordre nouveau.* Montréal: Éditions Fides, 1943.

Fruchaud, Louis-Damien. "Jacques Maritain, Michel Villey: Le thomisme face aux droits de l'homme." Memoire, DEA de droit public interne, Université de Paris II Panthéon-Assas, 2005.

Hittinger, F. Russell. "Maritain on Human Rights as Constitutional Limits." Paper presented at New York University, sponsored by Carnegie Council on Ethics and International Affairs and The American Maritain Association. Nov. 9, 1994.

Hittinger, John P. *Liberty, Wisdom, and Grace: Thomism and Democratic Political Theory.* Lanham, MD: Lexington Books, 2002.

Nielsen, Kai. "An Examination of the Thomistic Theory of Natural [Moral] Law." In *Natural Law Forum* 4 (1959): 44–71. Reprinted in Nielsen, *God and the Grounding of Morality*, 41–68. Ottawa, ON: University of Ottawa Press, 1991.

McCauliff, Catherine M. "Jacques Maritain's Embrace of Religious Pluralism and the *Declaration on Religious Freedom.*" *Seton Hall Law Review* 41 (2011): 593–624.

Meinveille, Julio. *Critica de la Concepción de Maritain sobre la Persona Humana.* Buenos Aires: Edn. Nuestro Tiempo, 1948.

Possenti, V. "Philosophie du droit et loi naturelle selon Jacques Maritain." *Revue Thomiste* 83 (1983): 598–608.

Sweet, William. "Maritain, Jacques." In *The Philosophy of Law: An Encyclopedia*, edited by Christopher B. Gray, vol. 1, 533–35. 2 vols. New York: Garland Press, 1999.

"Maritain's Criticisms of Natural Law Theories." *Études maritainiennes/Maritain Studies* 12 (1996): 33–49.

"The Metaphysical and Epistemological Foundations of Natural Law in Jacques Maritain" [in English and in Chinese]. *Universitas: Monthly Review of Philosophy and Culture* 388 (September 2006): 15–33; 83–98.

Viola, Francesco. "Jacques Maritain et les problems épistémologiques actuels de la science juridique." *Nova et Vetera* (1978): 279–90.

24

Robert Schuman

(1886–1963)

RAFAEL DOMINGO

INTRODUCTION

One of the founding fathers of the European Union, Robert Schuman embodies the most genuine spirit of European reconciliation. A convinced Christian Democrat of German education and French heart, and a profoundly committed Roman Catholic, he was raised in the contested border area of Alsace-Lorraine and thus experienced from his youth the desire for a Europe free of artificial boundaries and joined in cooperation and solidarity. Schuman's life coincides with one of the most extensive periods of crisis in European history. He was deeply marked by the consequences of the Franco-Prussian war, the two devastating World Wars, and the Cold War.

Early in life, Schuman was introduced to a trilingual culture, and in time he would hold two different citizenships – German and, later, French. He was able to defend without conflict of interest the particularities of Lorraine, the singularity of France, the special role of Germany in the construction of Europe, and the uniqueness of Europe as a supranational entity.

Visionary and realist, he brought to French diplomacy a new aim, a new dynamism, a new aspiration. Working in collaboration with West Germany, especially with its postwar chancellor Konrad Adenauer (1876–1967), and drawing on the creative work of French political economist Jean Monnet (1888–1979), Schuman was the leading advocate for and public author of the plan for the European Coal and Steel Community, which pooled French and German coal and steel industries and anticipated the European Union.

Illuminated by the Gospel, educated in Thomism, and fiercely influenced by Pope Leo XIII, Jacques Maritain, and Maurice Blondel, among others, Schuman tried to defend his political ideas from the viewpoint of Christian humanism. He felt that he was an instrument in the hands of divine providence to undertake a mission for his country rather than the designer of that mission.[1] Although much appreciated by his colleagues, he was neither a popular man nor a brilliant speaker. He was a hard worker with a pragmatic mind who exhibited legendary modesty, generosity, great capacity for listening, and a deep sense of humor.[2] He was an atypical French politician because of his double culture, "monkish ascetism,"[3] and lack of personal ambition. Perhaps that is why he spent so little time in the political arena. He dignified the governmental debate of his time. A man of great originality and imagination, he was able to take a simple approach to big ideas. He was a lover of dialogue and persuasion, a passionate reader, an admirer of Shakespeare, a great student of history, and a devoted collector of autographs of great men.

No full biography of Robert Schuman has been written in English. So far, the best accounts are provided by Alan Paul Fimister[4] and Margriet Krijtenburg.[5] In French, the leading biography is by Raymond Poidevin, published in 1986. Also useful is Christian Pennera's volume on Schuman's youth and early political years.[6] Schuman's colleagues and friends – especially Robert Rochefort, René Lejeune, and Jean-Marie Pelt – have left very useful information, as have the hagiographers François Roth and Hans August Lücker.[7] Rudolf

[1] See Robert Schuman, *French Foreign Policy towards Germany since the War.* Stevenson Memorial Lecture delivered on October 29, 1953 (London: Geoffrey Cumberlege; Oxford: Oxford University Press, 1954), 5. In a letter of 1942 to Robert Rochefort, Robert Schuman wrote (in French): "We are the very imperfect instruments of a Providence which makes use of them in the accomplishment of great designs which go beyond us. This certainty demands a lot of modesty but gives us a serenity that would not always be justified by our personal experiences considered from a merely human point of view." See François Roth, *Robert Schuman. Du Lorrain des frontières au père de l'Europe* (Paris: Fayard, 2008), 562.

[2] See some examples in Margriet Krijtenburg, *Schuman's Europe: His Frame of Reference* (Leiden: Leiden University, 2012), 52–53 available at: openaccess.leidenuniv.nl/bitstream/handle/1887/19767/fulltext.pdf?sequence=17

[3] Dean Acheson, "Robert Schuman," in Dean Acheson, *Sketches from Life of Men I Have Known* (New York: Harper, 1961), 31–59, at 32.

[4] Alan Paul Fimister, *Robert Schuman: Neo-Scholastic Humanism and the Reunification of Europe* (Frankfurt am Main, Bern: Peter Lang, 2011).

[5] Krijtenburg, "Schuman's Europe."

[6] Raymond Poidevin, *Robert Schuman, homme d'État (1886–1963)* (Paris: Imprimerie nationale, 1986); Christian Pennera, *La jeunesse et les débuts politiques d'un grand européen de 1886 à 1924* (Sarreguemines: Editions Pierron, 1985).

[7] Robert Rochefort, *Robert Schuman* (Paris: Cerf, 1968); René Lejeune, *Robert Schuman, père de l'Europe (1886–1963)* (Paris: Fayard, 2000); Roth, *Robert Schuman*; Hans August Lücker and Jean Seitlinger, *Robert Schuman und die Einigung Europas* (Bonn: Bouvier Verlag, 2000); and Jean-Marie Pelt, *Robert Schuman, Père de l'Europe – Father of Europe* (English version) (Thionville: General Council of Moselle, Serge Domini Publisher, 2001).

Mittendorfer's biography of Schuman, written in German, offers an especially good treatment of his European role.[8]

BIOGRAPHICAL INFORMATION

Jean-Baptiste Nicolas Robert Schuman was born on June 29, 1886, in Clausen, one of the oldest neighborhoods in Luxemburg City.[9] His father, Jean Pierre Schuman (1838–1900), was a French farmer born in Évrange, in the Moselle region of Lorraine, on the French border with Luxembourg. The father had fought with the French army for Napoléon III in the Franco-Prussian War of 1870, in which Prussia and its German allies overwhelmingly outnumbered the French.[10] After the war, as result of the Treaty of Frankfurt of May 10, 1871, some parts of Alsace-Lorraine, including Jean Pierre Schuman's birth village, were annexed to the German empire.[11] Jean Pierre decided not to exercise the option of retaining his French nationality, which would have required him to leave the annexed area and immigrate to the trimmed and humiliated France, thereby losing his small farm. Thus, Jean Pierre Schuman became a German citizen automatically by misfortune. To escape the German annexation, however, and to make up for the scanty yields of the farm, he decided to settle in Luxembourg in 1873 and to live off his rents. In 1884 he married a Luxembourger, Eugénie Duren (1864–1911), who also became German by the marriage and therefore lost her Luxembourgish citizenship. This explains why Robert Schuman, although born in Luxembourg from a Luxembourger mother, was born with German citizenship. Like every child born in Luxembourg to foreign parents, Robert was eligible for Luxemburgish citizenship when he reached the age of majority, but he never chose that possibility.

8 Rudolf Mittendorfer, *Robert Schuman. Architekt des neuen Europa* (Hildesheim, New York: Georg Olms, 1983).

9 For biographical details, see the biographies listed in notes 2–7 and the bibliography.

10 On the Franco-Prussian War, see Geoffrey Wawro, *The Franco-Prussian War: The German Conquest of France in 1870–1871* (Cambridge, New York: Cambridge University Press, 2003); and Michael Howard, *The Franco-Prussian War: The German Invasion of France 1870–1871* (2nd edn, London, New York: Routledge, 2001).

11 The territory was made up of 93% of Alsace and 26% of Lorraine; the remaining portions of these regions continued to be part of France. Since its complete reversion to France following World War I, the territory has been referred to administratively as Alsace-Moselle. Since 2016, Alsace and Lorraine have been a part of the new French administrative region in northeastern France called Great East. For an overview of the history of Alsace-Lorraine, see François Roth, *Alsace-Lorraine, de 1870 à nos jours: histoire d'un pays perdu* (Nancy: Place Stanislas, 2010).

Young Robert learned Luxembourgish at home because it was his mother's tongue.[12] He attended first the public school of Clausen-Luxembourg, where he mainly learned German, and at the age of ten he was admitted to the Luxembourg Athenaeum, where courses were taught both in German and, in the higher classes, in French. Trilingual from his youth, Robert also learned Latin, Greek, and English at the school (although his English was never fluent). The Catholic education he received in Luxembourg schools and especially at home from his beloved mother influenced his whole life. He also developed from a very young age a great love for his father's homeland, the Lorraine, where he spent seasons working on the family farm. All through his life, Schuman considered himself a Lorrainer like his father.

In 1900, when Robert was only 14, his father died. His mother died eleven years later as result of an accident with a horse cart. These losses deeply affected Schuman all his life. The preserved correspondence between mother and child – often weekly, and in French rather than Luxembourgish – testifies to the deep spiritual relationship between Schuman and his mother.[13] With her, Robert had traveled to Rome in 1909 to attend the beatification of Joan of Arc.

After finishing high school in Luxembourg, where there was no university, Robert moved to Lorraine. In 1903 he was admitted in the Kaiserliches Lyceum in the French city of Metz, just south of where France, Germany, and Luxembourg meet. One year later, he passed the German university-preparatory school exam (Abitur), which opens the door to German universities. As was customary at the time, Schuman attended different law schools to benefit from the scholarship of the most distinguish jurists: Josef Kohler, Otto von Gierke, Paul Laband, Lujo Brentano, Franz von Liszt, and Gustav von Schmoller, among others. He spent one semester in Bonn, two in Munich, and two in Berlin, and he finally graduated from the University of Strasbourg (then under German rule) in 1908, after passing the first state examination. In 1912, Schuman received his law doctorate with a thesis on civil litigation under the supervision of the young professor Wilhelm Kisch, and he passed the second state examination, which

[12] It is a West Germanic language, very close to German and Dutch, with borrowed words from French. In Luxembourg, children study in Luxembourgish at kindergarten level and in German and French at primary level.

[13] The letters received by Schuman from his mother (1906–09) are deposited in the Schuman Papers (34 J 1) at the Departmental Archives in the Moselle. See Charles Hiegel and Marion Duvigneau, *Papiers de Robert Schuman. Répertoire numérique détaillé des fonds déposés sous les cotes 34 et 36 J* (Saint-Julien-lès-Metz: Archives départamentales de la Moselle, 2002), 10. For a commentary about these letters, see Poidevin, *Robert Schuman, homme d'État*, 17–19.

allowed him to practice law in the German empire. Then Schuman decided to open a law firm in Metz.

Schuman also became actively involved in Catholic charities at this time. In 1912, the young lawyer of 26 met for the first time Bishop Willibrord Benzler. The prelate integrated Schuman into a group of lay diocesan leaders and put him at the head of an organization created specifically for him: the Diocesan Federation of Youth Groups. Benzler urged Schuman to deepen his Thomist thinking. This period in Metz convinced Schuman that he must consecrate not only his activity but also his whole person to God and to the service of others. He considered the possibility of becoming a priest but finally decided to live as a celibate lay apostle in the midst of the world. Increasing the frequency of his receiving the sacraments, he also devoted time to meditation on the Bible as well as concentrated study of the magisterium of the Church. He especially studied the teachings of the pope of his youth, Leo XIII, author of the first encyclical letter on social issues, *Rerum Novarum* (1891), and father of the social teaching of the Catholic Church.

In 1914, when World War I broke out, Schuman was not drafted into the German army because of poor health. Instead, he was assigned to administrative tasks in Boulay-Moselle. He never wore a German military uniform. In 1919, just after the entrance of French troops under Marshal Pétain into Metz, and once the imperial territory of Alsace-Lorraine had reverted to France, Schuman became a French citizen and was elected to the French National Assembly from the Department of Moselle. During his years as a deputy (1919–40), he worked to preserve the social legislation that had been applied in Moselle during the German annexation, because it was much more advanced and beneficial than the French policies: bilingualism in school and courts, special status of the railways, and moderate application of French secularism.[14] In 1924, Schuman purchased a piece of land in Scy-Chazelles, a

[14] In Alsace and Moselle, a local law is still in force. Established in 1919 after the end of World War I, it is applied in the French departments of Bas-Rhin, Haut-Rhin and Moselle, grouped under the generic name of Alsace-Moselle, which is now in the region Grand East. This local law retains the provisions set up by German authorities between 1871 and 1918 when those provisions are considered more favorable to the inhabitants of Alsace and Moselle. The local law also includes the pre-1870 French laws maintained by the German administration but abrogated by the French authorities before their return in 1918. Finally, the local law includes specific French laws after 1918 applicable only to these territories. The local law mainly affects professional regulations, credit institutions, statutory holidays, legislation on the reimbursement of health expenses, social assistance for the poorest, the organization of justice and the courts, civil procedures, bankruptcy, the land register, the law of hunting, and the law of association. The French law on separation of the churches and the state of December 9, 1905 is not applied in Alsace and Moselle. Instead, the Concordat with the Holy See of 1801 and the special laws of

Lorraine village in the Moselle valley. Today his house has been transformed into a museum and inspirational European convention center.

In March 1940, with World War II already begun, Schuman became a member of Paul Reynaud's government, as under-secretary of state for refugees. Just months later, on June 14, Paris fell to Nazi Germany. On June 22, Marshal Pétain signed the armistice with the Germans, and the French government moved to Vichy, 220 miles south of Paris.[15] Schuman was confirmed in his position by Pétain. On July 10, 1940, Schuman voted with the majority of the National Assembly to grant extraordinary powers to Marshal Pétain to reform the constitution of France, but, unhappy with the attitude and policies of the Petain government, Schuman resigned his ministry and returned to Metz at the end of August.

On September 14, 1940, Schuman was arrested by the Gestapo, the Nazi secret police, and on April 13, 1941, after the Nazis considered sending him to a concentration camp, he finally was placed under house arrest in Neustadt an der Weinstrasse, a German town in the Rhineland-Palatinate. This benevolent measure by gauleiter Joseph Burckel, the German party leader and governor of the annexed department of Mosele, may have been an attempt to persuade Schuman of the advisability of supporting the Nazi regime.[16] In Neustadt, Schuman enjoyed some degree of freedom, especially after gaining the confidence of the police. On August 1, 1941, helped by friends in Lorraine, he escaped to unoccupied France. Until the liberation at the hands of the Americans in August 1944, he lived secretly in twelve different hiding places, most of them religious houses, and worked for the French resistance. He also spent time improving his English and reading Shakespeare, Thomas Aquinas, and St John of the Cross. At that time, he experienced the need to do what was necessary to engage France and Germany in a common project of unifying Europe.

1802 remain in force. As result, religious education is compulsory in primary and secondary schools (with permission of the parents); the University of Strasbourg and the University of Metz are the only French public universities to teach theology; the remuneration of the ministers of the four recognized faiths (Catholic priests, Lutheran and Reformed pastors, and Jewish rabbis) is taken over by the state. The appointments of the archbishop of Strasbourg and the bishop of Metz are made by the president of the French Republic, the last head of state in the world to appoint Catholic bishops. For an overview of the local law in Alsace and Moselle, see Institut du Droit Local Alsacien-Mosellan (ed.) *Le guide du droit local: Le droit applicable en Alsace et en Moselle de A à Z* (4th edn, Strasbourg: Institut Du Droit Local Alsacien-Mosellan, 2015).

[15] On the so-called Vichy Regime, see Philippe Burrin, *France under the Germans: Collaboration and Compromise*, trans. Janet Lloyd (New York: New Press, 1996).

[16] See Poidevin, *Robert Schuman, homme d'État*, 137.

After the war, Schuman was officially declared a collaborator of the Vichy regime and therefore disqualified from public office. General Charles de Gaulle himself, undisputed leader of the French resistance, personally resolved the problem, however, and secured Schuman's rehabilitation, opening the door for Schuman to enter French political life again. Schuman made an enormous political contribution over the next eight years of the so-called French Fourth Republic (1948–56), marked as it was by governmental instability and social insurrection.

Schuman was almost sixty years old when he began his national and international career. He served as minister of finance (1946) under the governments of Georges Bidault, leader of a Christian democratic party called the Popular Republican Movement (MRP), and Paul Ramadier. In November 1947, the National Assembly elected Schuman himself as prime minister (only the Communists voted against him). Less than a year later, however, on July 27, 1948, Schuman stepped down as prime minister, unable to hold his political coalition together.[17] The new prime minister, André Marie, appointed Schuman as minister of foreign affairs, a post that Schuman retained through eight governments until January 1953. Later, Schuman was appointed minister of justice (1955) for less than a year.

As prime minister and, especially, as foreign minister, Schuman was instrumental in negotiating major treaties and international initiatives such as the Marshall Plan (1948–52), the Council of Europe (founded on May 5, 1949), and the North Atlantic Treaty Organization (NATO) (founded on April 4, 1949). Schuman believed that the North Atlantic Treaty, the European Convention on Human Rights (drafted in 1950 by the newly formed Council of Europe), and the European integration process itself would constitute the foundations of a new Western order.[18]

Schuman became internationally renowned for what is now called the Schuman Declaration,[19] which he issued on May 9, 1950, in Paris, at the Salon de l'Horloge (the Clock Room) in the Quai d'Orsay, headquarters of the French Ministry of Foreign Affairs. This declaration changed the history of Europe and is now considered the founding document of the European project that comprises the European aspirations of peace, solidarity, and cooperation.[20] There, just five years after the end of World War II, Schuman

[17] Schuman was prime minister once more for a week, September 5–11, 1948.

[18] See Lejeune, *Robert Schuman, père de l'Europe*, 153.

[19] The whole text is available at: europa.eu/european-union/about-eu/symbols/europe-day/schuman-declaration_en

[20] On the spirituality of the declaration, see Gary Wilton, "Christianity and the Founding: The Legacy of Robert Schuman," in Jonathan Chaplin and Gary Wilton (eds.), *God and the EU:*

launched his proposal for France and West Germany to work together on the production of coal and steel, "under a common high authority in an organization open to the other countries of Europe" – and in the process make "any war between France and Germany not merely unthinkable but materially impossible." The common high authority would have decision-making power in accordance with the statutes, and it would in effect be an authority protected by a supranational jurisdiction.[21] This plan would remove the means and incentives for new wars and would lay the foundation for a potential supranational Europe. The Schuman Declaration marked the beginning of post-World War II Franco-German cooperation and the reintegration of West Germany into Western Europe. Schuman was always aware of the relevance of the event: "In 1950," he wrote, "France was the forerunner of a new ideal. It was revolutionary in terms of its design and range, but it was peaceful in the way it was undertaken."[22]

The main architect of the plan had been Jean Monnet, the general planning commissioner.[23] With great humility, Schuman recognized the "exceptional merits of an exceptional man": Jean Monet, whom Schuman did not hesitate to call his friend.[24] Like all great men, Schuman discounted the significance of his own work: "It was the foreign minister's responsibility to

Faith in the European Project (London, New York City: Routledge, 2016), 13–32. As Fimister well pointed out, the 1950 declaration resulted from the "self-conscious application" by Schuman of Catholic social thought and neo-Thomistic political philosophy to international relations. See Alan Paul Fimister, *Robert Schuman: Neo-Scholastic Humanism and the Reunification of Europe* (Frankfurt am Main, Bern: Peter Lang, 2011), 17.

[21] See Robert Schuman, *For Europe* (Paris: Foundation Robert Schuman; Chêne-Bourg: Nagel, 2010), 110.

[22] Ibid., 20.

[23] Ibid., 119: "In a small hotel on Rue Martignac, it was Jean Monnet who, together with his collaborators, sketched out within a few months, discreetly and in the utmost secrecy – not even the government knew – the idea of the coal and steel community." See also Jean Monnet, *Memoirs* (London: Third Millennium, 2015), 318–35. The first draft was prepared by Paul Reuter, Schuman's colleague and the lawyer at the Foreign Ministry, and it was mainly revised by Jean Monnet, Étienne Hirsch, Pierre Uri, and Bernard Clappier. In her doctoral thesis, Margriet Krijtenburg tries to recover Schuman's leadership in the project. See Margriet Krijtenburg, "Schuman's Europe." In the same vein, see also David Heilbron Price, *Robert Schuman, Jalonneur de la paix mondiale* (Berlin: Brons Commuications, 2014), 61–62. On the role of Paul Reuter, see Antonin Cohen, "Le plan Schuman de Paul Reuter. Entre communauté nationale et fédération européenne," *Revue française de science politique* 48 (1998): 645–63. For a general overview, Paul Reuter, *La Communauté européenne du charbon et de l'acier* (Paris: Librairie Générale de Droit et Jurisprudence, 1953), foreword by Robert Schuman.

[24] Schuman, *For Europe*, 119. On this relationship, see Éric Roussel, "Les paradoxes de la relation Jean Monnet–Robert Schuman," in *Robert Schuman et les Pères de l'Europe* (Brussels: Peter Lang, 2008), 87–92.

provide his patronage and his backing, and to assume the political risks of the initiative."[25] Italy, Belgium, the Netherlands, and Luxembourg responded positively to the proposal and joined France and West Germany in creating the European Coal and Steel Community (ECSC) on April 18, 1951. The ECSC is considered the precursor of the European Economic Community established in 1957 and the beginning of what is now the European Union. May 9 has been celebrated annually as Europe Day since 1985, and it is commonly recognized as one of the great "European constitutional moments."[26] In some sense, it can be said that the Schuman Declaration is of similar importance to the Declaration of Independence of the United States. Both are at the heart of the birth of two important political and social projects: the United States of America and the European Union. Both documents were produced by great men in difficult circumstances. Both were firmly based on religious principles. Both constitute a call to the common sense of the people: the one to justify the independence of a new nation, the other to seek the union of a devastated continent. Similarities abound.

After May 9, 1950, Schuman the statesman became identified with the cause of European integration. With the fall of Antoine Pinay's administration in December 1952, Schuman's time at the ministry of foreign affairs ended. The German novelist Thomas Mann wrote to Schuman: "I cannot imagine that the country wants or can give up your services."[27] Schuman came back to government in 1955 for a short term as a minister of justice in the Edgar Faure government. In 1958, however, the return of General de Gaulle to power ended Schuman's political career in the French government. De Gaulle had never had great esteem for Schuman let alone for his particular European project.[28] Schuman then became the great defender of the European cause, traveling across the continent (Rome, Vienna, London, Athens) and around the world (Rio de Janeiro, Washington, Boston) promoting European reconciliation and unification. From 1955 to 1961 he was the president of the

[25] Schuman, *For Europe*, 119. A example of such risk is that two days before the declaration, on May 7, 1950, Schuman, without the consent of the French Council of Ministers, confirmed in a letter to Chancellor Konrad Adenauer that the proposal of declaration would be approved a few days later by the French government. The letter is available at: cvce.eu/content/publication/1999/2/10/5b2f4ed8-b98c-4dc3-b7de-0f53bf11ff55/publishable_en.pdf

[26] On such European constitutional moments, see J. H. H. Weiler, *The Constitution of Europe* (Cambridge, New York: Cambridge University Press, 1999), esp. 3–4.

[27] See Rochefort, *Robert Schuman*, 317; and Poidevin, *Robert Schuman, homme d'État*, 367.

[28] The lack of understanding between De Gaulle and Schuman was profound. See Fimister, *Robert Schuman*, 170–71, and Lejeune, *Robert Schuman, père de l'Europe*, 135–38. The divergences among the two politicians are examined by Hardev Singh Chopra, *De Gaulle and the European Unity* (New Delhi: Abhinav Publications, 1974), 35–39.

European Movement, and from 1958 to 1960, president of the European Parliamentary Assembly[29] (now the European Parliament) in Strasbourg.

Often honored, Schuman received honorary doctorates from the universities of Edinburgh, Birmingham, and Tilburg, the University of California, Los Angeles (UCLA), Fordham University, and the Catholic University of Leuven. In 1956, Pope Pius XII awarded him the Great Cross of the Order of Pius IX. In 1958, he received the Charlemagne Prize in Aix-la-Chapelle (Aachen), one of the most prestigious of European prizes. In 1959, he received the Erasmus Prize along with the German-Swiss philosopher Karl Jaspers. The European Parliamentary Assembly awarded him the title of Father of Europe at the end of his term of office (1960).

At the end of 1959, Schuman's health declined, and in 1962 he announced his retirement from political life. He then devoted much time to meditating on sacred scripture. He decided not to write his memoirs to avoid personal judgments about other people and circumstances, and because he did not want to feel the center of attention of European political life. Instead, he wrote a short essay on Europe, consisting of a brief summary of the essential ideas and convictions that had guided his political activity in favor of the European Union (see the next section).

Schuman died on September 4, 1963, at the age of 76. His death went largely unnoticed because Gaullism then occupied the whole political sphere. A few days before his death, the bishop of Metz, having administered the sacrament of the sick, read to him a telegram from Pope Paul VI. The old man was so much affected that he cried.[30] Schuman was buried in the twelfth-century fortified church of Saint-Quentin, adjacent to his house. The process of his beatification was officially opened in the diocese of Metz on June 9, 1990.[31]

The Robert Schuman Foundation was established in 1991 in Paris and Brussels to promote European research on the policies of the European

[29] After the establishment of the European Economic Community (ECC) and the European Atomic Energy Community (Euratom) in 1957, a single assembly was created with the powers and responsibilities assigned to it at the EEC and Euratom treaties. This assembly also replaced the Common Assembly of the European Coal and Steel Community. The single assembly held its first session on March 19, 1958. It was this new assembly that unanimously elected Schuman as president. The official and unified designation as European Parliament was made by Art. 2 of the Single European Act of 1986. For an overview of the history of the European Parliament, see: cvce.eu/en/obj/european_parliament-en-ad6a0d57-08ef-427d-a715-f6e3bfaf775a.html

[30] See Poidevin, *Robert Schuman, homme d'État*, 420.

[31] On the cause of Schuman's beatification, see Institut Saint-Benoît, *Actes des journées organisées à Metz du 4 au 8 septembre 2013* (Metz: Éditions des Paraiges, 2013), esp. 11–15.

Union, as well as to foster European values in accordance with the spirit and inspiration of the founding fathers of Europe. The European University Institute in Florence, Italy, is home to the Robert Schuman Centre for Advanced Studies (RSCAS), focusing on interdisciplinary, comparative, and policy research on the major issues on the European integration process.[32] In 2016, the University of Luxembourg inaugurated the Robert Schuman Institute of European Affairs, which focuses on the interdisciplinary study of European affairs and the European Union.[33] Schuman's papers are deposited at the departmental archive of the Moselle.[34] In addition, both the European Commission Library and the Robert Schuman Foundation hold abundant material. The archival collection of Hans August Lücker on the beatification process for Robert Schuman is now available for research at the Historical Archives of the European Union (HAEU).[35]

SCHUMAN'S EUROPEAN VISION

Schuman's vision of Europe has been reflected in the many speeches and lectures[36] he delivered throughout his life, but especially in what can be called his political testament – his essay *For Europe*.[37] Although written in the political context of the 1960s, Schuman's essay on Europe continues to have great value for our time because of the powerful inspiration of its perennial principles. Schuman did not look for a provisional solution to resolve the problems of a devastated Europe after World War II but sought to develop a long-term common project based on legal solidarity and constructive endeavor. He was realistic, believing that partial agreements and success should be the starting point for more relevant and lasting achievements. Schuman saw the need to politically organize interdependence and diversity as well as the need to maintain different levels of government, with different intensities, developing a healthy patriotism and solidarity among peoples.

[32] Information available at: eui.eu/DepartmentsAndCentres/RobertSchumanCentre/Index.aspx

[33] Information available at: en.uni.lu/recherche/robert_schuman_institute_of_european_affairs

[34] See Charles Hiegel and Marion Duvigneau, *Papiers de Robert Schuman. Répertoire numérique détaillé des fonds déposés sous les cotes 34 et 36 J* (Saint-Julien-lès-Metz: Archives départamentales de la Moselle, 2002), available at: archives57.com/phocadownload/6._FONDS_PRIVES/politique/frad57%2034-036j%20papiers%20schuman.pdf

[35] The inventory is available at: archives.eui.eu/en/fonds/153157?item=HALK

[36] A list of Schuman's more than sixty minor writings, lectures, and speeches can be found in Poidevin, *Robert Schuman, homme d'État*, 481, 484–86. Most of them can be consulted in the Schuman Papers (34 J) at the Departamental Archive of Moselle. Some are available at schuman.info, introduced by David Heilbron Price.

[37] Schuman, *For Europe*. The English translation of the essay must be improved.

The starting point for his project was the realization that the division of Europe had become anachronistic.[38] European borders had become an obstruction, a hindrance, or an impediment to the exchange of goods, the developing of ideas, and the mobility of people. More than a barrier, he believed, borders should constitute a venerable and respected meeting point of cultures and ideals. Union, cohesion, cooperation, and coordination between and among European nations was required. This new supranational level, illuminated by a universalist approach, should be founded on the principles of solidarity, international cooperation, majority rule freely accepted by the nation-states, and equality of rights among them. The aim would not be to join states to create a super-European state, but to allow people to live in different countries that are part of a supranational structure. Key to understanding Schuman's approach to the organization of Europe is supranationality. The supranational, Schuman explained,

> is situated at the same distance between, on the one hand, international individualism that treats national sovereignty as intangible, and accepts no more limit of sovereignty than contractual obligation; and, on the other hand, a state federalism that is subordinated to a super-state endowed with its own territorial sovereignty.[39]

Behind this project lie no hidden imperialistic goals or any kind of egoistic inclination, but only the firm desire to achieve peace among nations and to contribute to the development of humanity. The European project falls within a broader one that is the "rational organization of the world,"[40] of which Europe would become an essential part. It is therefore a peaceful endeavor, based on a matter of fact: countries need each other, regardless of the international power they might have. Isolation of countries means decline. Patriotism is not opposed to Europeism, because "the national can flourish within the supranational."[41] Nations have a mission not only in relation with their own peoples but also vis-à-vis other nations. Nationalism itself, therefore, is a bad refuge.

Europe is a "cultural community in the most elevated sense of the term"[42] before being a military alliance. It should to be thought to have developed a

[38] Schuman, *For Europe*, 15.

[39] Robert Schuman, "Préface," in Paul Reuter, *La Communauté européenne du charbon et de l'acier* (Paris: Librairie Générale de Droit et Jurisprudence, 1953), 3–8, at 7. The legal approach to the idea of supranationality was critically developed by Reuter.

[40] Ibid., 18.

[41] Ibid., 22.

[42] Ibid., 29.

soul in the diversity of its traditions and aspirations. Security is a necessary condition for peace and prosperity, and, like peace, has become indivisible. Thus, Schuman continues, a legitimate and constructive goal of Europe is to guarantee collective defense. Defending Europe is not enough, however, since mere defense of Europe does not necessarily imply building Europe. "The present feeling of insecurity," Schuman affirms, "will be the direct cause of the European unification, but it will not be its raison d'être."[43] European countries are interdependent. For better or worse, all countries are united in a single destiny, and this unity demands solidarity between and among nations. According to Schuman, solidarity is based on "the conviction that the real interest of all lies in acknowledging and accepting the interdependency of all,"[44] a reality incompatible with claims to hegemony or egoistic superiority. However, solidarity is also incompatible with any kind of political nationalism, autarchic protectionism, or cultural isolationism. True political solidarity requires "democratic equality."[45] The European project is not imperialistic but supranational and therefore democratic in essence. It implies majority decisions (avoiding any kind of dictatorial superiority), organized cooperation, and a free market, which in turn means competition, confidence, and automatic selection.[46] Finally, the European project demands the cultural development of a real community of ideas, values, and aspirations.

Christian Democracy constitutes the framework of Schuman's European ideal. According to him, democracy and Christianity are strongly linked because "democracy owes its existence to Christianity."[47] "Like Bergson," he pointed out, "I have come to the conclusion that democracy is essentially evangelic, since love is its mainspring."[48] As a doctrine, democracy is linked to human dignity, individual rights and freedoms, and brotherly love toward others. Democracy is an expression of civilized maturity. It took Europe over a thousand years to achieve democracy. "Christianity taught us that all men are equal by nature, children of the same God, redeemed by Christ regardless of race, color, social status, or profession [...]. The universal law of love and charity made every man our neighbor." All of these teachings, with crucial practical consequences, "have changed the world forever."[49] But Christianity should not be a part of the structure of a political system, nor should it be

[43] Ibid., 134.
[44] Ibid., 35.
[45] Ibid., 36.
[46] Ibid., 37.
[47] Ibid., 43.
[48] Ibid., 51.
[49] Ibid., 44.

identified with any form of government. Rather, it is necessary to distinguish what belongs to Caesar and what belongs to God. Administration of changing situations belongs to Caesar; immutable principles of natural law belong to God.[50] On the one hand, theocracy minimizes the necessary separation between the two domains. On the other hand, the nation-state, which seeks to separate the domains, cannot undermine the extraordinary value and moral authority of religious inspiration in public life and in protecting people against social disintegration. For this reason, democracy must define a positive approach to religion.

The last chapters of Schuman's essay on Europe are more circumstantial, but they also contain important statements that later history has confirmed. First, Schuman states that without Germany, just as without France, building Europe would be impossible.[51] More than any other country, perhaps, Germany has a deep sense of community that will make it a full player in a united Europe. Schuman firmly opposed the division of Germany into West and East, for one very practical reason: "The policy of constraint, applied by the victors, only brings flimsy and deceptive solutions; and it generates new conflicts. On the other hand, as long as there is room for revenge, the risk of war can arise again."[52] According to Schuman, neutralizing or even nullifying Germany is contrary to the European project. He anticipated a unified Germany fully integrated into European institutions.[53]

Second, Schuman foresaw that the United Kingdom would agree to join an integrated Europe only when forced by events. Schuman does not consider the United Kingdom as particularly identified with the new European spirit. The issues are psychological, cultural, and political. According to Schuman, "it was inconceivable for the British government to grant a European body more authority than the Commonwealth."[54] The Brexit vote of 2016 clearly harks back to the words of Schuman.

Third, Schuman believed that economic integration was inconceivable in the long term without its logical complement, political integration.[55] Political integration for Europe means federation in the noblest sense of the idea. European countries should be partner states working together through collective diplomacy and supranational institutions led by a parliamentary assembly

[50] Ibid., 46.
[51] Ibid., 61.
[52] Ibid., 79.
[53] Ibid., 139.
[54] Ibid., 86.
[55] Ibid., 93.

elected by universal suffrage,[56] with the capacity of imposing its will over national parliaments in serious decisions on war and peace, nations' independence, and integrity of territory.[57] This federation of states should avoid the mistakes of nation-states, particularly bureaucracy and technocracy[58]: "administrative paralysis," Schuman says, "is the basic danger that threatens any supranational organization."[59] Unfortunately, the European Union has disregarded the voice of one of its founders on a point as important as this.

CONCLUSION

Robert Schuman's life is closely linked to an international mission: bringing together France and Germany to lead the process of European unification. He believed in an organized and united Europe based on the leadership of Germany and France, acting as two powerful lungs under equal rights with other nations. The heart of Europe should be, however, Christian in character, because Christianity, according to Schuman, is the true inspirational source for forgiveness and love. He embodied and anticipated the values that Europe should develop politically: diversity, solidarity, forgiveness, magnanimity, and generosity. In this sense, Robert Schuman was the first citizen, the first founding father, of the European Union. He was a visionary but at the same time a very realistic politician. His proposals were courageous but accessible, without being lost in pure aspiration or abstraction. In all his political ideas and actions, he was guided and determined by his religious attitude. Out of his Christian outlook, he understood politics as a service to humanity, oriented to the common good, and in harmony between individuals and peoples.

RECOMMENDED READING

Acheson, Dean Gooderham. "Robert Schuman." In Dean Acheson, *Sketches from Life of Men I Have Known*, 31–59. New York: Harper, 1961.

[56] The Decision and Act on European elections by direct universal suffrage were signed in Brussels on September 20, 1976. The Act entered into force in July 1978, following ratification by all member states. The first elections took place on June 7 and 10, 1979. For information see: europarl.europa.eu/ftu/pdf/en/FTU_1.3.1.pdf

[57] Schuman, *For Europe*, 108.

[58] Around 33,000 people are currently employed by the European Commission. In the European Parliament, around 6,000 people work in the general secretariat and in the political groups. In the Council of the European Union, around 3,500 people work in the general secretariat. See information at: europa.eu/european-union/about-eu/figures/administration_en

[59] Schuman, *For Europe*, 106.

Adenauer, Konrad. *Memoirs, 1945–53*. Trans. Beate Ruhm von Oppen. London: Weidenfeld & Nicolson, 1966.
Benning, Hermann J. *Robert Schuman: Leben und Vermächtnis*. Munich: Verlag Neue Stadt, 2013.
Beyer, Henry. *Robert Schuman, L'Europe par la réconciliation franco-allemande*. Lausanne: Fondation Jean Monnet pour l'Europe, Centre de recherches européennes, 1986.
Bitsch, Marie-Therèse. *Robert Schuman: Apôtre de l'Europe 1953–1963*. Cahiers Robert Schuman 1, P. I. E. Brussels: Peter Lang, 2010.
Chaplin, Jonathan, and Gary Wilton, eds. *God and the EU: Faith in the European Project*. London, New York: Routledge, 2016.
Conzemius, Victor. *Robert Schuman: Christ und Staatsmann*. Hamburg: F. Witting, 1985.
Fimister, Alan Paul. *Robert Schuman: Neo-Scholastic Humanism and the Reunification of Europe*. Frankfurt am Main, Bern: Peter Lang, 2011.
Griffiths, Richard T. "The Founding Fathers." In *The Oxford Handbook of the European Union*, edited by Erik Jones, Anand Menon, and Stephen Weatherill, 181–92. Oxford, New York: Oxford University Press, 2012.
Heilbron Price, David. *Robert Schuman, Jalonneur de la Paix Mondiale*. Berlin: Bron Communications, 2014.
Hiegel, Charles, and Marion Duvigneau. *Papiers de Robert Schuman. Répertoire numérique détaillé des fonds déposés sous les cotes 34 et 36 J*. Saint-Julien-lès-Metz: Archives départamentales de la Moselle, 2002.
Institut Saint-Benoît. *Robert Schuman. Saintité et politique. Actes des journées organisées à Metz du 4 au 8 septembre 2013*. Metz: Éditions des Paraiges, 2013.
Kaiser, Wolfram. *Christian Democracy and the Origins of European Union*. Cambridge: Cambridge University Press, 2007.
Krijtenburg, Margriet. "*Schuman's Europe: His Frame of Reference*." Doctoral thesis. Leiden: Leiden University, 2012.
"Robert Schuman: Principal Architect of the European Union." Research paper. Markets, Culture and Ethics Centre Research Papers, 1(3)/2015. Rome: Pontifical University of the Holy Cross.
Lejeune, René. *Robert Schuman, une âme pour l'Europe*. Paris, Fribourg: Editions Saint-Paul, 1986.
Robert Schuman, père de l'Europe (1886–1963). Paris: Fayard, 2000.
Lücker, Hans August, and Jean Seitlinger. *Robert Schuman und die Einigung Europas*. Bonn: Bouvier Verlag, 2000.
McCauliff, C. M. A. "Union in Europe: Constitutional Philosophy and the Schuman Declaration, May 9, 1950." *Columbia Journal of European Law* 18 (2011–12): 441–72.
Milward, Alan Steele. *The European Rescue of the Nation-State*. Hoboken, NJ: Taylor & Francis, 1999.
Mittendorfer, Rudolf. *Robert Schuman. Architekt des neuen Europa*. Hildesheim, New York: Georg Olms, 1983.
Monnet, Jean. *Memoirs*. London: Third Millennium, 2015.
Monnet, Jean, and Robert Schuman. *Correspondence (1947–1963)*. Lausanne: Fondation Jean Monnet pour l'Europe, 1986.

Mowat, Robert Case. *Creating the European Community*. New York: Barnes & Noble Books, 1973.
Muñoz Martínez, María Ángeles. "El pensamiento europeo de Robert Schuman: el retorno lógico de la Unión Europea a la comunidad federación." Madrid: Universidad Complutense, 2012. Doctoral thesis available at: eprints.ucm.es/16322/1/T33942.pdf
Oreja, Marcelino, and Rafael Domingo. "Robert Schuman." In *Juristas Universales IV*, edited by Rafael Domingo, 141–45. Madrid, Barcelona: Marcial Pons, 2004.
Pelt, Jean-Marie. *Robert Schuman, Père de l'Europe – Father of Europe*. English version. Thionville: General Council of Moselle, Serge Domini Publisher, 2001.
Pennera, Christian. *La jeunesse et les debuts politiques d'un grand europeen de 1886 à 1924*. Sarreguemines: Editions Pierron 1985.
Poidevin, Raymond. *Robert Schuman, homme d'État (1886–1963)*. Paris: Imprimerie nationale, 1986.
Reuter, Paul. *La Communauté européenne du charbon et de l'acier*. Paris: Librairie Geénérale,1953.
La naissance de l'Europe communautaire. Lausanne: Fondation Jean Monnet pour l'Europe, 1980.
Rochefort, Robert. *Robert Schuman*. Paris: Cerf, 1968.
Roth, François. *Robert Schuman. Du Lorrain des frontières au père de l'Europe*. Paris: Fayard 2008.
Alsace-Lorraine: histoire d'un "pays perdu," de 1870 à nos jours. Nancy: Editions de la Place Stanislas, 2010.
Schirmann, Sylvain, edn. *Robert Schuman et les pères de l'Europe*. Brussels: Peter Lang, 2008.
Schreiber, Thomas. *Robert Schuman. De la déclaration Schuman à pour l'Europe*. Paris: Lignes de Repères, 2013.
Schuman, Robert. *For Europe*. Paris: Foundation Robert Schuman; Chêne-Bourg: Nagel, 2010.
Wahl, Jürgen. *Robert Schuman: Visionär, Politiker, Architekt Europas*. Trier: Paulinus, 1999.
Zin, Edoardo. *Robert Schuman: un padre dell'Europa unita*. Rome: AVE, 2013.

25

Gabriel Le Bras

(1891–1970)

KATHLEEN G. CUSHING

BIOGRAPHICAL INTRODUCTION

Gabriel Le Bras was one of the twentieth century's most important French scholars of medieval law and religious sociology and one whose research continues to be fundamental for the study of the medieval church, ecclesiastical institutions, religious sociology and especially canon and Roman law. Both on his own and through collaborations with his great teacher, Paul Fournier, and with Jean Gaudemet, Charles Lefebvre, Jacqueline Rambaud, and Fernand Boulard among others, Le Bras helped to pioneer a scientific approach to the study of canon and Roman law through meticulous attention to the manuscripts and their historical contexts and a collective approach for understanding the church through its institutions and *religion vécue* (lived religion). Along the way he created new methodological approaches for religious sociology and cemented its place as a scientific discipline.

Gabriel Le Bras was born at Paimpol in Brittany on July 23, 1891, into a maritime family, and as a child he planned for a career as a sea-captain.[1] After completing his primary studies at Saint-Joseph and at the seminary at Tréguier, Le Bras hoped to enter the naval school, Saint-Charles de Saint-Brieuc, but failed an eye test, which ended his plans for a naval career. As Gaudemet noted, the decision angered Le Bras, but ironically destined him for an academic career in which he brought an extremely perceptive eye to the

[1] The fullest biography of Gabriel Le Bras is by Jean Gaudemet, "Gabriel Le Bras (1891–1970)", *École pratique des hautes études, Section des sciences religieuses. Annuaire* 1970–1971, 78 (1971): 67–81. See also Raoul C. van Caenegem, "Legal Historians I Have Known: A Personal Memoir," *Rechtsgeschichte, Zeitschrift des Max-Planck Instituts für europäische Rechtsgeschichte* 17 (2010): 253–99, at 272–75.

deciphering of manuscripts, to the analysis of religious statistics, and to the appreciation of humanity.[2]

Le Bras studied classic law and literature at the University of Rennes between 1908 and 1911 and then continued his studies at the University of Paris (1911–14) where his passion for history and his first encounter with canon law was fostered by Paul Fournier[3] and Robert Génestal among others. Le Bras was mobilized on the Champagne front in 1916 before serving in Italy. Returning to Paris after the war, he received a doctorate in political and economic science in 1920, and in 1922 received his doctorate in law and his *agrégation de droit*. Le Bras then moved to take up the chair in Roman law at the University of Strasbourg, where he became associated with the Institute of Canon Law, established in 1920 within the faculty of Catholic theology, where he would teach from 1923 to 1929, although his association with the institute and the University of Strasbourg would last nearly forty years. This period saw his interest in history and sociology develop further through his friendship and intellectual exchange with colleagues at Strasbourg such as the historians Marc Bloch and Lucien Febvre and the sociologist Maurice Halbwachs (through whom Le Bras was introduced to the work of Emile Durkheim and Marcel Mauss). His teaching during these years inspired numerous students in canon law, including Jean Gaudemet with whom he would later collaborate.[4]

In 1929, Le Bras oversaw the teaching of the course on Justinian's *Digest* at the Faculty of Law in Paris, and two years later, following the death of Robert Génestal, he was appointed to the chair of the history of canon law, a chair that had been created in 1920 for his mentor Paul Fournier. Le Bras also became director of the study of canon law at Section V of the École Pratique des Hautes Études. With the outbreak of the Second World War, Le Bras was mobilized between 1939 and 1940 at Grand Quartier Général, which was disbanded following the German invasion of France and the signing of the Second Armistice at Compiègne in June 1940. During the remainder of the war, he was part of the French Resistance, about which he seldom spoke and for which he received a medal. During this time, he married Marthe Follain, a historian who had been his student, and with whom he had six children.

From 1942 to 1968, Le Bras served as president of the Société d'Histoire de L'Église de France, and in 1945, he became an adviser on religious matters at

[2] Gaudemet, "Gabriel Le Bras (1891–1970)," 67.

[3] On Paul Fournier, see Chapter 18.

[4] Gabriel Le Bras and Jean Gaudemet, eds., *Prolégomènes, Histoire du droit et des institutions de l'Église en Occident* (Paris: Sirey, 1955); 18 of a projected 35 volumes were published.

the Ministry of Foreign Affairs. In 1948, Le Bras also took over as director of Section VI of the École Pratique des Hautes Études, created to address economic and social sciences, a role in which he continued to just before his death. (In 1975, the section became a separate institution, L'École des Hautes Études en Sciences Sociales.)

Le Bras served as director of the Centre National de la Recherche Scientifique (CNRS) from 1945 to 1952, and as dean of the faculty of law from 1959 to 1962. He was elected a member of the Académie des Sciences Morales et Politiques as well as an officer of the Légion d'honneur. From 1942 to 1968, he also served as the president of the Société d'Histoire Religieuse. His renown and reputation was widely recognized beyond France, and he was awarded honorary doctorates from Liège, Louvain, Milan, and Bologna as well as being inducted into the Pontifical Academy of St Thomas and numerous scholarly societies in the United Kingdom, Belgium and the United States. He died in Paris on February 18, 1970, aged 81. His wife, Marthe Follain Le Bras, died on February 28, 2009.

SCHOLARLY CONTRIBUTION

Gabriel Le Bras was an extremely prolific scholar, whose research encompassed very different, if for him overlapping, disciplines. A complete bibliography of his works up to 1964 was published in a two-volume Festschrift in his honor in 1965 and itemized over four hundred titles.[5] His research encompassed the history of canon and Roman law, the history of ecclesiastical institutions, and religious sociology in both historical and contemporary contexts, and these were topics on which he worked simultaneously throughout his long career. For the sake of clarity, the consideration of his scholarly work will be addressed here in two parts.

LAW AND ECCLESIASTICAL INSTITUTIONS

In 1921, shortly after completing his doctorate, Le Bras published an article on Alger of Liège's *Liber de Misericordia et iusticia*. This was the first of many works by Le Bras devoted to the canonical sources of the classical age, including numerous studies on Gratian's *Decretum* on which he intended

[5] *Études d'histoire du droit canonique dédiées à Gabriel Le Bras*, edn. Georges Vedel (Paris: Sirey, 1965), 2 vols. A supplementary bibliography of work between 1964 and 1969 is found in Gaudemet, "Gabriel Le Bras (1891–1970)," 80–81. A monograph, *L' Église et le village*, was published posthumously in 1976. See below.

to produce a monograph, never completed. This research led to his collaboration with his former mentor, Paul Fournier, on a two-volume work, *Histoire des collections canoniques en Occident depuis les Fausses Décrétales jusqu'au Décret de Gratien* published in 1931 and 1932; his principal contribution concerned the development of canonical collections up to the eleventh century. The *Histoire des collections canoniques* was in many ways a groundbreaking piece of scholarship, not just in terms of the detailed archival work and consideration of the manuscript transmission of the canonical collections that informed the volumes – something in which both Fournier and Le Bras were consummate experts – but also for the ways in which Fournier and Le Bras sought to situate the collections in their historical contexts to understand their origins and rationales, and to use them as vehicles for understanding the religious preoccupations of their compilers across diverse periods of the history of the church.

Le Bras's chapter, focusing on the period from the early church to the eleventh century, underlined the extent to which conciliar canons, papal decretals and imperial law – by defining the organizational structures of the church, the temporal status of clergy, ecclesiastical property, and so on – introduced order, discipline, and unity even during the crises of the sixth and seventh centuries and amidst issues of regional dissonance, especially in Gaul. Here, while displaying his customary rigorous textual examination of the collections and their formal sources, especially with Regino of Prüm's *Libri duo de synodalibus causis et disciplinis ecclesiasticis*,[6] and the orientations of these collections, Le Bras clearly revealed a conception of the history of law that illuminated not just the development of the church as an institution but of Christianity as a lived religion – a vision that would underlie all his scholarly work. Le Bras was convinced that the study of law could not be undertaken as an abstraction but had to be rooted in an understanding of the lived experience of society.

This approach can be seen in the plans outlined in his *Prolégomènes* (1955) for a collective multivolume series under the title *Histoire du droit et des institutions de l'Église en Occident* with Jean Gaudemet and other former students of Le Bras. This series was intended to examine the history of the church's institutions in the West with extensive consideration of the law of the early church and the period before Gratian in general. Le Bras's approach, as detailed in the *Prolégomènes*, underlined the gaps in the historiography not

[6] For a critical edition of the text, see Wilfried Hartmann, ed., *Das Sendhandbuch des Regino von Prüm*. Freiherr vom Stein-Gedächtnisausgabe, 42 (Darmstadt: Wissenschaftliche Buchgesellschaft, 2004).

just in French scholarly work but elsewhere and offered a new vision for how the history of the law of the church should be written. For Le Bras, canon law was as vital and comprehensive as the church itself, at times expanding and contracting, at others changing with the church. Canon law, as he understood it, touched human life at every point and linked the temporal world with the unseen. In his comprehensive view of history, in which he had been influenced by his colleagues in the *Annales* school,[7] historians of canon law needed to address liturgy and theology as much as economics into order to understand "*la vie réelle des institutions.*" His new approach was nowhere more apparent than in the unusual chapter titles of the *Prolégomènes* – *speculum iuris, concordia discordantium, fortuna legume* – and Le Bras made it clear that subsequent volumes would not simply offer a traditional chronological narrative but would seek to explain chronological and local variations in the context of a universal church.

Le Bras followed this approach in his two volumes, *Institutions ecclésiastiques de la Chrétienté médiévale*, published in 1959 and 1964 in the series Histoire de l'Église, founded by Augustin Fliche and Victor Martin in 1934. Here, Le Bras again articulated his conception of a tripartite church comprising a complete society (its people, its leaders, its possessions, its relations with secular powers); of a spiritual (Le Bras used the term *supranaturelle*) society that existed to link this world and the next; and of an international (*supernationale*) society in which the church transcended political entities.[8] Here again, we can see the influence of his own Catholicism as well as his sociological and cross-disciplinary interests: for Le Bras, understanding ecclesiastical institutions entailed addressing not simply the organization of the church, and the growth of medieval ecclesiastical jurisprudence, but also its spiritual life and its provision of social order and discipline.[9]

Influenced by his work on religious sociology, Le Bras began the first volume with a sacramental framework (no doubt also influenced by his reading of the ordering of many medieval systematic canonical collections), focusing on how a Christian's life was shaped by baptism and the other sacraments. While recognizing the different types of members – lay, clerical,

[7] The *Annales* school, cofounded by Le Bras's colleagues at Strasbourg, Lucien Febvre and Marc Bloch, was a group of French historians who sought to break down the barriers between history and other disciplines, incorporating ideas from literature and psychology as well as the social sciences in an attempt to understand the *mentalités* of particular historical periods.

[8] Gabriel Le Bras, *Institutions ecclésiastiques de la Chrétienté médiévale*, vol. 1 (Paris: Bloud and Gay, 1959), 12–13.

[9] This vision clearly informed the collaborative project on parish visitations begun in 1944. See below.

monastic – he argued for interdependent solidarities among the different groups, and his discussion did much to reconfigure our understanding of the medieval clergy as shifting networks of interest and perception. In his analysis of the institutional structure, Le Bras necessarily focused on the role of the pope, cardinals, and papal administration, but he nuanced this analysis by addressing structures in the localities and the role of traditional monasteries, and the challenges and advantages presented by the mendicant orders. In so doing he underlined the tensions between an external-facing unity with its overarching sacramental framework and the internal, even disruptive, tensions that characterized the fabric of the medieval church and its institutions.

In 1965, with his former students Jacqueline Rambaud and Charles Lefebvre, Le Bras produced a second volume, *L'Âge classique (1140–1378): Sources et théorie du droit* for the series Histoire du droit et des institutions de l'Église en Occident, which he had begun ten years earlier. This volume traced the formation, transmission, and interpretation of canon law from Gratian until the Great Schism in 1378. The volume was intended to be just one of a six-volume series on the so-called classical age of canon law that was to trace the growth of the church's institutions and social order, sacramental doctrine and practice, and especially the circumstances of Christian society in which these canonists worked during this period. While providing an indispensable overview of this period in over six hundred pages and recognizing the interplay of institutions and persons, in the end, as reviewers of the volume noted, the canonists under consideration tended to be treated in isolation from the secular and historical events of their times. That said, while Rambaud's comprehensive survey on Gratian and the analysis of the *ius novum* by Lefebvre have been modified in subsequent and recent scholarship, *L'Âge classique* remains, much like Stephan Kuttner's *Repertorium der Kanonistik (1140–1234)*, fundamental for the study of law in this period.[10]

Up until his death, Le Bras continued to produce scholarly work on canon-law sources, the reconciliation of canonical and Roman law in the classical period, and the connections between theology and law in the eleventh century.[11]

[10] Stephan Kuttner, *Repertorium der Kanonistik (1140–1234)* (Vatican City: Biblioteca Apostolica Vaticana, 1937). An updated and invaluable digital resource is Kenneth Pennington, *Medieval and Early Modern Jurists: A Bio-Bibliographical Listing*, available at amesfoundation.law.harvard.edu/BioBibCanonists/HomePage_biobib2.php

[11] See the bibliography in Gaudemet, "Gabriel Le Bras (1891–1970)," 80–81.

LA SOCIOLOGIE RELIGIEUSE (RELIGIOUS SOCIOLOGY)

Le Bras's historical interpretation and analysis, especially the ways in which he sought to understand law and institutions within the context of the societies in which they operated – both as rules and as a set of social expectations – and his broader interest in *religion vécue* were profoundly influenced by an awareness of the value of sociological perspectives and methodologies for the study of the church and society. As noted, during his years in Strasbourg Le Bras was acquainted with notable sociologists such as Halbwachs, Gurevitch, and Mauss, and he became increasingly interested in religious sociology. Interest in lived religion was linked to the broader concerns about pastoral theology and reform that were part of twentieth-century Catholicism in general, which no doubt influenced Le Bras. Here, sociological work in the form of religious sociology (rather than that of a sociology of religion) sought – often statistically – to understand contemporary lay Christian belief and practice as part of a larger endeavor to comprehend the extent to which ordinary Catholics engaged with their religion in the past. Le Bras was often credited with establishing this new discipline, an attribution against which he always protested.[12]

In 1942, Le Bras published the first volume of his *Introduction à l'histoire de la pratique religieuse en France*, the second volume of which appeared in 1945. This was a synthesis of research undertaken since at least 1929 and was informed by phenomenal archival work and by numerous articles Le Bras had published in journals such as the *Annales sociologiques*, *Revue d'histoire de l' Église de France*, the *Revue du Folklore français*, and various regional journals.[13] The *Introduction* sought, in no small measure, to assess the allegiance of French Catholics to their religion from the time of the earliest preaching of Christianity and the baptism of Clovis in 496 to his own day. The volume and its companion offered both a methodology for evaluating the religiosity of the people of France and the documentary evidence of that allegiance to Catholicism.

[12] See Danièle Hervieu-Léger, "Gabriel Le Bras, 1891–1970,"*Dictionnaire des faits religieux* (Paris: Presses universitaires de France, 2010), repr. *Archives de sciences sociales des religions*, 2014 (electronic version); and Gaudemet, "Gabriel Le Bras (1891–1970)," 76–77.

[13] One of the most important of these, not least in methodological terms, was his "Statistique et histoire religieuse. Pour un examen détaillé et pour une explication historique de l'état du catholicisme dans les diverses régions de la France," *Revue d'histoire de l'Église de France* 77 (1931): 425–29. This was a topic to which he returned with articles under the same title in this journal in 1933, 1936, 1938, 1940, 1942, 1945, and 1949, most of which addressed specific regional statistics and their variations.

Le Bras argued for the originality of such an approach and its revolutionary impact on the broader discipline of sociology. He was not interested in sociology in terms of abstraction and theoretical approaches in isolation from lived experience. As a historian, he was above all immersed in studying the traditions of the practice of French Catholicism. He began first of all with what he termed the *tradition juridique* and the categories of Christians and how Christian practice (here using communion as the central Catholic sacrament) had evolved over the course of the centuries, sometimes encouraged, sometimes restricted by administrative and priestly authority. This approach enabled him to suggest ways of being more precise in terms of understanding Catholic identity (conformist, regular observers, and devout, for instance), which he argued provided a more nuanced understanding than that afforded by a simple identification as Catholic or non-Catholic. Through the scrutiny of parish registers, dossiers of parish visitations, and other ecclesiastical documents (which he called the administrative tradition), Le Bras sought to measure Catholic belief and practice both quantitatively and qualitatively over the *longue durée*, while always taking into account the sometimes transparent, sometimes less transparent nature of the documentation, especially responses to episcopal surveys.

In the final chapter of the first volume, titled the "Human Tradition," Le Bras offered on the basis of his previous analysis a challenge to a simplistic, Nietzschean-inspired narrative of an age of faith and its progressive decline from the end of the Middle Ages, weakened by the rise of Protestantism, the French Revolution and the separation of church and state by underlining patterns of continuity as well as change in French religious sensibilities. In the second volume, published in 1945, Le Bras addressed the causes and the effects of the variations in religious practice, and was concerned to assess the place of the humble as well as the learned within his conception of the church.

Le Bras's interest in quantifying religious practice led to a collaboration with Canon Fernand Boulard in 1947 and the establishment of a map of religious practice – the *Carte religieuse de la France rurale* – that displayed geographically the diffusion of Catholicism in France, in which Brittany, the east, and the Massif Central showed the greatest adherence to Catholicism.[14]

[14] Fernand Boulard and Gabriel Le Bras, "Carte de la pratique religieuse dans les campagnes,"*Cahiers du Clergé rural* (1947); reprinted in Fernand Boulard, *Premiers itinéraires en sociologie religieuse* (Paris: Les éditions ouvrières, 1966). Their map was subsequently analyzed to assess the extent to which political affiliation mapped onto religious practice. In his personal memoir of Le Bras, Raoul van Caenegem noted: "I remember a large map [in Le Bras's apartment] where various regions were coloured according to church

In 1949, in a brief article in the *Revue d'Histoire de l' Église de France*, Le Bras provided an update on an ambitious collaborative project, an investigation and inventory of parish and monastic visitations over the *longue durée*, first conceived in 1944.[15] In 1955, he published a collection of his articles produced over the preceding twenty-five years in a two-volume work, *Études de sociologie religieuse*, which underlined the range of his interests: statistical history, archival studies across time, the Ancien Régime, and sociological methods for other religions.

Le Bras continued to produce scholarly work on religious sociology from the perspectives of Buddhism and Islam and on sociological methodology more broadly.[16] *L'Église et le village*, published posthumously in 1976,[17] had its origins in 1925, when Le Bras was professor of law at Strasbourg, where his colleague Marc Bloch asked him to help his own research by locating the role of the sacred in rural history. The work was only published more than fifty years later through the efforts of Madame Le Bras, who assembled the volume from an early draft annotated by Bloch himself. In many ways, it was a fitting final publication that brought together Le Bras's scholarly interests in history, law, sociology, psychology, and topography, and which evoked a complex relationship between the church and the village in which the religious was closely interwoven with the profane. This was the civilization, according to one reviewer, in which Le Bras was born, lived, and conducted his life as a scholarly researcher.[18]

CHRISTIAN SCIENTIFIC SPIRIT

A very devout Catholic, Gabriel Le Bras was deeply influenced in his research and immense scholarly work by Catholic intellectual culture and numerous internal discussions within twentieth-century Catholicism in France and beyond. The trajectory of his career and his research interests combined diverse approaches, and he brought together a deep interest in religious sociology, an appreciation for the expansive history advocated by the *Annales* school (both of

attendance. Some were still clearly Catholic but others were almost 'heathen'. The interpretation of the map was open to debate." Van Caenegem, "Legal Historians I Have Known," 272.

15 Gabriel Le Bras, "Enquêtes sur les visites des paroisses," *Revue d'Histoire de l'Église de France* 125 (1949): 39–41.

16 See the bibliography in Gaudemet, "Gabriel Le Bras (1891–1970)," 80–81.

17 Gabriel Le Bras, *L'Église et le village* (Paris: Flammarion, 1976).

18 Gérard Cholvy, review of Gabriel Le Bras, *L'Église et le village* in *Revue d'Histoire de l'Église de France* 170 (1977): 107–09.

which were initially developed at his time in Strasbourg), a penetrating knowledge of canon and Roman law, and his own religious beliefs. In a series of radio broadcasts on religion and modern scientific methods in 1968, Le Bras noted that his interest had never been simply in understanding how laws were formulated in intellectual terms but rather in asking "why, for whom, for which society, in which social conditions they were made and in what measure did that society receive them, apply them and re-form them."[19]

It is undeniable that Le Blas's own Catholicism and his concern for the position of the Catholic Church in France underpinned many of his scholarly works. On one level, his ambition was to analyse – in a scientific sense by understanding the essential history of the French Church – the religious reality of a France in which church and state were separate and existed uneasily together, and which had been for too long characterized as *décatholicisée* from the time of the French Revolution and subsequent governments. He sought to achieve this ambition by establishing a precise accounting of believers, by mapping practice geographically, and by always maintaining a historical perspective on these findings. Like his mentor, Fournier, albeit in a different historical context, Le Bras served as an adviser for religious affairs for the Ministry of Foreign Affairs after 1945.[20] Following the law passed in 1905 separating the church and the state in France (apart from the dioceses of Strasbourg and Metz where a local right regarding episcopal elections was preserved after the end of the First World War and continues in a different form to the present day),[21] the French government had to be consulted by the Vatican about the appointment of French bishops. Although little was widely known or discussed about his precise role, Le Bras was clearly trusted by both parties to play a discreet role in composing the episcopate in France during this time.

Despite a rewarding, prestigious career and a happy family life, Gabriel Le Bras had for much of his life, according to Gaudemet, a deeply pessimistic view of human existence, something likely reinforced by his time in the French Resistance. For Le Bras, sadly, evil was a reality, and despite all of his achievements, he could not stop believing that the world was an empire of evil.[22] Although the devil appeared to be a constant part of Le Bras's

[19] Henri Desroche and Gabriel Le Bras, "Religion légale et religion vécue. Entretien avec Gabriel Le Bras." *Archives de sociologie des religions* 29 (1970): 15–20, here at 16.

[20] See Chapter 18 on Paul Fournier.

[21] See Chapter 18, note 45 and Chapter 24 on Robert Schuman, note 14.

[22] Gaudemet, "Gabriel Le Bras (1891–1970)," 72.

consciousness, he apparently frequently used him in his teaching. According to Raoul van Caenegem, on one occasion while lecturing, Le Bras noted: "It says in Scripture *omnis potestas a Deo* but I say *omnis potestas a diabolo*," on which van Caenegem commented that Le Bras well understood the temptations and hubris to which humans were victims.[23] Gaudemet noted that one of the doyen's favorite anecdotes concerned the visit of the devil to one of his lectures. Apparently, this unexpected visitor left sneering, and the attempt to pursue him in the corridors was futile.[24] Perhaps as a gifted lawyer as well as a devout Catholic, Le Bras understood better than anyone the constant need to dispute against the devil.

CONCLUSION

Le doyen Gabriel Le Bras, as he was known in later life, was one of the twentieth century's leading intellects, who inspired a generation of scholars working on the church, canon and Roman law and religious sociology. His formidable body of scholarly work in all these fields continues to be regularly cited, and remains a fundamental starting point for any scholarship in these fields, even if some of the specifics have been modified by the discovery of new canon-law manuscripts and advances in the methodologies of sociology. His towering intellect, humor, incessant scholarly activity, and humanity were frequently underlined by students of his such as Jean Gaudemet and Raoul van Caenegem, who noted that his office door was never closed, that Le Bras even received his students in his apartment on the Place du Panthéeon, that he was full of attention for them, even providing the means for them to attend conferences, and perhaps most strikingly, that he even took part (covertly) in organizing some of the contributors for his own Festschift.[25] Even in the final days of his life, he continued to speak of and plan for new research projects. The extent to which he continued to be held in esteem after his death in 1970 was evident at the widely attended Journée Le Bras, held in Paris at the Fondation Simone and Cino del Duca in April 2006, at which his widow, Marthe Le Bras, spoke. In the end, Gabriel Le Bras was a consummate scholar not just of law and sociology, but of humanity itself.

[23] Van Caenegem, "Legal Historians I Have Known," 272.
[24] Gaudemet, "Gabriel Le Bras (1891–1970)," 72.
[25] Van Caenegem, "Legal Historians I Have Known," 275.

RECOMMENDED READING

Arnold, John H. "Histories and Historiographies of Medieval Christianity." In *The Oxford Handbook of Medieval Christianity*, edited by John H. Arnold, 23–41. Oxford: Oxford University Press, 2014.

Desroche, Henri, and Gabriel Le Bras. "Religion légale et religion vécue. Entretien avec Gabriel Le Bras." *Archives de sociologie des religions* 29 (1970): 15–20.

Gaudemet, Jean. "Gabriel Le Bras (1891–1970)." *École pratique des hautes études, Section des sciences religieuses. Annuaire* 1970–1971, 78 (1971): 67–81.

Études d'histoire du droit canonique dédiées à Gabriel Le Bras. Edited by Georges Vedel. 2 vols. Paris: Sirey, 1965.

Hervieu-Léger, Danièle. "Gabriel Le Bras, 1891–1970." *Dictionnaire des faits religieux*. Paris: Presses universitaires de France, 2010; repr. *Archives de sciences sociales des religions*, 2014. Electronic version: assr.revues.org/25711

Le Bras, Gabriel. *Introduction à l'histoire de la pratique religieuse en France*. 2 vols. Paris: Presses universitaires de France, 1942; 1945.

Études de sociologie religieuse. 2 vols. Bibliothèque de Sociologie contemporaine. Paris: Presses universitaires de France, 1955; 1956.

Institutions ecclésiastiques de la Chrétienté médiévale. 2 vols. Paris: Bloud and Gay, 1959; 1964.

in collaboration with Paul Fournier. *Histoire des collections canoniques en Occident depuis les Fausses Décrétales jusqu'au Décret de Gratien*, vol. 1, *De la Réforme carolingienne à la Réforme grégorienne*. Paris: Sirey, 1931; vol. II, *De la Réforme grégorienne au Décret de Gratien*. Paris: Sirey, 1932.

with Jean Gaudemet, edn. *Prolégomènes. Histoire du droit et des institutions de l'Église en Occident*. Paris: Sirey, 1955.

with Charles Lefebvre and Jacqueline Rambaud. *L'Âge classique (1140–1378). Sources et théorie du droit*. Paris: Sirey, 1965.

Van Caenegem, Raoul C. "Legal Historians I Have Known: A Personal Memoir." *Rechtsgeschichte, Zeitschrift des Max-Planck Instituts für europäische Rechtsgeschichte* 17 (2010): 253–99, at 272–75.

26

Jean Carbonnier

(1908–2003)

LAETITIA GUERLAIN

BIOGRAPHICAL INTRODUCTION

Jean Carbonnier was one of the most influential twentieth-century French jurists. A specialist in civil law and founder of the discipline of legal sociology, he has acquired an international reputation owing to his vast classical learning and clear, simple, and elegant writing. Carbonnier is celebrated for his accurate sense of history and philosophy. He was eager to understand law by using other social sciences, and he claimed that law was fully a part of the functioning of the social world. Far from being a technical jurist, he was not so much interested in the technicalities of the law (though he mastered them perfectly) as in grasping its sociological essence. Carbonnier's unique position in French legal culture often impresses scholars so much that few dare critique his ideas in depth or study his works from a historical perspective. Jean Carbonnier has become a part of the cultural heritage of French legal scholarship and, actually, somewhat of a myth.

Jean Carbonnier was born in Libourne (Gironde) on April 20, 1908, to a Catholic family. He later became a Protestant by personal choice and faith, and married a Protestant woman. He was the second son of Thérèse and Joseph Fernand Carbonnier, a wine trader. He was very affected, as were his parents, by the death of his 13-year-old brother in 1917. After attending primary school in Libourne from 1913 to 1916 and in Andernos in 1917–18, Carbonnier completed high school away from home, mostly in Paris from 1918 to 1925, with a tutor who taught him German, English, Spanish, Latin, Greek, Hebrew, and literary Arabic. In 1924–25, he joined a philosophy class and developed an interest in the philosophers Théodule Ribot, Félix Ravaisson, Gabriel Tarde, Alfred Fouillée, Henri Bergson, Lucien Lévy-Bruhl, and Émile Durkheim. After studying law in Bordeaux from 1925 to 1928 (sojourning several times in Switzerland during those years), he specialized in Roman law and legal history (1929) and in political economy and private law (1930). He then defended his PhD dissertation under the supervision of French civil-law specialist Julien Bonnecase (*Le régime matrimonial, sa nature juridique sous le rapport des notions de société et d'association*, 1932). In 1933–34, Carbonnier completed his military service in the Service de Santé [the French Defense Health Service] in Paris. From 1934 to 1937, he trained in Geneva and Tübingen for the private-law *agrégation* examination, an extraordinarily competitive and difficult examination leading to highly selective careers in education and civil service.

After his success in the *agrégation*, he gained appointment in 1938 to a position of private-law professor on the Faculty of Law at the University of Poitiers, where he would later serve as dean, from 1950 to 1954. During World War II he was called up and worked again in the Service de Santé in Nantes, from September 1939 to November 1940. He was a member of the interim city council of Nantes in 1944–45 and of the city council in 1945–47. In 1947 he married Madeleine Hugues (1922–2001), a lawyer and granddaughter of Edmond Hugues, cofounder of the Musée du Désert, an important Protestant institution. The couple had seven children. In 1955, Carbonnier left Poitiers to accept a position on the faculty of law at the University of Paris, where he spent the rest of his career, until 1976. Just before retiring, he was named president of the private- and criminal-law *agrégation* examination, in 1975.[1]

Jean Carbonnier left many writings, both articles and books.[2] He is especially known for his famous civil-law textbook *Droit civil* (Paris: PUF, 1955), which was republished until 2004. He also wrote *Droit et passion du droit sous la Ve République* (1996), in which he criticizes French legislative inflation. Carbonnier indeed attached his name to the legislation of the French Fifth Republic. He helped modernize French family law by writing the draft

[1] For an overview of Carbonnier's life and work, see Jean-François Niort, "Carbonnier, Jean," in *Dictionnaire historique des juristes français, XXe–XXe siècle*, edn. Patrick Arabeyre, Jean-Louis Halpérin, and Jacques Krynen (Paris: PUF, 2015), 207–09. For more details, see Raymond Verdier, ed., *Jean Carbonnier. L'homme et l'œuvre* (Paris: Presses universitaires de Paris Ouest, 2011). A number of interviews with Jean Carbonnier have also been published: see "Entretien avec le doyen Carbonnier. Sociologie juridique et crise du droit," *Droits. Revue française de théorie juridique* 4 (1986): 65–73; "Paroles de Jean Carbonnier. Propos retranscrits par Raymond Verdier," *Droit et cultures* 48 (2004): 231–51; André-Jean Arnaud, ed., *Jean Carbonnier. Un juriste dans la cité* (Paris: LGDJ, 2012), and Olivier Abel, *Paul Ricoeur, Jacques Ellul, Jean Carbonnier, Pierre Chaunu: dialogues* (Genève: Labor et Fides, 2012), 75–97.

[2] Raymond Verdier has collected 203 of Carbonnier's writings, among which were several previously unpublished or difficult to access: Raymond Verdier, ed., *Jean Carbonnier. Écrits* (Paris: PUF, 2008).

legislation of several reforms from 1964 to 1975 (guardianship, 1964; matrimonial property regimes, 1965; adoption, 1966; legally incapacitated adults, 1968; parental rights, 1970; parentage law, 1972; divorce, 1975). He explained the spirit of those laws in his *Essais sur les lois* (1979).

These very important legislative achievements were made possible by the tools of sociology of law, especially opinion polls. Indeed, Jean Carbonnier is remembered as the founder of the sociology of law, not only as it is applied to legislation (*sociologie législative*) but also as a scholarly discipline.[3] He left a textbook dedicated to legal sociology (*Sociologie juridique*, 1972, reissued 2004). Yet his most famous book remains *Flexible droit. Pour une sociologie du droit sans rigueur* (1969, reissued 2001), a collection of essays blending sociology and law, or rather, a philosophical reflection on law.[4] He also published a great number of papers on legal sociology. Apart from this, he produced articles on civil law, a few on criminal law, and several studies of religious matters and legal history, especially one very well-known article arguing that the French civil code is fully part of French collective memory.[5] His fame led to his receiving degrees of doctor *honoris causa* from several universities (Athens, Bern, Brussels, Coimbra, Louvain, McGill in Montreal, Uppsala, and Utrecht). In 2005, a research prize was named after him (*prix Jean Carbonnier de la recherche sur le droit et la justice*), to reward the first work of a French-speaking scholar about law or justice.

JEAN CARBONNIER'S SOCIOLOGY OF LAW

The name of Jean Carbonnier has become attached inextricably to the discipline of sociology of law. Several jurists before him had tried to promote a sociological vision of law, for instance, French legal historian Henri Lévy-Bruhl, who wrote *Sociologie du droit* in 1961, or Georges Gurvitch whose *Eléments de sociologie juridique* was published in 1941. Yet sociology of law as a discipline is irrevocably linked to Carbonnier, who took advantage of

[3] For Jean Carbonnier's sociology of law, see principally Simona Andrini and André-Jean Arnaud, *Jean Carbonnier, Renato Treves et la sociologie du droit. Archéologie d'une discipline* (Paris: LGDJ, 1995), and *L'Année sociologique* 57, no. 2 (2007) (special issue dedicated to Jean Carbonnier).

[4] Two commentaries on *Flexible droit* are: Jean-François Niort, "*Flexible droit*," in *Dictionnaire des grandes œuvres juridiques*, edn. Olivier Cayla and Jean-Louis Halpérin (Paris: Dalloz, 2008), 77–82; and Laetitia Guerlain, "67. Observations sous *Flexible droit. Pour une sociologie du droit sans rigueur* (1969) de Jean Carbonnier," in *Les grands discours de la culture juridique*, edn. Julie Benetti, Pierre Egéa, Xavier Magnon, and Wanda Mastor (Paris: Dalloz, 2017), 830–39.

[5] Jean Carbonnier, "Le Code civil des Français dans la mémoire collective," in *Les lieux de mémoire. La Nation*, edn. Pierre Nora (Paris: Gallimard, 1986), 293–315.

favorable conditions to give the sociolegal approach its fame. Indeed, the 1960s and the 1970s saw the rising importance of human and social sciences, such as psychology, economics, sociology, linguistics, and philosophy. Carbonnier intended to take advantage of this intellectual context because at the beginning of the French Fifth Republic, the role of jurists in political and administrative life seemed to be declining rapidly. Even law faculties, in competition with other institutions, were losing their traditional role of educating elites. In those days, the government was trying to bypass the jurists and the French Parliament (that is, the legislative authority) to undertake important reforms. In this very peculiar context, a number of law professors, such as Pierre Catala, Paul Durand, Jean Foyer, François Terré, and Carbonnier, decided to offer the government their expertise by applying the tools of sociology to legal matters. By promoting an empirical sociology of law, they intended to restore the jurists' lost credibility and make them enlightened guides for legislators. Sociological surveys then became an essential prerequisite for any reform of private law.[6]

Carbonnier first took interest in sociology when he discovered the work of French philosopher Lucien Lévy-Bruhl (father of law professor Henri), who had written *La morale et la science des mœurs* in 1903. Carbonnier was also greatly influenced by Émile Durkheim's writings. Having read Durkheim, Carbonnier was convinced that law could be studied from the outside, that is, from a sociological point of view. The idea that law could be analyzed other than from an internal and dogmatic point of view appeared, at the time, as a major break in legal thought. Alongside Durkheim, who claimed that social facts should be treated as things, Carbonnier, applying this methodological rule to legal science, argued that law, too, could be treated as a thing, subject to outside empirical observation.

Carbonnier's appetite for sociology is visible even in his early works. Yet he really became involved in this field of research from the 1950s onward. Indeed, in 1955, the law faculties' reform led to the creation of a course on sociology of law at the faculty of law in Paris. The minister of higher education, Gaston Berger, immediately thought that Carbonnier, whom he had met in Poitiers, was the perfect candidate to teach this course. Ten years later, in 1965, Georges Gurvitch asked Carbonnier to replace him in teaching sociology of

[6] For this postwar high point of legal sociology, see Francine Soubiran-Paillet, "Juristes et sociologues français d'après-guerre: une rencontre sans lendemain," *Genèses* 41, no. 1 (2000): 125–42; and Antoine Vauchez, "'Quand les juristes faisaient la loi…' Le moment Carbonnier (1963–1977), son histoire et son mythe," *Parlement[s]. Revue d'histoire politique* 11 (2009): 105–16.

law at the Sorbonne. Carbonnier took this role until 1967, before agreeing to teach sociology of law to PhD students, from 1968 to 1976. Carbonnier was a major actor in the institutionalization of sociology of law, which then became a visible discipline within law schools. His textbook *Sociologie juridique* (1972) is based on his teachings.

Outside of legal education, he became a board member of the Durkheimian journal *L'Année sociologique* in 1962, before serving as president of the board at Gabriel Le Bras's request, replacing Henri Lévy-Bruhl, who had passed away in 1964. He also became codirector of the *Sociologie juridique et morale* book-review section.[7] Thus, Carbonnier managed to have an audience in the worlds of both general sociology and legal scholarship. But this double acquaintance is not the sole explanation for the flourishing of his sociology of law. Its success is also due to Carbonnier's promoting a very concrete form of sociology, unlike his predecessors, who, like Léon Duguit, Maurice Hauriou, or Gurvitch, had been developing a rather speculative sociology of law.

Indeed, in 1964, Carbonnier and Georges Levasseur created a research center dedicated to the sociology of law (*Laboratoire de sociologie criminelle et juridique*). The Ministry of Justice allocated funds to the center for Carbonnier to develop a program of sociology applied to legislation (*sociologie législative*).[8] Those empirical researches led to the liberalization of family law in the 1960s and 1970s, thanks to the use of opinion-polling techniques, which allowed the government to bring the laws into conformity with the thinking of mid-twentieth-century society. Far from wanting to reflect theoretically upon sociolegal matters, Carbonnier intended to build an efficient instrument that could serve the French legislator. Those reforms also incorporated statistical surveys, especially regarding matrimonial and inheritance practices (special issues of the scientific journal *Sondages* in 1967 and 1970). For example, Carbonnier published a short article in 1964 in *L'Année sociologique*, titled "Un essai de statistique de la répartition des régimes matrimoniaux à la veille de la réforme de 1965" (443–49). It was the first French statistical survey on matrimonial practices since 1898. Such studies shed light on the diversity of social life and took into account variables of age, gender, location, educational attainment, and social class. The methodology also offered a way to measure

[7] For Jean Carbonnier's involvement in *L'Année sociologique*, see François Terré, "Jean Carbonnier et *L'Année sociologique*," *L'Année sociologique* 57, no. 2 (2007): 555–69.

[8] For *sociologie législative*, see Jean-François Perrin, "Jean Carbonnier et la sociologie législative," *L'Année sociologique* 57, no. 2 (2007): 403–15.

the (in)efficiency of laws.[9] This new way of drafting legislation was later followed by other French-speaking countries, especially Switzerland.

This new *légistique* (the art of drafting legislation) went far beyond mere technical issues. It redefined the relationship between law and politics. By acting at the core of legislative power, it met the needs of the Gaullists, who wanted to benefit from direct legitimacy in lieu of the Parliament: *légistique* was about purposely ignoring the traditional filter function of the legal professions, which had claimed to be the sole holders of a legitimate opinion on law.

Carbonnier's practical sociology has suffered from a double criticism. It was first attacked by conservative colleagues of his, who thought he would blindly follow the polls' results. On the contrary, Carbonnier always insisted on the importance of the political and educational role of the law, and was very firm that polls should merely give an indication of the people's state of mind, never dictate the law. On the other side, his *sociologie législative* was also criticized by progressive scholars, who thought Carbonnier's reforms were too modest. This double critique is easily understood by the fact that Carbonnier tried to achieve a compromise between tradition and modernity.

Nevertheless, Carbonnier's practical vision of legal sociology does not mean that he did not reflect theoretically upon this discipline. In *Flexible droit*, Carbonnier advances what he calls the two fundamental theorems of legal sociology. The first theorem states that law is wider than its formal sources. From a sociological point of view, law should not be restricted to its formal sources but must take into account what François Gény called the *sources réelles du droit* [real sources of law], which contribute to the making of law: history, natural law, economics, social facts, etc. According to Carbonnier (following Eugen Erlich), law's true center of gravity lies within society itself, not in the legal system. Therefore, jurists, when seeking to go beyond formalism, ought to try to find the social facts lying below the legal system. The mistake of the early twentieth-century legal scholars was to look for social reality only by studying jurisprudence. On the contrary, Carbonnier stresses that judicial life and litigation only represent what he calls the "sick part of law," and therefore a tiny part of it, meaning by that that the mere existence of a trial proves that law has failed to organise social relationships properly. In his eyes, social reality does not lie solely in the courts' decisions but should be apprehended more broadly by studying law in everyday life with the tools of

[9] Jean Carbonnier, "Effectivité et ineffectivité de la règle de droit," *L'Année sociologique*, 3rd series (1957–58): 3–17. This famous and important article was later republished in *Flexible droit*.

legal sociology. In other words, one should also analyze the sound part of law, not only the sick part that leads to trials.

The second theorem states that law is smaller than human relationships. Carbonnier reacted strongly against the jurists' tendency to see law everywhere, in each interstice of social life. This second hypothesis is linked to Carbonnier's conception of law, and was greatly influenced by his faith.

JEAN CARBONNIER'S CONCEPTION OF LAW

Jean Carbonnier was born into a Catholic family, so his becoming a Protestant is the result of a personal choice, even if his father may have played a part in this conversion.[10] Carbonnier's father was an oppositional kind of Catholic, and mostly a Jansenist, sharing many views with Calvinists (on, for example, the role of the Bible, individualism, pessimism, moral austerity, and the doctrine of predestination). Yet Carbonnier's Calvinist faith mainly resulted from his intimate knowledge of the Bible, which led him to learn Hebrew in Bordeaux in the 1930s while writing his PhD dissertation.[11]

According to Carbonnier himself, religious action was one of his four professional concerns, alongside legal sociology, his work as a dogmatic scholar, and his legislative work.[12] His faith was fully part of his life: he assumed several responsabilities in Protestant institutions. From 1960 to 2003, Carbonnier was the curator of the Musée du Désert (a small village of the Cévennes, where Protestants used to take shelter under the hostile reign of Louis XIV[13]), in which the greatest gathering of French Protestants takes place each September. From 1961 to 2003, he was a member of the council of the Fédération Protestante de France. Moreover, he was vice president of the Société de l'Histoire du Protestantisme Français from 1965 to 1990 and was

[10] For an overview of Carbonnier's faith, see André Dumas, "Carbonnier, Jean," in *Dictionnaire du monde religieux de la France contemporaine. 5. Les Protestants*, edn. André Encrevé (Paris: Beauchesne, 1993), 115–16; and Patrick Cabanel, "Carbonnier, Jean," in *Dictionnaire biographique des protestants français de 1787 à nos jours* (vol. 1), edn. Société de l'histoire du protestantisme français, Patrick Cabanel and André Encrevé (Paris: Les éditions de paris Max Chaleil, 2015), 565–66.

[11] Marie-Thérèse Meulders-Klein, "Jean Carbonnier, l'homme, la foi et le droit," in *Hommage à Jean Carbonnier*, edn. Jean Beauchard, Alain Bénabent, and Pierre Catala (Paris: Dalloz, 2007), 84.

[12] Andrini and Arnaud, *Archéologie d'une discipline*, 61.

[13] In 1681, Louis XIV instituted the "Dragonnades," a French government policy intended to intimidate Huguenot families into either leaving France or reconverting to Catholicism.

part of the Committee on Legal Affairs of the Reformed Church of France.[14] Not only did Carbonnier actively participate in the life of the Reformed Church of France, but he also was the author of several papers on the history of the Protestant religion, on Calvin, and on theology. Among this prolific literature,[15] his most famous religious writing is *Coligny ou les sermons imaginaires. Lecture pour le protestantisme français d'aujourd'hui* (1982). In 1993, he also translated an 1806 play in relation with the history of the Protestant religion, written by Isaak von Sinclair: *La fin de la guerre des Cévennes. Drame romantique allemand.* Carbonnier's tireless devotion to Protestantism won him the title of doctor *honoris causa* of the faculty of Protestant theology of the University of Montpellier in 1989.

Carbonnier thought that the state and the church should be separated. This is not surprising, since Protestant jurists from the sixteenth century on favored secularization of the law. According to Luther's doctrine of the two kingdoms, which deeply influenced Carbonnier, faith should be separated from law. Law being the affair of men, not of God, there is no revealed law, so to speak. Carbonnier was accordingly much attached to secularism in the legal field – for example, in matrimonial law. For him, civil marriage since the admission of civil marriage for Protestants in 1787 by the Edict of Tolerance, was a key victory for minority religions. Indeed, one of Carbonnier's main concerns was the survival of religious minorities.[16] He was very eager to understand the legal persecution of the Protestants during the French Wars of Religion of the sixteenth century, and he wrote extensively about this period of history. He particularly wanted to understand the Edict of Fontainebleau (1685), the revocation of the previous Edict of Nantes (1598), which had put an end to the wars of religion by granting religious freedom to Protestants in France. The Edict of Fontainebleau appeared to him a major historical event, as important as the French Revolution. The date of the edict played an important role in Carbonnier's thought, inasmuch as it led him to reflect upon legal persecution and tolerance.[17] Indeed, in his notes on several judicial decisions,

[14] "Jean Carbonnier (1908–2003). Biographie établie par Marianne Carbonnier en février 2008," in *Jean Carbonnier. L'homme et l'œuvre*, edn. Raymond Verdier (Paris: Presses Universitaires de Paris Ouest, 2014), 688.

[15] A list of his religion-centered publications can be found in *Hommage à Jean Carbonnier*, edn. Jean Beauchard, Alain Bénabent and Pierre Catala (Paris: Dalloz, 2007), 230–32.

[16] Pierre-Yves Gautier, "Foi et droit. L'exemple de Jean Carbonnier," in ibid., 74–79.

[17] Christian Biet, "Carbonnier et les Camisards: la foi, la loi et la littérature," in *Jean Carbonnier. L'homme et l'œuvre*, edn. Raymond Verdier (Paris: Presses Universitaires de Paris Ouest, 2014), 189.

Carbonnier often took strong positions in favor of freedom of conscience and secularism, a subject he was very sensitive to.[18]

Even if he separated law from religion, it has often been noticed that, broadly speaking, Carbonnier's conception of law was much influenced by his faith, in at least two ways. First, it has often been remarked that his vision of law was *pessimistic*, from an anthropological point of view. According to the Lutheran doctrine of the two kingdoms, the Protestant Reformation freed religion from law by making law a purely human matter. Therefore, law, like humanity itself, is corrupted and sinful.[19] Yet law is absolutely necessary, lest the world destroy itself. Even if Carbonnier was convinced of the central role of the Decalogue and of the perfection of divine law, he was also fully aware that human laws can only work towards doing the good, but that good itself is variable. Law is full of contradictions and discord. Therefore, the jurist can only admit that his action is, in essence, limited. This explains why Jean Carbonnier always claimed that law should restrict itself and be modest, as his whole theory of the nonlaw (*non-droit*) shows.[20]

This is indeed one of Carbonnier's main ideas, influenced by Calvin: the state should avoid making laws whenever possible. Humanity being corrupted, human laws are a necessary evil. One is compelled to promote other kinds of normativities, such as morality or friendship, for instance. Carbonnier's most famous theory is that of the nonlaw (*non-droit*),[21] a concept influenced by religion and philosophy, dictated by a pessimistic vision of humankind and society. This concept does not refer to the absence or inefficiency of human laws: *non-droit* means that social life is wider than law, and that nonlegal

[18] Marianne Carbonnier-Burkard, "Note liminaire à la Table ronde du colloque 'Jean Carbonnier, le droit, les sciences humaines, sociales et religieuses,'" in ibid., 114–15.

[19] Martin Luther, *Œuvres*, vol. 2 (Paris: Gallimard, 2017). This idea is developed in the chapter entitled "Temporal Authority: To What Extent it Should be Obeyed? (1523)". On Carbonnier vision of this doctrine, see Thierry Revet, "Jean Carbonnier et la spiritualité," in *Hommage à Jean Carbonnier*, edn. Jean Beauchard, Alain Bénabent and Pierre Catala (Paris: Dalloz, 2007), 101.

[20] François Terré, "Jean Carbonnier, conservateur ou moderniste?" in *Jean Carbonnier. L'homme et l'œuvre*, edn. Raymond Verdier (Paris: Presses Universitaires de Paris Ouest, 2014), 425.

[21] On the *non-droit* theory, see André-Jean Arnaud, "Non-droit," in *Dictionnaire encyclopédique de théorie et de sociologie du droit*, edn. André-Jean Arnaud (Paris: LGDJ, 1988), 389–90; Alain Sériaux, "Question controversée: la théorie du non-droit," *Revue de la recherche juridique. Droit prospectif* 1 (1995): 13–30; Francesco Saverio Nisio, *Jean Carbonnier. Regards sur le droit et le non-droit* (Paris: Dalloz, 2005); and Gilda Nicolau, "La théorie du non-droit," in *Jean Carbonnier. L'homme et l'œuvre*, edn. Raymond Verdier (Paris: Presses Universitaires de Paris Ouest, 2014), 377–406.

systems of regulation exist to complete the laws. As Carbonnier states it, the *non-droit* is "the absence of law in a number of human relationships where law could theoretically have been present."[22] Therefore, *non-droit* means that humanity might not even need law at all. Carbonnier criticized what he called *panjurisme* (panlegalism), meaning the attitude of jurists who see law everywhere, enmeshed in every detail of everyday life. He voiced strong criticisms of the inflation of legislative texts typical of the French Fifth Republic. He was equally suspicious of *nomophilie* (the passion for laws), which he thought led to too much rationalism and uniformity and, eventually, to a kind of legislative paternalism.[23] In brief, Carbonnier stood in favor of an attitude of *legislative continence*. According to him, law is only an iceberg on the surface of social relationships. In a given society, the rules of conduct are usually much wider than law. What is important, regarding the *non-droit*, is the move from law towards the *non-droit*, namely the idea that law should abandon certain fields it was meant to occupy. The *non-droit* is therefore the withdrawal of the law.

Secondly, Carbonnier's conception of law has often been depicted as *pluralist*, influenced in this regard by both Georges Gurvitch and Eugen Ehrlich, even if he declined to follow all their conclusions. In his eyes, pluralism exists whenever, individually or collectively, a nonstate body of rules can be observed. Numerous jurisdictions thus produce their own regulation, both below the level of the state (trade unions, associations, public limited companies, churches, public administrations) and above it (the European Union, the United Nations). Carbonnier distinguishes between collective and individual aspects of legal pluralism. First, as a collective phenomenon, legal pluralism is a synonym of acculturation, as when a foreign culture encounters a local one. For instance, the colonial world, according to Carbonnier, is a perfect example of two legal cultures making contact. The legal acculturation that follows translates into legal pluralism. The two legal cultures (the foreign culture of a state body of laws contrary to the native legal culture) are then in conflict. In the eyes of sociologists, argues Carbonnier, both legal cultures are to be treated on the same level, whereas for "dogmatic jurists," the law of the state prevails. Further, legal pluralism can also be

[22] Jean Carbonnier, "Droit et non-droit," in Jean Carbonnier, *Flexible droit. Pour une sociologie du droit sans rigueur* (Paris: LGDJ/Lextenso éditions, 2014), 26.

[23] Jean-François Niort, "Jean Carbonnier, une philosophie juridique de la tolérance," in *Tolérance, pluralisme et histoire,* edn. Paul Dumouchel and Bjarne Melkevik (Paris: L'Harmattan, 1998), 195.

experienced from an individual point of view. In this case, it occurs as an internal conflict within the individual – for instance, when one experiences a conflict between a religious and a secular law, leading one to become a conscientious objector. In such cases, conscientious objection can be defined as the collision of two legal systems within the individual conscience.

Carbonnier's conception of pluralism has been criticized, inasmuch as pluralism makes sense only if those nonstate regulations lie outside the legal system. If they lie within the system, can one talk about pluralism any longer? In any case, Carbonnier terms such nonstate regulations the "infralaw" (*infra-droit*). According to him, the infralaw, being the emanation of subcultures, can be defined as phenomena that, like mores, resemble legal regulations enough to constitute an autonomous body of rules not sanctioned by the state. Carbonnier borrows this concept from Gurvitch. In Carbonnier's thought, it refers, for instance, to folk law, children's law, or common law. The infralaw, therefore, refers to all the legal systems parallel to state law.

Moreover, his pluralism has a second meaning. It is linked to his Protestant faith, which led him to a spirit of tolerance and civil peace. Even if he was very attached to the idea of a common law applicable to all French citizens, and believed that without common principles of justice, freedom would turn into chaos, he was also willing to give citizens as much freedom as possible regarding civil law. In his view, morals are a determining factor of law, and the legislator should take them into account. This is why Carbonnier, while working on the reform of family law in the 1960s and 1970s, acknowledged that French family patterns had evolved and were plural.

One example of Carbonnier's pluralism is the 1975 reform of divorce, which recognized several causes of marriage breakdown: not only on grounds of fault, but henceforth on account of a breakdown of cohabitation and, more importantly, by mutual consent. This liberalization of divorce law illustrates the fact that law is no longer at the service of a unique social pattern but accepts the coexistence of several family patterns. As Carbonnier stated, French civil law should be a law of peaceful and legal coexistence, meant to grant individuals enough room to organize their family life as they wish. This freedom granted by the law to invididuals has to be, according to Carbonnier, accompanied by the judge, whose function is to adjudicate on individual situations.[24] Therefore, genuine pluralism, in his eyes, is mainly to be found in jurisprudence and in the way laws are applied by judges.

[24] Ibid., 197–98.

CONCLUSION

In the eyes of many, Jean Carbonnier has become almost mythic, embodying the greatness of French civil law during the French Fifth Republic. Every first-year law student knows the name of this renowned jurist, who has often been called a modern Portalis (father of the French Civil Code). His sociology of law had a strong impact in Italy and Canada, and he benefited from an international reputation. Much has been written about Carbonnier, but this literature is of variable quality: most of it is merely hagiographical, and very few are the authors who have tried to discuss his ideas in depth. Moreover, even fewer articles are written by legal historians willing to undertake serious historical study of Carbonnier's contribution to French legal science. Carbonnier's thought is complex, because of the multiple cultural references on which it builds (philosophy, law, history, theology, and sociology). Let us hope that this gap will soon be filled, when historians will have access to his personal archives. Even though an autofiction was published posthumously in 2011,[25] Jean Carbonnier still awaits his biographer.

RECOMMENDED READING

Abel, Olivier. *Paul Ricoeur, Jacques Ellul, Jean Carbonnier, Pierre Chaunu: dialogues*. Genève: Labor et Fides, 2012.

Andrini, Simona, and André-Jean Arnaud. *Jean Carbonnier, Renato Treves et la sociologie du droit. Archéologie d'une discipline*. Paris: LGDJ, 1995.

L'Année sociologique 57, no. 2 (2007) (special issue dedicated to Jean Carbonnier).

Arnaud, André-Jean. *Critique de la raison juridique. 1. Où va la sociologie du droit ?* Paris: LGDJ, 1981.

"Non-droit." In *Dictionnaire encyclopédique de théorie et de sociologie du droit*, edited by André-Jean Arnaud, et al., 389–90. Paris: LGDJ, 1988.

"Carbonnier, Jean (1908–2003)." In *Encyclopedia of Law & Society: American and Global Perspectives*. Vol. 1, edited by David S. Clark, 158–60. Los Angeles, London: Sage Publications, 2007.

Jean Carbonnier. Un juriste dans la cité. Paris: LGDJ, 2012.

Beauchard, Jean, Alain Bénabent, and Pierre Catala, eds. *Hommage à Jean Carbonnier*. Paris: Dalloz, 2007.

Cabanel, Patrick. "Carbonnier, Jean." In *Dictionnaire biographique des protestants français de 1787 à nos jours*. Vol. 1, edited by the Société de l'histoire du protestantisme français, Patrick Cabanel, and André Encrevé, 565–66. Paris: Les éditions de Paris Max Chaleil, 2015.

[25] Jean Carbonnier, *Les incertitudes du jeune Saxon. Une autofiction de Jean Carbonnier*, edited by Anne Teissier-Esmeiger (Paris: LexisNexis, 2011).

Carbonnier, Jean. "Le régime matrimonial, sa nature juridique sous le rapport des notions de société et d'association." PhD thesis, University of Bordeaux, 1932.

Manuel de droit civil. 5 vols: *Introduction; Les personnes; La famille; Les biens; Les obligations*. Paris: PUF, 1955; last edn in two volumes, 2004.

"Effectivité et ineffectivité de la règle de droit." *L'Année sociologique*, 3rd series (1957–58): 3–17.

Flexible droit. Pour une sociologie du droit sans rigueur. 10th edn. Paris: LGDJ/ Lextenso éditions, 2014.

Sociologie juridique. Paris: Armand Colin, 1972; 3rd edn, 1994.

Essais sur les lois. Paris: Répertoire Defrenois, 1979; 3rd edn, 2005.

Coligny ou les sermons imaginaires. Paris: PUF, 1982.

"Le Code civil des Français dans la mémoire collective." In *Les lieux de mémoire. La Nation*, edited by Pierre Nora, 293–315. Paris: Gallimard, 1986.

Droit et passion du droit sous la Ve République. Paris: Flammarion, 1996.

Les incertitudes du jeune Saxon. Une autofiction de Jean Carbonnier. Edited by Anne Teissier-Esmeinger. Paris, LexisNexis, 2011.

De Vita, Anna, edn. *Giornata in onore di Jean Carbonnier, 13 ottobre 2000*. Turin: G. Giappichelli Editore, 2004.

Douchy, Mélina. "La notion de non-droit." *Droit prospectif. Revue de la recherche juridique* 49, no. 2 (1992): 433–76.

Dumas, André. "Carbonnier, Jean." In *Dictionnaire du monde religieux de la France contemporaine. 5. Les Protestants*, edited by André Encrevé, 115–16. Paris: Beauchesne, 1993.

"Entretien avec le doyen Carbonnier. Sociologie juridique et crise du droit." *Droits. Revue française de théorie juridique* 4 (1986): 65–73.

Guerlain, Laetitia. "67. Observations sous *Flexible droit. Pour une sociologie du droit sans rigueur* (1969) de Jean Carbonnier." In *Les grands discours de la culture juridique*, edited by Julie Benetti, Pierre Egéa, Xavier Magnon, and Wanda Mastor, 830–39. Paris: Dalloz, 2017.

Luther, Martin. *Œuvres*. Vol. 2. Paris: Gallimard, 2017.

Malaurie, Philippe. "Carbonnier, Jean. Libourne (Gironde) 1908." In *Anthologie de la pensée juridique*, edited by Philippe Malaurie, 281–86. Paris: 1996.

Niort, Jean-François. "Jean Carbonnier, une philosophie juridique de la tolérance." In *Tolérance, pluralisme et histoire*, edited by Paul Dumouchel and Bjarne Melkevik, 197–98. Paris: L'Harmattan, 1998.

"*Flexible droit*." In *Dictionnaire des grandes œuvres juridiques*, edited by Olivier Cayla and Jean-Louis Halpérin, 77–82. Paris: Dalloz, 2008.

"Carbonnier, Jean." In *Dictionnaire historique des juristes français, XIIe–XXe siècle*, edited by Patrick Arabeyre, Jean-Louis Halpérin, and Jacques Krynen, 207–09. 2nd edn. Paris: PUF, 2015.

Nisio, Francesco Saverio. *Jean Carbonnier. Regards sur le droit et le non-droit*. Paris: Dalloz, 2005.

"Paroles de Jean Carbonnier. Propos retranscrits par Raymond Verdier." *Droit et cultures* 48 (2004): 231–51.

Sériaux, Alain. "Question controversée: la théorie du non-droit." *Revue de la recherche juridique. Droit prospectif* 1 (1995): 13–30.

Soubiran-Paillet, Francine. "Juristes et sociologues français d'après-guerre: une rencontre sans lendemain." *Genèses* 41, no. 1 (2000): 125–42.

Terré, François. "Jean Carbonnier 1908–2003." *Archives de philosophie du droit* 48 (2004): 1–7.

Vauchez, Antoine. "'Quand les juristes faisaient la loi… '. Le moment Carbonnier (1963–1977), son histoire et son mythe." *Parlement[s]. Revue d'histoire politique* 11 (2009): 105–16.

Verdier, Raymond, edn. *Jean Carbonnier. Écrits*. Paris: PUF, 2008.

edn. *Jean Carbonnier. L'homme et l'œuvre*. Paris: Presses universitaires de Paris Ouest, 2011.

Von Sinclair, Isaak. *La fin de la guerre des Cévennes. Drame romantique allemand*. Translated by Jean Carbonnier. Montpellier: Les Presses du Languedoc, 1993.

27

Michel Villey

(1914–1988)

LUISA BRUNORI

BIOGRAPHICAL INTRODUCTION

Michel Villey was born in Caen (Normandy) in 1914, into an intellectual and cultured family. He was the grandchild of Edmond Villey, economist and dean of the faculty of law of Caen. He was also the grandchild of the Catholic neo-Kantian philosopher Émile Boutroux. Michel's father, Pierre Villey, was an eminent specialist in sixteenth-century literature, and his uncle was the prestigious polymath Henri Poincaré. His brothers Daniel and Raymond, respectively an economist and a doctor, were his interlocutors in a deep and constant dialogue throughout Michel Villey's life.

A music lover, to the question, "Why did you become interested in philosophy of law?" he once replied, "Because I wanted to be a musician. But my mother didn't allow it."[1] His father's blindness and Michel's love for music are perhaps the deep roots of his constant rejection of formalistic categorizations and *more geometrico* legal structures, as well as his incessant investigation into legal phenomena and the search for substantial justice as the ultimate goal of law.

Villey obtained a PhD in law in 1942, defending a thesis on "*La croisade: essai sur la formation d'une théorie juridique*" (The Crusade: Essay on the Formation of a Legal Theory)[2] under the supervision of Maurice Grandclaude. After a stay in Saigon, in 1949 Villey was appointed full professor at the faculty of law of Strasbourg, and then in 1961 at the University of Paris,

[1] François Vallançon, "Réflexion Biographiques sur Michel Villey," *Droits* 29 (1999): 119–24, at 119.

[2] Michel Villey, *La croisade. Essai sur la formation d'une théorie juridique*, L'Église et l'État au Moyen Âge 6 (Paris: Vrin, 1942).

where he remained until the end of his career. There he created with Henri Batiffol and Charles Eisenmann the Centre de Philosophie du Droit, which became the Institut Michel Villey pour la Culture Juridique et la Philosophie du Droit in 1998. In 1956 he succeeded Henri Motulsky as head of the journal *Archives de philosophie du droit*, still a reference today for the French legal philosophy community. Villey died in 1988, leaving unfinished a work on St Thomas Aquinas.

Michel Villey was the professor par excellence ("*toute sa carrière a été professorale*"[3]): polyglot, highly cultured, very much appreciated for his pedagogical talent and his commitment to the university, he always put his role as teacher before that of author.[4] His Catholicism came from a family tradition and represents the root of his opposition to the individualism and positivism of modern society,[5] one of the most important facets of Villey's thinking. Indeed, with the lively frankness that distinguished him, Villey constantly expressed harsh criticism towards the various forms of "modern legal thought," with objections to formalism, "unique thinking," and intellectual fashions. Actually, Villey's incessant struggle against the idols of his epoch is one of the most significant aspects of the philosopher's Christianity.[6] And "the list of idols is long," stresses Stéphane Rilas.[7]

Nevertheless, Michel Villey never ceased to dialogue with the legal philosophers of his time, notably Chaïm Perelman, Georges Kalinowski, Jean-Louis Gardies, and his French colleagues, among whom we find Henri Batiffol, Jean-Philippe Levy, Jean Gaudemet,[8] Jean Carbonnier,[9] Philippe Malaurie, and François Terré.[10]

Drawing from the observation that "the French jurist is considered to be rather allergic to the philosophy of law," Villey started drafting in the 1970s two texts for his students, *Définitions et fins du droit* (Definitions and Purposes of Law) and *Les moyens du droit* (The Means of Law), which were compiled, in their most recent versions, in his book *Philosophie du droit*. Despite the

3 Vallançon, "Réflexion biographiques sur Michel Villey," 123.
4 Sylvain Piron, "Congé à Villey," *L'Atelier du Centre de recherches historiques* [online] (uploaded November 18, 2008), accessed March 1, 2018, journals.openedition.org/acrh/314, p. 6.
5 Ibid., passim.
6 Stéphane Rials, *Villey et les idoles: petite introduction à la philosophie du droit de Michel Villey* (Paris: PUF, 1999).
7 Ibid., 26.
8 On Jean Gaudemet, see pp. 422, 424 and 431.
9 See Chapter 26.
10 Vallançon, "Réflexion Biographiques sur Michel Villey," 122.

high-sounding title (chosen by the publishers), in line with the author's style, it is a rather sober volume that collects Villey's main ideas.

Indeed, Villey's production is not extremely extensive, but in addition to the books edited by Villey himself, several studies, university courses, speeches delivered on various occasions, and his personal remarks in the notebooks he always carried with him have been published, thanks to the commitment of his colleagues and students. His works have been widely translated and disseminated abroad, countless conferences have been organized on his work, and many publications – monographs, collections of studies, theses – have been dedicated to his thought.

INFLUENCES AND METHODS

Villey's constant commitment to dialogue and dialogical methods guided his work, to the point of considering dialectics, understood as consideration of different positions, as the very essence of law.[11] Deeply consistent with the methodology of his two main references, Aristotle and Thomas Aquinas, Villey adopted a dialectical methodology in the analysis of legal phenomena.[12] This led Paul Dubouchet to use the term "negative epistemology" to indicate Villey's rejection of epistemological formalism and his approach to humanities as exact sciences,[13] and for Stéphane Rials to talk about the "'*pluralisme méthodologique*" of Michel Villey.[14] For Villey, "true method" bends to reality and recognizes its elusive mystery, so that thought, bending to the object, can only surround reality through controversy and dialectic.[15] According to Villey, that is precisely the great merit of Aristotle's approach to law: he analyzes the complexity of reality without bowing to a fixed and immutable law, and he trusts legal practice (in particular that of judges) in identifying what is just in various specific circumstances.[16] "Villey's Aristotelianism leads him to revisit St. Thomas, and also the whole erudite medieval experience, as a dialectical

[11] "The good use of dialogue" is the subtitle of Villey's book *Questions de Saint Thomas sur le droit et la politique* (Paris: PUF, 1987).

[12] Michel Bastit, "Un vivant aristotélicien: Michel Villey," *Droits* 29 (1999): 55–70.

[13] Paul Dubouchet, *Critique du droit chez Michel Villey et René Girard. Pour une épistémologie négative* (Paris: L'Harmattan, 2016).

[14] Rials, *Villey et les idoles*, 62.

[15] Michel Villey, *Réflexions sur la philosophie et le droit. Les Carnets*, posthumous edition prepared by M.-A. Frison-roche and C. Jamin, preface by B. Kriegel and F. Terré (Paris: PUF, 1995), book 10, n. 115; see also Daniel Gutmann, "Michel Villey, le nominalisme et le volontarisme," *Droits* 29 (1999): 89–104, at 95.

[16] Michel Villey, *La formation de la pensée juridique moderne*, 1st edn (Paris: PUF, 2003), 59–60; Bastit, "Un vivant aristotélicien," 68.

research," providing a reading of Aquinas much more Aristotelian than it is currently in fashion.[17]

It is indeed clear that Villey's thought on law was constantly nourished by his reflection on the history of legal thought. His works, even when they are strictly philosophical, often follow a chronological plan.[18] Endowed with a vast culture, perfectly at ease in Latin, Villey used legal history to demonstrate the progressive loss of the empirical and dialogical spirit of Roman law to achieve a supine veneration of law as the formal expression of self-styled human will. He develops this thesis, breaking with the idea, inherited from the nineteenth century, of a discontinuity with the Renaissance from the Middle Ages. Villey shows the continuity between the last medieval Scholastics (notably Duns Scotus and William of Ockham), the scholastics of the modern era (especially Suárez), and the first great modern political thinkers. According to Villey, in this continuum one can read the progressive imposition of law as an expression of a superior and external will, no longer as an intrinsic order in things. It does not matter whether Hobbes, Locke, and the other modern philosophers had secularized the thinking of the theological jurists of the Baroque era, since the result was in any case a "theology of law" for which the Second Scholasticism of the sixteenth century would be highly responsible.[19] This criticism of legalism – that is, of the veneration of law as a formal entity – is another pillar of Villey's thought. The fight against the "idolatry" of law[20] was one of Villey's constant battles. It is not surprising, then, that Villey harshly criticized Hans Kelsen, whom he considered the culmination of this exaltation of the will of the legislator. Villey's denunciation of modern idolatry, in the end, was not just restricted to law (understood in a formalist and absolute sense) but referred also to a "deification of Man" leading to the "great heresy" of human rights.[21]

From an epistemological point of view, the *Questions de Saint Thomas sur le droit et la politique* (Questions of Saint Thomas on Law and Politics, 1987) is of fundamental importance because it synthesizes Villey's criticism of law,

[17] Bastit, "Un vivant aristotélicien," 70.

[18] "In Villey the historian did not escape the philosopher, and the philosopher was nourished by the historian's discoveries": Gutmann, "Michel Villey, le nominalisme et le volontarisme," 89.

[19] Michel Villey, "La promotion de la loi et du droit subjectif dans la Seconde Scolastique," in Paolo Grossi (ed.), *La Seconda Scolastica nella formazione del diritto privato moderno* (Milano: Giuffré, 1973), 53–71, at 55; Franco Todescan, "Michel Villey et la Seconde Scolastique," *Droit & Philosophie* 8 (2016): 33–75.

[20] Villey writes about "La réligion de la loi" in *Philospohie du droit*, 276–86; see Rials, *Villey et les idoles*, 10.

[21] Rials, *Villey et les idoles*, 18.

philosophy, and the humanities.[22] The privileged role occupied by the legal doctrine of St Thomas within the thought of Villey implies that the entire doctrine of Aquinas, including the most theological and sacred, is an integral part of Villey's thinking. His main criticisms of the attitude of modern law are developed on the basis of this theological–legal background; thus follow the clear denunciations of the erroneous distinction between "being" and "ought to be," of a mistaken opposition between "theoretical reason" and "practical reason," and of the defective articulation of the particular and the universal in modern legal conceptions.[23] These epistemological faults led to deviations in the contents of law for which the successors of St Thomas are responsible, since, according to Villey, it is the same Thomism that betrayed St Thomas by causing these profound misunderstandings and inaugurating the attitude of modern legal thought that privileges analytical approach at the expense of the dialectical approach.[24]

Some scholars have questioned Villey's historical analyses: one can adhere to the author's theses concerning the formation of legal thought only by accepting *a priori* his main thesis on the fundamental division between classical natural law and modern thought, situated by Villey in the thought of William of Ockham.[25] In addition, according to Villey, it is from Ockham's philosophy that the notion of "subjective right" emerged: for some scholars this is an assertion that is difficult to verify and contested by some as a too rigid view of the evolution of the concept.[26]

Concerning Villey's method of analysis, Brian Tierney and Yan Thomas (among others) have pointed out that Villey deliberately selected certain doctrinal texts of medieval and Roman law and then constructed an overall interpretative theory, purposely leaving aside any theory that did not fit into the paradigm thus created.[27]

[22] Dubouchet, *Critique du droit chez Michel Villey et René Girard*, 85.

[23] Ibid., 86.

[24] Michel Villey, *Questions de Saint Thomas sur le droit et la politique* (Paris: PUF, 1987); Michel Bastit, "Villey et Perelman: argumentation avec ou sans ontologie?" *Droit & Philosophie* 8 (2016): 75–89.

[25] Piron, "Congé à Villey," passim.

[26] Annabel S. Brett, *Liberty, Right and Nature: Individual Rights in Later Scholastic Thought* (Cambridge: Cambridge University Press, 1997); Brian Tierney, *The Idea of Natural Rights: Studies on Natural Rights, Natural Law, and Church Law, 1150–1600* (Atlanta, GA: Scholars Press, 1997).

[27] Brian Tierney, "Villey, Ockham, and the Origin of Natural Rights," in John Witte, Jr. and Frank S. Alexander (eds.), *The Weightier Matters of Law: Essays on Law and Religion* (Atlanta, GA: Scholars Press, 1988), 1–31; and Tierney, *The Idea of Natural Rights*, 13–42; Yan Thomas, "Michel Villey, la romanistique et le droit romain," *Droit, nature, histoire*, IVe Colloque de l'Association Française de Philosophie du Droit, Université de Paris II, November 23–24, 1984

VILLEY'S THOUGHT

Regarding Villey's intellectual project, Sylvain Piron has stated that it cannot be described other than as a "Christian philosophy which does not openly say its name," applied only to the question of law; and even within the legal domain, Villey's general considerations on law are articulated via a subordination of human law to Christian revelation.[28] This project is explicitly inspired by St Thomas but is not without oscillations and tensions.[29]

ROMAN LAW

Almost unexpectedly, after his doctoral thesis, Villey's intellectual development begins with Roman law. In the immediate postwar period, he published *Recherches sur la littérature didactique du droit romain* (Research on the didactic literature of Roman law) and the collection *Le droit romain* in the series *Que sais-je?*[30] Villey's approach to Roman law is to underline the influence of Aristotelianism, rather than Stoicism, on its formation, especially as regards natural law.[31] These first publications on Roman law are in fact the first logical step in Villey's intellectual progression, with the main pillars of subsequent works already in place: the references to Thomas Aquinas and Aristotle, who would later become his favorite authors, and even more clearly, the notion of a contrast between classical law and modern law.[32] Roman law represents for Villey what law should be: dialogical rules, anchored in the reality of things, understood and expressed by juriconsults capable of understanding the balance necessary for each situation. This analysis of Roman law leads Villey to state that in Roman law subjective rights never existed, since

(Aix-Marseille: Presses Universitaires d'Aix-Marseille, 1985), 31–41; Michael P. Zuckert, "'Bringing Philosophy down from the Heavens': Natural Right in the Roman Law," *The Review of Politics* 51 (1989): 70–85.

[28] Piron, "Congé à Villey," 2; Bjarne Melkevik, "Michel Villey e la filosofia del diritto: una lettura di *Les Carnets*," *Rivista internazionale di filosofia del diritto* 83, no. 3 (2006): 487–514.

[29] Marie-France Renoux-Zagamé mentions an "Augustinian temptation" in Villey, especially in the *Carnets*, "Michel Villey et l'Augustinisme: les questions des *Carnets*," *Droits* 14 (1999): 71–87, at 80; "Michel Villey's relationship to philosophy thus appears as a strange mixture of sharpness and wave. Of asserted position and uncertainty," says Pierre-François Moreau, in "Michel Villey et les philosophes," *Droit & Philosophie* 8 (2016): 89–103, at 103.

[30] Michel Villey, *Recherches sur littérature didactique du droit romain (À propos d'un texte de Cicéron "De Oratore" 1 – 188 à 190)* (Paris: Montchrestien, 1945); Villey, *Le droit romain*, Que sais-je? 195 (Paris: PUF, 1945).

[31] Michel Villey, "Deux conceptions du droit naturel dans l'antiquité," *Revue d'histoire du droit français et étranger* 31 (1953): 475–97; Villey, *La formation*, 103–06.

[32] Piron, "Congé à Villey," 8.

they are considered instead a subsequent elaboration starting in the Late Empire and perfected by Cartesianism in modern times.[33] Thus begins the long investigation of law, subjective right, and natural law that will be one of the touchstones of Villey's thought.

LAW, NATURAL LLAW, INDIVIDUAL RIGHTS, AND HUMAN RIGHTS

The notion of natural law is one of the aspects of Villey's thought that are closest to Aristotle: law cannot and must not be limited to positive law, since human law is animated by a more intimate and natural reality. Law is born the same way as everything else: from nature, which is its cause. In particular, Villey joins Aristotle on a specific point of this axiom and draws legal consequences from it: nature is not immobile but variable, in constant movement; one can only recognize the variability of the laws of nature.[34] Consequently, natural law is not absolute and unchanging; on the contrary, the variability of legal institutions is the necessary reflection of natural law. Since nature is made up of a multitude of particularities, law therefore must correspond to these particularities.[35] For this reason, Villey's thought on natural law is associated with a veneration of classical law, in particular Roman law, *l'exemple romain*,[36] in which to express the "law" is to state "what is just" in the reality of things, not in the abstraction of a fossilized law.

This "classical" approach to legal institutions – as the most in harmony with true natural law – appears to Villey to be absolutely called into question by the modern regime of individual rights, understood as powers.[37] Villey gradually put this idea into shape through the writing of his university lectures, brought together in the volume *La formation de la pensée juridique moderne* [The Formation of Modern Legal Thought].[38] These ideas were later completed and developed in *Le droit et les droits de l'hommes* [Law and Human Rights], published in 1983 and considered by some scholars as Villey's philosophical and spiritual testament.[39]

[33] Michel Villey, *Le* 'jus in re' *du droit romain classique au droit moderne. Suivi des fragments pour un dictionnaire du langage des glossateurs* (Paris: Recueil Sirey, 1950); Villey, "Du sens de l'expression *jus in re* en droit romain classique," *Revue internationale des droits de l'antiquité* 3 (1949): 417–36.

[34] Villey, *Philosophie du droit*, 255–57.

[35] Bastit, "Un vivant aristotélicien: Michel Villey," 60–67.

[36] Villey, *Philosophie du droit*, 265–67.

[37] Piron, "Congé à Villey," 2.

[38] Michel Villey, *La formation de la pensée juridique moderne*, 1st edn (Paris: PUF, 2003).

[39] *Encyclopédie philosophique universelle, 3: les œuvres philosophiques, Vol. 2*, edited by Jean-François Mattéi (Paris: PUF, 1992).

According to Villey, the notion of subjective rights comes from an individualistic civilization that views the law from the perspective of the individual. On this point, Villey explicitly contests the position of Jacques Maritain, one of the most important Thomists of the twentieth century.[40] Following on from his *Humanisme Intégral* (1936), Maritain[41] assumed that human rights, expressing the purposes of human nature, were a heritage of Christian and classical thought.[42] Villey judged that, on this point, Maritain had unduly modernized the views of Aquinas, who had never taken an individualistic approach to law.[43] According to Villey, law is a social relationship, not an attribute of a person, nor a set of subjective rights.[44]

This is why Villey complains of the proliferation of "freedom rights" leading to a contradiction, since the affirmation of certain rights clearly implies the denial of other rights. Over the years, Villey increasingly and openly attacked the "religion" of human rights, contesting their "sacred texts," their "founding myths," their "mysteries," their "celebrations," and their "apologists."[45] The responsibility for the construction of the erroneous theory of human rights, according to Villey, dates back much earlier than Maritain and the Declarations of Rights. Taking a historical approach,[46] and with a "*furor* antihumanist,"[47] Villey affirms that the genesis of individualism derives from three factors: Christianity, humanism, and nominalism.

The great error, of which we are victims today, is the confusion made, under the influence of nominalism and voluntarism, introduced by Duns Scotus and William of Ockham,[48] between morality and law. This fatal confusion has a long history, Villey maintained: the "birth of human rights" dates to the fourteenth and fifteenth centuries and is particularly indebted to

[40] See Chapter 23.

[41] Ibid.

[42] Jacques Maritain, *Les droits de l'homme et la loi naturelle* (Paris: Hartmann, 1945).

[43] "Sur la politique de Jacques Maritain (à propos de Gregorio Peces Barba, *Persona, sociedad, estado. Pensamiento social y político de Maritain*, Madrid, Edicusa, 1972)," *Archives de philosophie du droit* 19 (1974): 439–45; Piron, "Congé à Villey," 10.

[44] Gregorio Peces-Barba, "Michel Villey et les droits de l'homme," *Droit et société* 71, no. 1 (2009): 93–100, at 95.

[45] Michel Villey, "Polémique sur les Droits de l'Homme," *Etudes philosophiques* 2 (1986): 191–98.

[46] "The main interest that there is today for a medieval historian to read Michel Villey is to observe the formation of a historiographical myth, endowed with a remarkable capacity of resistance to criticism": Piron, "Congé à Villey," 2; Moreau, "Michel Villey et les philosophes."

[47] Rials, *Villey et les idoles*, 9.

[48] "There would be an indissoluble link between nominalism and voluntarism, a link Villey wishes to underline as important": Gutmann, "Michel Villey, le nominalisme et le volontarisme," 89.

Ockham and Scotus.[49] But, according to Villey, it was above all the Second Scholastics of the sixteenth century who were responsible for the harmful diffusion of the ambiguous and sly notion of "subjective right," deviating as they did from the solid notions of antiquity[50] and basing their premodern vision of natural law on theology.[51] The seventeenth century, marked by Hobbes's anthropology, which was dominated by his concept of "right of nature," provoked the proliferation of these subjective rights; Locke insisted on economic rights; and liberalism, which had to admit "this marvel: the right to make mistakes," engulfed this perverse vision of humanity in "the philosophy of law." Consequently, the avalanche of human rights and citizens' rights is not an "admirable medicine" against absolutism or statism; rather, if taken seriously, these inflationary rights lead back to anarchy. "The emergence of human rights bears witness to the breakdown of the concept of law."[52] With them, the idea of justice and its tool, jurisprudence, were perverted. The triumph of rights in the twentieth century testifies to the confusions and illusions that make culture decay.[53] From the law of Rome to human rights, the story of a fall was sadly written,[54] because – as Peces-Barba observes – for Villey the new concept of human rights emerges from a Christian source but deviates from the source in three ways: (1) regarding its contents, because it is a theology of the laity and a deist religion of humanity; (2) regarding its form, since it is the development of formal logics opposing Aristotelian dialectic; and (3) because of the lack of knowledge of the value of Thomism or of the research spirit of truth, and the inclination, among Spanish scholastics, to pragmatism, to utility.[55]

So Villey condemns the "new rhetoric" that destroys the true natural law by denying the inherently dialectical character of natural law.[56] This is why the renaissance of natural law in the twentieth century seems to bode well. But it will be beneficial only if we really rediscover the concrete notion of nature. It is therefore important that the domination of the law and the passive

[49] Villey, *Philosophie*, 96–101.
[50] Villey, *Quanderni Fiorentini*, 53ff.
[51] Peces-Barba Martinez, "Michel Villey et les droits de l'homme," *Droit et société* 71, no. 1 (2009): 93–100, at 95.
[52] Michel Villey, *Le droit et le droits de l'homme* (Paris: PUF, 1983), passim.
[53] Alfred Dufour, "Michel Villey et les droits de l'Homme: la critique d'un Antimoderne?" *Droit & Philosophie* 8 (2016), 9–33.
[54] *Encyclopédie philosophique universelle*, 3; Peces-Barba Martinez, "Michel Villey et les droits de l'homme," 93–100.
[55] Peces-Barba Martinez, "Michel Villey et les droits de l'homme," 98.
[56] Michel Villey, "Nouvelle rhétorique et droit naturel," *Logique et analyse* 19, no. 73 (1976): 3–24.

acceptance of it cease. But the insurrection against the laws, as it appears in the free law school of Erlich, in the sociological jurisprudence inaugurated by Roscoe Pound in the United States, and in the modern spirit that manifests itself in America and Scandinavia, is far from sufficient, because it is, in fact, only a product of positivism and thus reveals its inadequacy. For these reasons, in the process of understanding natural law, the jurisprudential process is essential and necessary,[57] because law does not dwell in an ideal realm (hence an antiplatonism that is widespread in Villey),[58] and only jurisprudence can distinguish between law and morality.[59]

JUSTICE AND JURISPRUDENCE

According to Villey, all modern authors, from Hobbes to Rousseau, from Kant to Hegel, Marx, or Weber, have misunderstood the meaning of the term law, which they have considered from various points of view, but always extrinsically. In their philosophy, they do not know that law is an invention of the Romans, that it is based on the nature of things, that it expresses the just, and that it is manifested by *ars boni et aequi* (art of goodness and equity),[60] which has nothing to do with "the modern subjective idea of the right-freedom of a subject." Among the many theorists of the social contract, according to Villey, Hobbes is emblematic for the evidence of his break with the Aristotelian "science of the just."[61]

In fact, according to Villey, the idea of law is defined by the concept of "just partition."[62] The law appears not from an idea imposed by a sovereign but from the discoveries of jurists who act by taking small steps.[63] Law is an art that claims to achieve particular justice, which presupposes giving each one what is due to him or her. What is pursued is just distribution – not utility or the truth but the distribution of external goods (*suum cuique tribuere*).[64] Justice, expressed by jurisprudence such as Roman Law,[65] must realize this partition

[57] Michel Villey, "Le droit dans les choses," in Paul Amselek and Christophe Grzegorczyk (eds.), *Controverses autour de l'ontologie du droit* (Paris: PUF, 1989), 19.
[58] Michel Bastit, "Un vivant aristotélicien: Michel Villey," 61–62.
[59] Rials, *Villey et les idoles*, 34.
[60] Celsus-Ulpian, *Digest* 1.1.1.pr.
[61] Moreau, "Michel Villey et les philosophes," 107.
[62] Chantal Delsol et Stéphane Bauzon, eds., *Michel Villey: le juste partage* (Paris: Dalloz, 2007).
[63] Peces-Barba Martinez, "Michel Villey et les droits de l'homme," 98.
[64] Ibid., 94.
[65] Villey talks about "*Art judiciaire*" in *Philosophie du droit*, 313–33.

by identifying the part that belongs to each one; for this reason, the law is objective.[66] Justice, Villey writes in "Definitions and Purposes of Law," is the goal of law.[67]

When subjective law becomes the very purpose of law, as happens in Hobbes, justice is abandoned in order to conceive the law as solely at the service of the individual.[68] For Villey, Hobbes is "the founder of the philosophy of modern individualist law,"[69] and consequently of legal positivism.[70] Villey recognizes the durability of Hobbes and observes that his ideas may still be found in contemporary systems, as Hobbes is the foundation of modern legal thought.[71]

But even when the individual apparently disappears, because of the "emergence of collectivism" (represented by Hegel, Marx, and Comte), in reality the aims of law are distorted, causing injustice and sacrifice of individuals.[72] So a true philosophy of law is that which, without ignoring the *ius constitutuum*, also knows its limits, because it is aware of its origins. Its only means is the practice of dialectics, that is to say, questioning and controversy, so distant from dogmatism, which is the vice of the systems of modern rationalism.[73]

"WHY ST THOMAS?"

St Thomas's works, in which theology enables the understanding of law, constitute the main source of reference of Villey's thought. The fundamental *Questions de saint Thomas sur le droit et la politique* [Questions of Saint Thomas on Law and Politics, 1987] begins with a short introductory chapter: "Why St Thomas?" In these first pages, Villey defends, in open controversy with the intellectuals of his time, his choice of *Summa Theologiae* as the object of his course on philosophy of law. Villey underlines the global vision of the world of the *Summa* and St Thomas's vocation to regulate human actions, but also the theological character of his doctrine as well as his mystical character: "*Summa* is also a prayer."[74]

66 Villey, *Le droit et les droits de l'homme*, 48–52; Villey, *Questions de saint Thomas sur le droit et la politique*, 118–20; Rials, *Villey et les idoles*, 43–44.
67 Villey, *Philosophie du droit*, 39–70.
68 Ibid., 108.
69 Ibid., 105; Pierre-François Moreau, "Michel Villey lecteur de Hobbes," *Droits* 29 (1999), 105–17.
70 Villey, *La formation*, 635.
71 Ibid., 704.
72 Villey, *Philosophie du droit*, 122–32.
73 *Encyclopédie philosophique universelle*, 3.
74 Villey, *Questions de Saint Thomas sur le droit et la politique*, 20.

In Villey's thought, the convergence of epistemology and metaphysics explicitly springs from his reading of Aristotle and St Thomas.[75] Analytical formalism can only betray the dialectic inherent in the work of St Thomas, in which every preaching is intrinsically linked to ontology and theology. For this reason, St Thomas's dialectical itinerary between law and metaphysics is itself substantial, not only instrumental, and can never be circumvented. For this reason, Villey's veneration of the *Summa Theologiae* is accompanied by a profound criticism of Thomism, that is, the reception of the work of St Thomas by his successors. This criticism is so well argued that it represents a true history of St Thomas's reception from the Renaissance to the twentieth century[76] (not even the most illustrious of Villey's contemporary Thomists, Gilson and Maritain,[77] are exempt from criticism).

Indeed, Villey retraces the entire development of the betrayal of the thought of St Thomas without exempting from criticism Augustinianism, Franciscanism, and nominalism,[78] responsible for the triumph of individualism in the legal sphere and for introduction of the dangerous distinction between right and law. For Villey, there is nothing more to be condemned than legal individualism, for dogmatic but above all religious reasons, since individualism is contrary to nature, which is ordered by God and a reflection of God.[79]

It was especially from the sixteenth century, however, with the advent of the Second Scholasticism, that – according to Villey – the thought of St Thomas was distorted and misinterpreted. Vitoria, Suárez, Molina, and the other doctors of the Second Scholasticism had found ways to divert the dialectic objections of St Thomas, provoking a monolithic dogmatism. The result was a legal positivism[80] particularly visible in the *ius gentium* of Francisco de Vitoria and Francisco Suárez, based on human consensus and will, and on the harmful distinction between *ius* (right) and *lex* (law). Suárez, above all, was for Villey one of the deplorable founders of modern subjective law.[81]

But according to Villey, rationalism in the seventeenth century was the strongest moment of detachment from St Thomas: soaked in Euclid, rationalists (the most emblematic of whom was Hobbes) replaced an artificial *more*

[75] Dubouchet, *Critique du droit chez Michel Villey et René Girard*, 160ff.
[76] Ibid., 101.
[77] See Chapter 23.
[78] On Villey's doctrine on langage, see Rials, *Villey et les idoles*, 70–77.
[79] Villey, *Réflexions ... Les Carnets* 17, n. 54; Gutmann, "Michel Villey, le nominalisme et le volontarisme," 95.
[80] Michel Villey, *Le positivisme juridique moderne et le Christianisme* (Milan: Giuffré, 1984).
[81] "Villey has much more sympathy even for Hobbes than for Suarez," says Moreau, "Michel Villey lecteur de Hobbes," 116.

geometrico system of reasoning with the medieval *quaestio*.[82] The same mistake was made by the great French jurists of the seventeenth and eighteenth centuries, such as Boussuet and Domat,[83] and of course by the French Revolution and Napoleonic codes. It goes without saying that Kant and Kelsen, promoters of the deviant distinction between "being" and "ought to be" and of the more mature legal positivism, are strongly criticized by Villey, who drastically rejects this "epistemological dualism."[84]

In the name of "good use of dialogues" as a privileged approach to the study of humanities, in *Questions* Villey exposes how to "read an article" of the *Summa*.[85] For that purpose, Villey chooses an eminently legal article, the one on judgment, and proceeds to its reading following step by step the dialectical reasoning that constitutes it. It is an example of Thomistic "questioning": to pose the problem, to specify the adopted method, to examine the objections, to solve the question without closing it, to draw plural conclusions, to hear both parties (*audiatur et altera pars*).

According to Villey, this way of searching for the truth, the *quaestio*, is dead because of formal systematizations and intellectual dogmatism. However, "dialectical syllogism" is the specific instrument of the human sciences, as opposed to "analytical syllogisms," which respond only to pure formal logics. Hence, much of substance is asked in the *Questions*: should Catholic theology make room for secular philosophy? Can a social doctrine be found in sacred scriptures? Is there a "natural right"?

RÉFLEXIONS SUR LA PHILOSOPHIE ET LE DROIT. LES CARNETS [REFLECTIONS ON PHILOSOPHY AND LAW. NOTEBOOKS][86]

The *Notebooks*, in twenty-five "books of pages," record the reflections that, from 1958 through1988, the author pursued on philosophy and law and, in a broader theme, on humanity, the world, and God. Villey always carried his notebook with him, and wrote down his thoughts on a wide variety of occasions: while traveling, at international conferences, but also in the intimacy of his home in Paris and in his country residence. After his death, his wife and daughter found the notebooks and entrusted them to the friendly hands of their closest colleagues, who edited the publication. The topics dealt with are

[82] Villey, *Questions*, 43.
[83] See Chapter 12.
[84] Dubouchet, *Critique du droit chez Michel Villey et René Girard*, 122ff.
[85] Villey, *Questions de Saint Thomas*, 58ff.
[86] Villey, *Réflexions... Les Carnets*.

obviously heterogeneous and diversified, but what emerges from the *Notebooks* is that in an approach tinged with mysticism,[87] Villey reveals the sublime ideal of justice and virtue fed with love. Not being intended for distribution, the *Notebooks* show a more spontaneous dimension of Villey's Christianity. The presence of St Thomas in these notes is very important and shows how he was a reference for Villey from both the epistemological and the substantial points of view. Compared to the other works of Villey, where St Thomas is also preponderant, in the *Notebooks* his relationship to the great Aquinas is certainly more intimate and spiritual, although *Summa Theologiae* still remains the beacon illuminating legal phenomena.

As the preface to the *Notebooks* says, "his philosophical concern is dominant. It inspires his thoughts about man, the universe, God. As far as man is concerned, these thoughts are inseparable from the fact that Michel Villey has observed and reflected both as a philosopher and as a historian."[88] In this philosophical and historical perspective, Villey vigorously hurls charges against the impostures and artifices of the past and present. Substantialism, individualism, sociologism, scientism and technicism, Kantian criticalism, historicism, positivism, and legalism are all accused and deemed broken because, in an inexpiable imposture, they dispense hypocrisy, illusion, and error.[89]

Some eloquent passages in the *Notebooks* confirm the judgment made about Villey as a conservative Christian: indeed, he takes a stand against the return to the temporal sphere of the "new Christian religion."[90] In Villey's assessment, the evolution of humanity and society is not following the path of virtue and truth. However, contemplation of ideals – that is, Christian ideals – can be the light and movement that lead to God.

The patient meditation in the *Notebooks* expresses the moving spiritual iconography of a deeply Christian Villey,[91] for whom ethics becomes a crucial question that he poses first of all to himself.[92] This search for truth is accompanied by an incessant dialectic, learned from Scholastics – the exercise of the *disputatio*, so coherent with a scholar *par excellence*, as was Villey. In this perspective, the transmission of knowledge becomes necessarily fundamental, a task to which Villey dedicated himself with great talent and passion.

87 *Encyclopédie philosophique universelle*, 3.
88 Villey, *Réflexions… Les Carnets*, "Preface," v.
89 *Encyclopédie philosophique universelle*, 3; Dufour, "Michel Villey et les droits de l'Homme," 9–33.
90 Villey, *Réflexions… Les Carnets*, book 10, n. 3; Rials, *Villey et les idoles*, 8.
91 *Encyclopédie philosophique universelle*, 3.
92 Villey, *Réflexions… Les Carnets*, "Preface," vi.

In this recovered truth, humanity becomes again a "citizen of the city of God." What is the space for law in this "City of God"? Villey answers in his *Notebooks*: "The new world of Christianity, the kingdom of heaven, is the overcoming of law. But that integrates and supposes it."[93]

RECOMMENDED READING

Arnaud, André-Jean, edn. "Michel Villey, vingt ans déjà!" *Droit et societé* 1, no. 71 (2009): monographic number.

Association française de philosophie du droit. *Droit, nature, histoire: IVe Colloque de l'Association Française de Philosophie du Droit (Université de Paris II, 23–24 Nov. 1984): Michel Villey, philosophe du droit*. Marseilles: Presses Universitaires d'Aix-Marseille, 1985.

Bastit, Michel. "Villey et Perelman: argumentation avec ou sans ontologie?" *Droit & philosophie* 8 (2016): 75–89.

"Un vivant aristotélicien: Michel Villey." *Droits* 29 (1999): 55–70.

Bauzon, Stéphane. *Le métier de juriste: du droit politique selon Michel Villey*. Sainte-Foy, Québec: Presses de l'Université Laval, 2003.

Brett, Annabel S. *Liberty, Right and Nature: Individual Rights in Later Scholastic Thought*. Cambridge: Cambridge University Press, 1997.

Campagna, Norbert. *Michel Villey. Le droit ou les droits?* Paris: Michalon, 2004.

"Michel Villey: Die Zugeständnisse eines anti-modernen Rechtsphilosophen an die Moderne." *Archiven für Rechts und Sozialphilosophie* 87 (2001): 16–30.

Delsol, Chanatal, and Stéphane Bauzon, eds. *Michel Villey: le juste partage*. Paris: Dalloz, 2007.

Dubouchet, Paul. *Critique du droit chez Michel Villey et René Girard. Pour une épistémologie négative*. Paris: L'Harmattan, 2016.

Dufour, Alfred. "Michel Villey et les droits de l'Homme: la critique d'un Antimoderne?"*Droit et Philosophie* 8 (2016): 9–33.

Gutmann, Daniel. "Michel Villey, le nominalisme et le volontarisme." *Droits* 29 (1999): 89–104.

Institut Michel Villey. "Hommage à Michel Villey – pour le centième anniversaire de sa naissance." *Droit et Philosophie* 8 (2016).

Jacques, Francis. "Villey et les icônes." *Philosophie et Droit* 50 (2007): 315–30.

Mattéi, Jean-François, edn. *Encyclopédie philosophique universelle, III: les œuvres philosophiques*, Vol. 2 (Paris: PUF, 1992).

Melkevik, Bjarne. "Michel Villey e la filosofia del diritto: una lettura di *Les Carnets*." *Rivista internazionale di filosofia del diritto* 83, no. 3 (2006): 487–514.

Moreau, Paul. "Penser le droit de la famille avec Michel Villey." *Philosophie & Droit* 50 (2007): 331–42.

Moreau, Pierre-François. "Michel Villey et les philosophes." *Droit & Philosophie* 8 (2016): 89–103.

"Michel Villey lecteur de Hobbes." *Droits* 29 (1999): 105–17.

[93] Ibid., book 7, n. 4; Rials, *Villey et les idoles*, 40–41.

Niort, Jean-François, and Guillaume Vannier, eds. *Michel Villey et le droit naturel en question*. Paris: L'Harmattan, 1994.
Peces-Barba, Martinez Gregorio. "Michel Villey et les droits de l'homme." *Droit et société* 71, no. 1 (2009): 93–100.
Pfersmann, Otto. "Après Michel Villey, la philosophie du droit aujourd'hui." *Cités* 58, no. 2 (2014): 61–73.
Piron, Sylvain. "Congé à Villey." *L'Atelier du Centre de recherches historiques* 01/2008 (uploaded November 18, 2008). Accessed March 1, 2018. journals.openedition.org/acrh/314
Quiviger, Pierre-Yves. "Michel Villey et les formes contemporaines du droit naturel." *Droit & Philosophie* 8 (2016): 101–07.
"Michel Villey penseur de la sécularisation?" *Droits* 59, no. 1 (2014): 67–78.
Le secret du droit naturel ou après Villey. Paris: Classiques Garnier, 2012.
Rabbi-Baldi Cabanillas, Renato. *La filosofía jurídica de Michel Villey*. Pamplona: Universidad de Navarra, 1990.
Renoux-Zagamé, Marie-France. "Michel Villey et l'Augustinisme: les questions des *Carnets*." *Droits* 14 (1999): 71–87.
Rials, Stéphane. "Ne pas aimer fait comprendre aussi. Michel Villey, Thomas Hobbes et l'ontologie du droit de l'homme." *Droits* 41 (2005): 139–54.
"Présentation." In Michel Villey, *La formation de la pensée juridique moderne*, edited by Stéphane Rials, and Eric Desmons. 2nd edn. Paris: PUF, 2013.
Villey et les idole: petite introduction à la philosophie du droit de Michel Villey. Paris: PUF, 1999.
Sève, René. "Michel Villey et les évolutions contemporaines du droit." *Philosophie & droit* 50 (2007): 357–69.
Thomas, Yan. "Michel Villey, la romanistique et le droit romain." *Droit, nature, histoire*, 31–41. IVe Colloque de l'Association Française de Philosophie du Droit, Université de Paris II, 23–24 Nov. 1984. Aix-Marseille: Presses Universitaires d'Aix-Marseille, 1985.
Tierney, Brian. "Villey, Ockham, and the Origin of Natural Rights." In *The Weightier Matters of Law: Essays on Law and Religion*, edited by John Witte, Jr., and Frank S. Alexander, 1–3. Atlanta, GA: Scholars Press, 1988.
The Idea of Natural Rights: Studies on Natural Rights, Natural Law, and Church Law. Atlanta, GA: Scholars Press, 1997.
Todescan, Franco. "Michel Villey et la Seconde Scolastique." *Droit & philosophie* 8 (2016): 33–75.
Vallançon, François. "Réflexion Biographiques sur Michel Villey." *Droits* 29 (1999): 119–24.
Zuckert, Michael P. "'Bringing Philosophy down from the Heavens': Natural Right in the Roman Law." *The Review of Politics* 51 (1989): 70–85.

WORKS OF MICHEL VILLEY QUOTED

"Deux conceptions du droit naturel dans l'antiquité." *Revue d'histoire du droit français et étranger* 31 (1953): 475–97.

"Du sens de l'expression *jus in re* en droit romain classique." *Revue internationale des droits de l'antiquité* 3 (1949): 417–36.

"La promotion de la loi et du droit subjectif dans la Seconde Scolastique." In *La Seconda Scolastica nella formazione del diritto privato moderno*, edited by Paolo Grossi, 53–71. Milano: Giuffré, 1973.

"*Le droit dans les choses*." In *Controverses autour de l'ontologie du droit*, edited by Paul Amselek and Christophe Grzegorczyk. Paris: PUF, 1989.

"Nouvelle rhétorique et droit naturel." *Logique et analyse* 19, no. 73 (1976): 3–24.

"Sur la politique de Jacques Maritain (à propos de Gregorio Peces Barba, *Persona, sociedad, estado. Pensamiento social y político de Maritain*, Madrid, Edicusa, 1972)." *Archives de philosophie du droit* 19 (1974): 439–45.

"*Polémique sur les Droits* de l'*Homme*." *Etudes philosophiques* 2 (1986): 191–98.

La croisade. Essai sur la formation d'une théorie juridique. L'Église et l'État au Moyen Âge 6. Paris: Vrin, 1942.

La formation de la pensée juridique moderne. 2nd edn. Paris: PUF, 2003.

Le 'jus in re' *du droit romain classique au droit moderne. Suivi des fragments pour un dictionnaire du langage des glossateurs*. Paris: Recueil Sirey, 1950.

Le droit et les droits de l'homme. Paris: PUF, 1983.

Le droit romain. Que sais-je? 195. Paris: PUF, 1945.

Le positivisme juridique moderne et le Christianisme. Milan: Giuffré, 1984.

Philosophie du droit. Paris: Dalloz, 2001.

Questions de Saint Thomas sur le droit et la politique. Paris: PUF, 1987.

Recherches sur littérature didactique du droit romain (À propos d'un texte de Cicéron "De Oratore" 1 – 188 à 190). Paris: Montchrestien, 1945.

Réflexions sur la philosophie et le droit. Les Carnets. Posthumous edition prepared by M.-A. Frison-roche and C. Jamin; preface by B. Kriegel and F. Terré. Paris: PUF, 1995.

Index